# Customer Behavior:
## A Managerial
## Perspective

Jagdish N. Sheth

Banwari Mittal

**THOMSON**
™
**SOUTH-WESTERN**

Australia · Canada · Mexico · Singapore · Spain · United Kingdom · United States

**THOMSON**

**SOUTH-WESTERN**

## Customer Behavior: A Managerial Perspective, 2e

Jagdish Sheth and Banwari Mittal

**Managing Editor:**
Jack W. Calhoun

**Editor-in-Chief:**
George Werthman

**Acquisitions Editor:**
Steven W. Hazelwood

**Developmental Editor:**
Erin Joyner

**Marketing Manager:**
Nicole C. Moore

**Production Editor:**
Amy A. Brooks

**Manufacturing Coordinator:**
Diane Lohman

**Compositor:**
GGS Information Services, Inc.

**Printer:**
R. R. Donnelley Willard
Willard, OH

**Design Project Manager:**
Bethany Casey

**Internal Designer:**
Bethany Casey

**Cover Designer:**
Bethany Casey

**Cover Image:**
Digital Vision Limited

Library of Congress Control
Number: 2002112213

ISBN: 0-030-34336-4

*To my older brothers:*
*Himatlal N. Sheth and Gulabchand N. Sheth.*

*— JS*


*To the memory of my parents.*

*— BM*

# About the Authors

## Jagdish N. Sheth

**Jagdish N. Sheth** is the Charles H. Kellstadt Professor of Marketing in the Goizueta Business School and the founder of the Center for Relationship Marketing (CRM) at Emory University. Prior to his present position, he was the Robert E. Brooker Professor of Marketing at the University of Southern California and the founder of the Center for Telecommunications Management; the Walter H. Stellner Distinguished Professor of Marketing at the University of Illinois, and on the faculty of Columbia University, as well as the Massachusetts Institute of Technology. Dr. Sheth is nationally and internationally known for his scholarly contributions in Consumer Behavior, Marketing, Global Competition, and Strategic Thinking.

Jag has published more than 200 books and research papers in different areas of marketing. His book *The Theory of Buyer Behavior* (1969) with John A. Howard is a classic in the field. He is also a co-author of *Marketing Theory: Evolution and Evaluation* (1988), *Consumption Values and Market Choices* (1991), Clients for Life (2000), *ValueSpace: Winning the Battle for Market Leadership* (2001), and *The Rule of Three* (2002).

Jag is an American Psychological Association Fellow and past President of APA's Consumer Psychology Division and Association for Consumer Research (ACR). He was the recipient of the Viktor Mataja Medal from the Austrian Research Society in Vienna (1977) and the 1989 Outstanding Marketing Educator Award from the Academy of Marketing Science. Jag was also awarded the P.D. Converse Award for his outstanding contributions to theory in marketing in 1992 by the American Marketing Association. In 1996, Dr. Sheth was selected as the Distinguished Fellow of the Academy of Marketing Science. In November of 1997, Dr. Sheth was awarded the Distinguished Fellow award from the International Engineering Consortium.

Professor Sheth has worked for numerous industries and companies in the United States, Europe, and Asia, both as an Advisor and as a Seminar Leader. His clients include AT&T, BellSouth, Comstream, Cox Communications, Ford, Motorola, Nortel, 3M, Whirlpool, and many more. He has offered more than 6,000 presentations in at least 20 countries.

## Banwari Mittal

**Banwari ('Ban') Mittal** holds a Ph.D. in marketing from the University of Pittsburgh, with specialization in consumer choice process. Currently, he is a member of the management and marketing faculty at Northern Kentucky University where he teaches consumer behavior, advertising and promotion, services marketing, marketing management, and e-marketing. He has previously taught at University of Pittsburgh, State University of New York at Buffalo, and University of Miami. His research topics deal with consumer attitudes and response to marketing communications and promotions and to services marketing programs. His papers have been published in the *Journal of Marketing, Journal of Marketing Research, Journal of Economic Psychology, Psychology and Marketing, Journal of Retailing, Journal of Market-focused Management, Journal of Applied Social Psychology, Journal of Services Marketing, Health Care Marketing*, and *Journal of Consumer Marketing*, among others. He is an Associate Editor of *Journal of Business Research*, and also serves on the editorial boards of *Psychology and Marketing* and *the Journal of the Academy of Marketing Science*. Based on research on how *Fortune*'s "most admired companies" create value for the customer, Ban has co-authored a book: *ValueSpace: Winning the Battle for Market Leadership* (McGraw Hill, 2001).

# Preface

This is a book about the behavior of customers around the world. Customer behavior is an extremely dynamic field, increasingly exercising visible influence on corporations both small and large, domestic and global. There is a huge body of knowledge, both on theory and practice, often not published before. We have sought to bring together and give form to this knowledge, which has been accumulated through some 30 years of research, consulting, and teaching experience, and conversations with CEOs, senior executives, business and household customers, researchers, teachers, colleagues, and students on many continents.

Our goal has been to make the book comprehensive in its coverage, managerial in its focus, global in its orientation, and innovative in its organization and presentation. It dwells on the traditional issues in the field and then extends them to emerging topics both in theory and practice. The book goes beyond the conventional subject matter of "consumer behavior" textbooks in four ways:

- It covers the behaviors of customers both in the household market and the business market. The term *customer* is used to apply to both the individual household members as well as business units who buy products and services in the market.
- The person who pays for the product or service is not always the user, nor is the user always the buyer. This book reaches beyond the usual scope of this field by focusing not only on the buyer but also on the role of the user and the payer. The authors recognize that a person may play one or more of the three customer roles: user, payer, and buyer. Each role makes the person a customer.
- The book adopts a managerial, action-oriented approach to the study of customer behavior. It makes a connection between customer behavior principles and the elements of marketing strategy, allowing students to see how an understanding of customer behavior is crucial to successful marketing programs.
- The book also casts its view beyond packaged consumer goods which dominate in branding mass media advertising and promotion. In illustrations and applications, we constantly draw upon both products *and* services, consumers and business customers, and the domestic and international marketplaces. Specifically, we include significant knowledge about on-line customer behavior and impact of the Internet in customer behavior especially in business markets.

## A New Orientation: Customer Values

In this book, we have adopted a new perspective and framework: customer values. From this perspective, all customer behavior is driven by the market values customers seek. Six values are proposed, two for each of the three roles: user, payer and buyer. For each role, there is a "universal" value category, sought by all customers, and a "personal" value category, sought by customers as individuals. Specifically, for the user, the universal value is performance; personal value is social/emotional value. For the buyer, the universal value is service value; personal value is convenience and personalization; and for the payer, the universal value is price value, and personal value is credit and financing. This framework is used throughout to explain the significance of all concepts to diverse customers. The practice of marketing is shifting from a transaction focus to a relationship marketing orientation, and the kingpin of this orientation is the long-term customer retention. We believe that the six-values framework offers marketers an avenue to the practice of relationship orientation and, as a result, to achieving customer satisfaction and retention.

## Content and Organization

While striving for uniqueness in content and the three-customer-roles framework, the book is organized for easy understanding into four sections:

I. Customer Behavior: Power, Scope, and Impact
II. Foundations of Customer Behavior
III. Customer Decisions and Relationships
IV. Building Loyalty and Customer Value

### I. Customer Behavior: Power, Scope, and Impact

What is Customer Behavior? Who is a customer? Why should students of management study this subject? What role does an understanding of customers play in organizational performance? What do customers seek in market exchanges and how can organizations respond to customer search for value? What factors determine customer behavior and in what manner? And, how are customer behavior and its determinants poised to change in the coming years? These and related questions are addressed in this section.

In Chapter 1, we begin by defining the concepts of customer characteristics, customer behavior, customer needs and wants, customer value, and customer roles. We advocate that organizations must adopt customer-orientation and describe the competitive advantages of such a practice. We introduce the reader to a new view of the customer as playing not one role but three roles (user, payer, buyer) and as seeking a set of role-specific market values (performance, price, and service).

In Chapter 2, we explore the environment that surrounds the customer—environment that is economical, political, social, technological, physical, and ecological. We also explore the role of the consumer's personal characteristics such as genetics, age, gender, race, and personality. We describe how these environmental and personal factors determine customer behavior.

These determinants are not static; by nature, they change. In Chapter 3, we describe the expected changes in these factors—specifically in customer demographics, technology, and public policy—and map out the manner in which these will in turn alter the marketplace and the future behavior of customers.

### II. Foundations of Customer Behavior

Having discussed the nature of customer behavior and its external environmental determinants, we move in Part II to "internal determinants"—factors and processes that form the mindset of the customer. These include the processes of perception, learning, motivation, and attitude. In Chapter 4, under perception, we describe the perceptual process: biases and distortions in how customers view diverse marketplace offerings. And under learning, we cover the various mechanisms of human learning—from conditioning to modeling to cognitive—and apply it to customer learning about and adoption of new products and innovations.

In Chapter 5, we describe customer motives—the basic internal driver of all human behavior—and explore their nature and diversity—conscious as well as unconscious. These motives take the form of needs and wants, the entities that bring the customer into the marketplace, searching for satisfier products and services. Next, customer emotions are discussed as valuable motivators as well as outcomes of many consumption experiences. Finally, we describe customer psychographics—values, self-concept, and lifestyle. It is in enacting core values, fulfilling one's self-concept, and building and living one's chosen lifestyle that customers are constantly seeking out products and services.

In Chapter 6, we discuss customer attitudes as the sum total thoughts and feelings toward any product, service, person, and organization. Attitudes are the most direct precursor of behavior, and, consequently, the target of all marketplace communications. We describe various models of attitude and explain various processes underlying both attitude formation and change.

Based on this theoretical understanding of the mental processes—from perceptions to attitude, we are now ready to observe and measure these processes in real customers. In Chapter 7, we introduce the reader to the value of researching customer behavior and explain various research methods of uncovering the customer's mindset and overt behavior.

## III. Customer Decisions and Relationships

Having covered both external environmental factors and internal mind-set processes in the previous section, Part III moves to the core of customer behavior itself, the customer decision processes. We explore this process in individual customers in Chapter 8 and in consumers as groups in Chapter 9. In each chapter, we unravel the steps in the decision process, starting with need recognition and ending with the post-purchase consumption experience.

An important question for marketers is how, when faced with so many product and service alternatives, do customers choose what they buy. To answer this question, we describe elements of human information processing activity, or how customers take in marketplace information and what they do with it. Then we explain various decision and judgment models that help customers eliminate undesirable and less desirable alternatives in order to finally identify the one likely to be most satisfying.

These same intra-individual decision processes become more complicated when customers have to make decisions in groups such as spouses or whole families. In Chapter 9, we study decision making for three broad groups—families, business firms, and government organizations.

While 'decision-making' models and processes focus on individual instances of customer choice decisions, in practice, many customer choices are ongoing replications of prior choices, they are part of a relationship with vendors, brands, and marketers. In Chapter 10, we describe relationship-based buying, identifying customer motivations for relationship buying, explaining the importance of trust and commitment, describing how these motivations are engendered and sustained, and elaborating on the imperative of nurturing suppliers. This important chapter serves the valuable purpose of linking the study of customer behavior to the new paradigm of business, relationship marketing.

## IV. Building Loyalty and Customer Value

From a focus on marketplace decisions in the preceding section, we now move to post-choice experience of consumption and exchange. The satisfactions derived from consumptions and exchanges translate into customer loyalty for products, brands, and stores. We describe, in Chapter 11, various motivations for and distracters of customer loyalty. Knowledge of these favorable and unfavorable factors is valuable for marketers seeking to build customer loyalty, and also to achieve stronger brand equity.

Neither loyalty nor brand equity building can ignore the newest marketplace reality in the physical marketplace as well in cyberspace—the all-pervasive Internet. And customers are increasingly visiting the cyber marketplace, to learn about products and services, and to buy them. In Chapter 12, we describe customer behavior as it unfolds in cyberspace and shed light on the customer advantages of Internet shopping and how the cyber marketplace facilitates customer progress through the various decision making stages; we also describe various types of cyber markets and how they differ from the customer's point of view.

In the final chapter of the book (Chapter 13), we come back full circle to the concept of customer value (i.e., market values customers seek). Having already described the nature and types of customer value in the opening chapter, here we move to a detailed survey of organizational processes and actions needed to deliver specific customer value. We illustrate these value-driven processes from a recently published study of *Fortune*'s Most Admired Companies.

# Special Features

*Customer Behavior: A Managerial Perspective* goes beyond the conventional subject matter by examining such issues as:

- the notable influence of our physical environment: climate, topography, and ecology.
- government buying behavior.
- researching customer behavior.
- customer decisions by intermediaries such as resellers, buying clubs, and membership groups.
- relationship-based buying, reverse marketing, and supplier partnering.
- strategies for creating customer values.
- trends in customer behavior, such as anticipated developments in demographics, technology, and public policy on a worldwide basis.

The book also provides expanded and innovative treatment of such topics as models of customer loyalty; intergenerational influence in household buying behavior; simulation, virtual reality, and the Internet as research tools; the emotional basis of customer motivation; personality in business buying; the role of culture in business buying; major international cultures and subcultures; customer resistance to innovations; a model of customer store choice; and brand equity from the customer's point of view. A notable feature of the book is that, in addition to a full chapter (Chapter 12) on customer behavior in the cyber marketplace, it incorporates Internet applications of the concepts throughout the book.

# Illustrations and Applications

The subject matter is made relevant and practical for the student by describing applications and narrating stories. Each chapter features illustrative boxes called Window on Research and Window on Practice. In the former, we showcase current research on significant topics covered in the chapter. Examples include:

- the Zaltman Metaphor technique for customer research.
- perceived risk and the business buying behavior: 25 years of research findings.
- nutrients for a buyer-seller relationship.
- a virtual reality consumer research project.
- Windows on Practice is a unique collection of current practice stories, such as "Amazon.com—Implications for Dynamic Pricing" and "Relationship-Buying by Automobile Makers."
- global orientation: The book incorporates examples from around the world in every chapter. For example, we discuss the socialization of Chinese children as consumers, lifestyle clusters in Asian countries, and building relationships in Russia.

- Internet Applications: The text also incorporates Internet examples for all topics throughout the book, such as customer relationship management on the Web, motivations for Web usage, characteristics of early adopters of the Internet technology for online shopping, and the increased role of consumer factors in the perceptions of the Web.
- Opening Vignette: Each chapter opens with a vignette, narrated to engage the student from the very beginning, of such captivating stories as how one church in a suburb of Chicago makes religion relevant to churchgoers, the details surrounding a mass wedding ceremony where 250 customers wedded their cars, and how Century Plaza is using technology to become the hotel of the future.

Each topic, whether traditional or new, is presented with the current body of knowledge. Where knowledge is still emerging or gaps exist in the current literature, we develop new frameworks and concepts, extending the frontiers of knowledge in the field. The textbook is enriched with topics new to the field and is unprecedented in its comprehensive treatment. In this aspect, the book is unique; it educates the student mind with well-established knowledge, and then it piques student curiosity to question and explore the still-brewing pot of emerging knowledge.

# A Learning Experience

Writing a textbook is as much about learning the subject ourselves as it is about teaching the student. Our learning of customer behavior has spanned three decades. In gathering material for the book and in formalizing what we thought we knew, we were impressed to discover the vast amount of knowledge both in the academic writings and among the practitioners. It is our eclectic sourcing of materials, combined with our own endeavor to fill gaps in the current body of knowledge, which made us at once feel both humble and energized. Truly, we have learned a lot. But our learning has just begun. We expect to continue our journey by benefiting from the feedback from readers and adopters like you. We hope you would write, call, question, and advise us as you use this book.

*JS*
*BM*

# A Complete and Innovative Support Package

## Instructor's Resource CD (IRCD)

The Instructor's Resource CD delivers all the traditional instructor support materials in one handy place: a CD. Electronic files are included on the CD for the complete Instructor's Manual, Test Bank, computerized Test Bank, and computerized Test Bank software (Exam-View), and chapter-by-chapter PowerPoint presentation files that can be used to enhance in-class lectures.

### Instructor's Manual

The Instructor's Manual for the second edition of Customer Behavior contains many helpful teaching suggestions and additional student assignments to help instructors incorporate the text materials into their class. Each chapter includes the following materials designed to meet the instructor's needs.

- Learning goals & teaching suggestions
- Lecture outline
- Answers to review questions from text
- Suggested Comprehensive Projects
- Guest speaker suggestions
- Term paper suggestions

The Instructor's Manual files are located on the IRCD in Microsoft Word 2000 format.

### Test Bank

The revised and updated Test Bank includes 2,500-plus questions, including multiple choice, true/false questions, and short essays, which emphasize the important concepts presented in each chapter. The Test Bank questions vary in levels of difficulty so that each instructor can tailor his/her testing to meet his/her specific needs. The Test Bank files are located on the IRCD in Microsoft Word 2000 format.

### ExamView (Computerized) Test Bank

The Test Bank is also available on the IRCD in computerized format (ExamView), allowing instructors to select problems at random by level of difficulty or type, customize or add test questions, and scramble questions to create up to 99 versions of the same test. This software is available in DOS, Mac, or Windows formats.

### PowerPoint Presentation Slides

Classroom lectures and discussions come to life with the Microsoft PowerPoint 2000 presentation tool. Extremely professor friendly and organized by chapter, these chapter-by-chapter presentations outline chapter content and use figures, tables, and graphs pulled directly from the text. The eye-appealing and easy-to-read slides match the internal design of the text and make lectures more interesting. The PowerPoint presentation slides are available on the IRCD in Microsoft PowerPoint 2000 format.

# Web site

Visit the text web site at **http://sheth.swlearning.com** to find instructor's support materials as well as study resources that will help students practice and apply the concepts they have learned in class.

## Student Resources

- Online quizzes for each chapter are available on the web site for those students who would like additional study materials. After each quiz is submitted, automatic feedback tells the students how they scored and gives the correct answers to the questions they missed. Students are then able to e-mail their results directly to their instructor if desired.
- A list of glossary terms and definitions arranged by chapter is available for extra review of key terms found in the text.
- Students can download the PowerPoint presentation slides from the web site.
- Internet exercises and the direct web links needed to complete the exercises are on the Web for extra student practice and/or research.

## Instructor Resources

- Downloadable Instructor's Manual files are available in Microsoft Word 2000 format and Adobe Acrobat format.
- Downloadable PowerPoint presentation files are available in Microsoft PowerPoint 2000 format.

# Acknowledgments

A project of this magnitude cannot be completed without the support of many individuals. An important group among them is the colleagues and teachers of consumer behavior who reviewed the first edition of the book. As reviewers, they worked hard to (a) ensure the accuracy of facts, (b) improve readability, (c) suggest leads and research references, and (d) in general, serve as a "second opinion." Their valuable contribution is reflected in the significant improvement of the book.

Avery Abernethy, Auburn University

Ronald Adams, University of North Florida

Eric Arnould, University of South Florida

Russell W. Belk, University of Utah

Dennis Clayson, University of Northern Iowa

Dena Cox, Indiana University

Andrew M. Forman, Hofstra University

Ronald Goldsmith, Florida State University

Cathy L. Hartman, Utah State University

David E. Hartman, University of Virginia

Ronald Paul Hill, Villanova University

Jerome Kernan, George Mason University

Shanker Krishnan, Indiana University

Steven Lysonski, Marquette University

Shelley Rinehart, University of Oklahoma

Maria Sannella, Boston College

Linda Showers, Illinois State University

Patricia Sorce, Rochester Institute of Technology

Eric Spangenberg, Washington State University

Bruce Stern, Portland State University

Gerald Stiles, Mankato State University

Gail Tom, California State University—Sacramento

Stuart Van Auken, California State University—Chico

Meera Venkatraman, Suffolk University

Rhonda Walker Mack, College of Charleston

Other individuals contributed more directly to the contents of the second edition of the book and its accompanying support materials. Edward E. Ackerley, M.Ed. of University of Arizona worked diligently to produce the new Instructor's Manual. Fern Jones of Eli Jones & Associates created the content and template designs for the dynamic Power-Point presentations. Also, Eric Spangenberg and David Sprott, both of Washington State University, contributed their time and talent in authoring the Test Bank.

The book would have never seen the light of day but for the unflinching hard work of our good friends at Thomson/South-Western. Acquisitions editor Steve Hazelwood was instrumental in keeping us energized as well as focused. He brought to the project invaluable experience and organizational and leadership skills. Erin Joyner's contribution as developmental editor is unparalleled: her many thoughtful additions brought clarity and balance to the material, and her copyediting made the book much more readable for students. Equally helpful were the other members of the book team: editorial assistant, Christina Loehrke; production editor, Amy Brooks; designer, Bethany Casey; and marketing manager, Nicole Moore. To all these fine individuals, we express our sincere thanks.

Finally, we would like to thank our colleagues and associates for their help and support. Jag would like to thank Dr. Shobha Iyer who provided excellent leadership in making this revision possible. She was supported by Mr. Randhir Vieira and Ms. Nithya Narasimhan, two of Jag's graduate research assistants. Ban would like to thank Micky List and Vishal Melwani for their assistance in editing various drafts, and Mathew D. Shank (department chair) and Mike Carrell (dean) for moral and material support.

*Jagdish N. Sheth*               *Banwari Mittal*

# Brief Contents

Part 1    Customer Behavior: Power, Scope, and
          Context 1

Chapter 1    The Customer: Key to Market Success 2
Chapter 2    Determinants of Customer Behavior: Personal Factors and Market
             Environment 43
Chapter 3    Trends in Determinants of Customer Behavior 93

Part 2    Foundations of Customer Behavior 127

Chapter 4    The Customer as a Perceiver and Learner 128
Chapter 5    Customer Motivation: Needs, Emotions, and Psychographics 159
Chapter 6    Customer Attitudes: Cognitive and Affective 198
Chapter 7    Researching Customer Behavior 230

Part 3    Customer Decisions and Relationships 273

Chapter 8    Individual Customer Decision Making 274
Chapter 9    Institution Customer Decision Making: Household, Business, and
             Government 314
Chapter 10   Relationship-Based Buying 362

Part 4    Building Loyalty and Customer Value 388

Chapter 11   Customer Loyalty to Products, Brands, and Stores 389
Chapter 12   Online Customer Behavior 425
Chapter 13   Creating Market Values for the Customer 457

Glossary G-1
Index I-1

# Contents

## Part 1

## Customer Behavior: Power, Scope, and Context 1

### Chapter 1

*The Customer: Key to Market Success 2*

**Do Churches Have Customers? 2**

**Why Understanding Customer Behavior Is Important 3**

Satisfying the Customer 4

Adopting the Marketing Concept 4

Gaining Legitimacy in Society 4

**Customer Behavior and Customer Orientation 6**

Cost Efficiencies from Repeat Customers 8

Premium Prices from Established Customers 9

Protection Against Corporate Crisis 10

Increased Word of Mouth 11

One-Stop Shopping 11

New Product Innovations 12

Customer Orientation Creates Pride in Employees 12

**What Is Customer Behavior? 12**

**Three Roles of the Customer 14**

Role Specialization 14

Reasons for Role Specialization 15

**Customer Needs and Wants 17**

**Determinants of Needs and Wants 18**

**Market Values Customers Seek 19**

**Classification of Market Values 19**

Market Values Sought by Users 20

Market Values Sought by Payers 24

Market Values Sought by Buyers 25

**Characteristics of Customer Values 32**

Values Are Instrumental 32

Values Are Dynamic 33

Values Are Hierarchical 33

Diversity of Customer Values Increases with Hierarchy 33

Values Are Synergistic 33

Values Are Role-Specific 34

Values Vary Across Customers 34

**Conceptual Framework 35**

### Chapter 2

*Determinants of Customer Behavior: Personal Factors and Market Environment 43*

**Women Shop, Men Buy 43**

**Personal Factors 44**

Personal Traits 44

Personal Context 59

**Market Environment 69**

Market Traits 69

Market Context 73

**The Influence of the Determinants of Customer Behavior on the Three Customer Roles 80**

Personal Traits 80

Personal Context 84

Market Traits 85

Market Context 85

### Chapter 3

*Trends in Determinants of Customer Behavior 93*

**The Cyber Suite 93**

**Benefits of Anticipating Trends in Customer Behavior 94**

**Demographic Trends 95**

Aging of the Population 95

Women in the Workforce 97

Single-Person Households 99

The Declining Middle Class 100

Ethnic Diversity 101

Geographic Redistribution 102

**Technological Trends 104**

New Technologies 104

Customer Responses to New Technology 106

**Trends in Public Policy 108**

Economic Pragmatism Over Ideology 108

Rights of Passive Consumers 111

Regional Economic Integration 112

**Implications of the Trends for the Three Customer Roles 113**

Implications of Demographic Trends 113

Implications of Technological Trends 115

Implications of Trends in Public Policy 115

Overall Implications for Marketers 117

# Part 2

## Foundations of Customer Behavior 127

### Chapter 4

*The Customer as a Perceiver and Learner 128*

*Long Life* Perceptions 128
The Customer as a Perceiver 129
Factors that Shape Perception 130
Biases in the Perceptual Process 132
Perceptual Threshold 133
Managerial Uses of the Perceptual Process 134
The Customer as a Learner 136
Mechanisms of Learning 138
The Psychology of Simplification and Complication 142
Customer Acceptance of Change: The Ultimate Learning Experience 144
Innovation 144
Categories of Adopters 144
Adoption Process 147
Desirable Characteristics of Innovations 147
Innovation Resistance 149
The Perceptual and Learning Process and the Three Customer Roles 151

### Chapter 5

*Customer Motivation: Needs, Emotions, and Psychographics 159*

*Reacting to the Germ Scare 159*
Motivation 160
The Process of Motivation 162
Facets of Motivation: Needs, Emotions, and Psychographics 163
Customer Needs 163
Maslow's Hierarchy of Needs 164
Murray's List of Psychogenic Needs 165
Ernest Dichter's Consumption Motives 166
Needs Identified by Marketing Scholars 166
Needs for Arousal, Cognition, and Attribution 168
Evaluation of Need Categories 170

Customer Emotions 170
What Is Emotion? 170
A Model of Emotion 171
Types of Emotions 171
Customer Moods 173
Hedonic Consumption: Seeking Emotional Value 174
Deep Involvement 175
Psychographics 176
Values 176
Self-Concept 177
Lifestyle 179
Compulsive Buying and Consuming 187
Materialism 187
The Motivational Processes and the Three Customer Roles 190

### Chapter 6

*Customer Attitudes: Cognitive and Affective 198*

*Managing Attitudes 198*
Attitude: Definition and Characteristics 200
Attitudes as Evaluations 200
Three-Component Model of Attitude 201
Molding Customer Attitudes 207
Cognitive Route to Attitude Molding 207
Affective Route to Attitude Molding 208
Conative Route to Attitude Molding 209
The Psychological Processes Underlying Attitude Change 211
Learning Theories 211
Attribution Processes 212
Cognitive Consistency Theories 213
High- and Low-Involvement Information-Processing Modes 214
Multiattribute Models of Attitude 216
The Rosenberg Model 216
The Fishbein Model 216
Fishbein's Extended Model of Behavioral Intention 217
Use of Multiattribute Models 219
The Functional Theory of Attitude 220
Applications of the Functional Theory 220

Applying the Theory of Attitudes:
Planned Social Change 222
Choice of Strategy 223
**Customer Attitudes and the Three
Customer Roles** 224

Chapter 7

*Researching Customer Behavior 230*
*Internet Tracking Helps to Create
Value for Customers 230*
**Qualitative Research** 232
Focus Groups 232
Customer Visits 233
Motivation Research 234
Interpretative Research 240
**Quantitative Research** 242
Quantitative Research Methods 242
Applications of Quantitative
Research 246
**Information Processing Research** 252
Information Boards 254
Eye Movement 255
GSR 255
Brain Activity 256
Visual Image Profile 256
Protocol 256
**Secondary Research** 257
Public Data 257
Proprietary Data 258
Database Research 264
**Virtual Reality: New Tool of
Customer Research** 265
Virtual Reality Techniques in
Consumer Research 265
Advantages of Virtual Reality
Techniques 266
Data Trail from Shopping on the
Internet 266
**Customer Behavior Research and
the Three Customer Roles** 267

# Part 3

# Customer Decisions and
# Relationships 273

Chapter 8

*Individual Customer Decision Making 274*
*Cultural Differences in the Buying
Process 274*

**The Individual Decision Maker** 275
Roles of the Decision Maker 276
Location and Cost of an Individual's
Decision 276
**Customer Decision Process** 277
Step 1: Problem Recognition 278
Step 2: Information Search 282
Step 3: Alternative Evaluation 293
Step 4: Purchase 298
Step 5: Postpurchase Experience 301
**Individual Customer Decision
Making and the Three Customer
Roles** 305

Chapter 9

*Institution Customer Decision
Making: Household, Business, and
Government 314*
*Football Players for Sale 314*
**Household Buying Behavior** 316
**Families and Households** 316
**The Family Decision-Making
Process** 317
Steps in Family Buying Decisions 317
Husband-Wife Decision Roles 317
Children's Influence in Family
Decision Making 320
**Learning the Customer Roles** 322
Consumer Socialization 322
Intergenerational Influence 325
**Conflict in Family Decisions** 327
Types of Conflict 328
Conflict Resolution 328
**A General Framework for
Understanding Family Buying
Decisions** 330
Decision Process 330
Influences on the Decision
Process 330
**Business Buying Behavior** 332
**Components of the Business
Buying Process** 333
Nature of the Purchase 334
Organizational Characteristics 336
The Buying Center 338
Rules and Procedures 339
Decision Process 339
**A Comprehensive Model of
Organizational Customer
Behavior** 343
**Government Buying Behavior** 344
Government Buying Procedures 344

Procurement by State Governments 348
Similarities between Government and Business Procurement 348
How Government Customers Differ from Business Customers 349
**Future of the Government as Customer 351**
Downsizing and Restructuring the Government 351
Globalization 352
Economic Pragmatism 352
**Household, Business, and Government Decision Making and the Three Customer Roles 352**
Household Buying Behavior 352
Business Buying Behavior 355
Government Buying Behavior 356

## Chapter 10

*Relationship-Based Buying 362*
*It's More than Just a "Sale" 362*
**A Model of Relationship-Based Buying 364**
Customer Motivations for Relationship-Based Buying 364
The Supplier-Customer Relationship 370
Outcomes of Relationship-Based Buying 372
**Relationship Buying and Selling in Business Markets 372**
Process of Relationship Buying: The IMP Model 373
Reasons for Relationship Development in Business Buying 374
Determinants of Trust and Commitment from Business Customers 374
Determinants of Supplier Trust in Customers 376
Relationship-Based Buying: The Art of Nurturing Suppliers 377
Supplier-Customer Partnering 381
**Customer Relationship Management and the Three Customer Roles 383**

# Part 4

# Building Loyalty and Customer Value 388

## Chapter 11

*Customer Loyalty to Products, Brands, and Stores 389*
*Are You True to Your Brand? 389*
**Definition and Measurement of Brand Loyalty 391**
Behavioral Brand Loyalty 391
Attitudinal Brand Loyalty 392
Brand Loyalty as Attitude-Based Behavior 392
**A Model of Brand Loyalty 393**
Contributors to Brand Loyalty 393
Detractors from Loyalty: Attraction of Alternatives 397
**Brand Equity 399**
Two Views of Brand Equity 399
Brand Equity versus Brand Loyalty 399
Components of Brand Equity 400
Customer Loyalty 400
**Customer Loyalty to Stores 405**
A Model of Store Loyalty 405
**Store Choice 409**
How Customers Shop 409
**Planned, Unplanned, and Impulse Buying 412**
Nonfood Store Shopping 414
Shopping Motives 414
**One-Stop Shopping 415**
**Customer Loyalty to Products and Stores and the Three Customer Roles 417**

## Chapter 12

*Online Customer Behavior 425*
*Creating an "Amazon" Online Shopping Experience 425*
**The Internet and E-commerce: A Brief History 427**
History of the Internet and the World Wide Web 427
Projections for E-commerce 428
Characteristics of the Internet that Aid E-commerce 428
Who Is the Online B2C Customer in the United States? 430

Products and Services Customers Buy Online 432

**Online Decision Making— Pre-Purchase Stage 433**

Problem Recognition 433

Information Search 434

Evaluation of Alternatives 435

**Online Decision Making—Purchase Stage 437**

Personalization 438

Privacy Concerns in Online Purchase 439

Security Concerns in Online Purchase 440

Trust in Online Purchase 440

Turning Browsers into Buyers 441

**Online Decision Making— Post-Purchase Stage 442**

Tackling Returns 443

**Customer Behavior in Business-to-Business (B2B) Commerce 443**

**Value Creation in B2B Marketplaces 444**

**B2B Business Operating Models 444**

Straight Rebuy 445

Modified Rebuy 446

New Purchase 446

Learning New Behaviors in the B2B Marketplace 446

**Future Technology and the Internet Customer 447**

Mobile Commerce 447

Telematics 448

**Online Customer Behavior and the Three Customer Roles 448**

Chapter 13

*Creating Market Values for the Customer 457*

*Wanted: VALUE 457*

**Value Delivery 458**

Dimensions of Value Delivery 458

Tools for Creating Customer Values 459

**Creating Market Values for Users 459**

Performance Value 459

Social and Emotional Values 464

**Creating Market Values for Payers 466**

Price Value 466

Credit and Financing Values 469

**Creating Market Values for Buyers 470**

Service Value 470

Convenience Value and Personalization Value 474

**Measuring Value Delivery 475**

**Fulfilling the Business Purpose by Delivering Customer Value 480**

Glossary G-1

Index I-1

# Customer Behavior:
## A Managerial
## Perspective

# PART 1

## Customer Behavior: Power, Scope, and Context

Chapter 1     *The Customer: Key to Market Success*

Chapter 2     *Determinants of Customer Behavior: Personal Factors and Market Environment*

Chapter 3     *Trends in Determinants of Customer Behavior*

# CHAPTER 1

## The Customer: Key to Market Success

## Do Churches Have Customers?

This is the story of Willow Creek Community Church in the Chicago suburb of South Barrington, Illinois. William Hybels is the founder and senior pastor. Hybels' audience is different—an odd mix of true believers, along with atheists, agnostics, and those who once believed in Christianity but are now unsure. In their yearning for spiritual fulfillment, they have been disillusioned by conventional churches. Many have developed the attitude that the Bible and Christianity are not relevant to them.

Enter marketing. Hybels believes that the basic products—the Bible and Christianity—are good. What is needed is a way to present it that makes it relevant to these alienated folks' lives. So Hybels has revamped the typical ways the church sermons are offered. No more conventional religious props at Willow Creek, no more crucifixes, incense, or confessions; no more rituals. And he has devised new delivery platforms, the ones based on an intimate understanding of his target customers.

One such group of target customers is 20-year-olds, who are typically absent from the Sunday prayers. For these customers, Hybels has started a Saturday night service with rock music. The audience consists of young men and women—guys with faded jeans and goatees, girls in black boots with purple-streaked hair. To be sure, there is rock music. And then there is the sermon, delivered in ways that echo its young audiences' ethos. Dieter Zander, director of this service, stands up before the group and proclaims, "The leadership style of your generation is different from previous generations." Then he talks about the problems of drugs, divorce among parents, sex, and racial conflicts.

How does his young congregation take it? Very religiously, really. "God doesn't feel distant here," said one attendee. "They talk here about real life; it is dirty and it is grungy, and that is what I have been looking to hear about."

Willow Creek has 145 acres of lushly landscaped grounds with a man-made pond. The church complex has a food court and a bookstore. Also available are day-care services. The service is held in a stadium-like round with a seating capacity of 4,540.

Hybels got his marketing ideas from management guru Peter F. Drucker. After attending one of Drucker's seminars, Hybels started asking some hard questions: What is our business? Who is our customer? What does the customer consider value? His answers: People find church boring and sermons irrelevant to their lives. He discovered that most people believed in God but not in church. So he created a service using rock music, and he used skits to bring sermons to life. He invited people of all beliefs. No dress code, either. And he started ministries to deal with divorce, single-parenting, finding a potential spouse, and, with help from members, even offered car repair services to single parents. Thus, repairing psyches, marriages, and cars became part of the church's offerings.

Today, Willow Creek's success is being copied, with help from Hybels, by other churches. It has as affiliates some 2,300 churches in 15 countries. The average audience there is 400 worshippers, compared to 100 as a national average. At the heart of this success lies one fundamental lesson: understanding the customer's motivations, or needs and wants, and designing services so that they respond to those customer needs and wants.

Hybels is a pastor, but he is also a student of customer behavior par excellence. Nowhere else can one find a better showcase for the value of understanding customer behavior than in Hybels' church services. To students of customer behavior, Willow Creek is poignant proof that understanding customer behavior matters.[1]

The above example shows that marketing even the Bible and Christianity to customers in today's times is not easy. It requires a customer orientation. This is true of every company in the marketplace as well, whether it caters to household or business customers. When Kellogg's first entered the Indian market with its regular breakfast cereals in the late 1990s, it thought it could change customers' breakfast habits drastically. The company compared the healthy nature of the Kellogg's breakfast to the regular heavy and rich breakfast that the Indian customers were used to and thought that its rational arguments would win them over. It soon learned, however, that long-ingrained habits are difficult to change. The company then researched the Indian consumers and introduced cereals in flavors that Indian customers liked to consume with milk. This customer orientation helped Kellogg's garner a chunk of the Indian breakfast market. The case of Betamax versus VHS technology for VCRs also explains how a lack of customer orientation led to a complete wipeout of Betamax from the market. Betamax had the disadvantage of a short recording length of only one hour, one-half that for VHS, and hence, the customer would not be able to record a full movie on the Betamax tape or watch a movie without changing tapes. Moreover, the Betamax technology was also more expensive than VHS in the initial years. Several companies have failed in the market because their products were too complex or too expensive; in short, because they did not have a customer orientation, and consequently did not offer any value advantage to customers. Understanding customer behavior is critical for market success.

# Why Understanding Customer Behavior Is Important

Just as in the case of the Willow Creek community church, businesses everywhere are recognizing the importance of understanding customer behavior as a key to their success. It is the first step toward meeting the challenges of the exciting world of business. Specifically, it helps companies (a) *satisfy customers*, (b) *adopt the marketing concept*, and (c) *gain legitimacy in society*. Let us discuss each in turn.

## Satisfying the Customer

Peter F. Drucker, one of the leading management gurus in the world, believes that the purpose of business is to create and then retain a satisfied customer.[2] Although firms have to make money, Drucker argues that making money is a necessity, not a purpose. Moreover, a business makes money only if it satisfies its customers by catering to their needs. This realization has led companies to adopt a customer culture—a culture that incorporates customer satisfaction as an integral part of the corporate mission and utilizes an understanding of customer behavior as input to all its marketing plans and decisions. Lands' End, the second-largest catalog clothing retailer in the United States, operates with unusually high inventory levels. Its managers would rather carry excess inventory than fail to fill an order and risk losing a customer. "If we don't keep the customer for several years, we don't make money," said the company's CEO at the time, William End, in 1994. "We need a long-term payback for the expense of coming up with a buyer."[3] As we move from a traditional to an Internet economy, customers become more demanding, more time-driven, more information-intensive and highly individualistic.[4] They will evaluate marketers on their ability to deliver "total customer convenience"—hassle-free product information search (e.g., advertising-on-demand), hassle-free acquisition (e.g., home delivery), hassle-free consumption (e.g., products with built-in expert systems to enable maximum value extraction), and hassle-free disposal. A report by Boston Consulting Group (BCG) based on research with 12,000 consumers in the United States and Canada conducted in the fourth quarter of 1999 states that customers who have had a satisfying first purchase experience online are likely to spend more time and money online. The study reveals that the satisfied first-time purchaser typically engaged in 12 online transactions and spent $500 during the previous 12 months; the dissatisfied first-time purchaser engaged in only four transactions and spent only $140 on online transactions.[5]

## Adopting the Marketing Concept

According to Philip Kotler, professor of marketing at Northwestern University, the *marketing concept* is an improvement over the *selling concept*.[6] In the selling concept, the firm's principal focus is on finding a buyer for the product it makes and somehow "selling" that customer into parting with his or her cash in exchange for the product the firm has to offer. In contrast, under the marketing concept, the firm's obsession is to make what the customer needs or wants. The marketing concept gives a firm greater market success because its products and services meet customer needs better and customers seek out these products and services. Adopting the marketing concept entails the market-oriented firm focusing on understanding its customers' dynamic needs and wants. Instead of pushing a product on the customer, the firm now assumes a consultative role, helping customers identify products and services that would best meet their needs. The Window on Research presents the role that marketing will play in the network economy as a customer consulting function.

## Gaining Legitimacy in Society

If making money is the only goal of an organization, it does not provide a legitimate reason for society to support businesses. Rather, a society supports businesses because they serve its members by catering to their needs and wants. Focusing on the customer leads to better serving the society's needs. Paying attention to customer behavior and fashioning a business to respond to customer needs, desires, and preferences amounts to business democracy for a nation's citizens and serves both public and private interest.[7] In other words, we stand to create a more efficient system for both household and business customers if companies pursue the goals of business democracy, giving customers freedom of choice and depending for their own well-being on the economic patronage of their customers. The changes taking place in Eastern Europe demonstrate how

# WINDOW ON RESEARCH

## Marketing as Seller's Agent to Customer's Agent

Marketing professors Ravi S. Achrol and Philip Kotler specify the role of marketing in the network economy, and one of the levels at which they study the network phenomenon is in terms of *customer opportunity networks*. Customer opportunity networks are organized around customer needs and market opportunities and are designed to search for the best solutions to them. The core competency of the network is knowledge about product technology and the technology of use. Through a global network of offices and information centers, the network matches consumer needs and inquiries, market intelligence, and economic trends with a worldwide directory of suppliers of products, with all relevant information about product specification, custom design possibilities, prices, existing inventory and locations, production time, and terms of trade. These matches between customer needs and suppliers will be conveyed to the customers; the transaction will be negotiated and then simultaneously conveyed to the supplier's or the network company's distribution and delivery systems. Achrol and Kotler propose that, in this form, the marketing function may reach its highest level of development as a customer consulting function, making the marketing-consumer relationship dominant over the marketing-producer relationship. Organizing marketing around the consumer offers at least three important opportunities in the network economy.

First is the opportunity to capitalize on information about consumers as a business asset and, on the basis of its market value, realize appropriate economic rents for consumers for the use of this information. Infomediaries will emerge who collect information from consumers and make it available to companies willing to pay for the information in the form of price or value benefits for consumers. At the same time, they could also handle privacy concerns on the Internet by offering the consumer secure portals and protective software to facilitate financial transactions so that they could search commercial Web sites without their personal information being known to the sites. SuperProfile and PrivaSeek are among the first Web-based infomediary start-ups to emerge, and financial services companies such as Citigroup and First USA, with their large existing databases, are experimenting with the concept.

Second is the opportunity to provide consumers with content and usage information on products. Consumers would have access to product performance data, repair and warranty histories, customer comments, sale prices, and promotional offers. As the consumer is inundated with choices, the opportunity network would help to minimize the consumer's effort in searching for, evaluating, and negotiating the best value. The network company will screen suppliers, evaluate their products, compare and rate them, and collect information on product performance and consumer complaints. Thus, there will be a re-intermediation by consumer opportunity networks, and network companies could actually consolidate consumer needs (e.g., the travel or grocery needs of a network of consumers for a year) and could seek bids from qualified suppliers.

Third is the opportunity to facilitate such interaction by organizing consumers into lifestyle-related virtual communities, such as communities of

*(continued)*

retirees, sports fans, or outdoor enthusiasts. Hagel and Armstrong state that commercial success in the online arena will belong to businesses that organize electronic communities to meet multiple social and commercial needs. Electronic communities meet four types of consumer needs—they are communities of transaction, communities of interest, communities of fantasy, and communities of relationship. Communities of transaction primarily facilitate the buying and selling of products and services and deliver information related to those transactions. Examples are Travelocity or Virtualvineyards, Web-based services that sell flight bookings and wine respectively. Communities of interest bring together participants who interact extensively with one another on specific topics. GardenWeb is a community of interest where visitors can exchange gardening experiences and tips, share ideas, request seeds, and ask questions of one another. In communities of fantasy, people create new environments, personalities, or stories. On ESPNet, an Internet-based sports community, participants can indulge in their fantasy by creating their own sports teams (using names of real players), which then compete against teams created by other participants. Finally, communities of relationship, revolve around certain life experiences that are often intense and can lead to the formation of deep personal connections. The Cancer Forum on Compuserve or groups focused on widowhood or divorce are examples of such groups.

Companies develop customer communities who are involved with a company because the product represents a significant aspect of their lifestyle and because they can enhance their satisfaction by participating in information- and experience-rich exchanges with the company and among themselves. For example, marketers of recreational vehicles (RVs) hold large conventions at which thousands of RV owners congregate to socialize, exchange experiences, and participate in seminars on RV ownership and recreation. They organize sightseeing caravan tours that owners can join and enjoy as a community. Some other strong brand communities that customers identify with are Apple Computers, Harley-Davidson, Shiseido, and Nintendo. Opportunity networks integrated with customer communities represent the most dramatic scenario of change for marketing in the next millennium.

**Sources:** Adapted from Ravi. S. Achrol and Philip Kotler, "Marketing in the Network Economy," *Journal of Marketing*, Vol. 63, Special issue 1999, 146–63. Arthur Armstrong and John Hagel III, "The Real Value of Online Communities," *Harvard Business Review*, May–June 1996, 134–41.

economic democracy is taking a foothold in countries around the world, benefiting both businesses and newly liberated (in both political and economic terms) citizens (i.e., "customers").[8]

# Customer Behavior and Customer Orientation

The principles of customer behavior serve a company best when they are applied to developing and maintaining a customer orientation. **Customer orientation** (also referred to as **market orientation**) means a thorough understanding of customers' needs and wants, the competitive environment, and the nature of the market used to formulate all of the firm's plans and actions to create satisfied customers.[9]

Marketing scholar and Dartmouth College marketing professor Frederick E. Webster, Jr., has articulated the role of the marketing function and organization in the corporation as follows: "At the corporate level, marketing managers have a critical role to play as *advocates for the customer and for a set of values and beliefs that put the customer first* in the firm's decision making."[10] At this point, we ask you to take the quiz in the Customer Insight box.

## CUSTOMER INSIGHT

### How Customer-Oriented Is Your Firm?

If you are employed by a business firm, take the following survey from your business's perspective. If you are a customer, answer this survey for a company you do business with, based on whatever impressions you may have formed about the firm.
Scale:

| Not true | Partially true | True |
|---|---|---|
| −1 | 0 | +1 |

1. In this business unit, we meet with customers at least once a year to find out what products or services they will need in the future.
2. Individuals from our manufacturing department interact directly with customers.
3. We periodically review the likely effect of changes in our business environment on customers.
4. Marketing personnel in our firm spend time discussing customers' future needs with other departments.
5. Data on customer satisfaction are collected regularly and disseminated at all levels in this business unit on a regular basis.
6. Our business plans are driven more by customer research than by technological advances.
7. Customer complaints never fall on deaf ears in this business unit.
8. When we find out that customers are unhappy with the quality of our services, we take corrective action immediately.
9. According to top management, serving customers is the most important thing our business unit does.
10. Top managers keep telling all employees that they must gear up now to meet customers' future needs.
11. All managers' salaries and bonuses are partly linked to the levels of customer satisfaction.
12. At this firm, everything that is done is always done with the customer uppermost in mind.
13. The firm welcomes customer comments and complaints and tries to do whatever it takes to win over a customer.
14. The employees of this firm with direct customer contact treat their customers as if their pay depends directly on customer feedback.
15. Over time, the firm has offered its customers better value than the competitors.

*(continued)*

**Scoring:** The score could range from −15 to +15. If your score is negative, the firm is not customer-oriented. The firm is unlikely to retain its customers for long. For a score in the positive range, the closer to +15 the firm is, the more customer-oriented it is. Customers of this firm are probably very satisfied with its products and services. If you are a stockholder, you have reason to be happy, for the firm is likely to be profitable in the long term.

**Source:** Adapted from Ajay K. Kohli and Bernard J. Jaworski, "Market Orientation: The Construct, Research Propositions, and Managerial Implications," *Journal of Marketing* 54 (April 1990), p. 3. The first 10 questions are adapted from Professors Jaworski and Kohli's research. The last five questions, the scoring method, and suggested score range interpretations are based on authors' intuition and are offered here to advance student understanding of the customer orientation concept.

Following a customer orientation provides a company with competitive advantages that lead to higher corporate performance in the form of increased profitability and revenue growth. There are six advantages, three that increase profitability and three that generate revenue growth. The three advantages that increase profitability are (1) cost efficiencies from repeat customers, (2) price premiums from established customers, and (3) customer loyalty in corporate crisis. The three advantages that generate growth are (1) increased word of mouth, (2) one-stop shopping, and (3) new product innovations.[11] Figure 1.1 summarizes these six advantages, which contribute to corporate profits. Following a customer orientation also results in internal success for the company as it produces a work force that feels pride in its job.

## FIGURE 1.1     Competitive Advantages through Customer Satisfaction

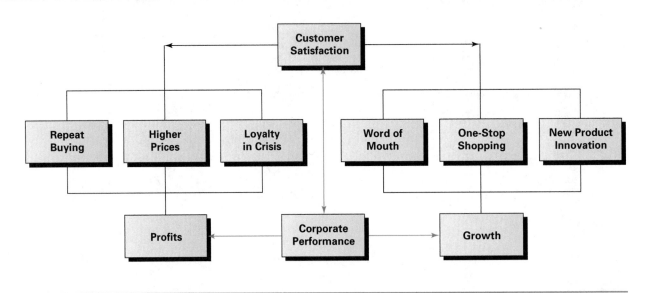

## Cost Efficiencies from Repeat Customers

Perhaps the best way a company can maintain a competitive advantage in a mature market is through retaining its customers. Competitive strategies for retaining existing customers tend to be less costly than those for gaining new customers. According to some estimates, it costs five times more to attract a new customer than to retain an existing one.

Repeat customers mean cost efficiencies. The cost of serving established customers is considerably less than the cost of serving new customers. This occurs due to several reasons. First, there are economies of scale in manufacturing. Accumulated learning and the resulting increased productivity make it less costly to produce the same item for the same customer. Further, for many products and services, one has to spend time and energy in offering pre-sale and post-sale service, which new customers require to a much greater extent than do continuing customers. Salespeople servicing new accounts need more time to familiarize themselves with the customers' operations. The second reason customer retention reduces costs is that dissatisfied customers increase the costs of doing business. At a minimum, dissatisfied customers slow down payments and elevate complaints to higher levels of management. Sometimes, the price a company pays for a dissatisfied customer goes beyond simply losing the customer. The costs of dissatisfied customers are staggering: 96 percent of unhappy customers don't complain about rude service people, but 90 percent who are dissatisfied will not buy again or will tell their story to at least nine other people,[12] and 13 percent of those unhappy former customers will tell of their experience to more than 20 people.[13] Dissatisfaction, in short, gets broadcast widely. It is also evident to marketers that it is impossible to satisfy all customers—some have unique requirements, their locations are too remote to serve them properly, and their user environments may not be conducive to proper product use. Hence, selecting the right customers and retaining them is an important goal for the company. Finally, it is better to prevent dissatisfaction than to correct it after it is created. It is, therefore, extremely important not to create unrealistic expectations through advertising, product packaging, or sales presentations. The higher the expectations a firm creates with aggressive sales and marketing tactics, the higher the cost of correcting them if customer expectations are not met by their product experience.

"Customer loyalty, measured in repeat purchases and referrals, is the key driver of profitability for online businesses, even more so than for offline companies," according to a study of 2000 online customers by Bain & Company and Mainspring. The study covered three online sectors—apparel, grocery and electronics. It shows that customers spend more money and generate more profits for online retailers as they visit the same site more frequently and stay loyal to the site. For example, at online apparel sites, customers were found to spend 67 percent more overall in the third year of their shopping relationship with the retailer than in the first six months. One-time customers are not profitable for online retailers. The study estimates that an online apparel customer would need to visit a site 4 times in 12 months for the retailer to break even. Hence, online retailers need to develop strategies to keep customers coming back to their site. Loyal customers tend to refer more people to the site and referrals from online grocery shoppers were found to spend an additional 75 percent of what the original shopper spent at the site. Therefore, providing existing customers with a fabulous shopping experience is a good way of acquiring new customers through positive word-of-mouth.[14]

## Premium Prices from Established Customers

Established customers are already satisfied with the firm. Unless there is a strong reason to do so, established customers are unlikely to switch their current suppliers. There are always some costs in switching, and sometimes these costs can be prohibitive. For example, if you have invested in a computerized ordering system linked directly to your supplier, switching to a new supplier would mean retooling your computer network or installing a new one. Thus, if a competitor wants to capture your satisfied customer, it must offer significantly better value in terms of lower price or higher performance. This was the experience of Airborne and Emery in competing with Federal Express in the overnight delivery business. Similarly this has been the experience of long distance telephone companies such as MCI, and U.S. Sprint as they try to capture AT&T's customer base. It is estimated that a minimum of 5 percent price advantage is generated through customer satisfaction. In niche markets and for specialty products, this premium could be as high as 30 percent. The price advantage occurs not only because the established customers are unwilling to go through the hassle of switching for a lower price but also because a customer-oriented firm is able to offer its customers value from four other avenues: (a) product excellence, (b) service excellence, (c) brand reputation, and (d) a customer-oriented culture in general.

A good example of price advantage through product excellence is provided by the 3M company. 3M has excellent products like Scotch® tape, Post-it® note pads, and 3M floppy disks, which have retained their performance superiority to command higher prices despite competition. On the other hand, IBM has maintained a price advantage in the mainframe business primarily through service excellence. A third source of price advantage through differentiation is brand reputation. In areas where quality varies significantly across competitors and the customer is unable to judge or control quality consistency, brand reputation becomes a significant price advantage. This is true for McDonald's in the fast-food business, for Marriott in the hospitality business, and for Boeing in the commercial aircraft business. Branding and trust are more important in the online context because there is a spatial and temporal separation between the customer and the retailer. Research by Erik Brynjolfsson and Michael D. Smith shows that consumers may be willing to pay a premium to the online retailer they trust instead of an unknown online retailer. They found that brick and mortar brand names with an online presence are actually able to charge a price premium of 8 to 9 percent on goods and services compared to pure-play Internet retailers.[15] A fourth source of price advantage through differentiation comes from a customer-oriented culture. There are several American and foreign companies where customer satisfaction is part of the corporate creed and practiced at the highest level of management. Examples include Nordstrom in the department stores business and Singapore Airlines in the airlines business.

## Protection Against Corporate Crisis

The third way a customer orientation enhances profits is by providing insulation against a corporate crisis. Four major sources of crises directly relevant to customer satisfaction are product tampering, unfair competition, operational breakdowns, and industry restructuring. When a company uses customer orientation to cultivate more committed customers, those customers will be willing to assist the company to ensure its survival.

Corporate crisis can come from product tampering; for example, when the Tylenol brand of analgesics was tampered with, company loyalty built up over the years prevented an erosion of the company's customer base. Tampering of software programs and planting of "viruses" are also a definite threat in today's times, which can cause a corporate crisis.

Loyal customers also will resist unfair and unethical business practices of competitors against a company they really like. Similarly, large and highly visible companies like Mc-Donald's, Coca-Cola, and Procter & Gamble are sometimes targets of rumors and social protests. For example, not too long ago, it was rumored that McDonald's products contain spider webs and that Coca-Cola is a narcotic. Loyal customers tend to ignore rumors and calls to boycott products and continue to patronize the firm. As the emphasis in computing moved from mainframes to desktops in the 1980s, IBM faced a corporate crisis. IBM controlled about 70 percent of the world's mainframe computer business and was losing the market to the distributed computing available on desktops. The company rallied with the IBM PC, and customers came back to the company in large numbers.

Another source of corporate crisis is internal operational problems that may be created by breakdowns, strikes, shortages, or sabotage. Again, loyal customers would, to the extent possible, patiently wait or postpone their purchases. UPS's recovery from its labor strike suggests that its customers are loyal. Instead of switching carriers permanently, they returned to UPS in large numbers.

In recent years, a common source of corporate crisis has been industry restructuring—the result of either consolidation within the industry or a government mandate. Industry restructuring has hit the oil industry and infrastructure industries such as telecommunications and airlines. Companies that have maintained a strong customer orientation and, consequently, a loyal customer base, have survived these changes while companies with high levels of customer dissatisfaction have not. For example, in the airline industry, Delta and United survived, but Eastern Airlines did not. Also noteworthy is the fact that the breakup of the Bell System by the government to induce more competition has not dampened the strong performance of the Bell operating companies and AT&T, largely because these companies have had a strong base of loyal customers.

## Increased Word of Mouth

The best way to grow a business is to gain new customers without significant investment of product, marketing, or sales resources. This is possible through word-of-mouth communication. For many years, the legal and medical professions have relied on a referral system to acquire new customers. A customer orientation produces satisfied customers, who will then be willing to invest their own time to tell others about your company. Word-of-mouth communication is a very powerful form of communication and influence since it is more credible and goes through less perceptual filters. Research indicates that satisfied customers talk to three other customers. However, dissatisfied customers talk to seven other customers. Word-of-mouth communication is especially important when the product or service is risky. Customers will want reassurance from others if there is a performance risk (e.g., What if the machine breaks down?), safety risk (e.g., What if the chemical is unsafe to handle?), economic risk (e.g., Is this a good economic investment?), or social risk (e.g., Is the style of this suit appropriate for the business interview?). For such risky products or services, new customers almost always look to word-of-mouth (W-O-M) advice from the company's current, satisfied customers. Hospitals, doctors, law firms, business consultants, and local service firms such as car mechanics, plumbers, construction crew suppliers, and recruitment firms gain new customers largely by W-O-M.

## One-Stop Shopping

The second source of business growth is the increase in the number of products a satisfied customer buys from the same company. Both household and business customers prefer to do one-stop shopping for several reasons. It is more economical for a customer to do business with the same firm because of volume discounts, favorable terms, better support service, and savings on procurement paperwork. It is also more convenient since the procedures for ordering, payments, and delivery are standardized. Finally, it eliminates the uncertainty that comes with doing business with a new company. For the company, the competitive advantage that comes with one-stop shopping is the ability of the company to expand its product line and generate more growth without significant risk. For example, McDonald's has expanded its product line from hamburgers to include a breakfast menu, chicken, salads, and other products. One strategy used by several marketers to increase their share of wallet is to issue cards with significant reward value. In the summer of 2000, Sears, Roebuck and Co.—the largest private-label card issuer in the United States, issued the Sears Gold MasterCard product. Customer research told Sears that customers wanted Sears card benefits and universal usability in a single credit product. Sears looked at this feedback as an opportunity to convert its inactive private-label accounts to active ones and offered its customers a card that could be used at Sears and other establishments, and increased Sears share of the customer's wallet. Several other department stores have followed suit with the same strategy now.

The fundamental concept underlying one-stop shopping is **lifetime revenues**. It represents the net present value of all products and services a satisfied customer is likely to buy from you over his or her lifetime. The lifetime revenue concept has interesting implications. It enhances respect, even for small accounts. Second, there is a significant amount of downstream revenues from value-added services. For example, once you sell machinery, you also can sell insurance, financing, maintenance, and repair services. Third, the customer puts his or her trust in the company and, therefore, expects comparable performance in value-added services or other products that he or she buys from the company.

Therefore, one-stop shopping will demand a high degree of consistency across diverse products and business units.

## New Product Innovations

A third way that a customer orientation generates revenue growth is by facilitating the introduction of new products. Customer input in the early stages of new-product development is one of the major reasons for success of an innovation because it allows the research and development departments to incorporate customers' wishes as they develop new technologies. This process is facilitated by satisfied and loyal customers who are more open to sharing their experiences with the firm.

## Customer Orientation Creates Pride in Employees

Customer orientation also has an effect on employee morale in the company. Front-line employees' job satisfaction depends greatly on the extent to which they are able to satisfy their customers. By doing well by the customer, employees feel a strong pride in their company. Hal Rosenbluth, co-author of *The Customer Comes Second*, says that companies should put their employees first if they want to offer stellar service. The reason is that satisfied employees create satisfied customers. But the influence flows in the reverse direction as well. Happy customers lead to employee happiness. Grudging, complaining, dissatisfied customers actually take a toll on employee morale. Bad employees drive out good customers, and bad customers drive out good employees. How often have we, as consumers, found ourselves switching hairdressers or dry cleaners because we were mistreated by an employee? Likewise, it is not uncommon for employees working in retail settings to leave their jobs as a result of harassment by dissatisfied customers.[16]

Interaction with satisfied customers and the feedback received from them in formal customer surveys, as well as ownership of quality work or service that a customer-satisfying organization necessarily produces, generate pride and happiness among employees.

# What Is Customer Behavior?

Now that we know the benefits that a firm can achieve through a customer orientation, let us formally define customer behavior. **Customer behavior** is the mental and physical activities undertaken by household and business customers that result in decisions and actions to pay for, purchase, and use products and services. Our definition of *customer behavior* includes a variety of activities and a number of roles that people can hold. Figure 1.2 illustrates the dimensions of customer behavior. These dimensions go beyond marketers' more traditional focus on consumer behavior.

Our definition covers the behaviors of customers in both the **household** and the **business markets**. Conventionally, the term **consumer** has referred to household markets, and the corresponding term for the business market has been "customer." We use the term "customer" to refer to both markets.

In a marketplace transaction, a customer can play one or all three of the following roles: (1) a buyer (i.e., selecting a product), (2) a payer (i.e., paying for a product), or (3) a user/consumer (i.e., using or consuming a product). This book, therefore, goes beyond the conventional subject matter of consumer behavior—the behavior of "end users" (in household or business markets)—to include the behavior of buyers and payers. The customer also can play other roles in the buying decision, such as the initiator (a person who suggests the idea of buying the product or service), influencer (a person whose view or advice influences the decision), decider (a person who decides on any component of the buying decision—when to buy, where to buy, what to buy, or how to buy), approver (a person who approves of the recommendations of the decider after considering the con-

## Customers: Types, Roles, and Behaviors     FIGURE 1.2

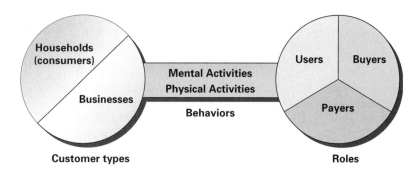

cerns of influencers and users), or gatekeeper (a person who controls access of information to any of the other roles). In this book, we concentrate on the three most important roles of the customer—namely, user, payer, and buyer.[17]

Our definition of customer behavior includes both mental and physical activities. Examples of mental activities are assessing the suitability of a product or service brand, making inferences about a product's or service's qualities from advertising information, and evaluating actual experiences with the product. Physical activities include visiting stores, searching for information on the Net, reading *Consumer Reports* (or accessing it online at **http://www.consumerreports.org**), talking to salespeople, and issuing a purchase order.

A customer's mental and physical activities are directed toward some type of product or service. Throughout this book, we discuss products and services that households buy and use regularly, both online, and in brick-and-mortar stores, such as automobiles, appliances, shirts, banking, dry cleaning, and insurance. But the discussion also goes beyond these typical household products and services and includes products and services that businesses use, such as office supplies, equipment, and bookkeeping services. Figure 1.3 presents the four types of products and services that constitute the domain of customer behavior discussed in this textbook.

In the upper left-hand quadrant are household products targeted exclusively to the household market. Items that are often replenished, such as food and milk, are examples of such products. Other products that are not replenished as often, such as clothing, electric razors, or an iron, are also listed in this category. Finally, major purchases, such as a home, car, and household appliances, are also part of this category.

## Customer Behavior Domain     FIGURE 1.3

|  | HOUSEHOLD | BUSINESS |
|---|---|---|
| PRODUCTS | Consumer Products | Business Products |
| SERVICES | Consumer Services | Business Services |

In the upper right-hand quadrant are business products that are sold exclusively to business firms or to individuals who use them for conducting their business. Examples include machine tools, corporate jets, internal power generators, office supplies, and raw materials.

In the lower left-hand quadrant are consumer services targeted exclusively to the household market. Examples include hair styling, dental cleaning, baby-sitting, home-cleaning service, and home-appliance repairs.

In the lower right-hand quadrant is the business services sector, targeted to businesses. Examples include management training and consulting services, employees benefit services, janitorial services, and document delivery services.

Of course, some products, like automobiles, are targeted to both household and business markets. Other examples of products used by both household and business customers include cellular phones, fax machines, desktop computers, bottled drinking water, and wall fixtures. In many instances, although the product categories are common, the design specifications might differ for the household and business markets. As with products, some services are used by both household and business customers. Examples include banking, security of physical premises, telecommunications, and insurance. While the same service company might target both markets, specific features are often tailored to each market segment.

# Three Roles of the Customer

A **customer** is a person or an organizational unit that plays a role in the consummation of a transaction with the marketer or an entity.

A customer can play three different roles in a marketplace transaction. The **user** is the person who actually consumes or uses the product or receives the benefits of the service. The **payer** is the person who finances the purchase, and the **buyer** is the person who participates in the procurement of the product from the marketplace. Each of these roles may be carried out by the same person or an organizational unit (e.g., a department) or by different persons or departments. For example, many teenagers buy groceries and household items for the entire family because both parents work. Parents pay for the purchases but do not always specify what specific food items to buy and/or which brands to purchase. Or they specify broadly, leaving the final decision to the teenager. Anyone who carries out at least one of these roles—end user, payer, or buyer—meets our definition of a customer.

Successful marketers are aware of the value of each of the above-mentioned customer roles. First and foremost, the user role is important in the design of the product or service. The features of the product or service have to be the ones that the user is seeking and that will best meet the user's needs or wants. The other two roles are equally important. The payer plays a critical role in that if the price or other financial considerations do not satisfy the payer, the user simply cannot buy the product. Without the payer, no sale will ever occur. Finally, the buyer's task is to locate the merchandise and find a way to order or acquire it. If the buyer's access to the product or service is constrained, the buyer will simply not buy the product, and thus, the user would not have the product available for use. Marketers must facilitate the buyer's task by making it convenient to buy and acquire the product/service. The Internet has played a crucial role in facilitating access to markets and products for the buyer.

## Role Specialization

Dividing the customer roles—user, payer, and buyer—among individuals or groups is called **role specialization**.[18] Regardless of whether the same person is the user, payer, and buyer, each role dictates a different set of values that are sought by the customer. For example, an office worker who is using a personal computer is concerned with the performance of the machine, whereas the purchasing agent for the company who buys the PC is more concerned with the price. Successful marketers are aware of the possible ways in which customers divide their roles among themselves. They adapt their marketing effort to the type of role specialization. Some scenarios of role specialization are discussed below.

## User Is Neither Payer Nor Buyer

In some cases, the user is distinct from both the payer and the buyer roles of the customer. For example, parents typically pay for and actually buy most of the products their children use. Pet foods are one product category and veterinary care one service category where the user is definitely different from a buyer and a payer. Other products and services can sometimes fall into this category (e.g., a car bought and paid for by parents for their son or daughter or a health insurance policy bought by the working head of the household and paid for by the employer, but used by the nonworking members of the household). Likewise, in a business setting, an employee is the user of office furniture, like a desk and chair, but the purchase and payment of these products are made by someone else, such as the purchasing and the accounts payable departments of the business. Products like office supplies, industrial raw materials, components, and machinery are also used by employees but bought and paid for by someone else in the organization.

## User Is Payer but Not Buyer

In other cases, the user is also a payer, but not a buyer. For example, in the financial markets, stockbrokers act as agents for clients who enlist them to buy stocks of various companies. In business markets, an office assistant may purchase office supplies for someone else's use that are paid for by the department budget. Travel services availed by different members of the organization are used and paid for by the organization but bought through an external travel agent.

## User Is Buyer but Not Payer

The user may be a buyer but not a payer of goods or services. A household example of this situation is a customer selecting and using a car towing service whose invoice is then reimbursed by an insurance company. Similarly, a business corporation might sponsor the building of a new wellness facility as an annex to an existing hospital. The hospital does the buying (of a construction contractor's services, for example) and will then be the user, both of the contractor's service and the end product of the contractor's work. Not-for-profit organizations purchase products and services for their clients using donations obtained from others.

## User Is Buyer and Payer

Finally, the user may also be both the buyer and the payer for a product or service, combining all three roles into a single person or department. Most consumers purchase and pay for products for their personal use, such as clothing, watches, airline tickets, haircuts, and colognes and perfumes. In the business markets, small business owners often combine all three roles when they acquire office equipment, furniture, and the services of an accountant or a bookkeeper.

## Reasons for Role Specialization

When a single customer carries out all the roles, marketers will likely use a different strategy than when different people act as user, payer, and buyer. Thus, it is helpful to be able to identify the conditions under which the various kinds of role specialization occur. In general, users are unlikely to play other customer roles when they lack expertise, time, buying power, or access to the market, or when the product is either unaffordable, subsidized, or free.

## Lack of Expertise

In many situations, the user just doesn't have adequate knowledge to make an informed choice. Whenever the user does not have the relevant knowledge and expertise, she or he is likely to delegate the buying task to someone else, who then becomes the buyer. For example, patients lack expertise and depend on their doctors for medication choice. Elderly persons who need a nursing home may not physically or mentally be able to evaluate, choose, and arrange for the nursing home; consequently, they may depend on their family to act as the buyer. In business markets, a firm may hire a consultant to give advice on and execute the buying task for a complex piece of machinery because the firm does not have the in-house expertise relating to evaluating alternative suppliers. The Internet has significantly reduced for the customer the risk of making uninformed purchase decisions; in fact, one can even say that it has led to a democratization of information to customers. Online information search is helping customers to gather a reasonable level of expertise before they visit a seller or a retailer, such as an auto dealer or even their doctor. Apart from the available wealth of information and easy comparison shopping, many Web sites such as AskMe.com and AskJeeves.com invite Internet users to write in questions that will be answered by intelligent search engines or human experts on the subject.

## Lack of Time

Another reason a user may delegate the purchasing task to someone else is lack of time. For example, executives delegate purchase decisions, such as making airline and hotel reservations or choosing a mail carrier service, to their assistants or secretaries. Likewise, more and more homemakers these days are delegating many household chores to their spouses, teenage children, or paid shopping consultants because they are too busy themselves. As customers face an information overload on the Internet, they use a new type of search intermediary called the *Infomediary*,[19] which helps them find products and services that match their personal preferences. DealPilot.com allows customers to search for best deals on books, videos, and CDs from more than 100 Internet retailers. The customer delegates the search task in buying to an intermediary and focuses on use and payment.

## Lack of Buying Power

Often users have to delegate the buying task to someone else because they lack the buying power. Corporations often adopt the "centralized procurement" practice to take advantage of economies of scale. Membership clubs like Sam's Club are examples of consumers delegating the buying responsibility to a professionally managed organization. According to a report by Access Markets International (AMI) Partners and *Inc. Magazine*, 670,000 small businesses have ventured into the online auction arena, bidding for products and services. Nearly 1 million small businesses planned to participate in online auctions in 2000. It also found that 1.3 million small businesses are interested in using the Internet to collaborate or pool with other small businesses to buy in groups to obtain better prices for products and services.[20]

## Lack of Access

Many times, the consumer is prohibited, either by law, by physical barriers, or simply by industry practice, from buying a product directly from the marketer. An example of prohibition by law is that of prescription drugs. Even though patients may know, based on past experience, what medicine works best for them, they cannot make the purchase decision; they need a doctor's prescription. A global supplier often presents a physical barrier. Because of language, distance, and other access barriers, the user has to go through a middleman, a trading or import/export agent, or a bank if it is a financial transaction. In such cases, customers must partner with other firms that have better access to markets in order to purchase a product or service. The Internet is fast reducing these physical barriers as customers gain access to the World Wide Web.

## Lack of Affordability

When a product is not affordable to the user, the role separation is between the user and the payer. The user may be the primary decider of what to buy, but the payer (who is also a customer by virtue of playing the payer role) may also influence the decision by restricting the choices that would qualify the payer's funds. College tuition is an obvious example: Parents are often the payers and influence the college their daughter or son chooses. Disadvantaged households that buy food with government stamps are restricted to buying from stores that accept food stamps. In this case, the food-stamp recipient is the user, and the government is the payer. The Internet has opened up options from the point of view of the buyer who now has access to a wide range of price points for each product.

## When the Product or Service Is Subsidized by Payers

In many situations, payers provide partial subsidies. An example is benefit programs offered by a company to its employees for health-care services. Another example is corporate cafeterias, where the employees' cost is only a percentage of the actual cost because of the subsidy paid by the company.

## When the Product or Service Is Free

Finally, the user and the other roles of the customer are separated when the product or service is given free to the user. The user accepts these products and services, not due to lack of affordability, but simply because of their free availability. Public parks, free music concerts, public libraries, and free coffee on some interstate highways represent instances of such free products and services. In these instances, the user of the service is not the same as the purchaser. As a publisher of books, a supplier of coffee, or a construction company engaged in building public parks, the marketer has to deal with city governments in their role as the purchaser and payer, separated from the role of the user. To the city government building the park, the important concerns are costs and ease of dealing with the contractor. In contrast, the residents who use the park will be more concerned with the performance and safety of the swing sets and the jungle gyms their children will be playing on.

# Customer Needs and Wants

It is important for businesses to know the needs and wants of users, payers, and buyers to be customer oriented. It is the needs and wants of customers that marketers have to satisfy.

A **need** is an unsatisfactory condition of the customer that leads him or her to an action that will make the condition better. A **want** is a desire to obtain more satisfaction than is absolutely necessary to improve an unsatisfactory condition. The difference between a need and a want is that need arousal is driven by discomfort in a person's physical and psychological conditions, whereas wants occur when humans desire to take their physical and psychological conditions beyond the state of minimal comfort. Thus, food satisfies a need, and gourmet food additionally satisfies a want. Just as any car satisfies a need for transportation from point A to point B, a Miata, Porsche, Lexus, or Mercedes, in addition, satisfies a want to get the excitement of performance, gain prestige among one's peers, or project the right image to significant others. In the business context, introduction of a new product may lead to a need for increase in plant capacity or a government regulation may lead to a need for improved safety standards. Club memberships for top executives, expensive furniture for the offices, and corporate jets are examples of wants. Only when needs are satisfied do wants surface. As the information revolution takes hold, we see a move toward "desires of a few" becoming "wants of all," and "wants of all" becoming "necessities," especially in the developed countries. Some examples of the second category are the television remote, microwave ovens, power locks, and cell phones.

## Determinants of Needs and Wants

Needs and wants also differ in terms of the factors that cause them. Customer needs are determined by the traits of the individual and the traits of the environment. The three personal traits that determine needs are genetics, biogenics, and psychogenics, and the three market traits are climate, topography, and ecology. In contrast, customer wants are determined by the individual context and the environmental context. The individual context consists of three dimensions: an individual's personal financial worth, institutions, and culture. The market context also consists of three dimensions: economy, technology, and public policy. These traits and context dimensions are discussed in detail in Chapter 2.

Figure 1.4 summarizes how each of the determinants shapes the needs and wants of customers in the marketplace. Their impact falls into four broad categories.

1. *Needs-driven markets.* When both personal and environmental characteristics are physical, pure needs drive customer behavior. Examples include climate-relevant clothing, allergy medicine during allergy season, and flood insurance for personal or business property in flood zones.
2. *Personal wants and environmental needs.* When the relevant environmental characteristics are physical, but personal characteristics are contextual, the driver of customer behavior is a personal want but an environmental need. Examples include product categories that are driven by climate, topography, or ecology but where brand usage reflects one's wealth, social standing, and self concept (e.g., name brand warm clothing, fur coat, a contemporary off-road vehicle).
3. *Personal needs and environmental wants.* When the relevant personal characteristics are physical but environmental characteristics are contextual (economy, technology, and public policy), customers seek something that will satisfy a personal need but an environmental want. Examples include microwavable food, home-shopping network or online shopping, and technological gadgets.
4. *Wants-driven markets.* Finally, when both personal and environmental contexts are salient, customer behavior is driven by pure wants. Examples include consuming

## FIGURE 1.4          Matrix of Personal and Environmental Characteristics

|  |  | Environmental Characteristics | |
| --- | --- | --- | --- |
|  |  | **Physical** | **Contextual** |
| **Personal Characteristics** | **Physical** | 1. Needs-driven markets (e.g., allergy medicine) | 3. Personal needs and environmental wants (e.g., microwavable food) |
|  | **Contextual** | 2. Personal wants and environmental needs-driven markets (e.g., fur coat) | 4. Wants-driven markets (e.g., theatre attendance) |

arts and theater, participating in political rallies, voting, buying designer clothing, and sporting the grunge look.

# Market Values Customers Seek

All customer behavior is driven by needs and wants, whose satisfaction customers seek and value. Thus, all customer behavior is driven by the value received through the acquisition and use of a product or service. The recognition of customers as seekers of problem solutions and the resulting value is fundamental to long-term business viability. As argued in a recent book, *Valuespace*, customer value is "the be-all and the end-all of all business activity; the only purpose of all organizations, all business enterprises. It is the only justifiable goal of all reengineering, organizational renewal, entrepreneurship and corporate innovation. And it is the only path for sustained growth, and for winning the battle for market leadership."[21] Indeed, it goes to the very core of how a business defines and views itself.

Marketing scholar Theodore Levitt has argued that many companies do not know what business they are in. They view themselves too narrowly and, thus, suffer from what Levitt calls "marketing myopia."[22] **Marketing myopia** refers to the narrow vision wherein firms view themselves in limited, product- or service-centered ways—as makers and sellers of products and services that they produce and sell. Consequently, firms that thought they were in the buggy business rather than in the business of providing their customers transportation solutions suffered from marketing myopia and were replaced by the automobile industry. Likewise, in obtaining a life insurance or a health insurance policy, customers are not seeking merely a paper document; rather, they are seeking "peace of mind"—freedom from anxieties about the unknown future. The problem-solving abilities of products and services are what constitute value to the customer.

A **market value** is the potential of a product or service to satisfy customers' needs and wants. Value is created only if the product or service has the capability to satisfy a customer's needs and wants. At the same time, since not all customers' needs and wants are identical, a product or service may be more valuable to one and less valuable to another because it satisfies one customer's needs and wants better than another customer's needs and wants. Furthermore, the customer's context or situation may make a product or service more or less valuable. For example, a product or service may be very valuable in one climatic zone but totally valueless in another climate (e.g., an umbrella is valuable when it rains).[23] Thus, value is created by the convergence of a product's capability with the context of the consumer. Market value differs among customer segments. For example, a business traveler is willing to pay more to be home by Friday evening than a leisure traveler who doesn't mind flying on the weekend.

# Classification of Market Values

In general, a product's or service's market values may be universal, personal, or both. **Universal values** are values that satisfy the *needs* of the customer. These pertain to the basic purpose of buying a product or service or for doing business with the firm. They are termed "universal" because all customers invariably seek them in a product or service, across nations and cultures.

**Personal values** are those that satisfy the *wants* of the customer. Personal values pertain to something beyond the basic or universal reason for buying a product or service or for doing business with a firm. They are called "personal" because wants are more diverse than needs and differ from person to person. Some personal values, called group-specific, are desired by and offered alike to a segment or a group of customers. Other personal values, called individual-specific, are more individualized, more internal, more related on one's own personal enjoyment or comfort.

Each class of values corresponds to a marketing strategy. Universal values are the basis of product differentiation strategies (those that distinguish a product from competition). Group-specific values are the basis of segmentation strategies (those that focus on subsets of the total market), and individual-specific personal values are the basis of one-to-one marketing as well as relationship marketing.

As shown in Figure 1.5, each of the three customer roles seeks a particular category of universal and personal values. For the user, the universal value is performance; the personal value is social at the group level and emotional at the individual level. For the payer, the universal value is price; the personal value is credit at the group level and financing at the individual level. Finally, for the buyer, the universal value is service; the group-related personal value is convenience, and the individualized personal value is personalization. Products and services deliver bundles of values to the various customer roles. This is true for each basic category of products and services, from consumer durables to business services.

## FIGURE 1.5          Matrix of Values and Customer Roles

**CUSTOMER ROLES**

| | User | Payer | Buyer |
|---|---|---|---|
| **UNIVERSAL VALUES** | Performance value | Price value | Service value |
| **PERSONAL VALUES**<br>Group-specific<br>Individual-specific | Social value<br>Emotional value | Credit value<br>Financing value | Convenience value<br>Personalization value |

## Market Values Sought by Users

### Universal Value: Performance

A product's or service's **performance value** is the quality of physical outcome of using the product or service, (i.e., it refers to how well a product or service serves its principal physical function consistently). The performance value resides in and stems from the physical composition of the product or from the design of the service. When customers buy detergents, for example, they seek such performance values as removal of dirt and stain from clothing and protection against color fading. Consumers with dandruff desire a strong shampoo that eliminates dandruff. For business products, performance consists in how accurately and reliably the products perform—for example, that blood testing equipment in a hospital gives correct measurements; that a machine tool cuts metallic surfaces within certain tolerance limits; or that the copier gives good color reproduction and does not jam the paper. In services, the performance value of a hair salon is simply cutting hair in patterns. The performance value of a travel agent is to find the traveler the most cost-effective travel plan.

## Personal Values: Social and Emotional

Products are bought and consumed not just for their physical function but also for social benefits. For the user, these benefits are termed social and emotional values. These include sensory enjoyment, attainment of desired mood states, achievement of social goals (e.g., social status or acceptance by one's reference groups), and self-concept fulfillment.

Some market choices may be determined primarily by social value. Users driven by social value choose products that convey an image congruent with the norms of their friends and associates or that convey the social image they wish to project. Social value exists when products come to be associated with positively perceived social groups. Users in both household and business settings are often concerned with the social meaning of the product or service they use (see Window on Research box to understand the symbolic value attached to the television in China). Certain types of clothing, for example, are associated with certain groups and are either embraced or avoided, depending on whether that group is desirable or undesirable. As a business person or as a corporate employee, the kind of clothes you wear, the kind of car you drive, and the kind of house you live in can signal to others whether you fit in. Other examples of products connoting social value in a business setting could be membership in country clubs, use of corporate jets, and first-class travel. Highly visible products lend themselves to acquiring positive or negative social value.[24] A New York restaurant called Daniel is fashionable, exclusive, and small. And it is expensive. But for the well heeled, the main obstacle to getting a table is not the cost but a lack of the right connections. You have to know the maitre d' Mr. Bruno Jamias by name, or at least know someone else who does. In late November 1996, a staffer for Bob Dole (then a U.S. presidential candidate) reportedly could not get a table at Daniel for her boss until she called again, asked for Mr. Jamias by name, and identified the guest by name. The same exclusivity reigns at New York's Mesa Grill or Coco Pazzo, Chicago's Frontera Grill, San Francisco's Bix, and New Orleans' Emeril. What do customers seek from restaurants such as these that they put up with this unwelcoming attitude? Superb performance value from the exotic cuisine for one; social value from being among the select celebrity circuit for another.[25] Customers may derive social value by going into a particular store to purchase a product. This value is removed when they buy prestige goods online.

# WINDOW ON RESEARCH

## Symbolic Consumption of Television in China

As the People's Republic of China emerges as a consumer market, certain products are taking on enormous symbolic meaning, and television sets are one such product. China's exposure to television has been brief by Western standards—about 10 years—but penetration is as high as 80 percent, with urban penetration approaching 98 percent of the homes. Due to the symbolic nature of the product, most of these sets are in color and are large (18 or more inches). Data on Chinese consumers and their interaction with this symbolic product was obtained from 15 consumers in three focus groups and 40 in-depth interviews in Beijing. An even mix of male and female consumers was drawn from a variety of occupations, with an age range of 23 to 81 years and with income levels of about 50 yuan ($60) to 10,000 yuan ($1,200) per month.

*(continued)*

Living conditions in China hold the key to understanding the importance of televisions in modern Chinese life. Products such as cars or houses seldom are symbolic in China, unlike in the West. Housing in China is provided by the employer, according to an established set of needs for the individual, and the rent is minimal. Consequently, savings rate for the Chinese run as high as 60 percent. But even so, the car remains unaffordable for most Chinese. However, a television set becomes an affordable indulgence. The average living space in China for a family of three is about 250 square feet, and in this small space, the television becomes a focal point. Hence, the size of the TV is of paramount importance to Chinese consumers, and they wish to buy the largest television that will fit into their home. The TV is often accompanied by a VCR to watch prerecorded movies and family videos and karaoke equipment since karaoke is very popular in China, even at home.

To the Chinese consumer, the television represents freedom from the past and access to information. It provides education, entertainment, and news programming to those who otherwise would have little access to them. It represents an escape from the crowding, noise, and dirt of everyday life in most of China. The choice of the television plays an important symbolic role in establishing one's financial image as well as projecting an aura of personal success. This symbolic importance also explains why the selection and purchase of a television plays such an important role in a couple's wedding plans and subsequent marital success. Saving for an appropriate make and model is an ordeal for most young adults, and it even influences when the wedding date is set. Moreover, they prefer a Japanese-made TV over a Chinese-made TV because of the status the former brings them. Naturally, given the symbolic importance of the product purchase, these Chinese consumers rely heavily on their reference groups for assistance and are also influenced by advertising.

The television you purchase in China is a representation of self-worth, freedom from oppression, and the wealth and promise of the "new" China.

**Source:** Adapted from Kathleen Brewer Doran (1997), "Symbolic Consumption in China: The Color Television as a Life Statement," *Advances in Consumer Research*, Vol. 24, pp. 128–131, http://www.acrweb.org.

Still other market choices are made primarily because of their potential to arouse and satisfy emotions (see Window on Research box—Utilitarian versus Expressive Product Appeals). **Emotional value** refers to the enjoyment and emotional satisfaction products and services offer their users. Many products and services offer desired emotions (e.g., feelings of attractiveness aroused by a special perfume or enhanced confidence from wearing attractive clothing). Most experiential consumption offers emotional value. **Experiential consumption** refers to the use of a product or service where the use itself offers value. Some examples are watching a movie, eating a favorite dessert, savoring a glass of wine, or traveling to an exotic place. In business settings, attending a convention can be, for some, an experiential consumption.[26] This experiential component of purchasing goods in a store where the individual customer is recognized by a sales person and bonds are forged is something that the customer will have to forego when purchasing goods over the Internet. Older, retired people may welcome the opportunity to purchase goods offline simply because this gives them the opportunity for social contact.

# WINDOW ON RESEARCH

## Utilitarian versus Expressive Product Appeals

If you would like to read some research literature on customer values or at least on user values, you will find it in the writings of several consumer researchers. In searching through the literature, you will meet such well-known consumer researchers as Russ Belk, Bill Bearden, Joel B. Cohen, Kenneth DeBono, Michael Etzel, Beth Hirschman, Morris Holbrook, Bernard Jaworsky, J. S. Johar, Jean Kepferer, Gilles Laurant, Debra MacInnis, Paul Miniard, Banwari Mittal, Jim Munson, Bruce Newman, C. W. Park, Paul Prabhakar, Brian Ratchford, Sharon Shavitt, Jagdish N. Sheth, Joseph Sirgy, Mark Snyder, and Michael Solomon, among others.

Several consumer researchers have argued that two major appeals of products and services for consumers are utilitarian benefits and value-expressive benefits. (In using the word *consumer*, they refer to what we call the user role of the customer.) These two values are analogous to our performance and socio-emotional user values, respectively. Consumer researchers have defined utilitarian appeals as those that stem from the functional features of the product or service (i.e., what physical job the product or service does). The value-expressive appeals are designed to create an image of the typical user of the product (i.e., what social image or self-image the product's use will give its user). It draws on the concept of self-concept, personality, and lifestyle research.

Various consumer researchers have argued that customers seek products whose functional benefits match their functional needs. Likewise, customers seek those products whose social image fits with consumers' self-concept.

In one research study, a sample of consumers were given the names of several products and asked to write down the associations they made with these products. Their thoughts were coded by independent judges who did not know what products elicited particular responses. For such utilitarian products as air conditioners and aspirin, the associations were mostly related to the product's attributes and objective benefits; in contrast, for such expressive products as wedding rings and the American flag, the associations were image- and emotion-related. In a follow-up experiment, consumers were shown advertising appeals that centered on functional benefits or, alternatively, on image appeals, each for both types of products. As expected, consumers found image appeals more persuasive for image products and functional appeals more persuasive for functional products. Furthermore, for such twin user-value products as watches and sunglasses, one type of appeal was more persuasive for one set of consumers, and the other type of appeal was more persuasive for another set of consumers. Further analysis revealed that consumers who were high in self-monitoring (i.e., those who are conscious of the impressions they generate on others) found image appeals more persuasive, whereas those low in self-monitoring found functional appeals more persuasive. This shows that consumers who seek performance value in a product find performance benefits more appealing; in contrast, those who seek socio-emotional values look for products that promise these values.

**Source:** Adapted from P. W. Miniard and J. B. Cohen, "Modeling Personal and Normative Influences on Behavior," *Journal of Advertising Research* 21 (1983), pp. 37–46; Banwari Mittal, Brian Ratchford, and Paul Prabhakar, "Functional and Expressive Attributes as Determinants of Brand Attitudes," *Research in Marketing* (JAI Press, 1989); J. S. Johar and Joseph M. Sirgy, "Value Expressive Versus Utilitarian Advertising Appeals: When and Why to Use Which Appeal," *Journal of Advertising* 20, No. 3 (September 1991), pp. 23–34; Morris Holbrook and Elizabeth Hirschman, "The Experiential Aspects of Consumption: Consumer Fantasies, Feelings, and Fun," *Journal of Consumer Research* 9 (September 1982), pp. 132–40; and Shavitt, 1990 (Ibid), and Sharon Shavitt and Tina M. Lawrey, . . . 1992, ACR.

## Market Values Sought by Payers

### Universal Value: Price

For a payer, the universal value is **price value**—the fair prices and other financial costs incurred in acquiring the product (e.g., shipping, maintenance). Catering to this universal value, there are several sites on the Internet that allow consumers to compare prices among vendors. In business settings, price value is of importance in commodity purchases. A new trend on the Internet is "reverse auctions" wherein qualified bidders compete on price in an anonymous online auction. This process drastically reduces the prices the company can get from suppliers and increases price value. When payers consider prices and costs, they, of course, also consider the payoffs they will receive. Thus, judgements about the reasonableness of price and costs are always made in the context of product benefits.[27] Note that the cost of obtaining the benefits that a product gives is more than the purchase price; it includes the operational and maintenance costs. For example, the major cost of an air conditioning unit is not the purchase price but rather the operating cost (i.e., the charges for electricity). So the marketer of an air conditioner or a refrigerator must use the higher operative efficiency of the unit and the installation and maintenance cost advantages of his unit as his selling point. True price value consists in computing the life-cycle costs of owning and using a product[28]—be it a car or a piece of machinery in a business.

### Personal Values: Credit and Financing

In their payer role, customers desire the freedom from having to exchange cash at the time of purchase or from becoming liable for immediate payment. They receive this value, called **credit value**, when the seller accepts a credit card issued by a third-party financial institution. Some sellers also issue their own credit cards (e.g., Sears credit card, Firestone credit card, or even a gas station credit card); thus, they offer credit value to customers who may not have been able to obtain bank-issued credit cards. The purpose of the credit value is not so much to offer long-term deferment of payment liability as it is to offer "convenience" to the payer in making the payment. Consider the American Express card, offered both to individuals and to corporations (i.e., Corporate Purchase card). The company requires payment of the entire outstanding amount upon receipt of the bill. Thus, the card offers the convenience of making payment only once for all of the purchases made during the preceding billing cycle. To business customers, their supplier's credit policy is crucial. The usual credit terms are 30 days, net 2 percent (i.e., 30 days' deferred payment, 2 percent discount if paid in cash). Most businesses will forgo a 2 percent price value advantage to avail themselves of the credit value. In some industries, customers are allowed a "float"—always carrying the credit equivalent to a given number of months' inventory. For example, in the diamond trade, the usual float is six months—if a customer's annual sale is $10 million, that customer is allowed to carry $5 million of outstanding dues.

Payers value affordability as well as convenience. **Financing value** consists of offering the terms of purchase that make the payment more affordable by distributing the liability over an extended period of time. Financing allows and often entails more "customized" payment schedules, designed with customer-specific requirements. The financing value becomes more salient in those choice settings where the price of a product or cost of a service is relatively high. Chrysler Credit Corporation and GMAC Financial Services are now separate profit centers of these automakers. Good sources of profit in their own right, they are also helping the car sales divisions sell more cars by offering the financing value. In recent years, leasing has become a very attractive option in automobiles, office equipment, and machinery, as it lowers the entry barrier, often requiring zero or a small amount in down payment. GE Capital, as the largest leasing company, provides this value to airline industries. Likewise, Lucent Technologies, a 1996 spin-off from AT&T, has won many business contracts on the basis of offering better financing value to its customers.

The Internet is significant in that it affords the potential customer far more accessibility to different financing options. According to a study by Brittain Associates, more than 15 million adults state that they have conducted research on mortgage and equity rates online. Approximately one in five of these shoppers has also obtained a mortgage or equity loan following an online search.[29]

## Market Values Sought by Buyers

### Universal Value: Service

For buyers, the universal value is **service value**—the assistance customers seek in purchasing a product or service. It has three elements:

1. Prepurchase advice and assistance.
2. Post-purchase advice and assistance in maintaining the product's use-worthiness.
3. Freedom from the risk of a mispurchase by being able to refund or exchange the merchandise.

Buyers value prepurchase assistance because they seek product or service information. For example, they want to know the technical features and performance information about various models of cellular phones, the itinerary and activity schedule of a cruise trip, or the availability of a vegetarian menu in a restaurant. Product demonstration and service explanations, key aspects of a salesperson's job, are also included in prepurchase service. Customers of Amazon.com can access media reviews of products and readers' comments and can get recommendations for gifts, thus aiding the buying process. Sites like epinions.com aim to consolidate buyer feedback and provide customer experiences to aid others in making a purchase decision. The reviewers are actually compensated based on how useful their reviews are rated by readers.

Second, customers seek post-purchase advice and assistance in keeping the product use-worthy. Thus, when they receive delivery of a car, appliance, or (for business-to-business customers) a production machine, they look to the salesperson or customer service engineer to explain the maintenance procedures. Furthermore, customers seek prompt and reliable repairs and maintenance service so that the product is always use-worthy—for example, the car is always in working condition and a substitute car is available during repairs; or the office copying machines are kept on an effective preventive maintenance schedule. Most software and hardware companies have sites on the Web where they "hand-hold" the customer through most post-purchase problems, either by accessing the FAQs or by e-mail interaction.

Third, customers seek freedom from risk of a mispurchase. They seek this value in the form of being able to easily return the purchased merchandise for refund or exchange if they later come to realize that they made a wrong decision or if the merchandise turns out to be defective after some use.

### Personal Values: Convenience and Personalization

Acquiring a product or service requires time and effort. The effort includes the distance the customer has to travel to acquire the product, the hours of operation during which the customer may conduct the exchange transaction, the ease with which the customer can locate the merchandise, and the ease with which the customer can acquire title to (i.e., take ownership of) the product or service and consummate the exchange. **Convenience value** refers to savings in the time and effort required to acquire the product. Three out of four shoppers in Hong Kong still buy fresh vegetables, fruits, meat, and poultry at their local wet market. However, now younger consumers and working women are opting for the convenience, time saving, and cleanliness of the supermarkets that provide these fresh products—all cleaned and packaged in serving sizes.[30]

Certain retailers specialize in offering convenience value. Convenience stores feature easy-to-reach locations, parking spaces near the door, and limited selection to make shopping fast and easy. Home shopping networks, banking by computer, shopping on the Internet, or home delivery of products such as a pizza are examples of easy physical access. ATM machines in grocery stores and 24-hour convenience stores appeal to "convenience shoppers." Besides convenient locations and hours, customers seek convenience value during the exchange transaction itself. They want the acquisition of title on goods and consummation of exchange made easy through short checkout lines, bar-coding of the merchandise so that it can be scanned quickly, and quick credit check procedures. Note that convenience in buying is different from convenience in use.

For services, customers seek convenience value in the way the service is provided. For example, in the installation of a phone or cable service, there was a time when the local cable company could not tell customers when the repair person would show up for service installation, forcing them to stay home and wait the whole day. Now, many cable and utility companies have improved their operations to give customers a two-hour time window during which the repair person will arrive. This has increased the convenience value for the buyer considerably. See Window on Research box to understand how all six values are equally applicable for services. For business-to-business customers as well, convenience value plays a significant role. They are increasingly seeking marketers who make it easy for them to do business. Small businesses operating out of home seek and appreciate (as indeed do employees in corporation) such wide-ranging products and services as office deliveries of packed lunches and office supplies (for example, Office Depot, a supplier of office supplies in the United States, offers this service), online ordering of office supplies, mail pick-up, delivery of car parts to repair mechanics, and windshield replacement at customers' premises (both homes and offices).

# WINDOW ON RESEARCH

## Values Customers Seek in Various Service Purchases

What market values do customers seek in various services they buy? Are these values equally important for different services? These questions were recently studied by two customer researchers, Banwari Mittal and Walfried Lassar. These researchers measured the extent to which various services offered three service attributes: reliability, responsiveness, and personalization. (They also measured a fourth attribute, the appearance of equipment, physical facilities, etc., which is not relevant to our present purposes.) Of these, reliability was measured by such questions as "The firm performs the service right the first time"; as such, it may be deemed to be equivalent of performance value in our framework. Responsiveness was measured by such questions as "Employees of this firm are always willing to help you"; as such, responsiveness can be deemed to be equivalent to the prepurchase and during-purchase assistance component of the service value in our framework. Finally, personalization was measured by such questions as "Employees are friendly and pleasant" and "They take the time to know you personally." These can be deemed to represent the personalization element of the service value in our framework.

The researchers studied customer satisfaction for two services: health care and car repair. They argued that since how well the car was repaired could always be credited to or blamed on the car mechanic, but recovery from illness did not always depend on the quality of the doctor, reliability (i.e., performance value) should be specially influential in customer satisfaction for car repair compared to health-care services. In sharp contrast, personalization should have the opposite influence. Since there was not much opportunity for interpersonal interaction in car repair services, personalization should not play much role in customer satisfaction for car repair services. On the other hand, since there were opportunities for extended interaction with health-care personnel, how well customers received the personalization value (i.e., service value in our framework) should have a strong influence on their satisfaction with the health-care service providers.

Their results supported the researchers' expectations. Personalization had a strong influence in satisfying health-care customers, whereas it played no role in car repair services. For car repair services, the performance value (reliability) was most influential in satisfying the customers.

**Source:** Adapted from Banwari Mittal and Walfried Lassar, "The Role of Personalization in Service Encounters," *Journal of Retailing* 72, No. 1, (1996), pp. 95–109.

Buyers also may want to be able to consummate the transaction in a personalized or individualized manner. This personalization value has two aspects: customization and interpersonal relation. **Customization** refers to receiving the product or service in a manner tailored to an individual customer's circumstance. Customization is common in business markets where schedules of deliveries are matched to the production schedule and delivered as close to the production site as possible. The second aspect of personalization is the desire for the transaction to occur in an environment of pleasant *interpersonal interaction.* Customers seek this value in the form of positive experience in interacting with the sales or customer service employees. Basically, the attitudes and behaviors of employees interacting with the customer determine this value. Some shoppers purposely seek positive interpersonal experience during shopping and were classified as "personalizing shoppers" in a classic study on shopper types.[31]

Several service companies are offering more customized customer services. For example, if you have an investment account with Merill Lynch, you can open a Cash Management Account (CMA). With this account, your account manager will automatically manage the portfolio—transferring funds as needed from cash/checking to investment accounts, or the reverse—to maximize your total return from the assets. According to a study by IBM and Louis Harris & Associates on consumers in the United States, Germany, and the UK, online retailers need to provide personalized services to customers and ensure privacy of their personal data to prevail on the web. Another survey, conducted by Opinion Research for Privacy and American Business, also found that customers were willing to part with preference information to receive personalized information tailored to their needs, provided online retailers gave them notice and choice.[32] Internet portals like Amazon.com and Yahoo.com deliver the personalization value to their customers by customizing their content based on the customer's tastes and preferences. Yahoo allows customers to develop a page called *My Yahoo*, which the customer can tailor to his or her interests, and Amazon. com greets the customer by name whenever he or she accesses the Web site and offers recommendations based on the customer's earlier purchases.

The Window on Practice presents some exemplary descriptions of how customers of selected market-leading companies are receiving extraordinary value.

# WINDOW ON PRACTICE

## Showcasing Customer Value

### Performance Value from Caterpillar

Caterpillar (CAT), a global manufacturer of farm and earth-moving equipment, offers to customers products that are reliable, durable, and most efficient in performance. Take the D11R carry dozer, CAT's latest, most advanced track-type tractor for mining applications, introduced at the Mine Expo in 1996. Charolais Coal, a coal mining company in Madisonville, Kentucky, leased a Komatsu D575A-2 "SD" tractor for 12 months. Within the first year, the tractor developed some engine problems, necessitating the installation of a replacement engine. Track bushings were worn 120 percent after only 2,500 hours of operation. After two years of trial operation, Charolais returned the tractor to the local Komatsu dealer and replaced it with the CATs D11R. At the time of writing (in 1999), Charolais is a very happy user of the D11R.

### Social Emotional Value from Fossil Watches

Fossil watches are popular among the 17-to-24-year-old youthful consumers. While the watches are of solid quality, the watch in and of itself is NOT the principal source of value to its core customers. Sure enough, were the watch of inferior quality, it would be hard to find a customer. But what really draws the consumer to Fossil is the brand's unique personality—it is an identity that is reminiscent of the 1950s. To cultivate this personality, the company has taken the images, visuals, and artifacts from that era and surrounded the brand with them. These images are everywhere—in the architectural style of its headquarters building, in the artwork that decorates its offices, in the in-store displays, in point-of-sale materials, and on company stationery. The company executives scout antique shops, flee markets, garage sales, old magazines, and the like for ideas as well as actual objects. Perhaps the most off-beat incarnation of this image is in its packaging. Fondly and simply called the *Tin*, it is a tin box with imprints of the images of the 1950s—about a hundred designs at any time. The customer chooses a watch, and then he or she chooses a tin (which is given free of charge). The company executives believe that choosing the tin after one has bought the watch adds immensely to the buying experience. Once home, it sits on the consumer's desk, dresser, or bookshelf, reminding the user of the brand's unique identity. The '50s style is executed by surrounding the brand with images, visual, and facts from that era. Fossil executives explain that "the images are unique and so different. They look like they are from—not just a different era—but a different planet; the artwork looks surreal—depicting people that are happy, people with a little goofy smile. There is a certain casual attitude about life in these characters and in these artifacts. And it has just caught the fascination of young people. It has become an aspirational brand. The target consumer thinks that if they buy this watch, they belong to a certain group of people, that they are part of some surreal culture, and are living a certain experience."

### Price Value from SYSCO

SYSCO, the largest food service marketing and distribution company in North America, has documented superior price value to its customer. Consider its supreme brand of some 20 indices, ranging from shorts and "mis-picks" to cases loaded per truck and quantity of product delivered per stop. Every week, the field level data are transmitted to Houston headquarters, and the corporate office looks for trends and exceptions. It ranks the operating units into quartiles for each index. All companies are then required to catch up to the top 25 percent on every index. One of the current cost reduction initiative is to reduce the SKUs (stock keeping units). In the year 2000, it reduced total SKUs from 614,000 to 597,000 (aggregate over 63 broadline facilities—or from 9,903 to 9,629 per operating unit.)

## Credit and Financing Value from AutoNation

Perhaps the most distrust customers have is about dealer financing and the perplexing payment amounts customers are given after they have agreed to buy a car. AutoNation is trying to overcome this distrust with a menu approach. "We have a menu-of-services approach. We present the customer with a menu of services with prices clearly identified for each service. Our pricing for these services is "open, honest, and transparent," says CEO Mike Jackson.

Menu of financial options? What could that be? We asked to see a demonstration, so we went to the Maroone-Toyota dealership on Sunrise Boulevard in Fort Lauderdale, Florida. Ric Gregson, Director of Finance at the dealership, took us through the menu. Basically, the "menu" is a pro forma that offers four preassembled packages of services—services like the Vehicle Protection Program (which is essentially an extended warranty program), Vehicle Care Program, which serves as a prepaid routine maintenance service, Theft Protection Program based on window engraving, Lojack Protection Program, which activates a specially installed transmitter in coordination with the local police, and Guaranteed Auto Protection (GAP), which makes up the gap between what you owe the bank and what your insurance company pays you in the event of a loss. The four preconfigured service packages include these in what the company considers most desired combinations. And the price of each is clearly mentioned. How is this different from the traditional practice? Explains Ric Gregson: "Traditionally, what the dealers would do is to give you a single final figure that incorporates the basic financing payment. Let us say you agreed to a 9% financing rate, so you will be given, say, a $600 monthly payment, and that payment included all the services and options, and you didn't know why the payment was so high. Then the negotiation process began, where the salesperson would delete a service here and a service there to come to a lower figure, and you still didn't know how much your basic payment would have been."

In the menu, we saw a box at the top left corner. It shows the base payment, which is exactly what you were told and what you agreed to when, a few minutes ago, the credit finance was discussed. And then in four columns, there are four different payment amounts depending upon which of the four preconfigured packages you desire. In one such demo sheet we reviewed, the base amount was $425 a month for 54 months. You can buy one of the four protection packages for a combined monthly payment of $460 a month, including the base payment of $425; or you can keep the payment constant at $425 (at the same amount as the basic payment) provided you can accept a 60-month payment period instead of the 54 months, and you still get all the protection. This form also included one other slightly reduced protection option that would cost $445 a month for 54 months but, in fact, cost only $410 a month (less than the basic payment of $425 on a 54-month option) for a 60-month period. Don't like any of the prepackaged option? The next page has a column for a totally customized protection plan, including the two insurance options (appearance protection and credit insurance) that were not included in the four preconfigured packages.

*(continued)*

Indeed, a menu of options! And a menu approach that is a far cry from the black-box approach of many other dealers (including, perhaps, some of the AutoNation dealers in their pre-AutoNation life). An open, honest, and transparent transaction indeed.

## Service Value from PPG Industries

### Easy Access

To make it easy for the customer to deal with it, PPG Industries attempts to establish lines of communication between the customer and each of its functional areas and departments—the lab, manufacturing, quality assurance, and marketing, for example. And these links are established early, during the development phase of the supplier evaluation by the customer. This is because a cross-functional team coordinated by a commercial development manager handles the account development process during the qualifying process. As a result, an R&D person from the customer organization can call PPG's R&D department directly if he or she has a question. And the customer's manufacturing department can directly call its customer service department to discuss a shipment.

### Rapid Response

However, these open lines of communication would be only half as useful if the people the customer communicates with were not empowered to fulfill the customer's request. At PPG, all customer service employees are authorized to do what is needed for their strategic and key customers. For example, illustrates Jim Faller, the Fine Chemical Unit's Commercial Development Manager, "one of our strategic customers can call one of our plants directly on a Saturday night for an emergency shipment, and the plant will ship it as soon as it is technically possible. Sales and Accounting will be notified on Monday but the plant won't hold the shipment for approval from Sales." This is rapid response, par excellence!

In fact, the company prides itself on being responsive and deems it as its differentiating feature. For example, initially in an RFP situation (where it answers a "Request for Proposal" from a prospective buyer), when the customer is trying to qualify its process, it is very quick with product samples and process data, and it helps the customer move quickly toward commercialization of its own new product in its end-markets. This level of responsiveness is epitomized in a slogan PPG uses in its advertising: "We make it difficult for you to know where your business stops and ours begins!"

To drive its customer-response level higher, it measures what it calls "customer action incident reports (CAIRs)." Every time a customer problem gets recorded, it gets into a system that analyzes the problems by categories; how and when the problem was resolved is also recorded. The CAIR summaries are regularly reviewed by management.

Another point of excellence is its service response. The company can customize delivery time, and it can even customize on package size. For example, if its usual packaging is in drums that contain 441 pounds of chemical, and a customer's process batch requires 1,200 pounds, so the customer might want three drums of 400 pounds each. That way he can pour three drums, and he doesn't have to worry about measuring and saving a partial drum. "Can you do that?" the customer asks. "We sure will," says Faller.

## Access Value from Rosenbluth International

Rosenbluth International takes great pride in its customer service, and the quality of its customer service positions it as a leader in Personalization Valuespace. Certainly, it offers its customers easy access. Many of its travel operations are located on client premises and work seamlessly with client organizations. Its reservation and customer service centers are accessible 24 hours a day, 7 days a week, and state-of-the-art equipment routes the calls to the next available representative anywhere in the world! Customers also have been given the ability to make a travel reservation themselves, using its E-Res® system on their PCs. A more recently launched system also allows customers to access the company online and complete the travel reservation with a few simple mouse clicks.

If you live in Europe, no matter which country you live in, to reach Rosenbluth International, you call a local number, and the call is automatically connected to its most recent Intellicenter in Killarney, Ireland. And don't worry about whether you will be able to follow the Irish accent of the service associate—the associate who answers your call will speak in your native language. Its automated call routing system, you see, automatically routes the call to an associate designated to receive calls from the country where the call originated. Such is the "access value" Rosenbluth International provides its customers.

## Personalization Value from XBS

For XBS, now reorganized as Xerox Global Services, work for a client begins with the design of a site operation. Rather than offering an off-the-shelf, canned solution, XBS configures a custom solution for each customer. Thus, XBS deploys customization as a key driver of performance value for the customer.

For example, consider a manufacturing company that makes sewing machines. The machines come packed with an owner's manual. The current practice is to print it in bulk and enclose it with the product being shipped to retailers. This practice is slated to change for many of the businesses. In the digital age, the manual can be stored and distributed digitally, and then printed by the dealer at the time of the product sale. The manual can even be customized for a specific model or for a specific customer. Now, as a supplier of this outsourced service, XBS can simply take over the current (traditional) manual printing service and run it more efficiently, or it can print more model-specific manuals in smaller quantities. Or, better still, it can distribute the manual to the retailer in a digital form for the retailer to customize it, incorporating value-added after-market services the dealership might offer, and print it on a "just-in-time" basis. This is, in fact, what it does for a number of clients.

Suppose XBS runs your company's mailroom services, and you want a certain category of mail distributed much earlier than currently delivered or even feasible. XBS can do it. One of its financial services clients, for example, wanted the mortgage applications distributed by 9 a.m. instead of the current delivery by 11 a.m. (Doing so would shorten the entire loan-approval cycle by one full day!) So XBS redesigned the whole document process for mortgage applications. It created a special return envelope that could be identified by sight, contracted with Fedex Corporation for a special 8:30 a.m. delivery of that envelope, and assigned an associate to deliver the envelope to the designated mortgage processing officer by 9 a.m.

*(continued)*

Thus, from initial service configuration for a new customer site to sub-process redesign on an ongoing site, XBS offers customization to enhance its total performance valuespace for its clients.

Relational attitude is the foundation of XBS's business model. Its three-part business model is "retain the present customer, grow the same-account revenues, and gain new customers." And XBS knows you can't retain and grow a client unless you develop, maintain, and grow a relationship with the client. Bill McDermott puts it this way: "I think that for Xerox to transform itself to a knowledge-based company, it has to be very much in partnering, in nurturing, in symbiotic relationships where both parties strategically need each other to get the job done."

The partnering relationship with clients begins at the very outset. XBS management outlines for its strategic clients (i.e., clients who seek enterprise-wide document management services) what kind of relationship it is seeking and how it works to win that relationship. The "retain and grow" objective colors all of its behavior and all of its attitude toward how it approaches specific industries and specific clients. Bill Patterson, XBS's senior VP of marketing, sums up that approach: "First, we understand the document-intensity and document-technology requirements by industries. Next, we move to understanding the client's critical success factors and mission-critical documents, and then we sort that out through conversations with the client. We absolutely ensure in the selling process that we have captured the requirements of the end-users. And with our existing customers, we spend a lot of time getting their feedback and ensuring that we are constantly building our capabilities to serve the client's long-term and emerging needs."

# Characteristics of Customer Values

There are several characteristics of customer values. Values are instrumental, dynamic, and hierarchical. As we move up the hierarchy of values, they become increasingly diverse. In addition, customer values are synergistic and role-specific, and they vary among customers.

## Values Are Instrumental

Instrumentality of market values refers to products and services being instrumental in fulfilling needs or wants of customers. Thus, it is important for marketers not only to create values in their offerings but also to link or associate these offerings to specific customer needs and wants.

A person will perceive a product, object, or idea to be useful only if the person can establish its instrumentality in achieving his or her goals. If recreation is not a particular customer's goal, then watching sports has no value for this customer. If you are thirsty, then water or other drinks, not a music CD, have value instrumentality. If you open any business magazine such as *Business Week* or *Fortune* or even a consumer magazine like *Newsweek* or *Time*, you can find an advertisement for one month's free trial of Prodigy, Compuserve, or America Online—interactive information services on your computer. Yet only some people take advantage of the free offer. Others do not respond to such free offers simply because they do not see how the free service meets any of their needs or wants; that is, they do not see any instrumentality in the free offer.

## Values Are Dynamic

Market values that customers seek change over time. First, they change because individual customers' needs and wants change due to alteration in their life stage and resources. Second, they change because of rising expectations of the entire market. As marketers meet or exceed market expectations, those expectations become the new baseline against which the marketers will be judged.

In business, network reliability of services is expected to be nearly 100 percent since many market suppliers have indeed met this level. American business people expect punctuality from the salespeople who call on them; in contrast, punctuality is an exception in third-world countries such as India.

## Values Are Hierarchical

Values are arranged in a hierarchy, with the universal values at the foundation. These are the market values a product or service must offer first. If the universal values are absent, the customer would not even care if the product or service provided personal values. Once universal values are met, customers look for personal values—first group-specific, then individual-specific.

This hierarchy of values is similar to classification of needs, such as Maslow's needs hierarchy (which ranks needs in order from physiological to safety to social status to self-esteem to self-actualization) and Katona's classification of needs (survival → comfort → convenience → spiritual). Need hierarchies will be described in detail in Chapter 5.

## Diversity of Customer Values Increases with Hierarchy

A market for any product or service category will be more homogenous if it is dictated primarily by universal values and more diverse if it is dictated by personal values. Commodities (e.g., grain, steel, coal, electricity) and necessities (e.g., medicines, vitamins, salt and pepper, detergents) serve universal values and, therefore, have limited potential for diversity among market offerings. Of course, even for products and services sought primarily for performance value, feature variations do exist because of customers' differentiation of needs (e.g., shampoo varieties for dry, oily, thin, thick, damaged, or sensitive hair). Yet, this variety is much greater for products and services sought for personal (e.g., socio-emotional) values.

In business markets, in buying raw materials and components, customers mainly seek universal values; in contrast, when buying personal office furnishings, customers seek socio-emotional values as well.

## Values Are Synergistic

**Value synergy** means that one value enhances the utility of another value. That is, performance value, price value, and service value (the three universal values) are highest when there is no trade-off among them. Likewise, the social or emotional value, convenience or personalization value, and credit or financing value work best without a trade-off among them.

Best Universal Value = (performance) × (price) × (service value); and

Best Personal Value = (social and emotional) × (convenience and personalization) × (credit and financing)

In other words, the relationship among universal values (and likewise among personal values) is multiplicative instead of additive. The idea is to create a synergistic relationship among the values. For example, performance should not be traded off at the expense of cost. The best strategy for the marketer is to keep costs low and to increase the performance.

## Values Are Role-Specific

The role-specific nature of values means that they differ among the user, payer, and buyer. Because of role-specificity, customers may change priorities among diverse values when they change their roles. For example, employees who are paying out of their own pockets may choose differently than when the company pays for travel and restaurants. Similarly, when children have to pay for the purchase of a product themselves, they choose differently than when someone else pays for them.

## Values Vary Across Customers

As we have already stated, what is valuable in a product or service to one customer may not be valuable to another. Consequently, a product or service is more versatile if it is capable of generating multiple values to satisfy different customers. For example, personal computers have a high degree of versatility because they must satisfy different needs: word processing, storage of information, communication with the outside world via e-mail, and so on. Nylon has multiple uses in both the consumer and business markets. During World War II, when there was a shortage of silk, nylon served as a substitute for silk stockings as it had the feel of silk. The government took over the production of nylon during the war and used it to make military parachute cords. Nylon has even been used for artificial ski slopes after the war. This product has a degree of versatility that allows it to be of value in various applications.

Finally, for a firm to assess how well it satisfies customer needs and wants, it needs to measure customer perceptions of the values its products and services offer. The Window on Research box provides a methodology for measurement of market values.

# WINDOW ON RESEARCH

## Measurement of Market Values

One way to measure customer perceptions is to ask a representative sample of customers whether specific choices possess any of the specified values. Here, customer choice refers to three levels of customer decisions:

1. Whether to buy a product or service category (e.g., whether to buy a computer).
2. Which brand or make to buy (e.g., should one buy IBM, Apple, Compaq, Dell, or some other make?)
3. From which supplier to buy it (e.g., from Computerland, Circuit City, mail order, or any other).

The values can be assessed at any of the three levels. The first step in generating a measurement scale is to specify the "content" of various values. This is best done by questioning a sample of customers (buyers, users, and payers), such as in a focus-group setting. The questioning would pertain to each of the values customers take into account while evaluating a set of choice alternatives. Some examples of the questions to be asked in the focus groups would be:

1. When people decide whether or not to buy a _____ (product name), what needs and wants are they expecting to satisfy?
2. When customers are deciding which brand of _____ to buy, what social associations (which brands of _____ would have) would they generally consider?

3. Sometimes people expect certain emotional satisfactions from their use of _____ (product name); what might be the various emotions people might look to experiencing in their selection and use of this product?

Note that these are merely examples, and such questions need to be framed for each of the values discussed in this chapter. The next stage would be to elicit from customers a rating of a given brand or supplier (i.e., an alternative) on the "value items" generated in the focus groups. Suppose focus groups generate five social associations from the ownership of a car; then we would list these five associations and ask customers (users, in this case) to check which associations apply for a given brand. For example, people who buy a Saab are: (1) successful, (2) financially prudent, (3) mature, (4) youthful, and (5) outdoorsy. Similarly one could list various emotions (the list generated from the focus groups) and ask which emotions are likely to be experienced by the user of a particular brand. For example, when you own and drive a Saab, you are likely to feel: (1) overjoyed, (2) confident, (3) embarrassed, and so on. In the same manner, we could measure performance value by asking the user to score Saab on (1) gas mileage efficiency, (2) maintenance needs, (3) road handling, and so on (the list of performance features based on focus groups).

Likewise, for the payer, the economic/price value can be measured by such items as: (1) this brand or store offers good value for money; (2) this brand at this price is a good bargain; (3) this brand is priced too high (reverse scored); and so on. The credit/ financing value can be measured by having payers rate the accuracy of statements such as: (1) the company or store offers good credit terms; (2) the installment payment system for this store/brand makes it possible for me to afford this item.

Finally, for the buyer, the service value can be measured by such aspects as: (1) this company (company or store name) makes it easy for me to do business with it; (2) I do not get the necessary assistance for purchasing the product at this store or from this firm (reverse scored); (3) it is a big hassle to deal with this firm (reverse scored). The convenience value can be measured as: It is convenient for me to shop at _____ (store name). The personalization value can be measured by rating statements such as: (1) the employees at this store or firm are very polite and friendly; (2) I enjoy talking to sales clerks at this firm or store; (3) employees at this firm or store make shopping a pleasure for me.

These examples are only an introductory outline, but they demonstrate that the various values discussed in this chapter need to be measured, and they show how these measures can be obtained from customers. To fully understand its markets, a firm would need to assess these values for its own brands as well as for competitors' brands. Moreover, these assessments need to be obtained from its customers as well as from the customers of the competing brands. These consumer data would then enable a firm to map its position on a value grid against its competitors. Such grids help identify which customer values the firm satisfies better and which it satisfies worse than its competitors. This, in turn, suggests which values need to be improved.

# Conceptual Framework

In the above section, we have discussed the three roles of the customer—user, payer, buyer—their needs and wants, and the values sought by each of these roles from products and services. Figure 1.6 presents a conceptual framework that identifies the factors influencing these three roles: 1) external determinants and 2) the internal mindset of the consumer. The influence of these factors on the three roles affects customer decision making, not only for individual and household-level customers but also for business and government customers.

This book is organized as follows. Chapter 2 focuses on the determinants of customer behavior; that is, the external influences on customer behavior. We examine four sets of external influence factors—personal traits (comprising genetics, race, gender, age, and personality), personal context (comprising culture, reference groups, and personal worth), market traits (comprising climate, topography, and ecology), and market context (comprising economy, government, and technology). Chapter 3 elaborates on the current trends in these determinants of customer behavior and discusses how these trends are likely to affect marketing strategy. We focus on three factors that are expected to cause the most significant change in future customer behavior—changes in demographics, advances in technology, and changes in public policy.

Chapters 4, 5, and 6 examine the "mind-set of the customer"—the internal influences on customer behavior. Chapter 4 explores what it means for customers to be perceivers and learners. It identifies elements of the perception process, customers' biases in the process, and the managerial uses of the perceptual process. The chapter also explains how learning occurs and how customers alter the basic process through simplification and complication. An important aspect of learning is customer response to product and service innovations, and the chapter examines this topic. Chapter 5 attempts to understand why people behave the way they do—the motivations for behavior. It identifies three facets of customer motivation—needs, emotions, and psychographics—and examines each facet in detail. Chapter 6 presents the current state of marketing knowledge about customer attitudes—the underlying psychological processes and the various theories that capture these processes. The chapter discusses the three-component view of attitudes and also explains attitude as a global concept. It dwells on the multi-attribute models of attitude formation and also explains the functional theory of attitudes. Knowing what functions an attitude serves helps us understand the deeper motivation of customer attitudes.

Having understood the different internal and external determinants of customer behavior, Chapter 7 describes how marketers conduct research to understand customer behavior. Several methods for conducting both qualitative and quantitative research are described in the chapter. The chapter also explores some recent innovations in marketing research—specifically, applications of virtual reality and the collection of data on the Internet.

Chapters 8 and 9 focus on "customer decision making." These chapters examine the choice process of individual customers, households, and business and government customers. Chapter 8 concerns individual decision making and identifies the steps in the customer's decision process, including the types of decisions relevant to customer behavior and the ways in which customers gather information. It presents several models for the process of evaluating alternatives and analyzes purchase and post-purchase behavior as part of the decision process. Chapter 9, on institution decision making, elaborates on the buying process of households, businesses, and government customers. Households are the basic unit of buying and consumption in a society, and the chapter discusses the influence of family members at various stages of the household buying process. Next, for business customers, the chapter discusses the components of the buying process, including the steps in, influences on, and participants in the process and their conflict resolution techniques. The government is a major customer in every country, and this chapter describes procedures and regulations that characterize government buying, as well as the challenges and rewards of doing business with the government.

Over a period of time, two important manifestations of customer behavior are relationship-based buying and customer loyalty. We discuss these topics in Chapters 10 and 11. Chapter 10 examines how and why household and business customers engage in relationship-based buying and how marketers need to respond to this emergent customer behavior. The model of relationship-based buying in this chapter discusses the antecedents (cost-benefit and socio-cultural factors) of and outcomes (customer loyalty to the supplier, increased buying, willingness to pay more, favorable word-of-mouth, and customer equity

## FIGURE 1.6    Conceptual Framework

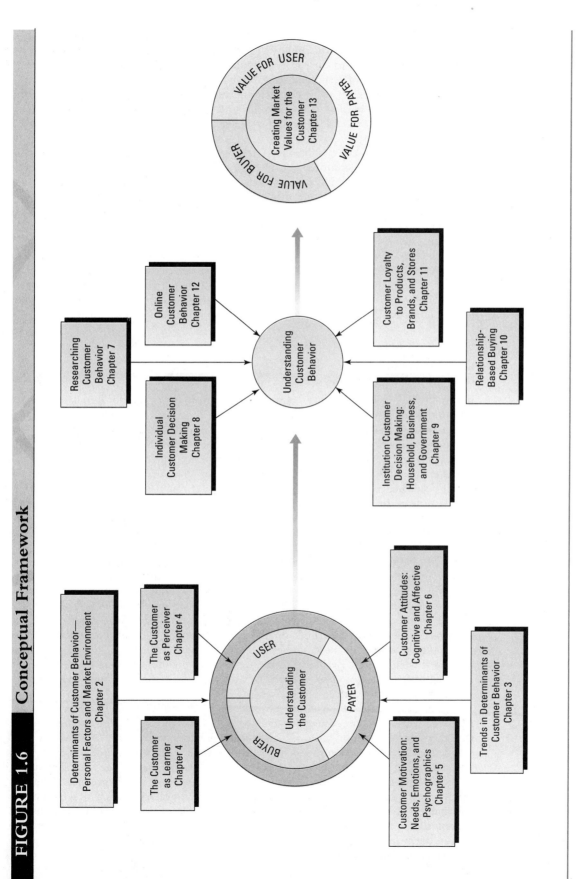

or goodwill) of relationship-based buying. The process of relationship buying in business markets is captured in the IMP (Industrial Marketing and Purchasing) model.

Marketers expect that their efforts should result in loyal customers, and Chapter 11 discusses the concepts of brand and store loyalty. The chapter presents a model of brand loyalty that brings together its diverse determinants. It also discusses the concept of brand equity and discusses its significance for marketers. Customers' shopping motives, store choice process, and the underlying factors determining customers' store loyalty are also presented in this chapter.

We have examined the influence of the Internet and the World Wide Web on customer behavior throughout the book. Chapter 12, on online customer behavior, looks at this burgeoning area in detail. It discusses the history of the Internet in brief and presents different facets of online customer behavior across the pre-purchase, purchase, and post-purchase stages of the customer decision-making process. Business-to-business models and e-procurement are also discussed, and, finally, some future trends in e-commerce are presented.

The final chapter, Chapter 13, identifies a set of action strategies for management to deliver each of the specific values sought by the three customer roles. Firms should attempt to differentiate themselves by exceeding on more than one type of customer value. The chapter urges customer-driven companies to constantly listen to the voice of the customer and continually strive to offer better value to their customers.

# Summary

In this chapter, you learned that a customer is a person or organizational unit that plays a role in the consummation of a transaction with the marketer or an entity. You learned why companies need to be customer-driven and what the managerial implications are to taking a customer orientation. First of all, creating and maintaining satisfied customers is the purpose of business. Second, according to the marketing concept, business should focus its efforts on the customer. Third, it leads to economic democracy by serving the society's needs better. Following a customer orientation results in a competitive advantage for the firm in the external market and success internally in producing a workforce that feels pride in its job. The competitive advantages in the external market are due to increased profits and revenue growth from satisfied customers. Increased profits come from the reduced costs of doing business with repeat customers, ability to maintain price premiums, and customer loyalty in corporate crisis. Revenue growth comes from increased favorable word-of-mouth, one-stop shopping, and new product innovations.

Customers play three roles: user (the person who actually consumes or uses the product or receives the benefits of the service), payer (the person who finances the purchase), and buyer (the person who participates in the physical exchange of the product with the marketer). The chapter then built on this role distinction to identify conditions under which the three roles of the customer are likely to be separated (i.e., the buyer and/or payer will be a different person from the user). The conditions include a lack of expertise, lack of time, lack of buying power, lack of access, lack of affordability, and situations where the product or service is free.

The next section of the chapter covered the needs and wants of customers—whether as users, payers or buyers. A need was defined as an unsatisfactory physical condition of the customer that leads him or her to an action that will satisfy or fulfill that condition. A want was defined as an unsatisfactory psychological or social condition of the customer that will lead him or her to an action that will satisfy or fulfill that condition. Needs are determined by the personal traits of the customer and by the physical traits of the environment. The personal traits of a customer are genetics, biogenics, and psychogenics. The physical traits of the environment are climate, topography, and ecology. Wants are determined by the individual context and by the environmental context of the customer. The individual context can be broken down into three areas: culture, institutions and groups, and net worth. The environmental context is shaped by the economy, technology, and public policy.

We then defined values as the potential of a product or service to satisfy customers' needs and wants. Two broad clusters of values were named—universal values and personal values. Each cluster has three values, one each for the three roles of the customer. The three universal values are performance value for the user, price value for the payer, and service value for the buyer. Analogously, the three personal values are social and emotional for the user, credit and financing for the payer, and convenience and personalization for the buyer. Consumer and business products and services offer a bundle of values in some or all of these categories.

We identified and described important characteristics of values. Values are instrumental, dynamic, and hierarchical; they work synergistically, are role specific, and vary across customers, and their diversity increases with hierarchy. We also introduced methods of measuring these values from a customer's viewpoint. This measurement would enable a firm to identify which values the firm needs to improve.

Finally, the last section of the chapter presented a conceptual framework that shows how the three roles of the customer are influenced by external and internal factors that, in turn, affect customer decision making.

The next chapter will look at the different determinants of customer behavior and how they affect the three customer roles.

# Key Terms

| | |
|---|---|
| Business Markets 12 | Market Orientation 6 |
| Buyer 14 | Market Value 19 |
| Consumer 12 | Marketing Concept 4 |
| Convenience Value 25 | Marketing Myopia 19 |
| Credit Value 24 | Need 17 |
| Customer 14 | Payer 14 |
| Customer Behavior 12 | Performance Value 20 |
| Customer Culture 4 | Personal Values 19 |
| Customer Orientation 6 | Price Value 24 |
| Customization 27 | Role Specialization 14 |
| Emotional Value 22 | Selling Concept 4 |
| Experiential Consumption 22 | Service Value 25 |
| Financing Value 24 | Social Value 21 |
| Household Markets 12 | Universal Values 19 |
| Instrumentality of Market Values 32 | User 14 |
| | Value Synergy 33 |
| Lifetime Revenues 11 | Want 17 |

# Discussion Questions and Exercises

1. Some consumer groups and consumer rights advocates have accused marketers of unfairly creating needs and wants by offering customers unnecessary and often

high-priced items. How would you defend the marketers' point of view that needs and wants cannot be artificially created?

2. You are the new marketing assistant to the vice president of admissions at a premier liberal arts college. Historically, the marketing program of this college has consisted of sending a college team to visit the various high schools around the country. On these visits, the college team meets with students during their class periods. This arrangement does not make it feasible for parents to be present, nor has the team considered it necessary. Write your boss a memo explaining why she should consider others (rather than merely high school students) as prospective customers and outlining the appeals that would make sense to these other customers.

3. Describe the process of measuring values. Design a questionnaire for measuring all customer values for the following products:
   a. Washing machine for household use
   b. Long-distance phone service in household markets
   c. Employee recruitment and outsourcing services for business customers
   d. Babysitting services in hotels for guests from diverse foreign countries where parents' child-rearing goals differ vastly

4. Find three friends or classmates to interview. Ask each of them about their recent purchases of the following items:
   a. Jeans or slacks
   b. Athletic shoes
   c. Jewelry or watch
   Ask them what value(s) they were most concerned with as they chose from different brands and whether they made trade-offs between values in their decision making.

5. As the director of marketing of a major international hotel chain, you are faced with increasing competition in your home country (the UK) as well as in other countries in which you are currently doing business and in those that you wish to enter. Your main concern is that customers be fully satisfied with the diverse customer values they seek from your offerings. Design a hotel management manual (which will also serve as a basis for all staff training) that would enhance your value-delivery potential to diverse groups of guests.

6. Using a toll-free telephone number or the Internet, call or access three international airlines that fly from the United States to Europe, Asia, and Latin America, and get a list of the different types of special meals that can be ordered. Use that information to discuss the importance of taking a customer orientation and how this might influence the prosperity of these airlines.

7. Interview the marketing managers of two companies, one that is operating in a very competitive environment and the other in a relatively monopolistic industry. Ask them to answer the customer orientation survey. Which company's scores are higher? Is your finding consistent with your expectations? Please comment.

# Notes

1 Katrina Burger, "Jesus Christ.com," *Forbes*, May 7, 1997, pp. 76–83.

2 Peter F. Drucker, *Management: Tasks, Responsibilities, Practices* (New York: Harper & Row, 1973).

3 Robert Blattberg and John Deighton, "Manage Marketing by the Customer Equity Test," *Harvard Business Review*, July–August 1996, pp. 136–45.

4 Jagdish N. Sheth, Rajendra S. Sisodia, and Arun Sharma, "The Impact of Demographic Shifts and Facilitating Technology trends on Future Customer Behavior," *Journal of the Academy of Marketing Science*, Special Issue 1999, http://www.jagsheth.com.

5  David Pecaut, Michael Silverstein, and Peter Stanger, "Winning the Online Consumer: Insights into Online Consumer Behavior," *BCG report*, 1/1/00 http://www.bcg.com/publications–search type =word and topic =ecommerce.

6  *Chicago Tribune*, January 13, 1994, Section 3, p. 3.

7  This was echoed by Adam Smith in his work, *The Wealth of Nations*. For a more recent discussion of Smith's thinking, see Athol Fistzgibbons, *Adam Smith's System of Liberty, Wealth, and Virtue: The Moral and Political Foundations of The Wealth of Nations* (New York: Oxford University Press, 1995).

8  For a very provocative essay on the role of consumers in business democracy, see Roger A. Dickinson, *Consumer Citizenship: The United States, Business and the Contemporary World* (in press), and also Roger A. Dickinson and Stanley C. Hollander Dickinson, "Consumer Votes," *Journal of Business Research* 23 (1991), pp. 9–20.

9  Ajay K. Kohli and Bernard J. Jaworski, "Market Orientation: The Construct, Research Propositions, and Managerial Implications," *Journal of Marketing* 54 (April 1990), p. 3.

10  Frederick E. Webster, Jr., "The Changing Role of Marketing in the Corporation," *Journal of Marketing* 56, No. 4 (October 1992), pp. 1–17.

11  Jagdish Sheth, "Competitive Advantages through Customer Satisfaction," *BMA Review* 2, No. 1 (January–February 1991), pp. 13–25.

12  Robert G. Cooper, "New Products: What Distinguishes the Winners?" *Research-Technology Management* 33 (November/December 1990).

13  Roger L. Desatnick, *Keep the Customer* (Boston: Houghton-Mifflin Co., 1990), p. 4.

14  "Customer Loyalty-Key to E-commerce Profitability," March 30, 2000, http://cyberatlas.internet.com/markets/retailing/article/0,,6061_331431,00.html.

15  E. Brynjolfsson and M. Smith (1999), "Frictionless commerce? A comparison of Internet and conventional retailers," Working paper January, http://ecommerce.mit.edu/papers/friction/friction.pdf.

16  Hal Rosenbluth with Diane McFerrin Peters, *The Customer Comes Second* (New York: Morrow Publishing Co., 1992).

17  Adapted from Philip Kotler, *Marketing Management, Analysis, Planning, Implementation and Control*, 9th ed. p. 190 (New Jersey: Prentice Hall, 1997), Richard P. Bagozzi, Jose Antonio Rosa, Kirti Sawhney Celly, and Francisco Coronel, *Marketing Management* p. 252 (New Jersey: Prentice Hall, 1998).

18  Berkman and Gilson (1986) recognize the terms *consumer* and *buyer* but align this distinction with the household versus institutional settings, respectively; we view the terms to be separate in both settings. Runyon and Stewart (1987) also recognize that sometimes the buyer may be different from the user, but they elect to use the single term *consumer* to include both the roles. Likewise, Solomon (1992), while recognizing the separation of the buyer and user roles in some situations, uses the term *consumer* inclusively to encompass the processes of buying, having, and being. See Harold W. Berkman and Christopher Gilson, *Consumer Behavior: Concepts and Strategies* (Boston: Kent Publishing Company, 1986), p. 7; Kenneth E. Runyon and David W. Stewart, *Consumer Behavior And the Practice of Marketing* (Columbus: Merrill Publishing Company, 1987), p. 5; Michael R. Solomon, *Consumer Behavior: Buying, Having, and Being* (Boston: Allyn and Bacon, 1992), pp. 4–5.

19  John Hagel III and Marc Singer, *Net Worth*, (Boston, Mass.: Harvard Business School Press, 1999).

20  "Small Businesses Buy, But Shy to Sell, Online," May 17 2000, http://cyberatlas.internet.com/markets/smallbiz/article/0,,10098_365281,00.html.

21 Banwari Mittal and Jagdish N. Sheth, *ValueSpace, Winning the Battle for the Market Leadership, Lesson from the World's Most Admired Companies*, (McGraw Hill, 2001).

22 Theodore Levitt, *Marketing Imagination* (The Free Press, 1985).

23 Vast consumer research literature exists on the role of situation in consumer behavior. For example, see Russell W. Belk, "Situational Variables and Consumer Behavior," *Journal of Consumer Research* 2 (December 1975), pp. 157–64; Richard J. Lutz, "On Getting Situated: The Role of Situational Factors in Consumer Research," *Advances in Consumer Research* 7 (1980); Joseph A. Cote and John K. Wong, "The Effect of Time and Situational Variables on Intention-Behavior Consistency," *Advances in Consumer Research* 11 (1984), pp. 374–75; U. N. Umesh and Joseph A. Cote, "Influence of Situational Variables on Brand Choice Models," *Journal of Business Research* 16 (March 1988), pp. 91–100.

24 Roger S. Mason, *Conspicuous Consumption: A Study of Exceptional Consumer Behavior* (New York: St. Martin's Press, 1981).

25 Amy Stevens, "Does Monsieur Have a Reservation? Let Me See. . . ," *The Wall Street Journal*, December 6, 1996, pp. B1, B10.

26 Morris B. Holbrook and Elizabeth C. Hirschman, "The Experiential Aspects of Consumption: Consumer Fantasies, Feelings, and Fun," *Journal of Consumer Research* 9 (September 1982), pp. 132–40; Elizabeth C. Hirschman and Morris B. Holbrook, "Hedonic Consumption: Emerging Concepts, Methods, and Propositions," *Journal of Marketing* 46 (Summer 1982), pp. 92–101; Peter Weinberg and Wolfgang Gottwald, "Impulsive Consumer Buying as a Result of Emotions," *Journal of Business Research* 10 (March, 1982), pp. 43–57.

27 Valarie A. Zeithaml, "Consumer Perceptions of Price, Quality, and Value: A Means-End Model and Synthesis of Evidence," *Journal of Marketing* 52 (July 1988), pp. 2–22.

28 Milind M. Lele and Jagdish N. Sheth, *The Customer Is Key* (John Wiley, 1991).

29 Net Used for Financial Research, November 17, 1998, http://cyberatlas.internet.com/markets/finance/article/0,,5961_152971,00.html.

30 Cecile Leonard, "Hong Kong Supermarkets Woo Wet-Market Clients," *The Wall Street Journal*, 11/13/2000.

31 Edward M. Tauber, "Why Do People Shop?" *Journal of Marketing*, 36 (October) 1972, pp. 46–59.

32 "Consumers Will Provide Information for Personalization," November 10, 1999, http://cyberatlas.internet.com/markets/advertising/article/0,,5941_236141,00.html.

# CHAPTER 2

## Determinants of Customer Behavior: Personal Factors and Market Environment

## Women Shop, Men Buy

In April 1991, a new magazine for men—*Full-time Dads*—appeared on the newsstand. It contained stories about the joys and frustrations of child rearing. Utterly familiar to women, these topics were largely new to men. At least until the 1970s, men in much of the Western world didn't spend much time shopping, cooking, or changing diapers. But in the 1980s, and much more so in the 1990s, men started sharing more and more in the home-making chores, partly because women were increasingly in the labor force, and partly because of a movement toward equality of the sexes. The old adage *Real men don't . . .* changed into *Enlightened men do. . . .*

According to a survey by Maritz Marketing Research, a U.S. marketing research company, only 45 percent of men buy all of their personal items, compared to 82 percent of women who buy or control all of their personal purchases. Retailers generally believe that while women shop, men buy—meaning that men don't enjoy shopping and that they don't do comparison shopping. Moreover, the objective men and women expect their purchased product to satisfy differs. As one clothing retailer has put it, "Women shop to look beautiful; men shop not to look stupid." Men are also less likely to be buyers of household products—cleaning supplies, for example. Only 28 percent of men buy these products, as opposed to 77 percent of women. Men have a greater motivation for knowing how things they buy work. Dubbed the "must-know" segment of men (some 25 percent of those with an annual income of $20,000), these men are good at do-it-yourself jobs and influence others about products.

In media, men read more newspapers while women read more magazines and books. Men also read more nonfiction, whereas women read more fiction. On TV, men watch more sports, action, or scientific programs, whereas women watch more daytime dramas, feature films, game shows, and sitcoms. Men are becoming more savvy about household products. And women are learning to buy cars, electronics, and power tools. Still, some activities remain mostly the "men thing," like watching sports or drinking beer. Eighty-five percent of beer drinkers in the U.S. are men.[1]

According to U.S. Census 2000, the number of single-father households rose 62 percent between 1990 and 2000. The increase in single dads outpaced the growth of single moms, which increased 25% in the same 10-year period. As more men join the ranks of full-time dads, household products previously bought mostly by women will increasingly be bought as much by men. The trend shows that gender as a personal trait will continue to affect customer behavior in a more profound manner in the twenty-first century.

Gender is only one of the personal traits that influences customer values and preferences. Personal traits refer to the characteristics customers possess as individuals. These can be grouped into three broad categories: genetics, biogenics, and personality. Race, gender and age are the three biogenic personal traits affecting customer behavior. The second set of personal factors affecting the customer is the personal context—the social, economic, and cultural environment in which the customer has lived and is living. The dimensions are culture, groups and institutions, personal worth, and social class.

Apart from the personal factors, two facets of market environment—natural (the market traits) and man-made (the market context)—also affect customer behavior. Market traits refer to the physical characteristics of the marketplace. Where customers live, purchase, and use products and services affect customer's needs and wants in all areas of life (food habits, clothing, tastes, leisure choices, to name a few). These influences are not merely weather-related, but are related more broadly to customers' habitat, including the climate, topography, and ecology.

In contrast to the three market traits, the economy and other aspects of the marketplace are created by humans as members of an organized society. We explore the influence of economy, government policy, and technology on customer behavior. We begin with the impact of economy—in particular, financial resources, customer sentiment, and business cycles. We then consider how various types of government policies and technology influence customer wants and behavior. Figure 2.1 presents the different external determinants, both personal and market-related, that affect the three roles of the customer—user, payer, and buyer.

Finally, we summarize how the dimensions of market environment and personal factors affect these three customer roles. With all this valuable information and statistics, this chapter covers some of the most important aspects that a marketer must realize in understanding customer behavior.

# Personal Factors

Personal factors can be divided into two broad classes—personal traits and the personal context.

Personal traits refer to the characteristics customers possess as individuals. The personal context refers to the characteristics of the social, economic, and cultural environment in which the customer has lived and is living.

## Personal Traits

Personal traits include those biological and physiological features a person is born with and those that develop as a person grows but whose origin derives from biological heredity. There are two types of personal characteristics: individual traits and group traits.

## Framework

FIGURE 2.1

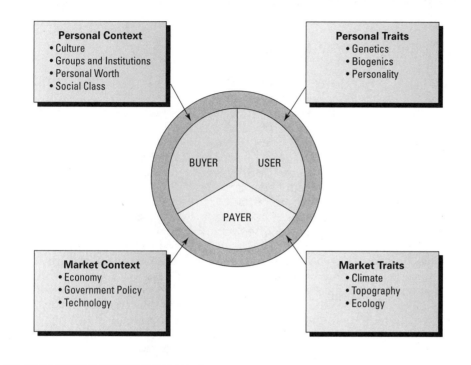

Individual traits consist of unique biogenic and pyschogenic aspects of an individual customer. The biogenic individual trait is called *genetics*. The psychogenic individual traits are called *personality traits*. Genetics are ascribed (i.e., a human inherits them from birth), while personality traits are produced by a combination of genetics, group traits, and a person's external environment.

Group traits consist of common biogenic categories including race, gender, and age. These are considered group traits because they are not unique to an individual; rather, they are shared by and describe a group of persons such as "all men 25 years of age." A person is born with these traits and does not have the ability to alter them. These group traits allow researchers to analyze customers at a group or segment level to see whether trends or significant differences exist between groups of customers with different traits.

## Genetics: The Cards We Are Dealt at Birth

Genetics refers to the biochemical heredity of an organism, specifically to sequences of chemical compounds in DNA. DNA, an acronym for deoxyribonucleic acid, refers to the chemicals in cell nuclei that form the molecular basis of heredity in organisms. Genes, or segments of DNA, synthesize the proteins of which the human body is made. In so doing, the 100,000 or so genes within each human cell provide the code that determines our characteristics. Currently, research is in progress on genetics and DNA, seeking to discover secrets of the human condition and behavior. The Window on Research provides information on the Human Genome Project that is currently extending the frontiers of research in this area.

Advances in neurology are uncovering various chemicals that regulate human emotions and behavior. These discoveries support the idea of **biological determinism**—the belief that human behavior is determined by biological factors such as genetics and DNA.

# WINDOW ON RESEARCH

## The Human Genome Project

Started in 1990, The Human Genome Project (HGP) is a 13-year project to map completely the entire spectrum of genetic materials that can be found in all human beings. It is a research effort initiated by the Department of Energy (DOE) and jointly managed by the DOE and the National Institutes of Health (NIH). The main goals of this project are to identify all of the approximately 30,000 genes in human DNA and to determine the sequences of the three billion chemical base pairs that make up human DNA.

Some of the most significant benefits of the HGP lie in the area of medicine. With the complete sequence of the DNA from a human cell, the HGP provides detailed genome maps to understand the critical differences that differentiate individuals and that often contribute to diseases. This information provides inputs to earlier detection of genetic predispositions to diseases such as inherited colon cancer, Alzheimer's disease, and familial breast cancer. At the same time, medical researchers will also be able to devise new treatments for these diseases with new classes of drugs, immunotherapy techniques, and possible augmentation or even replacement of defective genes through gene therapy. In 1994, the DOE initiated the Microbial Genome Program to sequence the genomes of bacteria useful in energy production, environmental remediation, toxic waste reduction, and industrial processing. This project is likely to provide information on development of new energy sources (biofuels) and on products and processes that decrease environmental pollution. It will also help pharmaceutical researchers understand how these pathogenic microbes cause disease, thus helping to discover better solutions to tackling these diseases.

Use of DNA information in forensics for criminal investigations is already well-known in the United States. Research on the HGP will aid this process by making it easy to use DNA-related evidence in exonerating innocent people and identifying criminals in trials. It also will help establish paternity and provide help in other family-related cases.

Genome identification for agriculture, livestock, and poultry also will help us create more disease-resistant plants and animals, increasing outputs in agriculture and providing the customer with more nutritious foods.

The Consulting Resources Corporation newsletter projects the large-scale commercial use of this data, and sales of DNA-based products and technologies in the biotechnology industry are pegged at $45 billion by 2009.

The presence of genome technology is bound to have societal implications, which are already evident in the discussions on cloning of humans. Hence, a program devoted to the ethical, legal, and social implications (ELSI) of genome research has been set up. As a part of this effort, a model genetic privacy bill was introduced into the U.S. Senate in November 1995, and parts of it have been incorporated into the Genetic Confidentiality and Non-Discrimination Act introduced by Senator Pete Domenici in June 1996.

There is no doubt that the Human Genome Project is a vast resource of information for consumer researchers on how genetic traits will ultimately affect consumers' marketplace behavior.

**Source:** The above section is adapted from several reports on the Human Genome Project information site funded by the DOE on the Internet. Please see http://www.ornl.gov/hgmis/ for detailed information on the project.

However, we need to note that other nonbiological factors, such as culture, perception, learning, and individual motivation, determine much of adult behavior as well.

Genetics affects customer needs and behavior by establishing the following four factors: (1) physiological differences, (2) diseases and mental disorder, (3) circadian rhythm, and (4) emotions and behavior.

The most direct and vivid effect of genetics is on a person's physical features and *physiological characteristics*—height, weight, skin color and tone, color of eyes, color and texture of hair, and bodily reactions to variations in temperature and other environmental changes (e.g., allergies), which are all caused by genetics. Genetics and biological makeup immediately affect human susceptibility to certain diseases. Diseases like Huntington's chorea, hemophilia, Alzheimer's disease, and schizophrenia also are caused by genetic factors. The effect of genetic makeup causes customers to seek special products and services, environments, and possible medical services and treatments to alleviate or cure genetics-produced diseases. All living creatures, humans included, have a daily cycle of activity, called their *circadian rhythm*. This biological "clock" governs rhythms like sleep-wake cycles. People's rhythms affect, among other things, when shoppers like to shop, and research also is examining whether consumers might process advertisements differently at different times of the day according to their circadian rhythm. Finally, many emotions or emotional disorders and behaviors also are rooted in biological factors. Twelve percent of U.S. children and teenagers suffer, for example, from brain disorders,[2] and many of these problems are based in brain chemistry.

An interesting debate concerns whether human behavior is determined by **nature** (biological factors) or **nurture** (the familial and social environment). Those who favor nurture argue that behavior is determined by a person's upbringing, family life, parental values, peer group influences, school, and church groups. The nature argument, on the other hand, credits a person's genetic makeup for much of human behavior: our emotions, sexual preference, tribalism, love of status, notions of beauty, sociability, creativity, and morality itself. Adherents to the nurture-based argument insist that we learn these behaviors by observing how we and others are treated. On the nature side of the debate, one particular factor that researchers have studied is the birth order of children. Birth order is the sequence among all siblings born of the same mother. Frank Sulloway, a science historian at MIT, has studied thousands of famous people of the last five centuries and has concluded that birth order matters. Specifically, older children are control freaks—aspiring, ambitious, and driven. Having no younger siblings in their family during the initial years, they identify with adults and learn to act responsibly and to maintain and enforce law and order. Younger siblings, in contrast, take themselves much less seriously and are more sociable, less judgmental, more risk taking, and more open to new things and to change.

## Race

*Race* refers to a person's genetic heritage group. A related concept is *ethnic identity*, which refers to one's ethnic heritage. In the United States, the Bureau of the Census specifies the following four race categories: (1) Caucasian, (2) African American, (3) American Indian and Alaskan Eskimos, and (4) Asian and Pacific Islanders. The U.S. Census asks for ethnic identity separately, and Hispanics are included as a category there, although they are not identified as a separate race. Another point to note is that not all Asians have the same genetic heritage and, therefore, are not the same race. Asians tend to mark the fourth category because they interpret it as a geographic identity group rather than a race. Thus, the U.S. government's race identification is an administrative designation rather than a scientific or cultural classification.

In the 1980 census in the United States, one in five persons was of nonwhite, non-European origin; in the 1990 census, this number had risen to one in four. According to a report by the U.S. Census Bureau, in 2000 there were 33.9 million African Americans (12.1 percent of the population), 35.3 million Hispanics (12.5 percent), 10.1 million Asians (3.6 percent), and 2.1 million American Indians (0.7 percent).[3] By 2010, one in three American children will be a member of a minority group.

Given such diversity, marketers need to understand the ethnic makeup of U.S. customers. The marketing literature identifies four race/ethnic groups in the United States: European Americans, African Americans, Hispanics, and Asian Americans.

European Americans—Americans of European descent—number about 200 million, about 4 million of them foreign born, representing some 15 countries of origin. Median household income is highest among those of French origin (<$75,000 for 40 percent of them), the majority of whom have been in the United States for more than 10 years.[4] The lowest income is among those of Polish origin (<$25,000 for about 40 percent of them), the majority of whom have had a U.S. residence for fewer than 10 years. European Americans are very competitive, aggressive, and explicit and direct in their communications. They seek and desire change and value youth and materialism. Not all Europeans think of themselves as ethnic, but many do, and this group exhibits different marketplace behavior from the other European Americans.[5] The ethnic Europeans work longer hours and spend the fruits of their labor liberally on material goods and on recreation such as cruises and gambling. Marketers have to adapt their mainstream strategies to reach ethnic Europeans.

African Americans number 33.9 million (12.1 percent of the total U.S. population) and are expected to grow to 40 million by 2010. Their median age is 30.6 years (compared to 38.6 years for whites).[6] In 1998, their average household size was 3.42 (compared to 3.02 for whites).[7] Many children live in single-parent families, and most of them are female-headed families. The median annual household income (3-year average 1997–99) of this group is $26,608 compared to $43,287 for whites.[8] The U.S. Department of Commerce has found that a child in a low-income white family is three times more likely to have Web access than a low-income African-American child. African Americans are the smallest group online (32 percent) compared to whites (45 percent).[9] Apart from income and education differences that lead to the smaller online population, another reason could be that general purpose search agents may not be perceived as an effective way to locate Web content that is compelling to African-American users.[10] Some exclusive sites on the Net for African Americans are **http://netnoir.com**, and **http://www.everything black.com**. Family and religious values are very important to African Americans. They are self-image conscious and like to display style. They tend to buy premium brands; they buy premium liquor and gold as status symbols. African Americans enjoy shopping, using it as a social occasion. Compared to the general population, they spend disproportionately more on clothing, shoes, and home electronics. African Americans tend to drink regular colas, flavored drinks, and high-sugar drinks. They also account for one-third of the U.S. consumption of malt liquor. Marketers have not directed much of their resources to African Americans in products, or in TV or print advertisements. Until recently, cosmetic companies marketed the same makeup products for whites and African Americans, and their children had to make do with white dolls, white cartoons, and white fairy tales. Now, however, there are special media such as the Black Entertainment Television (BET) network and magazines such as *Ebony, Essence, Black Enterprise, Emerge,* and *YSB.*

With over 35.3 million in number in 2000, Hispanics are an important customer group in America. Growing at the highest rate of any ethnic majority, they are estimated to become the single largest ethnic minority group in the United States by 2010. They are the youngest of all groups, with a median age of 26.6 years. There are four major subgroups—Mexicans, Puerto Ricans, Cuban Americans, and Dominicans. Hispanic median income (1997–1999 average) is $29,110. Though these groups share a broadly common language, cultural values, and customs, there are many important differences in tastes and activities. On Web penetration parameters, Hispanics are just slightly better than African Americans with an online presence of 38 percent.[11] Some exclusive Web sites for Hispanics are *Hispanic Online* (**http://www.hispaniconline.com**), which offers chat rooms, message boards and news, events, job availabilities and issues of interest to the Latino community based on its publication, *Hispanic* Magazine, a monthly for and about Latinos. Family and children are very important to Hispanics and take precedence over work. Hispanics, both men and women, have a strong interest in appearance, and they are fascinated by technology. Since good looks and appearance are important to Hispanics, they are heavy buyers and users of cosmetics and toiletries, much more than mainstream America. Since

Hispanics are close-knit and community-oriented, word of mouth is very effective for them; hence, event marketing (sweepstakes, music festivals, sporting events, religious holidays) is a good tool. In mass media, Spanish TV and magazines such as *Hispanic* and *Hispanic Business* are important. From a marketing communications standpoint, the most significant common factor among the Hispanic customers of different origins is their common language, Spanish. To account for differences among Hispanic groups, Donnelley Marketing Information Services (DMIS) in Stanford, Connecticut, has identified as many as 18 segments. For example, two of those segments are "Puerto Rican, high-income, younger, established homes" and "Mexican, lowest-income, younger, low-mobility, Hispanic neighborhoods."[12] Such micro-segmentation helps local, regional, and national marketers temper national campaigns with local variations.

Between 1980 and 1990, the Asian-American population more than doubled, and it doubled yet again by 2000 to 10.8 million. According to the U.S. 2000 Census, Asian Americans' median age is 32.4 years, and they have the highest median household income, $48,614 (3-year average, 1997–1999). They also have a high rate of completing college, 39 percent compared to 17 percent U.S. average. Forrester Research estimates show that about 74 percent of Asian Americans were online by the end of the year 2000. They lead the digital revolution primarily because they are wealthier and better educated than any other ethnic group in the United States, even whites.[13] The Asian-American group comprises immigrants from several countries: Chinese Americans (23 percent), Filipinos (19 percent), Japanese (12 percent), Asian Indian (11 percent), Korean (11 percent), and Vietnamese (14 percent).

Confucianism has a big influence on many Chinese. This system of beliefs values hard work, long-term reciprocal relationships, respect for authority (especially teachers and parents), harmony in all things, and discipline or delaying gratification. Core Japanese-American values are hard work, loyalty to the group (work, employer, family, community, or whichever group they join), an obligation to return favors, and respect for age and tradition. Education is also valued highly. Filipinos share many cultural traits with Hispanics: family values, courtship rituals, and allowing enough "play" time; they are outgoing and sociable. Korean Americans are very hardworking and value family loyalty, education, frugality and respect for elders. Koreans prefer *Kye*, a system of borrowing from individuals rather than from banks or government. More than any other minorities, Koreans prefer to maintain their own culture, resisting assimilation. Among Asian Indians, one of the most remarkable traits is a faith in the Hindu philosophy of Karma. Karma, a gospel from Hindu Lord Krishna, emphasizes two seemingly contradictory dictums: (1) a person is predestined to get and achieve whatever is his or her due, based upon his or her deeds in a previous life, or, otherwise, whatever the God has willed for him or her; and (2) at the same time, it is a person's duty to do his or her work diligently since the work, too, is willed by God. Karma does not imply fatalism; it urges people not to shirk effort but to make peace with whatever is the outcome of their effort. Asian Indians value their families, are deeply religious, and like to maintain their traditions and customs. They are also hardworking and ambitious. Among Asians in general, humility and self-denial for the sake of the group are valued.

Marketplace behavior of Asian Americans differs from the mainstream population as well as from other racial/ethnic minorities. Some examples are:

- Japanese Americans are very sophisticated consumers, have a good deal of money to spend, and buy high-quality mainstream brands.
- Many Asian Indians are vegetarians. But even among those who are not, Hindus will not eat beef, and Muslims will not eat pork or drink alcohol. Many Indians prefer Pizza Hut to McDonald's.
- Saving face is important to Asians. Therefore, they do not take kindly to advertisements that disparage a competitor's product. It is considered bad to make someone (e.g., a competitor) lose face.
- In Hawaii, Chinese tend to pay cash for a car, whereas Japanese tend to finance it.
- Koreans prefer a soft sell and face-to-face shopping. Koreans will, however, say "no" more directly than other Asians.

Language obviously is a key factor in targeting ethnic customers. Marketing communications need to be in the language with which minorities feel the most comfortable. But targeting ethnic groups goes beyond a simple language translation; communications should reflect the particular minorities' cultural values and marketplace norms. Local marketers should organize their promotions around ethnic events like the Moon Festival banquet for Chinese and Deepawali for Asian Indians.

## Gender

Gender is a biogenic group trait that divides customers into two groups—males and females. This group trait remains constant throughout a person's life, and it influences customer values and preferences. Concerning food, gender differences exist in health-oriented perceptions of foods and beverages. Women tend to buy fresh vegetables, lo-cal foods, and diet drinks more than men do.

In clothing, men-women differences exist with respect to color, fabric, and style. Certain fabrics, like chiffon or silk, are predominantly used in women's clothing. Bright full-spectrum colors are usually used for women, whereas men are mostly clothed in white, blue, black, brown, and gray.

Men-women differences in shelter preferences also are well known. In the purchase of a house, women are generally more concerned with such functional features as the amount of closet space in bedrooms, the size and shape of the kitchen, and the proximity of the house to a playground. Men, on the other hand, have historically been more concerned about the heating, cooling, and electrical systems and the kind of building material utilized. Marketers should, however, be watchful for changes in gender-based preferences since many of the traditional gender roles in the United States are changing. Today, a large number of men are buying groceries, and women are buying cars. By the early 1990s, women had become 49 percent of all new car buyers, and they exercise an influence on some 80 percent of all new car sales. So car makers are paying attention to women's needs in terms of design and customer contact.[14]

In businesses, men-women differences also are relevant to career paths, benefits, and support services. Men-women differences are moderated by life cycle, education, and income. Sex differences between pre-puberty children are very minimal, but they begin to materialize significantly as a child moves into the teenage years, and even more significantly as the person moves into young adulthood and parenthood. However, as a person moves into retirement, the differences become less acute as the pressures to conform to societal norms become less important. Education also moderates gender differences so that the role differences between men and women tend to be less pronounced with education. Finally, income also may mediate gender differences. Higher-income groups (with better education and occupation) are likely to show reduced men-women differences.[15]

Internet usage seems to be quite gender-balanced, with women accounting for about 49 percent of the online population in the U.S. and men accounting for 51 percent. However surveys show that "women are 'seekers' online, meaning they go online for a specific reason, while men tend to be surfers or browsers." It follows that men tend to spend more time online while women visit fewer sites for shorter periods of time, and are loyal to these sites. Portal sites like *iVillage.com*, *Women.com*, and *Oxygen.com* provide information on all issues that women are interested in. Studies show that women in the United States make 80 percent of health-care decisions and 60 percent of the health-care purchases, and sites like *OnHealth.com*, *Allhealth.com* (an iVillage site) and *ThriveOnline.com* (owned by Oxygen Media) target women with health related information.[16]

## Age

A person's age, like the preceding two biogenic group traits, has monumental influence on customer behavior. In this context, age refers to the length of time elapsed since a person's birth. This is the chronological age, different from psychological age (how young a person feels) or mental age.

Age is perhaps the most pervasive influence on customer behavior. It is an important personal determinant to study for three reasons. First, both needs and wants vary immensely by age. Young people's needs and preferences in clothing, food, and automobiles differ significantly from those of older adults. Second, age helps determine the lifetime revenue from a customer. **Lifetime revenue** is the estimated revenue a firm may expect to receive from a customer over the customer's lifetime. For example, in the insurance industry, a firm makes money on a policy only after the policy has been in effect for seven years. In such instances, the lifetime revenues from a customer, rather than the initial sale, become the key consideration. The estimation of lifetime revenues obviously depends on a customer's age. The final reason for studying age is that changes in a population's age composition imply massive shifts in markets and in the values and demands of consumers in the aggregate. In particular, the aging of the population in the United States is creating great age diversity, with corresponding diversity in the kinds of products the market demands, and this diversity is likely to pervade in cybermarkets as well. A recent Annual Internet Shopper Study by Ernst & Young found that the online buyer age profile closely parallels the age distribution of U.S. households as a whole, except for a few percentage point differences in the under-30 and 65+ age groups.[17] See Figure 2.2.

**Identifying the Age Groups.**  There are three ways to classify customers by age groups. The first and most direct measure of age is to anchor the counting to the birth year, that is, chronological age-based grouping. The book *Generations* identifies four age groups in the U.S. population.[18] These are (1) The G.I. Generation—born from 1901 to 1924; (2)

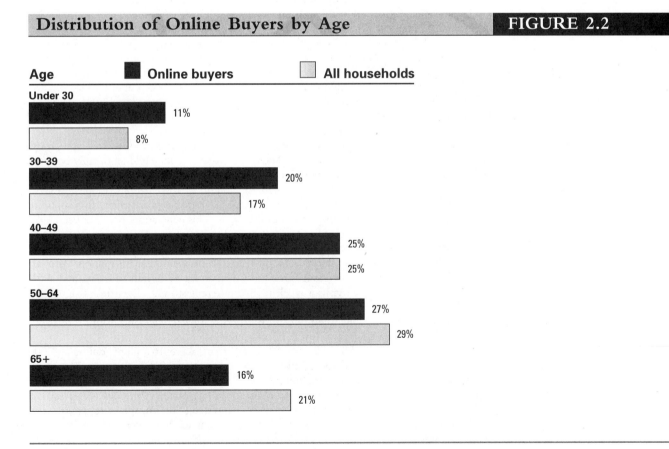

## Distribution of Online Buyers by Age                 FIGURE 2.2

Silent Generation—born between 1925 and 1945; (3) Baby Boomers—born between 1946 and 1964; and (4) Generation X—born after 1964. In addition, teenagers and children are important age segments for many marketers. Values and marketplace behaviors vary greatly among these different groups.

The *G.I. Generation* accounted for some 16.6 million persons in the United States in 2000 (of the total 63 million born). This generation has lived through the Great Depression in the late 1920s and World War II and has emerged triumphant and optimistic. Aided by the G.I. Bill, they have a financially secure life in their senior years. According to a survey done by Georgia State University's Center for Mature Consumer Studies, 32 million Americans aged 65 or over have discretionary incomes of roughly $7,000 a year, and a record number participate in leisure activities, travel, investing, and extending loans and gifts to youngsters in their extended families. For details on values of this age group, read the Customer Insight box.

The *Silent Generation* (some 42.7 million in 2000) faced the Depression and the World War crises during its youth. They believed in the success of the system rather than in individual enterprise, seeking secure careers in big corporations. This generation has enjoyed a life of prosperity and the lowest rate of any sociological evils (e.g., crime), all with minimum initiatives.

The *Baby Boomers* (82.8 million in 2000) are the most self-absorbed of all four generations. They desire anti-aging, anti-fat products, cosmetics, body shapers, and so on. As a group, they are more educated and affluent; their household income is higher than the average U.S. household income. Most of them are in the parenting trap with children under the age of 18. Employment rate among baby boomers is high among both sexes, and time is a major constraint, increasing the demand for convenient time-saving.

*Generation X*, the age segment born between 1965 and 1975 (39.9 million in 2000), is so named because of their negation of most Boomer values. Today, the early cohorts are young adults (ages 25 to 35) while the latter cohorts are youth (ages 20 to 24). Most of the Xers in the younger cohort are found on college campuses, military bases, and in their parental homes. Their music is not rock 'n' roll or classic rock or retro; it is rap, urban rhythm and blues, and industrial dance music. They are serious about education and enhancing their job prospects. They are more accepting of diversity in race, ethnicity, religion, language, and lifestyles. They support social issues, dislike hype in advertising, and reject conspicuous consumption.

Beyond the four age groups described in the book *Generations*, two more age groups deserve attention: teenagers and children. Today's teenagers are the children of baby boomers and are about 31 million in number. They spent an estimated $103 billion of their money in 1996 and, in addition, spent an estimated $33 billion of their parents' money.[19] Savvy marketers recognize the potential teens represent and have made special efforts to respond to their needs and offer them the market values they seek. This generation, born between 1977 and 1995, is also being recognized as Generation Y by marketers and is extremely Internet-savvy. The Window on Practice presents a profile of Generation Y.

In the United States, children 5 to 13 years old now number 35 million. According to a national survey of this group, children spend about $9 billion annually, and a 10-year old averages about five visits a week to five different stores.[20] Even more significant than their own purchases is the amount of influence they exercise on their parents' purchase decisions. This influence stems both from personal preference and from product expertise and is estimated at upward of $150 billion a year.[21]

Of the 31 million U.S. kids ages 12 to 19, there were 16 million online in 2000 (Simmons Market Research), and 31 million will be online in 2005 (*Computer Economics*). Teens spend 10-plus hours a week online and 20 percent have shopped online (Jupiter Communications). Some popular teen portals are *Alloy, Scour, iTurf, Bolt, Snowball and Bluetorch,* and they offer various features such as chat, email, fashion, sports, entertainment, e-commerce and more. A product's "cool image" tends to draw teens to sites and they share this information with their peers thereby bringing referrals to sites. An important problem with teen e-commerce is lack of payment options. Sites like *IcanBuy.com* and *Cybermoola.com* enable parents to create online accounts for their children, so that teens

# CUSTOMER INSIGHT

## How Mature Adults Differ from Young Adults

According to David B. Wolfe, the author of *Serving the Ageless Market*, as a person matures, his or her modes of thinking change. In early childhood, his or her cues to thinking come from within. During adulthood, the person is more oriented to cues from the external world. During mature years, the person tends to turn again toward internal cues, assimilating the external information within the internal cues from experience and values one holds.

Based on his research, David Wolfe believes that mature persons hold five key values:

- Autonomy and self-sufficiency
- Social and spiritual connectedness
- Altruism
- Personal growth
- Revitalization

Thus, to mature adults, direct benefits of products (e.g., clean hair) are less appealing than a product's role in fulfilling these values. Some examples illustrate this distinction:

1. Kimberly-Clark's promotion of Depend undergarments was hugely successful by showing an actress playing golf and going about her active life; in contrast, competitors promoted the functional features such as absorbency and were not as successful.
2. Freedom Group of Florida developed a senior housing community and recruited residents by having a mortgage-burning party signifying self-sufficiency and autonomy.
3. Mature adults tend to patronize mom-and-pop stores to a greater degree because their owners are able to offer them personalization and social connectedness.
4. Thrifty Car Rental Co. found that a donation to a social project was more appealing to seniors than a direct discount.
5. Elderhostel offers mature adults travel programs in conjunction with educational programs at universities worldwide; close to 300,000 adults participate annually in this personal growth and revitalization opportunity.

These examples show that marketers can benefit greatly by being aware of these values. Each communication and advertising campaign and each product offering should be preassessed on how well it reflects the values mature adults hold.

**Sources:** Adapted from David B. Wolfe, *Serving the Ageless Market* (McGraw Hill, 1990); David B. Wolfe, "Targeting the Mature Adults," *American Demographics*, March 1994, pp. 32–36.

without credit cards can still purchase goods. Teens have also been known to research products online and purchase offline because of a lack of credit cards. Hence, marketers need to focus on making the Web a branding and information vehicle for teen products.[22]

# WINDOW ON PRACTICE

## Generation Y

Generation Y, those born between 1977 to 1995, is the largest population sector in the United States since the baby-boomer era. Also known as the Echo Boomers, Digital Generation, and the Millenniums, they account for 21 percent of the U.S. population. They are racially diverse, one in three is not Caucasian, and one in four lives in a single-parent household.

"This generation is destined to eat, breathe, and sleep online." According to a survey by the Fortino Group, Generation Y kids (aged 10 to 17) will be associated with the Internet for an average of 23 years of their lives. The adult cohort of Generation Y (young adults aged 18 to 23) is adept at using the Internet for information search and e-commerce. As Bob Reiner, unit manager of Enterprise Internet Services with State Farm puts it—"This is the first generation to truly internalize the Internet, as opposed to other generations that have adopted it."

Marketers are cognizant of this characteristic when they deal with Generation Y members. More and more companies are using the Internet as a marketing tool to target young people. Given the sophisticated nature of the digital media that they are exposed to, they are more tuned to merchandise concepts that involve "exploring the unknown" or focus on "co-production" in terms of developing their own products.

In terms of their Internet usage, Generation Y and Generation X customers are quite similar. Brand loyalty is important to Generation Y and they prefer ordering online to ordering on the phone. However, Generation Y customers are "harder to please" and account for higher product returns compared to older customers. Most of the Generation Y consumers have Internet access

Another approach to classifying the age is based on a person's school year. Categories include preschoolers (under 6 years of age), primary and secondary schoolers (6 to 18 years old), college students (18 to 25 years old), adults (26 to 45 and 45 to 65), and mature adults (over 65). This approach to classifying age is a good approach if the interest is in measuring the impact of outside influences (as well as continuing family influences) on the development of a person.

The third approach is the **family life cycle concept**. This concept captures the movement of individuals and families as they go through major life events (e.g., marriage, divorce, birth of a baby, death, and so on). Some of these stages are, illustratively, single persons, families with young children, and empty nesters whose children are living on their own. Each of these and other stages characterize the commonalties that exist among the families in that stage. For example, a young single person is characterized by having relatively low earnings and, therefore, very little discretionary income. Newly married couples are more financially well off if both spouses work, and they buy such products as automobiles, clothing, and vacations. However, married couples with very young children tend to experience tremendous time pressure (particularly if both spouses are working) and consequently seek time-saving products and services. Empty nesters tend to spend a greater part of their discretionary income on vacations and recreation and also become more health oriented. Thus, the family life cycle-based classification of age offers marketers valuable insights into the consumption patterns of customers as they move from one age group to the next.

and convenience is a key motivation for shopping on the Internet. More than 33 percent are satisfied with their online shopping experience.

A Saatchi & Saatchi study found today's youth to be "confident, self-reliant, optimistic, and positive." Despite being the 'cool' generation, they retain family values—they want to marry, have children, and own a home. They admire attributes such as honesty, caring in others as against ambition or fashion ability, and pride themselves on their determination. They are looking for strong successful careers and want to play a meaningful role in the companies that they work in. They are very strong on the concept of "work/life balance."

Marketers' research processes to study Generation Y need to take a more indirect approach than direct. Projective techniques could be used to gather information about Generation Y peers and focus groups can be conducted with groups of friends in their homes, or malls, music festivals, and clubs where the generation normally hangs out. It would be worthwhile for marketers to look for Generation Y opinion leaders and interview them to get an idea of trends. As John Almash, president of Stratcom, a Massapequa, N.Y.-based marketing consultancy puts it—"Marketing campaigns to Generation Y would be best low-key and sincere, as this group does not want to be controlled—they would like to be addressed as people who can figure out things for themselves."

**Sources:** Adapted from "Generation Y Web Shoppers Emerge as Mini-Baby Boomers," *Business Wire*, May 9, 2000; Caela Farren, "Gen Y: A new breed of Values and Desires," *Philippine Daily Inquirer*, February 21, 2001, 10; Lori Chordas, "A New Generation in the Cross Hairs," *Best's Review*, February 1, 2001, 49; Kenny MacIver, "Connectivity from a Lifetime of Clicks," *The Times of London*, November 22, 1999, 19; "Generation X and Y Reveal the Future of Home Improvement and Repair," *PR Newswire*, September 16, 1999; "Landmark Study Identifies Generation Y Preferences," *Children's Business*, 32(1), March 1, 1999; "Key to Marketing Successfully to Gen X And Y? Break All Your Rules," *Card News*, Vol. 15, Issue 3, February 9, 2000.

**Intergenerational Differences in Household and Business Markets.**   The intergenerational differences among the age groups affect their customer behavior with regard to basic consumer goods—food, clothing, and shelter. There has been a significant change over the last 80 years with respect to what customers value. In regard to universal values that customers seek, there has been a general shift from a functional and economic orientation for the pre-war (G.I.) segment to a preoccupation with personal values by successive generations. With respect to food, the universal value of product quality is a driving force for all segments, except that the value of convenience-in-use is also very important for the Baby Boomers and Generation-X segments. The ability to use a credit card at the supermarket is a credit value sought by the Baby Boomers and Generation-X segments, in contrast to the two older segments. For clothing, the pre-war segment is more concerned with performance values like durability, quality, and universal price/economic value, whereas the younger segments, while not ignoring the universal values, tend to place greater importance on the nonfunctional personal value of social image associated with various items and styles of clothing. Among services, insurance is a good example of an industry where age plays a significant role in shaping customer desire for diverse market values. Customers from the pre-war segment have little need for life insurance because their dependents have already grown up. However, Silent Generation and Baby Boomer segments place much greater emphasis on the universal value for financial coverage as well as the personal value of the security for their loved ones in case of an eventuality.

In business markets, age has an influence on a service like payroll benefits, since employees look for different benefits from a company as they grow older. For example, a Generation X customer will want to start building a pension; in contrast, a younger employee, such as a Generation Y member, would be concerned with life insurance and disability insurance.

## Customer Personality

As mentioned in the beginning of the discussion on personal traits, personality is an individual psychogenic trait that affects customer behavior. *Personality* refers to a person's consistent ways of responding to the environment in which he or she lives. Everyday descriptions of people as innovative or tradition-bound, dogmatic or open-minded, sociable or aloof, aggressive or meek, are all references to these persons' personalities. Humans develop personality because it is efficient to build a standard repertoire of responses to one's environment, as opposed to developing a new response every time a situation arises. Some of these standard responses will apply to a person's behavior as a customer.

**How Is Personality Developed?**   Customer personality is a function of two factors: genetic makeup and environmental conditioning.

$$\text{Personality} = \text{Genetics} \times \text{Environment}$$

These two factors have emerged from separate streams of research: environmental determination and genetic determination. The leading proponent of environmental determination was American psychologist B. F. Skinner, and the leading proponent of genetic determination was British psychologist Hans Eysenck. Skinner's theory, known as **behaviorism theory**, is that a person develops a pattern of behavioral responses because of the rewards and punishments offered by his or her environment. Therefore, personality—a consistent pattern of behavioral responses—is formed and can be molded by a society by means of environmental shaping. Eysenck, on the other hand, considered biogenetic factors as important causes of individual differences. As an illustration of the genetic origins of personality, consider the trait of introversion/extraversion. Eysenck demonstrated that a person's relative introversion/extraversion depends highly upon arousal of the brain as mediated by the body systems. Introverts exhibit a more intense state of arousal than extraverts. With intrinsically lower levels of stimulation, extraverts tend to seek it in their external environment, "whereas introverts tend to avoid additional stimulation because their internal mechanisms are chronically switched to a 'high-gain' position."[23] For an example of research behind these views, see the Window on Research box.

In the psychology literature, two of the dominant theories for explaining the concept of personality are the Freudian theory of personality and the personality trait theory.

Sigmund Freud, the founder of psychoanalysis, was the first to argue that the human personality is driven by both conscious and unconscious motives (i.e., desires). He proposed three divisions of the human psyche: **id**, **ego**, and **superego**. The *id* is the basic source of inner energy directed at avoiding pain and obtaining pleasure and represents the unconscious drives and urges. The *superego* is the moral side of the psyche and reflects societal ideals. The *ego* is the conscious mediator between the id and the superego; that is, between the unconscious and impulsive desires of the id and the societal ideals internalized by the superego. The ego helps the person respond to the world in many societally acceptable ways, and such behaviors are called "defense mechanisms." For example, the id may want to own an expensive car, but the superego would remind the ego that, given the person's financial means, it would be unwise to buy an expensive car. To resolve this anxiety, the person saves his or her ego (sense of self) by arguing, for example, that an expensive car is a status symbol, used by people with not enough confidence in their inherent ability or talent. This argument, made to others or to oneself, is an example of a defense mechanism.

# WINDOW ON RESEARCH

## Genetics and Personality Traits

Why are some people thrill seekers while others lead a more subdued life? The answer lies in chromosome 11. Thrill-seeking behavior is affected, according to a recent discovery, by how brain cells process a neural messenger chemical called dopamine. The transmission of that chemical message is determined by a gene called D4DR. Individuals who have a certain kind of extra-long DNA sequence on part of chromosome 11 also score much higher on psychological tests measuring a personality trait called "novelty seeking."

This is the finding of two independent researchers. Richard P. Ebstein and colleagues at Herzog Memorial Hospital in Jerusalem examined 124 unrelated Israeli subjects, giving them a test that measures four personality dimensions—novelty seeking, harm avoidance, reward dependence, and persistence. The researchers took blood samples from each subject for genetic analysis. They found that subjects who scored highest on novelty seeking, characterized as impulsive, exploratory, fickle, excitable, quick-tempered, and extravagant, were much more likely to have the long seven-segment component of D4DR. In contrast, subjects with the shorter version scored significantly lower and tended to be reflective, rigid, loyal, stoic, slow-tempered, and frugal. The same findings were obtained in another study, conducted by Jonathan Benjamin and colleagues at the Laboratory of Clinical Science at the National Institute of Mental Health, who tested 315 American subjects.

The studies do not indicate that novelty seeking is controlled by a single gene or a number of genes. Upbringing, life experience, and numerous environmental factors clearly play a major role in complex human behaviors. Indeed, the researchers note that the genetic factor had a relatively minor impact, accounting for some 10 percent of the variance in the novelty-seeking behavior.

In another study of nearly 2,300 twins, psychologists at the University of Minnesota found that on a rating scale for happiness, genetically identical twins scored more similarly than even fraternal twins. A person's proclivity for being happy is explained, according to psychologists, only 3 percent by such factors as level of education, family income, marital status, and religious belief; in comparison, it is explained as much as 50 percent by our genetics.

**Sources:** Adapted from "Genetic Studies Suggest Connection between Heredity and Behavior," *The Buffalo News*, January 2, 1996, Tuesday, City Edition, p. 3A; Curt Suplee, "Researchers Find Personality Gene: Chromosome Pattern Markes People Seek Thrills," *International Herald Tribune*, January 3, 1996; Kathleen McAuliffe, "Born to Be Happy," *Self*, December 1996, p. 33.

To prevent anxiety, by keeping the unacceptable id impulses or other threatening material from reaching consciousness, the ego employs a variety of unconscious tactics:

- *Aggression*—To display anger or inflict pain on someone out of frustration and without justification. Example: A customer who suspects the retailer of taking advantage of a market shortage spoils merchandise in the store.

- *Rationalization*—To explain some action by a motive that is more acceptable than the actual motive, which is suppressed from consciousness. The use of corporate jets and country club memberships are rationalized as needed for business efficacy although the real motive and reason in many cases is prestige and a personal sense of vanity.
- *Projection*—To blame others for a person's own shortcomings or to attribute personal feelings to others. For example, a customer breaks an appliance by wrongful use and then blames the manufacturer or the workmanship.
- *Repression*—To devote a great deal of energy to keeping a particular thought or feeling at the unconscious level. Examples of repression include situations in which consumers avoid products that are associated with unattractive situations and, at the same time, deny that association to be the reason for their choice. For example, products associated with a person's ex-spouse may be avoided.
- *Withdrawal*—When not successful in a situation, to simply withdraw from the situation. Thus, both household and business customers literally withdraw from associations, conferences, book clubs, and so on, if they believe they are not respected in those gatherings.
- *Regression*—To "revert" to childhood behaviors. At special sale events in stores where supplies are limited, many adults resort to fighting like children to get to the merchandise.

In the **trait theory of personality**, a person is viewed as a composite of several personality traits. A **personality trait** is a consistent, characteristic way of behaving.[24] Thus, compulsive people consistently and characteristically act compulsively; people with the personality trait of dogmatism consistently hold on to their beliefs; and variety-seeking individuals are constantly changing their preferences. Catell, a leading trait theorist, identified 16 fundamental traits that account for a person's behavior.[25] He termed these "source traits" since, in his view, these were the source of other "surface traits" or overt behavior.

Another set of personality traits is the Edwards Personality Preference Schedule (EPPS), which consists of the 15 traits. In fact, early personality research in consumer behavior used the EPPS to identify brand preferences of different consumer segments.

Yet another classification is made by psychologist Karen Horney. Horney grouped people into three categories: compliant, aggressive, and detached (CAD). The **compliant** type seeks others' friendship, acceptance, appreciation, and love, and tries to be likable and agreeable. The **aggressive** type, on the other hand, values personal accomplishment over friendship and seeks power and admiration from others. Finally, the **detached** person is independent-minded, entertains no obligations, and admits little social influence on personal choices.

The first reported study of personality traits in marketing was conducted by Franklin B. Evans in 1959. Evans used the EPPS measures to examine whether Ford and Chevy owners differed in their personality traits, but he failed to find any personality differences. Three years later, another researcher, Westfall, attempted the same study with a different personality measure and found no difference between owners of Ford and Chevrolet brands. However, he did find personality differences between owners of convertible and standard/compact models. For example, owners of convertibles were more active, sociable, and impulsive, as we would intuitively expect. Another researcher, Joel B. Cohen, used Horney's CAD typology of personality to check for product purchase and consumption differences across the three personality types. Though differences were found for just 7 of the 15 categories used in the study, the study did reveal some interesting findings. For example, mouthwash and Dial soap were used substantially more often by compliants than by the detached group. Old Spice was the favorite deodorant of the aggressive type, whereas the leading brand, Right Guard, was the choice of the other two types. Aggressives used colognes more and preferred Coors beer, whereas the detached types drank tea more than the other groups.

Some consumer researchers have studied the personality trait of *tolerance for ambiguity*, which, as the name implies, refers to how comfortable a person feels with uncertainty and lack of complete information. Researchers Charles M. Schaninger and Donald

Sciglimpaglia found that consumers with low tolerance for ambiguity and higher self-esteem tended to use more product information in their brand-choice decision.[26]

Personality research in earlier years has suffered from (1) a lack of personality scales specifically developed for consumer behavior and (2) a lack of understanding on which personality traits should matter for which consumer choices.[27] Today, trait-oriented personality research has fallen out of favor with consumer researchers, who increasingly use a lifestyles view of personality.

**Personality of the Business Customer.**  In business organizations, people are not simply employees, co-workers, managers, or subordinates. In addition to their job titles and job responsibility, they have a personality that they bring to the work they do and, for our purposes, to how they play their customer role. They could be aggressive or subdued, fast or slow in their speech and movement, emotional or unemotional, and task-oriented or relationship-oriented. One apt personality typology for business customers is the "social styles" classification, proposed by Dr. David W. Merill of the research group at Tracom Corporation, Denver, Colorado.[28] This classification uses two personality traits:

1. *Assertiveness*—the aspect of behavior that measures whether a person tends to tell or ask and the degree to which others see that person as trying to influence their decisions. Assertive people take a stand and make their position clear to others. They are demanding, aggressive, and forceful. In social situations, they are likely to initiate conversation and display a take-charge attitude. In contrast, unassertive people are unassuming, contented, quiet, and easygoing. They tend not to express their ideas or beliefs, but instead to listen to others and to be supportive of others' ideas. The "telling" kind of individuals, when placed in an uneasy social situation, tend to "fight" or confront the situation. The "asking" kind prefer "flight" or avoiding the situation.
2. *Responsiveness*—a person's tendency to emote rather than control feelings and the extent to which others can see that person as an individual who displays feelings or emotions openly in social situations. A more responsive individual readily expresses anger, joy, or hurt feelings and tends to be warm, emotional, or lighthearted. The unresponsive, or the controlling types, tend to be reserved, cautious, and serious; to be independent of or indifferent to others' feelings; and to use reason or logic more in making decisions. An unresponsive person is more task-oriented rather than relationship-oriented, and the reverse is the case with the responsive person.

By combining these two traits, we can identify the four social styles shown in Table 2.1: driving, expressive, amiable, and analytical. The driving types want to dominate in interpersonal situations, want their opinion to prevail, demand compliance with their wish, and do so in a "cold" manner, without any regard for others' feelings. The expressive types also are opinionated and demanding of compliance with their requests, but they do so with emotions, using persuasion rather than authority. The amiable types are unassertive, undemanding, and easygoing, but they also are warm, openly show their feelings, and are desirous of establishing personal relationships with those they deal with. Finally, the analytical types are neither demanding and assertive nor emotional. They tend to ask questions, collect information, and study the data carefully before forming an opinion. This classification has been used in employee selection and in employee training to increase effectiveness in working with co-workers, subordinates, and superiors.

The following four social types display distinct behaviors, both verbal and nonverbal, that can be used to identify the social style of a customer in business negotiations.

## Personal Context

Our personal context—the characteristics of the socio-econocultural environment in which we have lived and are living—has intimately influenced our resources, tastes, and preferences. It therefore affects our behavior as customers by helping to define what we can and

| TABLE 2.1 | Classification of Personality Into Social Styles |
|---|---|

LOW
RESPONSIVENESS

LOW
ASSERTIVENESS

HIGH
ASSERTIVENESS

| Analytical | Driving |
|---|---|
| Slow reaction | Swift reaction |
| Maximum effort to organize | Maximum effort to control |
| Minimum concern for relationships | Minimum concern for caution in relationships |
| Historical time frame | Present time frame |
| Cautious action | Direct action |
| Tends to reject involvement | Tends to reject inaction |
| Amiable | Expressive |
| Unhurried reaction | Rapid reaction |
| Maximum effort to relate | Maximum effort to involve |
| Minimum concern for effecting change | Minimum concern for routine |
| Present time frame | Future time frame |
| Supportive action | Impulsive action |
| Tends to reject conflict | Tends to reject isolation |

HIGH
RESPONSIVENESS

**Source:** Adapted from David W. Merrill and Roger H. Reid, *Personal Styles and Effective Performance: Make Your Style Work for You* (Radnor, PA: Chilton Book Company, 1981).

want to use and buy. Personal context has four dimensions that affect customer behavior: culture, institutions and groups, personal worth, and social class. Of these, culture and reference groups influence customers' tastes and preferences, and personal worth influences resources. This quartet of contextual factors forms the conduit through which all customer behavior is channeled. Without an understanding of these contextual factors, it is nearly impossible to understand why customers from different countries, subcultures, economic means, religions, families, and other institutions seek different values from the marketplace.

## Culture

*Webster's New Collegiate Dictionary* defines culture as "the integrated pattern of human behavior that includes thought, speech, action, and artifacts and depends on man's capacity for learning and transmitting knowledge to succeeding generations." Thus, culture is everything a person learns and shares with members of a society, including ideas, norms, morals, values, knowledge, skills, technology, tools, material objects, and behavior. Culture excludes genetically inherited instincts, since these are not learned, as well as individual behaviors, norms, knowledge, and so on, not shared with other members of society.

We learn our culture by the processes of enculturation and acculturation. **Enculturation** is the process of learning one's own culture. **Acculturation** is the process of learning a new culture. Learning a culture entails becoming knowledgeable about its various elements.

- *Values*—Values are conceptions of what is good and desirable versus what is bad and undesirable.
- *Norms*—Norms are rules of behavior. They are a guide of do's and don'ts. Norms are more specific than values and dictate acceptable and unacceptable behavior.

- *Rituals*—Rituals are a set of symbolic behaviors that occur in a fixed sequence and tend to be repeated periodically. Being symbolic behavior, they have a meaning in culture.
- *Myths*—Myths are stories that express some key values of society. For example, the story of Santa Claus is a myth in much of the Christian world.

**National culture** refers to the culture prevalent in a nation. It comprises the norms, rituals, and values common to everyone in that nation regardless of the subgroup affiliation. A related concept is that of popular culture. **Popular culture** is the culture of the masses, with norms, rituals, and values that have a mass appeal. For example, Hollywood and the movie industry has had an influence on the popular culture in the United States. **Subculture** is the culture of a group within the larger society. The group may be based on any common characteristics (such as nationality of origin, race, region, age, religion, gender, social class, or profession) identifying that group as distinct from other groups or from the society at large.

Corporations have culture, too,[29] and it is reflected in a company's rituals and customs and even in corporate myths and celebration of its heroes. Values such as "People are important," "Merit matters," and "Prosper through diversity" define what success means in the corporation. Cultural heroes, such as Henry Ford at Ford Motor Co., Thomas Watson at IBM, Jack Welsh at GE, Richard Bronson at Virginia Atlantic, Herbert D. Kelleher at Southwest Airlines, and Steve Jobs at Apple, personify the culture's values and provide tangible role models for others. The current dot.com era has spawned its own culture in corporations, where 20-somethings in their faded jeans and pony-tailed hair teach their 60-something bosses how to communicate via the Internet as well as how to loosen their tie a bit!

**Characteristics of Culture.**   The concept of culture has the following six characteristics.

1. *Culture is learned.* We are not born with it, and instinctive behavior, which we possess since birth, is not culture. Thus, the act of crying or laughing is not culture; however, knowing when it is proper to cry or laugh in public is culture, since that is something we have to learn.
2. *Culture regulates society.* It does so by offering norms and standards of behavior and by sanctioning deviations from that behavior. Everyone in a culture knows the rules to live by.
3. *Culture makes living more efficient.* Because culture is shared (by definition), we don't have to learn things anew as we encounter new people and new situations within the same culture.
4. *Culture is adaptive.* Culture is a human response to the environment, and as the environment changes, culture is likely to adapt itself to the new environmental demands. Survival makes adaptation imperative. A U.S. firm doing business in Latin America, for example, would have to adapt its ways of dealing with Latin American customers or else face failure.
5. *Culture is environmental.* It envelops everyone's life alike and always. Like environment, we take culture for granted until something unexpected happens. That is, if a cultural norm is broken, only then is our attention drawn to the otherwise quiet existence of culture.
6. *Multiple cultures are nested hierarchically.* The culture of a larger group constrains and shapes the culture of the smaller groups within it. For example, the culture of a middle-income Hispanic family in the United States is actually the culture of the middle class, nested inside the culture of the Hispanics, in turn nested in the U.S. culture.

**Dimensions of Cross-Cultural Values.**   Although culture includes a host of shared beliefs and behaviors, the bedrock of culture is values. Cultural values may apply to things, ideas, goals, and behaviors. Based on research in a number of countries, Dutch social scientist Geert Hofstede has developed a classification of value orientations with the following five dimensions: individualism/collectivism, power distance, uncertainty avoidance, masculinity/femininity, and abstract or associative thinking.[30]

*Individualism versus collectivism* concerns the value individuals place on their own individual advancement and benefits versus the good of the groups and institutions of which they are members. Cultures marked with individualism exhibit loose ties among individuals, self-interest over the group interest, a large amount of personal freedom, and survival of the fittest. Contrarily, cultures of collectivism exhibit close ties between individuals, group interest over self-interest, a limited amount of personal freedom, and group protection. The United States is an example of individualism, whereas Asian societies value collectivism. One implication of this cultural value is the kinds of emotional appeals that will influence consumers in these two societies. Emotional appeals can be ego-focused— associated with the internal state such as pride, happiness, anger, and frustration. Or emotional appeals can be other-focused—associated with others in a social context and including such emotions as empathy, peacefulness, indebtedness, and shame. It is well documented that in collectivist cultures (e.g., China, Japan, Taiwan), the self is considered to be inseparable from others and the social context. Hence, in an emotional experience, members of a collectivist culture would be expected to focus on interpersonal aspects of the experience, weaving the individual with interpretations of what other people notice, think, and feel about the experience. Consequently, in the collectivist cultures, other-focused emotional appeals would be expected to be more persuasive than ego-focused appeals; the converse would be expected for individualistic cultures. However, at least one research study found this not to be true. Researchers Jennifer Aaker and Patti Williams examined the persuasive effect of emotional appeals on members of a collectivist culture (China) versus an individualistic culture (the United States). They found that ego-focused emotional appeals led to more favorable attitudes for the members of the collectivist culture than other-focused emotional appeals. In this study, when the Chinese participants from the collectivist culture encountered the ego-focused emotional appeal (on a one-to-one basis, as a form of a print advertisement rather than in the presence of others), it actually prompted them to access several parts of their independent self, thus leading to an increase in individual thoughts. Hence, the ego-focused appeal led to more favorable attitudes than the other-focused appeal. The reverse was true of the U.S. participants in the study.[31] Obviously, the way in which the individualistic and collectivist values play out depends on a number of other factors.

*Power distance* refers to the extent of social inequality and the extent of submissive relationship with authority. In cultures with large power distance, there is greater authoritarianism among persons of different strata in the larger population, among members of the family, and among managerial hierarchy in organizations. Whereas in cultures with small power distance, there is greater egalitarianism among those same groups. Consequently, decision making is more participative.

Power distance also refers to the extent to which personal relationships are allowed to be formed between members holding different levels of power and authority. In societies with large power distance, subordinates are required to maintain a distance from their superiors and always act in a subservient way. In societies with small power distance, relations between members at different vertical ranks are not as formal. Some countries with large power distance are Egypt, Guatemala, India, Iraq, and Malaysia. Some countries with small power distance are Canada, the United States, Germany, Great Britain, Israel, and Switzerland, to name a few.

*Uncertainty avoidance* can be defined as the extent to which people in a society feel the need to avoid ambiguous situations. They try to manage these situations by providing explicit and formal rules and regulations, rejecting novel ideas, and accepting the existence of absolute truths and superordinate goals in the context of work organization.

Uncertainty avoidance is directly related to the importance of quality assurance and service guarantees. People who cannot tolerate uncertainty would be expected to seek greater dependability, reliability, and guarantees when buying products and services.

*Masculinity versus femininity* refers to the extent to which male and female roles are segregated and the degree to which masculine roles are considered superior (masculine culture) or inferior (feminine culture). The United States is becoming a society free of this dimension, with greater equality between the genders. In contrast, Asian societies are markedly masculine. In a masculine society, dominant values are money, success, and material things. A feminine society more strongly values improving quality of life, preserving the environment, helping others, putting relationships before money and achievement, and thinking "Small is beautiful."

The fifth dimension is *abstract versus associative thinking*. Thinking cultures also differ in terms of the thinking associated with the creation of values in products or services; that is, whether values are engineered into them or added by associative processes, such as celebrity endorsement of the products and services. In abstract cultures, cause-and-effect relationships and logical thinking are dominant. Abstract cultures emphasize the use of the cause-and-effect relationships, face-to-face communication, field independence, and eagerness to change and innovate.

In associative cultures, people utilize associations among events that may not have much logical basis. For example, associative cultures tend to link events to the influence of gods or the supernatural or to link a personality (e.g., Michael Jordan) to a product or service.

Researchers Johnston and Johal map the Internet culture on four of Hofstede's cultural dimensions. On the dimension of power distance, the Internet culture leans toward low power distance since it is informal in nature, promotes interaction, treats every user as equal in status and power, and has no differential barriers for access to information. On the individualism-versus-collectivism front, the Internet is slowly moving from being of a collective nature (with cooperation, sharing, and free information to all) to being of an individualistic nature that is more commercial. As to uncertainty avoidance, the Internet culture scores low on this dimension as it is innovative, constantly changing with the introduction of new technology and tools, and it encourages interaction rather than acceptance. The final dimension against which the Internet is matched is that of masculinity/femininity. Johnston and Johal find it difficult to brand the Internet as one or the other since it reflects characteristics of both. The aggressive, competitive masculine nature is certainly present on the Internet as illustrated in e-commerce activity, and, at the same time, communities on the Net also exhibit all the caring, nurturing feminine characteristics for its members.[32]

## Institutions and Groups

Besides being part of a culture, customers are members of various institutions and groups, which form the second part of the customer's personal context. **Groups** can be defined as two or more persons sharing a common purpose. **Institutions** are more permanent groups with pervasive and universal presence in society, such as schools, religions, and the family.

Since institutions and groups influence individual behavior by serving as points of reference, as sources of norm, value, and conduct, they are also called reference groups. Reference groups are persons, groups, and institutions that individuals look to for guidance regarding their own behavior and values and whose opinion they respect.

**Types of Groups.**  Groups have been classified in many ways. The common classifications divide groups according to frequency of contact, nature of membership, formality, and group members' ability to choose whether they belong. Within the category of *frequency of contact*, there are two divisions: primary groups and secondary groups.

Primary groups are those a person interacts with frequently (not necessarily face to face) and considers their opinion or norms important to follow. In secondary groups, the contact is infrequent, and the norms of the group are considered less binding or obligatory. Examples of primary groups are family, work organization, church groups, business cartels, and so on. Examples of secondary groups are distant relatives and occupational groups such as doctors, lawyers, musicians, and theater artists.

A second dimension to differentiate groups is according to whether the membership is real or symbolic (the *nature of the membership*). Membership groups are the ones where an individual claiming to be a member is recognized as such by the head or leader or the key members of the group. In symbolic groups, on the other hand, there is no provision or procedure for granting membership, and the group leader or key members may even deny membership. However, the individual regards himself or herself to be a member and voluntarily and unobtrusively adopts the group's norms and values and identifies with the group. Examples of membership groups are family, the YMCA, and warehouse clubs, while celebrities and heroes as sources of inspiration may be symbolic groups to customers who emulate the norms, values, and behavior of their hero. As shown in Table 2.2 (the nature of membership and frequency of contact), these two bases for classifying groups can be combined to describe many groups.

## TABLE 2.2　Types of Groups

| | PRIMARY | SECONDARY |
|---|---|---|
| MEMBERSHIP | • Family<br>• Work organizations<br>• Church groups<br>• Fraternities/sororities | • Professional associations<br>• Credit unions<br>• Political campaign volunteers<br>• YMCA |
| SYMBOLIC | • Personal role model<br>• A significant other<br>• The person one "secretly admires" | • Celebrities<br>• Fortune 500 companies<br>• Other artists (for an artist) |

Groups differ on the degree of *formality* and whether or not the person has the *freedom to choose the group*, the other two ways to classify groups. In formal groups, conduct and behavior tend to be highly codified. Informal groups, in contrast, have few explicit rules about group behavior. A choice group, as the name implies, is a group a person voluntarily chooses to join. An ascribed or assigned group is one in which membership is automatic for someone who has the characteristic that defines the group. Together, these two dimensions lead to four types of groups as depicted in Table 2.3.

## TABLE 2.3　Classification of Groups for Household Customers

| | TYPE OF INSTITUTIONS/GROUPS | |
|---|---|---|
| | INFORMAL | FORMAL |
| CHOICE | • Volunteer groups<br>• Community<br>• Friendship groups<br>• Cultural heroes | • School<br>• Workplace<br>• Fraternities/sororities |
| TYPE OF MEMBERSHIP | | |
| ASCRIBED OR ASSIGNED | • Family<br>• Relatives<br>• Tribes | • Religion<br>• Prison |

Choice-based informal groups include neighborhood, community, social, and volunteer groups while formal choice-based groups include school, workplace, fraternities, and sororities. Membership in the assigned or ascribed group is usually by birth (family, relatives, or a tribe) or by some formal process, such as becoming a prisoner or being declared a minority for receiving government benefits. Since most people stay in their religion of birth, we consider religious groups as well as families as ascribed groups—the family being an informal institution, and the religious group being a formal institution.

This typology of groups applies to business customers as well. Informal but choice-based groups are "best in class" companies with which a business customer firm may consider itself to be affiliated. Informal ascribed groups are committees and task forces. Choice-based formal groups are professional associations, such as the American Marketing Association (AMA) or corporate country clubs. An example of a formal but ascribed group in a business setting is a business being identified as a small business and then being accorded all the privileges and responsibilities of the small businesses as a group.

**Family and Religion as Reference Groups.**  As stated above, the family is an ascribed informal group and also a primary membership group. It is undoubtedly the most influential reference group for any individual customer. Family can be defined as a group of people related by marriage and biology. Family is the institution in which children, the future adults of the society, receive their precepts and guidance. In families, members interact continually in intense and face-to-face communications, and member preferences and desires get constant feedback and are channeled and shaped by reinforcement or sanctions from other members. Families are important and influence customer behavior across cultures. The influence of family members on one another's buying decision process is discussed in a later chapter.

Like family, religion is a reference group that exercises substantial influence on customers' values, customs, and habits. Religion refers to a system of beliefs about the supernatural and spiritual world, about God, and about how humans, as God's creatures, are supposed to behave on this earth. Religious affiliation affects customer behavior principally by influencing the customer's personality structure—his or her beliefs, values, and behavioral tendencies. These personality structures, in turn, affect customers' marketplace behaviors.

**Conditions for Reference Group Influence.**  Behavioral scientist Francis S. Bourne addressed the question, "When or under what conditions does reference group influence occur?" He proposed that a product's or service's conspicuousness is the principal factor that affects whether or not users of that product of service will be susceptible to reference group influence.[33] Bourne proposed that there are two dimensions of conspicuousness: exclusivity and public visibility. If everyone owns and uses a product or service, then the ownership and use of that product or service has no exclusivity. Hence, there is no basis for being concerned about others' opinions of it. The second dimension, visibility, is critical because a product or service has to be visible and identifiable in order for reference group members to approve or disapprove it.

Based on Bourne's ideas, marketing professors and consumer researchers William O. Bearden and Michael J. Etzel have suggested that the reference group influence may occur for the ownership of the product per se, for the choice of a specific brand, or for both. This will depend on whether a product is a luxury or a necessity (capturing the "exclusivity" dimension in Bourne's proposal) and whether the product is used in private or in public (capturing the "visibility" dimension of conspicuousness). The following four combinations are presented in Table 2.4.[34]

1. *Publicly consumed luxuries*—In this case, reference groups will influence both whether or not the product will be owned and which brand will be purchased.
2. *Privately consumed luxuries*—Here, reference group influence will be strong for the ownership of the product (because it is a luxury) but weak for the brand choice (since it will be used in private, out of public visibility).

| TABLE 2.4 | Private–Public, Luxury–Necessity, Product–Brand Influences |
|---|---|

PUBLIC

| | | WEAK REFERENCE GROUP INFLUENCE (−) | STRONG REFERENCE GROUP INFLUENCE (+) |
|---|---|---|---|
| | Strong reference group influence (+) | *Public necessities*<br>• Influence: Weak product and strong brand<br>• Examples: Wristwatch, automobile, man's suit | *Public luxuries*<br>• Influence: Strong product and brand<br><br>• Examples: Golf clubs, snow skis, sailboat |
| | Weak reference group influence (−) | *Private necessities*<br>• Influence: Weak product and brand<br><br>• Examples: Mattress, floor lamp, refrigerator | *Private luxuries*<br>• Influence: Strong product and weak brand<br>• Examples: TV game, trash compactor, icemaker |

NECESSITY                                                                                                    LUXURY

PRIVATE

**Source:** William O. Bearden and Michael J. Etzel, "Reference Group Influence on Product and Brand Purchase Decisions," *Journal of Consumer Research* 9 (1982), pp. 183–94. Reprinted with permission of the University of Chicago Press.

3. *Publicly consumed necessities*—In this case, product ownership influence will be absent or weak since everyone owns it, but brand-level influence will be strong due to public visibility.

4. *Privately consumed necessities*—Finally, for products that are necessities and, in addition, are consumed privately, neither product ownership nor the choice of specific brands is likely to be influenced by reference groups.

**Types of Reference Group Influence.** Whether the reference group influences decisions about a brand or a product category, the influence may operate through several types of power. The nature of influence power exercised by reference group members may be of three types: expertise, reward and sanction, and attractiveness. Corresponding to each type of power is a type of reference group influence: informational, normative, and identificational, respectively.[35]

*Informational influence* occurs when a consumer seeks and accepts advice from someone else because of the latter's expertise on the performance characteristics of the product or service being bought. Professional advisors such as doctors, lawyers, or product enthusiasts among your informal groups are examples of informational reference groups. Business customers also seek and accept informational influence from legal, technical, and management consultants.

*Normative influence* occurs when a consumer's decision is influenced by his or her desire to conform with the expectations of someone else. This influence stems from the reference group's power to reward or sanction the consumption behavior of others. Family members exercise normative influence on our behaviors as customers, and businesses are subject to normative influence from the government.

*Identificational influence* occurs when a consumer buys something because it helps him or her to be like someone else. Everybody has a role model, and the consumer emulates, to the extent possible, the lifestyle of people he or she admires, buying products associated with, used by, or endorsed by these admired people. Entertainment, sports, or political celebrities serve as reference groups for multitudes of consumers. In business markets, identificational influences are at work when companies look to other corporations as "best in class," or the most admired companies, and emulate these companies to gain their advantages.

## Personal Worth

Along with culture and reference groups, the customer context that influences the market values a customer seeks includes personal worth. Personal worth is equivalent to the financial worth of a person.

**Measurement of Personal Worth.**   Personal worth has three components: income, wealth, and borrowing power.

A person's income is the amount of monetary earnings that person receives periodically on a more or less regular basis. Although no two families spend their money in exactly the same way, there is, on average, quite a consistent pattern of how income is allocated over expense categories. Statistical analyses of data from families with diverse income groups show that poor families spend their income largely on food, housing, and basic clothing. As income increases, people tend to eat more food, and more of the food is less staple, but the proportion of income spent on food declines. Proportion of income spent on housing rises with income in the very low income range, but then it remains fairly constant. Expenditures on clothing, automobiles, and luxury goods rise sharply with income until a very high upper limit is reached. Finally, savings rise dramatically with income, and they never decline. Similarly, in business markets, cash flows influence what will or will not be bought. Many small business failures can be traced directly to cash-flow problems. On the other hand, rapid growth also can create cash-flow problems from corporate acquisitions. For example, General Foods was built on buying out small local or regional brands and making them national brands, including Yuban, Maxwell House, and Sanka coffees and Bird's Eye frozen vegetables.

The second component and measure of personal worth is wealth. In household markets, wealth is assessed as the net worth of the individual. Net worth of an individual is defined as the current monetary value of all assets owned minus the current monetary value of all liabilities. Wealth is created by five means: (1) inheritance; (2) high-income accumulation, including "passive income" from investment of one's wealth; (3) employee stock option plans and 401K savings; (4) accumulation of nonmonetary wealth such as equity in home ownership, jewelry, or art; and (5) lottery winnings.

The counterpart of net worth for a business market is the concept of shareholder equity. Net worth is the book value of the business and may or may not be commensurate with the business's market value as captured in shareholders' equity.

**Borrowing power** is the final indicator of a customer's economic condition. In consumer markets, borrowing power is the anticipated level of income of the person (lifetime disposable income and asset accumulation through savings). Consumer credit cards, home mortgages, and automobile financing are based upon an accounting of the customer's borrowing power. The business market equivalent is the firm's ability to repay debt in the future and is measured by creditworthiness of the organization based on ratings by A. M. Best Company and Standard & Poor's.

Customers can be divided into three groups on the basis of their personal worth: poor, middle-class, and affluent, and customer behavior differs widely across these groups.

In general, poverty is a level of personal wealth at which a household cannot even pay for all its basic needs, such as food, clothing, and shelter. In 1999, this figure was $15,569 for a U.S. family of four.[36] The number of people below the poverty line was 32.3 million, representing 11.8 percent of the U.S. population.[37] Studies show that the poor do not follow wise purchasing strategies and actually pay more for goods and services than do the rest of society. This occurs because poor consumers do not have the skills and transportation to shop for bargains and because merchants exploit their weaknesses. There is no single definition of "middle income." One conventional grouping deems income levels of less than $25,000 as low income, from $25,000 to $75,000 as middle income, and greater than $75,000 as upper income. There is no universal definition for affluence. A convenient definition is to designate the top one-fifth of households as affluent. In the United States, this group's annual income exceeds $70,000, with the average income exceeding $100,000. The top one-fifth of the households account for 35 percent of all wine consumption in the United States, more than 60 percent of all airline travel, and 54 percent of all new car sales.

The income distribution of Internet users is slowly reflecting the economically privileged and unprivileged classes. Though research on the Internet population has found that Internet users, in the aggregate, have higher household earnings than the general public, this econo-digital divide seems to be closing. In 1999, according to *eMarketer*, the average Net household earned $57,000. In August 2001, the largest income group on the Internet was the $60,000–$100,000 bracket comprising about 28.4 percent of the population online. However, from about 1995 to 1996, the Internet population was divided almost equally among the income classes, with about 27.8 percent of the Internet population having an annual income of under $40,000, 25.8 percent having between $40,000 and $60,000, and about 18.1 percent having an income above $100,000.

Yet, it is evident that the higher-income group is more tuned to purchasing via the Internet. A comparison of U.S. households purchasing via the Internet in 1999 and 2000 shows that 53 percent of the respondents in the $50,000-plus income bracket purchased via the Internet in 2000 compared to 40 percent in 1999. The overall percentages have increased in the $35,000–$49,999 bracket (29 percent in 2000 versus 18 percent in 1999) and in the $25,000–$34,999 bracket (35 percent in 2000 versus 27 percent in 1999). However, as PC costs decrease, penetration of the Internet will increase in lower-income households, and online purchasing also will become prevalent in the lower-income groups.[38]

## Social Class

Many sociologists, consumer economists, and consumer researchers consider social class, rather than personal worth, to be a more meaningful characteristic to understand and predict customer behavior. Income is an important factor in deciding a person's social class, but it is not the only determinant. Social class also depends considerably on one's education and occupation so that, despite relatively low income, a highly educated person or someone in a more prestigious occupation could be accorded a higher social class, and vice versa. Social class is the relative standing of members of a society so that a higher position implies a higher status than those in the lower social class.

**Social Class Characteristics.** Some characteristics of the concept of social class are as follows:

1. *Rank ordering*—Social classes are ranked in terms of social prestige.
2. *Relative permanence*—Social classes are relatively permanent characteristics of the family. A person's social class does not change from day to day or even from year to year.
3. *Intergenerational class mobility*—It is possible for a person to move out of the social class of his or her birth and into a higher or lower class by acquiring the values, resources, and behaviors of the new class.
4. *Internal homogeneity*—Classes are homogenous within each strata. Persons belonging to the same social class tend to be similar in terms of the types of occupations, the kinds of neighborhoods they live in, their food habits, socializing, and so on.
5. *Distinct from income*—Though income is an important determinant of social class, there is no one-to-one correspondence between the two. Since social class depends as much on other factors, such as education, occupation, and personal tastes, it is not uncommon for a person of relatively middle income to be in the upper social class and vice versa. For example, priests, politicians in power, and educators command prestige and status significantly disproportionate with their income earnings.

**Social Classes in America: A Brief Profile.** Sociologist Richard P. Coleman and his colleague Lee P. Rainwater have developed a social-class grouping based on a study of 900 residents in the Boston and Kansas City areas.[39] They questioned respondents on their perceptions of the social hierarchy and their own participation in it. They found that the middle mass of citizens most readily talk in terms of "people like us in the middle," "people above," and "people below." The broad social groups in Coleman's scheme— Upper, Middle, and Lower Americans—differ markedly in their marketplace behaviors.

Typically, Lower Americans are "family folks," deriving their emotional and psychological support from family members and relatives. "Locational narrowness" marks their preference in housing, travel, sports, and news. They live close to their kin, travel nearby or to meet relatives, favor local sports heroes, and take interest more in local news than national news.

On the other hand, Middle Americans are most concerned with wanting to "do the right thing" and buying what is popular. Middle-class persons tend to emulate the lifestyles of the Upper Americans, and this "upward gaze" makes them patronize dinner theaters and other trickle-down culture. Physical activities are becoming core to middle-class life "in which possessions-pride has yielded to activities-pleasure."

Upper Americans are, as a whole, concerned with buying quality merchandise, favoring prestige brands, and spending with good taste. Two points about the Upper American group are noteworthy. First, a subdivision of this group has been identified and referred to by sociologist Irving Kristol as "The New Class." Consisting of media influentials (TV anchor persons, talk-show hosts, newspaper editors and journalists) and nonprofit professionals (educators and government officials), the members of this subgroup tend to be anticapitalists, and their basic thrust in ideology and consumption style has been to establish themselves above the Middle American classes. Marketing scholar Fred Webster calls them "socially conscious consumers."[40]

The second point Coleman makes is that, more than any other group, Upper Americans are a more heterogeneous group today: "Upper America is now a vibrant mix of many lifestyles, which might be labeled post preppie, sybaritic, counter-cultural, conventional, intellectual, political, etc. Such subdivisions are usually more important for targeting messages and goods than are the horizontal, status-flavored, class-named strata."[41]

# Market Environment

In addition to the personal factors described above, the market environment presents the second group of determinants that affect customer behavior. We divide market environment into two broad classes: market traits and market context. Market traits refer to the physical characteristics of the surroundings in which consumers select, use, and pay for products and services in both household and business markets. There are three physical characteristics of a place: climate, topography, and ecology.

Market context refers to the man-made market forces (as opposed to the nature-made forces) of the market as a physical place that affects customer wants and needs. It has three components: economy, government policy, and technology.

## Market Traits

The market traits—climate, topography, and ecology—influence customers' needs as opposed to wants.

## Climate

Climate is the first major component of the geophysical market environment. It consists of temperature, wind, humidity, and rainfall in the area. The patterns of these four elements vary on different locations of the earth, depending on latitude, the distance north or south from the equator. Research in the area of homeostasis (a process by which the body seeks to regulate its internal environment) reveals that certain consumer behaviors, such as mood and expressed affect, are influenced by variations in the intensity and duration of sunlight and temperatures across climates and seasons, respectively. Several other consumption behaviors, such as stimulation and sensation seeking, novelty and variety seeking, risk taking, and impulsivity, are related to the optimal stimulation level of an individual. The optimal stimulation level is a function of the interaction of three neurotransmitters in the brain whose release and synthesis is caused by different levels of sunlight and temperature (heat) in our atmosphere.[42]

In an attempt to maintain a thermoregulatory balance (an internal core body temperature of about 37°C), humans learn to cope with climate and climate-dependent availability of food, plants, animals, and building materials. This, in turn, intimately influences people's consumption of food, use of clothing, housing patterns, and the geographical distribution of population itself. Food consumption patterns differ dramatically between the tropical and arctic countries. Colder arctic countries rely heavily on animals for food as well as for clothing. Northern Europeans eat more red meat and fewer fruits and vegetables than do southern Europeans.

Striking differences in clothing are apparent across different climates with respect to materials, design, and style. People living in colder climates rely on wool and leather, while those living in warmer climates rely on cotton, silk, and other lighter fabrics.

Differences are found in customer needs for shelter. Colder countries utilize wood and stone as materials, compared to warmer countries that use clay and brick.

Climate also affects business customers' needs and purchases. All industrial machinery and equipment must be designed to withstand the climatic conditions in which the business customer is located. For example, heat, humidity, and dust affect the performance of trucks, tractors, and farm equipment. Computers and other machinery often need climate-controlled environments to perform.

In addition to climatic changes from one location to another, climate in any one place also varies throughout the year, causing the annual cycle of seasonality. Business sales vary from month to month in a calendar year. This seasonal variation is caused by three factors: (1) annual climate changes; (2) calendar events such as school year, football season, and so on; and (3) holidays and festivities. To a degree, the last two factors are themselves related to or influenced by the first factor.

The effects of annual climate changes on customer purchases are obvious. Customers need and buy warm clothing during winter and cool clothing during summer. Around the world, coffee, tea, and other hot beverages are purchased more during cold months, and soft drinks and ice creams are bought more during warm months. Calendar-year events impel other purchases. Some examples of purchases for a typical calendar year in a North American family with children are cold remedies during the January–February flu season, and allergy medications during March, the start of allergy season when pollen counts start. May begins the four-month-long summer season, where customers embark on outdoor activities, such as bicycling, gardening, swimming, and sports. Accordingly, they buy products related to these activities throughout these four months. June is peak season for weddings and graduations, both inducing purchases of party goods and other celebration merchandise. July and August are peak months for family travel, both vacationing and moving. August is back-to-school month, and sales of school supplies and children's clothing peak. November begins the early holiday shopping season, and December peaks the purchase of all kinds of retail items, including clothing, toys, books, shoes, and gifts. Holiday spending online for the year 2000 was $10.7 billion, more than double the 1999 total of $5.2 billion. Convenience (avoiding crowds), easier price comparison, wider product selection, and lower prices online are some of the reasons for this boom in online spending in the holiday season.[43]

## Topography

Another major component of the geophysical environment is **topography**—the terrain, altitude, and soil conditions of the market where customers buy and use the product or service. In addition to differences in food, shelter, and clothing across topographical regions, a number of other products and services also are needed principally due to topographical conditions. These include flood insurance, erosion-resistant foundations for homes, special water treatment plans, and different means of transportation based on terrain.

Consumption varies across different regions of the world, and indeed within a single country. Regional consumption differences are due to two factors: (1) geophysical conditions comprising climate, topography, and ecology and (2) cultural and/or ethnic heritage. To capture regional preference differences, it is illuminating to draw and study maps of regional variations in product consumption. These maps show **geographical variation**— different patterns of consumption in different regions. If we consider bicycling as a mode of commuting to work, the Pacific region has the greatest concentration, with more than 10 bike commuters per 1,000 commuters; Alabama, Mississippi, Tennessee, and Kentucky show the lowest rate, with fewer than 2 bike commuters per 1,000 commuters. These differences occur due to variations in climate, topography, and facilitative infrastructure such as biker lanes in city traffic.[44]

As against topography, cultural and ethnic heritage plays a major role in the variation in pretzel consumption in the United States. A significant proportion of the population of New York and the Mid-Atlantic states is of European heritage, accounting for the greater consumption of pretzels there.[45]

To address such differences, marketers may use a strategy of **regional marketing**— the practice of adapting marketing programs according to segmentation based on geographic differences among customers. The marketer recognizes customer diversity from one region to another and tailors the entire marketing mix to each region. For example, Campbell's Soup, whose chicken noodle soup is a runaway national success, has revamped its entire marketing infrastructure along regional lines. The sales and brand management is also set up along regional lines, and brand managers serve as the company's "listening post" on its consumers' regional preferences.[46]

## Ecology

The third market characteristic, **ecology**, refers to the natural resources and the delicate balance and interdependence among vegetation, animals, and humans. It also includes concepts related to the food chain. One of the recent concerns in the United States is what has been referred to as the greenhouse effect and global warming. **Global warming** is the theory that the earth's climate is becoming warmer due to increases in hydrocarbons in the atmosphere, which are released with increased industrialization.

Ecology affects customer behavior by making certain market options less convenient or less attractive and by customers exercising their environmental values, which then bear upon their market choices. Market choices become less attractive, in turn, by two mechanisms: (1) the deteriorating ecology makes certain modes of consumption less convenient or less satisfying, and (2) government disincentives make ecologically undesirable behaviors personally more costly. As an example of the ecology itself hindering certain behaviors, consider pollution. To avoid polluting the air, many consumers will reduce the amount of driving they do. On the other hand, as an example of the second mechanism of government disincentives, the government could impose a higher tax on fuel or require certain pollution-reducing equipment to control pollution. Apart from these two options, customers' own environmental values affect customer choices in that they voluntarily seek ecologically friendly options.

**Ecology: Consumers Who Want to Save Nature.** Some have called the 1990s "the age of the **green consumer**"—the consumer who is concerned about the deteriorating environment and is willing to take action to save it, including sacrificing personal consumption. In a 1991 survey of U.S. adults, the environment was the fourth most mentioned problem, after the economy, homelessness, and education. People who show some commitment to the environment in their marketplace choices are termed **environmentally conscious consumers**, defined as "those who actively seek out products perceived as having relatively minimal impact on the environment."[47] Depending on the degree of "greenness," consumers have been defined segmented as shown in Table 2.5. The Window on Research box presents a profile of the green consumer.

**TABLE 2.5**     **Environmental Segments**

1. True-Blue Greens (9 percent)—The most deeply committed to environment, they are in the forefront of the green movement in America, and they express their concern both by advocacy and by pro-environmental consumption behavior, such as recycling and buying products made from recycled materials.
2. Greenback Greens (6 percent)—This group backs its commitment to environment by showing willingness to pay more for environmentally friendly products.
3. Sprouts (31 percent)—This group shows a moderate level of commitment to environmental issues with a limited amount of pro-environmental behavior.
4. Grousers (19 percent)—They display a lack of pro-environmental attitudes and behavior and rationalize their inaction by blaming others.
5. Basic Browns (33 percent)—Environment is not a concern to them, and they do not want to be bothered with environmental issues. The majority of them are poor and are more preoccupied with just making ends meet than with worrying about anything else.

**Source:** *The Environment: Public Attitudes and Behavior,* a report by RoperASW and S.C. Johnson & Sons, Inc. (New York, June 2002).

# WINDOW ON RESEARCH

## Profile of the Green Consumer

What is the profile of green consumers? Demographically, according to various polls, the typical green consumer is a woman who is likely to be 30 to 49 years of age; who has children six years or older; is educated, affluent, politically liberal; and lives in a northeast, west, or midwest suburb. Pyschographically, green consumers are very interested in news and politics and are active in their communities. They are not afraid to express their opinions and will do so by writing letters to newspapers. They think pollution is a serious threat to people's health and are willing to reduce their standard of living in an effort to tighten pollution standards. They do believe that the individual can make a difference in making the environment healthier. An intercept sample survey of 704 shoppers in Hong Kong shows that the demographic profile of the green consumer in Hong Kong is very similar to that of the green consumers in the West. They were more likely to have a higher education and higher household income. Heavy green consumers perceived influence from other persons, the government and other green groups; possessed a strong self-identity; and used the mass media for environmental news.

**Sources:** Adapted from Jacquelyn A. Ottman, *Green Marketing* (Lincolnwood, Ill.: NTC Business Books, 1992); Joseph Winski, "Lifestyle Study," *Advertising Age,* October 5, 1990, in Ottman, *Green Marketing*; Kara Chan, "Market Segmentation of Green Consumers in Hong Kong," *Journal of International Consumer Marketing,* 12 (2), 1999, pp. 7–24.

Envirolink network (**http://www.envirolink.netforchange.com**) is an online community forum that provides comprehensive resources (Web site and domain name hosting for environmental and animal rights organizations, discussion forums, educational and government resources) for individuals, organizations, and businesses working for social and environmental change. Despite consumer interest in the environment, environmental products remain a small fraction of the retail market, mainly because shopping for green products is not easy. Reading *Consumer Reports* and other literature to find the most energy-efficient appliance or the safest microwave is laborious and impractical for day-to-day shopping. Moreover, studies have found that consumers are skeptical of claims made on the labels of green products. With the growth of e-commerce, online shops will be able to empower consumers by providing them with fast and easy information and access to green goods. E-tailers like *EcoMall.com* and *GreenMarketplace.com* have seized the business opportunity provided by green consumers to set up sites that offer a wide array of environment-friendly products and services to customers on the Net. The next generation of sites will rely on sophisticated search engines—or "green bots"—to scan and screen for environmental features of products. Brokers, agents, and buyers' clubs could use these search engines to ferret out the best products for their clients and members. Some search criteria that could be used are published energy and water efficiency ratings of appliances, toxic chemicals used as product ingredients, publicly available information on chemical releases or accidents at manufacturing facilities, and products that use tropical hardwoods or other scarce resources.[48]

**Business Response to Environmentalism.** In their effort to respond to the consumer demand for a healthier environment, marketers engage in **environmental marketing**, which refers to the marketing of products and services in a manner that attempts to minimize the damage to the environment. This might entail conservation of scarce resources such as trees and energy; prudent use of pesticides in agricultural production; use of recycled, recyclable, or biodegradable materials in the production of the product as well as in its packaging; product design changes to reduce air or water pollution due to product use; and adapting manufacturing processes to minimize air or water pollution. For example, DuPont, an American firm, has promised that within a decade it will slash its emissions of greenhouse gases by nearly two-thirds compared to 1990 levels, while holding total energy use flat and using renewable resources for one-tenth of its energy worldwide. Britain's BP has also accepted voluntary targets for reduction of carbon-dioxide emissions through use of an innovative emissions-trading scheme among its dozens of divisions worldwide. The board of directors at Royal Dutch/Shell, an Anglo-Dutch energy giant, now require that all big projects must not only meet the company's required internal rate of return, but also consider the future cost of carbon emissions. This cost will be $5 per ton of carbon dioxide in 2005–2009, rising to $20 per ton from 2010.[49]

## Market Context

The market context—economy, government policy, and technology—are the three other environmental determinants of consumer behavior. In contrast to the market characteristics, these aspects of the market context are created by humans as members of an organized society. The economic conditions in your own country, state, or city affect your purchase behavior—stimulating it in prosperous times and dampening it during economic downturns. Government policy can create or collapse markets and their competitive structures with the stroke of a pen. Finally, technology can revolutionize both what and how customers buy. If you could visit your mom, for example, on the videophone, or if you could confer with your business associates via a videoconference, you would be less likely to give much business to the airlines.

## Economy

As a component of the market context, the **economy** refers to the state of the national economy with respect to levels of employment, wages, inflation, interest rates, currency exchange rates, and aggregate household savings and disposable income. The economic climate affects customer behavior by three mechanisms:

1. By directly expanding or shrinking the financial resources of a household, or the buying power of these resources, the national economy encourages or constrains

customer purchases at the individual household levels as well as for business customers. Take the case of the slump in the IT industry with the current recession in the economy. Companies are downsizing, and as customers lose jobs, the financial resources in their households shrink drastically.

2. By influencing customer sentiment—optimism or pessimism about the future—it encourages or dampens consumer spending.

3. By driving business cycles the economy influences a customer's spending and saving behavior.

Speaking of financial resources, George Katona, a well-known economist, classified all household expenditures as either necessary or discretionary. **Necessary expenditures** entail the purchase of products and services needed for minimal sustenance, while **discretionary expenditures** entail the purchase of goods and services to make life physically or psychologically more comfortable beyond sustenance. In hard economic times, consumers would cut down on what they consider to be discretionary purchases, limiting their purchases to necessary items.[50]

The effect of the national economy on household purchase behavior occurs through **customer expectations**. The customer's economic outlook can be optimistic or pessimistic, which will either spur or curb household spending. The economic optimism/pessimism of consumers has been tracked since 1946 by the University of Michigan Survey Research Center. Termed "**The Index of Consumer Sentiment**," the measure is based on monthly surveys in which a national probability sample of households are asked the following questions:

1. We are interested in how people are getting along financially these days. Would you say that you (and your family living there) are better off or worse off financially that you were a year ago? Why do you say so?

2. Now looking ahead—do you think that a year from now you (and your family living there) will be better off financially, or worse off, or just about the same as now?

3. Now turning to business conditions in the country as a whole—do you think that during the next 12 months we'll have good times financially, or bad times, or what?

4. Looking ahead, which would you say is more likely—that in the country as a whole we'll have continuous good times during the next five years or so, or that we'll have periods of widespread unemployment, depression, or what?

5. About the big things people buy for their homes—such as furniture, a refrigerator, a stove, television, and things like that. Generally speaking, do you think now is a good time or a bad time for people to buy major household items? Why do you say so?[51]

In addition, the survey asks respondents about their plans to purchase automobiles over the next year. Thus, the general state of a nation's economy influences customer behavior by affecting customers' sense of optimism. Another such survey is the Consumer Confidence survey conducted for The Conference Board by NFO Research, Inc. Each month, questionnaires are mailed to different nationwide representative samples of 5,000 households, of which roughly 3,500 typically respond. The Index is based on responses to five questions included in the survey:

1. Respondents' appraisal of current business conditions.
2. Respondents' expectations regarding business conditions six months hence.
3. Respondents' appraisal of the current employment conditions.
4. Respondents' expectations regarding employment conditions six months hence.
5. Respondents' expectations regarding their total family income six months hence.

For each of the five questions above, there are three response options: *positive, negative,* and *neutral*. The response proportions to each question are seasonally adjusted. For each of the five questions, the *positive* figure is divided by the sum of the *positive* and *negative* to yield a proportion, which is called the "*Relative*" value. For each question, the average "*Relative*" for the calendar year 1985 is then used as a benchmark to yield the Index value for that question. The Indexes are then averaged together as follows: Consumer Confidence Index: Average of all five Indexes; Present Situation Index: Average of Indexes for Questions 1 and 3; Expectations Index: Average of Indexes for Questions 2, 4, and 5.[52]

A measure of business performance is the total retail sales of all goods and services in the economy. When total retail sales are rising, the economy is said to be in a boom; with declining sales, the economy is said to be in recession. Often a nation's business goes through a cycle of boom and recession; this is called a business cycle. The business cycle works like this: When the economy is doing well and is growing, the unemployment rate is low, and total production is high. Consumer spending is on the rise, causing high demand. Due to rising demand as well as rising wages (which raise the cost of production), consumer prices increase, resulting in inflation. With inflation, interest rates go up, which makes consumers want to save more and reduce spending. Reduced spending leads to a manufacturer inventory buildup, which in turn leads to manufacturers cutting back on production and laying off workers. Consequently, unemployment rises, and consumer spending is further reduced, leading to recession. Eventually, piled-up inventories begin to deplete, and manufacturers begin to return to prerecession levels of production, giving the economy its recovery, and later a boom. Thus, the business cycle is completed.[53]

## Government Policy

Another market context factor—government policy—comprises monetary policy, fiscal policy, and public policy. Monetary policy includes decisions on interest rates, the money supply, regulating financial institutions, and so on. Fiscal policy deals with government trade practices, procurement, spending, borrowing, taxing, and the like. Finally, public policy comprises such government acts as economic regulation, environmental regulation, product safety, mergers and acquisitions, and other government policies. Internet marketers are still relatively free of customary and legal restrictions, but new global commercial instruments and laws will soon evolve to support the global cyberspace market.

**Monetary and Fiscal Policy.**   Government influences market behavior by managing the national economy through adjustments to federal interest rates, money supply, taxation, and other instruments of monetary and fiscal policy. In the United States, the Federal Reserve (the nation's central bank) may raise its prime lending rate (the rate at which it loans funds to other commercial banks), which discourages borrowing (e.g., home-refinancing market slows because interest rate hikes cause customers to abandon their refinancing plans). A hike in interest rate also causes customers to reduce their overall spending. This happens for two reasons. First, an increase in interest rate translates to higher mortgage payments, which reduces money that the customer will have available for other spending. Second, the higher rates also cause customers to reduce their use of credit cards, which again reduces their purchasing power.

The effect of the Fed's policy on business customers is just the opposite. Because of lowered consumer demand due to a decline in cash available to the consumer, businesses cannot command the price they require to keep up with the rising costs. They must rely on cost reduction via productivity gains, so they need to invest in new equipment that may improve productivity. This results in capital outlays despite the high interest rates for borrowing.

A change in the income tax or sales tax similarly causes shifts in customer purchases. Depending on the nature of tax changes and the expected permanency of it, customers would postpone or advance their purchases of products and services. In October 1998, then-President Bill Clinton signed the Internet Tax Freedom Act, creating a three-year moratorium on state and local taxation of Internet access. A special commission studied the recommended tax policies for the cyber environment in this time, and this moratorium has been extended for two more years. The moratorium now expires on November 1, 2003. The decision of this committee could influence e-commerce in a big way.[54]

**Public Policy.** Governments at the federal, state, and local levels enact various laws that influence both business and customer behavior. These laws establish public policy that influences customer behavior in four ways: (1) by constraining choices, (2) by mandating certain products or services, (3) by protecting the consumer in his or her purchases, and (4) by setting up facilitative infrastructure.

*Constraining Choices.* When constraining choices, the government creates regulations that monitor negligent consumer behavior. Negligent behavior puts a person or others at risk and imposes heavy costs on society or otherwise deteriorates quality of life in the long run. At an individual level, these include behaviors such as driving under the influence of alcohol, smoking, using steroids and other drugs, and littering along highways. For businesses, such behaviors include environmental pollution, sale of unsafe products, or use of harmful ingredients or processes in manufacturing. Government bans or controls the sale and use of what it considers to be harmful products, such as drugs, alcohol, tobacco, and firearms. Government also controls what products may be consumed in public places, for example, by prohibiting smoking, drinking, and gambling in schools.

*Mandating Choices.* Though the government forbids some choices, it mandates others. Compliance refers to the government mandate for customers to obey defined rules and regulations with respect to purchase, payment, and, more important, product usage, including disposal. To obtain customer compliance with these mandates, governments pass laws and issue regulations with penalties for failure to comply. For example, in the United States, the federal and state governments require the use of certain products, such as helmets by motorcycle riders and seat belts by drivers and passengers of automobiles.

*Protecting the Consumer.* The government also can play an intense role in enacting and enforcing laws to protect consumers against personal injury or fraud. In effect, all elements of the marketing mix (product, promotion, price, and place) are covered in various laws meant to protect the consumer.

In 1914, the U.S. Congress established the Federal Trade Commission (FTC— **http://www.ftc.gov**) as a body of specialists with the power to investigate and enforce laws that require businesses to engage in fair business practices. One of the FTC's most important duties is to oversee advertising and ensure that no company engages in deceptive advertising. The FTC defines deceptive advertising as that which "has the capacity to deceive a measurable segment of the public." A classic example of the regulation of deceptive advertising is the case of Listerine. Warner-Lambert, the manufacturer of Listerine, claimed in its advertising from 1921 to 1975 that Listerine would prevent or lessen common colds and sore throats. In 1975, the FTC determined that the claim was misleading and ordered corrective advertising (advertising whose message includes a correction of previous deception). Accordingly, the company was required to insert the following disclaimer in its future advertising: "While Listerine will not prevent colds or sore throats or lessen their severity, . . ." (This was followed by whatever new selling appeal it wanted to employ, such as countering bad breath). The FTC requires that companies substantiate any claim made in an advertisement by documenting all verifiable benefits in company files. A verifiable benefit is one that can be verified by independent laboratory tests, such as whether a brand cleans clothes better than a competitor's brand, or whether a shampoo will prevent hair thinning. The FTC is also authorized to monitor manufacturers' adherence to warranty promises and consumer redress for failed warranties.

In the online marketplace, commercial Web sites collect personal information explicitly through a variety of means, including registration pages, user surveys, online contests, application forms, and order forms. Web sites also collect personal information through means that are not obvious to consumers, such as "cookies." Surveys show that "privacy" of personal information submitted is a major concern for consumers who participate in the electronic marketplace. The FTC endorses industry self-regulation in the context of consumer privacy in the online environment. It has developed five fair information practice principles to protect consumers in the collection, use, and dissemination of their information:

1. *Notice/Awareness*—covers the disclosure of information practices, including a comprehensive statement of information use—information storage, manipulation, and dissemination.

2. *Choice/Consent*—includes both opt-in and opt-out options and gives consumers the choice to trade information for benefits, depending on the value consumers place on the benefits.

3. *Access/Participation*—allows for the confirmation of accuracy of information, necessary when information is aggregated from multiple sources.

4. *Integrity/Security*—controls for theft or tampering.

5. *Enforcement/Redress*—provides a mechanism to ensure compliance by participating companies; this mechanism is an important credibility cue for online companies but is extremely difficult to accomplish effectively.[55]

Of these principles, the Notice/Awareness principle is the key to privacy since it informs the consumer of the kind of information collected at a site and its use. However, presently, under self-regulation, it is left to the online company to decide the degree of information collection and use along with the type and structure of the disclosure statement.

In addition to issues of individual and organizational privacy, the government also will need to address the issues of information security, controlling the intrusiveness of information technologies, and ensuring universal access (to prevent the creation of information "haves" and "have-nots").[56] The Digital Signature and Electronic Authentication Law, passed by the federal government in 1998, allows financial institutions and businesses to use secure electronic authorization in the conduct of business.

The FTC plays an important role in protecting children from unfair advertising practices by applying special regulations to children's advertising. With regard to the online environment, privacy is even more important in the case of children because the information posted by them on Web sites can be used to identify them by name, e-mail, or postal address. Such information can be misused by predators and by companies for marketing purposes. To address this concern, The Children's Online Privacy Protection Act (COPPA) and its implementing Rule went into effect on April 21, 2000. The Rule requires commercial Web sites and online services that collect personal information from children under 13 to post privacy policies, notify parents of their information practices, obtain verifiable parental consent, and provide parents with access to their children's information.[57]

The U.S. Congress also has passed many laws designed to protect the customer from being misled by a business. Different agencies also have been created to protect customers against businesses' possible wrongdoing. Third-party entities also have emerged online to provide legitimacy and trustworthiness to Web sites with their seals of approval that confirm adequate privacy compliance. TRUSTe, Council for Better Business Bureaus (BBBOnline), and Alliance for Privacy are three such organizations. TRUSTe is an industry-launched initiative with support from AT&T, America Online, Netscape, Oracle, Wired, and Tandem Computers. Alliance for Online Privacy is an alliance of 85 marketers, technology firms, and associations. BBBOnline has the Reliability Seal Program and the Privacy Seal Program that it awards to companies meeting its requirements. It also has a special seal for sites with advertising for children.[58]

*Facilitative Infrastructure.* The final mechanism by which government policy shapes customer behavior is the development of infrastructure. Governments can establish incentives and infrastructures to encourage certain customer behaviors. One example is the Electric Vehicle initiative in California. Another example is the program to encourage bicycling as a means of commuting. The U.S. government's 1990 Clean Air Act and 1991 Intermodal Surface Transportation Efficiency Act (ISTEA) give local communities a mandate to build bicycling into their transit plans. The Clean Air Act specifies air quality standards and requires metropolitan areas to develop methods of maintaining air quality, including the encouragement of bicycling for commuting purposes. The ISTEA requires states and local governments to develop plans that would encourage the use of nonmotorized transportation. The federal government has earmarked nearly $155 billion to support this mandate. Similarly, in the corporate context, the Occupational Safety and Health Act (OSHA) of 1970 ensures safe and healthful working conditions for men and women by enforcing standards specified under the act. Another U.S. government agency, the EPA (Environment Protection Agency), sets standards to protect human health and to safeguard the natural environment—air, water, and land—upon which life depends.

Singapore illustrates how government, through facilitative infrastructure, affects customer behavior. Its government has allocated millions of dollars to build a technology infrastructure to convert Singapore from an economy built on trade and services to one built on information technology. Singapore officials have launched a host of new electronic services that make the government more efficient. Central databases allow bureaucrats to track everything from immigrant work permits to detailed information on the population. The education, hospital, and legal systems are seeing changes, and online training courses are being held for government officials. The infrastructure is being set up to prepare Singaporeans for a Web life so that they become the netizens of tomorrow—super-connected, technologically savvy, civic-minded, and knowledgeable.[59]

## Technology

In terms of customer behavior, technology is the dimension of market context that consists of the applications of new technology to the development, distribution, and consumption of products and services that increase the quality of life for all customers. Technological breakthroughs can significantly change market behaviors and customer expectations, affecting customer behavior through several avenues:

- By altering the flow of and access to information about marketplace alternatives.
- By making available newer generations of products and services.
- By automating processes that give customers greater flexibility and control as well as improve productivity.
- By making customized products economically feasible.

**Increased Access to Information.**  Technology brings new mass media into being, media that offers consumers information about the marketplace. Before the advent of newspapers, the only sources of market information were town criers, billboards, and word of mouth, and the first two were out-of-home media. With newspapers and television, advertising has come into consumers' homes, thus increasing consumer access to market information.

The role of conventional mass media in bringing market information to customers has been remarkable, but it pales in comparison to the implications of the most recent advancement in technology—namely, the Internet and the so-called information superhighway. You can buy a car on the Internet today; business travelers can find deals on airlines and hotels worldwide, and students can learn about various colleges and universities. The AOL/Roper Starch Cyberstudy of 1,004 adult (ages 18 and over) Internet users in August 2000 shows that four out of five (80 percent) research products online prior to purchase, 76 percent read the news, 70 percent search for health information, and 50 percent get local entertainment information online.[60] Thus, the first avenue of the impact of technological advances on customer behavior is through increasing customer access to marketplace information.

**Product Innovation: New Options.**  The second way that technology impacts customer choices is via the availability of new products and services based on advances in technology. Consider the advent of cable TV, with its multichannel offerings and services such as pay-per-view and video on demand. Now, customers can order a movie on their television, without leaving their home. Obviously, this cuts into sales at movie theaters and video rental stores. For a business person, computerized reservation systems, online information services, electronic libraries, database marketing, and cable shopping are changing the way they do business with their customers as well as with suppliers.

**More Flexibility and Control.**  Technology also affects customer behavior by delivering freedom from the confines of space and time. That is, you can do business *anytime, anywhere.* You can bank at the ATM (automatic teller machine) 24 hours a day or reach your account via toll-free telephone numbers from anywhere in the United States at any time. You can order flowers online rather than going to the neighborhood store, and you can receive a college degree without leaving home.

Among business-to-business customers, one noteworthy use of computer technology has been **electronic data interchange (EDI)**, a computer link between a supplier and its business customer that transmits customer inventory data to the supplier as it is being used and depleted, which sets into motion an automatic reorder and shipping of the depleted product. Retailing giant Wal-Mart and its supplier Procter & Gamble have an EDI system; the use of the system results in lowered costs of ordering and order filling, as well as eliminating costly stock outages on the Wal-Mart shelves.[61] Several automobile manufacturers have similar systems with their suppliers. The EDI technology frees the business customer from the effort of monitoring inventory and reordering, and thus lowers costs.

**Customized Products and Services.**  One of the most exciting technological developments in recent years is in the manufacturing arena, namely flexible manufacturing. The marketing benefit of technology is **mass customization**—producing a product after the customer order is received and tailoring the product to the customer's specific needs without sacrificing the speed or cost efficiencies of conventional mass production methods.

Many companies have capitalized on the use of mass customization. Here are some selected examples.

- Hallmark uses computer technology to offer custom-made cards. By using simple on-screen instructions, you can choose from a selection of graphics, write your own message, and instantly print the card, all for about the same price as off-the-rack cards.
- The John Deere Harvester Works manufacturing plant in Moline, Illinois, is a good example of customization for business customers. The company sells a wide variety of crop planters priced at more than $100,000. The company has revamped its mass-production manufacturing process to respond to customized orders, and it now keeps only about 20 planters in finished goods inventory. Thus, customers can now choose from hundreds of options (such as row counter, liquid or dry fertilizer, and depth of planting) and can purchase a crop planter that matches their individual needs more closely than ever before.[62]
- Companies like IMIXrecords (**http://www.imixrecords.com**) allow users to customize music CDs and DVDs over the Internet and then have the product shipped directly from the company. Customers are presented with a list of choices and can pick and choose by title, album, artist, or genre.

**Technophilia versus Technophobia.**  Customers differ in their attitude toward technology. While many customers benefit from and welcome new technology, a sizable proportion show a distaste for it. This is explained by:

1. *Preference for human interaction:* Some consumers desire the "human touch" rather than high tech.
2. *A lack of aptitude for technology:* Some consumers simply find themselves ill-equipped to handle new technology and, indeed, feel a degree of technophobia.

**Technophiles**, or "**techthusiasts**," are people who get excited about technology; love to buy new technological innovations as soon as they appear on the market; have early knowledge about technology; and invest substantial time and energy in learning about, acquiring, and using new technological gadgets. **Technophobes**, on the other hand, are the exact opposite. They hate new technology, feel overwhelmed and confused by it, and find themselves ill-equipped to operate even common household and marketplace gadgets.

According to a survey by Backer, Spielvogel, and Bates (BSB) Research Company of New York, one in five Americans is a technophile. Technophiles are younger, more affluent, and somewhat better educated than the average American. They act as advisors, shopping pals, and decision makers for their colleagues, friends, and relatives. Technophobes make up about one in three Americans. These people have never used a computer or programmed a VCR. To appeal to this segment, technological products ought to be user-friendly and very simple to operate.

In business-to-business markets, too, adopting a new technology requires a new investment from customers as well as a degree of comfort with the new and the unfamiliar. Consider the new technology that Eastman Kodak can offer its customers for their printing needs. Eastman Kodak's Professional & Printing Image Division (which has been sold to Danka) has advanced beyond the traditional photographic imaging using silver-halide film to digital systems for more speed and creative flexibility. Digital applications now complement and, in some cases, even replace, the more traditional silver-halide film imaging. Yet, the reason that Kodak and other companies are holding onto the silver-halide technology is because all customers are not ready to switch completely to the newer technology. There is an important customer behavior lesson here: breakthrough technology that runs ahead of its customers' ability to invest in it or their aptitude for using it will never work from a marketing standpoint.

# The Influence of the Determinants of Customer Behavior on the Three Customer Roles

Table 2.6, on pages 82–83, summarizes the effect of each of the determinants on the three customer roles.

## Personal Traits

The five personal traits influence the three roles in distinct ways.

### Influence of Genetics

A person's genetic makeup determines his or her biological needs as well as physical constitution and hence the need for products necessitated by those biological needs or by special physiological constitution. Beyond performance, genetics also affect a person's emotional state and personality, and this, in turn, affects a person's desire for emotion-producing experiential or hedonic products. The payer role is not much affected by genetics directly, but the buyer role is affected in that certain genetic disorders might incapacitate customers from going to the market, making convenience a more dominant value.

### Influence of Race

Some of the effects of race and genetics are similar, while others differ. Due to related genetic differences, race affects skin color and hair type and texture. Therefore, customers from different races need personal care items with specific performance characteristics. Beyond physiology, a customer's race also implies differences in values, lifestyle, and tastes. Then, race influences the payer role for two reasons. First, economic conditions are distributed differently across races due to historical differences in access to opportunities and to race-based cultural differences in individual achievement motivation and belief in upward mobility. Second, there has been a systematic bias against certain ethnic minorities in credit approval. Both of these limit the buying power of some ethnic minorities. Finally, the buyer role is affected by race in at least two ways. First, many ethnic groups prefer to patronize vendors, store owners, and service agents (e.g., insurance agency representatives, real estate agents) of the same race and ethnic background. Second, as buyers, ethnic groups differ in the kind of interaction they seek from suppliers and from store operators. Some races expect mere politeness in commercial transactions and, hence, behave accordingly, while others may expect personal warmth.

## Influence of Gender

Gender, too, has a pervasive effect on customer roles. For the user, gender implies the purchase of some gender-specific products and services, based either in some biological or physiological needs or in culture-generated gender-specific customs and tastes. Many performance-related values differ between men and women, such as the ergonomics in the design of the driver seat in cars or the extra security needs in hotel rooms for women business travelers. But men-women differences also spill over to social and emotional values in purchase of products to satisfy these values. The payer role is affected only insofar as there exists, in a given society or in a given family unit, sex-role-based bias in the allocation of the payer role. The buyer role is affected by gender, both in allocation of the responsibility and in gender differences in the specific values the customer seeks as a buyer. Regarding role allocation, again, there are norms about who should be the buyer, which differ across families and cultures. In traditional societies, women do the shopping for routine household items, while men do the shopping for major purchases. In modernized societies and families, the sex roles are more egalitarian, so both sexes assume an equal share of purchasing. Women seek more convenience and time-saving means of shopping due to their being strapped for time, and men are learning the necessary purchasing skills as they are being forced to assume more of that role.

## Influence of Age

As users, the needs and wants for product and service categories obviously differ across different age groups. As users in business markets, older workers can't use heavy equipment or parts, and, thus seek different performance value from raw material, parts, and equipment. Moreover, social and emotional values are likely to be more important to youth than to elderly and middle-age customers. As payers, customers are affected by age because age influences their station in their career and, accordingly, their financial resources. Age also affects the separation of the payer and the user role. Generally, these two roles are separated for youth and, again, for many elderly, who now depend on the government for Medicare and retirement benefits. Finally, age influences the buyer role. Elderly purchasers need and seek more service and more convenience and build relationships with sellers. Word-of-mouth communication about shopping is the highest among youth.

## Influence of Personality

The role of personality is overarching, affecting all domains of customer behavior. Outgoing persons would participate in outdoor and social activities more and, therefore, would consume products and services relevant to these recreational activities. Similarly, pleasure-seeking individuals would like experiential products more. As payers, some customers would be extravagant, and others would be very frugal and conservative. Some would like to live on credit; others would stay well within current cash resources. Customer personality also affects the buyer role. Brand loyalty and, likewise, store loyalty vary from person to person. These individual differences in brand and store loyalty are basically personality differences. Some individuals like to stick with the tried and tested; others like to explore new options. Another manifestation of personality is in the shopping style—some are browsers, while some are focused shoppers. The personality of the business customer is influential, likewise, across the three roles. The choice of office decor, airline and hotel during business trips, and performance features such as speed versus memory in a computer (impatient users want more speed), as well as the safety factor in design specifications are dependent on the personality of the user. As payers, the long- versus short-term perspective definitely affects the business customer's choice between options or allocation of funds

# TABLE 2.6 Personal Characteristics and the Three Customer Roles

| CHARACTERISTIC | CUSTOMER ROLE | | |
|---|---|---|---|
| | USER | PAYER | BUYER |
| **Genetics** | **PERSONAL TRAITS**<br>• Customers' genetic makeup determines biological needs and the specific performance features sought.<br>• Genetics determines personality and emotional makeup to influence specific social and emotional values sought. | | • Certain genetic disorders might incapacitate customers from making shopping trips, so value is more desirable. |
| **Race** | • For personal care items, customers seek products that are compatible with their skin and hair needs.<br>• Ethnic tastes in food, clothing, and homes differ.<br>• Some minority groups seek social values as compensation. | • Economic means are unevenly distributed across races and ethnic groups.<br>• Race-based discrimination in credit limits affordability for some customers. | • Many customers prefer ethnic stores and suppliers.<br>• Race and ethnic group influence the preferred modes of interaction with vendors. |
| **Gender** | • Many products and services are gender specific, due to either physiology or culture.<br>• In some cultures, women might use emotional products more. | • Sex roles may be the basis for allocating the payer role. | • Sex roles may be the basis for allocating the buyer role.<br>• Where sex roles include women in the workforce, they might seek convenience and time saving in shopping.<br>• In some cultures, men are still learning shopping skills. |
| **Age** | • Product/service usage in many categories is contingent on age.<br>• Social and emotional values are more important for youth.<br>• Product/service needs are influenced by the physical limitations related to aging (such as inability to lift heavy weights or read fine print). | • Age influences the amount of financial resources.<br>• The payer's role is more separate from the user's among youth (dependent on parents) and the elderly (dependent on government for income). | • Elderly buyers need more service and convenience.<br>• Word-of-mouth communication about shopping is highest among youth.<br>• Older buyers (in both businesses and households) prefer to buy based on relationship with the seller. |
| **Personality** | • At onset of need, some personality types may either delay or rush use of the product or service.<br>• Some personalities will be more open to cross-gender product use.<br>• Some personalities will have more need for mood and emotional products. | • Some personalities will be frugal; others extravagant.<br>• Some personalities (of business and household payers) will focus on long-term investment; others on immediate price. | • Personality types will differ in their loyalty to brands and stores.<br>• Some personalities enjoy browsing; others focus on obtaining target merchandise.<br>• Some personalities focus more on seeking relationships with sellers. |
| **Culture** | **PERSONAL CONTEXT**<br>• Cultures differ in their insistence on flawless performance.<br>• Conspicuous consumption is frowned upon in some cultures.<br>• Different cultures permit emotional expressiveness to different degrees.<br>• Corporate culture constrains what people wear and drive. | • Cultures vary significantly in sanctioning borrowing and in living in debt.<br>• Cultures allocate the payer role to specific members of the household. | • Cultures assign the buyer role according to their sex-role norms.<br>• Negotiations and bargaining practices are governed by cultural norms. |

| | | | |
|---|---|---|---|
| **Institutions and groups** | • Families differ on seeking materialism and in emphasis on performance versus social and emotional values.<br>• Religion prohibits consumption of certain products and services.<br>• Employers and work groups exercise norms on clothing, cars, and business travel options.<br>• Economic classes have distinct cultures of consumption. | • Families differ in using credit and in individual versus joint responsibility for managing financial matters.<br>• Islam prohibits borrowing.<br>• Employers affect the payer by assuming partial or full financial burden. | • Families differ in blending versus separating the buyer role from the user and/or payer roles.<br>• Some religions disallow women to go shopping.<br>• Employers' purchasing policies constrain the purchaser. |
| **Personal worth** | | • By enabling or limiting the resources, economic conditions affect the payer role most directly. | • Greater personal worth supports a more confident approach to vendors.<br>• Economic means may limit access to vendors.<br>• Higher economic condition leads customers to seek more convenience and personal shopping experience. |

**MARKET TRAITS**

| | | | |
|---|---|---|---|
| **Climate** | • Certain types of food, clothing, and shelter are needed.<br>• Weather-related products are needed.<br>• Suitable packaging is required. | • Out-of-place products cost more.<br>• Out-of-season products cost more. | • Climate-appropriate storage facilities affect accelerated buying.<br>• Bad weather may require postponement of purchase.<br>• Pickup/delivery services may be needed in bad weather. |
| **Topography** | • Products adapted to local conditions (e.g., flood insurance, bottled water) are needed.<br>• Available means of transportation may be limited. | • Special-needs products must be budgeted for. | • Transportation difficulties may require minimizing trips, buying in bulk, or delegating purchase to others. |
| **Ecology** | • Pollution control products are needed.<br>• Environmentally friendly products/services are needed. | • Ecologically friendly products may cost more. | • Ecologically friendly products may require special search effort. |

**MARKET CONTEXT**

| | | | |
|---|---|---|---|
| **Economy** | • Financial resources affect definition of necessities as opposed to luxuries. | • Poor economy requires postponement of major purchases. | • Demand and supply imbalances affect choice options.<br>• Interest rates influence desirability of borrowing decisions, such as home refinancing. |
| **Government** | • Government incentives and disincentives influence choice. Use of some products is forbidden or mandated. | • Tax laws affect net price. | • Government protection and laws of commerce (e.g., blue-sky laws) make purchasing secure.<br>• Laws provide protection against a deceptive or unfair price. |
| **Technology** | • New products are available.<br>• Products may be more customized to the user. | • New payment options such as credit card infrastructure or payment via Internet may be available. | • Purchaser may have access to "anytime, anywhere" shopping.<br>• Market information may be more readily available, for example, on the Internet. |

to a business activity or service. Finally, the four social styles—driving, expressive, amiable, and analytical—directly bear on the kind of interactions buyers would seek with sellers and business negotiators.

## Personal Context

Let us see how the personal context factors influence the various market values customers seek in their user, payer, and buyer roles.

# Culture

The influence of culture on the market values that users seek (performance, social, and emotional) is pervasive and immense. Cultures vary in their insistence on performance and quality. Social value is also differently interpreted in different cultures. Conspicuous consumption is frowned upon in some cultures, such as in more egalitarian societies. Likewise, cultures differ in whether emotional expressiveness is considered proper and natural. Corporate culture constrains the kinds of clothes we wear and the kinds of cars we drive. Culture influences the payer role in at least two ways. First, it is a determinant of who plays the payer role. In some cultures, it is the female head of the household; in others, it is the male head. Second, cultures influence the payer role in that they differ significantly in their prescription for borrowing money. In non-Western cultures, for example, borrowing is a sign of being poor; the well-to-do don't borrow money. In Western cultures, in contrast, even millionaires may borrow money, since borrowing is a sign of managing money (e.g., in investment portfolios) rather than a sign of not having money. Finally, culture influences the buyer role both in terms of who plays the buyer role and what specific values the buyer may tend to seek. In many cultures, there is a clearer allocation of gender roles, including a norm as to what kinds of products will be shopped for mainly by the female members of the household and what kinds by the male members. In addition, expectations about personal service and convenience differ across cultures. Cultures also vary in negotiating tactics and in allowing the practice of bargaining. Similarly, in business negotiations, the level of direct confrontation considered prudent differs across cultures. These cultural nuances make playing a buyer role an art form in many societies.

# Institutions and Reference Groups

Let us consider institutions and groups and their influence on the three roles. The larger culture of a society or country shapes all families in it, but each family also has its own culture, norms, and practices. Thus, different families differ in the value they place on materialism and on simplicity versus indulgence, in permitting debt, and in the extent to which the user, payer, and buyer roles are blended or separated.

Religion certainly influences what people may or may not consume, as detailed earlier in the chapter (e.g., kosher food by Jews). Religion also affects the payer role by sanctioning the practice of borrowing. Islam, for example, forbids the practice of borrowing and lending, since usury is considered a sin. Again, certain religions prohibit women from going to the market, so the buyer role becomes the exclusive prerogative of men.

Employers and work groups influence all three roles. Beyond a norm about clothes and cars, employers also influence other user decisions, such as what kind of personal computer you can buy for your office desk, what airlines and which fare class you may fly, which hotels you may stay at, and whether or not you may take your spouse on business trips. Employers affect the payer role in letting or not letting employees manage their own budget, in terms of allowing certain business expenses (e.g., entertainment, social club membership), and in the extent to which they partially or fully assume the financial burden for the things you buy as an employee and as a consumer (e.g., health-care insurance, company car, housing rent subsidy, home phone, paid annual vacation). Finally, purchasing practice is dictated by employers—some allow individual employees to do their own purchasing while others mandate centralized purchasing (e.g., using your own travel agent versus using the corporate travel agency).

## Personal Worth

Finally, consider the influence of personal worth on the three customer roles. Personal worth influences customers' behavior primarily by constraining their resources. Its influence is greatest, therefore, on the payer role. Not only is the amount of money (whether equity or credit) available for market transactions relatively abundant or scarce, but it also affects the extent to which money is tightly controlled among the user, buyer, and payer roles.

Personal worth affects the other two customer roles as well. Economic classes acquire their own consumption cultures, so there is the consumption culture of the poor, of the middle class, and of the rich, for example. As to the buyer role, personal worth affects both the broad mindset of customers and their specific purchase strategies. In broad terms, it influences the confidence versus timidness with which buyers can approach their suppliers and vendors, and it influences their choice of vendors. In general, then, low personal worth focuses customer attention on universal values in each of the three roles. Only when economic conditions are better does the consumer move up to seeking individual values, whether as a user, a payer, or a buyer.

## Market Traits

The three market traits affect all three customer roles. Climate affects the users' need for food, clothing, and shelter. Topography affects needs for particular means of transportation (e.g., the camel in the deserts of Saudi Arabia) and insurance against topography-based mishaps (e.g., floods or hurricanes). Ecology makes ecology-unfriendly products nonviable and channels customer needs toward environment-friendly products and services. For the payer role, some physical environment factors imply greater expense—buying warm clothing in a tropical country is going to be more expensive because of the specialty nature of the products. Similarly, out-of-season merchandise costs more and ecology-friendly products also are more expensive. The buyer role is also affected by the physical market characteristics. If you live in a very hot climate, either you have a good cold storage facility or else you buy products in quantities sufficient for immediate consumption. Accelerated buying to take advantage of price and promotional deals is made infeasible if the storage facilities are inadequate for the climate of the place. Bad weather also leads purchasers to postpone a shopping trip and order home delivery rather than make in-store acquisitions.

## Market Context

In this section, we pull together the diverse effects of the three market context factors on the three customer roles. For the user, the economy affects the purchase of discretionary products and luxuries (wants). Government incentives and disincentives (including mandatory prohibition against certain products) influence customer choice. Technology makes new products available and, thus, influences desire for them. It also enables more customized products, and, consequently, it promotes a desire for more individualized products or service. For the payer, poor economic climate induces postponement of major purchases. Interest rates influence home refinancing decisions. Government influences the payer role by means of taxation and protective laws. Laws against deceptive and discriminatory pricing practices serve as assurance to payers that their money will not be taken fraudulently. Technology enables credit card infrastructure, such as the widespread use of technology by merchants across a nation to seek instant credit authorization from credit card vendors. For the buyer, the economy affects the supply and demand, which, in turn, affects the choices available for consideration and the ease or difficulty of acquiring the product or service. Government laws affect the buyer (as they do the user and payer) by making the purchase activity secure. Finally, technology affects the buyer role by enabling shopping "anytime, anywhere." Technology also has empowered the buyer by making more information more conveniently available, for example, on the Internet, so that you as a buyer can make more informed decisions.

# Summary

This chapter focused on the influence of the external determinants—namely, personal and market factors—on customer behavior.

There are two facets of the personal factors affecting customer behavior—personal traits and personal context. We first discussed personal traits, and showed how they affect customer behavior, and the three roles of the customer—user, payer, and buyer. These traits are genetics, the three biogenic features of race, age, and gender, and personality, which is a function of genetics, biogenics, and the environment. The influence of genetics is through its determining role in the physiology of the individual, the diseases to which a person is made susceptible, circadian rhythms, and moods and emotions. Race and ethnic background influence customers' needs for skin-specific personal care items, taste, and differences in food and clothing. We discussed the profiles of major races and ethnic groups in the United States, such as Hispanics, African Americans, and Asian Americans. We then discussed customer behavior differences between the two genders with respect to consumption of clothing and personal items. We discussed the diverse categories of age: the G.I. generation, the Silent Generation, Baby Boomers, Generation X, teenagers, and children. These customers need and want different products and services, because their physical characteristics are different and their tastes are different according to the age of their subculture. Finally, we explained what personality is and how it is formed. The Freudian theory illuminates the nature of personality as a set of conscious and subconscious motives and urges. Trait theory views personality as a pattern of behavior. Defense mechanisms were described as the ego's attempt to manage anxiety and to protect the self from being slighted. For a business customer, we introduced a specific personality typology—social styles—and we showed the relevance of this typology on customer behavior in business interactions.

We then discussed the second facet of the personal factors—personal context. The personal context is the cultural, social, and economic environment that a customer is a member of and in which the customer resides. We described three context factors—culture, institutions and groups, and personal worth. We defined what culture is and discussed its characteristics and components. We described national and popular culture. On the business side, we said that corporate culture also has a significant bearing on the behaviors of individuals or departments. We identified five dimensions of cross-culture value orientations. Institutions and groups, the second context factor, act as reference groups for individuals. Depending on frequency of contact, groups can be primary or secondary, membership or symbolic, choice or ascribed. Their influence depends on the conspicuousness of consumption, and as such, it can occur at the product or brand-choice level. Finally, the last context is the economic condition surrounding the consumer. Its components are income, wealth, and borrowing power. The concept of social class was discussed. It was argued that social classes are motivational in that they motivate customer behavior toward certain activities and possessions. The three major social classes (lower, middle, and upper) were contrasted in regard to their consumption behavior.

The first dimension of the market environment is market traits (i.e., the characteristics of the market as a physical place). You learned that there are three geophysical characteristics—climate, topography, and ecology. Climate plays an important role in shaping the market values customers would seek, and it affects the three basic necessities of life: food, shelter, and clothing. Businesses are also affected by climate, including different types of packaging required for warm and cold climates, and the fact that there is a seasonality with products and services. Topography, the second market trait refers to the terrain, altitude, and soil conditions where customers use products and services. Topography also affects choices that households and businesses make with respect to food, clothing, and shelter. For example, consumption of snack food varies, and office designs in businesses vary based on topography of the region. Ecology is the final market trait, and it refers to the natural resources and the balance that exist among humans, animals, and vegetation. You learned that ecological changes, such as global warming, air and water pollution, and ozone layer depletion, are affecting household and business customers. As an outcome, there are activist movements around the world to save the environment, and marketers are responding to these demands put on them.

The second dimension of the market environment is the market context, which refers to the context created by humans—namely, economy, government policy, and technology. You learned that the general state of a country's economy impacts customer behavior through the sense of optimism that is measured by the spending patterns of businesses and households. Businesses also follow business cycles, and these have a dramatic impact on the behavior of customers. Government policy affects customers through the monetary and fiscal policies that are enacted and through the public policies that are passed. You learned that through government policies, customer choice is sometimes constrained, mandated, or protected. A brief overview was given of various governmental agencies that play a role in either constraining, mandating, or protecting the user, payer, and buyer in the marketplace. The last determinant of the market context is technology. We discussed how technological breakthroughs significantly change market behaviors and shape customer expectations. You also learned that businesses also are affected by technology. Wal-Mart is one example that was used to show how businesses are using technology to partner with their suppliers in an effort to create better value for the user, payer, and buyer.

These external determinants, both personal and market-based, shape a person's psychological makeup—his or her motives, emotions, and lifestyles.

# Key Terms

Acculturation 60

Aggressive 58

Behaviorism Theory 56

Biological Determinism 45

Borrowing Power 67

Business Cycle 75

Climate 69

Compliance 76

Compliant 58

Corrective Advertising 76

Customer Expectations 74

Deceptive Advertising 76

Detached 58

Discretionary Expenditures 74

Ecology 71

Economy 73

Ego 56

Electronic Data Interchange (EDI) 79

Enculturation 60

Environmental Marketing 73

Environmentally Conscious Consumers 71

Family Life Cycle Concept 54

Geographical Variation 71

Global Warming 71

Government Policy 75

Green Consumer 71

Group Traits 45

Groups 63

Id 56

The Index of Consumer Sentiment 74

Individual Traits 45

Institutions 63

Lifetime Revenue 51

Mass Customization 79

National Culture 61

Nature 47

Necessary Expenditures 74

Negligent Consumer Behavior 76

Nurture 47

Personality Trait 58

Popular Culture 61

Regional Marketing 71

Social Class 68

Subculture 61

Superego 56

Technology 78

Technophiles (or Techthusiasts) 79

Technophobes 79

Topography 70

Trait Theory of Personality 58

Verifiable Benefit 76

# Discussion Questions and Exercises

1. Cosmetic companies have product lines targeted specifically to African-American women. In contrast, under public pressure, R.J. Reynolds canceled its plan to introduce Uptown, a cigarette targeting African Americans. Do companies have the right to use a subculture's unique characteristics to increase the sales of products? Was R.J. Reynolds simply following the marketing concept, which states that companies should design products to meet the needs of specific market segments? What are the ethical issues involved in subcultural market segmentation?

2. Describe some of the general gender differences that affect consumers in both household and business markets. What have marketers done to handle these differences? Recently, companies like Calvin Klein have tried to minimize gender differences. Do you think this strategy is a good idea?

3. How can marketers use the information in this chapter to develop promotional campaigns designed to increase market share among Asian-American, Hispanic, and African-American consumers for the following products:
   * Cameras
   * Ready-to-eat cereals
   * Fragrances (perfume or cologne)

4. Identify five consumers who come from different national cultures. Interview them to identify how their customer behaviors are different in each of the three roles.

5. Select two households featured in two different TV series or sitcoms. First, classify each household into one of the social classes discussed in the chapter. Then, analyze each household's lifestyle and consumption behavior. Compare the two households if they fall into different social classes.

6. As the Director of Product Development for a medium-sized international producer of soap, lotion, and detergent, you are fundamentally concerned with the movement worldwide toward protecting and preserving the environment. In many countries, specific raw materials have been banned and certain packaging materials have been discontinued. In addition to consumer and government pressure to become a "green" marketer, your major competitor, The Body Shop, has exhibited its commitment to the environment in several meaningful ways. What will you do to move your company toward being more environmentally friendly, and how will you communicate this to your customers?

7. Interview five consumers to rate them on how "environmentally conscious" they are. Then ask them about how their environmental consciousness affects the products and services they have bought within the past year. Verify whether "environmental consciousness" relates to customers' purchasing behavior.

8. Assume you are an entrepreneur and you are about to introduce to the market a revolutionary new product—an interactive kiosk—which enables convenient, easy, Internet access and offers a host of value-added services for business travelers. In general, your target group will be fairly computer savvy and will be familiar with most office equipment, such as faxes, e-mail, and voice-mail systems. What specific customer values will this new technology product satisfy? How will you introduce your new technology given the barrage of new innovations in the marketplace? How will you show that your product has the ability to appeal to both technophiles and technophobes?

# Notes

1 Quoted in Bill Saporito, "Unsuit Yourself," *Fortune*, September 20, 1993, pp. 118–20; Diane Crispell, "The Brave New World of Men," *American Demographics*, 14, no. 1 (January 1992), pp. 38–43.

2 Harold Koplewicz, *It's Nobody's Fault: New Hope and Help for Difficult Children and Their Parents* (Arlington, VA: National Alliance for the Mentally Ill, 1996).

3 Census 2000 population tables and reports, http://www.census.gov/population/census2000/phc-t1/tab04.xls.

4 This 1994–1995 survey was done by Paul Sladkus International, Inc. (PSI), a New York-based multicultural advertising and marketing firm. The survey results are reported in *American Demographics*, March 1997 issue.

5 This section is based on a report published in *American Demographics*, March 1997. See Shelly Reese, "When Whites Aren't a Mass Market," *American Demographics*, March 1997, pp. 51–54.

6 Age estimates: http://www.census.gov/population/estimates/nation/intfile3-1.txt.

7 Household and Family characteristics—March 1998, http://www.census.gov/prod/3/98pubs/p20-515.pdf.

8 Median Income of households 1997–99—http://www.census.gov/hhes/income/income99/99tableb.html.

9 e-Demographics Report, www.emarketer.com, 2000.

10 Donna Hoffman, Tom Novak, and Ann. E. Schlosser, "The Evolution of the Digital Divide: How Gaps in Internet Access May Impact Electronic Commerce," *Journal of Computer Mediated Communication*, Vol. 5 (3), March 2000, http://www.ascusc.org/jcmc/vol5/issue3/hoffman.html.

11 e-Demographics Report, http://www.emarketer.com, 2000.

12 Patricia Braus, "What Does Hispanic Mean?" *American Demographics* 15, no. 6 (June 1993), pp. 46–51.

13 e-Demographics Report, http://www.emarketer.com, 2000.

14 Adapted from Frieda Curtindale, "Car Dealers Give the Lady Some Respect," *American Demographics*, 14 no. 9 (September 1992), p. 25.

15 For further reading, see Bernd H. Schmitt, France Leclerc, and Laurette Dube-Rioux, "Sex Typing and Consumer Behavior: A Test of Gender Schema Theory," *Journal of Consumer Research* 15 (June 1988), pp. 122–28; Barbara B. Stern, "Sex Role, Self-Concept Measures and Marketing: A Research Note," *Psychology and Marketing* 5 (Spring 1988), p. 85; Janeen Arnold Costa, ed., *Gender Issues and Consumer Behavior* (Thousand Oaks: Sage, 1994).

16  e-Demographics Report, www.emarketer.com, 2000, http://www.digitrends.net.

17  Second Annual Internet Shopping Study, The Online Shopper: Profile of the On-line Shopper, Ernst & Young, 1999 http://www.ey.com/global/gcr.nsf/US/1999_Internet_Shopping%7EProfile_-_Retail_%26_Consumer_Products_-_Ernst_%26_Young_LLP.

18  William Strauss and Neil Howe, *Generations: The History of America's Future, 1584–2069* (New York: William Morrow & Company, 1991).

19  Estimate by Teenage Research Unlimited (TRU), reported in Shelley Reese, *The Quality of Cool, Marketing Tools*, July 1997.

20  "Children as Customers," *American Demographics*, September 1990, pp. 36–39.

21  S. Selina Guber and John Berry, *Marketing to and through Kids* (New York: McGraw Hill, 1993).

22  Teens Online, http://www.emarketer.com, 2000. Michael Pastore, *New Payment Options Will Open E-commerce to Teens*, September 7, 2001, http://cyberatlas.internet.com/markets/retailing/article/0,,6061_880271,00.html.

23  Hans J. Eysenck, *The Biological Basis of Personality*, C. C. Thomas (Springfield, IL, 1967); and *The Structure of Human Personality* (London: Metheun, 1970); also, Hans J. Eysenck, *Personality, Genetics, and Behavior: Selected Papers*, (New York: Praeger Publishers, 1982).

24  For a more formal definition and treatment of personality and trait theory, see Ernest Hilgard, Richard Atkinson, and Rita Atkinson, *Introduction to Psychology*, 6th ed. (New York: Harcourt Brace Jovanovich, Inc., 1975); and Walter Mischel, "On the Future of Personality Measurement," *American Psychologist*, 32 (April 1977), p. 2.

25  R.B. Cattell, H.W. Eber, and M.M. Tatsuoka, *Handbook for the Sixteen Personality Factor Questionnaire* (Champaign, IL: Institute for Personality and Ability Testing, 1970).

26  Raymond L. Horton, "Some Relationships between Personality and Decision Making," *Journal of Marketing Research* 16 (May 1979), pp. 233–46; Michael B. Mazis and Timothy W. Sweeney, "Novelty and Personality with Risk as a Moderating Variable," in B.B. Berkers and H. Becker, eds., 1972 *Combined Proceedings* (Chicago: American Marketing Association, 1973), pp. 401–11; Charles M. Schaninger and Donald Sciglimpaglia, "The Influence of Cognitive Personality Traits and Demographics on Consumer Information Acquisition," *Journal of Consumer Research* 8 (September 1981), pp. 208–16. For a review of personality studies, see Girish N. Punj and David W. Stewart, "An Interaction Framework of Consumer Decision Making," *Journal of Consumer Research* 10 (September 1983), pp. 181–96.

27  Harold H. Kassarjian, "Personality and Consumer Behavior: A Review," *Journal of Marketing Research* 8 (November 1971), pp. 409–19.

28  David W. Merrill and Roger H. Reid, *Personal Styles and Effective Performance: Make Your Style Work for You* (Radnor, PA: Chilton Book Company, 1981).

29  Parts of this section are adapted from Terrence E. Deal and Allan A. Kennedy, *Corporate Cultures: The Rites and Rituals of Corporate Life* (Reading, MA: Addison-Wesley Publishing Co., 1982).

30  Geert Hofstede, *Cultural Consequences: International Differences in Work-Related Value* (Beverly Hills, CA: Sage., 1980); Geert Hofstede and Michael H. Bond, "Hofstede's Culture Dimensions: An Independent Validation Using Rokeach's Value Survey," *Journal of Cross-Cultural Psychology*, 15 (December 1984), pp. 417–33.

31 Jennifer L. Aaker and Patti Williams, "Empathy versus Pride: The Influence of Emotional Appeals across Cultures," *Journal of Consumer Research*, 25 (December 1998), pp. 241–61.

32 Kevin Johnston and Parminder Johal, "The Internet as a 'virtual cultural region': are extant cultural classification schemes appropriate?," *Internet Research: Electronic Networking Applications and Policy*, Vol 9, Issue 3, 1999, http://www.emerald-library.com.

33 Francis S. Bourne, "Group Influence in Marketing and Public Relations," in *Some Applications of Behavioral Research*, eds. R. Likert and S.P. Hayes (Basil, Switzerland: UNESCO, 1957).

34 William O. Bearden and Michael J. Etzel, "Reference Group Influence on Product and Brand Purchase Decisions," *Journal of Consumer Research* 9, (1982), pp. 183–94.

35 See C. Whan Park and V. Parker Lessig, "Students and Housewives: Differences in Susceptibility to Reference Group Influence," *Journal of Consumer Research* 4, no. 2 (1977), pp. 102–10; and Robert E. Burnkrant and Alain Cousineau, "Informational and Normative Social Influence in Buyer Behavior," *Journal of Consumer Research* 2 (December 1975), pp. 206–15.

36 Poverty Thresholds 1999, http://www.census.gov/hhes/poverty/poverty99/pv99thrs.html.

37 Income and Poverty 1999—Press Briefing on September 26, 2000—http://www.census.gov/hhes/income/income99/prs00asc.html.

38 Statistics on the use of the Internet and Purchasing via the Internet for U.S. households, 2000, http://www.emarketer.com., "The Rise of I-Commerce," Supplement to *The Wall Street Journal*, October 29, 2001.

39 Richard P. Coleman, and Lee P. Rainwater, with Kent A. McClelland, *Social Standing in America: New Dimensions of Class* (New York: Basic Books, 1978).

40 Frederick E. Webster, Jr., "Determining the Characteristics of the Socially Conscious Consumer," *Journal of Consumer Research* 2 (December 1975), pp. 188–96.

41 Coleman, "The Continuing Significance of Social Class to Marketing," *Journal of Consumer Research*, 10 (December 1983), pp. 265–80.

42 Philip M. Parker and Nader T. Tavassoli, "Homeostasis and Consumer Behavior Across Cultures," *International Journal of Research in Marketing*, 17 (2000), pp. 33–53.

43 Dick Kelsey, "Online Holiday Spending more than doubles." *PC Data*, January 9, 2001, http://www.emarketer.com/estatnews/enews/newsbytes/20010109_Online_Holiday.html.

44 *American Demographics*, March 1995, p. 50.

45 Adapted from Marcial Mogelonsky, "The Geography of Junk Food," *American Demographics*, July 1994, pp. 13–14.

46 Ottman, *Green Marketing*.

47 Larry Carpenter, "How to Market to Regions," *American Demographics*, November 1987, pp. 44–48.

48 Nevin Cohen, "eGreen: Efficient Web Shopping for Environmentally-Safe Products," *eMarketer*, April 21, 2000, http://www.emarketer.com/analysis/ecommerce_b2c/042400_green.html.

49 "Big business bows to global warming; Energy firms and global warming," *The Economist* (US), December 2, 2000: p. 4.

50 George Katona, "Consumer Saving Pattern," *Journal of Consumer Research* 1 (June 1974), pp. 1–12.

51 Richard T. Curtin, "Indicators of Consumer Behavior: The University of Michigan Survey of Consumers," *Public Opinion Quarterly* 46 (1982), pp. 340–52. Also see, E. James Jennings and Paul McGrath, "The Influence of Consumer Sentiment on the Sales of Durables," *Journal of Business Forecasting*, 13 (Fall 1994) pp. 17–20.

52 Consumer Confidence Index, http://www.crc-conquest.org/.

53 W. Fred van Raaij, "Economic Psychology," *Journal of Economic Psychology* 1 (1981), pp. 1–24. Alf Lindquist, "A Note on Determinants of Household Saving Behavior," *Journal of Economic Psychology* 1 (March 1981), pp. 39–57.

54 H. Robert Wientzen, "What Is the Internet's Impact on Direct Marketing Today and Tomorrow?," *Journal of Interactive Marketing*, 14 (3), Summer 2000, pp. 74–78.

55 Federal Trade Commission, *Privacy Online: A Report to the Congress*, June 1998; Eve M. Caudill and Patrick E. Murphy, "Consumer Online Privacy: Legal and Ethical Issues," *Journal of Public Policy and Marketing*, 19(1), Spring 2000, pp. 7–19.

56 Jagdish N. Sheth and Rajendra S. Sisodia, "The Information Mall," *Telecommunications Policy*, July 1993, pp. 376–89.

57 Child Online Privacy Protection Act (COPPA), http://www.ftc.gov.

58 Eve M. Caudill and Patrick E. Murphy, "Consumer Online Privacy: Legal and Ethical Issues," *Journal of Public Policy and Marketing*, 19(1), Spring 2000, pp. 7–19.

59 Michelle Levander, "New Economy in Asia: Singapore Is Pushing Populace to the Internet," *The Wall Street Journal Europe*, October 28, 1999.

60 "Demand for E-Commerce Activities and New Devices Surges Ahead," According to 2000 America Online/Roper Starch Cyberstudy, October 24, 2000, http://www.roper.com/news/content/news218.htm.

61 "Chain Store Age Executive with Shopping Center Age," *Going beyond EDI* 69, no. 3 (March 1993) pp. 150–51.

62 Jeff Moad, "Let Customers Have It Their Way," *Datamation* 41, no. 6 (April 1, 1995), pp. 34–37.

# CHAPTER 3

## Trends in Determinants of Customer Behavior

## The Cyber Suite

You need not insert the key card to open your hotel room; simply hold it, and the proximity-sensitive lock will flip open. You can hold real-time videoconferencing via the Internet right from your room. You can play interactive video games on the flat-screen TV right in your room, using the virtual-reality headgear connected to that TV. You will also find the "butler in the box," ready to obey all your orders via voice recognition, controlling such room functions as lighting, temperature, draperies, and appliances. Finally, your room comes with a cellular phone with the same number as the hotel room number so that you can wander anywhere and still receive all your calls. Welcome to the Los Angeles Century Plaza Hotel. Welcome to the hotel of the future. This is the Cyber Suite in the hotel, built as a prototype for the hotel of the future. The introduction of these innovative technologies is just a sampling of what will eventually become the industry standards for accommodating business travelers in the twenty-first century, says Jim Petrus, the managing director of the Century Plaza.[1]

Predicting future customer behavior, just as Jim Petrus has done for Century Plaza, requires predicting the factors that influence customer behavior. Almost any of the diverse factors discussed in Chapter 2 is capable of changing and, in turn, changing customer behavior. In this chapter, we focus on the three factors that are expected to cause the most significant change in future customer behavior: (1) changes in demographics, (2) advances in technology, and (3) changes in public policy (see Figure 3.1). Changes in other customer factors are likely as well, but less discernible and perhaps less dramatic. This chapter elaborates on each of these trends and how they affect customer behavior. It closes with a discussion of how these trends are likely to affect marketing strategy.

**FIGURE 3.1**     **Conceptual Framework**

# Benefits of Anticipating Trends in Customer Behavior

Anticipating trends in customer behavior can give companies a key strategic advantage. Foreseeing the coming trends in customers' needs and wants offers companies several advantages. First, if you see a market need first, you can be the first to start working to meet that need. Consequently, it reduces the fulfillment time, making the economic payback a lot quicker. For example, Sony anticipated the Walkman phenomenon, and, similarly, Netscape anticipated the impact of the Internet. Both companies were the first to come out with their respective products and services, and both succeeded in the marketplace.

Second, by sighting a trend, the industry can create a market by channeling a latent need. One example is the cellular phone industry. Being able to communicate without being grounded in one location (i.e., wireless communication) is certainly on many people's wish list, but not everyone can afford the high initial equipment costs. The industry responded by offering a free phone with a service contract, and the market for cell phones has skyrocketed.

Third, anticipating trends in customer needs and wants and responding to them creates positive public opinion for the company and the industry, portraying them as responsive. Examples include smoke-free facilities, such as airports, airplanes, and restaurants, and environmentally friendly products, such as organically grown foods, recyclable paper products, and cosmetics developed without animal testing.

# Demographic Trends

Changing demographics of the customer serve as a good indicator of the future marketplace. As explained in Chapter 2, such demographic characteristics as age, income, race and ethnicity, and geographic location of a customer intimately influence his or her customer behavior. Studying projections or trends in the demographic makeup of a population can, therefore, help marketers anticipate the needs and wants of their customers. Six demographic trends have already begun to transform the marketplace:

1. Aging of the population
2. Rise in number of working women
3. Increase in single-person households
4. Decline of the middle class
5. Increase in ethnic diversity
6. Geographic redistribution.

## Aging of the Population

In all of the advanced countries of the world, the population is aging. As of the year 2000, Sweden has the oldest population in the world, with 17.2 percent of its people being 65 years of age or older. In comparison, 12.6 percent of the people in the United States are 65 years of age or older, and 17 percent of the Japanese people are over the age of 65. However, by the year 2025, Japan is likely to become the oldest nation in terms of its people, with 27.5 percent of the population being 65 years of age or older.

Populations age for two key reasons: (1) their birthrate is declining and (2) their life expectancy is rising. In the early 1900s, the birthrate in the United States was approximately seven children per woman. At that time, the U.S. economy was driven by farming, and children were an economic asset. However, in the industrial society, children became more of an economic burden. (In fact, the current estimates are that the net present value of all the future costs of having and raising a child today, including four years of college, amounts to approximately $220,000!) Consequently, by 1980, the U.S. birthrate had dropped to 1.6 children per woman; in the year 2000, it stood at 2.1 children per woman. When fewer babies are born, the average age of the nation's population goes up.

The second, and more significant, factor behind the aging of the U.S. population is the rising life expectancy. A good indicator of the aging of the population is the rise in the number of people 65 or more years old. In 1960, there were 16.6 million people 65 years of age or older; in 2000, the number had risen to 34.8 million, and it is expected to be 62.6 million by 2025.[2] The two fastest-growing segments in the U.S. population are centenarians and people 85 years of age, further adding to the average age in the United States.[3] Similarly, almost all of the European countries are also aging as the proportion of young people is decreasing, with the exception of Ireland, which has a considerably larger population of young people.[4]

These two factors are behind most of the aging of the Japanese population also. In Japan, the life expectancy in the year 2025 will be 82.9 years, compared with 82.2 in Sweden and 80.6 in the United States. At the same time, the annual growth rate of Japan is expected to be −0.6 in the year 2025, compared with rates of −0.1 in Sweden and 0.8 in the United States.[5] These two factors imply that Japan will have the oldest population in the next century.

The aging of the population is creating new needs and wants. In particular, an aging population is relatively concerned about wellness, financial well-being, safety and security, and recreation. Seniors also are using the Internet to address these concerns today. Adults 55 and older represent the fastest-growing group of U.S. Internet users, according to International Data Corp. (IDC). It found that the number of seniors will more than triple from 11.1 million in 1999 to 34.1 million in 2004 and that they will account for 20 percent of all new Internet users.[6] Researchers McMellon and Schiffman conducted a study with online members of SeniorNet—a group of older adults on America Online—and with Retirement + and AARP—two groups accessible through CompuServe. They suggest that there may be a relationship between the limited out-of-home mobility of seniors and the amount of time they spend on the Internet. Seniors might be using the Internet to keep in touch with their social circle and to keep themselves informed, thus compensating for their limited out-of-home mobility.[7] In confirmation of this study, Greenfield Online found that seniors are getting on to the e-commerce bandwagon. Of the 1265 Web users aged 55 and above, 92 percent have used the Internet for window-shopping and 78 percent have made a purchase online. Seniors use e-mail to stay in touch with family, friends, and also exchange digital photos of children and grandchildren. Surprisingly, they buy more books and software over the Internet than drugstore items. Marketers need to personalize the shopping experience for this segment, which has high purchasing power and plenty of time to spend on the Internet. They are faced with the challenge of converting the seniors' recreational and informational usage of the Internet into profits for their sites, keeping in mind the simple fact that seniors may be looking for a compelling retail experience online to substitute for their limited out-of-home mobility.[8]

## Wellness

One of the most important implications of an aging society is a rise in the costs of health care. In the United States, health care costs made up less than 7.5 percent of the gross domestic product in 1970. By 1991, the share had increased to nearly 15 percent. The most conservative projections (i.e., based on assuming a robust economic growth, improved demographic trends, and a moderation in the rate of health care price inflation) are that the health-care sector will consume more than a quarter of the national output by the year 2065. A less conservative scenario (i.e., a continuation of current trends) places health-care expenditures between one-third and one-half of national output by the year 2065.[9]

Inevitably then, cost containment will be a priority. The healthcare programs will need to emphasize not only caring for the ill but also prevention and health-promotion programs. As more people age and live longer, their need for physical well-being will significantly increase demand in the nutrition, drug, and physical fitness industries. Marketers will need to respond to customer needs in these three product/service areas as well as to educate customers about their importance and proper usage. Already, the concern over health has changed people's food habits and smoking behavior dramatically. Internet sites like WebMD.com provide customers with complete healthcare information and education—health news, a directory of physicians, question-answer sessions with specialists, and provision for chatting on message boards with regard to specific health interests.

All three customer roles will be involved in these wellness needs of the elderly. For the user, the most important value will be performance value. Food products will have to offer nutritional and dietary value, and drugs will need to offer efficacy as a value in addition to cure and prevention. The personal value of social and emotional kinds will also be relevant to some degree. Marketing communications will have to present these foods and nutrients as part of a healthy and active lifestyle that would need to be supplemented by physical fitness programs tailored to the elderly.

The payer role is affected as the costs of medicine and vitamin and health supplements increase. In their payer role, end-user customers will be concerned with the price value, even if they pay only a part of the cost. But government and health-insurance agencies will be concerned primarily as a payer. Already, health maintenance organizations are demanding from physicians and hospitals that they use generic or less expensive substitutes for brand-name or more expensive drugs.

Finally, the convenient availability of drugs, food products, and fitness programs will be a concern of the elderly in their buyer role. Buyers will want service (e.g., advice on ingredients) as well as convenience (e.g., locations close to home or work and open longer hours). Walgreen Pharmacies in the United States now offer home drop-off of prescription drugs, creating precisely the value elderly buyers will seek even more. As mentioned before, seniors are going online in big numbers and studies show that one-third of online seniors have visited online drugstores. Twenty-seven percent of them have bought over-the-counter products on the Internet, but only 9 percent of those that have visited an on-line drugstore have bought prescription drugs. They are not comfortable with buying drugs online; only 17 percent of seniors said they are extremely or very likely to purchase from an online drugstore in the future and 56 percent said they were not very likely to purchase this type of item online.[10]

## Financial Well-Being

As people grow older, their concerns also center around financial well-being. Financial products and services such as financial planning, wills and trusts, and mutual funds and stocks acquire new significance in aging customers' lives. The elderly begin to build and draw on their wealth; wealth, rather than income, therefore, becomes the source of what customers buy and pay for in their buyer and payer roles.

## Safety and Security

As people grow older, they become increasingly concerned about physical safety at home, at the workplace, and on the street. Concern also grows about security of possessions. Personal safety has been the concern of many Americans. For example, in recent years, gun possession has skyrocketed. In 1980, $1.35 million was spent on firearms and hunting equipment; by the 1990s, that increased to $14.4 million, a tenfold increase over an approximately 15-year period.[11] Likewise, the use of antitheft security devices in cars, houses, and even neighborhoods has increased dramatically. As nations age, antitheft devices, security alarm systems in cars and homes, cell phones for emergencies on the road, and even self-defense classes will increase in popularity.

Recent surveys have shown that concerns about safety on the Internet are quite similar between the older and younger population. Safety was defined in the studies as the possibility of other people reading personal e-mail or tracking visits to Web sites and so on. It does not look like the older population is unduly concerned about this aspect and hence, it cannot be used as a differentiator between the two segments. Seniors are however, more concerned about e-commerce security in relation to banking or making purchases over the net than the 25–50 age group and this is reflected in the value of their Internet transactions. Over 60 percent of the aging population spent less than $50 on Internet transactions while 74 percent of the 25–50 group spent more than $100 per transaction.[12]

## Recreational Needs

With homes paid for and children's college education completed, the elderly find more discretionary income available for travel, eating out, and other recreational activities. As their recreational needs increase, they will fuel growth in the travel and restaurant industries. Other beneficiaries will be the businesses involved in manufacturing and marketing bicycles, athletic shoes, and other sporting and recreational equipment.

With the aging population, recreation also will shift from active to passive. Examples are (1) replacing team contact sports with individualized sports and (2) going out or staying at home and watching TV or listening to the radio. This causes a demand for sporting goods for individualized sports and a change in TV and radio programming to include more reality-based programs and programs of interest to elderly at the time that they are most likely to watch.

## Women in the Workforce

A second demographic shift is the increasing number of households that have women working outside the home. In 1960, only 37 percent of all adult women (between the ages of 18 and 68) were working outside the home. Their numbers have risen steadily over the past three decades, to 43 percent in 1970, 51.5 percent in 1980, 57.5 percent in 1990, and 60 percent in 1998. By the year 2006, the number of households with working women is projected to rise to 61.4 percent.[13]

The increase in the number of working women has resulted in a significant change in the resources of a household, specifically the time resource. There are two effects on time as a resource: time shortage and time shift. Time shortage refers to lack of free time; time shift refers to the time when nonwork-related activities may be pursued. Because dual-income families are spending close to 60 hours per week in work-related activities, adults have discretionary time left only in the evenings and on weekends. This time shift has made it more difficult for businesses to service this segment. For example, automobile repair, store hours, delivery of packages, or even having repair and maintenance done to the home has been made more difficult for many businesses. This makes weekends and evenings a more desirable time for businesses to cater to their customers. A study by America Online and the Business Women's Network (BWN) found that working women are accessing the Internet in large numbers. They spend more than 14 hours a week online and more than half of working women access the Internet at least once a day. Seventy-two percent of working women would prefer a computer with Internet access on their desk than a telephone. They use the Internet for work, for career advancement, and to find jobs. In fact, the study found that 84 percent of women say "the Internet saves them time in every aspect of their lives." Almost all women surveyed had also researched products on the net and a sizeable number had even purchased online.[14] Working women tend to shop and buy online more frequently than the female online population in general. Leisure products, computer equipment, and travel equipment are the most popular online purchases for businesswomen.[15]

Another effect of the working women trend is the shift in the lifestyle of families. With both spouses working, households have turned into roommate families, where parents and children are reluctant to share anything, including food served at mealtime, television shows, and other activities that take place in the household. There is a movement towards highly individualized preferences, especially when it comes to food and television.

Finally, time shortage is resulting in the outsourcing of a typical homemaker's duties—namely, cooking, cleaning, and childcare. As a result of more women working outside the home, consumption patterns are changing dramatically. People are eating out more, estimated at two meals a day among adults. In addition, 50 percent of the time, the one meal eaten at home is prepared by someone other than the woman in the household. This has resulted in dramatic changes in the layout of kitchens and a subsequent change in the suppliers to kitchens. Telephones, cable television, security systems, and even personal computers are finding their ways into the kitchens of households today. As the kitchen becomes the family activity center, customers are demanding larger kitchens. As women work outside the house during the day, housecleaning is being outsourced, that is, provided by contractors. By one estimate, there will be an 18 percent increase in the number of cleaners, maids, and janitors—up to 3.6 million by the year 2005. According to a recent estimate, more than 11 percent of all U.S. households use either a maid or professional cleaning service.[16] Child care is another industry that is booming in response to the need to care for children whose parents are not able to stay home. In 1991, 23 percent of all children under five years of age were in an organized child-care facility while 31 percent were cared for in another home. Approximately 5 million preschool children in the United States attend some form of child-care service. At a cost of around $6,000 a year per child, child-care services account for a $30 billion industry in the United States. An interesting development is the increasing role of grandparents in babysitting their grandchildren. A recent estimate is that of the children receiving child care at the child's own home or another home (i.e., not counting school-based, place of employment-based, or commercial day care centers), fully one-fifth to one-fourth of them receive it from their grandparents.[17]

Some new patterns also are emerging wherein there seems to be a growth in home-based work and independent contracting for women, flexible schedules, back-to-back shifts among parents, and "sequencing," or moving in and out of the work force. This shift is not seen statistically yet, but there is a trend towards parents considering options such as part-time work or one parent quitting work so that they get to spend more time with children.[18] Some parents prefer one parent to be around when the child is young, while some feel that more support and guidance is needed during a child's teen years and hence they need to cut back on work at that time.

## Single-Person Households

Living alone by choice represents a shift in the family unit. A number of factors are responsible for this trend. First, as people delay marriage, it forces them to live alone. Second, a significant part of the adult population is in transition. They are between marriages due to situations such as divorce or separation. Third, dual careers split homes. Career opportunities often require the physical separation of spouses. Fourth, as we age, more people in their older age will be living alone. Finally, as both men and women have more economic independence, they may prefer to live alone to enjoy personal lifestyles and freedom.

An increase in single-person households is not limited to the United States. In Europe, too, household sizes are decreasing as the countries age, resulting in fewer children being born, young people leaving home, and older people staying single after becoming divorced or widowed. The average household size in the European Union is now 2.7 people. The smallest household sizes can be found in Denmark (2.0 on average), and the largest in Spain (3.7). This shift has increased demand for more appliances, telecommunication equipment such as telephones, and electronics goods.[19]

Living alone shifts the society from a nuclear family unit (households of parents plus children) to an atomistic family unit (households of individuals). The unit of analysis will become the individual and not the household. People will share less and personalize more. More specifically, implications of the living alone trend include loneliness, self-respect and autonomy, cocooning, and impulse buying.

## Loneliness

One of the consequences of living alone is loneliness. This fast-growing disease is generating a significant need for belongingness. Institutions and objects will become methods and symbols of belonging replacing the kinship methods of belonging. Not having family members available in day-to-day life, people will identify increasingly with the workplace, homes, pets, automobiles, and membership clubs. Drug and alcohol abuse or suicide could be considered an escape from loneliness. On the positive side, people also will join social causes and contribute their time to volunteer organizations in order to escape loneliness.

The marketplace will feel the impact of this trend with a shifting emphasis in products and services. Products and services will be sold more on the basis of symbolism and social group values rather than merely on their functional or performance values.

## Self-Respect and Autonomy

As people live alone and are financially self-sufficient, they will demand more autonomy (power to control their own lives) and self-respect from others. They want to be treated correctly as customers, workers, and citizens. To the user, this trend will result in more customized products and services that are appealing. To the buyers in the household, businesses will have to be careful to offer them the best service value possible. Bored at home, many will visit stores for socializing. They will value retail stores whose personnel are friendly and engage in small talk. Customers also will prefer stores and service establishments (e.g., hair salons, restaurants) where sales staff or service employees are similar to them in demographics and lifestyle.

## Cocooning

In contrast to the trend for single people to leave their homes to socialize is the demand for new services and products to be available at home. Cocooning is the habit of staying at home rather than going out. Businesses are increasingly providing services and activities in customers' homes to meet the convenience value of the customer. Suppliers of products and services will have to be as physically close to the customer as possible, offering such conveniences as direct marketing, one-stop shopping, neighborhood shopping centers, and home deliveries. A study by the Peppers and Rogers Group and the Institute for the Future states that the consumer direct channel will account for 12 percent of all U.S. retail sales by 2010. The study shows that consumers are already using this channel extensively with 83 percent of consumers making a purchase through direct-to-home channels in 1999. Twenty-five percent of these consumers used the Internet to buy products and the online channel is expected to account for a large portion of consumer direct sales by 2010. Consumers will use the Internet to buy products and services in all categories. Estimated online spending for groceries in 2004 is $8.8 billion, up from less than $200 million in 1999. It is also expected that U.S. customers will spend up to $10 billion on health related products online by 2004.[20]

## Impulse Behavior

As people live alone, they tend to make choices more impulsively. This occurs because there is no social norm or control to slow down the urge or desire. Consequently, they will have greater desire for instant gratification, or immediate satisfaction of their wants and needs. For example, as customers do their food shopping, they will be attracted to the performance value of prepared foods.

## The Declining Middle Class

Between 1970 and 1997, the middle class shrunk as a percentage of U.S. households, even though it grew in total numbers. When measured in 1997 dollars, households with incomes between $25,000 and $50,000 dropped from 38 percent to 30 percent of all households (although it increased in numbers from 25 million to 30 million). The most often cited reason for the decline of the middle class in the United States is stagnant wages. The stagnation in real wages has hit the middle class the hardest since they (in contrast to the upper class) rely on their wages to pay the bills.[21]

The same compression of the middle class is occurring in other advanced economies as well. However, the middle class is growing in Asia due to the recent and continuing business boom there. For example, in India, the demand from the rapidly expanding middle class is fueling its economy. These middle-class citizens have increasingly higher aspirations and more disposable income and purchasing power. The largest middle class is found in China, with 300 million middle-class citizens fueling industrial growth in that country by 10 percent a year.[22]

In advanced nations such as the United States and Western Europe, the declining middle class has transformed the economics of survival. This trend has four key implications: an increasing range in prices of products, more customer militancy, affordability, and the neo rich.

## Increasing Range of Prices of Products

One major consequence is that the price range from minimum to maximum prices for the same product category, across a range of different brand names, will begin to increase. Generally, when there is a very tight, large middle class, the maximum to minimum price ratio is no greater than five. However, with the decline in the middle class and corresponding growth at the extremes of the income range, the price range becomes much larger to fit with a diverse range of customer resources, increasing up to 20 to 25 times. For example, the price of fresh fruits and vegetables ranges widely, from low-cost vegetables like lettuce and carrots to very fancy vegetation from far-flung parts of the world being sold in supermarkets today. The same is true for automobiles, where there are mass-produced cars priced as low as $8,000 to $10,000, to special super-premium cars like the Bentley, priced at $300,000.

## More Customer Militancy

A second major consequence is the rise in customer militancy—vocal and physical protest if expectations are not met. One reason for customer militancy is the frustration of the lower socioeconomic classes, who are finding it almost impossible to survive. There is an increase in marketplace violence because people are unhappy about the income gap that exists.

Customer militancy can also be attributed to a sense of hopelessness as people see their bills climbing, incomes stagnating, and future prospects for paying college bills worsening. A lack of control can ultimately lead to a sense of unhappiness, which influences customer behavior. Buyers of products will seek service-oriented businesses that are receptive to their mood. Unhappy customers will seek stores that have uplifting environments, ones that give them a reason to get out of the house to go shopping.

## Affordability

A shrinking middle class implies a growth of the low-income class. A large segment of the society will be unable to afford what is considered to be an acceptable middle-class lifestyle— owning a home, raising children, and having retirement plans. This affordability issue will become extremely important in the marketplace; it will require marketers to generate creative financing, not only for durables such as automobiles and appliances but even for consumables. It also will require marketers to bring in low-cost, high-quality products and services, even if it means offshore manufacturing and procurement. Finally, this trend also implies increased problems with shoplifting, bad debts, and customer fraud in general. Income has been shown to be one of the most important reasons for the "digital divide" among households in Internet access and use. However, recent studies show that computer and Internet access is increasing for American households at all income levels, specially the middle-income levels. Internet access among households earning $35,000 to $49,000 rose from 29.0 percent in December 1998 to 46.1 percent in August 2000. Low-income groups seem to also use the Internet for job search.[23]

## The Neo Rich

As the affluent class grows to 30 percent, the wealthy (or what some have referred to as neo rich) will abandon old symbols of affluence and will patronize new symbols of conspicuous consumption. The lifestyle of the rich and famous will become more and more unique through customized behavior. In the marketplace, customized (totally unique, not duplicated) products and services will rise significantly in homes, property, vacations, and so on.

## Ethnic Diversity

Because of the economic integration in Europe, people are migrating to obtain better living standards. This migration is causing an increase in cultural and ethnic diversity. The United States, of course, has historically been ethnically diverse, and that trend is on the rise. For example, it is estimated that the Hispanic population, whose rate of growth is at least three times faster than that of the average population, will represent nearly 16 percent of the total U.S. population by the year 2020.[24] The African-American population is expected to retain its approximately 12 percent share of the total population, and the Asian population will increase significantly, becoming the third largest ethnic minority group in the United States.

From around 20 percent noncaucasian, the U.S. population has increased to around 30 percent noncaucasian and will continue to increase even more in the future. By the year 2050, the movement toward greater ethnic diversity in the United States will result in the country having a majority of people who are noncaucasian. Ethnic groups are no longer coming only from Europe, but from Latin America, the Caribbean Islands, Asia, and Africa, bringing to the United States a greater number and wider diversity of people from all over the world.[25] Increasing globalization of the economy, job opportunities and lenient immigration laws are some of the factors accounting for this diversity.

This trend has two distinct implications: First, markets must be more segmented. Second, marketers must meet the requirements of increasing cultural diversity. As discussed in Chapter 2, each of these ethnic groups also have a presence on the Internet catering to their own specific tastes and interests.

## Segmented Markets

In a more diverse population, markets will require more careful segmentation to serve each of the distinct ethnic groups. More choices will be available for food, shelter, and clothing through the mainstream retail institutions. For example, restaurants and supermarkets will carry a wide range of ethnic foods. Department stores will carry ethnic merchandise. Of course, in order to cater to diverse segments, marketers would have to study their customers closely.

## Cultural Diversity

With ethnic diversity comes cultural diversity, bringing with it changes in products and marketing communications. For example, it is not uncommon to see many product labels around the United States printed in both English and Spanish. As the proportion of Hispanic customers increases in the marketplace, for example, so will the marketer's sensitivity toward incorporating the language and cultural differences of these segments. The Internet is said to be the ultimate vehicle for globalization of business and has broken all geographical barriers that bound business locally. Yet, language is an important issue to be tackled to truly harness the full potential of the Internet. With more than 57 percent of Internet users expected to speak a language other than English by 2005 (Computer Economics estimates), businesses operating in different countries will need to mirror their sites in different languages and customize them with local content to make them interesting.[26] Table 3.1 gives statistics on web pages by language. In the year 2000, English pages accounted for 68.3 percent of total web pages on the Internet, followed by Japanese at 5.85 percent, German at 5.77 percent, and Chinese at 3.87 percent. However, Chinese pages are slated to be second only to English on the Web in a few years as the number of Internet users in China increase and more and more of the English content is being translated into the Chinese language for use.

## Geographic Redistribution

In the future, marketers also can expect geographic redistribution, or shifts in population density from one region of a nation or world to another. Currently, the United States is experiencing such a movement, such as the breakup of big cities and a move to the Sunbelt. This is the result of several forces:

- As more people come from Asia and Latin America, they prefer to settle in warmer climates comparable to where they grew up. This was true of the early European settlers, and it continues to be true of new immigrants.

## Web Pages by Language     TABLE 3.1

| Language | Number of Web Pages | Percent of Total |
|---|---|---|
| English | 214,250,996 | 68.39 |
| Japanese | 18,335,739 | 5.85 |
| German | 18,069,744 | 5.77 |
| Chinese | 12,113,803 | 3.87 |
| French | 9,262,663 | 2.96 |
| Spanish | 7,573,064 | 2.42 |
| Russian | 5,900,956 | 1.88 |
| Italian | 4,883,497 | 1.56 |
| Portuguese | 4,291,237 | 1.37 |
| Korean | 4,046,530 | 1.29 |
| Dutch | 3,161,844 | 1.01 |
| Sweden | 2,929,241 | 0.93 |
| Danish | 1,374,886 | 0.44 |
| Norwegian | 1,259,189 | 0.40 |
| Finnish | 1,198,956 | 0.38 |
| Czech | 991,075 | 0.32 |
| Polish | 848,672 | 0.27 |
| Hungarian | 498,625 | 0.16 |
| Catalan | 443,301 | 0.14 |
| Turkish | 430,996 | 0.14 |
| Greek | 287,980 | 0.09 |
| Hebrew | 198,030 | 0.06 |
| Estonian | 173,265 | 0.06 |
| Romanian | 141,587 | 0.05 |
| Icelandic | 136,788 | 0.04 |
| Slovenian | 134,454 | 0.04 |
| Arabic | 127,565 | 0.04 |
| Lithuanian | 82,829 | 0.03 |
| Latvian | 60,959 | 0.02 |
| Bulgarian | 51,336 | 0.02 |
| Basque | 36,321 | 0.01 |

- The United States is a service economy and is, therefore, less dependent on natural resources. This means that new businesses can locate in all areas of the country.
- Geographic boundaries are less relevant because information technologies overcome or reduce space and time barriers.
- The quality of life, as measured by crime, traffic, pollution, and education, in big cities is very poor. This has resulted in an exodus out of big cities to nearby towns.
- Corporations are relocating in remote locations due to the economic incentives available there, many offered by local and state governments trying to attract new businesses into their territory.
- As both the federal and state governments invest in infrastructures such as highways, utilities, and other public services, they are bridging the gap between big cities and small towns.

Geographical redistribution affects families directly in that it separates different generations in different space and time zones. This will increase gaps both within generations (i.e., between siblings) and between generations (i.e., between grandparents, parents, and children) as people living in different areas of the country reflect different values, lifestyles, and attitudes. Since families will be split both between generations and within generations, there will be a trend toward fractured families, or a decline in extended families. There also will be less intergenerational influence. No longer will customers buy and use a brand simply because their parents used it. Finally, there will be greater heterogeneity within each region. Every region will have a greater mix of people born elsewhere.

Regional marketing both responds to and feeds these differences by exposing newly arrived residents to regional tastes. Consequently, procurement and consumption patterns are likely to become more divergent in different regions of the country. National manufacturers and national store chains will have to adapt to the regional differences. Therefore, regional marketing will acquire increasing significance.

# Technological Trends

A second force shaping future customer values is technology. As discussed in Chapter 2, advances in technology have already given customers increased access to information, newer generations of products, automation of transaction processes to provide customers with greater flexibility and control, and access to some customized products. Future developments will further change products and the very nature of customer behavior.

## New Technologies

In particular, technological advances are expected to include products that give customers more control over information and information access-smart products, automation of processes that liberate customers from operations-driven processes, and products and services that enable customized lifestyles.

### Increased Control Over Information

The information age is already upon us. The computer storage of information has made widespread distribution and access to marketplace information a reality. And yet, the information infrastructure is still evolving, and what we see today is barely the tip of the iceberg. What will the full-blown information age be like? According to information technology strategy experts Jagdish N. Sheth and Rajendra S. Sisodia:

> The vision of the future information infrastructure is that there will be an interactive broadband digital highway terminating in very high resolution multimedia display terminals in consumer homes and workplaces. . . . Today's World Wide Web (WWW) represents a crude approximation of the capabilities and functionality that are expected to be widely deployed by the middle of the next decade. It is serving as a very large test bed for companies and as a training platform for consumers to learn new modalities of interaction and consumption.[27]

This prophesy is already unfolding. The appendix in this chapter gives us the status of the Internet information infrastructure across different regions and countries in the world.

The equipment that gives you the combined capabilities of TV and computer is already available, such as WebTV or network computers. In the future, these will become more powerful, sophisticated, portable, easy to use, and affordable (i.e., smarter, easier, smaller, and cheaper). Already currently available handheld computers, such as the latest gizmo, Sony Clie, PEG-NR70V, combine phone, digital camera, and PDA (Personnel Digital Assistant) and cost just $599. These smart terminals, along with the much broadened bandwidth and multimedia experience capabilities, will enable consumers to select the information they want, when they want it. Advertising messages will not be broadcast anymore; rather, they will have to be narrowcast (targeted to a narrow group of customers) or even monocast or pointcast (targeted to a single customer). Information will be stored in digital video servers to be viewed or downloaded *on demand*. The viewer will be in control of content scheduling and selection. The customer will view, hear, and attend to the market communications of his or her choosing, at a time and place of his or her choosing. In such an environment, information invitations may become a common practice companies will have to seek permission to present their case to customers—a far cry from the uninvited barrage of advertising messages cluttering the mass media today.

## Smart Products

The newer generation of products will increasingly become smart products—products that can communicate their functioning status to an outside agent or receive communication from an outside agent to adapt their function within predefined limits. Thus, they contain elements both of some artificial intelligence and built-in adaptability. For example, smart copiers that communicate impending breakdown to a remote repair agency already are available; the repair person comes and fixes the machine even without the customer making the repair request. Moreover, beyond just communicating their function status and impending breakdown, they could receive instructions from the remote site and recycle the set-up procedures to correct the software-related problems.

Smart products also are being developed with voice-recognition capabilities. Voice-recognition technology, when incorporated into smart products, offers customers ease of use and assurance against theft or fraud since voice is the most unique identification of an individual. For example, automated teller machines will be able to receive voice instructions from the customer, making them very user-friendly.

Smart products are being designed to store the selected preferences of their owners and users; in other words, they will have memory. Thus, if you sat in a car or chair once, it might store the ergonomic profile in its memory so that the next time you sit in the same seat, it will, based on a voice code, or, better still, based on a tactile code, automatically shape itself into that ergonomic profile. This profile will, of course, be more customized than the current versions of memorized seat positions available in many automobiles. Such technology is already in use in Mercedes' new line of S-Class cars, which features a front passenger seat that automatically recognizes when a child safety seat is being used and reduces the air bag power. The line also features a chip-card key equipped with a profile of the driver. Smart products also will adapt to the intended usage by incorporating a feedback loop. Consider, for example, the water temperature you prefer in the shower. A smart shower will set itself to give you the temperature consistency on the second and later usages. Moreover, it also will adapt the water temperature according to the room temperature. Motorola, the world's leading producer of embedded semiconductor solutions, has donated $5 million to establish the Motorola DigitalDNA Laboratory at the MIT Media Lab in Cambridge by 2003. The Motorola DigitalDNA Laboratory will focus on linking several smart products, such as set-top TV boxes, automobiles, household appliances, personal digital assistants, and wireless communications systems, thus integrating several independent gadgets into one intelligent mechanism.[28]

## Access to Products Anytime, Anywhere

In the industrial age, the customer became a hostage to the marketer and was forced to buy the mass-produced goods at a time and place chosen by the marketer. If the stores were open only from 10 A.M. to 5 P.M., or if the car repair facility was open only on the weekdays, then that was when the customer could buy store products or take the car for repairs. Technology has liberated this hostage customer. Now the customer can buy anytime and anywhere. Moreover, due to mass customization, the customer can better fit the products to his or her needs. Thus, whatever, wherever, and whenever will be the new tenets of customer behavior. Anytime, anywhere purchasing and consumption will become commonplace. One consequence of this will be that customer desire for instant gratification will increase.

Consumers will engage in a new way of shopping, mainly, mobile shopping. A study from Strategy Analytics estimates the mobile e-commerce market in the United States at $200 million by 2004. The study expects radical shifts in consumer behavior as transactions using mobile phones increase dramatically in the coming years. Mobile phones are expected to be used to purchase goods from vending machines, buy cinema and train tickets and shop on the Internet.[29] The wireless boom in Japan has already made this scenario a reality in 2002 as services such as *I-mode* (**http://www.nttdocomo.com**) allow consumers to reserve airline and concert tickets, find restaurants, check bank balances, read news, check train schedules, send e-mail and access the Internet from their mobile phones. Technology is a major facilitator for anytime, anywhere m-commerce.

## Mass Customization

Mass customization will expand exponentially. With technology, houses, shoes and clothing, and food could all be customized and delivered almost at the speed and cost of mass-produced products. Moreover, customization will diffuse to services. Imagine that the hairstyle you got the last time can be stored in computer memory, and a visual image can be recalled on a computer screen the next time you visit the salon. You could even carry this image with you on a disk. Even more dramatically, using a virtual reality platform, you could see yourself with simulated hairstyle options and choose or create your own style.

Your preferences when you visit a restaurant or hotel can be recorded and stored. When you return for another visit, the same amenities and services would be available to you, with options to make modifications.

## Customer Responses to New Technology

Technological developments will, in turn, stimulate changes in customer behavior. Customers will increasingly take on the role of coproducers. In addition, they will engage in disintermediation, outsourcing, and automation of consumption.

## Customers as Coproducers

As described in Chapter 2, because of flexible manufacturing technology in the production stage and computer capabilities in managing customer-specific preferences, it will be possible to mass-customize products. Customers will be able to routinely offer direct input into the making of the product, called coproduction. But this is barely the beginning of customer input. The real customer participation will come with virtual reality.

Imagine an architect sitting down with you and, based on your initial specifications, drawing a picture of the house you want to build. Now, you can walk into this building, feel the materials utilized, and sense the light variations as you move from one room to another. As you suggest changes, the architect can modify the building, and you can walk into it again. You can repeat this process until you eventually have designed the house of your dreams. All this is possible with virtual reality. Virtual reality will enable you to coproduce the design for your home. Likewise, you would be able to install appliances, put together modular equipment, and repair machines, all guided by realistic graphics beamed from a remote location. Similarly, telemedicine will allow you to consult with your doctor, show your physical condition, transmit information about your vital signs (e.g., heart rate and temperature), and follow your physician's advice to medicate yourself.

Thus, for a variety of products and services, by linking directly into production systems, customers will engage in self-service, self-design, and self-ordering and provisioning. Learning from the problems faced by e-tailers in the 1999 holiday shopping season, Fedex revamped its Internet-based package return systems in 2000 to involve the customer. Ease of returns to an online retailer has been identified as an important aspect in defining the customer's shopping experience with the online retailer. In 2000, Fedex's NetReturn upgrade, allowed customers to print package return labels from their personal computers, and also specified a list of drop-off locations for depositing the packages, which would speed up the crediting procedures for the returned merchandise. This makes the customer a co-producer in the returns process, and at the same time increases the efficiency of the online retailer since he is able to track returns online.[30]

## Disintermediation

Because information technology will allow you to communicate directly with the factory, you would be able to deal with manufacturers without any intermediaries. Since enhanced graphics capability of home computers/TV terminals and video transfer of product information will allow you to get a realistic view of the product, you would not have to visit a store. Since advances in distribution technology will allow producers to ship the product to individual customers directly without much loss of speed and economy, there will be no need for intermediaries who maintain inventory closer to where customers live. In other words, customers would make their purchases without intermediaries. This manner of direct transactions between the producers and customers is called **disintermediation**. Disintermediation also accompanies greater control by customers and coproduction. ATMs are a familiar example; another noteworthy example is FedEx Ship, a software program that customers can run on their PC. Using this software, business customers of FedEx can now self-ship, self-track, and self-invoice shipping of time-sensitive documents. FedEx Ship is an example of both disintermediation and coproduction of service.

## Customer Outsourcing

Technology will make it increasingly possible for household customers to cope with rising time pressure by outsourcing what was previously produced in the home. Because customers will be able to order products and services from anywhere around the country or even from around the globe, outsourcing will not have to depend on whether the suppliers are available nearby. More and more cooked food will be outsourced, for example. Instead of cooking at home, customers will order, using their computer terminals, largely precooked food that merely needs reheating or defrosting. And this ordering will be automated with a prespecified weekly menu, with provision for spur-of-the-moment alterations.

Home-based businesses will continue to grow because technology enables operations to be set up on a small scale, and more people will find it convenient to telecommute. Telecommuting, or the more appropriate term, *teleworking*, blurs the boundaries between home and office so that, for example, office suppliers will have to deliver increasingly to workers' homes. Pizza-style delivery will spread to a wide range of home-office products as well as household-related products. Conversely, to attract and retain qualified workers, offices will be more like homes. Many products and services not traditionally considered part of an office setting will be delivered to and consumed at the office. For example, more offices will have child care, health and fitness facilities, cooking facilities, and carry-out foods for their employees.

## Automated Consumption

Thanks to new technology, time-pressed customers also will be able to benefit from an increasing degree of automation of product purchasing processes. Just as electronic data interchange (EDI) automates the ordering process in business markets, so, too, household customers will be able to automate their order processing. The home pantry will be similar to a store shelf in terms of stock replenishment, equipped with a small home computer. Every time an item is consumed, the user scans it to record stock depletion. When the stock falls to a prespecified level, the computer automatically locates the store with the best price and orders the product, getting the best deal!

In sum, future customers, emboldened by what technology will make feasible, will demand hassle-free product information (e.g., advertising on demand), hassle-free product acquisition (e.g., home delivery), hassle-free consumption (e.g., self-correcting smart products), and also hassle-free disposal. They will seek greater value in terms of (a) better fit of products and services with their needs and (b) greater savings in time, effort, and money. Armed with user-friendly access to marketplace information, future customers will no longer be the *targets* of marketing activity. Rather, they will be knowledgeable and demanding *drivers* of it.

Technological revolution in all spheres of life will undoubtedly unleash customer behavior that is more liberated as well as more demanding. As people start to change the way they work, communicate, and spend their leisure time, they will demand a change in the way companies do business with them. They will resent the high costs (both in time and effort) of acquiring the goods and services they seek and will shun marketers who cannot meet their preferences. They will be more demanding, more information-driven, and more individualistic.[31]

There is a flip side to technology and the customer's response to it. A study conducted by the Stanford Institute for the Quantitative Study of Society (SIQSS) of 4,113 adults in 2,689 households, including both Internet users and non-users, shows that "the more hours people use the Internet, the less time they spend in contact with real human beings." The Internet could be the "ultimate isolating technology" as it draws people away from social interaction.[32] Research at Carnegie Mellon University examined the social and psychological impact of the Internet on 169 people in 73 households during their first one to two years online. Longitudinal data was used to examine the effects of the Internet on social involvement and psychological well-being. In this sample, the Internet was used extensively for communication. Nonetheless, greater use of the Internet was associated with declines in participants' communication with family members in the household, declines in the size of their social circle, and increases in their depression and loneliness.[33]

# Trends in Public Policy

Several projected trends in public policy are relevant to a study of customer behavior. First, economic pragmatism is prevailing over ideology. In addition, many governments are concerned with protection of passive consumers. **Passive consumers** are those who are not consuming a product themselves, but are merely bystanders, consuming the product secondhand, or otherwise being negatively affected by the action of those who consume. Finally, governments on an international level are pursuing **regional economic integration**, the realignment of nations into region-based economic blocs.

## Economic Pragmatism Over Ideology

Many governments are altering their view of the government's role in the national economy. When it comes to business, ideology is giving way to economic pragmatism in country after country. The governments are recognizing, in increasing degrees, the inherent power of free markets and the market economy, and they are getting out of its way, shunning their long-cherished ideologies. This is not to say that economic goals are the only goals with which societies should be concerned or that values other than consumerism are not valid. Instead, freeing economic systems to function will, over the long run, provide benefits such as increased productivity, better allocation of resources, and higher standards of living.

Historically, three ideologies—political, religious, and central planning—have shaped government's role in national economic affairs. Each has favored other goals over economic progress, but each is being abandoned in favor of economic pragmatism. Figure 3.2 summarizes the implications of these two approaches.

**Implications of Ideology versus Economic Pragmatism** | **FIGURE 3.2**

## Political Ideology

The former communist bloc countries, like the USSR, Eastern Europe, and China, have realized that their central control of economy and commerce choked their economy rather than promoted it. The ideological divide between Eastern Europe and the West during the Cold War era was matched by the economic divide—the Western economies flourished while the centrally controlled communist economies suffered. This was a glaring lesson in the power of free-market economies. These once-communist countries are now welcoming foreign investments with open arms, and state control is being replaced with entrepreneurial initiative.

This trend toward greater economic freedom will continue. The remaining holdouts against capitalism and free-market economy, like Cuba, will increasingly open their economies to international investment and entrepreneurial influence.

## Religious Ideology

Some countries are secular, upholding a separation between the government and religion. In many other countries, the government follows a religious ideology. Religious ideology has proven to be a hindrance to modernization and economic development. For instance, Arab countries have historically boycotted doing business with the Jewish nation. Muslim countries with nonsecular governments also have looked at foreign investment from nonmuslim nations as undesirable. The Israel airline has been under a government-imposed prohibition of refraining from business on Saturday (Sabbath), a burden on its ability to compete with other international airlines. Now these governments are realizing the dysfunctional role of allowing religious ideology to dictate to the business world and are loosening their religious ideological grip.

## The Ideology of Central Planning

The third ideology is that of centrally planned economies like India, or, until recently, the United Kingdom. Under this ideology, sectors of economy considered crucial to public well-being were either government-owned or heavily regulated. Thus, in India, for example, all the infrastructure (railroads, airlines, utility, postal service, insurance, and so on) and basic industries (steel, coal, and defense production) have been either exclusively or dominantly in the public sector. Its state-run banking industry has almost been bankrupt, now barely surviving with constant government bailouts. But the tide is changing; the domestic airline industry has been opened up to private competition. The most dramatic test case of privatization is Britain, where only a decade ago the Margaret Thatcher government rescued a crippled economy by giving up state control of industry after industry—airlines, utilities, and telecommunications. The privatized British Telecom has now become the most competitive communications network, even offering cable TV to its phone subscribers. And even Heathrow Airport in London is privatized, a first in the aviation industry anywhere in the world.

This trend toward privatization and deregulation will continue. A related development will be the decreasing role of government as a welfare state. Market-based insurance and public assistance programs will replace the straight dole-out welfare programs of today. In the United States and Western Europe, government welfare is already being reduced; an example is the U.S. Medicare program.

## Implications for Customer Behavior

In effect, then, all three ideologies are giving way to market control of economies. This trend has several implications for customer behavior:

- There will be greater competition. In order to compete, it will become increasingly important for firms to become customer-oriented.
- Competition generally results in better products and services at lower prices; moreover, with increased competition, firms will have to make it easier to do business with them. Thus, all three customer roles will benefit—the payer by lower prices, the user by better products, and the buyer by ease of doing business.
- Because of more international flow of capital, products, and services, there will be greater internationalization of products and services. A product or service available in one corner of the world also will be available in other corners. Due to global markets, there will be more standardization.

Thus, for business customers and household customers alike, there simply will be more choices, without barriers of distance and time. In consumption terms, we will become what Marshall McLuhan called a global village. Consumers everywhere will be able to have access to the same goods and services, facilitated both by changing public policy and more empowering information technology. Government will use technology like the Internet to make consumers aware of public policy. Former president Bill Clinton launched a World Wide Web site called FirstGov (**http://firstgov.gov/**) on September 20, 2000, that gives citizens access to government information and services 24 hours a day, seven days a week, 365 days a year. "FirstGov allows users to browse a wealth of information—everything from researching at the Library of Congress to tracking a NASA mission. It also enables users to conduct important business online, such as applying for student loans, tracking Social Security benefits, comparing Medicare options, and even administering government grants and contracts."[34] On the other hand, governments of some countries such as Saudi Arabia, Qatar, Bahrain, Oman, Kuwait, and China have censored the Internet and this obviously has implications in terms of unexploited purchasing power and propensity to buy. Saudis obtained access to the Internet in 1999 and total number of Internet users was expected to be 300,000 by the end of 2000. Some forbidden topics for Saudis on the Internet are offensive rap music and discussions of opposition to the royal family. The 200 Internet cafés in the kingdom are the primary means for consumers to access the Internet.

In Syria, only 5,000 of the country's 17.5 million people have Internet access, and the only ISP in United Arab Emirates' filters selected Web sites. The Chinese government has rules to prevent "subversive" content entering China via the Internet.[35] Recently, the Chinese government came under fire from media freedom groups for blocking access to the popular search engine Google for 10 days.

## Rights of Passive Consumers

Even in free-market economies, where governments have given free rein to businesses, they have not given up their control on protection of the public. Consumer protection from unfair business practices and the public's well-being have been a concern of most democratic governments.

While government's direct control of businesses will decline, its protectionist role will increase to protect the innocent victims of reckless consumption. Governments will increasingly come to the rescue of the passive consumers. One of these bystander victims is, of course, the physical environment. Damage to the environment, in turn, affects consumers, whether or not they caused the damage in the first place.

As western economies shift from a production orientation to a consumption orientation, governments have to step in and monitor consumption. Therefore, governments' role in protecting the environment and protecting passive consumers is going to intensify. The U.S. government is likely to promote something akin to the Bill of Rights for passive consumers, for example. Four U.S. agencies are going to increasingly assume an activist role: the Environmental Protection Agency (EPA), the Federal Trade Commission (FTC), the Federal Communications Commission (FCC), and the Food and Drug Administration (FDA).

Governments can protect and promote the interests of passive consumers and the general public by three means:

1. *New laws and stricter enforcement.* Governments will resort to more new lawmaking in the area of protection of the public interest from reckless consumption, and they will enforce stricter compliance. For example, California's auto emission law is the strictest in the country, and more and more states will adopt similar laws. Other examples are the "V" chip on U.S. television sets (which allows a display of program ratings to protect children from exposure to unsuitable programs) and the monitoring of indecent content on the Internet. Finally, John F. Kennedy's Bill of Rights for Consumers will be extended to a Bill of Rights for Bystanders. The Child Online Privacy Protection Act (COPPA) requires commercial web sites and online services that collect personal information from children under 13 to post privacy policies, notify parents of their information practices, obtain verifiable parental consent, and provide parents with access to their children's information.

2. *Financial disincentives.* To discourage consumption deemed not to be in the public interest, fines of ever-increasing amounts will be imposed both on the offending consumers (e.g., an adult carrying a child in a car without a child restraint, thus endangering the child) and on the businesses that facilitate that consumption (e.g., tobacco and cigarette companies).

3. *Consumer education.* More and more public money is likely to be expended on educating the consumer (e.g., promotion of antidrug education programs in schools). Some of that public money will come from increasing fines on the offending companies.

Concerns have been raised with regard to the content on the web and the privacy of personal information collected by commercial web sites explicitly through a variety of means, including registration pages, user surveys, online contests, application forms, order forms, or cookies. In most countries, the government has no direct restrictions on the content; it is up to the individuals to monitor the sites visited by their children.

## Regional Economic Integration

More and more national governments are embracing regional economic integration. In 1992, 12 nations of Europe formed a common market, called the European Union (EU). Its member nations are Belgium, Denmark, France, Germany, Greece, Ireland, Italy, Luxembourg, the Netherlands, Portugal, Spain, and the United Kingdom. By uniting these megaeconomies of Europe into a single supranational entity, the EU is becoming a major world market with substantial cross-border investment and trade. Similarly, under the European Free Trade Association (EFTA), Austria, Finland, Iceland, Norway, Sweden, and Switzerland have formed a single trading bloc. With the collapse of the communist regime in the USSR, Eastern European countries like Hungary, the Czech Republic, Slovakia, Poland, Romania, Bulgaria, Bosnia, and Croatia are opening up to Western-style economies. With the reunification of Western and Eastern Germany, Europeans are projecting a future when the countries of Eastern and Western Europe will be marching toward a common economic destiny.

Similarly, in the Western Hemisphere, the United States, Canada, and Mexico are now a single trading bloc, uniting under NAFTA (the North American Free Trade Agreement). By 2015, all of the countries in South America, Central America, and the Caribbean Islands are expected to join this alliance. But even without such a formal alliance, the countries in South America are already wide open to North American trade. In Brazil, for example, American fast-food franchises and direct-selling companies like Amway and Tupperware are a popular presence.

Yet another notable alliance is the Association of South East Asian Nations (ASEAN), incorporating such countries as Malaysia, Indonesia, Singapore, Brunei, Thailand, and the Philippines. While Japan is not a formal partner, it is moving toward integrating its economy (e.g., permanently locating some of its manufacturing facilities in these low-cost countries) with the ASEAN bloc. Eventually, Australia and China are likely to join this alliance.

Across continents, then, the trading partnerships are shifting from the East-West axis to the North-South axis; that is, trade among the countries was limited to those above the equator and likewise to those below the equator, but it is now on a trend of changing to countries *above and below* the equator (e.g., North America and South America within the same bloc). And, the new alliances are more than trading partnerships. Production facilities are being integrated, producing something for the entire bloc wherever it is most economic or feasible to produce; the tariff barriers are being pulled down; and even currencies are being integrated. Each bloc is increasingly acting as a single producing and consuming unit. And this phenomenon will continue. Regional economic integration is going to become more widespread, occurring across cultural and climatic boundaries.

### Impact on Customer Behavior

Because of the shift along the North-South axis, climatic boundaries are going to be blended within economic blocs. As a result, products will be available year-round. Seasonality (in the availability of products) will vanish. Consumers will be able to enjoy all goods in all seasons. Furthermore, because production facilities will be located where it is most economical, with free trade within regions, consumers will be able to obtain better price value. As international trade is liberalized, products and services will be available from all over the world to consumers anywhere in the world. The user will have more choices, and the buyer will be able to buy conveniently from a vendor at hand.

For business customers, also, regional economic integration will have far-reaching implications. Free trade will allow faster, cheaper, and better sourcing, and sourcing of parts, materials, and components will be global. Within-region sourcing flexibility will increase. Businesses will be able to relocate their manufacturing, procurement, and marketing functions on a distributed basis. Global infrastructure will speed up logistics for such things as transport, payment, and insurance, further enabling global sourcing.

This third customer benefit—global choices to consumers anywhere—is going to further feed into a trend already mentioned, the globalization of the consumer. More and more, the world is going to become a global village. This will give rise to an interesting related phenomenon. Local diversity is going to increase. No longer will there be homogeneous communities, uniform within but different from others. Rather, each nation, each community, each local population group will become more heterogeneous within itself, but as a unit will more and more resemble similarly heterogeneous communities. National, geophysical, climatic, and cultural boundaries are going to exist merely as administrative units but will collapse when it comes to consumption.

In this global village, retailers will buy their merchandise from all over the world. A visit to any Pier 1 Imports store in the United States (whose eclectic home-furnishing merchandise comes from craftsmen in developing countries) or to your Dekalb Farmers Market in Atlanta, Georgia (which buys its rare collection of produce and food products from far-off countries), is merely a window on the markets of the future. An industrial tools manufacturer will be able to buy spare parts from countries historically isolated by time, distance, political system, and cultural barriers. Franchise businesses will open new stores in new countries. A household in a tribal town of Africa will be able to get U.S.-based television shows like MTV and Home Shopping Network, not to mention its own shopping network, which it is likely to have. A custom tailor in a remote village in Romania is likely to have merchandise from the fashion streets of Milan and Paris. A traditional Brahmin family in Madras, India, will be able to savor a Japanese dish.

In such multicultural global consumption villages, who will be opinion leaders for new-product adoption? What kind of influence will institutions like the family, school, and religious institutions exercise on consumers? What gender roles will prevail? Who will be whose reference group? Indeed, each community is going to be a laboratory for the observation of consumption. The future is going to be a fascinating time for the study of customer behavior worldwide!

# Implications of the Trends for the Three Customer Roles

The foregoing trends in demographics, technology, and public policy will influence all three customer roles. These influences are briefly outlined in Table 3.2.

## Implications of Demographic Trends

The projected demographic changes will influence the needs and wants as well as the resources (time, physical energy, and money) of future customers, and they will do so with respect to all three customer roles. As users, the aging population will need and want increased and improved health care and security (financial and physical) and recreational products and services suitable for their ages and bodies. Cost containment for escalating health-care needs will become a heightened concern for payers (e.g., government, employers, and insurance agencies). Finally, as buyers, the aging population will want more and more home delivery of products and services and will seek greater service and convenience value in the buying process.

The impact of women in the workforce will be on time availability, thus creating a demand for time-saving products and services; as examples, cooking, cleaning, and baby-care services will be increasingly outsourced. As payers, affordability will improve somewhat, especially where both spouses work, enabling them to buy the products and services they want and value. As buyers, the traditional male-female role specialization (e.g., men

| **TABLE 3.2** | **Influence of Major Trends in Demographics, Technology, and Public Policy and Their Influence on the Three Customer Roles** |
|---|---|

| | User | Payer | Buyer |
|---|---|---|---|
| **DEMOGRAPHICS** | | | |
| Aging population | • Increased health and security and recreational needs. | • Cost containment for health-care needs a high concern. | • Home delivery and convenience in buying important. |
| Working women | • Time-saving appliances; cooking, cleaning, child care outsourced. | • Affordability somewhat improved. | • Male-female role specialization in buying further diluted. |
| Single-person households | • Social and emotional values in products acquire prominence. | • Better affordability. | • More impulse and experiential buying. |
| Declining middle class | • Demand for extreme upscale and downscale merchandise. | • Financing progressively more important. | • More diligent buying effort among the expanded downscale customer groups. |
| Increasing ethnic diversity | • Greater ethnic diversity in customer tastes. | • Cross-ethnic differences in affordability. | • Expected customer service levels differ across ethnic groups. |
| Geographic redistribution | • Greater regional diversity in customer tastes. | | |
| **TECHNOLOGY** | | | |
| Access to information | • More customized products. | • Better information on competitor prices. | • Product search on the Internet. <br> • Product information on demand. |
| Smart products | • Smart products with memory for users preferences. | • New methods of identity verification ensure security against frauds. | • Automated purchase. <br> • Buying direct from the factory. |
| Liberated customer behavior | | | • Buyers will need to be technology-savvy. |
| Mass customized lifestyles | | | |
| **PUBLIC POLICY** | | | |
| Economic pragmatism | • Better products due to open-market economy. | • Better prices due to competitive economy. | • Easier access to global products. <br> • Easier to do business with companies. |
| Rights of passive consumers | • Consumers assured protection against passive consumption. <br> • Consumers assured protection against passive consumption. | • Financial penalties for offensive consumption. | • Access to societally harmful products/services made more difficult. |
| Regional economic integration | • Seasonal products available for year round consumption. <br> • Exposure to diverse consumption cultures. | • More economically produced and more economically priced products and services. | • Easier to acquire products and services from diverse consumption cultures. <br> • Local availability of global products. |

buying tools, women buying groceries) will be further diluted so that marketers must cater to either gender's service and convenience needs.

Next, the trend of more single-person households implies greater demand for social and emotional value in products and services users seek and in the market transactions the buyers would prefer. For the payer, the single-person trend implies greater affordability as household and per-capita income become one and the same thing. In search of social interaction and self-reward, single individuals also will engage, as buyers, in impulse and experiential buying.

The declining middle-class trend implies, in contrast, a bipolar status in affordability—easy for payers in the expanding affluent class, but more difficult among the expanding poor classes. For the latter, financing will become increasingly important. As users, these bipolar groups separately will demand more upscale and more downscale products and services. The expanding poorer class of customers also will engage, in their buyer roles, in a more diligent buying process.

The two remaining demographic trends, geographic redistribution and increased ethnic diversity, are interrelated in their impact on customer roles. To users, the two trends will bring greater exposure to regional and ethnic diversity in consumer tastes. As payers, within each market territory, customers will experience greater cross-ethnic differences in affordability. Finally, as buyers, diverse ethnic and geographic customers will bring divergent expectations regarding the desirable level of service and convenience.

## Implications of Technological Trends

As described earlier, advances in technology will bring forth new capabilities to customers with respect to all three of their roles. (See the Window on Research box for more examples.) We described four customer behavior-related technological advances: increased access to information, smart products, liberated customer behavior, and mass-customized lifestyles. These advances imply, for the user, a desire for and availability of more customized products and smart products and services that memorize the user's preferences on the previous-use occasions and adapt their performance accordingly for the next-use occasion.

For the payer, technology will make available better information about price levels in the market, and credit payment methods will become more secure. For the buyer, marketplace information will be more customized and be available for perusal on customers' terms (at the time and place of customers' choosing). Technology will make intermediaries redundant, and buyers will be able to convey their product and service specifications directly to the factory and receive direct delivery. Items of daily consumption will be re-ordered by an automated purchase system installed in customers' homes. Of course, these technology-based market transactions also would imply that customers will need to become more technology-savvy and learn the skills for technology-mediated commerce.

## Implications of Trends in Public Policy

Three trends for public policy are economic pragmatism, rights of passive consumers, and regional economic integration. Each is going to affect each of the three customer roles. Economic pragmatism will bring forth open-market economy, which, in turn, will bring forth better products and services to users. Due to open-market competition, payers will also benefit by receiving better prices. The same competition also will imply better customer service, which means that buyers will find it easy to do business with companies. Greater public policy attention to the rights of passive consumers will offer value to users by giving them increased protection against harmful and undesired consumption of others. Payers will incur heightened costs should they or the users whose consumption they fund choose not to curb their use of societally harmful products and services. And buyer access to harmful products will become more difficult.

# WINDOW ON RESEARCH

## High-Tech Forecast

Stephen Millett and William Koop are two of the most visionary technology experts and forecasters associated with the Battelle Technology Intelligence Program. For *The Futurist* magazine, they forecasted the top 10 innovative products in the year 2006. Here is a brief introduction of three we consider most relevant to customer behavior:

*Personalized computers.* The personal computer we all know today will become a powerful personalized computer. It will be versatile and mobile, sending and receiving data from wireless remote sites. It will recognize your voice commands, will include advanced security features, and will be equipped with intelligent agents. These agents will automatically show information of your interest; ask you questions about your needs; remind you of things you need to do and buy; automatically shop for needed items, finding the best deals and ordering them; and electronically transfer money from your bank account.

*Home health monitors.* An electronic medical team will live with you in your home, complete with a chemical analysis laboratory. The machines will analyze your urine or blood, for example, and advise you about the status of various physical functions (e.g., liver, heart). They will be nonintrusive, bothering you only when they need to serve you a health alert. Eventually, they also will be able to recommend changes in your diet, exercise, and lifestyle.

*Never-owned products.* Within the next 10 years, we will begin to lease most household appliances, computers, and most durable goods. We will buy the function rather than the item. Manufacturers and distributors will retain ownership and responsibility for repairs as well as eventual disposal and recycling. Leasing practice will grow exponentially, and the leases themselves will be customized packages of equipment and related service. For example, from a utility company, you will be able to lease a home-environment package, customized to provide the temperature settings in different rooms of the house according to your personal preferences.

According to Millett and Koop, these products will be ready for commercial use by the year 2006 although not everyone will find them of value immediately.

**Source:** Adapted from Stephen Millett and William Koop, "The Top 10 Innovative Products for 2006: Technology with a Human Touch," *The Futurist*, July–August 1996, pp. 16–20. Additional information available at http://www.battelle.org.

Finally, regional economic integration will give to users products both in and out of season. Users also will be exposed to diverse consumption cultures as the marketplace will carry products from local and foreign cultures alike. Within the broadened and integrated region, production facilities will be located to yield the lowest costs of production, and as a result, payers will find products and services more economically priced. Buyers, seeking to meet users' broadened and more culturally diverse needs and wants, will find easier access to products and services from far and wide, all in the nearby local market. In overall terms, both the changing government policy of economic pragmatism and regional economic integration will fundamentally enhance the market values both the user and buyer seek by assuring increased local availability of global products and services.

## Overall Implications for Marketers

Anticipation of the changes outlined in this chapter will bring about significant shifts in marketing strategies and practices. Continuing the current trend, the economy will become much more service-oriented; this will occur not only because the current service sectors will grow but also because customers' need for anytime, anywhere purchasing and consumption will add a significant component of service to the marketing of physical products. This shift from a product orientation to a service orientation will require companies to make significant changes: from supply-driven to demand-driven operations, from centralized operations to more widely distributed locations, and from customer-isolated to customer-participative production (i.e., coproduction). Marketers will have to learn to measure customer value of products and services in terms of time as well as money, as customers continue to make trade-offs that save them time.

In terms of marketing practices, safety and quality, as well as courteous efficiency, will become an integral part of the service offered by all companies. One-stop shopping is certainly the trend of the future, generating growth of superstores. However, the current dominant avenue of one-stop shopping—the regional shopping mall miles from home—will no longer be perceived as convenient. Instead, neighborhood minimalls and shopping via catalogs and the Internet are the wave of the future.

More and more firms will have to adopt mass customization to respond to the market discontinuities described in this chapter. A good example of the mass-customization strategy is the concept of the franchise, such as the McDonald's fast-food chain. McDonald's, found today around the globe, became a success because it was the first fast-food chain to standardize its business processes on such a large scale, and yet adapt the menu to local tastes. Although the quality of the product and service at McDonald's is virtually identical worldwide, the menu is somewhat customized to accommodate regional differences—even different neighborhoods in the same metropolitan area address ethnic differences. Such franchise-based mass customization will spread to a diverse set of industries.

The time-starved customer will be highly stressed and will demand that services be carried out dependably. Without the time to supervise or adjust schedules, service personnel will have to deliver service reliably without the customer being physically present to scrutinize the quality (e.g., landscaping while the customer is not at home) and in a manner that engenders customer trust. Security will also be a desirable attribute, as customers would have to leave their homes unattended for service personnel to come in and make the repairs (e.g., cable TV installation or service) while the homeowner is away.

The delivery of services and products to the home and place of business will become increasingly more prevalent. Customers will want all kinds of services delivered to their doorsteps, including health care, accounting, and other professional services. The winning marketing position will be **instant marketing**—being ready when the customer is. All services must be organized around the concept of no delay (i.e., instant reservations, 24-hour shopping, cash and carry, in-and-out, and so on). Products will have to be designed for hyperspeed: convenient packaging and ease of consumption also will become valuable attributes.

Since the customers of tomorrow will be time- and stress-driven, they will want not only hassle-free service but also empathy. Consequently, the psychological supports of empathy and courtesy will be important market values. Marketers must, then, address the customer from the attitude of "I understand who you are, and I understand your problem."

# Summary

In this chapter, we have demonstrated how customer needs and wants change over time as a consequence of changing demographics, advances in technology, and the applications of public policy. We described six important demographic changes taking place in the United States today and the implications to the customer in the marketplace as a result of these changes. The six changes include the aging of the population, more working women, more single-person households, a declining middle class, a geographic redistribution, and increasing ethnic diversity.

Advances in technology also will alter the customer-behavior landscape. We described how four trends in technology, already on the horizon, will further alter customer behavior in the future. These trends were described as a shift from mere increased customer access to information toward greater customer control over the information, from newer products to smarter products, from operations-driven processes to anytime/anywhere purchasing, and from merely offering customized products to offering customized lifestyles. As an example of the last trend, consider the forecast made by some technology futurists that the consumer of the future will rent, rather than own, most of the durable goods.

Finally, changes taking place in public policy were identified. These were a shift in government's economic policy from ideology to market economy, increased protection of passive consumers, and greater regional economic integration. These pro-market trends in public policy, combined with the advances in technology, will enable consumers to satisfy their new set of needs and wants, altered and shaped by changing demographics.

# Key Terms

Affordability 101

Atomistic Family Unit 99

Autonomy 99

Changing Demographics 95

Cocooning 100

Coproduction 106

Customer Militancy 101

Disintermediation 107

Financial Well-Being 97

Geographic Redistribution 102

Instant Gratification 100

Instant Marketing 117

Neo Rich 101

Nuclear Family Unit 99

Outsourced 98

Passive Consumers 108

Personal Safety 97

Quality of Life 103

Recreational Needs 97

Regional Economic Integration 108

Roommate Families 98

Smart Products 105

Time Shift 98

Time Shortage 98

# Discussion Questions and Exercises

1. Review Table 3.1 about the relevance of the trends to the three customer roles. Add at least one example in each of the cells in this table, thus exhibiting your understanding of these concepts.

2. What implications will changes in demographics, changes in technology, and changes in public policy have on market values discussed in Chapter 1? In other words, what is the link between these emerging customer behavior trends and the market values customers seek?

3. Visualize how technology will have changed the market place in the year 2010. Now, in this marketplace, visualize yourself as a consumer. Describe whether your experience in this marketplace will be one of a happy or a confused consumer. Explain your answer.

4. As a marketing director of home furniture, you have just read about how technology will enable customers to be co-producers. You realize, of course, that this does not mean you will be able to transfer some of your production labor to customers, thus saving on labor costs. How exactly would it affect your company? How can you take advantage of this trend?

5. With the advent of the Internet as a mode of shopping, customers are now realizing the impact that this new technology has on their marketplace behaviors. Describe the pros and cons of Internet shopping from the perspective of a marketer of greeting cards and gifts and for the customers of these products.

# Appendix: Status of the Internet in Different Regions and Countries in the World

## The Internet in Europe

The number of active adult Internet users in Europe (14 years of age or older online for at least an hour a week) was 70 million in 2000 and expected to be 255 million by 2004. By 2002, Europe will overtake the United States in the percentage of worldwide Internet users and will have more Internet users than any other region in the world. In 1999, 69 percent of the Internet users in Western Europe were male and 31 percent were female. The gender gap is more prominent in Germany, Denmark, and Spain than it is in France and the UK. The online population is significantly younger, more upscale, and more educated than the general population, but as more and more people go online, this profile will mirror the profile of the general population.

European B2C (business-to-consumer) e-commerce will double, from about $8 billion in 2000 to about $16 billion in 2001. Yet there are several problems that plague B2C e-commerce in Europe. Secure servers—used for secure transmission over the Internet of information like credit card numbers—are an indicator of e-commerce readiness, and as of March 2000, Netcraft measured approximately six times as many secure servers, per capita, in the United States as in the entire European Union (EU). It is less cost-effective to shop online in the EU because of the sales tax and the high delivery charges. Apart from this, telephone connection costs are high, and a low level of credit card usage among customers makes payment difficult for online purchases. For example, as of 1998 (the latest statistics published by the Bank for International Settlements), the UK had roughly half the number of credit or debit cards per capita as the United States, despite being the most credit card-carrying country in Europe. Finally, fear of fraud is one of the major deterrents to shopping online. European Internet penetration by country in the year 2000 is presented in the table below.

## European Internet Penetration, 2000 (as a % of total households and number of wired households)

| Country | Penetration |
|---|---|
| Denmark | 50% (1,650,000) |
| UK | 30% (7,000,000) |
| Germany | 25.7% (8,900,000) |
| France | 17.5% (4,200,000) |
| Spain | 12.7% (1,650,000) |

Source: eMarketer, 2000

©2000 eMarketer, Inc.                                    www.eMarketer.com

**Source:** Estats, Etopics—http://www.emarketer.com.

## The Internet in Hungary

Hungary's Internet market has benefited from the country's robust telecommunications sector, which boasts one of the most developed networks in Central and Eastern Europe. According to data from the International Telecommunications Union (ITU), the total number of Internet users has grown from fewer than 300,000 in 1998 to 715,000 in October 2000. Much of this growth has come from academic users, who account for more than half of the Internet-user market, according to ITU data.

By 2001, Carnation Research estimates that 969,000 Hungarians will be regular Internet users. According to eMarketer's 2000 eEurope report, the number of active (one hour or more of surfing per week) 18 and older Internet users in Hungary will reach nearly 1.3 million by 2003, up from 10,000 in 2001.

The average age of a Hungarian Internet user is under 30, generally 20–25 years old, according to Carnation Consulting. Not surprisingly, most Internet users live in cities, and a large share of the user population lives in Budapest. eCommerce is not well-developed in Hungary. Based on research conducted in 2000, Carnation Consulting predicts that total e-commerce revenues in Hungary will rise from $441 million in 2000 to $1.28 billion in 2002, when consumers will be spending $5.6 million online, and businesses will spend $1.27 billion.

## The Internet in Asia

According to eMarketer estimates, the total number of active Internet users (age 14 or older online for at least an hour a week) in Asia in 2000 was 48.7 million and should increase to 173 million by 2004. Asia accounted for less than 14 percent of the entire global e-commerce revenues in 2000 and is estimated to account for about 10 percent of global e-commerce revenues by 2004. Japan alone generates almost 70 percent of the region's e-commerce revenues and will continue to maintain its dominance in the future. China presently accounts for about 2.1 percent of the revenues but is expected to experience the fastest growth and will climb to third place in the region, following Japan and Australia. Asian e-commerce sites are, however, more cost-efficient in attracting visitors and retaining customers than their U.S. and European counterparts, according to a survey by consulting firm McKinsey & Co. A survey of more than 50 e-commerce and content sites in Asia found that Asian business-to-consumer sites spend an average of 10 U.S. cents in marketing expenses to attract a visitor each month, compared with US$1.50 in Europe and US$2.30 in the United States. Asian customers are also more likely to revisit the e-commerce sites they have used, compared to U.S. and European customers. The lower costs and high customer-retention rate are largely due to cautious spending and heavy use of direct marketing to existing customers. Asian e-commerce sites have zeroed in on specific niches rather than large markets and leverage the brand's presence in the offline world to build higher profitability on the Internet. McKinsey found that such a site has a five to eight times higher conversion rate (of visitors to customers) as compared to pure-play etailers in Asia.

## The Internet in India

Compared to an urban population of 250 million or a population of 30 to 40 million in the upper and upper middle-income segments, NASSCOM's (National Association of Software and Service Companies') latest estimates peg the Internet user base in India at 7.5 million by March 2001. Yet, it is almost equal to the 20 percent of the C&S (cable and satellite) television households in the country, and the compounded growth rate of Internet usage is in excess of 100 percent per year.

Internet users in India are predominantly young (77 percent are below 40, according to NASSCOM). Users have a higher SEC and income profile than nonusers (according to market research agency TNS-Mode). Studies in India show that Internet users are online at home during TV prime time too. Hence, marketers are using the Internet in conjunction with other media to target the young affluent consumer. Car manufacturer Maruti launched its new model "Alto" with an aggressive mass media campaign, but it also used the Net for a creative and well-executed teaser campaign that generated curiosity and inquiry. The "hottest little thing" theme was driven home by the combination of all media channels. The Net is better suited for marketing of some product categories than others, and a diverse mix of organizations is active on the Indian Internet scene including Ericsson, Samsung, HLL, Intel, ICICI, Citibank, Parle, and Maruti.

E-commerce revenues were expected to reach $2.17 billion in 2001–2002 compared to $1.4 billion in 2000–2001, according to NASSCOM. The Indian government also is playing its part in this technological revolution. It is teaming up with the Massachusetts Institute of Technology (MIT) to develop a Media Lab that will cost between $500 million and $1 billion over 10 years. India will fund 20 percent of the project that's designed to help Southeast Asia boost its technological potential. IBM also has opened a software development lab in India with plans to invest $100 million in it over a span of three years. This is IBM's fourth Indian facility.

## The Internet in East Africa

The East African sub-region comprises the three states of Kenya, Uganda, and Tanzania, which belong to the sub-regional economic bloc, the East African Cooperation (EAC). The states see the need for regional integration in the development of information systems and information networks to help in the realization of a single market and investment area. However, several problems plague Internet access and use in East Africa:

1. Public universities are short of funds, and the introduction of Internet to university campuses is considered expensive.
2. High costs of hardware—computers and telephones—coupled with bureaucracy and corruption in license giving (leading to collusion among businessmen to maintain high prices) make it impossible for institutions and individuals to purchase computers and connect to the Internet.
3. Inadequacy and unavailability of telephone lines in the sub-region is perennial. According to the International Telecommunications Union, Tanzania had 0.29 main phone lines per 100 inhabitants in 1992, compared with figures of 0.77 in Kenya and 0.45 in Uganda. This telecommunication infrastructure also is concentrated in the cities, and rural areas are neglected.
4. Dial-up is costly because of the high local call rate, and limited bandwidth, resulting in low data rates, is unsuitable to support effective Internet access.
5. The East African sub-region has high levels of illiteracy, and education programs are a higher priority for the government than investment in Internet technologies.
6. Conservative managers in organizations are not keen on adopting modern communication technologies.

Despite these problems, the three East African governments have recognized the role of the Internet in national development. Some efforts in this area include setting up various policy frameworks, liberalizing the telecommunication sector, licensing a number of ISPs, engaging in market-driven policies, setting up regulatory bodies to oversee the privatization of the telecommunications sector, and reducing the import duty and other tariffs on software and hardware. Individual organizations like The University of Dar es Salaam (**http://www.udsm. ac.tz**) and Makerere University (**http://www. muk.ac.ug**) have established Web sites. Many public telephone operators in the sub-region, as a result of user needs, have recently installed public-access packets switching services. Political and economic association between Kenya, Uganda, and Tanzania has led to some positive reduction in tariffs. The three countries only charge direct long-distance calls without any international tariff for calls among them. The World Bank has funded the establishment of the African Virtual University, with campuses in Kenya and Uganda. There are efforts to rehabilitate the existing telephone infrastructure in the three countries. In Dar es Salaam, a Japanese company is already undertaking extensive rehabilitation of the telephone lines. There is a lot more to be done by the governments to address legal, regulatory, and institutional practices that hinder the information revolution, but pooling resources by the three East African countries is the first step forward.

## The Internet in Russia

According to a report based on a study by the Russian National Institute of Social and Psychological Research (NISPR), the active Internet user base (one hour or more of surfing per week) in Russia was 2 million as of November 1999. The regular Internet user base (those who have used the Internet at least once during the last 3 months, or not less than 3 times in their entire lifetime) was about 2.5 million, accounting for about 2.3 percent of the total Russian population.

The representative regular Runet user is a young male (less than 34 years old) living in big cities like Moscow or St. Petersburg and is a student or white-collar professional. Low penetration of household PCs and telephone lines restricts access to the Internet for a majority of the people to the workplace (49 percent). News, science/education, information about goods and services, entertainment, music/literature, chat, and business/finance are some of the top interests of the online population. Forty-seven percent of the total Internet user population has an e-mail address, and 99 percent of the active Internet user base receives e-mails.

E-commerce activity is really not very well developed, with Internet revenues in 1998 not exceeding $161.5 million, most of it from the B2C segment. An absence of a strong legislation system and Internet payment problems are some of the main constraints hindering e-commerce development in Russia. Yet, B2C online consumer activity increased 9 times during the period from October 1999 to January 2000. The dominant categories in the segment are computer goods (75 percent of retailers), books, CDs, videotapes, and flowers/gifts. Low credit-card penetration (just 5.3 percent of the Russian population is a credit- or debit-card holder, according to American trading chamber statistics), low solvency of the population, and overall insecurities about Russian reality also add to the problems in online e-commerce. Ninety-five percent of online shops accept cash (customer pays at pick-up location or pays the company courier or the Russian State post service on delivery); other modes of payment are money orders through Sberbank or some of the new digital money payment systems.

## The Internet in China

Increasing numbers of organizations and individuals are getting connected to the Internet either in offices or at home in China. According to the 5th Survey on the Internet in China issued by the China Network Information Center (CNNIC) in January 2000, 3.5 million computers and 8.9 million users had been connected to the Internet by the end of December 1999. There are about 15,153 Web sites operating in China. In China, a three-step procedure has been launched to promote a networked society— government online, business online, and family online.

The Chinese Government Online project (**http://www.gov.cn**) was officially launched on June 22, 1999, and 1999 was named Government Online Year in China. The objective of the project was to develop the information industry, increase government efficiency, and promote political reform. The project will establish Web sites of Chinese government departments; conduct civil services such as tax transactions, over these Web sites, to bring about as much convenience as possible to the public; and encourage other sectors of the economy to get on the Internet, promoting the development of a networked society.

Some of the problems that this project faces are a) lack of information resources in the Chinese language, b) an imbalance of network facilities (there is a concentration of network facilities in the south-eastern coastal areas where economic progress and living standards are higher than those of the northern and western areas), and c) a lack of policy and coordination with regard to issues such as the selection, processing, and storage of government information, the management and updating of the government Web sites, the interface of the government Web sites, and the security of the information on the government Web sites.

The Business Online project was officially launched in China on July 7, 2000 along with its Web site (**http://www.lianmeng.com.cn/ alliance_intro/englishversion.htm**). Eighteen large enterprises and 300 small enterprises connected to the Business Online project on the first day. The year 2000 was named Business Online Year, and the long-term objective of the Business Online project is to link all the enterprises in China to facilitate economic reform. Lack of relevant knowledge and experience is the major problem in this project.

The final step of the three-step procedure in China is Family Online (**http://www.sino home.com**). The China Family Online Web site presented a free Internet connection CD-ROM to families in May 2000. This CD-ROM will guide novices through the procedure of connecting to the Internet and also offer three hours' connection to the Internet free of charge. The Family Online Web site mainly offers information regarding entertainment, stock exchange, medical consultation, online shopping, and free downloads to cater to households.

# Notes

1 Hotel Room of the Future, *The Futurist*, March–April 1997, p. 59.

2 U.S. Census Bureau, *IDB Summary Demographic Data*, updated May 10, 2000 (http://www.census.gov/cgi-bin/ipc/www/idbsum.html).

3 Jagdish N. Sheth, "Changing Demographics and the Future of Graduate Management Education," *Selections: The Magazine of the Graduate Management Admissions Council*, Spring 1988, p. 22.

4 S. H. Peter Leeflang and W. Fred van Raaij, "The Changing Consumer in the European Union: A Meta-Analysis," *International Journal of Research in Marketing* 12 (1995), pp. 373–87.

5 U.S.Census Bureau, *IDB Summary Demographic Data*, updated May 10, 2000 (http://www.census.gov/cgi-bin/ipc/www/idbsum.html).

6 "Demographics of the Net Getting Older," August 29, 2000 (http://cyberatlas.internet.com/big_picture/demographics/article/0,1323,5901_448131,00.html).

7 Charles A. McMellon and Leon G. Schiffman, "Cybersenior Mobility: Why Some Older Consumers May Be Adopting the Internet," *Advances in Consumer Research*, Volume 27, 2000, pp. 139–44.

8 "Seniors Use Internet for Shopping," August 31, 1999 (http://cyberatlas.internet.com/big_picture/demographics/article/0,,5901_192461,00.html).

9 Mark J. Warshawsky, "Projections of Health Care Expenditures as a Share of the GDP: Actuarial and Macroeconomic Approaches," *Health Services Research* 29, No. 3 (August 1994), pp. 293–303.

10 "Seniors Use Internet for Shopping," August 31, 1999 (http://cyberatlas.internet.com/big_picture/demographics/article/0,,5901_192461,00.html).

11 U.S. Bureau of the Census, *Statistical Abstract of the United States: 1995*, 115th edition (Washington, D.C., 1995), pp. 260–61.

12 GVU's Tenth WWW User survey; (http://www.gvu.gatech.edu/user_surveys/survey-1998-10/).

13 U.S. Bureau of the Census, *Statistical Abstract of the United States* (http://www.census.gov/prod/www/statistical-abstract-us.html), data revised July 27, 1999, p. 411.

14 "Women Taking the Internet Lead," November 11, 1999 (http://cyberatlas.internet.com/big_picture/demographics/article/0,,5901_221541,00.html).

15 Claudine Thompson, *Americans Online—Part 3: Gender*, http://www.emarketer.com/etopics/gender/.

16 Shannon Dortch, "Maids Clean Up," *American Demographics* 18, No. 11 (November 1996), pp. 4–8.

17 U.S. Bureau of the Census, *Statistical Abstract of the United States: 1995*, 115th edition (Washington, D.C., 1995), p. 261.

18 Sue Shellenbarger, "Work and Family: The Heralded Return of Traditional Families Is Not What It Seems," *The Wall Street Journal*, May 31, 2000.

19 S. H. Peter Leeflang and W. Fred van Raaij, "The Changing Consumer in the European Union: A Meta-Analysis," *International Journal of Research in Marketing* 12 (1995), pp. 373–87.

20  "Direct-to-Consumer Sales Seen Increasing," June 28, 2000 (http://cyberatlas.internet. com/markets/retailing/article/0,,6061_404851,00.html); "Net Trends from Web Business" (http://www2.cio.com/webbusiness/metrics/).

21  U.S. Bureau of the Census, *Statistical Abstract of the United States* (http://www.census.gov/ prod/www/statistical-abstract-us.html), data revised July 27, 1999, p. 474.

22  Ravi Marphatia, "Painting Consumers Fuel Industry Boom; Capacity Plays Catch-up," *Chemical Week* 158, No. 34 (September 11, 1996), pp. 49–51.

23  "Digital Divide Shows Signs of Narrowing," October 18, 2000 (http://cyberatlas. internet.com/big_picture/demographics/article/0,,5901_487971,00.html).

24  Jagdish N. Sheth, "Changing Demographics and the Future of Graduate Management Education," *Selections: The Magazine of the Graduate Management Admissions Council*, Spring 1988, p. 26; U.S. Bureau of the Census, *Statistical Abstract of the United States*, p. 19 (http://www.census.gov/prod/www/statistical-abstract-us.html), data revised July 27, 1999.

25  U.S. Bureau of the Census, *Statistical Abstract of the United States* (http://www.census. gov/prod/www/statistical-abstract-us.html), data revised July 27, 1999.

26  Nevin Cohen, "Eurobabel: Language and the Web," May 28, 2000 (http://www. emarketer.com/etopics/articles/052900_eurobabel.html).

27  Jagdish N. Sheth and Rajendra S. Sisodia, "Consumer Behavior in the Future," in Robert A. Peterson, ed., *Electronic Marketing and the Consumer* (Sage Publications, 1997) pp. 17–37.

28  Erica Noonan, "Making Smart Tech Mainstream," *The Associated Press*, March 15, 1999 (http://www.abcnews.go.com/sections/tech/DailyNews/smarttech990315. html); "Motorola Donates $5 Million to Create Motorola DigitalDNA Laboratory at MIT," *MIT News*, March 15, 1999 (http://web.mit.edu/newsoffice/nr/1999/ motorola.html).

29  "Mobile Ecommerce to Revolutionize Shopping," January 13, 2000 (http://www. nua.ie/surveys/index.cgi?f=VS&art_id=905355523&rel=true).

30  Clare Saliba, "Fedex Revamps Online Return System," October 10, 2000 (http:// www.ecommercetimes.com/news/articles2000/001010-2.shtml).

31  A significant part of material in this section is adapted from Sheth and Sisodia 1997; also see Jagdish N. Sheth, "Call It Anytime, Anywhere Future: Telecommunications in the Next 10 Years," *BellSouth Magazine* 7, No. 1 (January–February 1994), pp. 3–5; Jagdish N. Sheth and Rajendra S. Sisodia, "The Information Mall," *Telecommunications Policy*, July 1993, pp. 376–88; Ripley Hotch, "Communications Revolution," *Nation's Business*, May 1993, pp. 20–32.

32  Norman Nie and Lutz Erbring, "How Internet Is Changing Daily Life—Social Aspects of Web Usage," April 2000, http://www.stanford.edu/group/siqss/.

33  Robert Kraut et.al. "A Social Technology That Reduces Social Involvement and Psychological Well-Being?" *American Psychologist*, selected article at http://www.apa. org/journals/amp/amp5391017.html.

34  William Peters and Charlene Porter, "E-Government: No Walls, No Clocks, No Doors," *Global Issues, An Electronic Journal of the U.S. Department of State*, November 2000, Volume 5, No. 3 (http://www.usinfo.state.gov/journals/itgic/1100/ijge/ijge 1100.htm).

35  "Internet Still Censored in Saudi Arabia," September 28, 2000 (http://www.nua.ie/ surveys/index.cgi?f=VS&art_id=905356072&rel=true); "Increased regulation for

Chinese Internet Use," October 9, 2000 (http://www.nua.ie/surveys/index.cgi?f=VS&art_id=905356091&rel=true).

## Appendix Sources

Nevin Cohen, *Hungary's Healthy Outlook*, February 13, 2001, http://www.emarketer.com/analysis/eeurope/20010213_europe.html?ref=wn.

Estats, Etopics—http://www.emarketer.com, Ling, Connie "Asian E-Commerce Sites Need Niches—While Efficient in Luring Visitors, Most Aren't Profitable, McKinsey Says—Best Strategies May Be Specialization and Joining With Offline Businesses," *The Asian Wall Street Journal*, December 5, 2000.

http://www.asia.internet.com/cyberatlas/001123india.html, Internet Marketing, A&M, November 30, 2000, http://www.aandm.com.

Adapted from Stephen M. Mutula (2001), "Internet Access in East Africa: A Future Outlook," *Library Review*, Vol. 50, Issue 1, http://www.emerald-library.com.

Galina Kan, "The Internet in Russia," Working paper, eLab, Owen Graduate School of Management, Vanderbilt University, May 8, 2000, http://www.ecommerce.vanderbilt.edu/papers/Internet_in _Russia.htm.

Jinhong Tang, "Recent Internet Developments in the People's Republic of China: An Overview," *Online Information Review*, Vol. 24, Issue 4, 2000, http://www.emerald-library.com.

# PART 2

## Foundations of Customer Behavior

Chapter 4    *The Customer as a Perceiver and Learner*

Chapter 5    *Customer Motivation: Needs, Emotions, and Psychographics*

Chapter 6    *Customer Attitudes: Cognitive and Affective*

Chapter 7    *Researching Customer Behavior*

# CHAPTER 4

## The Customer as a Perceiver and Learner

## *Long Life* Perceptions

Milk. You find it in the refrigerated section of the supermarket, and you store it in your refrigerator, not in your pantry. Right? Not necessarily. Parmalat, the world's largest milk producer, markets a type of milk called *Long Life*, which is specially processed without any preservatives. The processing technology is ultra-high temperature, which neutralizes bacteria and thus prevents spoilage. The milk is then packaged in aseptic cartons. It does require refrigeration after opening. But until then, it can be stored on dry-goods shelves for up to six months. The advantages to customers are substantial. It saves refrigerator space, which in most households is scarce. Customers can stock extra milk in their pantry so that they don't have to run to the store at midnight because they just discovered they are out of milk. When Parmalat introduced *Long Life* in the United States, it expected that customer acceptance of this revolutionary new product would be immediate and high. The product concept sounded great in theory. However, the actual product sales have been extremely slow. Somehow, U.S. customers just can't fathom fresh milk in a dry-goods can or box. This is one innovation where customers' preexisting perceptions and learning are at odds with the new product concept.

This example of conflict between preexisting perceptions and learning is not an isolated case. Individuals and businesses face such situations regularly as customers. Take the case of the "beef flavor in french fries at McDonald's." Vegetarian customers who consumed the fries perceived that if the french fries were made in pure vegetable oil they had to be completely vegetarian. However, when the company confirmed that beef extract is used as a natural flavor for the fries, these customers filed a lawsuit against the company for misleading them. Likewise, a business customer expects accountants from his audit firm to be in business suits; if they show up in jeans, he would suspect their professional qualifications. This is because this reality is at odds with preexisting perceptions.

When we buy, use, or pay for a product or service, it is not our first exposure and response to the marketplace. Rather, it is one in a sequence of other marketplace decisions we have made in the past. As customers, we bring to each decision a lifetime of learning about the world in general and about the marketplace in particular. This stock of knowledge guides how we respond to new information in the marketplace, as in the case of *Long Life* milk in the above example, and it deeply affects what we learn about various products and services. These activities characterize the customer's tasks of perceiving and learning.

This chapter explores what it means for customers to be perceivers and learners—the internal influences on customer behavior (Figure 4.1). It defines perception and identifies elements of the perception process. We then describe how customers perceive, including common distortions of information. Next, we define what it means for customers to be learners. We explain how learning occurs and how customers alter the basic process through simplification and complication. Finally, we discuss an aspect of learning that is crucially important to marketers: customer response to product and service innovations.

## Perception and Learning         FIGURE 4.1

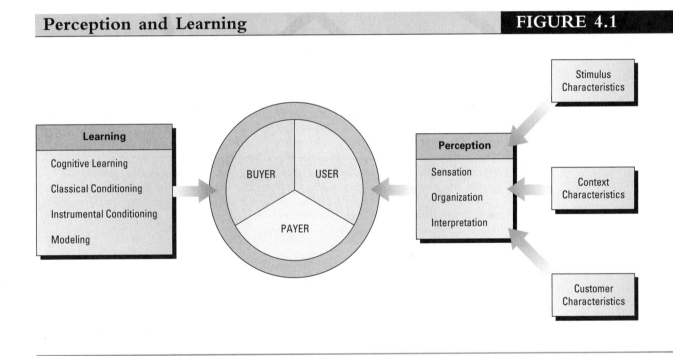

# The Customer as a Perceiver

The objective reality of a product matters little; what matters is the customer's perception of a product or a brand. **Perception** is the process by which an individual selects, organizes, and interprets the information he or she receives from the environment. For example, cereals use darker colors to make them look more masculine. Similarly, mouthwashes are colored green or blue to connote a clean, fresh feeling. One brand, Plax, makes its mouthwash red to distinguish it from competing brands but also to create the impression that it is medicinal and, therefore, more effective. Similarly in the business context, colors, shapes, and corporate logos are used to aid customer perception. For example, Caterpillar relies on a yellow color, John Deere on green, and Techtronics on blue to register themselves immediately to the customer. The color and shape of the IMAC Apple computer is designed to appeal to the creative user. The process of perception has three steps:

1. Sensation—Attending to an object or an event in the environment with one or more of the five senses: seeing, hearing, smelling, touching, and tasting. Examples include the sensation of an aircraft taking off, or feeling the texture and taste of a hot, juicy hamburger at a particular restaurant. The object or event in the environment is technically called a stimulus. Engendering rich sensation is comparatively difficult for Internet sites to achieve, but e-tailers are identifying this as a potential source of differentiation. As a result, a site such as Indulge.com has created an ambience reminiscent of the beauty store that it is meant to represent. It creates a soothing ambience with a background in different shades of blue, and customers can use a 1-800 number or live-chat to chat with a customer representative as they would in an off-line store.[1]
2. Organization—Categorizing by matching the sensed stimulus with similar object categories in one's memory. In the example of eating a hamburger, organization occurs as the consumer identifies all the ingredients and classifies it as a specific type similar to or different from the ones he or she has eaten before.
3. Interpretation—Attaching meaning to the stimulus, forming a "ruling" as to whether it is an object you like and of what value it would be to you, the perceiver.[2] In the hamburger example, interpretation occurs when the consumer judges whether the hamburger tastes good and whether he or she likes it more or less than those eaten before.

To further clarify these perceptual processes, consider an example from everyday life. When you see two straight headlight beams coming at you in the dark, you fill in the rest of the detail and "organize" these two discrete pieces of information (namely, two light beams) as parts of an oncoming car rather than two motorcycles. A little later, judging from its speed—depending on whether it is controlled and slowing down as it approaches you or it is astray, uncontrolled, and approaching you with accelerated speed—you "interpret" it to be a friendly or threatening vehicle. At a customer-service center, when there is a customer call, the operator first asks the consumer to classify his or her problem among several categories of problems available and then, depending on the problem details, interprets the information to provide a solution.

## Factors that Shape Perception

Three factors shape customer perceptions:

1. *Stimulus characteristics*—The nature of information from the environment (objects, brands, stores, marketers, friends, government, and so forth).
2. *Context characteristics*—The setting in which the information is received; this includes social, cultural, and organizational contexts.
3. *Customer characteristics*—Personal knowledge and experiences, including the customer's expertise on the relevant topic and prior experience with similar stimuli.

### Stimulus Characteristics

People perceive a stimulus differently according to its characteristics, and marketers need to consider both the sensory characteristics and the information content of a stimulus.

A characteristic is sensory if it stimulates any of the five senses. For example, strong sensory characteristics include bright colors, loud noises, and strong aromas. Such strong characteristics tend to attract more attention and are perceived more than weak sensory characteristics. Getting attention is important because most customers face a flood of stimuli in today's world. For example, a typical customer faces more than 3,000 advertisements in a week.[3] Marketers strive to break through this clutter with stimulus novelty—incorporating new elements in advertisements such as visually distinctive polar bears in the Coca-Cola campaign, handwritten copy in a print advertisement, or a likable celebrity. Supermarkets address the problem of clutter on a supermarket shelf with attractive package designs, point-of-purchase display materials, and eye-level shelf displays. The aesthetic responses toward a product also have an important influence on product preferences. Sensory elements like unity of the product design (congruity among elements of the design such that they look as though they belong together)[4] and prototypicality of the design (the degree to which an object is representative of a category)[5] are important in determining a customer's aesthetic responses toward the product.[6] Communicating sensory characteristics is difficult for services (such as electricity, phone, and insurance), and a recommended solution is the use of accompanying tangible facilities to create an identity for the service.[7] For example, Traveler's Insurance Company uses the trademark of an umbrella to connote coverage and protection, and Merrill Lynch uses a bull as a trademark to connote its aggressive investment strategy. Similarly, with more and more business being carried out on the Internet, it is also important for marketers to design Web sites so that customers are not bogged down by unwieldy graphics and big blocks of text that make navigation difficult. Audio and video links that enhance perceptions need to be used with care so that they do not hinder the overall purpose and objective of the site. Web advertising, like TV or print advertising, has also come into its own and interactive banner ads and sponsorships help to draw customers to the respective corporate sites.

The other characteristic of a stimulus that shapes perception is its information content. After an advertisement has achieved sense perception, by its sense characteristics, informational content moves the perceptual process beyond sensation or stimulus selection toward organization and interpretation. For example, information about an automobile engine's horsepower, acceleration, and style enables one to classify (i.e., organize) it as a performance car or a family sedan; information about the car's country of origin, manufacturer, and price allows inferences about its quality. Research by Cyber Dialogue shows that factors such as site navigation, personalization features, responsiveness to inquiries, user education features, and the ability to compare other consumer opinions are important in shaping perceptions of customers towards online financial service brands. In fact, the study states that Internet based information search has not only influenced customers' opinions about financial service providers, but in some cases it has been instrumental in the customer's switch between providers.[8] Information content has been identified as one of the key elements by which B2B e-marketplaces can differentiate themselves and create loyal buyers and sellers. Since most B2B marketplaces will be able to facilitate transactions between buyers and sellers, value-added content relating to the transaction, the industry, and all other services related to the transaction will be a major plus for the site.[9]

## Context

In perceiving a stimulus with a given set of characteristics, customers also will be influenced by the context of the stimulus.[10] The clearest illustrations of the context effect on the perceptions of marketing stimuli are blind-taste test studies (for example, studies of beer taste). In these tests, customers pick the brand they think is their usual or favorite brand, even when the brand names have been switched. The taste perceptions are influenced by the context the brand name provides.

## Customer Characteristics

Finally, perceptions are influenced by customer characteristics, notably what customers already know and feel about the stimuli. Such prior knowledge and feelings become expectations—prior beliefs about what something will possess or offer. Expectations influence perceptions in that we often end up seeing what we expect to see. Students who come to a course having heard good recommendations about it or about the instructor end up liking the course much more than those who enroll having heard criticism about it. The principle underlying this phenomenon is that expectations bias the perception of reality. This principle was tested in a recent consumer behavior study that showed that customers who were led to have positive expectations about the service level at a hotel actually perceived the service level as higher (after having a simulated service experience in an experimental condition) than those who had been led to expect a lower level of service.[11] The dominant influence of prior expectations on perceptions occurs within specific conditions: (1) when the stimulus is vague and open to interpretation, and (2) when the perceiver does not have the expertise to evaluate the stimulus objectively. Thus, if the hotel's service levels were very different from expectations, then vivid reality (rather than prior expectations) will drive perception, and the hotel will be perceived unfavorably despite prior expectations. Similarly, a doctor's prior reputation influences a patient's perceptions of his or her skills only when the patient is not knowledgeable about disease diagnosis and treatments.

Since customer expectations color the perception of reality, users, payers, and buyers are also likely to see a product or service differently. Consider a mother shopping with her 19-year-old son to decide which car to buy for him. The son (who will be the user) is delighted about a sports car symbolizing fun and excitement. Mom, the buyer, sees it as an unsafe car. She is also mindful of Dad, who has promised to pay for the insurance, and from his standpoint, a sports car would mean big insurance payments.

Researchers Coupey and Sandgathe state that the Internet as a medium is different from the traditional media like the print, radio, and television, in terms of its increased media richness (media with more cues for developing meaning), interactivity, and selectivity. The features of interactivity and selectivity on the Internet allow a customer to choose the format for information received via the Internet, both in terms of the content and in terms of information needed for decision making.

Hence, they suggest that *consumer factors* should be more important than *task/stimulus factors* (communication modalities and media features) and *context factors* (message characteristics) on the Internet. With respect to traditional media, understanding how modality of communication interacts with messages to influence information search and attention is essential to understand how this information will be used by the consumer in the alternative evaluation and purchase stages of his/her decision making. However, in the Internet environment, search for information is a result of the consumer's active interest, and this ensures exposure and attention to the message. Thus, the focus shifts from information search to information use and the outcomes in terms of decision making. Consumers will use the modality that best balances effort and achieves the accuracy of their goals. Their *own level of knowledge* will determine which mode of communication—plain text, audio, or audio-visual—will be best suited for their decision-making process. The authors state that Internet based marketers must keep their marketing objectives (such as brand awareness, persuasion, purchase, and knowledge enhancement) in mind while creating information displays and be cognizant of the customer's expected effort/accuracy tradeoffs while designing features at Web sites.[12]

## Biases in the Perceptual Process

To cope with the barrage of marketing information (and other information in everyday life), customers become "selective." They ignore some stimuli and some possible interpretations of stimuli, thus biasing their perceptions of incoming information through three processes: selective exposure, selective attention, and selective interpretation.

### Selective Exposure

Of the more than 3,000 marketing communications to which a typical customer is potentially exposed during a typical week, only a small number achieve actual exposure depending on the customer's needs and interests. Customers seek out some advertisements, some shelf displays, some salespersons, or other sources of information if they are contemplating a purchase. On the other hand, customers not planning a trip may skip the travel section of a newspaper altogether; those not contemplating a computer purchase will skip an entire special advertisement section on computers in a magazine. This selective exposure (also called gatekeeping) is practiced by customers in any of the three roles. For example, a store selling costumes for Halloween (a custom celebrated yearly in North America on October 31 when everyone wears a mask or scary costume) advertises its special promotions on the radio; however, the customer playing the buyer role tunes out the ad because she knows the store location is too far and she has no chance of going there. In contrast, the child user may have gone out of the way to seek information from classmates about the store where a particular kind of costume might be available. Likewise, a customer who, in her payer role, judges a particular store to be too expensive would not enter the store even if it has big signs screaming merchandise clearance savings and even though she happens to pass it while strolling in the mall. U.S. Web advertising in the form of banner ads, text ads, pop-up ads, rich media ads (with sound and animation effects), and other forms has increased from $650 million in 1997 to about $6.1 billion in 2000. Marketers are interested in the click-through rates for advertising on the Web, which is a measure of "how many people who saw the banner ad or hyperlink, actually clicked on it." Though Web advertising has increased from 1997 to 2000, click-through rates have dropped from 1.35 percent in May 1997 to 0.39 percent in March 2000. Customers are becoming more selective as ad clutter increases and as they become more savvy in searching the Web for their particular needs and requirements.[13]

## Selective Attention

Even if an advertisement or product display manages to come face to face with a customer, the customer may still choose to ignore it if it does not relate to his or her interests. A person's attention may be initially impelled by the stimulus characteristics of contrast or vividness, but beyond the initial attention, a person's further processing of a stimulus advertisement or display depends on personal interest that the featured product or service arouses. Thus, tennis enthusiasts will read through or continue to watch or listen to an entire advertisement on tennis equipment while a business customer considering purchasing a computer will fully process the computer advertisement. On the Internet, advertisers are placing customer-specific ad-banners on related Web sites. For instance, data from media research firms Media Matrix and AdRelevance shows that marketers of pet supplies, personal care products, and home and garden products are targeting their core audience of women by advertising heavily on sites that are specifically geared towards women. It benefits both the marketers and the sites as it increases click-through for marketers and advertising revenues for the sites.[14]

## Selective Interpretation

Customers also interpret the content and message of marketing communications selectively. People generally view a political message or a political candidate, for example, positively or negatively based on their political affiliation. Similarly, after an important purchase, customers seek communication that will reassure them about the wisdom of their selection. Customers also distort negative information that might threaten their ego. This phenomenon, called **perceptual distortion**, refers to information being encoded by a person in a manner that makes it more congruent with his or her prior beliefs than it objectively is. Customers learn certain tricks, so to speak, to cope with the barrage of information available every day and to more easily solve the purchase-decision problem. Perceptual distortion is one such trick or tactic wherein people distort, whether intentionally or inadvertently, the incoming information to quickly encode it for immediate use or to file it away for later use.

## Perceptual Threshold

Of the three steps of the perception process (sensation, organization, and interpretation), sensation is the most important since the marketing stimulus is rendered inconsequential if it fails. But not every stimulus is sensed. Consider sitting in a classroom for every week in a semester and taking a look around the room. Are the lights today somewhat dimmer than before? No? Are you absolutely sure? What if the university authorities were to lower the lights just a tad in all the campus buildings? The small decrease in illumination would save them a bundle, and you wouldn't even notice it. You did not notice the change because it was below your perceptual threshold, the minimum level or magnitude at which a stimulus begins to be sensed. A related concept is the just noticeable difference (j.n.d.). This refers to the magnitude of change necessary for the change to be noticed. Marketers use this principle to marginally reduce product quantity or size in order to keep the prices constant in the wake of rising costs. Some years ago, M&M/Mars successfully reduced the size of its candy bars by keeping the size of the change small.

The magnitude of change needed for it to be noticed depends on the base quantity. The larger the base quantity, the larger the magnitude of change needed for the change to be noticed. This is known as Weber's Law, named after the German scientist Ernst Weber.[15] For example, a one-half-inch reduction in the size of a five-inch candy bar perhaps will not be noticed, but the same reduction in a two-inch-long stick of chewing gum is likely to be noticed.

## Managerial Uses of the Perceptual Process

Customers' perceptual processes are relevant to all aspects of marketing communications—product design, brand names, packages, in-store displays, and mass-media advertisements.

Three special areas of managerial concern where customer perceptual processes are complex and highly consequential are:

1. The psychophysics of customer price perceptions.
2. Country-of-origin effects.
3. Perceived corporate image.

### Psychophysics of Price Perceptions

The psychophysics of price refers to how customers psychologically perceive prices. Noteworthy aspects of the psychophysics of price are reference price, assimilation and contrast, and price as a quality cue. Reference price is the price that consumers expect to pay.[16] If the actual price is lower than the reference price, it is perceived as good economic value. The customer who accidentally walks into the store has the full price as a reference price; in contrast, the customer who has seen advertisements of "huge savings" has a much lower reference price and is, therefore, disappointed. Another important perceptual construct is assimilation and contrast. This principle states that customers have a latitude of acceptance and rejection, so prices (or other information) that fall within the acceptance latitude are assimilated and those that fall within the rejection latitude are contrasted and, hence, rejected. For example, a customer who is willing to spend up to $10 to purchase a gift might assimilate $9 or $11 but will reject other prices as either too low or too high. Another way this principle works is that customers have certain cut-off levels for accepting a price and prices below that level are viewed as acceptable. While those above it are rejected though the latter may exceed the former by just two cents. That is why marketers adopt the odd pricing method—a practice wherein prices are set just below the next round number. For example, a price of $9.99 falls below the $10 range and is acceptable, while a price of $10.01 would not. Customers often use price as a quality cue—as a basis for making inferences about the quality of the product or service. Such use of price is particularly likely where quality cannot be independently judged.[17] In a review of literature of this topic, researchers Kent B. Monroe and R. Krishnan (professors, respectively, at the University of Illinois and California Polytechnic State University) concluded that "a positive price perceived quality relationship does appear to exist."[18] Again, this is especially the case when other clues for inferring quality are unavailable.

## Country-of-Origin Effects

Country-of-origin effects refer to the bias in customer perceptions of products and services due to the country in which these products and services are made. For example, customers who would be happy to purchase a VCR from Japan, a fashion suit from Italy, a machine tool from Germany, and management consulting from a U.S. firm are driven by "country-of-origin" image.[19] Today, Korean companies face a negative country-of-origin effect for their automobiles (e.g., Hyundai) and electronic products (e.g., Goldstar TV). While countries with a poor overall image suffer from this bias, those with a good image benefit from it. The Window on Research shows how this perception of country-of-origin can vary across cultures and across processing conditions.

# WINDOW ON RESEARCH

## Country-of-Origin Effects

In two studies, researchers Zeynep Gurhan-Canli and Durairaj Maheswaran show that perceptions of country of origin are not uniform across cultures and across processing conditions.

Their first study shows that country-of-origin perceptions vary across countries, and these variations can be attributed to culture-specific factors. Customers in an individualistic culture, the United States, and a collectivist culture, Japan, were given attribute information about a mountain bike made either in Japan or the United States. The target product was described as being either inferior or superior to the competition. They found that U.S. customers (individualists) evaluated the home-country product more favorably only when it was superior to the competition. In contrast, Japanese customers (collectivists) evaluated the home-country product more favorably regardless of its superiority. Thus, the cultural dimension of individualism-collectivism is an important dimension in accounting for country-of-origin differences between the United States and Japan. Marketers must know that in collectivist cultures, a country-of-origin based advertising strategy is likely to benefit home products while in individualistic cultures, this would be true only if the home product is superior to competition. U.S. consumers tend to prefer home or foreign products based on the perceived quality differences, and a simple appeal to "buy American" may not be very effective.

In a second study, Zeynep Gurhan-Canli and Durairaj Maheswaran determine the factors that influence customers' country-of-origin perceptions. They show that motivation, processing goals, and the type of information presented, affect country-of-origin evaluations. Their study shows that customers use country of origin in making judgments only when the motivation is low or when their processing goal is to evaluate the country of origin itself. Under these conditions, customers direct attention toward country of origin when the information is dispersed across several products manufactured in a country. If unfavorable country-of-origin information is present in only a few products, then customers tend to think of these products as exceptions and do not consider this information in making a judgment about products made in that country in general. However, if such information is

*(continued)*

present in every product manufactured from the country, it is used in making judgments. Thus, the type of information presented also affects how the country-of-origin information is used in making judgments.

Under high motivation conditions, or when the customer's attention is drawn away from the country-of-origin information, customers do not utilize the country-of-origin information in making judgments. The study provides pointers to marketers about conditions that foster a focus on country-of-origin information. If marketers want the consumer to use the country-of-origin information in making a judgment, they need to draw attention to the same in advertising.

**Source:** Adapted from Zeynep Gurhan-Canli and Durairaj Maheswaran, "Cultural Variations in Country of Origin Effects," *Journal of Marketing Research*, Vol. 37, Issue 3 (August 2000), pp. 309–317; Zeynep Gurhan-Canli and Durairaj Maheswaran, "Determinants of Country-of-Origin Evaluations," *Journal of Consumer Research*, Vol. 27, Issue 1 (June 2000), pp. 96–108.

### Perceived Corporate Image

Corporate image refers to the public perception of a corporation as a whole.[20] Customer perceptions of corporate image affect everything a firm does. Thus, companies are known to be producers of high- or low-quality products or healthy products, users of high-pressure tactics or of soft-selling approaches, and socially conscious or utterly selfish merchants. The Window on Research shows that cultural differences and differences in processing of linguistic information can lead to differential perceptions of brand image and corporate image for Asian and Western consumers.

Sometimes, a company's image concerns not the main product the company produces but, rather, some other business actions. To many, Benetton, an Italian clothing company, stands for young and trendy clothing with vibrant colors; but to others, the first image that comes to mind is Benetton's ad campaign in support of controversial contemporary social issues, such as racial prejudice and AIDS. Some companies indulge in deceptive advertising or selling techniques; this is true especially in selected industries where the customer may be more vulnerable, either due to a lack of expertise or of time to understand the nuances of marketers' claims. The healthcare and insurance industries are often cited as examples, where elderly customers are sometimes taken advantage of by unscrupulous marketers engaged in deceptive practices.

# The Customer as a Learner

Consider the following customers and their behaviors:

- As you exit the Service Merchandise store, you run into your friend Sally walking out with her purchase—a VCR. She bought a Hitachi, four-head VCR-plus. What is a VCR-plus? And what do the four heads do? Besides, how did Sally know all this? How did she learn it?
- You present an expensive cologne, Polo, to your friend Miguel on his birthday. He tells you that he uses Woods. Polo is a little loud and stuffy, he tells you, like flaunting your riches. Woods is subtle. How can he say that? You are actually wearing Polo yourself, but he has never been able to tell! Where did he learn this notion about Polo anyway?
- Your friend Christele always flies with Delta Air Lines. Once, she had to take a flight at 6:00 a.m. even though American Airlines had a more convenient 7:00

# WINDOW ON RESEARCH

## Differences in Corporate and Brand Perceptions between Asian and Western Consumers

Research on Asian consumers shows that they respond to brand names, logos, corporate advertising, and branding communications differently than consumers in the West. Three factors contribute to these differences.

1. *Differences in the processing of linguistic information due to the structures of languages used in the West and in the Region.* Corporate and brand names are linguistic labels for a company and its products. Languages in the Asian region—Chinese, Japanese, Korean, and Vietnamese—are ideographic in origin and are largely based on Chinese characters, which are sign symbols composed of strokes. Characters are visual in nature, and, hence, visual processing would be the primary mode of remembering information in an ideographic system. It follows that Asian consumers pay close attention to the writing/spelling of the name and are strongly affected by the writing system in which a name appears.

2. *Differences in how corporate and branding information is categorized.* It is argued that Asian consumers might not evaluate brand extensions on the basis of category fit in terms of attributes or concepts (between parent and extension brands) as in the Western context. They are more likely to use a very simple process in evaluation of extensions—use of the company image as an heuristic. This is likely because of the differences between Asians and Westerners in the perceived abstraction between company name and brand name.

3. *Differences in value structures resulting from broader socio-cultural characteristics.* Several explanatory concepts such as individualism vs. collectivism, attitudes toward risk taking, gender roles, and time perceptions lead to differences between consumers in the West and in Asia. However, in the case of brands, two other differences lie in the concepts of aesthetic values of Asian consumers and mystical beliefs. Confucian ideals and religious backgrounds seem to have developed a far greater aesthetic of naturalism in Asian consumers than is seen in the West, and this affects the way they respond to brand and corporate communications. Further, corporate and brand names also are judged by Asians in terms of whether they are "lucky names." This concept of luck has been applied to colors, numbers, geometric positions, and names.

**Source:** Adapted from Bernd H. Schmitt (1994), "Corporate and Brand Identities in the Asia-Pacific Region: Theoretical and Applied Perspectives," *Asia Pacific Advances in Consumer Research*, Vol. 1, 1994, pp. 1–3. http://www.acrweb.org.

a.m. flight available. She explains that she is trying to collect a free travel certificate on Delta. How does Delta get her to show such loyalty?

- Your neighbor's son, Wolfgang, is in high school, and he wears oversized flannel shirts, baggy pants, baseball hats turned backwards, beads, headbands, and earrings. So do his friends. Where did they learn to dress this way?

Each of these customers is typical of many others, and their behaviors represent instances of learning. None was born with the knowledge, attitude, or behavior depicted in these examples. Each learned these things as a customer.

**Learning** is a change in the content of long-term memory. As humans, we learn because what we learn helps us respond better to our environment. Thus, a child who accidentally puts his hand on a hot electric bulb learns never again to touch anything resembling that object. A business learns not to hire a consultant again after finding out the consultant was trading the firm's secrets with competitors. Thus, human learning is directed at acquiring a potential for future adaptive behavior. In the context of consumer navigation behavior in an online environment, researchers Hoffman and Novak define "flow" "as a cognitive state occurring during network navigation (1) characterized by a seamless sequence of responses facilitated by machine interactivity, (2) intrinsically enjoyable, (3) accompanied by a loss of self-consciousness, and (4) self-reinforcing." One of the key consequences of flow is increased learning. When the customer is surfing the net without a purposive goal (experiential activity), flow produces latent learning. As a part of latent learning, the consumer learns about the Internet environment in general—sources of information, products/services, prices, and so on. This translates into higher recall and word-of-mouth activities. However, when the customer surfs the net to complete a particular task (goal-directed activity), flow leads to more informed decisions.[21]

## Mechanisms of Learning

As customers, we face a marketplace environment of a multitude of product and service choices; we learn to adapt and respond to this environment. Sally, Miguel, Christele, and Wolfgang represent four different mechanisms of learning: cognitive learning, classical conditioning, instrumental conditioning, and modeling.

### Cognitive Learning

When people talk about learning, they are often thinking of **cognitive learning**, or acquiring new information from written or oral communication. When we acquire information about something, whether incidentally and passively or deliberately and actively, we learn. Cognitive learning occurs on two levels: rote memorization and problem solving. With **rote memorization**, we rehearse the information until it gets firmly lodged in our long-term memory. Rote memorization can result from active rehearsal (as in trying to rehearse a phone number) or from passive, repeated exposure to the information. A great deal of advertising aims simply to create a rote memory of the brand name by repeated presentation. Top-of-the-mind brand awareness helps customers efficiently make everyday purchase decisions. **Problem solving** is a type of cognitive learning that occurs when the customer is actively processing information (weighing it, discounting some, combining and integrating disparate pieces of information) to reach certain judgement. In the business context, CISCO and SAP certifications are an example of cognitive learning by individuals to be able to perform better in their workplace.

### Classical Conditioning

Almost everyone has heard about Pavlov's dog. Ivan Petrovich Pavlov was a Russian psychologist interested in understanding the learning process among humans and animals. A giant in his field in his time (1849–1936), with a Nobel Prize in physiology, Pavlov studied human learning processes by experimenting on animals. In his experiments, Pavlov harnessed a dog, gave him some meat powder, and observed that the dog salivated. This salivation is an inherent reflex. Next, he rang a bell just before giving the meat powder, repeating this sequence several times. Then, he merely rang the bell without giving any meat powder. The dog, however, still salivated. The dog was said to have been conditioned to salivate to the bell ringing.

Note that the salivating response to the meat powder itself did not have to be learned since it already existed as an instinctual response. Rather, the transfer (i.e., conditioning) of this response to a previously neutral bell stimulus is what constitutes "learning." In this experiment, the meat powder is called an unconditioned stimulus, and the bell is called the conditioned stimulus. **Unconditioned stimulus (UCS)** refers to a stimulus toward which a customer already has a preexisting specific response, so the response to it does not have to be conditioned. **Conditioned stimulus (CS)** is a stimulus to which the customer either does not have a response or has a preexisting response that needs modification, so a new response needs to be conditioned.[22] In the Pavlov experiment, the sound of the bell is not inherently appealing for the dog, and the dog had never before salivated on hearing it. But the dog's involuntary reflexive new reaction now is to salivate. This is classical conditioning at work. **Classical conditioning** is the process in which a person learns an association between two stimuli due to their constant appearance as a pair. Because of this constant contiguity (pairing), customers tend to attribute to the previously unknown stimulus (product or service) whatever they think or feel about the paired other stimulus.

Classical conditioning is pervasive in our everyday lives. It has been proved in marketing in a number of laboratory experiments. In what by now has become perhaps the best-known experiment on this topic, Professor Gerald Gorn of the University of British Columbia demonstrated that the classical conditioning principle works in advertising. In this experiment, Professor Gorn selected two musical tunes, one from the movie *Grease* (which customers in his experiment liked) and the other from classical Indian music (which the same customers disliked). Then he showed slides of two pens that were identical except for their colors, which were pretested to ensure that the chosen colors were preferred equally. The slide for one pen advertisement was paired with the music from *Grease* while the other was paired with the Indian music. The pen paired with the liked music was preferred by more customers than the other pen. Thus, pairing liked and disliked musical stimuli with two virtually identical pens conditioned customers to prefer the pen that was shown in conjunction with the liked music.[23]

In another experiment at a supermarket, the music pace was varied on different days from slow to fast. On the slow-music days, shoppers spent more time in the store and bought more products than on faster-music days.[24] (See Window on Research box for yet another example).

# WINDOW ON RESEARCH

## Seeking Evidence that Classical Conditioning Really Works!

Terence A. Shimp, a well-known consumer researcher and marketing professor at the University of South Carolina, joined with Randall W. Engle, a professor of psychology at the same university, and Elnora W. Stuart, a marketing professor at Winthrop College, to perform a series of 21 experiments demonstrating, in by far the most rigorous way, the classical conditioning effect in the context of the marketplace.

These researchers used four unknown brands of colas (Cragmont, Elf, My-te-Fine, and Tiger) that were not sold in the region where the experiment was conducted, two moderately known brands (Royal Crown [RC] and Shasta), and two well-known brands (Pepsi and Coke). Each of these served as the conditioned stimulus (CS). For the unconditioned stimulus (UCS), the researchers employed four attractive water scenes: a mountain waterfall, a

*(continued)*

sunset over water, a boat mast against the sky, and a lavender-hued island. An important consideration in classical conditioning experiments is that the UCS have at least some degree of relevance to the CS. Here, water scenes do have relevance to colas because both have a refreshing mood effect.

Subjects were randomly assigned to either an experimental or control group. The experimental group was shown slides of the cola product and of the water scenes in tandem. Specifically, one cola slide was shown for 7.5 seconds, followed immediately by a scene slide for 7.5 seconds, and then a two-second blank screen. This 17-second showing was termed a "trial." Each subject was shown a total of 80 such trials. Of these, 20 were conditioning trials, in which a cola slide featuring a specific cola brand was followed by a specific water scene slide; the other 60 were nonconditioning trials that paired a cola slide (other than the cola brand that had been paired with the water scene slide) with the slide of a neutral stimulus (e.g., license plate, landscape, and so on). The control group was shown all the cola slides and all the scene slides at random—none were paired.

Afterward, subjects answered questions pertaining to the evaluation of the brand under study (i.e., the brand paired with the water scene). When the colas were paired *consistently* with the water scenes, the rating of colas was more favorable than when the colas were accompanied by water or neutral scenes in random fashion. This effect occurred the most for completely unknown brands and the least for previously well-known brands. For moderately known brands, the effect was in between.

Since, in the real world, brands are exposed along with other competing brands, the experiment also used a design in which the 20 slides of the same focal brand (paired with a water scene) were interspersed with 60 slides of the other cola brands (which were paired with neutral scenes). These other colas served as the surrounding context for the focal brand. The favorable rating of the focal brand was always higher when the surrounding context was made up of unknown colas rather than known colas.

This research (comprising 21 separate experiments) was significant both from theory and practice standpoints. In terms of theory, although classical conditioning effects have been demonstrated before, none of the previous research had used a surrounding context (which in this case consisted of competing brands). Thus, it captured the real marketplace conditions better. Moreover, the experiments compared the conditioning effect for well-known, moderately known, and previously unknown brands.

In terms of practice, the research implications are that (1) pairing an unknown brand with a likable audio or visual scene or person can indeed help develop consumer liking for the brand; (2) once the brand is already well known, the brand stands on its own, and pairing it with new likable scenes or persons does not do much for its already favorable rating; and (3) for a relatively unknown brand, it is easier to take advantage of the classical conditioning effect when competitive brands are not being advertised heavily than when intense competitive advertising is occurring.

The classical conditioning effects obtained here are with relatively pallid unconditioned stimuli (UCS) of water scenes. In the real world, much more powerful UCS are typically employed; brands are paired with intense, emotionally arousing, alluring audiovisuals and with highly attractive models with a fan-like following.

**Source:** Adapted from Terence A. Shimp, Elnora W. Stuart, and Randall W. Engle, "A Program of Classical Conditioning Experiments Testing Variations in the Conditioned Stimulus and Context," *Journal of Consumer Research* 18, No. 1, (June 1991), pp. 1–12. Additional information available at http://www.usc.edu. Reprinted with permission of the University of Chicago Press.

Marketers put this principle to use when they pair their brand with a likable celebrity. The celebrity's personality, by classical conditioning, rubs onto the product itself. Similarly, products are packaged to look expensive or more basic, natural or fancy, healthier or indulgent, special or everyday, environmentally friendly or not, and aesthetically appealing. Manufacturing firms exploit the prestige of the distributors and retailers who agree to carry their products. Companies try to associate themselves with other programs with certain public appeal. Some firms even boast about their major clients, hoping that such name dropping will boost their own public image. The practice of using their association with famous clients is common among advertising agencies and consultants and many business-to-business marketers. In a field like medicine, classical conditioning is at work during the residency training period for doctors when they are trained to prescribe drugs for specific symptoms and conditions.

## Instrumental Conditioning

The third learning mechanism is **instrumental conditioning**, whereby we learn to respond in certain ways because they are rewarding; that is, a response is instrumental to obtaining a reward. For example, we frequent a particular restaurant because we find the food there satisfying. We visit the same barber because the haircut is always perfect. We eat our vegetables, even if not always to our taste, because they are "good for you."

No lesson about instrumental learning is complete without at least a brief glimpse into the work of B. F. Skinner, a legendary figure among American psychologists. In 1931, with a Ph.D. in psychology from Harvard University, he began experiments to understand the causes of human behavior. He was uncomfortable with the prevailing explanation that human behavior was caused by unobservable "inner forces," such as desires and motives. He felt that since these inner forces could not be observed, they could not be scientifically verified. Instead he proposed a simpler theory, verifiable by direct observation: Behavior occurs because it is reinforced or rewarded. This theory has been called behaviorism, and Skinner is popularly known as the "father of behaviorism."

In a typical experiment with pigeons, Skinner would place a pigeon in a box (now referred to as a "Skinner box") equipped with a key or switch wired to a data recorder as well as a food dispenser. Every time the bird pecked the switch, a premeasured quantity of food was dispensed. Once the pigeons discovered this contingency, they would consistently display this pecking behavior every time they were in a state of food deprivation. Reporting on experiments such as this one in his scholarly work *Science and Human Behavior* (1953), Skinner argued that the pecking behavior of pigeons can be explained by "external" reinforcements or rewards and that there was no need to invoke "internal drivers and states." Likewise, Skinner argued that human behavior can be shaped or modified by rewarding that behavior. In other words, by reinforcements or rewards, humans can be made to learn a behavior.

How do marketers use this learning mechanism? First, they use instrumental conditioning naturally, and most effectively, when they make the product its own intrinsic reward. But when a brand becomes a parity brand with no intrinsically superior rewards compared to its competing brands, marketers offer extrinsic rewards to attract customer patronage. Examples are coupons, sweepstakes, and rebates. The best examples of instrumental learning are the frequent flier programs that accumulate mileage toward future free flight awards.

## Modeling

The fourth mechanism of learning is **modeling**, whereby we learn by observing others. Children learn much of their social behavior by observing the elders around them. We also learn from teachers and other people we admire or who we believe are experts. We owe much of our understanding of modeling to psychologists Neal E. Miller and John Dollard, who called this type of learning **imitation** or **imitative behavior**. These scholars explain that we imitate the behavior of those whom we see rewarded, because we expect to be rewarded ourselves by adopting that behavior, either by the person we model or by others who admire that person. Based on their studies of imitation, Miller and Dollard identified four classes of people likely to be imitated by others: (1) persons superior in age-grade hierarchy, (2) persons superior in social status, (3) persons superior in intelligence ranking system, and (4) superior technicians in any field.[25]

The choice of models varies from culture to culture. The age hierarchy works more in Eastern countries like Japan, India, and most of the Arab countries where elders are always respected and emulated. In the Western cultures, grade hierarchy is influential; for example, sixth graders emulate the tenth graders in school. Similarly, in most societies, the more educated are imitated by the less educated, superior technicians are imitated by the less-skilled technicians, and people often imitate those higher in social status. This is the basis of middle-class consumers aspiring to the lifestyles of the upper class. The modeling phenomenon works in a similar fashion for businesses, too. Small hospitals will adopt new surgical procedures after the larger, more reputed hospitals or renowned surgeons have adopted them. The whole management practice of benchmarking dramatically exemplifies organizational imitation or modeling.

## The Psychology of Simplification and Complication

In practice, customers do not always follow a standard path in the learning process. For various reasons shown in Table 4.1, they may engage in simplification or complication.

| TABLE 4.1 | Conditions Leading to the Psychology of Simplification and Complication |
|---|---|

| Psychology of Simplification | Psychology of Complication |
|---|---|
| Problem routinization | Boredom |
| Habitual purchasing | Maturation |
| Desire to limit decision problems | Forced irrelevance of current alternatives |

### Simplification

As a lifetime learner of market-related information from diverse sources (marketers, media, and self-experience), the customer develops what has been termed the *psychology of simplification*, the customer strategy of simplifying the task. Customers do this by avoiding further information-gathering effort and by relying primarily on what is already learned.

Cumulative learning from past experiences helps a customer solve problems more efficiently. When encountered repeatedly, problems are "routinized" with respect to their solution. **Problem routinization** refers to defining a decision problem so that no new decisions need to be made. As customers recall previously made decisions from memory, they simply purchase the same brand as before, a buying strategy termed **habitual purchasing**. Thus, one underlying cause of brand-loyalty repeat purchase of a brand is habit formation, and customers adopt this procedure because it simplifies life; it is the psychology of simplification at work.[26] Customers' natural calling is habituation, routinization, simplification, and inertia. With some exceptions (to be discussed), customers want to reduce choices, not enlarge them. This is needed to navigate the twenty-first century marketplace, which proliferates with choices.[27] Customers are fundamentally creatures of habit; incentives to switch come from dissatisfaction with current brand, lack of distinction among brands, and offers of distinctly superior value from competing brands or firms.

## Complication

The psychology of complication, or customer desire to redefine a problem so decisions have to be made anew, occurs due to three factors: (1) boredom, which causes exploratory or diversive activities, (2) life status changes and maturation, and (3) forced irrelevance of current solutions.

**Boredom.** Desire for variety is an inherent motivation for humans. As boredom sets in from repeated experience with the same stimulus (product or brand) and its utility declines, customers indulge in variety seeking or novelty seeking.[28] The desire for variety is sought principally from products with social/emotional value rather than mainly performance value. Thus, one doesn't get bored using the same vacuum cleaner daily, but one seeks variety in foods (sensory/emotional value), clothing, perfume/cologne, and other recreational products. Companies satisfy this desire by building variety in their offerings. Thus, Campbell's soup comes in different flavors, and airlines increase satisfaction of their frequent travelers by varying some part of the service experience (e.g., meals, movies, décor).

**Maturation.** Sometimes, customers outgrow old tastes, such as in music, art, or wine. In formal terms, we call this maturation, meaning a self-perceived obsolescence of prior preferences. Maturation is not so much a case of getting bored with the old; rather, it is a feeling that past tastes were poor choices and that they are no longer appropriate to the current time and age.

Change in life-status is one source of maturation. Life-status change refers to a major event in a customer's life that changes his or her status—events such as changes in location (e.g., moving to a new city), family composition (e.g., a marriage, divorce, death, birth), resources (e.g., getting a job or a degree), and position (e.g., a promotion, an appointment). These changes bring forth two kinds of needs. The first type of need is for products previously not needed, like a bridal gown or baby furniture. The second type of need is to modify the prior solutions to the same need. For example, a promotion to an executive position might require a fundamental change in your wardrobe.

Maturation also results from a change in a person's self-concept, which usually stems from acquisition of new reference groups. An example is a teenager who may suddenly dissociate himself from the "grunge clothing type" or a middle-aged person attempting to redefine his or her identity in the face of a midlife crisis.

The third source of maturation is the phenomenon of rising expectations. Customers hold all market offerings to certain expectations, and as these expectations are met, new expectations arise. New expectations make the previous solutions look unsatisfactory, and they search for better products and services.

**Forced Irrelevance of Current Solutions.** While boredom and maturation are internal sources of the psychology of complication, forced irrelevance refers to an external environment source that renders prior solutions irrelevant. Three environmental sources that can force people to give up current solutions and look for alternatives are marketer, business organizations, and the government.

Marketers can rekindle new choices by phasing out certain products, by going out of stock of the regular brand that the customer purchases, or by actually closing the business down, forcing the customer to look for other choices. Businesses also alter available choices. For example, an employer changes its health insurance agency, which forces employees to choose their provider anew. Schools may ban certain clothing styles, necessitating new purchases. Government enacts new regulations that make prior solutions irrelevant and force new decisions for the same customer need. By banning smoking on airplanes, government has forced customers to seek alternatives like the nicotine patch or chewing gum. Similarly, a ban on import of certain brands and products makes purchase of those brands infeasible.

# Customer Acceptance of Change: The Ultimate Learning Experience

Some products are entirely new to the world. Such a product is called an **innovation**— a product, a service, or an idea that a customer perceives to be new. VCRs, computers, compact disc players, electronic toothbrushes, patches for smokers, and laser surgery were all innovations when they were first introduced. Among the products that are still innovations today are hair transplants, laser keratotomy (an eye surgery operation), male birth control pills, melatonin (an anti-aging pill), and digital photography cameras. Customers do not rush to purchase these products, no matter how promising they look. Rather, they adopt an extensive process of deliberation, sometimes actively resisting the new product. Customer response to these new products and services is referred to as innovation adoption. The Internet has grown much faster than previous media innovations like telephone, television, radio, and the cable. Morgan Stanley Dean Witter Technical Research states that it has taken radio 38 years to reach 50 million users; television, 13 years; cable, 10 years; and the Internet just 5 years.[29]

## Innovation

A product is an innovation if it is new in some sense. "Newness" has two dimensions: (1) uniqueness—how different it is from existing products, and (2) age—how long it has existed in the marketplace. For uniqueness, what matters more than the absolute newness is whether the customer perceives it as unique. Likewise, what matters more than the product's chronological age is when the customer was first exposed to it. Thus, a product or service that has existed for a long time is still an innovation to a group of people if it was introduced to that subculture or group only recently.[30] Some examples of innovations are computers, televisions, and cellular phones in developing countries.

Uniqueness is also a matter of degree. Some products and services are marginally dissimilar from their existing forms while others are substantially dissimilar. Based on the degree to which they are unique, marketers classify innovations as continuous, dynamically continuous, and discontinuous. Both for business and individual customers, where the innovation falls on the continuum depends on prior exposure to it and on experience with the forerunners of specific innovations. Thus, to a computer savvy user, a new computer software application service, such as banking by computer, may appear to be a continuous innovation, in contrast to a consumer, totally unaccustomed to computers, who may perceive it as a discontinuous innovation. Hence, marketers must define as their initial target markets those customers who would perceive an innovation as continuous. In addition to the user role, marketers introduce innovations for the buyer and payer roles as well. For example, debit cards (which have a cash reserve against which a merchant draws the amount for the current purchase) or prepaid phone cards are innovations for the payer role. Shopping on the Internet or by computer are innovations for the buyer role.

The Internet itself can be categorized as a discontinuous/radical innovation and a process innovation in specific since it alters the internal operations of a firm, changes their mode of transaction with the various stakeholders—customers and suppliers—and modifies their responses to the market forces—industry and competition.[31]

## Categories of Adopters

There are various categories of adopters among customers. The categories are defined through the diffusion of an innovation across a population. The **diffusion process** refers to the spreading of an innovation's acceptance and use through a population. If one plots all the acceptors of an innovation over time, the diffusion follows a bell curve (see Figure 4.2).

## Adopter Categories: Some Customers Are Quick to Adopt; Some Are Very Slow                    FIGURE 4.2

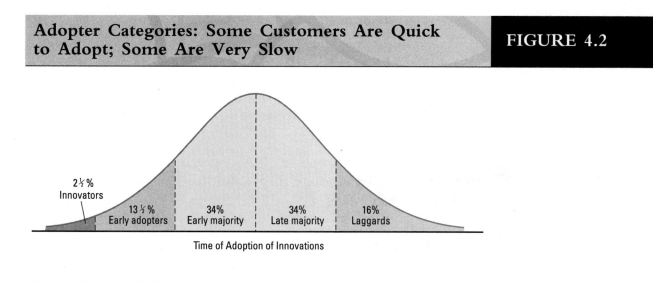

Time of Adoption of Innovations

On this curve, the first adopters are called **innovators**, and normally constitute 2.5 percent of the population. They adopt independently of other people. Those who adopt later are **imitators**; namely, early adopters, early majority, late majority, and laggards in that order. The innovators and early adopters are risk takers because they are the first groups to adopt. Those who adopt later are risk avoiders, and they wait to see if the risk takers' experience has been satisfactory. Thus, communication between the early groups of adopters and the later adopters is central to the diffusion of innovations.

## Innovators and Opinion Leaders

Innovators and early adopters may be opinion leaders. **Opinion leadership** is the giving of information and advice, leading to acceptance of the advocated position by the recipient of the opinion. This definition has two implications. First, not only must information be given, but it must be accepted frequently or by a majority of those who receive the opinion. Second, the information given by the opinion leader must pertain to a recommended action, and the recipients of the opinion must act on the recommendation.

Opinion leaders have two qualities, both necessary for their success: expertise and trustworthiness. **Expertise** is possessing knowledge about the innovation that is not yet common knowledge. Since a person cannot be an expert on everything, opinion leadership is by necessity interest-area specific. **Trustworthiness**, the second requisite for opinion leadership, refers to the perceived benevolence and dependability of the opinion giver. It is founded on the requirement that the opinion giver has no vested interest in promoting a position.[32]

What are characteristics of innovators and opinion leaders? According to scholarly research in the field, these are the characteristics of innovators:[33]

* Risk takers
* Variety seekers
* Upper socioeconomic status
* Product interest
* Less well integrated with other members of the society
* More individualistic and independent in their thinking

Opinion leaders have the following characteristics:

* High product involvement
* Recognized as leaders

- Socially well integrated
- More exposed to a variety of media sources, especially news and information media programs (rather than merely entertainment-oriented media)
- Leaders and formal office holders in social, political, and community organizations.

Figure 4.3 presents some illustrative measures that customer behavior researchers recommend for measuring opinion leadership and innovativeness. The Window on Research (pages 148–149) outlines some characteristics of the early adopters of Internet technology for online shopping.

## FIGURE 4.3  Illustrative Measures of Opinion Leadership and Innovativeness

### Opinion Leadership

**Q.** Compared to your friends, are you more likely to be asked, less likely to be asked, or about as likely to be asked about ____?

**Q.** During the past six months, how many people have you told about ____?
**a)** Told no one. **b)** Told a number of them.

**Q.** In your discussions with your friends and neighbors about ____, are you more likely to
**a)** give information/receive information?
**b)** be used as a source of advice/not used as a source of advice?

**Q.** My friends and neighbors often ask my advice about ____ (agree/disagree).

**Q.** I influence the types of ____ my friends buy (never/sometimes/often).

**Q.** I look to my friends for advice on ____.

### Innovativeness (Yes or No or a five-point agree/disagree scale)

- I like to take a chance.
- I like to try new and different things.
- When it comes to taking chances, I would rather be safe than sorry.
- I like to wait until something has been proven before I try it.
- If people would quit wasting their time experimenting, we would get more accomplished.
- When I see a new brand on the shelf, I usually pass right by.
- In general, I am the first (last) in my circle of friends to buy a new ____ when it appears.
- I like to buy new ____ before others do.

**Sources:** Items compiled from Goldsmith and Hofacker, 1991; Reynolds and Darden, 1971; and Ronald E. Goldsmith and Charles F. Hofacker, "Measuring Consumer Innovativeness," *Journal of the Academy of Marketing Science*, 19 (1991), 209–221; Fred D. Reynolds and William R. Darden, "Mutually Adaptive Effects of Interpersonal Communication," *Journal of Marketing Research*, 8 (November 1971), pp. 449–454. See also Leisa Reinecke Flynn, Ronald E. Goldsmith, and Jacqueline K. Eastman, "Opinion Leaders and Opinion Seekers: Two New Measurement Scales," *Journal of the Academy of Marketing Science* 24, Spring 1996, 137–47.

Innovation orientation differs not only among consumers but also among countries. Research by Steenkamp, Hofstede, and Wedel in a cross-cultural study in 11 countries of the European Union shows that consumers in countries that are high on individualism and masculinity and low on uncertainty avoidance tend to be more innovative than countries that are collectivist, feminine, or high on uncertainty avoidance. You might recall that these are three of the five dimensions of cross-cultural values that we discussed in Chapter 2. Consumer innovativeness was also affected by the importance that the consumer attached to the value domain of conservation (security, conformity, and tradition) as compared to the domain of openness to change. Further, innovation also decreased with higher ethnocentrism (beliefs held by consumers about appropriateness/morality of purchasing foreign-made products),[34] a more favorable attitude towards the past, and age. These differences across countries gives marketers a better idea about the kind of countries that they need to target when introducing an innovation and also how to design strategies such as sampling, liberal return policies, or advertising so as to overcome these obstacles to innovation adoption.[35]

## Innovators among Business Customers

Innovators and opinion leaders are just as important among business customers. Marketing expert Eric Von Hippel calls them "lead users." Lead users use the products of today in ways that predict how those products should be modified to meet the needs of tomorrow. Thus, lead users use existing products to their maximum capacity with some unmet needs. Marketers can study these users and their needs and can implement innovations in those products. Von Hippel cites the example of college students as the lead users of personal computers. The students had access to time-sharing terminals linked to mainframe computers at the university; these terminals were functional equivalents of what would be later known as personal computers. By studying their usage, marketers could have predicted the future popularity of desktop-based computer games among college youth.

## Adoption Process

The adoption of an innovation refers to customer acceptance of an innovation for continued use. Two principal factors that distinguish innovations from current products and cause people to be cautious are: (1) as new product categories, innovations lack evaluation criteria, so customers don't know how to appraise them; and (2) their benefits and negative outcomes are unknown or unestablished by experience. Therefore, customers engage in a long deliberative process before adopting the innovation. This adoption process has been characterized by the acronym, AIDA, which signifies a sequence of four stages, or four mental states, an adopter goes through: awareness, interest, desire, and action. Thus, customers first become aware of the innovation, then they become interested in and feel a desire for it, and finally they take the necessary action to acquire it.

A related depiction of this process, emphasizing the customer's active mental processing has five steps: exposure, information gathering, evaluation, trial adoption, acceptance or rejection. The customer on exposure to an innovation, gathers information, evaluates the innovation, decides to try it, and then finally accepts or rejects it. Contrary to the popular view, rejection does not make a person non-innovative. A true nonadopter is one who, following exposure, resists further evaluative processing of the innovation.

As one might expect, the incidence of early adopters in the general population declines as people get older, yet recent Web measurement reports show that highest growth rates for Internet usage in the U.S. are now among seniors. Seniors are using the Web to keep in touch for socialization with family and friends. They are also planning vacations and shopping online. As computers become more user-friendly and seniors get more comfortable using the Web, their adoption rates will increase further.

## Desirable Characteristics of Innovations

Innovations vary along certain characteristics that render them easy or difficult for customers to adopt. The characteristics that consumers desire in innovations are as follows:

- *Relative advantage*—The relative advantage refers to how much better the innovation is compared to the current product that it will substitute. For example, customers would adopt digital answering machines only if they perceive them to satisfy the value they seek better than the machines with conventional tapes do.

# WINDOW ON RESEARCH

## Characteristics of Early Adopters of the Internet Technology for Online Shopping

Data from the sixth GVU survey of 1996 was analyzed with reference to the adoption of online shopping as an innovation on the Internet. Respondents were classified as buyers/innovators based on the number of different product categories in which they had made online purchases within the last six months. Of the 17 product categories, skeptics had not bought in any categories, triers had bought in fewer than three categories, and buyers/innovators had bought in three or more categories.

Three factors underlie people's perception of online vendors versus off-line vendors:

1. *Post-purchase expectations*—The post-purchase expectations dominate people's perceptions of online shopping in terms of timely receipt of goods, billing, etc., and this concern is similar across buyers, triers, and skeptics.
2. *Benefits of purchasing online*—Buyers and triers tend to feel that there are greater benefits to buying online compared to the skeptics.
3. *Transaction costs*—Once again, buyers and triers have a more favorable perception of online transaction costs.

The distinguishing characteristic among the innovators (buyers), triers, and skeptics in adoption of online shopping was their primary reason for using the Web. Forty-six percent of innovators considered online shopping as their primary reason for using the Web, compared to 21 percent for triers and 8 percent for skeptics. Buyers represented 48 percent of those who

- *Perceived risk*—**Perceived risk** of innovations refers to the uncertainty about whether their relative advantage will accrue and whether unanticipated harm will occur. Customers are less likely to adopt innovations with high perceived risk, such as laser surgery or irradiation of foods.
- *Complexity*—Customers prefer an innovation that is easy to comprehend. The easier it is to comprehend, the less **complexity** it has. For example, many customers may find the Internet too complex to understand, so they may decide not to adopt it.
- *Communicability*—**Communicability** refers to the extent to which an innovation is socially visible or is otherwise easy to communicate in social groups. The greater the ease with which customers can communicate about an innovation, the more rapidly they are likely to adopt it. For example, taboo topics such as personal hygiene products have low communicability while hairstyles are more visible and, therefore, naturally more communicable.
- *Compatibility*—Customers want products that are compatible with their behavior and values. **Behavioral compatibility** consists of qualities that do not require customers to alter their behavioral routine. **Value compatibility** is consistency with customers' deeply held values. Examples of behavioral incompatibility are vans that do not fit in the garage and electric cars that may require frequent bat-

spent 20 or more hours per week on the Internet, compared to 30 percent and 22 percent for triers and skeptics. Thirty-eight percent of buyers had more than 100 bookmarks on their browser, compared to 21 percent and 15 percent for triers and skeptics respectively. They found that in terms of demographic characteristics, buyers were more likely to be male, married, have higher incomes, and work in computer-related jobs. In a survey of on-line users in 1998, Ernst and Young also profiled the online shopper to be the male head of the household (49 percent), be 40 years of age or older, have an annual income of over $50,000, and be better educated than the average householder.

In another survey posted on TechWeb, Yahoo!, Hermes, and 50 other sites between October and November 1996, the authors explored risk perceptions of users about the online medium and its impact on their intention to shop online and provide information online. They collected data from users on financial risks, privacy risks, and overall risks of shopping on-line. Data was also collected on the users' attitudes toward web vendors, their willingness to buy from that vendor, and their willingness to provide information to the vendor. The authors found that perceived financial risk was a major determinant of perceived overall risks online. These risk perceptions influenced users' attitudes toward online vendors. When users had a negative attitude toward an online vendor, it affected their willingness to purchase from the vendor and their willingness to provide information to the vendor.

**Source:** Adapted from Arvind Rangaswamy and Sunil Gupta, "Innovation Adoption and Diffusion in the Digital Environment: Some Research Opportunities," *eBRC Working Paper*, February 1999, http://www.ebrc.psu.edu/pubs. html; The Second Annual Ernst & Young Internet Shopping Study, 1999.

tery charging. An example of value incompatibility is contraceptives for customers whose religion may prohibit contraception.

- *Trialability*—**Trialability** refers to the extent to which it is possible to try out the innovation on a smaller scale. For example, among the birth-control methods, oral pills have trialability, whereas a vasectomy does not. Therefore, customers are likely to adopt vasectomy less rapidly.

## Innovation Resistance

The marketing terms that describe the diffusion of innovation have a pro-innovation bias.[36] Somehow it is assumed that adopting the innovation is good while resisting it is bad. But as Edward Rogers, the pioneer in innovation diffusion research, has pointed out, "Many individuals, for their own good, should not adopt them."[37] In fact, people who desire not to change may be more rational than those who seek change for its own sake. The research evidence suggests that true innovators, for many innovations, are more likely to be social deviants, abnormal in their drive to explore new things forever, always seeking change, and adopting innovations indiscriminately without any rational choice calculus. Therefore, marketers should understand the psychology of resistance for those individuals who resist change and focus on offering innovations that offer true value to customers, presented in a manner that responds to the customers' motivations for resistance.

Two factors account for resistance to innovation: habit and perceived risk. Habit is a learned sequence of responses to a previously encountered stimulus. Habits are efficient means of task execution since, by repetition, the skill has been perfected. The second factor, *perceived risk*, was defined before as the uncertainty about whether there would be any advantage and whether some unanticipated negative outcome might occur. These risks may take the form of performance risk (the probability that the product may not perform as expected or desired or that there may be physical side effects or unwanted consequences) or social risk (the probability that significant others may not approve of the innovation adoption).

Based on these two factors, four types of innovation resistance can be found, as depicted in Table 4.2.

---

| TABLE 4.2 | A Typology of Innovation Resistance |
|---|---|

|  |  | RISK | |
|---|---|---|---|
|  |  | Low | High |
| H A B I T | WEAK | 1.<br>NO RESISTANCE INNOVATIONS<br><br>(New and improved versions of established products; fads and fashions) | 3.<br>RISK RESISTANCE INNOVATIONS<br><br>(Discontinuous and replacement innovations) |
|  | STRONG | 2.<br>HABIT RESISTANCE INNOVATIONS<br><br>(Continuous and replacement innovations) | 4.<br>DUAL RESISTANCE INNOVATIONS<br><br>(Social programs) |

**Source:** Jagdish N. Sheth, "Psychology of Innovation Resistance: The Less Developed Concept," *Research in Marketing* 4 (1981), pp. 273–282.

---

When risk is low and habits are weak, there is likely to be virtually no resistance. Examples of these "no resistance innovations" are soft soap or soap jelly instead of the soap bar, better shaped razors and toothbrushes, change in a package design for sending overnight mail to business customers and so on. Some of these "no resistance innovations" may be fads, and there would be no reason for rational consumers to adopt them.

Even when risk is low, habit for the old product may be well entrenched, and a new habit may be required for the new product. This category, called the "habit resistance innovations," includes many continuous innovations: for example, cars that work on electric power rather than gas and that would require consumers to recharge their batteries regularly. For consumers to learn this new habit, they would need substantial incentive, such as the prospect of significant savings in the costs of energy.

When habit for the existing alternative is weak (or the new alternative requires no habit), the risk may be high. An example of such "risk resistance innovations" would be for consumers to switch to solar-energy home-heating systems. Once installed, using one or the other system entails no physical action, so habits do not come into the picture. But, there is risk that the solar system may not work. Documentation of risk-free performance of new technology is required before rational consumers can be expected to adopt these innovations.

Finally, there are innovations that entail overcoming old habits as well as high risks. These "dual resistance innovations" are the hardest for consumers to accept. Examples include social programs in developing countries, such as contraception practices. Consumers in these societies perceive health risks in the use of contraceptives, and using them requires learning new routines. Marketers should reengineer these innovations to minimize both the learning of new habits and the perceived risk.

For instance, research by the National Consumer Council in UK shows that Internet security concerns are an important reason for consumers' slow adoption of e-commerce. Consumers are skeptical about providing their credit card and personal details to suppliers who might turn out to be fraudulent. Also, the inability to touch and feel products before purchase is a serious concern. These fears can be addressed by marketers and credit card companies by providing information about consumer liabilities in case of online fraud and legal recourse available to consumers in these cases.

The research showed that consumers try to minimize the risks of online shopping by relying on the trusted nature of brand names and well-known retailers. Twenty-eight percent of consumers surveyed stated that they would look for a well-known brand name when shopping online.[38]

## The Perceptual and Learning Process and the Three Customer Roles

The perceptual and learning processes described in this chapter are experienced and exhibited by the customer in all three of his or her roles. Table 4.3 illustrates major areas where they apply.

### Influence of Perception Processes

The general perceptual process depends on stimulus characteristics, the context, and the perceiver characteristics of prior knowledge and expectations. User evaluations of product usage experience are perceptions inevitably biased by their knowledge of the brand name or price or the consumption situation. Many consumers swear how much they love their favorite brand and how they could never enjoy another brand, yet in blind tests they can't tell which brand is their favorite brand.

Similarly, payers are intimately influenced in their perception of the price value by the context and their expectations. A price of $200 for a suit in a very upscale store such as Neiman Marcus would appear a steal while the same price for the same suit in a discount store like T.J. Maxx or Value City would look unattractive. The psychophysics of price perceptions, discussed at length in this chapter, exemplifies the relevance of perceptual processes to the payer role.

Finally, the buyer role is also subject to the perceptual processes. The buyer's judgment of product quality from brand name, price, or store name is an indicator of the perceptual biases at work. Similarly, buyers perceive certain store locations to be too far compared to others despite equal distance and/or travel time. For example, in a city, stores accessible by an interstate highway or expressway are perceived by some to be farther away than those reachable by city roads, even though it might take longer to drive to those stores reachable by city roads.

The specific concepts we discussed in the perceptual process are also applicable to all three roles. For example, consider the concept of j.n.d. Users will not notice subtle differences (those that fall below the j.n.d. levels) between brands or the product or service from the same vendor. The new and improved product versions should be improved beyond the j.n.d. levels rather than merely objectively. Similarly, buyers will not notice reductions in product size or quantity (a strategy marketers sometimes use instead of changing

| TABLE 4.3 | The Perceptual and Learning Processes among the Customer Roles | | |
|---|---|---|---|

| Process | User | Payer | Buyer |
|---|---|---|---|
| **PERCEPTION PROCESS**<br>General process | • Usage experience biased by prior expectations based on brand name, price, or consumption situation. | • The price-value perception depends on brand-name and store contexts. | • Perceptions of alternative brands biased by price, brand name, store, etc. Store distance perceptions are often biased. |
| Just noticeable difference (j.n.d.) | • "New and improved" products must cross the j.n.d. barrier. | • Price variations below j.n.d. are not noticed. | • Package size reductions below j.n.d. are not noticed. |
| Assimilation and contrast | • Distance to destinations, wait in service settings, etc., are assimilated or contrasted. | • Price discrepancies from expected levels may be assimilated (acceptable) or contrasted (not acceptable). | • Store distances and customer service variations may be assimilated or contrasted. |
| **LEARNING PROCESS**<br>Cognitive learning | • User learns about the use of products and services by reading about them. | • Payer learns about used-car prices from the NADA used-car price book. | • Buyers learn about new stores by word of mouth and about brand ratings from *Consumer Reports*. |
| Classical conditioning | • Food preferences are acquired in early childhood. | • Perceived fairness of price levels is classically conditioned. | • Buyers are conditioned through continued patronage of the same vendors. |
| Instrumental conditioning | • Users adopt new products and services if they find them beneficial. | • Payers "buy cheap" at first, then experience shoddy performance and learn to "invest" more. | • Buyers learn they can get better terms by changing vendors. |
| Modeling | • Users model their clothing and car choices after people they admire. | • Budgeting decisions mirror those of admired companies. Payers learn norms for tipping by observing others. | • Buyers may switch preferences to stores and vendors that are trendy. |
| Adoption of innovation | • Users adopt product and service feature innovations. | • Payers adopt financing innovations (e.g., leasing, debit cards). | • Buyers adopt purchase procedure innovations (e.g., buying through the Internet). |

the price) as long as they are within the j.n.d. range. Finally, payers will not notice price variations across brands or for the same brand across purchase occasions if these variations are maintained within the j.n.d. levels. Similarly, the concepts of assimilation and contrast apply to all three roles. Will a patient expecting to wait at the doctor's office for about 15 minutes assimilate or contrast a 21-minute wait? Will a customer in the payer role, when confronted with a new product at a higher price, assimilate that price into his or her zone of acceptance, or, instead, contrast and reject it? These are the questions marketers need to consider when designing product and price changes and destination locations.

### Influence of Learning Processes

The four models of learning are also general in nature, applicable to all three customer roles. However, the type of things the three roles need to learn differs. Users learn about the meaning and personal utility of product and service attributes by reading information about them. Buyers learn about new stores and new vendors by word-of-mouth information and about brand ratings from *Consumer Reports*, for example. And payers learn what is a good price value also by reading the price information. For example, suppose you wanted to buy a used car; you would learn the appropriate price by looking up a used-car price guide book, such as the one published by the National Association of Automobile Dealers (NADA).

Next, consider the other three models of learning: classical conditioning, instrumental conditioning, and modeling. As users, the examples of these learning modes abound and were cited earlier in the chapter. We all acquire our preferences in foods, for example, in early childhood by classical conditioning. We adopt new products and services and use them repeatedly due to the rewards we obtain (instrumental conditioning), and we model our choice of clothing, houses, and cars after certain referents we admire.

As buyers, we continue to buy from the same vendors (classical conditioning) or decide to change vendors to obtain better terms (instrumental conditioning), or we mold our vendor choices following the trend leaders (modeling). The popularity of particular coffee houses, restaurants, and nightclubs soars and wanes, for example, based on which celebrities are or are not patronizing them. Business companies tout the identity of their illustrious customers, hoping to attract new customers for whom the current customers might serve as models.

Finally, as payers, we learn to view certain price levels as customary and fair (classical conditioning). For example, a cup of coffee for $2 in a gourmet coffee shop would not make us raise our eyebrows, but at a vending machine it would, even when labeled "gourmet coffee." Poor experiences teach us to spend more for better quality and consider the higher amount an investment (instrumental conditioning). Also, in many cases how much the admired others pay becomes our own guideline through the process of modeling. For example, how much the business firm we admire spends on advertising might guide our own budgeting decisions, or our notions of how much to tip in a restaurant might have been molded by friends we consider to be socially savvy (or by those whose frugality we admire).

## Customer Roles in Innovation Adoption

The last topic we discussed was the adoption of innovations. The applicability of the concepts within this topic to all three roles is rather obvious and straightforward. Innovations occur in relation to product and service features (for the user), in financing arrangements such as leasing and debit cards (for the payer), and in new modes of buying such as through the Internet (for the buyer). Innovators would adopt these due to the desirable characteristics we discussed earlier (e.g., relative advantage, trialability, and so on). Contrarily, users, payers, and buyers would resist their adoption if the innovation does not overcome the barriers of habit and perceived risk. For example, in regard to buying through the Internet, habit will not be a resistance factor for those who are already using the Internet for other purposes.

# Summary

In this chapter, we have described three processes of customer behavior: perception, learning, and innovation adoption. In the perceptual process, we identified the influence of the characteristics of the stimulus, the context, and customers themselves. Next, we described three biases in the perception process: selective exposure, selective attention, and selective interpretation. We also illustrated these biases for marketing stimuli, such as perception of price and its biased association with quality.

In discussing the customer as a learner, we described four models of learning: cognitive learning, classical conditioning, instrumental conditioning, and modeling. Classical conditioning occurs when a preexisting customer response to a stimulus (product, service, or person) is transferred to another object, product, or service the stimulus is constantly paired with. Instrumental conditioning occurs when customers learn to engage in a behavior repeatedly because the behavior is rewarding. Cognitive learning occurs when customers obtain new information. Modeling occurs by observing other customers whose behavior we find worth imitating. Marketers take advantage of these learning models by structuring their market offerings and communications about them in a fashion conducive to most customer learning of desired responses.

Next, we discussed the customer as a responder to change. The market offers customers change in the form of new products and services, and the process of responding to the change is discussed in the context of diffusion of innovations. Customers desire certain characteristics in innovations—relative advantage, low perceived risk, low complexity, easy communicability, behavioral and value compatibility, and trialability. Customers adopt innovations easily when they conform to these characteristics. However, there are customers who resist innovation adoption, and two factors underlying this psychology of resistance are habit and perceived risk. Such resistance is overcome by redesigning the innovations to minimize both the learning of new habits and the perceived inherent risks.

Finally, we also discussed the roles and distinct qualities of innovators and opinion leaders, suggesting ways to measure who is or is not an innovator or an opinion leader. Opinion leaders play a significant role in promoting innovations. The customer perspective—how customers perceive, learn, accept or reject change, and make marketplace decisions—is detailed in this chapter. As marketers and students of customer behavior, we will serve our purposes well by understanding this customer perspective and by using it as the basis of our response to customers.

# Key Terms

Adoption 147

Assimilation and Contrast 134

Behavioral Compatibility 148

Classical Conditioning 139

Cognitive Learning 138

Communicability 148

Complexity 148

Conditioned Stimulus (CS) 139

Corporate Image 136

Country-of-Origin Effects 135

Diffusion Process 144

Expectations 131

Expertise 145

Forced irrelevance 143

Habit 150

Habitual Purchasing 142

Imitation/Imitative Behavior 141

Imitators 145

Information Content 131

Innovation 144

Innovators 145

Instrumental Conditioning 141

Interpretation 130

Just Noticeable Difference (j.n.d.) 134

Lead Users 147

Learning 138

Life-Status Change 143

Maturation 143

Modeling 141

Odd Pricing 134

Opinion Leadership 145

Organization 130

Perceived Risk 148

Perception 129

Perceptual Distortion 133

| | |
|---|---|
| Perceptual Threshold 134 | Sensation 130 |
| Performance Risk 150 | Sensory 130 |
| Problem Routinization 142 | Social Risk 150 |
| Problem Solving 138 | Stimulus 130 |
| Psychology of Complication 143 | Trialability 149 |
| Quality Cue 134 | Trustworthiness 145 |
| Reference Price 134 | Unconditioned Stimulus (UCS) 139 |
| Relative Advantage 147 | Value Compatibility 148 |
| Rote Memorization 138 | Weber's Law 134 |

# Discussion Questions and Exercises

1. Why does classical conditioning work better for unknown brands than for known brands? What characteristics would you use to select a celebrity to pair with your brand? Or to be a spokesperson for your company?
2. What are the psychology of simplification and the psychology of complication? Think about your own life as a customer and identify two examples of each. Again, considering your marketplace behavior, do you find yourself engaging more frequently in the psychology of simplification or in the psychology of complication? How? Why?
3. Evaluate the following products or services in terms of the characteristics of innovation that facilitate their adoption:
   a. Caller identification
   b. A shopping service where an employee from the firm will go to the supermarket with your phone order, buy your groceries, and deliver them to your home
   c. A clothing fashion such as the recently introduced collarless shirts
   d. The business practice of just-in-time inventory management
   e. The ISO-9000 standard of quality (assume it is not mandatory).
4. You are the marketing director of a local museum. You recall the concepts of instrumental conditioning, psychology of simplification and complication, boredom, maturation, and so on, and wonder if any of these can help you develop ideas for getting your member patrons to visit the museum more often. List some ideas with their concepts.
5. Assume a clothing company in Russia has appointed you as a country marketing manager for introducing the designer clothing in your own country, Canada. The clothing line has sold well among Russian consumers—young adults, who view it as their own national alternative to a Western brand like Tommy Hilfiger or Calvin Klein. You also recall the concepts of innovators and opinion leaders and want to use these to define your target markets. As you ponder the differences between consumers in the two countries, you also recall reading about "global youth," the idea that youth everywhere are becoming quite alike in their tastes as consumers. Prepare a marketing memorandum for the host country's top management, outlining your initial thoughts on these issues.

# Notes

1 "Top 10 Beauty Sites," *emarketer 2000*, http://www.emarketer.com/elist/t10beauty/t10beaut_1.html.

2 For further discussion on this process, see Joel B. Cohen and Kunal Basu, "Alternative Models of Categorization: Toward a Contingent Processing Framework," *Journal of Consumer Research* 13 (March 1987), pp. 455–72.

3 Quoted in Banwari Mittal, "Public Assessment of TV Advertising: Faint Praise and Harsh Criticism," *Journal of Advertising Research* (January–February) 34, No. 1 (1994), pp. 35–53.

4 David A. Lauer, *Design Basics*, 1979, New York: Holt, Rinehart & Winston.

5 L. W. Barsalou, "Ideals, Central Tendency, and Frequency of Instantiation as Determinants of Graded Structure," *Journal of Experimental Psychology: Learning, Memory and Cognition*, 11, October 1985, pp. 629–54.

6 Robert W. Veryzer Jr. and J. Wesley Hutchison, "The Influence of Unity and Prototypicality on Aesthetic Responses to New Product Designs," *Journal of Consumer Research*, 24, March 1998, pp. 374–94.

7 Valarie A. Zeithaml, A. Parasuraman, and Leonard L. Berry, "Problems and Strategies in Services Marketing," *Journal of Marketing* 49 (Spring 1985), pp. 33–46.

8 "Internet Changing Financial Service Brand Perceptions," January 18, 2000, http://cyberatlas.internet.com/markets/finance/article/0,,5961_287291,00.html.

9 "Building the B2B Foundation: Positioning Net Market Makers for Success," ATKearney Report 2000, http://www.atkearney.com/main.taf?site=1&a=5&b=3&c=1&d=4.

10 Abhijit Biswas and Edward A. Blair, "Contextual Effects of Reference Prices in Retail Advertising," *Journal of Marketing* 55 (July 1991), pp. 1–12.

11 William Boulding, Richard Staelin, Ajay Kalra, and Valarie Zeithaml, "A Dynamic Process Model of Service Quality: From Expectations to Behavioral Intentions," *Journal of Marketing Research* 30 (February 1993), pp. 7–27.

12 Eloise Coupey and Erin Sandgathe, "Rethinking Research on Communications Media: Information Modality and Message Structuring," *Advances in Consumer Research*, Vol. 27, 2000, pp. 224–29.

13 eAdvertising Report, http://www.emarketer.com, June 2000.

14 "Internet Advertisers Target Women," January 19, 2000, http://cyberatlas.internet.com/markets/advertising/article/0,,5941_288371,00.html.

15 See Stuart Henderson Britt, "How Weber's Law Can Be Applied to Marketing," *Business Horizons*, February 1975, pp. 21–29.

16 See Robert Jacobson and Carl Obermiller, "The Formation of Reference Price," *Advances in Consumer Research* 16 (1989), pp. 234–40; Joel E. Urbany, William O. Bearden, and Dan C. Weilbaker, "The Effects of Plausible and Exaggerated Reference Prices on Consumer Perceptions and Price Search," *Journal of Consumer Research* 15 (June 1988), pp. 95–110.

17 See Valarie A. Zeithaml, "Consumer Perceptions of Price, Quality, and Value: A Means-End Model and Synthesis of Evidence," *Journal of Marketing* 52 (July 1988): pp. 2–22. See also Steven M. Shugan, "Price Quality Relationships," in Thomas C. Kinnear, ed., *Advances in Consumer Research* 11 (Association for Consumer Research, 1983), pp. 627–32; and Carl Obermiller and John J. Wheatley, "Price Effects on Choice and Perceptions under Varying Conditions of Experience, Information, and Beliefs in Quality Differences," in Thomas C. Kinnear, ed., *Advances in Consumer Research* 11 (Association for Consumer Research 1983), pp. 453–58.

18 Kent B. Monroe and R. Krishnan, "A Procedure for Integrating Outcomes across Studies," in Richard P. Bagozzi and Alice M. Tybout, *Advances in Consumer Research*, Vol. 10, (Ann Arbor, Mich.: Association for Consumer Research, 1983), pp. 503–8.

19 For further reading on country-of-origin effects, see W. Li and R. S. Wyer, Jr. "The Role of Country of Origin in Product Evaluations: Informational and Standard-of-Comparison Effects," *Journal of Consumer Psychology* 3, No. 2 (1994), pp. 187–212; Sung-Tai Hong and R. S. Wyer, Jr., "Effects of Country of Origin and Product-Attribute Information on Product Evaluation: An Information Processing Perspective," *Journal of Consumer Research* 16, No. 2 (September 1989), pp. 175–87; E. Kaynak and T. Cavusgil, "Consumer Attitudes Towards Products of Foreign Origin: Do They Vary Across Product Classes," *International Journal of Advertising* 2 (1983), pp. 147–57; M. Wall and L. A. Heslop, "Consumer Attitudes Toward Canadian-made Versus Imported Products," *Journal of the Academy of Marketing Science* 14 (Summer 1986), pp. 27–36; M. Wall, J. Liefeld, and L. A. Heslop, "Impact of Country-of-Origin Cues on Consumer Judgments in Multi-Cue Situations: A Covariance Analysis," *Journal of the Academy of Marketing Science* 19, No. 2 (Spring–Summer 1991), pp. 105–14; Chih-Kang Wang and Charles W. Lamb, Jr., "Foreign Environmental Factors Influencing American Consumers' Predispositions Toward European Products," *Journal of the Academy of Marketing Science* 8 (Fall 1980), pp. 345–56; D. Tse and G. J. Gorn, "An Experiment on the Salience of Country-of-Origin in the Era of Global Brands," *International Marketing Review* 9 (1992), pp. 57–76. W. K. Li, K. B. Monroe, and D. Chan, "The Effects of Country of Origin, Brand, and Price Information: A Cognitive-Affective Model of Buying Intentions," *Advances in Consumer Research* 21 (1994), pp. 449–57. J. K. Johansson, "Determinants and Effects of the Use of Made in Labels," *International Marketing Review* 6 (1989), pp. 47–58. Murray A. Young, Paul L. Sauer, and H. Rap Unnava, "Country-of-Origin Issues," in Salah H. Hassan and Roger D. Blackwell, *Global Marketing: Perspectives and Cases* (Fort Worth, Tex.: Dryden Press, 1994), pp. 196–210; Sevgin A. Eroglu and Karen A. Machleit, "Effects of Individual and Product-Specific Variables on Utilizing Country-of-Origin as a Product Quality Cue," *International Marketing Review*, 6 (November 1998), pp. 27–41; G. Erickson, J. K. Johansson, and P. Chao, "Image Variables in Multiattribute Product Evaluations: Country-of-Origin Effects," *Journal of Consumer Research* 11 (September 1984), pp. 694–99. C. M. Han, "Country Image: Halo or Summary Construct," *Journal of Marketing Research* 16 (May 1989), pp. 222–29.

20 Jay S. Niefeld, "Corporate Advertising," *Industrial Marketing* (July 1980), pp. 64–74; "Two Different Animals: Brand Awareness and Corporate Image," *Forbes* 6 (March 1989), p. 20.

21 Donna L. Hoffman and Thomas P. Novak, "Marketing in Hypermedia Computer-mediated Environments: Conceptual Foundations," *Journal of Marketing*, 60 (July 1996), pp. 50–68.

22 For a fuller description of the Pavlov experiments, see Leland C. Swenson, *Theories of Learning: Traditional Perspectives/Contemporary Developments* (Belmont, Calif.: Wadsworth Publishing Company, 1980), pp. 13–30.

23 See Gerald J. Gorn, "The Effects of Music in Advertising on Choice Behavior: A Classical Conditioning Approach," *Journal of Marketing* (Winter 1982), pp. 94–101.

24 Ronald E. Milliman, "Using Background Music to Affect Behavior of Supermarket Shoppers," *Journal of Marketing* (Summer 1982), pp. 86–91.

25 Neal E. Miller and John Dollard, *Social Learning and Imitation* (New Haven, Conn.: Yale University Press, 1941).

26 See John A. Howard and Jagdish N. Sheth, *The Theory of Buyer Behavior* (New York: John Wiley and Sons, 1961).

27  Jagdish N. Sheth and Atul Parvatiyar (1996), "Relationship Marketing in Consumer Markets: Antecedents & Consequences." *Journal of the Academy of Marketing Science* 23, No. 4 (Fall 1995), pp. 255–71.

28  P. S. Raju, "Optimum Stimulation Level: Its Relationship to Personality, Demographics, and Exploratory Behavior," *Journal of Consumer Research* 7 (December 1980), pp. 272–82.

29  Arvind Rangaswamy and Sunil Gupta, "Innovation Adoption and Diffusion in the Digital Environment: Some Research Opportunities," eBRC Working Paper, February 1999, http://www.ebrc.psu.edu/pubs.html.

30  For further reading, see E. Hirschman and M. Wallendorf, "Some Implications of Variety Seeking for Advertising and Advertisers," *Journal of Advertising* 9 (1980), pp. 17–25; W. D. Hoyer and N. M. Ridgway, "Variety Seeking as an Explanation for Exploratory Purchase Behavior: A Theoretical Model," *Advances in Consumer Research* 11 (1984), pp. 114–99; L. McAlister and E. A. Pessemier, "Variety-Seeking Behavior: An Interdisciplinary Review, *Journal of Consumer Research* 9 (December 1982), pp. 311–22.

31  Arvind Rangaswamy and Sunil Gupta, ibid.

32  Pamala L. Alreck and Robert B. Settle, "The Importance of Word-of-Mouth Communications to Service Buyers," in David W. Stewart and Naufel J. Vilcassim, eds., *1995 AMA Winter Educators' Proceedings* (Chicago: American Marketing Association, 1995), pp. 188–93. Lawrence F. Feick, Linda L. Price, and Robin A. Higie, "People Who Use People: The Other Side of Opinion Leadership," in Richard J. Lutz, ed., *Advances in Consumer Research* 13 (Provo, Utah: Association for Consumer Research, 1986), pp. 301–5; Ronald E. Goldsmith, Melvin T. Stith, and J. Dennis White, "Race and Sex Differences in Self-Identified Innovativeness and Opinion Leadership," *Journal of Retailing* 63, Winter 1987, pp. 411–25. Pamela Kiecker and Cathy L. Hartman, "Predicting Buyers' Selection of Interpersonal Sources: The Role of Strong Ties and Weak Ties," in Chris T. Allen and Deborah Roedder John, eds., *Advances in Consumer Research* 21 (Provo, Utah: Association for Consumer Research, 1994), pp. 464–69.

33  For further reading, see Frank M. Bass, "A New Product Growth Model for Consumer Durables," *Management Science*, 15 (January 1969), pp. 215–27.

34  Terence A. Shimp and Subhash Sharma, "Consumer Ethnocentrism: Construction and Validation of the CETSCALE," *Journal of Marketing Research*, 24 (August 1987), pp. 280–89.

35  Jan-Benedict E. M. SteenKamp, Frenkel ter Hofstede, Michel Wedel, "A Cross-National Investigation into the Individual and National Cultural Antecedents of Consumer Innovativeness," *Journal of Marketing*, 63 (April 1999), pp. 55–69.

36  This section is adapted from Jagdish N. Sheth, "Psychology of Innovation Resistance: The Less Developed Concept (LDC) in Diffusion Research," *Research in Marketing* 4 (Greenwich, Conn.: Jai Press Inc., 1981), pp. 273–82.

37  Everett M. Rogers, "New Product Adoption and Diffusion," in R. Ferber, ed., *Selected Aspects of Consumer Behavior*, Washington, D.C.: NSF Government Printing Office, 1977, pp. 223–38; Everett M. Rogers, *Diffusion of Innovations*, 3rd ed. (New York: Free Press, 1983), pp. 281–84.

38  "U.K. Consumers Wary of Online Security," August 3, 2000, http://cyberatlas. internet.com/big_picture/geographics/article/0,,5911_429671,00.html.

# CHAPTER 5

## Customer Motivation: Needs, Emotions, and Psychographics

## Reacting to the Germ Scare

In one of its routine consumer surveys a few years ago, Colgate-Palmolive Co. discovered something unexpected: an unusually high level of consumer concern over germs and bacteria. Recent events, both real and fictional, had fueled the consumer paranoia of germs. First, there was the sudden death of moviemaker Jim Henson from a bacteria-related illness. Then an *E. coli* (a type of bacteria) outbreak from undercooked hamburger killed three children and one adult. Finally, new outbreaks of tuberculosis and cholera were reported in the United States. In April 1994, the Centers for Disease Control (CDC) issued a startling warning: the country's ability to detect and monitor infectious diseases was in jeopardy.

To top it off, in 1995, Hollywood released a movie called *Outbreak*, the story of a diseased monkey roaming the streets of New York City. And a made-for-TV movie called *Virus* aired on all major networks.

With all this news as well as hype, consumer fears about germs increased. In response, Colgate and a host of other companies raced to the market with a bevy of antibacterial products. Playskool Frog Waterpal is a children's bath friend on the outside, but from the inside, it releases a powerful chemical defense that destroys the cell walls of bacteria, leaving them crippled and unable to multiply. Other antigerm weapons include Palmolive Ultra dish soap with "antibacterial" splashed across the label, Dial Corp.'s Brillo cleaning pads with a patented microbe shield, Bristol-Myers Squibb Co.'s Keri antibacterial hand lotion, and Playskool's bacteria-fighting version of Soft Bear.

Consumer phobia runs so high that one consumer in the Bristol-Myers study for the lotion is reported to have asked, "If I rub it on my nose, will it stop me from getting a cold?" This is just as psychologist Abraham Maslow proposed: physiological safety is one of human beings' most basic motivations.[1] Companies like Colgate-Palmolive, Bristol Myers, and Playskool developed products to meet this consumer motivation for physiological safety. In fact, newer products are introduced regularly to meet this need, with Clorox and Lysol antibacterial wipes being the most recent additions.

Marketers ask a number of questions in an attempt to understand why people behave the way they do: Why do customers in their roles as users, payers, and buyers use, pay for, and purchase what they do? What goals are they trying to achieve? What needs are they trying to satisfy? What feelings and emotions are they experiencing? How do these needs and emotions shape their lifestyles? How do their lifestyles relate to and explain their behavior as customers?

This chapter addresses the ways in which marketers have attempted to answer such questions (See Figure 5.1). It begins by defining motivation and identifying three facets of customer motivation: needs, emotions, and psychographics. We then explore each facet. First, we summarize several models that categorize customer needs. Next, we define emotions and discuss their role in influencing customer behavior. Finally, we define psychographics and introduce the major methods for classifying customers according to their values and lifestyles.

## FIGURE 5.1 | Conceptual Framework

## Motivation

Dr. Leeflang, how come you are still prescribing *Zovirax* rather than *Valtrex*, the leading brand from our company? Ms. Neuno, why did you change the specs on this purchase order? Mr. Suboto, the CFO (chief financial officer), wants to know why you are recommending this vendor over the lowest-price bidder for the computer network installation contract.

What do these questions have in common? They all are looking for the underlying motivations for behaviors. The Window on Research explores the motivations for Web usage by customers.

**Motivation** is what moves people, the driving force for all human behavior. More formally, it is defined as the state of drive or arousal that impels behavior toward a goal-object. Thus, motivation has two components: (1) drive or arousal and (2) goal-object. A **drive** is an internal state of tension that produces actions purported to reduce that tension. A **goal-object** is something in the external world whose acquisition will reduce the tension. Arousal or drive provides the energy to act; goal-object provides the direction for one to channel that energy. A person with goal-objects but without the drive is just a daydreamer; one with energy but no goal-object is akin to a hyperactive child. When energy is expended to attain some goal-object, we call that use of energy **purposive behavior.**[2]

# WINDOW ON RESEARCH

## Motivations for Web Usage

Researchers Pradeep K. Korgaonkar and Lori D. Wolin explore the motivations and concerns of web users in three usage contexts: a) number of hours spent per day on the Web; b) percentage of time spent for business versus personal purposes; and c) purchases made on the Web; in specific, the number of purchases made in the past year. The study lists the following reasons as motivations for Web usage, and these motivations correlate positively and significantly with the number of hours of Web usage and whether purchases are made on the Web. The Social Escapism, Interactive Control, and Economic Motivation factors also correlate positively with the actual number of purchases made in the last year. The Interactive Control motivation correlates with the percentage of time spent on the Web for personal purposes. (Korgaonkar and Wolin, 1999, Table 2, pgs. 57–59)

1. *Social Escapism motivation*—Escape from reality; diversion and aesthetic enjoyment; relief from day-to-day boredom, stress, and loneliness.
2. *Information motivation*—Use of the Web for information and self-education needs.
3. *Interactive Control motivation*—Using the interactive nature of the Web to control, customize, and personalize their experience on the medium.
4. *Socialization motivation*—Facilitate interpersonal communication and activities through e-mail, chat rooms, and virtual communities.
5. *Economic motivation*—Shopping and buying motivations—price savings, freebies.

The respondents of the study also voiced transaction-based security and privacy concerns (fear of providing credit-card information on the Web for purchase of products and concerns on privacy of personal information) and nontransactional privacy concerns (overall concerns of privacy in terms of unsolicited e-mail, hackers).

**Source:** Adapted from Pradeep K. Korgaonkar and Lori D. Wolin, "A Multivariate Analysis of Web Usage," *Journal of Advertising Research*, March–April 1999, pp. 53–68.

Consumption without direction, such as alcoholism, and unrestrained materialism are non-purposive in nature.

## The Process of Motivation

The motivational process, shown in Figure 5.2, begins when a stimulus engenders arousal or drive. The arousal can be autonomic (felt physiologically), such as when you suddenly sight a bear. It can be emotive: for example, when you are feeling lonely. Or it can be cognitive, such as when you are struggling with finding a way out of a deal that you no longer find attractive.

---

**FIGURE 5.2**          **A Model of the Motivation Process**

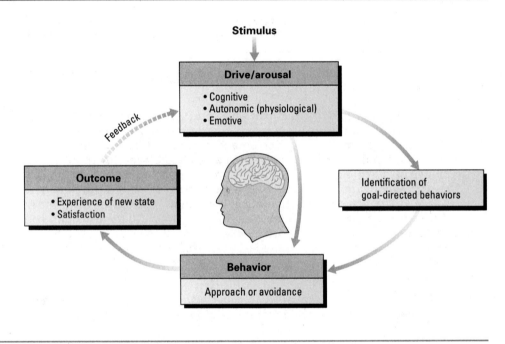

---

The arousal leads a person to act (i.e., to behavior). Autonomic (physiological) or emotive arousal can elicit the relevant behavior directly. For example, the sight of a bear will autonomically (i.e., automatically) make you flee, and seeing something funny may make you immediately smile or laugh. Similarly in a business context, when an executive sees in the mail an express mail envelope, his or her automatic response is to open that envelope first. Emotive feelings are aroused when we buy products that are made in our home country versus foreign countries. These feelings are magnified when there are tensions between the home country and a foreign country. For example, the recent case of U.S. soldiers being held in China has aroused negative feelings toward Chinese products in the United States. Cognitive arousal also would elicit behavior but generally only after further cognitive activity to figure out possible goal-directed behaviors; for example, a person seeking a way out of a commitment will identify and deliberate available options. Or a person with a car breakdown will deliberate alternative ways of getting to the destination. In business, the onset of a new project causes cognitive arousal, and there is a request for proposals that are scanned and deliberated upon.

Following the automatic or selected behavior, the final outcome will be the experience of a new state and a possible sense of satisfaction. This outcome, if positive, feeds back to calm the drive. If the new state was not satisfactory, the feedback recycles the process.

## Approach/Avoidance Motives

Depending on whether the identified goal is something to embrace or avoid, the person will use either an approach or an avoidance behavior. **Approach motivation** is the desire to attain a goal-object. Approach goal-objects (i.e., objects that attract us) are sought or even longed for. For example, most people seek vacations and good food. Their deprivation creates unhappiness.

**Avoidance motivation** is the desire to protect oneself from an object. Avoidance goal-objects might include traffic tickets and the measles. E-tailing tries to cash into the avoidance motivation of the buyer by building on his or her desire to avoid traveling long distances to purchase a product, paying high prices for a product, or conducting time-consuming comparison searches.

Marketers want to make their products and services approach objects. "No money down" purchase of products and pre-approved credit cards are examples of marketer approach features, and the high interest rates charged on these purchases and cards are the avoidance motives. Often, a trade-off is involved—the product contains some approach and some avoidance outcomes. For example, the taste and sensory pleasure in candies elicit approach, but their fat and calorie content evoke an avoidance motive. Part of the consumer conflict is between immediate approach outcomes and distant, long-term negative side effects; for example, between the thrill of driving a car and its relatively low safety or between an appliance that is low in initial purchase price but high in its cost of maintenance or vice versa. More and more, the marketer's challenge is to minimize avoidance features while maximizing approach features, such as offering reduced-fat or reduced-calorie snacks without sacrificing the taste, or improving product quality without letting the costs rise.

In the business context, Application Service Providers (ASPs) provide services that make them approach objects for small- and medium-sized businesses. They provide the company with access to every required software application, from the simplest e-mail program to a sophisticated customized database that could, for example, track daily change in a company's sales figures by store or zip code and deliver it to wireless laptops anywhere in the country, all for a monthly fee. For the payer, it eliminates the cost of purchasing software and its upgrades. For the user, there is no headache of customizing, maintaining, integrating, and supporting software, yet there is access to all the software needed and the upgrades. Finally, for the buyer, it eliminates the hassle of evaluating suppliers and reduces risk.

## Facets of Motivation: Needs, Emotions, and Psychographics

Whatever the direction of motivation, it manifests in three facets: needs, emotions, and psychographics. Needs are gaps between the desired and the current state, and they lend themselves more readily to cognitive consciousness and appraisal. Emotions are more autonomic and engender more personal experience. Psychographics combine behaviors driven by both needs and emotions.

# Customer Needs

The concept of needs and wants is closely aligned to the concept of motivation. In Chapter 1, we defined *need* as a felt deprivation of the desired state. The desired state provides the goal-object, and its deprivation provides the drive. Psychologists and consumer researchers have suggested various *categories* of needs. Among the most relevant to marketers are Maslow's need hierarchy, Murray's psychogenic needs, Dichter's consumption needs, and various marketing scholars' lists of customer needs.

## Maslow's Hierarchy of Needs

According to psychologist Abraham Maslow, human needs and wants are arranged in a hierarchy. Higher-level needs are dormant until lower-level needs are satisfied.

**Maslow's hierarchy of needs** consists of (from lowest to highest):

1. Physiological needs (hunger, thirst)
2. Safety and security needs (security, protection)
3. Belongingness and love needs (social needs)
4. Esteem and ego needs (self-esteem, recognition, status)
5. Need for self-actualization (self-development, realization)[3]

A person progresses to higher-level needs if the lower-level needs are satisfied; he or she regresses back to lower-level needs should these needs become unsatisfied again. Maslow does not distinguish between needs and wants, but most contemporary books on marketing do. According to this distinction, only the first two needs in Maslow's hierarchy would be needs while the last three are wants.

## Maslow's Needs for Household Customers

Physiological needs lead customers to strive for, purchase, and use food, clothing, and shelter. For many, such as those below the poverty line, these needs remain perpetually less than adequately met so that they never rise to higher-level needs. Furthermore, many of the differences in what customers use and buy are due to physiological differences, as we read in Chapter 2 (i.e., physiological differences due to genetics, race, gender, and age).

At the next level, safety and security needs are responsible for many people's fear of flying, for example, and for buying insurance against various uncertainties of life. Personal safety is a motive as old as survival itself, and in modern times, purchase and use of guns is on the rise in major urban centers to ensure personal safety. Likewise, other safety concerns relate to automobile safety and safety with regard to health as consumers develop a germ phobia.

Social motives of belongingness and love are evident when customers want to buy products that are well regarded by others so that the use of those products brings the customers' peer approval, affection, and a sense of belonging. The kind of neighborhood you choose to live in, the kind of car you choose to drive, the designer logos on the clothes you wear, what school you send your youngster to, and the places you vacation are at least in part determined by how your peers and significant others will look upon these choices. Many products, such as greeting cards, flowers, and other kinds of gifts, are bought specifically to promote relationships between individuals.

Next, we all work hard to gain success in our individual sphere of activity and to acquire the qualities others consider desirable and virtuous so that we may win our own and others' esteem. We also buy products and services we deem fitting of our esteem. Beyond impressing others, for example, we drive a car that, in our judgment, reflects who we are; we visit stores where we are treated with respect; and we even buy and give gifts to ourselves because we feel we deserve them.

Finally, once these physiological, social, and esteem needs are satisfied, people begin to explore and extend the bounds of their potential—that is, seek self-actualization. This self-actualization motive is what is behind a person engaging, for example, in self-improvement activities, such as taking an adult-education course or tenaciously pursuing a skill toward perfection, like in competitive sports, or even doing meditation to, according to Eastern philosophy, meet one's creator, to become what one was supposed to be, in a cosmic sense.

## Maslow's Needs for Business Customers

Like customers in household markets, customers in the business markets experience Maslow's hierarchy of needs. This can be visualized at two levels: business customer as an enterprise and business customer as individuals working in firms. First consider business as an enterprise. As an enterprise, business firms need, for their physical survival, at least three resources: money, employees, and raw materials and equipment. Banks and venture capitalists who supply cash, recruitment agencies who supply employees, and suppliers of raw materials and equipment are catering to the survival needs of the business enterprise, akin to physiological needs of the individual.

Security needs for business firms translate into insurance against loss of property and assets and against liabilities that may arise in various business transactions. Indeed, safety and security are key concerns in government and business buying; for example, the safety features are of paramount importance when city governments procure vehicles for their police forces. In office buildings, elevators need to be inspected and maintained for safe operations. In Department of Defense contracts, all vendors must assure and abide by data security requirements.

Belongingness for business enterprises refers to recognition by peer organizations and being admitted to formal or informal membership groups of other similar organizations. Thus, to belong to *Fortune 500* or to Silicon Valley, to be listed on the stock exchange, to belong to the Better Business Bureau, to be recognized as a leading contender in the field, or to be certified and recertified by formal certification agencies are examples of an enterprise's sense of belonging.

Esteem comes partly from being recognized by various bodies but also partly from one's own sense of accomplishment, such as winning the Malcolm Baldrige award or obtaining the AACSB accreditation by a business school (American Assembly of Colleges and Schools in Business). Qualifying to belong to a group of enterprises or to attain certain status and awards, businesses need to buy, use, and pay for a range of products and services—for example, tightly controlled quality in raw materials, training for its employees, or reengineering services.

Finally, self-actualization is seen in business firms' striving to become what they want to be, such as 3M as the innovative company, Ben & Jerry's as the environmental company, Levi Strauss as the diversity company, and Benetton as the social consciousness company. Firms that have these and similar other business firms as their customers must themselves reflect these values and deal in ways that further or help the customer companies to actualize their selves.

Now consider business customers as individuals working in organizations. Whatever they want to buy, they want to feel secure that it is a wise decision and be assured that the product or service will perform well and to the specifications. Whoever is making the purchase decision for the organization is held accountable for it, and often he or she is at risk of being perceived as being incompetent should an unwise purchase decision be made. Thus, business customers are likely to buy from someone they feel secure in dealing with. Next, many products are bought simply to satisfy a person's belongingness and esteem needs; for example, corporate membership in country clubs, corporate jets, the kind of hotel one chooses on business travel, and even the location and address of business premises. Finally, self-actualization reflects a person's personal value system and affects what he or she buys and whom he or she buys from—for example, buying from local or minority suppliers.

## Murray's List of Psychogenic Needs

Psychologist Henry Murray proposed a list of 12 primary (or viscerogenic) and 28 secondary (or psychogenic) human needs. An illustrative sample of those psychogenic needs is shown in Table 5.1, along with an example. As can be seen from that list, Murray looks at human needs more microscopically so that each need is more focused, narrow, and specific compared with Maslow's needs, which are more broadly defined and, therefore, have fewer categories. Murray's list can be very useful in identifying more precisely the

| TABLE 5.1 | Murray's List of Needs: Examples of Psychogenic Needs |
|-----------|-------------------------------------------------------|

| Need | Definition | Examples |
|------|------------|----------|
| • Autonomy | To be independent and free to act according to impulse; to be unattached, irresponsible; to defy convention. | Impulse buying, wearing unconventional clothing |
| • Dominance | To direct the behavior of others | Aggressively demanding attention in service establishments |
| • Nurturance | To give sympathy and to feed, help, and protect the needy | Giving to humanitarian causes |
| • Exhibition | To make an impression; to excite, amaze, fascinate, entertain, shock, intrigue, amuse, or entice others | Wearing high-fashion clothing |
| • Cognizance | To explore, to ask questions, to seek knowledge | Visiting museums, learning about new technology and products |
| • Exposition | To give information and explain, interpret, and lecture. | Playing opinion leaders. |

**Source:** From *Explorations in Personality* by Henry A. Murphy, copyright 1938, renewed 1966 by Henry A. Murray. Used by permission of Oxford University Press, Inc.

motivation underlying customers' specific marketplace behaviors, such as compulsive consumption (discussed later in this chapter).

## Ernest Dichter's Consumption Motives

Ernest Dichter was a psychoanalyst trained in Vienna in the early part of the century. A strong believer in Freud's theory of personality, he believed that unconscious motives play a significant role in people's consumption decisions. Based on in-depth interviews with consumers for some 200-plus products, he identified a set of motives/needs that underlie an individual's consumption of diverse products (see Table 5.2). Since many of these motives are thought to influence consumption decisions unconsciously, the list is most useful for incorporating symbolism in product advertising.

## Needs Identified by Marketing Scholars

Working more directly on marketing problems and reflecting specifically on an individual's behavior in the marketplace, several marketing scholars have identified and proposed their own classification of needs. Consumer researcher Geraldine Fennel identified consumer motives for product use based on use-situation—for example, aversive (to avert an adverse situation) or positive (to gain a reward) product-use situation. Consumer researcher Morris Holbrook has discussed the hedonic (i.e., pleasure seeking) consumption motive, distinguishing it from the more utilitarian consumption. Similarly, marketing professor Olli T. Ahtola has described utilitarian and hedonic consumer attitudes toward products. (Hedonic motive is discussed later in this chapter).

Sheth, Newman and Gross have proposed that individual choice behavior stems from five needs:[4]

1. *Functional*—A product or service satisfies its physical or functional purpose (for example, soaps for cleansing and medicines for alleviating physical ailments).
2. *Social*—A product or service satisfies the social need through its association with selected demographic, socioeconomic, or cultural-ethnic segments of society (for

| Dichter's List of Consumption Motives | TABLE 5.2 |

| Motive | Examples of Consumption Decisions |
|---|---|
| Mastery over environment | Kitchen appliances, power tools |
| Status | Scotch, owning a car in third-world economies |
| Rewards | Candies, gifts to oneself |
| Individuality | Gourmet foods, foreign cars, tattoos |
| Social acceptance | Companionship: sharing tea drinking |
| Love and affection | Giving children toys |
| Security | Full drawer of neatly ironed shirts |
| Masculinity | Toy guns, heavy shoes |
| Femininity | Decorating (products with heavy tactile component) |
| Eroticism | Sweets (to lick), gloves (to be removed by women as a form of undressing) |
| Disalienation | Listening to and calling in talk shows (a desire to feel connected) |
| Moral purity/cleanliness | White bread, bathing, cotton fabrics |
| Magic-mystery | Belief in UFOs, religious rituals, crystals (having healing power), visiting Elvis Presley museum and buying related products. |

**Source:** Constructed by authors based on Ernest Dichter, *Handbook of Consumer Motivations* (New York: McGraw, 1964); and Jeffrey F. Durgee, "Interpreting Dichter's Interpretations: An Analysis of Consumption Symbolism in the Handbook of Consumer Motivations," in Hanne Hartvig-Larsen, David Glen Mick, and Christian Alstead, eds., *Marketing and Semiotics: Selected Papers from the Copenhagen Symposium* (Copenhagen, 1991).

example, wearing a Polo brand of shirt to identify with upper-income, successful people). Online communities like ivillage.com are attempting to fulfil social needs and, thereby, create strong emotional associations with the brand.

3. *Emotional*—The product or service satisfies this need by creating the appropriate feelings and emotions, such as joy, love, or respect that a person experiences upon receiving a gift.

4. *Epistemic*—The product or service satisfies the human need to know or learn something new (for example, buying and reading a newspaper, watching a TV news program, or purchasing an encyclopedia or books on history, science, and commerce). On the Internet, web sites such as AskMe.com and ExpertCentral.com satisfy this need by inviting surfers to ask questions on any subject and having them answered by experts.

5. *Situational*—Certain products or services satisfy needs that are situational or contingent upon the time and place (for example, an emergency car repair on an out-of-town trip).

These classifications are valuable to study because they have been used in a number of consumer studies. Sheth and his colleagues, for example, have applied the classification to consumers' transportation choice, to people's voting behavior, and to an individual's smoking behavior.

Finally, reviewing the entire literature on consumer needs, consumer researcher Janice Hanna has proposed a list of seven consumer needs:[5]

1. *Physical safety*—The need to consume products so as to avoid harm or danger in their use, and to preserve clean air and water in the environment.

2. *Material security*—The need to consume an adequate supply of material possessions.

3. *Material comfort*—The need to consume a large and/or luxurious supply of material possessions.

4. *Acceptance by others*—The need to consume products in order to be associated with a significant other or a special reference group.

5. *Recognition from others*—The need to consume products in order to be acknowledged by others as having gained a high status in his or her community.
6. *Influence over others*—The need to feel one's impact on others' consumption decisions.
7. *Personal growth*—The need to consume products in order to be or become one's own unique self.

## Need for Arousal, Cognition, and Attribution

Marketing scholars also have identified some specific needs that are especially influential in marketing. Three of these are the need for arousal, need for cognition, and need for attribution.

### Arousal Seeking

One of the human needs that underlies a considerable number of marketplace transactions is the need for arousal. The motive underlying hedonic consumption is the need to seek arousal. Humans have an innate need for stimulation. Psychologists James Olds and Peter Milner demonstrated that when subjects were deprived of all sensory experiences, they could not survive this environment for long; some of them reported hallucinations after enduring the environment for a few hours.[6]

There is an **optimal level of stimulation** or a level at which a person feels neither bored nor overwhelmed. The process works like this: When we encounter a new stimulus, it interests us and holds our attention. However, as we continue to be exposed to it, we become used to it, or adapt to it, and this condition is called the **level of adaptation** for any stimulus, the level of stimulation perceived as normal or average. Once adaptation level is reached, there is no longer interest in the stimulus object. If new stimuli are all within the adaptation level, they arouse no interest, and the individual is starved of stimulation. If, on the other hand, he or she encounters too many new stimuli, the individual becomes overwhelmed and stressed and spontaneously acts to shut off additional sensory input (e.g., our eyes shut when watching a scary movie). Conversely, when the stimulation level falls below the optimum level, we feel bored and seek stimulating experiences.[7]

The **arousal-seeking motive** is the drive to maintain a person's stimulation at an optimal level. Some people are characteristically more arousal-seeking than others. Consumer researchers P. S. Raju, Jan-Benedict E. M. Steenkamp, Hans Baumgartner, and others studied this motivation in consumers. They found that arousal-seeking consumers were more risk taking in life activities in general (e.g., gambling) as well as in their buying behavior. They tended to adopt new products and switch brands just to try out a different brand. They also looked for more information about products and got bored when exposed to repetitive advertisements. Arousal seekers were also users of a greater assortment of options within the same product category, such as fast food.[8] Although no research has especially established this, we would expect arousal seekers to use more diverse products—perfumes and colognes, restaurants, clothing, vacation spots; likewise among business customers, arousal seekers are likely to be open to alternative suppliers' pitches, be predisposed to attend trade shows and professional conferences, and actively search for better products and services.[9]

### Curiosity: Need for Cognition

All humans are equipped with means for gathering and processing information for purposes of survival. The need for information, need for understanding the world around us, and need for knowledge are derivative needs, i.e., needs in the service of the basic need for survival and safety.[10] This need for knowing is called **need for cognition**.

A related concept is **tolerance for ambiguity**. This trait refers to the degree to which lack of information or uncertainty makes a person anxious. Consumers intolerant of ambiguity are less likely to adopt new products and services than those with a high degree of this trait. Business executives and business customers low in this trait are likely to feel threatened meeting other business associates and salespersons without a specific agenda and predeliberated items of information to be exchanged. The Internet has begun to play a crucial role in satisfying the need to obtain information and avoid ambiguity. The consumer is now able to very easily conduct comparison shopping across various purchase options and there are also a number of general and specialized web sites that make it simple for the consumer to obtain information about any topic. Retail banking and brokerage customers consider the Web a top media source for financial information and use it on a regular basis, according to a study by Harris Interactive.

Need for cognition is real, and it has a vivid presence in the marketplace. The volume of news stories in the papers, on TV and radio, and the very survival of 24-hour Cable News Network (CNN) and C-Span assumes a high need for cognition. So do more than a thousand nonfictional magazines, both general news and editorial material on special topics (e.g., *Popular Mechanics*, *Wired*, *Chemical Engineering*).

We refer here not just to the need for knowing in order to make a purchase decision, such as the features of two vendor offerings or the timetable for the train between Geneva and Milan; rather, we refer also to the need to know for its own sake, like the game statistics for all the past games, the new developments in computer technology, or a visit to the National Archives museum. All the various gossip magazines with news and gossip about celebrities (e.g., *People*, *Entertainment Weekly*, *National Enquirer*) also satisfy the need for cognition—knowing for its own sake.

One specific significance of this phenomenon in marketing is the role of what have been called *market mavens*. **Market mavens** have been defined as individuals who have information about many kinds of products, places to shop, and other facets of markets and initiate discussions with consumers and respond to requests from consumers for market information.[11] Market mavens differ from opinion leaders (discussed in Chapter 4) in that opinion leaders' expertise and influence is limited to a specific product category or a group of related products (e.g., electronics) or a set of related topics. In comparison, market mavens are knowledgeable about the marketplace in general—what new products are available, what price deals are being offered, where you can find specific products or deals, and so on. To fulfill this self-assumed role, market mavens attend to diverse sources of marketplace information, window shop more, enjoy shopping, use coupons more, and frequently engage in market-related conversations with others.

## Need for Attribution

Human beings are scientists. They want to know why something happened, the cause for someone's particular behavior, or, for that matter, for their own behavior. The process of assigning causes is called making attributions. **Attributions** are inferences that people draw about the causes of events, others' behaviors, and their own behavior.[12]

The motivation to assign causes is called **attribution motivation**. This motivation has implications for marketing. For example, when an appliance salesperson recommends a particular model, we in our buyer roles wonder why he or she is recommending it. We may attribute the cause to the salesperson's personal interest (e.g., a bigger commission), or to his or her genuine desire to serve our interests in order to build a long-term business relationship with us. This attribution will influence whether we patronize or shun the salesperson.

We assign the cause of a person's behavior either to the person himself or herself (internal) or to the situation (external). **Internal attributions** ascribe the cause of someone's behavior to personal dispositions, traits, abilities, or motivations and feelings; **external attributions** assign the cause to situational demands or environmental constraints that were beyond the control of the individual.

Psychologist Harold H. Kelley proposed a theory to explain when internal versus external attributions are made. He identified three conditions:

1. *Consistency*—If a person does something only once rather than consistently, we would be disinclined to attribute the cause to the person.

2. *Consensus*—If this person is the only one who does something (low consensus), then we will assign it to him or her.

3. *Distinctiveness*—If this person singles out this particular setting to behave this way, then we would not blame the person.

To summarize, in conditions of low consensus, high consistency, and low distinctiveness, we will tend to attribute the cause to the person (i.e., an internal attribution). In conditions of low consistency, or in conditions of high consistency accompanied by high consensus and high distinctiveness, the situation is likely to be blamed (i.e., an external attribution).[13]

## Evaluation of Need Categories

In the classical literature on human needs, many more perspectives and classification schemes are presented, applying perspectives ranging from economics and organizational behavior to social psychology and cultural anthropology.[14] We have barely presented a few of these. A few points will help marketers evaluate the various models. First, different classification schemes are simply different ways of dividing the same pie. Second, the models differ in the level of detail. Finally, it is possible to cross-classify these need categories and, thus, relate one to the other. Maslow's need hierarchy is perhaps the best known and most universal and general, but other schemes (e.g., Murray's list, Dichter's list) provide a more detailed and richer view of the tapestry of the complex web of human needs. We offer them here to enrich reader perspectives and to encourage a deeper reflection of your own needs and motivation as a customer.

# Customer Emotions

Needs and emotions are closely related. Similar to needs, emotions are also capable of energizing the person toward relevant goal-objects. Felt deprivations of desired goal-objects (which engender the drive) are experienced in consciousness as negative emotions, and their attainment (which subsides the drive) is experienced in consciousness as positive emotion. We all seek positive emotional experiences and avoid negative emotional experiences. Thus, positive emotions serve as approach motivations and negative emotions as avoidance motivations. Among several metaphors used to describe how consumers consume, the *Consuming as Experience* metaphor examines consumers' subjective emotional reactions to common objects (see Note 43 for reference). Therefore, it will be useful to gain some basic understanding of what emotions are and how they explain customer behavior.

## What Is Emotion?

As humans, we are creatures of emotion. Emotions lace our lives and guide everyday actions. Emotion is a complex set of processes, occurring concurrently in multiple systems of humans (i.e., both in the mind and in the body). **Emotions** are consciousness of the occurrence of some physiological arousal followed by a behavioral response along with the appraised meaning of both. This definition implies that emotions have three components: physiological, behavioral, and cognitive.[15]

Let's say you are going about your day. Suddenly a stimulus appears before you (e.g., the shadow of some intruder in the dark or your lottery number on the TV screen). Instantly and automatically, your nervous system is aroused: that is, you feel a tremor in the visceral system, butterflies in your stomach; you perspire; or your body feels a sudden burst of energy. This is the physiological component, and because it occurs by reflex, almost automatically, it is called autonomic arousal. Then follows cognitive interpretation or meaning analysis—what does the stimulus mean? For example, is the intruder a friend or a foe? Is the winning lottery number real? Is it really the number on your ticket? This is the cognitive component.

Depending on your cognitive appraisal and the meaning you make of the initial stimulus, there can be further autonomic arousal (or reduced arousal, when the nervous system is calming down). If the intruder is a friend, your arousal calms down; if a foe, you experience more arousal. Next, but almost instantly, you act out a physiological response (or a behavior). Thus, you flee if the intruder is a foe and approach if he or she is a friend. This is the behavioral component.

While all this autonomic and physiological arousal and response is going on, you also experience a consciousness of these changes in your body, and you also perceive the response you are making and interpret its efficacy and meaning, including the perception that a response is unavailable (i.e., that you can do nothing about it). This consciousness, these perceptions of arousal and response, are accompanied by, and further produce feelings of, pleasure or pain. These feelings are called emotions.[16] For example, when a consumer faces a dissatisfying marketplace experience, the cognitive appraisal process starts first with the consumer's assessment of the significance of the dissatisfaction for his or her own well being (whether the dissatisfying experience is relevant to deeply held goals, whether it inhibits goals or, whether it hurts his or her ego/self-esteem), and if the experience is dissatisfying on these parameters, it causes stress. This cognitive appraisal of stress may lead directly to coping actions to manage the dissatisfying market experience or to emotions which then lead to coping actions. Negative emotions arise due to the stress involved, and depending on who the entire experience is attributed to, the emotions are different. Anger, disgust and contempt emotions arise when the dissatisfying experience is attributed to external factors and they lead to problem-focused coping strategies, wherein people complain about the experience. Believing that the event could not have been helped leads to situational attribution and emotions of sadness and fear, while blaming oneself for the situation (internal attribution) leads to emotions of shame and guilt. The consumer does not complain when he or she uses an emotional coping strategy (uses some self-deception tactic such as denial of the problem, self-blame, or self-control in not complaining) or an avoidance coping strategy (quits the situation).[17]

## A Model of Emotion

Although a number of psychologists have tried to explain emotions, the most contemporary theory is **Schachter's two-factor theory**.[18] According to psychologist Stanley Schachter, the experience of emotion depends on two factors, autonomic arousal and its cognitive interpretation, or meaning analysis. In this model, we recognize that the initial stimulus can come from the external environment as well as from the inside of the organism, such as hunger pangs or a headache.

Marketers can adapt or respond to customer emotions by (1) designing the stimulus and (2) aiding the meaning appraisal. The first intervention takes the form of making product or service designs to fit appropriate consumption emotions. The second takes the form of communication, such as in attaching symbolism to products or services in advertising or in explaining certain aspects of the market offering or certain deviations from the expected marketplace events or outcomes. For example, positive attempts to help a customer's meaning appraisal process might include a physician explaining treatment procedures to a patient or a server explaining why there is a delay in serving food at a restaurant.

## Types of Emotions

Psychologist Robert Plutchik has proposed eight primary emotions (see Figure 5.3), each of which can vary in intensity:

   1. *Fear*—Ranging from timidity to terror. An individual customer might experience this if, when driving on the expressway, he or she discovers the car's brakes are not working. A business customer might experience fear upon learning that top management is looking into the problems experienced with the lower-cost computer network he or she was responsible for buying.

## FIGURE 5.3    Emotions Typology: Plutchik's Circle

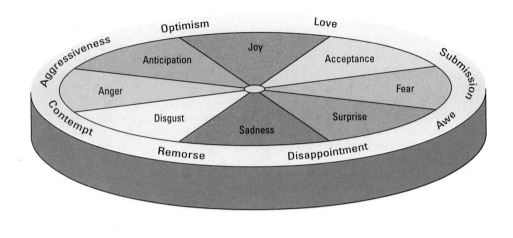

**Source:** Adapted from Wayne Weiten, *Psychology: Themes and Variations,* 4th ed. (Pacific Grove, CA: Brooks/Cole, 1998), p. 413.

2. *Anger*—Ranging from annoyance to rage. For a household customer at the desk of a car rental agency, anger might result when the agency employee explains that the car the customer reserved is not available. A business customer might become angry upon realizing that the company's insurance agent sold the company a policy for more coverage than necessary.

3. *Joy*—Ranging from serenity to ecstasy. An individual customer might experience joy in an auto dealership when the customer spots a rare model he or she has been looking for. A business customer might experience joy when the company's advertising agency delivers an awesome TV commercial.

4. *Sadness*—Ranging from pensiveness to grief. For a household customer, sadness might result from calling the airline for a last-minute reservation, only to be informed that the last seat was just sold. For a business customer, a cause of sadness might be the news that a favorite supplier has gone out of business.

5. *Acceptance*—Ranging from tolerance to adoration. For a household customer, acceptance might involve feelings about a favorite restaurant. For a business customer, the feeling might be preference for working with a particular salesperson.

6. *Disgust*—Ranging from boredom to loathing. A household customer might feel disgust at finding an insect in his or her cola. A business customer might be disgusted to learn that no insurance firm covers the risk of loss due to an act of war.

7. *Anticipation*—Ranging from mindfulness to vigilance. For a household customer, anticipation might include the wait for the announcement of the winning lottery number. For a business customer, it might include waiting for the results of a marketing research effort.

8. *Surprise*—Ranging from uncertainty to amazement. A household customer might feel surprise when his or her waiter announces that dessert will be on the house. For a business customer, surprise might be the response to a call from the company's media buying agency, saying that a long-sought television spot on the final championship game has become available.

These eight human reactions are based in the evolutionary process and define, according to Plutchik, basic human emotions. Hence these are called **primary emotions.** Other emotions we experience are combinations of these; for example, joy and acceptance combine to produce the emotion of love; disgust and sadness combine as remorse. A way to measure these emotions is shown in Table 5.3. The Window on Research discusses the Consumption Emotions Set associated with consumption of products.

## Scales to Measure Plutchik's Eight Emotions                    TABLE 5.3

Plutchik's emotions can be measured by rating the following triads of adjectives, each rated on a five-point scale, ranging from "not at all" to "very strongly." How do you feel at the moment?

Fear: threatened, frightened, intimidated
Anger: hostile, annoyed, irritated
Joy: happy, cheerful, delighted
Sadness: gloomy, sad, depressed
Acceptance: helped, accepted, trusting
Disgust: disgusted, offended, unpleasant
Anticipation: alert, attentive, curious
Surprise: puzzled, confused, startled

**Source:** William J. Havlena and Morris Holbrook, "The Varieties of Consumption Experience: Comparing Two Typologies of Emotion in Consumer Behavior," *Journal of Consumer Research* 13, No. 3, (December 1986), pp. 394–404. Reprinted with permission of the University of Chicago Press.

# WINDOW ON RESEARCH

## The Consumption Emotions Set

In a series of six extensive studies, consumer researcher Marsha L. Richins has developed a Consumption Emotions Set (CES) that reflects directly experienced emotions that result from consumption of products and excludes vicarious (aesthetic) emotions that are associated with artistic works like books, plays, and movies or that may be induced by advertising. Consumers were asked to generate emotions that they experienced during six different types of consumption situations: use of a favorite possession; a recent important purchase; recent purchase of a clothing item, food item, a durable good or service. The CES comprises a list of sixteen emotions—namely, anger, discontent, worry, sadness, fear, shame, envy, loneliness, romantic love, love, peacefulness, contentment, optimism, joy, excitement, and surprise.

**Source:** Adapted from Marsha L. Richins, "Measuring Emotions in the Consumption Experience," *Journal of Consumer Research*, 24, September 1997, 127–146.

## Customer Moods

**Moods** are simply emotions felt less intensely; they are also short-lived. They are easy to induce, and they appear and disappear frequently and readily. They are pervasive in that we are always in some kind of mood—happy mood or sad mood, pensive mood or careless mood, irritated or pleased, amused or bored. Moods affect our behavior of the moment in general and our response to the marketing activities to which we might be exposed at the time. For this reason, moods are important for marketers to understand.

Moods are induced by external stimuli as well as internally by autistic thinking; that is, recalling some past incident or fantasizing about some event. Among the marketing stimuli that can induce positive or negative moods are:

- the ambiance of the store or service delivery facility
- the demeanor of the salesperson
- the sensory features of the product
- the tone and manner of advertising
- the content of the message itself from a salesperson or in the advertisement whether it frustrates or fulfills one's goals in attending to that message (e.g., if the salesperson is not knowledgeable or if the advertisement is vain, the customer may feel frustration at having wasted the time).

Mood states have consequences in terms of favorable or unfavorable customer response to marketer efforts. In research studies done by consumer researchers, customers have also been found to linger longer in positive mood environments, recall those advertisements more that had created positive moods, and feel more positive toward brands based on advertising that created feelings of warmth.[19]

Mood affects the strategies used to process information by consumers. However, there is one stream of research that states that positive mood reduces the processing of stimulus information, and there is another that states that positive mood enhances the learning of brand names better in comparison to a neutral mood. Brand name recall is a prerequisite for the choice of the brand and recall depends on the process by which the brand was first encoded into memory. Researchers Lee and Sternthal state that two factors important in the encoding process are *brand rehearsal*—"how frequently and recently the brand has been exposed in the memory as a member of a particular category"—and *relational elaboration*—"the process by which consumers link the brands to the specific categories they belong to." In a brand-learning task, they found that being in a positive mood helps consumers to cluster the brands that they are exposed to, by the categories they belong to. When the respondents are asked to recall as many brands as possible after this exposure, a positive mood helps them recall more categories and more brands as members of these categories, thus increasing the number of brands recalled compared to when they are in a neutral mood.[20] Corroborating this finding, is the research study by Barone, Miniard, and Romeo on the effect of positive mood on brand extension evaluations. They show that a positive mood influences the perceptions of similarity between the brand extension and the core brand (particularly for extensions that are moderately similar to the core brand) and the perceived competency of the manufacturer in producing the extension. Both of these factors are important determinants of extension evaluations, and positive mood enhances evaluation of brand extensions by influencing these determinants. Thus, marketers could use advertising, point-of-sale material, celebrity endorsements, free gifts, and several other strategies to induce positive moods in consumers to enable a more positive evaluation of a brand extension, thereby influencing choice.[21]

Marketers on the Internet attempt to overcome their inability to actually bring the customer into the store by creating the mood or ambience within the web site. This might include the incorporation of store colors and background music aimed at creating a favorable mood in the customer.

## Hedonic Consumption: Seeking Emotional Value

Emotions and moods drive a host of consumption behaviors. While detergents, lawn mowers, microwave ovens, chain saws, insurance policies, investment portfolios, and computers are purchased and used for some utilitarian/functional end-states, such products and services as perfumes/colognes, diamonds, and bubble baths and such activities as sports, theater, movies, music concerts, and amusement parks are used or engaged in purely for the emotional or hedonic values they provide. In Chapter 1, we introduced the concept of emotional value as a discretionary value.

Hedonic consumption refers to the use of products or services for the sake of intrinsic enjoyment rather than to solve some problem in the physical environment. More specifically, hedonism refers to sensory pleasure. Thus, hedonic consumption is the use of products and services that give pleasure through the senses, that help create fantasies, and that give emotional arousal.[22] Here are some examples:

- *Sensory pleasure*—taking a bubble bath; relaxing in a jacuzzi or sauna; using perfume and colognes; wearing exciting colors in clothing; enjoying strobe lights in a discotheque; choosing office decor; landscaping the corporate office building.
- *Aesthetic pleasure*—reading poetry; visiting an art gallery; taking a course in Greek history; having original works of art in the corporate offices.
- *Emotional experience*—watching movies or soap operas on TV; taking a roller-coaster ride; sending gifts; receiving gifts; visiting relatives; making or receiving long-distance social calls; dating; attending class reunion; celebrating silver wedding anniversary; celebrating winning a major business contract from a highly coveted client.
- *Fun and enjoyment*—video game arcade; playing sports; dancing; vacationing; attending a business convention; entertaining a business customer in a game of golf; attending office Christmas parties.

It is interesting to note that while American teenagers are enamored by the newness and hedonic value of technological gadgets, European teenagers are concerned with their functional utility. They look at technology as a means to an end. The "end" they are interested in is social connectivity. They want to keep in touch with friends and develop relationships with peers, and they consider devices such as computers and cellphones to be a means to achieving this end.[23]

## Deep Involvement

One special case of hedonic consumption is deep involvement in a product, service, or activity. This describes customers' relationships with a select few products that are consumed with interest, pausing to savor their taste, smell their aroma, feel their texture, or hear their sound. We like them; we enjoy them; we love them.

Everyone has a favorite activity, a favorite product, a favorite brand. Some of us are fashion experts; others, car buffs; still others, computer jocks. We are eager to get to know these products (e.g., fashions, cars, and computers) and find out everything there is to know; we get excited whenever the topic comes up, and, of course, we want to be using them whenever possible. This relationship we develop as users with selected products and services is called deep involvement. It can be defined as a customer's extreme interest in a product or service on an ongoing basis.

Involvement is a general term that can be defined as the degree of personal relevance of an object, product, or service to a customer. Furthermore, involvement is a matter of degree—how relevant or how central a product is. Involvement, defined as the degree of interest, can be viewed as having two forms: enduring involvement and situational involvement. Enduring involvement is the degree of interest a customer feels in a product or service on an ongoing basis. In contrast, situational involvement is the degree of interest in a specific situation or on a specific occasion, such as when buying a product or when consuming something in the presence of an important client or friend. Thus, Celia Fernandez is not much interested in dishwashers; she takes the one in her kitchen for granted. But the last time she was buying one, she became extremely interested (i.e., involved) in dishwashers, attempting to learn about them, deliberating over various options, and weighing them vis-a-vis her own needs. In contrast, she is enduringly involved in gardening and in garden-related products, taking considerable interest in them and enjoying them. In a business context, a major infrastructure project in a company is an object of high situational involvement, and maximizing the lifetime value of its customers would be a matter of enduring involvement. (The general roles that enduring and situational involvement play in customer attitudes and decision making will be discussed in later chapters.)

The extreme form of enduring involvement is deep involvement. Deep involvement affects customer behavior in a number of ways. First, deeply involved consumers are knowledgeable about the product or service and, thus, can act as opinion leaders. Second, they consume a greater quantity of the product and also buy related products. Third, they are less price sensitive for that product and are willing to spend well. Fourth, they seek constant information about products and services. Fifth, they want to spend more time in related activities. It is easier to build more extended relationships with these customers. Consider, for example, Harley-Davidson motorcycle owners; there is a Harley Owners Club (HOG), and members participate in a wide range of activities, including charity work. The fanatic loyalty that favored IBM at one time but now favors the Apple Mac shows the deep involvement that these users have for the product. Finally, deeply involved customers can act as lead users for new products; they try products in innovative ways and, thus, are sources of new-product ideas.[24]

# Psychographics

Along with needs and emotions, the third facet of motivation is psychographics. **Psychographics** are characteristics of individuals that describe them in terms of their psychological and behavioral makeup—how people occupy themselves (behavior) and what psychological factors underlie that activity pattern. They are a manifestation of an individual's underlying motivations, and they, in turn, define them. For example, a person's need to seek affiliation or peer approval makes him or her engage, say, in going to theaters or playing golf. Theater going or playing golf, thus, becomes part of his or her psychographics. This psychographic, in turn, drives customer behavior toward buying golf equipment or doing whatever is needed to implement that particular psychographic; it becomes motivational.

Psychographics have three components: values, self-concept, and lifestyles.

## Values

When you think about what is important to you in life, you are thinking about your values. **Values** are end-states of life, the goals one lives for. Psychologist Milton Rokeach has identified two groups of these: terminal and instrumental. Terminal values are the goals we seek in life (e.g., peace and happiness) whereas instrumental values are the means or behavioral standards by which we pursue these goals (e.g., honesty). Rokeach developed these lists of values for understanding human psychology.[25]

Consumer researchers felt a need for values more directly relevant to everyday consumer behavior. For this purpose, consumer researcher Lynn Kahle and his associates developed a List of Values (LOV), consisting of nine terminal values:

1. Self-respect
2. Self-fulfillment
3. Security
4. Sense of belonging
5. Excitement
6. Sense of accomplishment
7. Fun and enjoyment
8. Being well respected
9. Warm relationships with others.[26]

This list of values corresponds well to the needs in Maslow's hierarchy, except that Maslow includes physiological needs, and LOV adds values of fun and excitement. Kahle argues that the nine values in LOV relate more closely to the values of life's major roles, such as marriage, parenting, work, leisure, and daily consumption, than do the values in Rokeach Value Survey.

In a number of studies, LOV has been found to be well related to consumer activities. For example, consumer researcher Sharon Beatty and her associates found that people who value a sense of belonging especially like group activities. Those who value fun and enjoyment especially like skiing, dancing, backpacking, hiking, and camping, and they consume a lot of alcohol. People who value a warm relationship with others tend to give gifts to others for no reason at all.[27]

## Linking Product Attributes to Customer Values

One of the basic tenets of marketing has been that customers don't buy products or services; rather, they buy benefits. Thus, when consumers buy an automobile, they are not buying simply 5,000 pounds of sheet metal. Rather they are buying transportation. They want a car with ergonomic seats because they want their body to feel comfortable, or they want a car with acceleration from 0 to 60 miles per hour in 7 seconds versus 10 seconds to experience the driving thrill. If we go one step further, transportation, comfort, or driving thrill is important to consumers so that they can overcome the physical distance barrier, or escape to a more desirable place, or master the machine. Ultimately, then, the product or service features make sense only because they serve some more fundamental needs (such as the needs in Maslow's hierarchy) or values (as in the List of Values). Identifying the connections between product or service features on the one hand and customers' fundamental needs and values on the other is important if marketers are to design features that would offer value to customers.

This linking is accomplished by drawing means-end chains. **Means-end chains** are simply linkages between the product's physical features and customers' fundamental needs and values. They are identified by a research technique called **laddering**, in which potential customers are asked repeatedly in iterative sequence, "Why is that feature important to you?" For example, "Why is quick acceleration important to you?" If the answer is, "to maneuver out of traffic situations," we next ask, "and why is that important?" and so on.[28] Figure 5.4 shows an example of a means-end chain for a hypothetical customer.

## Self-Concept

Everyone has a self-image of who he or she is. This is called **self-concept**. Furthermore, the self-concept includes an idea of what the person currently is and what he or she would like to become; these two concepts are respectively called **actual self** and **ideal self**. For some, the self-concept pertains to their intellectual and/or career accomplishments; for example, one wants to be a successful writer or an engineer or a Wall Street financial executive.[29] For many, the self-concept pertains to the kind of material life they want to live.

The self-concepts influence a person's consumption deeply, for people live their self-concepts in large measure by what they consume. The *Consuming as Integration* metaphor describes how consumers are able to integrate their self-concepts and objects through a variety of consumption rituals, self extension and personalizing rituals. For example, business students who are about to enter the corporate world start dressing more seriously in their senior year, or employees who are promoted to executive cadre change their wardrobe to include suits. Marketers can apply the principle of self-concept by obtaining a self-concept profile of customers in terms of selected personality traits, then obtaining the consumer's perceptions of a brand on the same traits, as shown in Table 5.4. From these two profiles, it is possible to identify the match or gaps between consumers' self-concept and their perceptions of the personality of the brand.[30] If the gaps are significant, the marketer may want to make changes to the product or to marketing communications about the product.

Businesses, too, have a self-concept. Some think of themselves as a company at the forefront of technology; others view their essence to be in communications wherever and in whatever form it may exist; still others define their essence as innovation. For example,

| FIGURE 5.4 | A Means-End Chain for a Hypothetical Customer |

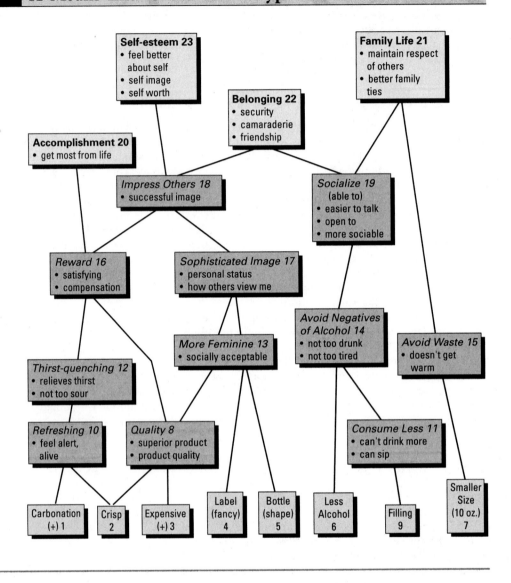

**Source:** Thomas J. Reynolds and Jonathan Gardner, "Laddering Theory, Method, Analysis, and Interpretation." Reprinted from the *Journal of Advertising Research* 28 (February/March 1988), p. 19. © 1988 by the Advertising Research Foundation.

Benetton's self-concept can be described as a clothing company for the young that promotes social issues. Basically, corporate self-concepts are expressed in mission statements.

## Self-Concept as Users, Payers, and Buyers

Individuals have their self-concepts as individuals in general, of course. But they also have a self-concept of themselves in their specific roles of user, payer, and buyer. Illustratively, a user could have the self-concept of a very discerning connoisseur user or a very involved (or alternatively, very detached) user. The payer could have the self-concept of being thrifty or financially prudent, or of having the attitude of "money is no object to me." Finally, the buyer could have the self-concept of being a convenience seeker or service seeker or of being very time conscious.

| A Scale to Measure Self-Image and Product Image | | | | | | | | TABLE 5.4 |
|---|---|---|---|---|---|---|---|---|

*Instruction:* Please rate yourself, as you see yourself, on the following descriptive word pairs, by circling a number in each row closer to the word that describes you.

| | | | | | | | | | |
|---|---|---|---|---|---|---|---|---|---|
| 1. | Rugged | 1 | 2 | 3 | 4 | 5 | 6 | 7 | Delicate |
| 2. | Exciting | 1 | 2 | 3 | 4 | 5 | 6 | 7 | Calm |
| 3. | Uncomfortable | 1 | 2 | 3 | 4 | 5 | 6 | 7 | Comfortable |
| 4. | Dominating | 1 | 2 | 3 | 4 | 5 | 6 | 7 | Submissive |
| 5. | Thrifty | 1 | 2 | 3 | 4 | 5 | 6 | 7 | Indulgent |
| 6. | Pleasant | 1 | 2 | 3 | 4 | 5 | 6 | 7 | Unpleasant |
| 7. | Contemporary | 1 | 2 | 3 | 4 | 5 | 6 | 7 | Uncontemporary |
| 8. | Organized | 1 | 2 | 3 | 4 | 5 | 6 | 7 | Unorganized |
| 9. | Rational | 1 | 2 | 3 | 4 | 5 | 6 | 7 | Emotional |
| 10. | Youthful | 1 | 2 | 3 | 4 | 5 | 6 | 7 | Mature |
| 11. | Formal | 1 | 2 | 3 | 4 | 5 | 6 | 7 | Informal |
| 12. | Orthodox | 1 | 2 | 3 | 4 | 5 | 6 | 7 | Liberal |
| 13. | Complex | 1 | 2 | 3 | 4 | 5 | 6 | 7 | Simple |
| 14. | Colorless | 1 | 2 | 3 | 4 | 5 | 6 | 7 | Colorful |
| 15. | Modest | 1 | 2 | 3 | 4 | 5 | 6 | 7 | Vain |

**Source:** Adapted from Naresh K. Malhotra, "A Scale to Measure Self-Concepts, Person Concepts, and Product Concepts," *Journal of Marketing Research*, Vol. 18 (November 1981), pp. 456–464.

**Note:** To measure product or brand image, the entire scale is repeated with instructions to rate the specified product or brand.

## Lifestyle

Along with what we think of ourselves and what we value, psychographics describes us in terms of **lifestyles**, or the way we live. Consider two consumers with very different lifestyles. Thelma is a home- and family-oriented, traditional, religious, educated, politically active, nonworking mother of two children. She likes to cook, spend most of her time at home, and entertain relatives and friends over the weekend. Candice, in contrast, is a very outgoing, career-oriented, fashion-oriented, nonreligious, single mother of a five-year-old. She likes to go out rather than stay at home and dislikes household chores. Given different lifestyles, these customers have very different customer behaviors as well.

Lifestyles are determined by (a) a customer's personal characteristics (discussed in Chapter 2), namely, genetics, race, gender, age, and personality; (b) his or her personal context, namely, culture, institutions and reference groups, and personal worth; and (c) needs and emotions. These three sets of factors together influence the pattern of our activities—how we spend time and money.

How do consumers live their lifestyles? How else but by doing activities that inevitably entail marketplace exchange and choices. Thelma obviously eats out less but buys more of the food items from the market than does Candice. Candice uses babysitting services more than Thelma does. Candice also uses drycleaning services more while Thelma buys laundry detergents more. Candice is a frequent visitor to the fashion boutiques while Thelma buys all of her own and her family's clothing at a department store. Because commercial products play a major role in customers' enactment of their lifestyles, lifestyles can explain customer behavior significantly.

For instance, some consumers are extremely frugal in their consumption of goods and services. "Frugality is a unidimensional consumer lifestyle trait characterized by the degree to which consumers are both restrained in acquiring and resourcefully using economic goods and services to achieve long-term goals." Empirical research shows that the frugal are less susceptible to interpersonal influence, less materialistic, less compulsive in buying, and more price and value conscious. The frugal are not found to use coupons more often than regular customers; frugality affects customer decisions about "whether to buy" and "what to buy." Beyond buying, it also affects customers as users since the frugal are more resourceful in using products and services (for example—timing showers, packing lunch for work).[31]

Catering to different lifestyles of consumers are **lifestyle retail brands** like Gap, Benetton, and Laura Ashley. Their basic retail proposition is augmented with a set of added values that have symbolic value and meaning for the lifestyles of a specific consumer group. In shopping at these stores, the consumer is projecting these lifestyles on his or her purchases, and with each different store the expectation is completely different, including store atmospherics. Laura Ashley represents "gentile English country lifestyle," while the Gap represents a "classic American, casual lifestyle" and the Polo/Ralph Lauren experience is the realm of "an exclusive gentleman's club and the country house."[32]

Even in business, clothing can signify lifestyles. A professor is encouraged to wear semi-formal clothing at school campuses while an investment banker is likely to wear suits, and software professionals are likely to be dressed in business casuals. Some companies like IBM and Andersen Consulting ask their employees and consultants to dress conservatively in dark suits and white shirts that makes them look older than their real age and, thereby, adds credence when they meet with top executives of their client organizations.

## Psychographics As AIO Profiles

The appeal of psychographics in marketing from the outset has been its quantifiability—like demographics, psychographics were derived based on quantitative measures. To measure psychographics (i.e., values, self-concepts, and lifestyles), researchers present a series of statements about possible activities, interests, and opinions. Respondents indicate their agreement or disagreement with these statements. A sample of these statements is presented in Chapter 7.

To analyze and interpret data from measures based on AIO statements, researchers group together people with similar responses. These groups, considered to have relatively similar lifestyles, values, and self-concepts, can then be described using certain AIO profiles, called psychographic profiles. These profiles are excellent indicators of how people are thinking and where they are going with their lives.

In an attempt to profile online shoppers, Ernst & Young charted their psychographic profile. They found that leisure time activities of the study's online buyers were not much different from the average household. Some differences were visible in movie attendance (37 percent of online shoppers go to movies frequently or regularly compared to 26 percent of the average household), recreational travel (42 percent versus 32 percent), performing arts attendance (25 percent versus 17 percent), and family-time pursuits (57 percent versus 50 percent). A smaller percentage of online shoppers watched television (61 percent) compared to 65 percent of average households. Online shoppers are, however, similar to all households in volunteer activities, gardening, gourmet cooking, photography, and attending sporting events.[33]

## VALS™

One of the most used psychographic profiling schemes is called VALS™. Developed by SRI International, Inc., its first version groups the entire U.S. population into nine groups, based on the identities they seek and implement via marketplace behaviors. According to SRI, people pursue and acquire products, services, and experiences that provide satisfaction and give shape, substance, and character to their identities.[34] Even though this scheme has been replaced by a new VALS system with an eight-segment classification, the original scheme, introduced in 1978, is important to understand for us as students of consumer psychology. That scheme used two dimensions for its conceptual foundation: (1) Maslow's hierarchy—the theory that people rise from physiological, to safety, to social belonging, to self-esteem, to self-actualization motivations; and (2) Riesman's Social Character Theory that a person is either inner directed or outer directed, deriving one's code of conduct respectively from oneself or from others. Inner-directed persons are more independent minded, whereas outer-directed persons are concerned with others' opinion of them. See Figure 5.5.

## VALS 1: Nine Lifestyle Segments in the United States     FIGURE 5.5

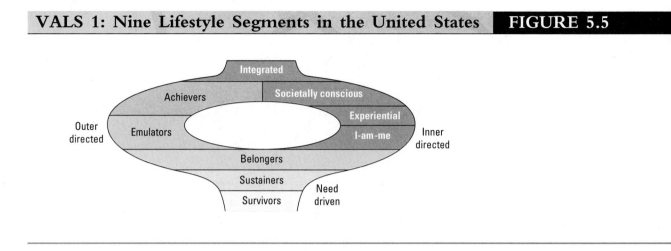

Source: *Advertising: Principles & Practice* by Wells/Burnett/Moriarty, p. 191, ©. Reprinted by permission of Pearson Education, Inc., Upper Saddle River, NJ.

At the bottom of the VALS hierarchy are *Survivors* and *Sustainers*, who are, respectively, the elderly poor and unemployed youth. *Belongers* is the next group, the largest of the nine groups and comprising middle-aged, middle-class, outer-directed Americans. Along with the Belongers, two other outer-directed groups are called *Emulators* and *Achievers*. Achievers are the most affluent, successful professionals and businesspeople. In contrast, Emulators don't have as much money or success, but they try to emulate the lifestyles of Achievers. On the other side are three inner-directed segments, *I-am-me's*, *Experientials*, and *Societally Conscious*. I-am-me's are teenagers with rebellion against the established ways as their principal motto. Experientials are big on experiencing all the sensory and recreational experiences life has to offer—mountaineering, skiing, sports, travel, bungee-jumping, and so on. The Societally Conscious are concerned about and work for larger, societal issues, such as the environment, world peace, and racial harmony. Finally, the group at the top is the Integrateds, a small group that has gained material well-being and success in the material world and is, at the same time, working for larger issues or in jobs that give some intrinsic meaning to life rather than merely fame and wealth.

## Today's VALS™

The current version of VALS groups U.S. customers into eight groups (see Figure 5.6). This grouping is based on two dimensions: self-orientation and resources.

**Self-Orientation.** According to SRI, people are motivated by one of three powerful self-orientations: principle, status, and action. Principle-oriented consumers are guided in their choices by abstract, idealized criteria, rather than by feelings, events, or desire for approval and opinions of others. Status-oriented consumers look for products and services that demonstrate the consumers' success to their peers. Action-oriented consumers are guided by a desire for social or physical activity, variety, and risk taking.

**Resources.** Resources refer to the full range of psychological, physical, demographic, and material means and capacities people have to draw upon. It encompasses education, income, self-confidence, health, and energy level. It is a continuum from minimal to abundant. Resources generally increase from adolescence through middle age but decrease with extreme age, depression, financial reversal (e.g., layoff), and physical or psychological impairment.

| FIGURE 5.6 | Eight American Lifestyles: VALS |

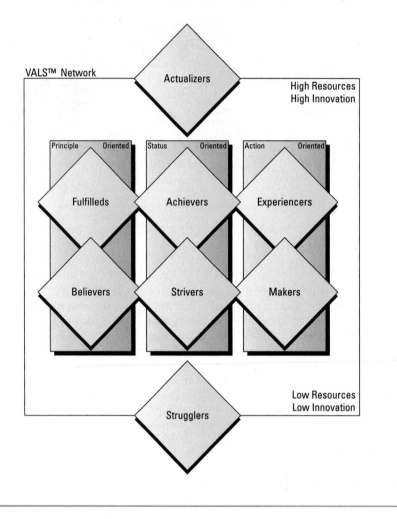

**The Eight VALS™ Groups.** Using the self-orientation and resources dimensions, VALS defines eight segments of adult consumers who have different attitudes and exhibit distinctive behavior and decision-making patterns. These segments are Actualizers, Fulfilleds, Achievers, Experiencers, Believers, Strivers, Makers, and Strugglers. (Table 5.5 presents a list of questions that can be used to classify consumers into these VALS groups. You can try the survey yourself on the Internet at **http://www.sric-bi.com/vals/presurvey.shtml**.

*Actualizers* are successful, sophisticated, active, take-charge people with high self-esteem and abundant resources. They are leaders in business and government and are interested in growth, innovation, and change. They seek to develop, explore, and express themselves in a variety of ways, sometimes guided by principle and sometimes by a desire to have an effect or to make a change. Image is important to them, not as evidence of status or power but as an expression of their taste, independence, and character. They possess a wide range of interests, are concerned with social issues, and show a cultivated taste for the finer things in life.

*Fulfilleds* are mature, satisfied, comfortable, reflective people who value order, knowledge, and responsibility. Most are well educated and in (or recently retired from) professional

## Questionnaire To Assess VALS Type                    TABLE 5.5

Reply to the following statements, using the response categories of

| | Mostly Disagree | Somewhat Disagree | Somewhat Agree | Mostly Agree |
|---|---|---|---|---|
| 1. I am often interested in theories. | ___ | ___ | ___ | ___ |
| 2. I like outrageous people and things. | ___ | ___ | ___ | ___ |
| 3. I like a lot of variety in my life. | ___ | ___ | ___ | ___ |
| 4. I love to make things I can use every day. | ___ | ___ | ___ | ___ |
| 5. I follow the latest trends and fashions. | ___ | ___ | ___ | ___ |
| 6. Just as the Bible says, the world literally was created in six days. | ___ | ___ | ___ | ___ |
| 7. I like being in charge of a group. | ___ | ___ | ___ | ___ |
| 8. I like to learn about art, culture, and history. | ___ | ___ | ___ | ___ |
| 9. I often crave excitement. | ___ | ___ | ___ | ___ |
| 10. I am really interested only in a few things. | ___ | ___ | ___ | ___ |
| 11. I would rather make something than buy it. | ___ | ___ | ___ | ___ |
| 12. I dress more fashionably than most people. | ___ | ___ | ___ | ___ |
| 13. The federal government should encourage prayer in public schools. | ___ | ___ | ___ | ___ |
| 14. I have more ability than most people. | ___ | ___ | ___ | ___ |
| 15. I consider myself an intellectual. | ___ | ___ | ___ | ___ |
| 16. I must admit that I like to show off. | ___ | ___ | ___ | ___ |
| 17. I like trying new things. | ___ | ___ | ___ | ___ |
| 18. I am very interested in how mechanical things, such as engines, work. | ___ | ___ | ___ | ___ |
| 19. I like to dress in the latest fashions. | ___ | ___ | ___ | ___ |
| 20. There is too much sex on television today. | ___ | ___ | ___ | ___ |
| 21. I like to lead others. | ___ | ___ | ___ | ___ |
| 22. I would like to spend a year or more in a foreign country. | ___ | ___ | ___ | ___ |
| 23. I like a lot of excitement in my life. | ___ | ___ | ___ | ___ |
| 24. I must admit that my interests are somewhat narrow and limited. | ___ | ___ | ___ | ___ |
| 25. I like making things of wood, metal, or other such material. | ___ | ___ | ___ | ___ |
| 26. I want to be considered fashionable. | ___ | ___ | ___ | ___ |
| 27. A woman's life is fulfilled only if she can provide a happy home for her family. | ___ | ___ | ___ | ___ |
| 28. I like the challenge of doing something I have never done before. | ___ | ___ | ___ | ___ |
| 29. I like to learn about things even if they may never be of any use to me. | ___ | ___ | ___ | ___ |
| 30. I like to make things with my hands. | ___ | ___ | ___ | ___ |
| 31. I am always looking for a thrill. | ___ | ___ | ___ | ___ |
| 32. I like doing things that are new and different. | ___ | ___ | ___ | ___ |
| 33. I like to look through hardware or automotive stores. | ___ | ___ | ___ | ___ |
| 34. I would like to understand more about how the universe works. | ___ | ___ | ___ | ___ |
| 35. I like my life to be pretty much the same from week to week. | ___ | ___ | ___ | ___ |

**Source:** http://www.sric–bi.com/vals/presurvey.shtml. Used with permission of SRI Consulting Business Intelligence.

occupations. Content with their career, families, and station in life, their leisure activities tend to center around the home. Fulfilleds have a moderate respect for the status quo institutions, but they are open-minded to new ideas and social change. They tend to base their decisions on firmly held principles and, consequently, appear calm and self-assured. Fulfilleds are conservative, practical consumers, and the universal values of performance, service, and price are more important than personal values (e.g., social and emotional values).

*Achievers* are successful career and work-oriented people who like to feel in control of their lives. They value predictability and stability over risk. They are deeply committed to work and family. Work provides them with a sense of duty, material rewards, and prestige. Their social lives are structured around family, church, and career. Achievers live conventional lives, are politically conservative, and respect authority and the status quo. Image is important to them; they favor established, prestige products and services that demonstrate success to their peers.

*Experiencers* are young, vital, enthusiastic, impulsive, and rebellious. They seek variety and excitement, savoring the new, the offbeat, and the risky. Still in the process of formulating life values and patterns of behavior, they quickly become enthusiastic about new possibilities but are equally quick to cool. At this stage in their lives, they are politically uncommitted, uninformed, and highly ambivalent about what they believe. Their energy finds an outlet in exercise, sports, outdoor recreation, and social activities. Experiencers are avid consumers and spend much of their income on clothing, fast food, music, movies, and video.

*Believers* are conservative, conventional people with commitment to family, church, community, and the nation. Living by a moral code is very important to them. As consumers, Believers are conservative and predictable and favor American products and established brands. Their income, education, and energy are modest but sufficient to meet their needs.

*Strivers* seek motivation, self-definition, and approval from the world around them. They are striving to find a secure place in life. Unsure of themselves and low on economic, social, and psychological resources, Strivers are concerned about the opinions and approval of others. Money defines success for Strivers, who don't have enough of it and often feel that life has given them a raw deal. Strivers are impulsive and easily bored. Many of them seek to be stylish. They emulate those who own more impressive possessions, but what they wish to obtain is often beyond their reach.

*Makers* are practical people who have constructive skills and value self-sufficiency. They live within a traditional context of family, practical work, and physical recreation and have little interest in what lies outside that context. Makers experience the world by working on it—building a house, raising children, fixing a car, or canning vegetables—and have enough skill, income, and energy to carry out their projects successfully. Makers are politically conservative, suspicious of new ideas, respectful of government authority and organized labor, but resentful of government intrusion on individual rights. They are unimpressed by material possessions other than those with a practical or functional purpose (such as tools, utility vehicles, and fishing equipment).

*Strugglers* tend to be chronically poor, ill-educated, low-skilled, elderly, and concerned about their health. Preoccupied with the urgent needs of the present moment, they do not show a strong self-orientation. Their chief concerns are for security and safety. Strugglers are cautious consumers. They represent a very modest market for most products and services, but they are loyal to favorite brands.

## Applications of VALS™

Although SRI Consulting Business Intelligence (SRIC-BI), the company that currently runs VALS, has identified product consumption differences among the segments in each of the two VALS systems, the best use of VALS is in targeting marketing communications. Advertisers can use VALS to depict particular lifestyles the brand is attempting to target. SRIC-BI is also researching the generalizability of VALS to other cultures. One such application is for consumers in Japan (see the Window on Research box).

Likewise, to understand European customers as a unit, in the wake of unification, the ad agency Backer Spielvogel Bates Worldwide runs a Global Scan, a program of surveys

# WINDOW ON RESEARCH

## The Japan VALS: A Portrait of Japan in Change

Japan VALS is the same scheme of grouping customers according to a psychographic profile developed by SRI International specifically for understanding Japanese consumers. Japan VALS divides society into segments based on two key consumer attributes: life orientation and attitudes to social change. Life orientation is simply what interests or animates a person the most—life goals, occupational duties, or recreational interests. Japan VALS identifies four primary life orientations: Traditional Ways, Occupations, Innovation, and Self-Expression. Each orientation provides a life theme around which activities, interests, and personal goals are woven.

Cross-cutting the variety of life orientations, changing attitudes stratify society into distinct layers, like overturned bowls nested one inside another. The change-leading segments are found in the outermost layers of society, while the change-resisting segments are located at the center. Change diffuses from one layer to the next, primarily along the channels created around different life orientations. The resulting classification identifies the following six groups of Japanese consumers: Integrators, Self-Innovators, Self-Adapters, Ryoshiki Innovators and Ryoshiki Adapters, Tradition Innovators and Tradition Adapters, High Pragmatics and Low Pragmatics, and Sustainers.

- *Integrators* (4 percent of population)—Highest on the Japan VALS measure of Innovation, these consumers are active, inquisitive, trend leading, informed, and affluent. They travel frequently and consume a wide range of media print and broadcast, niche and foreign.
- *Self-Innovators and Self-Adapters* (7 percent and 11 percent of population)—These consumers score high on self-expression, desire personal experience, seek excitement and daring ideas, are fashionable, and engage in social activities.
- *Ryoshiki Innovators and Ryoshiki Adapters* (6 percent and 10 percent of population)—These groups score highest on occupations; education, career achievement, and professional knowledge are their personal focus, but home, family and social status are their guiding concerns.
- *Tradition Innovators and Tradition Adapters* (6 percent and 10 percent of population)—These consumers score highest on the measure of traditional ways and adhere to traditional religions and customs, prefer long-familiar home furnishings and dress, and hold conservative social opinions.
- *High Pragmatics and Low Pragmatics* (14 percent and 17 percent of population)—These groups do not score high on any life-orientation dimension. They are not very active and not well informed; they have few interests and seem flexible or even uncommitted in their lifestyle choices.
- *Sustainers* (15 percent of population)—These consumers score lowest on the innovation and self-expression dimensions. Lacking money, youth, and advanced education, these consumers dislike innovation and are typically oriented to sustaining the past.

of consumers in 17 countries. It has identified five global psychographic types: Strivers, Achievers, Pressureds, Adapters, and Traditionals. It measures 250 attitudes (130 specific to one country, and 120 cross-culturally pertinent). Likewise, the advertising agency DMB&B did a 15-country survey and found four European groups: Successful Idealists, Affluent Materialists, Comfortable Belongers, and Disaffected Survivors.[35] The Window on Research box presents an attempt at identifying lifestyle clusters in the Asian region. Thus, marketers are using VALS-based classifications and other psychographic measures to understand the customer worldwide.

# WINDOW ON RESEARCH

## Lifestyle Clusters in Asian Countries

Researchers Jiuan, Jung, Wirtz, and Keng review lifestyle research conducted in Japan, Malaysia, Singapore, Taiwan, and Thailand to develop Asian styles—that could mirror the Eurostyles common to fifteen European countries.

In Japan, the Dentsu Consumer Value Survey presented four lifestyle clusters: Achievers, Intelligent, Group Merit, and Membership Dependent. The clusters were derived based on Japanese consumers' attitudes towards changes and norms in life. Some other clusters such as the New Teenager, the New Singles, the New Jitsunen (those in their 50s and 60s), and the New Rich represent the changing lifestyle in Japan.

In Malaysia, the Survey Research Group (SRG) identified seven clusters: Yesterday People, Village Trendsetters, Chameleon, Loners, the new Breed, Yuppies, and Sleepwalkers.

Seven clusters were identified in Singapore, but they are different from the seven clusters in Malaysia: Aspirer, Pragmatist, Entrepreneur, Independent, New Age Family Oriented, Traditional Family Oriented, and Materialist.

In Taiwan, the eight clusters defined by SRG are: The Traditional Homebodies, The Confident Traditionalists, The Family-Centered Fatalists, The Lethargic, The Middle-Class Hopefuls, The Discontented Moderns, The Rebellious Young, and The Young Strivers.

Finally, in Thailand, nine distinct segments were derived: Today's Women, The Comfortable Middle Class, We Got The Blues, Mainstream Belongers, Young Achievers, Young At Heart, Trying To Make It, The Left Outs, and Almost.

These clusters actually describe market segments and the vast differences in the labels of such clusters across the countries shows that there are enormous differences in attitudes, traits, and values between these market segments. At the same time, descriptive characteristics of the clusters will also help to link these different countries together with respect to some attitudes, values, and traits. Yet, it is important for Western marketers in these countries to be cognizant of the many differences between such countries as they market products and services to their customers.

**Sources:** The review of lifestyle research across Asia is from "Special Session Summary: Lifestyle Research, Macro Trends and Consumer Behavior in Asia," by Jochen Wirtz, in *Asia Pacific Advances in Consumer Research*, Vol. 3, K. Hung and K. Monroe, Eds., Association for Consumer Research, 1998, pp. 1–3; the Singapore-specific results are from Kwon Jung, Jochen Wirtz, Ah Keng Kau, and Soo Jiuan Tan, "The Seven Faces of Singaporeans: A Typology of Consumers Based on a Large-Scale Lifestyle Study," *Asia Pacific Journal of Management*, Vol. 16, No. 2, 1999, pp. 229–248. Reprinted with permission from the author.

## Compulsive Buying and Consuming

The psychographic profile of some customers includes behavior we call compulsive buying and consuming. These two categories of behavior are distinct but related.

### Compulsive Buying

We all know people who are compulsive buyers, always shopping, always buying things they may never use, or things they already have more of than they can use, and buying it even if they can barely afford it or even when they are short on money. Thus, we define compulsive buying as a chronic tendency to purchase products far in excess of both a person's needs and resources.

Benign compulsive buyers buy things whenever they are on sale, accumulating them for future use, but they are deliberative as to the value of the purchase, buying it only if the item represents a good bargain or a rare find; the compulsiveness resides in constantly looking for opportunistic merchandise. The less benign consumer buys without evaluation of future need and without regard for available means. Such people often accumulate huge debt and a large stock of unused products. For them, the act of buying becomes a thrill in itself.

It is this negative behavior that detracts from individual welfare and, thus, deserves study. Consumer researchers have defined this negative compulsive behavior as chronic, repetitive purchasing that becomes a primary response to negative events or feelings.[36] (To try a measurement scale for compulsive buying, see the Window on Research box.)

Compulsive buyers have been found to differ from other customers in a number of respects. Compared with others, compulsive buyers have a lower self-esteem, are more depressed, show a greater tendency to fantasize, experience greater emotional lift at the time of purchase, experience remorse in the post-purchase phase, and accumulate a much higher debt. Moreover, research has found that compulsive buying is motivated less by a desire to possess things and more as a means of maintaining self-esteem.[37]

### Compulsive Consumption

Beyond purchasing, some consumers are compulsive users of products and services. Whereas compulsive buying occurs for a broad range of products, compulsive consumption is limited to one or two related product or service categories (e.g., compulsive eating, drinking, or gambling). Compulsive consumption can be defined as an uncontrolled and obsessive consumption of a product or service frequently and in excessive amounts, likely to ultimately cause harm to the consumer or others. Here is how one consumer described her compulsive consumption behavior:

> When I was using drugs, they were the focal point of my whole life. They were all I thought about. Every two hours I would think, How can I do my drugs? . . . They were what I allocated my time to first, my money to first. . . .  (a research respondent in consumer researcher Elizabeth Hirschman's study[38])

In the consumer research literature, three characteristics of compulsive consumption have been reported. Compulsive consumers experience a drive or urge to engage in a behavior, deny harmful consequences, and face repeated failure in attempts to control that behavior.[39] A number of behaviors are examples of compulsive consumption: alcoholism, eating disorders, compulsive gambling, compulsive exercising, and compulsive sexuality.[40]

## Materialism

Do you want to own a lot of things, indulge in luxuries, live a very rich and comfortable life, and have lots of money, and do you consider your possessions an important aspect of your self-identify? If so, then you are what social scientists and consumer researchers call materialistic. The *Oxford English Dictionary* defines materialism as a devotion to material

# WINDOW ON RESEARCH

## Are You a Compulsive Buyer?

Consumer researchers Ronald J. Faber and Thomas C. O'Guinn have developed the following measurement scale to score customers on compulsive buying. If you want to score yourself, answer the questions, and then apply the formula given at the bottom of the table.

1. Please indicate how much you agree or disagree with each of the statements below. Place an X on the line that best indicates how you feel about each statement.

| | STRONGLY AGREE (1) | SOMEWHAT AGREE (2) | NEITHER AGREE NOR DISAGREE (3) | SOMEWHAT DISAGREE (4) | STRONGLY DISAGREE (5) |
|---|---|---|---|---|---|
| a. If I have any money left at the end of the pay period, I just have to spend it. | — | — | — | — | — |

2. Please indicate how often you have done each of the following things by placing an X on the appropriate line.

| | VERY OFTEN (1) | OFTEN (2) | SOME-TIMES (3) | RARELY (4) | NEVER (5) |
|---|---|---|---|---|---|
| a. Felt others would be horrified if they knew of my spending habits. | — | — | — | — | — |
| b. Bought things even though I couldn't afford them. | — | — | — | — | — |
| c. Wrote a check when I knew I didn't have enough money in the bank to cover it. | — | — | — | — | — |
| d. Bought myself something in order to make myself feel better. | — | — | — | — | — |
| e. Felt anxious or nervous on days I didn't go shopping. | — | — | — | — | — |
| f. Made only the minimum payments on my credit cards. | — | — | — | — | — |

To score yourself, enter your responses into the scoring equation and calculate the total:

Scoring equation = $-9.69 + (Q1a \times 0.33) + (Q2a \times 0.34) + (Q2b \times 0.50)$
$+ (Q2c \times 0.47) + (Q2d \times 0.33) + (Q2e \times 0.38) + (Q2f \times 0.31)$.

If your final score is less than or equal to 21.34, you are classified as a compulsive buyer. If you score this low, you may want to reflect on your motivations and resolve to identify strategies to overcome this psychographic aspect of yourself.

**Source:** Adapted from Ronald J. Faber and Thomas C. O'Guinn, "A Clinical Screener for Compulsive Buying," *Journal of Consumer Research* 19 (December 1992), pp. 459–69. Additional information available at http://www.sltrib.com/98/feb/020298/utah_lif/20581.asp. Reprinted with permission of the University of Chicago Press.

needs and desires, to the neglect of spiritual matters; a way of life, opinion, or tendency based entirely upon material interests. Consumer researcher Russ Belk defines **material-ism** as the importance a consumer attaches to material possessions.[41]

Marsha L. Richins and Scott Dawson, marketing professors, respectively, at University of Missouri and Portland State University, studied this consumer psychographic. Based on the review of literature in psychology, sociology, economics, and philosophy, these consumer researchers identified three dimensions of materialism as follows:

1. *Acquisition centrality*—The tendency to place material possessions and their acquisitions at the center of one's life.
2. *Acquisition as the pursuit of happiness*—All consumers pursue happiness. However, some pursue it through other things, such as personal skill accomplishment; in contrast, materialists pursue happiness through acquisition of possessions.
3. *Possession-defined success*—This is a tendency to judge one's own and others' success by material possessions.

Based on extensive research, Richins and Dawson designed a scale to measure these three dimensions of materialism (see Table 5.6).

## A Scale to Measure Materialism                    TABLE 5.6

### SUCCESS SUBSCALE
I admire people who own expensive homes, cars, and clothes.
Some of the most important achievements in life include acquiring material possessions.
I don't place much emphasis on the amount of material objects that people own as a sign of success.
The things I own say a lot about how well I'm doing in life.
I like to own things that impress people.
I don't pay much attention to the material objects other people own.

### CENTRALITY SUBSCALE
I usually buy only the things I need.
I try to keep my life simple as far as possessions are concerned.
The things I own aren't all that important to me.
I enjoy spending money on things that aren't practical.
Buying things gives me a lot of pleasure.
I like a lot of luxury in my life.
I put less emphasis on material things than most people do.

### HAPPINESS SUBSCALE
I have all the things I really need to enjoy life.
My life would be better if I owned certain things I don't have.
I wouldn't be any happier if I owned nicer things.
I'd be happier if I could afford to buy more things.
It sometimes bothers me quite a bit that I can't afford to buy all the things I'd like.

**Source:** Marsha L. Richins and Scott Dawson, "A Consumer Values Orientation and Its Measurement: Scale Development and Validation," *Journal of Consumer Research*, 19, 3 (December 1992), pp. 303–17. Reprinted with permission of the University of Chicago Press.

Richins and Dawson also suggested several characteristics of materialistic persons. First, materialists value acquisition of possessions more than they value other life goals and more than relationship with others. Second, materialistic people are self-centered and, hence, are less likely to be sharing and giving. Furthermore, materialists lead a life of material complexity—reliance on technology, positive attitude toward growth, and a lack of concern for things of nature. **Voluntary simplicity**, a tendency to simplify life and to adopt economic behaviors of low consumption and ecological responsibility, will be contrary to the spirit of materialism. Materialists tend to be less satisfied with life than others, for the lust for goods is insatiable; it always leaves materialists wanting more.

Using their scale of materialism, Richins and Dawson divided consumers into high and low materialists. They had these respondents choose and rank-order the four most important values out of a standard list of nine and also indicate how much they would be willing to spend on such categories as buying things, giving to church organizations, and so forth. As expected, materialists tended to value financial security much more than nonmaterialists and to place less value on warm relationships with others and a sense of accomplishment. Materialists were also likely to spend more on buying things than non-materialists but less on giving to church organizations or charity and lending friends money.[42]

We have already referred to two metaphors related to consumption when we looked at the topics of emotions and self-concept; namely, *consuming as experience* and *consuming as integration*. Researcher Douglas B. Holt develops a typology of consumption practices with two other metaphors—namely, *consuming as classification and consuming as play*—and then conceptualizes materialism as a consumption style. When consumers use meanings associated with a consumption object (classifying through objects), or their interactions with the consumption object (classifying through actions) as means to classify themselves against relevant others, the *consuming as classification* metaphor is in use. With reference to spectators of a baseball game as consumers who are consuming the experience of a baseball game, classifying through objects would imply use of souvenirs, photos, and insignia clothing to classify spectators into groups while classifying through actions would imply participating in conventions, predicting, mentoring, and expressing tastes with fellow spectators. *Consuming as play* involves using consumption objects to interact with fellow consumers. Spectators of a baseball game would commune as they share mutually felt experiences with one another and socialize as they make use of experiential practices to entertain each other. (This baseball game example is a case study woven in the paper to explain the four metaphors.)

The author conceptualizes materialism as a "consumption style that emphasizes integrating practices over experiential practices (since integrating links possessions to the individual) and classifying through objects rather than classifying through actions (because objects are perceived as value laden) and demphasizes playing practices (because playing focuses on people rather than objects)." Thus, materialism is a distinctive consumption style in which "the focus is on consumption objects rather than experiences or other people."[43]

# The Motivational Processes and the Three Customer Roles

Needs, emotions, and psychographics are general characteristics of customers, applicable to all three roles. (See Table 5.7.) Consider needs first. For users, needs drive product usage. For example, locks and guns are used for security needs, and flowers are sent as gifts for emotional value. Many of these same needs also motivate customers as payers. Payers often feel anxious about being cheated (which relate both to one's security and esteem needs). Donors often donate to worthy causes for self-esteem. Payers for gifts seek to satisfy social needs as well as esteem; for example, the price of the gift might be viewed as reflecting on the value or worth of the gift giver. Donors to charity organizations satisfy their need for belonging and view themselves being actualized as the cause of charity is furthered. Finally, as buyers, customers are concerned with their personal safety in the shopping areas, which is why buyers shun high-crime areas. Also, many buyers seek social interaction with salespersons or service-provider employees. Also they expect to be respected by salespersons and seek to maintain or bolster their self-esteem by interacting with polite and courteous service employees. For business customers in their buying roles, patronizing socially responsible vendors satisfies their self-actualizing needs.

| The Motivational Processes and the Three Customer Roles | | | TABLE 5.7 |
|---|---|---|---|

|  | **User** | **Payer** | **Buyer** |
|---|---|---|---|
| NEEDS | • One or more needs constitute the primary purpose of product or service usage. | • Fear of being ripped off (security, esteem).<br><br>• Donors to worthy causes (esteem).<br><br>• Payers for gifts (esteem, social needs). | • Personal safety in shopping areas.<br><br>• Seek social interaction with salespersons and service providers.<br><br>• Need to protect and look to enhancing self-esteem in marketplace experiences. |
| EMOTIONS | • Emotional value from products and services. | • Emergency expenses and involuntary expenses cause negative emotions.<br><br>• Debt causes grief to many payers.<br><br>• Spending on self and for loved ones causes positive emotions. | • Shopping activity is sometimes enjoyable, and, at other times, boring.<br><br>• Finding a deal gives a thrill. |
| PSYCHOGRAPHICS | • Users seek and use many products and services to live their lifestyles, to fit in with their psychographics. | • Being a spendthrift or a big spender, being a credit card user, accumulating debt or being eager to stay debt-free are psychographics. | • Comparison shopper, shop-'til-you-drop shopper, and late-night shopper types. |

Emotions also surround and suffuse all three roles. Illustratively, talking to a parent or a close friend long-distance on the phone is joyful; attending a church mass is spiritually uplifting; wearing a diamond necklace for the first time is ecstatic; or flying in an airplane is, for some, fearful. For a business traveler, traveling first class or using a corporate jet is an emotional experience. As payers, customers experience negative emotions when faced with some emergency expenses (e.g., a sudden breakdown of the transmission in the car) or involuntary spending (e.g., a heavy fine for speeding or a steep increase in tuition fee). Likewise, mounting debt causes grief to many payers. On the flip side, positive and pleasant emotions are experienced by payers for spending money on self and on loved ones. Finally, in their buyer roles, customers sometimes enjoy shopping while at other times they find it boring. Many encounters with sales and service employees are emotionally rewarding. And, buyers get a thrill in finding a deal.

Psychographics, the third facet of customer motivations, applies to all three customer roles as well. Customers use many products and services to put together a lifestyle, to weave a psychographic profile, so to speak. Many product categories (e.g., mountain bikes, golf equipment, Western clothing, nature trips, tattoo parlors) are targeted to users with specific lifestyles, and many brands in mature product categories are differentiated by the lifestyles and psychographics of their purported users (e.g., Brooks Brothers for the upscale corporate executives and Armani for the upscale celebrities). For the payer, relevant elements of psychographics are such individual traits as being a spendthrift or a big spender, being or not being a credit-card user, accumulating a debt or being eager to stay debt-free. Finally, for the buyer, such traits as being a comparison shopper or an impulse buyer or being a compulsive shopper (i.e., shop 'til you drop), late-night shopper, and so on, are aspects of the buyer's psychographics. Buyers in business markets might have the self-concept of being very successful negotiators. Similarly, the shopper classification mentioned in Chapter 1 (i.e., personal shopper, convenience shopper) are also elements of psychographics for buyers.

# Summary

This chapter dealt with customer motivations—why customers buy, pay for, and use specific products and services. We organized this topic into three sections, one each on needs, emotions, and psychographics. Needs are felt deprivations of desired states. We discussed some of the prominent classifications of needs by scholars. Maslow's hierarchy of needs classification is perhaps the most well known of these, but we also outlined Murray's social needs system and Dichter's list of subconscious needs (or motives). Finally, we discussed some needs classifications adapted by marketing scholars such as Sheth and Holbrook, with a synthesis by Hanna.

Human emotions also play a significant role in motivating human behavior. We explained Plutchik's emotional classification system and discussed the concept of hedonic consumption and the related phenomenon of product-use involvement. Hedonic consumption offers customers intense emotional satisfaction and makes them highly involved in product or service use. This involvement turns into enthusiasm and accounts for heightened participation by customers in marketplace activities related to those products and services (e.g., Harley Owners Group).

Psychographics, the third facet of customer motivation, describes customers' profile of needs, emotions, and resulting behaviors, and as such explains much of customer behavior. Psychographics includes self-concept, personal values (what aspects of life are important to us), and lifestyles (how we spend time and money and what activities we participate in). We discussed ways of measuring lifestyles or ways of graphing the psychological makeup of the customer (hence, the name psychographics). Finally, we discussed one particular classification of lifestyles (called the VALS system) for both the United States and Japan. In conclusion, we reviewed all the concepts covered in the chapter and illustrated their applicability to each of the three roles of the customer.

# Key Terms

Actual Self 177

Approach Motivation 163

Arousal-Seeking Motive 168

Attribution Motivation 169

Attributions 169

Avoidance Motivation 163

Compulsive Buying 187

Compulsive Consumption 187

Deep Involvement 175

Drive 161

Emotions 170

Enduring Involvement 175

External Attributions 169

Goal-Object 161

Hedonic Consumption 175

Ideal Self 177

Internal Attributions 169

Involvement 175

Laddering 177

Level of Adaptation 168

Lifestyle retail brands 180

Lifestyles 179

Market Mavens 169

Maslow's Hierarchy of Needs 164

Materialism 189

Means-End Chains 177

**Moods** 173

**Motivation** 161

**Need for Cognition** 168

**Optimal Level of Stimulation** 168

**Primary Emotions** 172

**Psychographics** 176

**Purposive Behavior** 161

**Schachter's Two-Factory Theory** 171

**Self-Concept** 177

**Situational Involvement** 175

**Tolerance for Ambiguity** 168

**Values** 176

**Voluntary Simplicity** 190

# Discussion Questions and Exercises

1. Compare and contrast terminal and instrumental values. Give five examples of each of these two types of consumer values, and, for each one, provide an example of a company that stresses the achievement of that value in its advertising messages.

2. What is attribution theory? Why is it so important to consumer researchers? How would you use this theory if you were a marketing manager for
   **a.** A weight-reduction exercise and diet plan
   **b.** A car dealership's car service division.

3. Do you anticipate any major changes in your lifestyle five years from now? If so, what are these likely to be and into which VALS segment are you likely to belong five years from now? Explain your rationale.

4. Construct a hypothetical means-ends chain model for the purchase of an engagement ring. How might a jeweler use this approach to develop a promotional strategy?

5. Assume that you are the director of marketing for a major credit-card company. You are interested in sending more targeted promotions to your customers and have been able to analyze your best customers in more depth. On the surface, it appears that a comparison of customer groups reveals a number of similarities in terms of several demographic variables, such as age, gender, and income (e.g., a 40-year-old male plumber and a 40-year-old male lawyer, each making $80,000 per year). However, upon more careful analysis, you find that their spending patterns and choice of goods and services vary greatly. Upon consulting your consumer research staff, you realize that this is due to psychographical differences. What might some of these differences be for the lawyer and the plumber segments, and why is understanding these differences important for you?

# Notes

1   Adapted from Tara Parker-Pope, "Fear of Disease Has Consumers Resorting to Germ Warfare," *The Wall Street Journal*, February 7, 1997, pp. A1, A4.

2   Any description of this concept in the space allowed here is necessarily oversimplified and lopsided. For fuller appreciation of this topic, see John W. Atkinson, *An Introduction to Motivation* (New York, NY: D. Van Nostrand Company, 1964); Edward J. Murray, *Motivation and Emotion* (Englewood Cliffs, NJ: Prentice Hall, 1964).

3   Abraham H. Maslow, "A Theory of Human Motivation," *Psychological Review* 50 (July 1943), pp. 370–96; also, Abraham H. Maslow, *Motivation and Personality* (New York: Harper & Row, 1970).

4 See Jagdish N. Sheth, Bruce I. Newman, and Barbara L. Gross, *Consumption Values and Market Choices: Theory and Application* (Cincinnati: South-Western Publishing Co., 1991) pp. 16–79.

5 Janice Hanna, "A Typology of Consumer Needs," *Research in Marketing*, 3, Jagdish N. Sheth, ed. (Greenwich, Conn.: JAI Press, 1980), pp. 83–104.

6 James Olds and Peter M. Milner, "Positive Reinforcement Produced by Electric Stimulation of Septal Area and Other Regions of Rat Brains," *Journal of Comparative and Physiological Psychology*, 47 (1954), pp. 419–27.

7 See Lyle E. Bourne and Bruce R. Ekstrand, *Psychology: Its Principles and Meanings* (New York, NY: Holt, Rinehart, and Winston, 1979), pp. 255–57.

8 P. S. Raju, "Optimum Stimulation Level: Its Relationship to Personality, Demographics, and Exploratory Behavior," *Journal of Consumer Research*, 7 (December 1980), pp. 272–82; Jan-Benedict E. M. Steenkamp and Hans Baumgartner, "The Role of Optimum Stimulation Level in Exploratory Consumer Behavior," *Journal of Consumer Research* 19 (December 1992), pp. 434–48.

9 Maslow, *Ibid.* Meera P. Venkatraman and Deborah J. MacInnis, "The Epistemic and Sensory Exploratory Behaviors of Hedonic and Cognitive Consumers," *Advances in Consumer Research* 12, Elizabeth C. Hirschman and Morris B. Holbrook, eds. (Provo, Utah: Association for Consumer Research), pp. 102–7.

10 Maslow, *Ibid.*

11 Lawrence F. Feick and Linda L. Price, "The Market Maven: A Diffuser of Marketplace Information," *Journal of Marketing* 51, No. 1, (January 1987), pp. 83–97.

12 Wayne Weiten, *Psychology: Themes and Variations* (Belmont, Calif.: Wadsworth, 1989), p. 596.

13 Harold H. Kelley, "Attribution Theory in Social Psychology," *Nebraska Symposium on Motivation*, 15 (1967), pp. 191–241; Harold H. Kelley, "The Process of Causal Attribution," *American Psychologist* 28 (1973), pp. 107–28.

14 For an illuminating review, see Janice Hanna, *Ibid.*

15 As for motivation, so too for emotions; our treatment is necessarily oversimplified due to space limitations. For fuller discussion, see P. T. Young, *Motivation and Emotion* (New York: John Wiley and Sons, 1961); Edward J. Murray, *Motivation and Emotion* (Englewood Cliffs, NJ: Prentice Hall, 1964).

16 For further reading, see George Mandler, *Mind and Body* (New York: Norton, 1984); Carroll E. Izard, *Human Emotions* (New York: Platinum, 1977).

17 Nancy Stephens and Kevin P. Gwinner, "Why Don't Some People Complain? A Cognitive-Emotive Process Model of Consumer Complaint Behavior," *Journal of the Academy of Marketing Science*, 26 (3), 1998, pp. 172–89.

18 See Wayne Weiten, *Psychology: Themes and Variations* (Belmont, Calif.: Wadsworth, 1989), pp. 374–77.

19 See, for example, Rajeev Batra and Douglas M. Stayman, "The Role of Mood in Advertising Effectiveness," *Journal of Consumer Research* 17, No. 2 (September 1990), pp. 203–14.

20 Angela Y. Lee and Brian Sternthal, "The Effects of Positive Mood on Memory," *Journal of Consumer Research*, 26, September 1999, pp. 115–12.

21 Michael J. Barone, Paul W. Miniard, and Jean B. Romeo, "The Influence of Positive Mood on Brand Extension Evaluations," *Journal of Consumer Research*, 26, March 2000, pp. 386–400.

22 Morris Holbrook and Elizabeth Hirschman, "The Experiential Aspects of Consumption: Consumer Fantasies, Feelings, and Fun," *Journal of Consumer Research* 9 (September 1982), pp. 132–40; Elizabeth Hirschman and Morris Holbrook, "Hedonic Consumption: Emerging Concepts, Methods, and Propositions," *Journal of Marketing* 46 (Summer 1982), pp. 92–101.

23 Becky Ebenkamp, "The Ugly American URL? (European Teens Not Interested in Generic Web-Marketing)," *Brandweek*, Vol. 41; Issue 36, September 18, 2000.

24 For further reading on involvement, see John H. Antil, "Conceptualization and Operationalization of Involvement" in T. C. Kinear, ed., *Advances in Consumer Research* 11 (1984), pp. 203–9.

25 See Milton Rokeach, *The Nature of Human Values* (New York: Free Press, 1973); David E. Vinson, Jerome E. Scott, and Lawrence Lamont, "The Role of Personal Values in Marketing and Consumer Behavior," *Journal of Marketing* 41 (April 1977), pp. 44–50.

26 Lynn R. Kahle, Sharon E. Beatty, and Pamela Homer, "Alternative Measurement Approaches to Consumer Values: The List of Values (LOV) and Values and Life Style (VALS)," *Journal of Consumer Research* 13 (December 1986), pp. 405–09; Sharon Beatty, Lynn R. Kahle, Pamela Homer, and Shekhar Misra, "Alternative Measurement Approaches to Consumer Values: The List of Values and the Rokeach Value Survey," *Psychology & Marketing* 2 (Fall 1985), pp. 181–200.

27 *Ibid.*

28 This technique has been applied in extensive research done by marketing professors Thomas J. Reynolds and Jonathan Gutman. See Thomas J. Reynolds and Jonathan Gutman, "Laddering Theory, Method, Analysis, and Interpretation," *Journal of Advertising Research* 28 (January–February 1988), pp. 11–31; also see Thomas J. Reynolds and Alyce Byrd Craddock, "The Application of the MECCAS Model to the Development and Assessment of Advertising Strategy: A Case Study," *Journal of Advertising Research* (April/May 1988), pp. 43–54.

29 For a state-of-the-art review of self-theory in the context of people's work life, see Robert A. Snyder and Ronald R. Williams, "Self-Theory: An Integrative Theory of Work Motivation," *Journal of Occupational Psychology* 55 (1982), pp. 257–67.

30 For discussions of self-concept, see M. Joseph Sirgy, "Self-Concept in Consumer Behavior: A Critical Review," *Journal of Consumer Research* (December 1982), pp. 287–300; also, Harold H. Kassarjian, "Personality and Consumer Behavior: A Review," *Journal of Marketing Research*, Vol. 8 (November 1971), pp. 409–18; M. Joseph Sirgy, "Using Self-Congruity and Ideal Congruity to Predict Purchase Motivation," *Journal of Business Research*, Vol. 13 (June 1985), pp. 195–206; Warren S. Martin and Joseph Bellizzi, "An Analysis of Congruence Relationship between Self Images and Product Images," *Journal of the Academy of Marketing Science*, December 1982, pp. 473–88.

31 John Lastovicka, Lance A. Bettencourt, Renee Shaw Hughner, and Ronald J. Kuntze, "The Lifestyle of Tight and Frugal: Theory and Measurement," *Journal of Consumer Research*, 26, June 1999, pp. 85–98.

32 Deborah Helman and Leslie De Chernatony, "Exploring the Development of Lifestyle Retail Brands," *The Service Industries Journal* 19, April 1999, pp. 49–68.

33 The Second Annual Ernst & Young Internet Shopping Study, 1999, p. 9.

34 VALS description on the Internet, at http://www.sric-bi.com.

35 Rebecca Piirto, "Global Psychographics," *American Demographics* 12, No. 12 (December 1990) p. 8.

36  Thomas C. O'Guinn and Ronald J. Faber, "Compulsive Buying: A Phenomenolog-ical Exploration," *Journal of Consumer Research* 16 (September 1989), pp. 147–57.

37  *Ibid.*

38  Elizabeth C. Hirschman, "The Consciousness of Addiction: Toward a General The-ory of Compulsive Consumption," *Journal of Consumer Research* 19 (September 1992), pp. 155–79.

39  See Faber and O'Guinn; also Dennis W. Rook, "The Buying Impulse," *Journal of Consumer Research* (September, 14, 1987) pp. 189–99; and Dennis W. Rook and Steven J. Hoch, "Consuming Impulses," *Advances in Consumer Research* 12, E. C. Hirschman and M. B. Holbrook, eds. (Provo, Utah: Association for Consumer Re-search), pp. 23–7.

40  For a fascinating theoretical understanding of compulsive consumption, see Hirschman.

41  Russell W. Belk, "Materialism: Trait Aspects of Living in the Material World," *Jour-nal of Consumer Research* 12 (December 1985), pp. 265–80.

42  Marsha L. Richins and Scott Dawson, "A Consumer Values Orientation and Its Mea-surement: Scale Development and Validation," *Journal of Consumer Research*, 19, 3 (December 1992), p. 385.

43  Douglas B. Holt, "How Consumers Consume: A Typology of Consumption Prac-tices," *Journal of Consumer Research*, 22, June 1995, pp. 1–16.

# CHAPTER 6

## Customer Attitudes: Cognitive and Affective

## Managing Attitudes

As with any e-transformation, technology is not the only stumbling block; user attitudes create significant problems as well. Joe Lejander, a training consultant at the Office of the Clerk of the Superior Court in Maricopa County, Arizona did nothing as drastic as implementing an e-learning initiative. As a start, he changed the older paper-based registration process to an online registration process for the office's classroom-based training. The online form at the Web site was very similar to the paper-based form, yet instead of completing it online and hitting the "send" button, 20 percent of the users filled out the form, printed it, and sent it through inter-office mail. And, 30 percent of the users refused to access the site.

Air Canada faced a similar challenge in getting computer novices to accept e-learning. "What's a mouse?" was a question that arose more than once. In Montreal, Air Canada held open houses, serving coffee and doughnuts in the same area where the computers were set up so that users could become more comfortable with the technology. The younger employees who frequently accessed the Net at home and were more comfortable with computers helped their older colleagues through this technology-adoption process.

John Deere & Co. had similar hurdles regarding user adoption of online courses. Dealers were pleased with the online courses offered by the company for their technicians, but many of the technicians had never worked on a computer, making the most basic tasks of opening a new file or using the mouse a major hurdle to the adoption of the online course. An innovative solution used by several dealers was to have the technicians play computer games for half an hour every day for a certain period of time. Clicking soon became second nature. (Sandra Swanson, 2001)[1]

All of the above examples show how managing user attitudes is extremely important for the success of technology in business. Likewise, managing customer attitudes is important in every sphere of business. When the sweatshop crusade began against several retailers like Nordstrom, Gap, and Kathie Lee Gifford's line of clothing at Wal-Mart, these organizations had to take concrete steps so that they could make customer attitudes toward their products favorable again.

Marketers are interested in knowing customer attitudes about their products and services and other elements of the marketing mix since it helps predict customer behavior. This chapter introduces the current state of marketing knowledge about attitudes. (See Figure 6.1 for framework.) First, we define and discuss attitude as a global concept. Next, we present a three-component view of attitude and discuss three hierarchies in which the three components are organized. Following this, we discuss various strategies of influencing customer attitudes, utilizing current knowledge of how the three components are interrelated. This description of attitude-influence strategies is then followed by an explanation of the underlying psychological processes and the various theories that capture these processes. Next, we discuss a class of models (called multiattribute models) that account for how customers might combine several beliefs about something into a global attitude. In one of these models, we also discuss how global attitude combines with social pressures to produce customer action. Next, we discuss the functional theory of attitude. Knowing what functions an attitude serves will help us understand the deeper motivation for customer attitudes. Finally, we discuss a special application of attitudes to marketing; namely, how to utilize knowledge of customer attitudes in order to plan and promote social change. In the concluding section, we outline the relevance of various topics covered in this chapter to each of the three customer roles.

## Conceptual Framework                          FIGURE 6.1

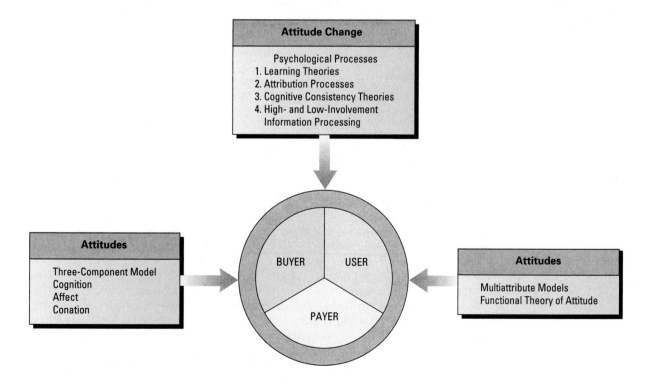

# Attitude: Definition and Characteristics

To fully understand the significance of attitudes, let us first review a classic definition of attitudes, offered by psychologist Gordon Allport:

> **Attitudes** are learned predispositions to respond to an object or class of objects in a consistently favorable or unfavorable way.[2]

This definition has several implications:

- Attitudes are learned. That is, they get formed on the basis of some experience with or information about the object.
- Attitudes are predispositions. As such, they reside in the mind.
- Attitudes cause consistent response. They precede and produce behavior.

Therefore, attitudes can be used to predict behavior. For example, if you show a favorable attitude toward a new product concept, then marketers predict that when the new product is made available, you are likely to buy it.

Alternatively, behavior can be used to infer the underlying attitudes. For example, if you buy a ticket for a fine arts show, marketers infer that you have a favorable attitude toward fine arts; a fundraising letter is then sent to you in the hope that your attitude (inferred to be favorable) toward the fine arts implies support for the arts category in general. Thus, your purchase of the ticket has been used to infer your underlying attitudes toward arts in general.

## Attitudes as Evaluations

Attitudes, then, are our evaluations of objects, people, places, brands, products, organizations, and so on. People evaluate these in terms of their goodness, likability, or desirability. As such, it is easy to measure attitudes by getting customers to rate statements such as the following:

> Please check how you feel about Olestra, [a fat substitute used by Procter & Gamble as a cooking medium for snack products]:
>
> I dislike Olestra very much        ☐ ☐ ☐ ☐ ☐  I like it very much.
>
> Toward Olestra, I feel unfavorably    ☐ ☐ ☐ ☐ ☐  I feel favorably.
>
> My opinion about Olestra is: Negative ☐ ☐ ☐ ☐ ☐ Positive

Attitudes are held by customers both in household and business markets. In household markets, many customers hold an attitude toward salespersons in general (for example, "Salespeople are basically all hucksters"), and a business customer might hold an unfavorable attitude toward off-shore companies or toward vendors as a group (e.g., "Vendors are, in general, opportunistic").

With e-commerce burgeoning on the Web, the customer's attitude toward the web site is an important consideration. Attitude toward the site is "the Web surfer's predisposition to respond favorably or unfavorably to Web content in natural exposure situations." Researchers Chen and Wells developed a six-item scale to measure consumer's attitudes toward the site (Table 6.1). They also determined the factors leading to a favorable attitude toward the site and found that Entertainment (fun, exciting, cool, imaginative, entertaining, flashy), Informativeness (informative, intelligent, knowledgeable, resourceful, useful, helpful) and Organization (not messy, not cumbersome, not confusing, and not irritating) are most important.[3]

Independent home and garden products chain Robert Dyas in Britain, is defining new ways of using its floor space to augment the customer's Internet experience. It has created a showroom in the dead space of the store's basement, where customers can experience the products. Customers then take the specifications, and go home to check if

| Measures for Attitude Towards Site | | | | | | TABLE 6.1 |
|---|---|---|---|---|---|---|

The following statements measure your general favorability toward the web site you just visited. Circle the number that best indicates your agreement or disagreement with each statement.

|  | Definitely disagree | | | Definitely agree | |
|---|---|---|---|---|---|
| The web site makes it easy for me to build a relationship with this company. | 1 | 2 | 3 | 4 | 5 |
| I would like to visit this web site again in the future. | 1 | 2 | 3 | 4 | 5 |
| I am satisfied with the service provided by this web site. | 1 | 2 | 3 | 4 | 5 |
| I feel comfortable in surfing this web site. | 1 | 2 | 3 | 4 | 5 |
| I feel surfing this web site is a good way for me to spend my time. | 1 | 2 | 3 | 4 | 5 |
|  | One of the worst | | | One of the best | |
| Compared with other web sites, I would rate this one as | 1 | 2 | 3 | 4 | 5 |

**Source:** Qimei Chen and William D. Wells, "Attitude towards the Site," *Journal of Advertising Research*, September–October 1999, pp. 27–38.

the product will fit in their home space. If they are satisfied, they can purchase the product from the store's web site and the product is delivered to the home in 24 hours. Thus, the store has taken the risk out of the Internet purchase and, at the same time, provided the customer with the convenience of electronic shopping. The physical environment also helps create brand presence. This is, therefore, an example of using the physical and virtual environment to create a favorable attitude about the brand in the mind of the customer.

Another example of managing different customer attitudes towards a brand can be seen at John Lewis department stores in UK. Adjacent to the women's dressing rooms, the "boyfriend area" has been introduced, where partners can sit down and listen to records, read newspapers, and have coffee. Thus, the store is not only making sure that the actual customer has a fantastic retail experience, but is also ensuring that the person accompanying the customer also feels good about the shopping experience, thus creating positive attitudes for the brand for both parties.[4]

## Three-Component Model of Attitude

The previous view of attitude as an overall evaluation of objects treats attitude as a single dimensional global concept. This view informs us how a person feels in overall terms about an object but not why he or she feels that way or what underlies that specific attitude. Psychologists have identified three underlying dimensions to global attitude: cognition, affect, and conation or, respectively, knowledge, feeling, and action. That is, when we hold an attitude about an object, typically it is based on some knowledge and beliefs about the object. We feel some positive or negative emotion toward it, and we want to act in a certain way toward it—either embracing it or spurning it, for example.

Cognitions or thoughts about brands or objects are also called beliefs. More specifically, **beliefs** are expectations as to what something is or is not or what something will or will not do. Statements of belief connect an object (person, brand, store) to an attribute or benefit. Accordingly, a **brand belief** is a thought about a specific property or quality of the brand. Customers' beliefs about purchasing foreign and domestic products are captured in a construct called ethnocentrism. The Window on Research elaborates on the characteristics of ethnocentrics and draws pointers for marketers to tackle these attitudes.

# WINDOW ON RESEARCH

## Ethnocentrism

Researchers Shimp and Sharma use the consumer ethnocentrism construct "to represent the beliefs held by American consumers about the appropriateness, indeed morality, of purchasing foreign-made products." Ethnocentric consumers believe that purchasing foreign-made goods hurts the domestic economy through loss of jobs, and, hence, it is unpatriotic to purchase foreign-made goods. Shimp and Sharma developed an instrument called the CETSCALE that measures consumers' ethnocentric tendencies toward purchasing foreign-made versus American-made products. They found that consumer ethnocentrics had significantly lower educational achievements, incomes, and social class attainments compared to nonethnocentrics. Consumer ethnocentrism affected consumers' attitudes toward domestic and foreign-made products.

Researchers Netemeyer, Durvasula, and Lichtenstein measured ethnocentric tendencies using the CETSCALE with samples from the United States, France, Japan, and Germany. They found that the attitude-towards-home country had a significant effect on consumer ethnocentrism. People with strong positive attitudes towards their home country were likely to display more ethnocentric tendencies than others.

After the fall of the communist bloc in Russia, Netemeyer, Andrews, and Durvasula conducted studies across samples in the U.S. and Russia. Russian consumers were found to be less ethnocentric than U.S. consumers. They were more positive about foreign-made products and also more accepting of them than the U.S. consumers. Another study of Polish customers after the removal of trade barriers in Central Europe shows that patriotism as a dimension of ethnocentrism is related to preference for Polish products. However, social status demonstration, as a dimension of conspicuous consumption, is related to a preference for Western products.

How is knowledge of "ethnocentrism" useful for multinational firms? It follows from the above discussion that if consumers in a country are highly ethnocentric, the firm should focus on product and brand attributes and not on the product's country of origin. Multinationals can also apply the ethnocentrism scale within a country to determine which regions are more ethnocentric and tailor marketing strategies accordingly within a country. The scale could also help retail chains make store-location decisions.

**Sources:** Adapted from T. A. Shimp and S. Sharma, "Consumer Ethnocentrism: Construction and Validation of the CETSCALE," *Journal of Marketing Research*, 24 (August 1987), pp. 280–289; R. G. Netemeyer, S. Durvasula, and D. R. Lichtenstein, "A Cross-National Assessment of the Reliability and Validity of the CETSCALE," *Journal of Marketing Research*, 28 (August 1991), pp. 320–327; S. Durvasula, J. C. Andrews, and R. G. Netemeyer, "A Cross-Cultural Comparison of Ethnocentrism in the United States and Russia," *Journal of International Consumer Marketing*, 9(4) (1997), pp. 73–93; J. S. Marcoux, P. Filiatrault, and E. Cheron, "The Attitudes Underlying Preferences of Young Urban Educated Polish Consumers Towards Products Made in Western Countries," *Journal of International Consumer Marketing*, 9(4) (1997), pp. 5–29.

There are three types of beliefs: descriptive, evaluative, and normative. **Descriptive beliefs** connect an object or person to a quality or outcome; for example, "This computer has a large memory," or "This airline is often late." **Evaluative beliefs** connect an object to personal likes or dislikes, preferences, and perceptions. Some statements expressing evaluative beliefs are: "This computer is very user-friendly" or "The service at this store is outrageous." **Normative beliefs** invoke moral and ethical judgments in relation to someone's acts, as in the following examples: "Cigarette companies should not advertise in a way that would appeal to youth," and "It is unfair for businesses to take advantage of innocent customers."

**Affect** is the feelings a person has toward an object or the emotions that object evokes for the person. Finally, **conation** is the action a person wants to take toward the object.

Table 6.2 presents examples of each attitude component for attitudes about two services. Researchers can measure attitudes by asking respondents to rate how well each statement describes them or their beliefs.

---

**Illustrative Measures of the Three-Component Model of Attitude**                                    **TABLE 6.2**

| | Attitude Object | |
|---|---|---|
| **Attitude Component** | **DHL, for Shipping a Business's Small Packages** | **Shopping for Airline Tickets on the Internet** |
| Cognitions or Beliefs | • DHL is very reliable in its service. <br> • DHL is more economical than other package-carrier services. <br> • DHL is able to customize its service to my shipping needs. | • For my airline tickets, shopping on the Internet is very convenient. <br> • You can find the cheapest fares by shopping on the Internet. <br> • Internet-based travel agents do not offer you a comprehensive set of airline and flight options. |
| Affect or Feelings | • When I ship by DHL, I feel secure. <br> • I am very happy to be using DHL for my shipping needs. <br> • I don't care if DHL goes out of business. | • Shopping on the Internet is: <br> (please circle as many as apply) <br> Totally cool    Confusing    Boring <br> A pain in the neck    Enjoyable    Terrible |
| Conations or Actions | • I use DHL for my shipping more than I use other carriers. <br> • I often recommend DHL to other business associates. <br> • I am looking for alternative carriers. | • I have used the Internet for my travel airline tickets recently. <br> • I often search the Internet for planning my travel itinerary. |

---

## Hierarchies in Attitude

If attitudes have three components, we need to know how, if at all, they are related. Do you think first and then act, or do you act first and think afterward? Marketers have addressed such questions by looking for an attitude hierarchy. **Attitude hierarchy** refers to the sequence in which the three components occur.

**Learning Hierarchy.** The most commonly discussed hierarchy is the learning hierarchy. In the learning hierarchy, cognitions come first, affect next, and action last. (See Figure 6.2.) That is, you think first, feel next, and act last. The learning hierarchy assumes that brand beliefs underlie our feelings toward the brand. Brand beliefs lead to brand feelings, which then cause brand purchase and use (or avoidance).

---

## FIGURE 6.2    Learning Hierarchy of Attitude

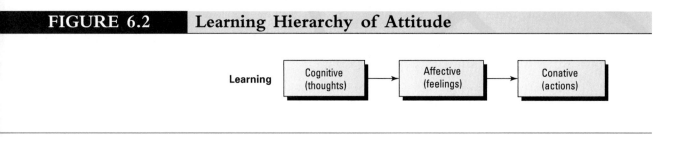

---

Consider an example. Let us say that you need to decide where to go for spring break: Panama City, Florida; Los Angeles; Cancun; or Steamboat Springs, Colorado. Suppose you were to first collect information, such as how far these places are in terms of the travel time, the cost of travel, hotel room cost, and the kinds of activities offered by each site. Then you make a judgment based on such information about the destination that will be good for you, whether you like Los Angeles better or Panama City, whether the idea of going to Cancun excites you or not, or whether it is Steamboat Springs that you really feel the urge to visit. Based on these feelings, you then choose one of these four destinations. You are using the learning hierarchy, also known as the rational hierarchy. In business, you may attend a trade show and collect several brochures from different vendors for some products that you intend to purchase. You could evaluate each of these vendors on several parameters and then make a rational decision as to whom you should award your contract. This is the learning hierarchy.

**Emotional Hierarchy.** However, if you said, "The last time I decided on my spring break plan . . . well, what happened was that we were a bunch of friends watching this show on cable TV, called *MTV Spring Break*; it was basically a live scene from Panama City Beach, where lots and lots of college students were having one big party on the beach. And we said, 'That is it. That is where we are going.'"

This description of your attitude feelings, action, and thoughts toward the Panama City Beach illustrates a different process, the emotional hierarchy of attitude. Here you *feel* first, then act, and think last. Based on your emotions—attraction or repulsion toward certain brands or persons or things—you embrace or avoid them, buy them, and use them. Finally, through experience, you learn more about them. Thus, in this hierarchy, affect comes first, conation next, and cognition last. (See Figure 6.3.)

These hierarchies happen just as much for business customers. The same scenarios could be observed, for example, for a business manager choosing a site for the next

---

## FIGURE 6.3    Emotional Hierarchy of Attitude

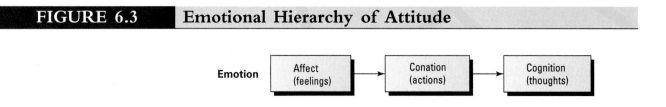

national sales meeting. The manager could follow the rational route, choosing the site primarily on cost considerations, for example. Alternatively, he or she could follow an emotional route, choosing the site primarily based on the lure of the place.

**Low-Involvement Hierarchy.** The learning and emotional hierarchies are *high-involvement hierarchies* because the attitude object generates high involvement. As we defined *involvement* in Chapter 4, it can be viewed as the degree of importance of an object to you. It is the stakes you have in the object. It is how much owning the object matters to you. The spring break site or an international trip is a high-involvement object for you, and, hence, you want to have the attitude that you can feel committed, whether you reached this attitude state via the rational or the emotional hierarchy.

In contrast is the *low-involvement mode* where not much is at stake, and it would not matter much if your attitude happened to be wrong. **Low-involvement attitude hierarchy** refers to the sequence in which the three attitude components occur in a person's acquisition of attitude toward objects that are of low salience or importance in his or her life. This model has the sequence of conation, affect, cognition, as shown in Figure 6.4.

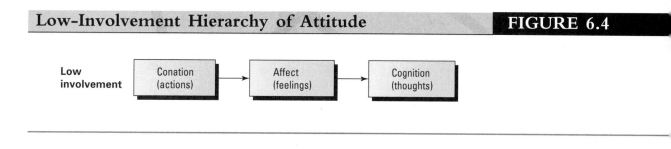

**Low-Involvement Hierarchy of Attitude**        **FIGURE 6.4**

Low involvement → Conation (actions) → Affect (feelings) → Cognition (thoughts)

Suppose that you are in the neighborhood bakery and you notice a new kind of bread; it has multigrains and some seeds in it, and the appearance looks inviting. The bread is new, so you don't have an attitude toward it. Now, do you have to know a whole lot about it or really feel attracted to it before you buy it? Not likely. Thus, neither the rational nor the emotional hierarchy is likely to apply. Instead, what you are likely to do is just put it in your shopping basket, bring it home, take the first bite, and say that it is good and that you like it. Then you pause to feel what grains it has and what flavor it has, and then maybe you even read the ingredients label and the nutrition information. Thus, in this case of a low-involvement product, action comes first (buying and using the bread), feelings next (the bread is good), and cognitions or thoughts last (noticing the ingredients). A similar example is the case of some demonstration software that you might receive in the mail. Action comes first since you use it first. Depending on whether it is of use to you, you feel good or bad about it, and then you check for various features included in the software, thus forming cognitions about the product.

Two clarifications are in order. One, involvement is not a property of the product or service; rather, it is the importance of it to a customer. Thus, the same product could be low-involving for some and high-involving for others. In our example, bread could indeed be a high-involvement product for some consumers. These consumers will then first read the label and try to learn as much as possible about the bread. Based on this information, they will like it or not like it, and then, based on this feeling, they will choose to buy it or not. That, of course, is the high-involvement attitude acquisition process described earlier.

The second clarification is that involvement is not dichotomous (a strict choice between very high and very low). Rather, it is a matter of degree. The low-involvement hierarchy occurs at the very low-involvement end when something is utterly of no consequence to the consumer. In the middle range, the high-involvement hierarchies occur, but with less intensity of processing. The emotional hierarchy still begins with affect, but at the middle range, it is likely to begin with a mood rather than a deep emotion. And the rational hierarchy is still relevant, except that instead of the extensive cognitions of the high-involvement condition, fewer cognitions will drive the affect. (See Figure 6.5.) This is why relatively lower-involvement products are advertised by citing only one or two features.

**FIGURE 6.5**

## Degrees of Involvement and Types of Attitude Hierarchy

## Consistency Among the Three Components

Although the three components develop in terms of hierarchies, they imply one another. A person tries to make the three components consistent and to maintain consistency among them. Certain cognitions inevitably give rise to certain affect and certain action tendencies, and vice versa.

The consistency can be related to two factors: valence and intensity. **Attitude valence** refers to favorable and unfavorable thoughts, feelings, and actions. Thus, favorable cognitions will be associated with positive affect, and unfavorable cognitions with negative affect, regardless of the sequence in which they might have arisen initially. Likewise, favorable action tendencies will be associated with positive affect and positive cognitions. If one of them needs to be modified, then the other components will need to be modified as well. For example, suppose that you have recently tried a new kind of multigrain bread, and after several uses, you don't like its taste anymore; then you will have to modify some cognitions (e.g., the grains don't really taste as good as they first did) and conation, too (e.g., I won't buy it in the future).

The second dimension on which the three components have to be consistent is intensity: the *strength* with which they occur. Some beliefs are strong; others are weak. Likewise, some feelings are deep; others are mild. Finally, there is strong action commitment toward some things and "take it or leave it" stance toward others. **Attitude strength** refers to the degree of commitment one feels toward a cognition or feeling or action. Just as on valence, so too on strength: the three components have to be balanced. Strong beliefs produce strong feelings and very committed action tendencies, and vice versa.

Since these three components must be mutually consistent, regardless of their initial sequence or hierarchy, they continue to mold one another. Accordingly, it is informative to depict them as mutually interdependent and mutually influential. Thus, in contrast to the previous hierarchy models, Figure 6.6 shows the arrows going in both directions among all three of the components.

## Three Attitude Components in Mutual Interdependence          FIGURE 6.6

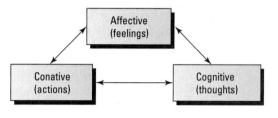

# Molding Customer Attitudes

The two dimensions of consistency—valence and intensity—have implications for how marketers may help mold customer attitudes. Since the three components—cognition, affect and conation—are mutually consistent, it is possible to mold an attitude (all three components) by first molding or changing any component. By attitude molding, we mean both helping to form an attitude where none existed before and changing a preexisting attitude. Accordingly, there are three avenues of attitude molding: (1) via cognitive change, (2) via affective change, and (3) via behavior change.

### Cognitive Route to Attitude Molding

To follow the cognitive route, the marketer provides an association (e.g., Brand A has property X) about the product or service; if the consumer accepts that association, then a brand belief is formed. Brand belief is a unit of thought that associates a brand with a property: for example, that Head and Shoulders brand of shampoo is really effective in eliminating dandruff or that Makino brand of hydraulic controls is very reliable. When a brand belief is formed, the cognitive component of attitude is formed. This component then produces compatible affective and conative components. The same process works in altering a cognition if the customer already had one; that is, if you give the customer new facts on something, he or she would likely change his or her old beliefs. Suppose you thought that a potato is fattening and has no good qualities. Now, suppose we were to tell you that it is fattening only when fried (as in potato chips or french fries) and not by itself and that, further, it has much-needed carbohydrates. This is likely to change your prior beliefs about potatoes (cognitive attitude *change*). As commerce grows on the Internet, a similar change in beliefs about security and privacy issues on the Internet is occurring among Internet users. They were initially wary of providing credit card and personal information to vendors on the Web. But with marketers providing information on secure encryption methods for transmitting credit card information and also posting statements protecting privacy of personal information, customer beliefs on these issues are undergoing change.

## Affective Route to Attitude Molding

The marketer may also mold attitudes by attempting to create an emotional connection with the consumer in the context of the product or service being promoted. (See the Window on Research box for an example of how antismoking ads shape adolescents' long-term attitudes toward smoking.) Domestic marketers of both household and industrial products could appeal to a sense of patriotism. Products such as soft drinks, colognes, and food are often presented with mood-inducing upbeat music. Some car models appeal to the customer's sense of exploration and fun, shown by the Saab campaign titled "Find your own road." For business customers, IBM had long played upon what came to be known as the FUD factor—fear, uncertainty, and doubt—promoting its computers as the safest bet.

Just as affect is generated by any of the above methods that result in evaluation of an alternative, research shows affect is generated by engaging in the processing activity involved in the evaluation—termed as process-induced affect. As cognitive effort involved in the processing of an alternative increases, negative process-induced affect is generated. Hence, between equivalent alternatives, consumers tend to choose the alternative that is less effortful to evaluate. This effect is intensified under time pressure and, hence, has implications on the ways in which marketers should present information to consumers for evaluation in a time-constrained world.[5]

# WINDOW ON RESEARCH

## What Makes Kids Think Smokers Are Cool?

Is it possible to change customers' attitudes toward something—a product, service, or category of persons—by giving them information on the undesirable aspects of it? Is it possible, for example, to modify adolescents' attitudes toward smoking and smokers by exposing them to antismoking messages in advertising? This question was researched in a pair of studies by attitude researchers Cornelia Pechman and S. Ratneshwar of the University of California at Irvine and the University of Florida, respectively.

In Study 1, Pechman and Ratneshwar showed seventh graders either antismoking advertisements, smoking advertisements, or advertisements not related to smoking. Each seventh grader saw only one type of advertisements, and research participants were randomly assigned to see one of these ads. The ads were embedded in a mock-up magazine, and the research was presented as an evaluation of the magazine.

After rating the magazines, respondents participated in a second study. A computer presented information about an unnamed person. This student (Student A) was described to all the respondents as having three habits: watches TV, rides a bike, and goes to the mall. The interesting twist on this research design was that half of the seventh graders in each of the three groups from Study 1 were told of only these three habits while the other half were additionally informed that Student A was a smoker. All the participants were told certain traits of Student A; the traits were a mix of positive and negative traits, and every seventh grader was told the same traits.

Did the viewing of the antismoking ads in Study 1 affect participants' perceptions of Student A when Student A was described as a smoker versus

## Conative Route to Attitude Molding

Finally, in this third approach, behavior is influenced directly, for example, by free product sampling or by giving incentives such as rebates, coupons, and discounted price. Once the behavior is influenced (e.g., the consumer buys a brand due to coupons), the cognitions and feelings will fall into place. Part of the appeal of this approach is that it can be easier to get someone to try a sample (or mandate that they do something) than to convince them to think or feel in a new way. "Just try it," marketers urge, confident that the experience will win the customer over. Risk-free trials are becoming more common in business markets. Marketers urge customers to try a product completely free for 30 days and if dissatisfied, the customer can return it, no questions asked. Netscape used this strategy to corner the browser market. Methods of influencing the customer's behavior directly are incentives, structuring the physical environment, business procedures, government mandates, and information structuring.

## Incentives

As already mentioned, special price promotions, coupons, rebates, and so on, are a frequently used means of inducing the desired behavior. Three cases of behavioral change due to incentives can be distinguished:

1. In low-involvement choices, such as for many supermarket items, where the customer has no preference for one brand or the other and hasn't thought much, he or she buys the brand on sale.

a nonsmoker? Pechman and Ratneshwar measured this by asking participants to rate Student A on such characteristics as smart, intelligent, healthy, grown-up, mature, good-looking, attractive, exciting, adventuresome, popular, has friends, and cool. They were also asked whether they (the seventh graders) might personally like the target. The results? Seventh graders who had seen the antismoking ads rated Student A much lower when Student A was described as a smoker than when he or she was described as a nonsmoker. This deterioration in the rating of Student A was much greater for the participants who had seen the antismoking ads than for those who had seen either the pro-smoking ads or the smoking-unrelated ads.

Each student saw only one type of ad and was asked to rate only one instance of Student A. Thus, each seventh grader was totally unaware of the experimental manipulation (that Student A was being presented in two different ways). Seventh graders were also unaware that the two studies were related (they were conducted by different research staff). Rather than seek reactions to the ads or to the idea of smoking, researchers measured consumer reactions to a person who happened to be a smoker or a nonsmoker.

This clever research procedure went to the heart of the issue in antismoking advertising: Can antismoking advertising shape adolescents' long-term attitude toward smokers so that they don't view smokers in attractive terms as the cigarette advertising purports to show? The answer, based on this research, is a reassuring yes.

**Source:** Adapted from Cornelia Pechman and S. Ratneshwar, "Advertising versus Prior Beliefs: Does Cigarette and Antismoking Advertising Alter Young Adolescents' Perceptions of Smokers?" *Report No.*, pp. 93–125, December 1993 (Cambridge, Mass.: Marketing Science Institute). Additional information available at http://www.tobaccofreekids.org.

2. If a product is not necessarily low in involvement, but two or more brands are comparable and the customer is equally likely to buy either of them, the price incentive would channel the behavior for many. For example, some people buy either Coca-Cola or Pepsi, depending on which brand is on sale during a particular week. This strategy may be even more common in business markets as companies switch between carriers such as FedEx and UPS depending on the deals available.

3. If the attitude is already favorable but not yet strong enough to impel action, the financial incentive gives that extra push; it tilts the customer preference toward the brand with the incentive. Cash rebates on cars are an example. A consumer doesn't buy just any car because of a rebate; rather, only the car he or she was already considering buying.

## Structuring the Physical Environment

The physical facility surrounding the customer may be designed to induce behavior directly, either as an impulse purchase or as subconscious behavior.[6] Examples of the former are the display of candies, magazines, or novelties in the checkout lines in the supermarket. Examples of physical environments designed to induce subconscious behaviors are store designs that are inviting, with pleasing colors, spaciousness of aisles, and lighting conditions.

In an experiment by consumer researcher Ronald E. Milliman, a supermarket played fast-paced music on certain days and slow-paced music on certain other days.[7] The days of fast and slow music were rotated so that each type of music was played on each of the weekdays (say, on Wednesday of one week fast music was played, and on Wednesday of the next week slow music was played, and the same with other weekdays or weekend days). Guess what happened to customer behavior? Compared to fast-paced music days, on slow-paced music days, customers themselves moved with a slower pace, spent more time in the store, and had a larger average bill! And all of this occurred without their being aware that they were doing so. This strategy of molding behavior is called **ecological design**.

On the Internet, the physical environment is created with the text, graphics, colors, and layout on the web site. An attempt is often made to recreate the store-feel on the web site by use of relevant colors, symbols, and layout. Companies such as Dell.com, a pure online company, compensate for the assistance provided by a store assistant by prominently displaying a toll-free number on every page in their web site.

## Government Mandates

An important means of eliciting some desired behaviors is *government mandates*.[8] Making consumption or disconsumption mandatory might be the only means available when (1) consumers lack the knowledge/competence to judge their own interests (e.g., automobile insurance policies and seatbelts are examples of mandated consumption, and a smoking ban is an example of mandated disconsumption) and (2) individual benefits are remote and are outweighed by collective public benefits, such as with recycling, observing speed limits, and using unleaded gasoline.[9] Among business customers, many workplace environmental and hiring practices are followed because of the presence of possible legal penalties.

## Business Procedures

Customer behaviors can also be modified by business procedures.[10] Marketers mold customer behavior by instituting business procedures that prescribe certain behaviors and by prominently bringing them to customers' attention. These behavioral prescriptions include store hours of operations, which force customers to shop during certain hours; "take a number" queue-management procedures; visibility of in-store surveillance devices; and dress requirements for participating as customers (e.g., shoes and shirts required to enter a store).

## Information Structuring

Finally information also can be structured in such a way as to channel the customer behavior toward the desired target. Some salesmen or retailers adopt the practice of selectively presenting information, such as declaring the item as being the last one in stock, or they display the store brand in conjunction only with those brands that would make the store brand seem a better choice. In the business context, information can be structured in presentations to prospective clients.

**Foot-in-the-Door versus Door-in-the-Face.** A particularly interesting variant of this information-structuring method is what has been called the twin procedures of foot-in-the-door and door-in-the-face methods. In the **foot-in-the-door strategy**, the customer is first asked for a small favor. Since the favor is really small, the customer typically complies, even if unenthusiastically. Later, he or she is asked for a somewhat bigger favor. Research has found that when a favor is presented after a small request, the bigger request is generally granted more often (or by more customers) than if the bigger request had been made at the outset. An example of this is charity organizations' seeking help from volunteers and donors. Typically, they begin by asking for small help, too small to be refused, and then follow it up by a subsequent appeal for larger assistance.

The opposite to the foot-in-the-door strategy is the **door-in-the-face strategy**. Here the first request is large, almost certainly to be refused (hence called "door-in-the-face"). This is then followed by a much smaller request. The assumption is that the customer would have denied the smaller request, except that he or she feels bad, maybe even a little guilty, about the first refusal. That feeling increases the chance of the second request being granted. Not much research has been done to identify the conditions under which one approach would be much better than the other.

# The Psychological Processes Underlying Attitude Change

The approaches to attitude molding or change are descriptions of what an external agent (such as the marketer) does to elicit the desired attitude changes. For example, the marketer provides information, presents emotion-arousing stimuli, structures the environment, imposes procedures or government mandates, and manages information. In response to such actions, certain *internal* (i.e., psychological) processes occur to produce these attitude changes. The effort to explain these processes has generated four major groups of theories:

1. Learning theories
2. Attribution theory
3. Cognitive-consistency theories
4. High- and low-involvement information processing

## Learning Theories

The four learning theories described in Chapter 4 explain how attitudes are *formed*. In addition, learning is a pathway to attitude *change*. These four learning theories are classical conditioning, instrumental conditioning, modeling, and cognitive learning.

Classical conditioning methods can be used to reposition a brand by associating it with new celebrities and situations. Thus, milk was repositioned recently from an image of being a children's drink to being an adult drink by advertising that paired it with adult celebrities. This learning method is the explanation for (a) creating new associations (i.e., beliefs) by presenting the brand in constant conjunction with desired celebrities, situations, or user groups; (b) influencing the affective component directly by presenting emotional stimuli, such as the Saab campaign mentioned earlier; and, (c) using the environmental structuring method, which was described earlier. IBM has successfully repositioned itself from being a "hardware provider" to a supplier of e-business solutions through an e-business ad campaign. It spent millions of dollars on the campaign and targeted businesspeople, IT decision makers, and their related influencers such as business partners and software developers. The campaign has helped establish IBM as the company that can help businesses move to the next generation of e-business with the help of its specialists in areas of strategy, digital branding and marketing, interactive design, Web application development, knowledge management, and system integration.[11]

Instrumental conditioning can also be used to change attitudes. For example, the marketer might offer frequent-use rewards on a previously disliked product or service. Also, giving a free sample induces initial behavior; the outcome of this behavior, if positive, is then instrumental in sustaining that behavior. If a computer manufacturer were to sell computers with a free one-year maintenance contract thrown in, this company would be more favorably viewed compared to the competitors vying for the same business.

Similarly, modeling can change attitudes. For example, fashions come and go, and then they reappear. Their fast diffusion upon reappearance is a prime example of attitude change by modeling. This method creates desired association (e.g., clothing with the grunge look is cool), and/or emotional arousal, such as the urge to wear clothes like rap musicians whose song lyrics feature themes of rebellion. In businesses, the lead customer of an organization usually prompts attitude change for other customers through a process of modeling. For example, once a new software has been adopted by a well-respected organization, other companies follow suit.

Finally, the cognitive-learning method is a very potent method to alter attitudes because of its capacity to engage the attitude holder in a conscious re-examination of his or her beliefs underlying his or her old attitude. Information from external sources and from one's own experience acts to change beliefs. Information is also generated by the customer himself or herself by a process of reasoning. This is called **inference making**. For example, a consumer may reason, "This pair of shoes is twice as expensive, so it must be more durable." Offshore software is usually subject to such inference making as well—"Since it is offshore software, it must be cheap." In this manner, based on some initial information and some logical expectations, the person generates further information internally in order to fill in missing information. Thus, whether from an external source or internally generated, new information influences our attitude.

## Attribution Processes

In Chapter 5, we described the attribution motivation as motivation to assign causes and motivation to explain things. In the context of attitude molding, attribution processes are set in motion when the customer first engages in some behavior that is incongruent with his or her initial attitude. The respondent then resolves the inconsistency between what his or her initial attitude supposedly was and the attitude-incongruent behavior. This forces the consumer to reread and reinterpret his or her attitude, bringing it more in line with the behavior.

A marketer can get the customer to engage in an attitude-incongruent behavior if the prior attitude is not overly negative or is only mildly unfavorable and the incentive given to engage in the behavior is not large. Under these circumstances, the inferred post-behavior attitude is likely to swing in the positive direction. This process is explained by psychologist Daryl J. Bem's **self-perception theory**, which proposes that sometimes people do not know or are unsure of what their attitudes really are. When queried about their attitudes, they reflect on their behavior and infer what their attitude must be. For their behavior, they could assign the causality to an external agent or to themselves—that they did it on their own volition. When they assign it to themselves, they consequently infer that their attitude must have been positive, even at the outset.

A marketing implication of this is that when consumers buy a less-preferred brand due to a coupon, their attitude toward the purchased brand will become more positive only if the coupon was for a small amount. If the coupon has a large face value, people tend to make the external attribution that they bought because of the coupon. If the coupon has a small face value, they tend to see the small savings as insufficient cause for purchase, so they assign the cause to their own volition, rereading their attitude as being more positive than it might otherwise have been.

Attribution theory provides explanations to the foot-in-the-door strategy and the door-in-the-face strategy to attitude change. In the foot-in-the-door strategy, the consumer complies with a small request first, even if somewhat unenthusiastically. Later, he or she attributes (i.e., credits) this accommodation to his or her own volition and, hence, to his or her own favorable attitude. Subsequently, when he or she is asked for a bigger favor, the re-interpreted positive attitude impels further accommodation. This accommodation, in turn, readjusts the attitude further.

In the door-in-the-face strategy, cognitive processes are set in motion following a behavioral act of the customer shutting the door in the marketer's face. Specifically, two theories can be advanced, both based on cognitive processes: One theory, advanced by consumer researchers John C. Bowen and Robert Cialdini, is called norm of reciprocity.[12] **Norm of reciprocity** refers to an expectation that an act of favor or concession toward someone must be returned by a comparable act of favor. In effect, the customer says, "If you are willing to give up something, then I will give up something." Thus, when the marketer makes a large request and then follows it up by a smaller request, he or she creates the impression that what was really needed was the large request; however, the marketer is making a big sacrifice in now making a substantially reduced request. The customer feels obligated, in turn, to make some concession and accede to that second request.

The other cognitive theory that can account for this phenomenon is the attribution theory. At the initial refusal of the large request, the customer embarks on self-scrutiny of his or her refusal behavior and surmises two possible reasons for refusal—that he or she, is too selfish or mean or is not a helpful person, or that the request was too unreasonable. The customer is not willing to consider that he or she is mean and, hence, reasons that he or she would have acceded to the request if it had been reasonable. In the wake of this self-serving attribution, one's helpfulness is reaffirmed in one's consciousness. A smaller request then challenges the person to prove that helpfulness, thus making it likely that the smaller request will be granted.

## Cognitive Consistency Theories

The general concept of cognitive consistency is that various cognitions people hold have to be consistent with one another. Inconsistency among ideas causes tension or drive, which people are moved to reduce by bringing the inconsistent cognitions into consistency. People accomplish this by changing one of the cognitions in order to make it consistent with another. Two specific theories based on the cognitive-consistency principle are Festinger's dissonance theory and Heider's balance theory.

### Festinger's Dissonance Theory

When you buy something, do you sometimes feel some uncertainty as to whether you made the right choice? If you do, this is quite normal—most customers experience it. In popular language, it is called **buyers' remorse**. In psychology, it is called **cognitive dissonance**. Psychologist Leon A. Festinger observed that the customer first makes a decision based on a certain evaluation of the object; next, post-decision doubt arises. Finally, the customer resolves that doubt by upgrading the evaluation in the positive direction.

This happens, according to **Festinger's dissonance theory**, because two cognitions are in dissonance: the cognition that the decision *has been* made (i.e., that the brand has been bought) and the cognition that the decision may not have been the best (i.e., the brand may not be the best choice). Assuming that the behavior cannot be undone (the purchased brand cannot be returned, or there is no certainty that another brand would be better), the only way to achieve consistency is to think that the decision is actually much better than previously realized (e.g., that the brand is actually a very good choice). That is why the post-decision evaluation becomes more favorable.[13]

One frequently observed customer behavior is that customers become more attentive to product or brand information after they have already bought the product. This is explained by the dissonance theory. Customers are looking for positive information to resolve their dissonance.

Rationalization to overcome dissonance is common in business, too. There is statistical evidence that 80 percent of acquisitions are deemed failures.[14] Yet, there are few companies that admit to an acquisition being a failure. They generally try to rationalize the whole decision with arguments and figures and make it appear as if the acquisition was one of the wisest decisions ever taken. So, also, is the case with the multimillion-dollar Enterprise Resource Planning (ERP) systems adopted by companies. Sometimes, the systems do not provide the company with the benefits expected, but companies rationalize their decision by stating that the systems are a must to be competitive in the twenty-first century.

## Heider's Balance Theory

According to **Heider's balance theory**, based on the principle of *cognitive consistency*, when a respected opinion leader endorses an issue not initially favored by a person, the person would either lower the opinion leader in his or her esteem or become more favorable toward the endorsed issue. If the issues are value laden and if the initial opinions are deeply negative, the endorser must be held in strong esteem to overcome the negative opinion.

For example, in business markets, consider a small company that buys machine tools from a Japanese supplier, believing that domestic machines are of poor quality. One day it learns that the industry leader whom it respects actually patronizes a domestic supplier. As a result, it stops respecting the industry leader, at least as far as the latter's opinion about the quality of the domestic supplier goes. Alternatively, of course, the firm could modify its opinion in favor of the domestic supplier.

## High- and Low-Involvement Information-Processing Modes

Within the cognitive explanation of attitude formation and change, the second mode is the information-processing mode. When customers are exposed to an ad or other marketing communications, they process the information in either of the two modes: central or peripheral routes. In the **central processing route**, the customer attends to and scrutinizes message *content* actively and thoughtfully. This has been termed *Elaboration Likelihood Model* (ELM). The consumer elaborates upon the message to examine and interpret it. Therefore, the quality of evidence presented to support the product claims plays a key role.

In contrast, in the **peripheral processing route**, the consumer attends to the message only cursorily and tends to make quick inferences by simply looking at the elements in the ad (such as the quality of music, the setting, the spokesperson). The *form* of the message determines consumer attitude more than does the message substance. The central route is followed in a high-involvement mode, and the peripheral route in a low-involvement mode. See the Window on Research box on central and peripheral routes to attitude formation.

Researchers J. L. Aaker and D. Maheswaran assessed the cross-cultural generalizability of the persuasion effects predicted by the above dual-process models. They conducted a comparative study using data sets from Hong Kong (collectivist culture) and the U.S. (individualistic culture), and found that the central and peripheral processing models are effective in predicting persuasion effects across cultures. Attitudinal and behavioral differences across cultures are explained by the differences in the perceived importance of heuristic cues across cultures. In collectivist cultures, opinions of others, or group norms (consensus-related heuristic cues), are more emphasized, and, hence, play a larger role in persuasion (compared to attribute-related information used in individualistic cultures). Therefore, even under high-motivation conditions, when faced with incongruent information from consensus and attribute-related cues, members of the collectivist culture tend

# WINDOW ON RESEARCH

## Central and Peripheral Routes to Attitude Formation

To test the occurrence of central and peripheral routes to attitude formation, psychologists Richard E. Petty, John T. Cacioppo, and David Schumann did an experimental research. They prepared an ad booklet containing 10 ads—some familiar, others new. The sixth ad was for a fictitious brand (brand name Edge) of shaving razor blades. This sixth ad was different in two versions of the booklet: In one booklet, the ad featured a famous endorser (e.g., "Professional athletes agree . . .") and five strong and product-relevant message arguments: new advanced honing method creates unsurpassed sharpness; special chemically formulated coating eliminates nicks and cuts; handle is tapered to prevent slipping; in tests, Edge blade gave twice as many close shaves; and unique angle placement of blade provides a smooth shave. The other version featured ordinary citizens and weak message arguments: floats in water without rusting; comes in various colors, sizes, and shapes; designed with bathroom in mind; in direct-comparison tests, Edge gave no more of a close shave than the competition; and can only be used once, but will be memorable. Half the respondents were given one version of the booklet, and the other half were given the second version.

Subjects were placed in either the high-involvement or low-involvement mindset (without the subjects realizing this) by telling them a cover story. Half of the respondents were told that the product would be available in their part of the country soon while the other half were informed the opposite. Furthermore, the first group was offered a free gift of a disposable razor while the other group was offered a free gift of an unrelated product. The first group was called a high-involvement group, and the second was a low-involvement group.

After they had looked through the booklet, respondents answered a questionnaire pertaining to their evaluation of the advertised brands. Logically, the strong-arguments ad produced a more favorable brand attitude, but the absolute power of the argument's strength and quality was not under research here. What was of interest was how the low- and high-involvement groups differed in their attitude. The findings here were most fascinating: Strong arguments produced a positive attitude both among the low- and high-involvement groups; however, the weak arguments produced a more favorable attitude among the low-involvement group compared to the high-involvement group! The reason, argue Petty and Cacioppo, is that the weakness of the weak arguments was transparent only to high-involvement respondents since only they processed the ad in the central route.

**Source:** Adapted from Richard E. Petty, John T. Cacioppo, and David Schumann, "Central and Peripheral Routes to Advertising Effectiveness: The Moderating Role of Involvement," *Journal of Consumer Research*, Vol. 10 (September 1993), pp. 135–146.

to use consensus–related information to form attitudes because they perceive these cues to be more important than the individual attribute–related information. However, when the attribute and consensus cues are congruent, the attribute–related information is used to form attitudes just as is expected in individualistic cultures.[15]

After initial attitudes are formed through exposure to ads, it is imperative that these attitudes must persist over time until the actual purchase decision is made. This is attitude persistence. **Attitude persistence** is more associated with high-involvement processing than low-involvement processing because the customer goes through a more thorough interpretation of the message in the high-involvement condition. However, since most advertising is processed in the low-involvement condition, it is important for marketers to find out the conditions under which attitude persistence occurs, even under conditions of low involvement. Research shows that peripherally processed cues, like brand names and celebrity endorsers, can lead to attitude persistence when they are related to the product category advertised. Hence, marketers need to be careful about choice of these cues in advertising.[16]

# Multiattribute Models of Attitude

In the cognitive route to attitude change, how do various cognitions or beliefs about a product or brand combine to produce a global attitude? This question is answered by multiattribute models. The **multiattribute models of attitude** suggest that overall attitude is based on the component beliefs about the object, weighted by the evaluation of those beliefs. There are three such models: the Rosenberg model, the Fishbein model, and the extended Fishbein model.

## The Rosenberg Model

Psychologist Milton Rosenberg developed a model based on cognitive consistency theory. According to the **Rosenberg model**, an object may be instrumental in helping us achieve certain values (things that we value). Our attitude toward that object is a function of the extent to which the object is instrumental in obtaining various values, weighted by the relative importance to us of those values:

$$A_o = \sum_{j=1}^{n} I_j \times V_j$$

where $A_o$ is the overall attitude toward the object, $I$ is the importance of value $j$, $V$ is the instrumentality of the object in obtaining value $j$, and $n$ is the number of values.

Consider a business customer's attitude toward buying from a minority or domestic supplier. To find the customer's attitude, add together each of the values this behavior satisfies (e.g., patriotism, encouraging the disadvantaged, rewarding the spirit of enterprise, nurturance, and so on), weighted by the importance of the value to him or her.

## The Fishbein Model

Martin Fishbein, a professor of psychology at the University of Illinois at Champaign-Urbana, tried to explain the formation of overall attitude by seeing the object as having a set of consequences, which could be desirable or undesirable. In the **Fishbein model**, attitude is the sum of these weighted consequences, where each consequence is weighted by the evaluation of that consequence (i.e., how good or bad that consequence is):

$$A_o = \sum_{i=1}^{n} B_i \times E_i$$

where $A_o$ is the overall attitude toward the object,

$B_i$ is the belief that object $i$ has a certain consequence,

$E_i$ is the evaluation of that consequence, and $n$ is the number of consequences.

As an example, assume a customer rates two Internet service providers, America Online and AT&T, as shown in Table 6.3. Using the data from the table, we can compute the customer's attitude toward each service provider by using Fishbein's formula:

$$A_{AOL} = 3(3) + 2(4) + -3(3) + -1(2) = 6$$

$$A_{AT\&T} = 3(5) + 2(3) + -3(3) + -1(5) = 7$$

In this example, the customer's attitude toward both services is positive, but it is more positive toward AT&T. Other customers would have different perceptions about the four attributes, as well as different values for the attributes so that they would have different attitudes.

## Example of Customer Attitudes: Two Internet Service Providers · TABLE 6.3

| | Evaluation of Attribute (Unlikely 1 2 3 4 5 Likely) | | |
|---|---|---|---|
| **Attribute** | **America Online** | **AT&T** | **Evaluation of Consequences** |
| 1. Connection will be established successfully every time. | 3 | 5 | +3 |
| 2. The connection will be established speedily. | 4 | 3 | +2 |
| 3. The connection will be dropped in the middle of the session. | 3 | 3 | −3 |
| 4. The price (monthly fee) will be high. | 2 | 5 | −1 |

(Very bad  −3  −2  −1  0  +1  +2  +3  Very good)

## Fishbein's Extended Model of Behavioral Intention

Psychologist Martin Fishbein has also proposed an augmented model of attitude, which emphasizes behavior. Fishbein's extended model measures attitudes toward behaviors and defines the role of these attitudes in determining behaviors. Figure 6.7 is a schematic of this model. In general, a person's attitudes and subjective norms about a behavior lead to a behavioral intention, and that behavioral intention is the impetus for a behavior.

To examine this model in more detail, begin at the upper left of Figure 6.7. A person's beliefs about the consequences of a behavior, multiplied by his or her evaluation of the consequences, generate an attitude.

This is similar to the previous multiattribute model, except that the model is not concerned with attitude toward the object per se, but with attitude toward a specific *behavior*. This distinction is important in Fishbein's view because we may hold multiple attitudes toward different behaviors for the *same* object. For example, suppose a city wants to build a new stadium for its football team and is holding a referendum on it. A person (1) may dislike the idea of a stadium, (2) may approve of the stadium but does not like the idea of campaigning for it, (3) may not like to contribute to it, or (4) may not mind contributing but does not want a mandatory tax levy. Thus, rather than measuring customer attitude toward the stadium (or the idea of having it in the city), Fishbein's model measures attitude separately toward each of these behaviors in relation to the stadium.

# FIGURE 6.7      Schematic of Fishbein's Extended Model

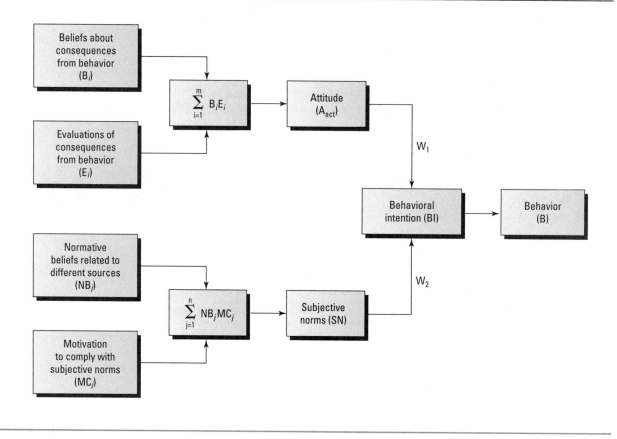

Along with attitude, a person's behavior depends on social norms, called **subjective norms,** or others' desires or expectations from us. Thus, someone may *personally* have an unfavorable attitude toward giving donations to an abortion clinic, but may end up doing so due to the expectations of his or her co-workers or neighbors. Subjective norms are the product of beliefs about others' norms or expectations multiplied by one's motivation to comply with these norms (see the bottom left of Figure 6.7). In a business context, a purchasing agent might disregard the plant engineer's wishes concerning the vendor choice because there may be no motivation to comply with the plant engineer's wish.

To find the person's behavioral intention, the person's attitude and subjective norms are each weighted; then the two are added together. (For a particular situation, the weight would be obtained through empirical research.) Finally, the model uses behavioral intention as an approximation of behavior. The reason is that attitude and subjective norms can only predict an intention; actual behavior also depends on the specifics of the situation. Table 6.4 summarizes the equations used in this model.

The distinctive advantage of Fishbein's extended model is that it accounts for social normative pressures as well as one's own internal beliefs about the consequences of the behavior. Explain to a teenager all you want about how utterly injurious to health smoking is, yet if the teenager's peers consider smoking cool, your fact-laden pleadings are probably going to fall on deaf ears.

Social norms influence business behavior as well. A firm buying legal and auditing services, for example, may be expected to sign a contract with the most prestigious firms

## Fishbein's Extended Model of Behavior                    TABLE 6.4

| B | = | $f[(BI) = f(A_{act})w_1 + (SN)w_2]$ |
|---|---|---|
| *where* | | |
| B | = | overt behavior (i.e., brand purchase) |
| BI | = | behavioral intention or purchase intention |
| $A_{act}$ | = | attitude toward purchase of brand |
| SN | = | subjective norm |
| $w_1$ and $w_2$ | = | empirically determined evaluation weights |
| | | |
| $A_{act}$ | = | $\sum_{i=1}^{m} B_i E_i$ |
| *where* | | |
| $B_i$ | = | belief that performance of a certain behavior brand purchase will lead to an anticipated outcome |
| $E_i$ | = | evaluation of an anticipated outcome, either a positive benefit or the avoidance of a negative consequence |
| $i$ | = | anticipated outcome 1, 2, ... m |
| | | |
| SN | = | $\sum_{j=1}^{n} NB_j MC_j$ |
| *where* | | |
| SN | = | subjective norm—the motivation toward an act as determined by the influence of significant others |
| $NB_j$ | = | normative beliefs—belief that significant others ($j$) expect the consumer to engage in an action |
| $MC_j$ | = | motivation to comply—the extent to which the consumer is motivated to realize the expectations of significant others ($j$) |
| $j$ | = | significant other 1, 2, ... n |

in town, even if, on objective performance, other firms are comparable or better. Thus, normative expectations mold, in important ways, customers' own internal desires for specific products and services. It is important for marketers, therefore, to understand social sanctions and rewards surrounding their products and services.

In a qualitative study of prostitute patronage and the resulting problem of AIDS in Thailand, researchers Belk, Ostergaard, and Groves challenge the underlying assumptions of Fishbein's beliefs-based extended model of behavioral intention. The study shows that although a high level of knowledge on HIV risks leads to a change in beliefs, it still does not affect actual condom use behavior among tourists and students in Thailand. This inconsistency between beliefs and behavior can be attributed to cultural values (pertaining to fidelity, romance), rituals (consumption of alcohol before visiting a brothel, unprotected sex), sex roles (culturally stronger for men than for women), and emotions in the Thai context.[17]

## Use of Multiattribute Models

Whether or not they are extended to include social norms, the multiattribute models of attitude have advantages over the models of global attitude, which could have been measured by a couple of simple scales such as dislike/like, favorable/unfavorable, and so forth. In the global attitude measure, we know only that the customer attitude is favorable or unfavorable, but we do not know why. In the multiattribute models, we know what beliefs underlie customer attitudes and how those beliefs are weighted to yield overall attitudes. Thus, multiattribute models *explain* attitudes, rather than simply index them. They add diagnosticity—the ability to diagnose why certain attitudes are the way they are.

Since the multiattribute models specify what underlies attitudes, they offer us a handle on how, in the cognitive mode, we can change or influence customer attitudes. According to the multiattribute model, we can change customer attitudes in three ways:

1. By changing a specific component belief, which can be done by changing the perception of the corresponding attribute level or associated consequence.
2. By changing the importance customers assign to an attribute or the evaluation of that consequence.
3. By introducing a new attribute (i.e., evaluation criteria) into customers' evaluation process.

These three strategies can be applied to the preceding example of America Online (AOL). Suppose AOL wants to influence a particular customer's attitude toward itself relative to AT&T. It can improve its connection success rate and communicate this improvement to the customer. (If its connection success rate is already comparable to that of AT&T, then it can communicate this to correct the current misperception.) Since, in the example, AOL has a superior rating on speed, it can try to emphasize the desirability of high speed, thus raising the speed's evaluation from the current rating of +2 to, say, +3. Finally, if AOL offers very good customer support, it could communicate that customer support should be an important consideration in choosing an Internet service provider. In the face of a competitive bid for business, an account executive from an advertising agency would use these three strategies to convince the customer that his or her agency is a better choice compared to the competition.

# The Functional Theory of Attitude

The process of forming attitudes does not fully explain differences in attitudes and in people's willingness to change them. Some of this variation is related to the reasons behind people's attitudes.

Psychologist Daniel Katz called this perspective the functional theory of attitude. According to Katz's theory, people hold certain attitudes (or come to acquire those attitudes) because the attitudes serve certain functions. Katz proposed four such functions: utilitarian, ego defense, value expressive, and knowledge. Table 6.5 provides the definitions and examples for each of the four functions.

## Applications of the Functional Theory

An understanding of these functions of attitudes helps explain why certain attitudes are resistant to change, as well as why attitudes about the same object, person, or brand vary from one customer to another. Someone may have a prejudiced attitude about immigrants, for example. This person might view immigrants as taking jobs away from native-born people (utilitarian function). Someone else may hold a favorable attitude toward immigrants because they provide a cheap source of labor, particularly for menial household chores, such as for babysitting or cooking and cleaning (again, a utilitarian function). Yet another person may hold a favorable attitude toward immigrants because they offer a window on another culture (knowledge function). Similarly, offshore software made in Singapore or India might be preferred by businesses since it is relatively cheaper than the U.S. software (utilitarian function).

| Functions of Attitudes | | **TABLE 6.5** |
|---|---|---|
| **Function** | **Definition** | **Example** |
| Utilitarian | Related to whether the object serves some utility | I prefer no-crease jeans because they are easy to care for. |
| Ego-defensive | Held to protect a person's ego | My income may not be high, but I can buy this luxury car. |
| Knowledge | Related to whether the object adds to a person's knowledge | I like to work with this salesperson because he spends a lot of time learning my needs and explaining how his company's products will help our company. |
| Value-expressive | Manifesting one's existing values | Every year I donate to the art institute and a local dance theater because the arts are a vital part of this community. |

Stereotypes themselves are attitudes toward a *category* of objects or persons. We hold them toward a category of people (e.g., Asian Americans) and toward a group of products, such as those made in Hong Kong. Customers use stereotypes to efficiently order the world around them—to give some structure to the world, to understand it in terms of what is what. Stereotypes serve the knowledge function of attitudes. For example, depending on your vantage point, you might hold the stereotype that immigrants from Russia are hard to understand, unsophisticated, and spendthrift people or that they are hard working, very intelligent, and successful career professionals. Traditionally, customers and marketers alike have stereotypes. For example, there has been a broad stereotype of Internet users as "computer geeks." Early business web sites were designed with these so-called "geeks" in mind. But as Internet demographics change and the Internet user resembles more and more the common American, it is necessary for Web content to cater to the regular customer and new adopter of the Internet. The regular customer has concerns about security of credit card information, privacy of personal data, shipping costs, disclosure of return policies etc. and web sites need to provide this information upfront. If businesses on the web do not move away from their stereotype of the Internet user, they will lose business.[18] Stereotypes are even more prevalent in business. American car makers once believed that the Japanese could not make good quality cars, and they lost the market. India is in the same situation today with respect to the software business. It was considered to be an avenue for basic coding of U.S. software, but now companies in India are competing against the U.S. software companies with their own software solutions. Once formed, stereotypes help you deal with newer instances. In other words, stereotypes as attitudes help you deal with the world efficiently (but not always accurately).

Even in modern societies, there are plenty of people who are unfamiliar or unaccepting of explanations provided by modern science and who look to scriptures or mythology for answers. To these people, Greek mythology or the Hindu scriptures are valuable sources of knowledge about the workings of the universe. In many founder-driven or family-owned companies, one sees the nonacceptance of modern management principles. This knowledge function of the scriptures accounts for a very favorable attitude these people hold toward the scriptures and toward the myths.

Thus, it is difficult to alter people's attitudes because they are often rooted in some critical function they serve for the individual. Only by understanding what function it is can we hope to mold that attitude in the desired direction.

# Applying the Theory of Attitudes: Planned Social Change

In every society, some individual behaviors are not in the long-term interests of the society as a whole. Examples include individuals not practicing contraception in high-population countries, producing excessive garbage, littering, driving beyond speed limits, and polluting the environment. Sometimes individual behaviors are not even in the long-term interest of the individuals themselves, even though these individuals may enjoy them at the moment. Examples include unhealthy eating, smoking, drinking and driving, and not taking preventive health measures, such as vaccinations or breast examinations for cancer.

Governments and other agencies that want to protect the societal and individual interests engage in programs designed to alter these individual behaviors. These programs are called planned social change programs. Planned social change refers to active intervention by some agency with a conscious policy objective to bring about a change in some social or consumption behavior among the members of a population. The agency implementing such programs is called a change agent, and people whose behavior is sought to be altered are called change targets. Marketing scholars Gerald Zaltman and Philip Kotler have argued that principles and tools of marketing can be applied to planned social change. This application is termed social marketing. Social Marketing is even more important in the social era. The Internet could promote unwanted customer behavior by allowing free trade of goods that may be subject to social controls in the offline world. For instance, selling cigarettes over the Internet allows minors to purchase them freely while simultaneously allowing purchasers to avoid high taxes that the government has been employing as a tool to discourage smoking.[19]

Planned social change programs utilize a number of strategies, and we review them here to understand how they relate to the attitude change models we have discussed in the preceding section. The social marketing literature has identified eight strategies of planned social change:

1. *Informing and educating*—This strategy consists of dissemination of objective information without drawing conclusions. Examples would be information about daily nutrition requirements or how to perform a breast self-examination. To promote energy conservation, utility companies offer to audit a business customer's production and office faculty and recommend steps to conserve energy.

2. *Persuasion and propaganda*—This entails a dramatic, and sometimes biased, presentation of information while stressing the recommended behavior. Government, especially in nondemocratic societies, has often used this strategy to get the cooperation of its people in nation building.

3. *Social controls*—This entails using group and peer pressure to adopt the group's values, norms, and behaviors. Examples include a blood drive by a work group in which co-workers would communicate their expectation of each co-worker, or a neighborhood campaign for fundraising or recycling, and so forth. With regard to the Internet, the United States favors self-regulation and is pressing the Better Business Bureau to develop a set of codes for advertising and marketing on the Internet. This is akin to using social controls to make users conform to a specified set of behaviors.

4. *Delivery systems*—This entails making it easy for individuals to engage in prosocial behavior. Examples include convenient placement of trash cans to prevent littering, mobile blood collection, or vaccination units, and more flexible public health clinic hours.

5. *Economic incentives*—This entails giving monetary incentives for prosocial behavior, such as giving tax credit for home insulation or use of a solar heating system, or even offering a cash incentive for undergoing a surgical procedure for birth control.

6. *Economic disincentives*—This strategy entails adding to the financial costs of continuing with the undesirable behavior. Examples include increased tax on cigarettes and liquor and increased fines for speeding and littering.

7. *Clinical counseling and behavior modification*—This entails psychiatric and psychoanalytic programs for individuals one-on-one, or programs of small-group therapy that bring about the unlearning of socially undesirable behaviors or learning of socially desirable behaviors. Examples include quit-smoking clinics and Alcoholics Anonymous, a group in which persons with severe drinking habits discuss their problems and seek social support in their effort to overcome their addiction.

8. *Mandatory rules and regulations*—The government may enact laws to restrict the undesirable behavior, specifying punitive measures for noncompliance. Examples include mandatory reproduction restriction, smoking prohibition in public buildings, and fire safety codes in building construction.[20]

## Choice of Strategy

How does a manager know which strategy is appropriate for a specific social change program in a specific population? This question is answered by considering a person's attitudes about the change program. Basically, a person's attitude may be positive or negative; for each case, moreover, the person may or may not be engaged in the desired behavior. Using these attitude and behavior statuses, customers can be classified into four groups, as shown in Table 6.6. A different strategy is appropriate for each of these groups.

| A Typology of Strategy Mix for Planned Social Change | | TABLE 6.6 |
| --- | --- | --- |

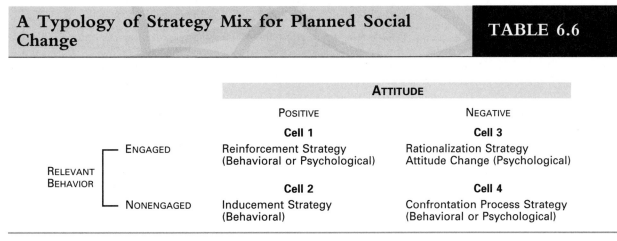

| | | **ATTITUDE** | |
| --- | --- | --- | --- |
| | | POSITIVE | NEGATIVE |
| **RELEVANT BEHAVIOR** | ENGAGED | **Cell 1**<br>Reinforcement Strategy<br>(Behavioral or Psychological) | **Cell 3**<br>Rationalization Strategy<br>Attitude Change (Psychological) |
| | NONENGAGED | **Cell 2**<br>Inducement Strategy<br>(Behavioral) | **Cell 4**<br>Confrontation Process Strategy<br>(Behavioral or Psychological) |

**Source:** Jagdish N. Sheth and Gary L. Frazier, "A Model of Strategy Mix for Planned Social Change," *Journal of Marketing,* Winter 1982, 46(1), pp. 15–26.

When attitude is positive and behavior is present (Cell 1), what is needed is a reinforcement strategy, a strategy that will reward the person for his or her behavior and encourage him or her to maintain the positive attitude. The reinforcement may be either behavioral (e.g., economic incentives for participation in the prosocial program) or psychological (e.g., praise).

If attitude is positive but behavior is absent (Cell 2), then an inducement strategy is needed. Basically, the behavior needs to be facilitated (since the attitude is already positive). Therefore, the social-change programs should try to remove whatever is holding back the behavior, such as some organizational, socioeconomic, time, or place constraints. Delivery systems become important, making it convenient for the customer to engage in the proattitude behavior.

When attitude is negative and yet the person is engaging in the desired behavior (Cell 3), a rationalization strategy is called for. This situation may occur due to lack of choice (e.g., wearing a helmet while riding a motorcycle because that is the law) or due to a temporary situation (e.g., carpooling due to a temporary shortage of fuel). Social change agents need to aid and stimulate the rationalization of the behavior; that is, the person tries to justify the behavior as desirable rather than merely necessary under the circumstances.

Finally, in Cell 4 is the situation where attitude is negative and the behavior is absent. Here, a confrontation process strategy is needed. Two types of confrontations are behavioral and psychological. In the behavioral confrontation, the change agency utilizes its power to block the current behavior, thus leaving the desired behavior as the only viable option. In the psychological confrontation, the change agency directly attacks the person's existing attitudes toward the desired behavior. Although the ultimate goal is to move change targets from Cell 4 to Cell 1, this may be too radical to attempt in one step. If so, the change targets may be moved first to Cell 2 or Cell 3 and then, in the next phase, to Cell 1.

The general lesson of the foregoing discussion is that it is important to understand the attitudes underlying a particular behavior and also to recognize the nature of the attitude-behavior gap. Depending on the direction of any discrepancy, the task may be to mold the attitude first or the behavior first. In either case, certain strategies may be more appropriate than others.

# Customer Attitudes and the Three Customer Roles

The concepts of attitudes discussed in this chapter apply to all three customer roles. Customers hold attitudes relevant to each of their roles (see Table 6.7). As users, for example, we like certain products and services (e.g., vegetables if we are health-conscious and power tools if we are do-it-yourselfers) and dislike others (e.g., cigarettes if we are nonsmokers). As payers, we have attitudes toward credit—some of us like it while others don't like it. Finally, as buyers, we like certain stores, vendors, and purchase methods while we dislike others.

In each of these foregoing instances, our attitudes exist in their three components. As users, our attitudes comprise beliefs we hold about products and services (e.g., "Toyota cars are reliable," or "Sun Microsystems have versatile connectivity"), have feeling toward them (e.g., "I love my Toyota," or "I like doing business with Sun Microsystems"), and manifest corresponding approach or avoidance behavior (e.g., "I will always buy a Toyota," or "My current preferred network service provider is Sun Microsystems"). Then, as payers, we have beliefs about specific credit cards, have favorable predispositions toward them, and we use certain cards and reject others. Finally, as buyers, we have beliefs about certain vendors, like some and dislike others, and patronize those we like and avoid those we dislike. For example, some of us may like to shop at warehouse club stores, believing that they offer good selection and price while others among us may avoid them because of the belief that they offer a low level of service. Fishbein's extended model points to the role of subjective norms—the expectations of significant others—and these norms also influence each of the three roles. As users, we are concerned about whether significant others will like what we use. We buy the cars our neighbors will not frown upon, wear clothing our friends and co-workers will admire, eat our vegetables to appease our parents, and (as business customers) fly economy class to comply with the company's new cost-saving measures. As payers, our debt behavior is shaped by parents' expectations during our teenage years when we first acquire our own credit cards. Furthermore, we are expected to spend money within a normative range for specific products; for example, our spouse would expect us not to be spendthrift, and gift recipients would expect us to spend at least a certain amount on the gift. Finally, subjective norms also influence our choice of vendors as well as our shopping strategy. For example, we shop at stores our friends and people of our

## Attitudes and the Three Customer Roles　　　TABLE 6.7

| | User | Payer | Buyer |
|---|---|---|---|
| Customer attitudes | • Users like products/services they use, and dislike products they avoid. | • Payers have attitude toward credit. | • Buyers like some vendors more than others. |
| Three-component-model | • Users hold beliefs about products and services, have feelings toward them, and manifest approach or avoidance behavior. | • Payers have beliefs, feelings, and behaviors toward specific credit cards and other forms of payment methods. | • Buyers have beliefs about the attributes of vendors, have feelings of like or dislike toward them, and patronize or ignore them accordingly. |
| Fishbein's extended model | • Subjective norms dictate customer use or nonuse of many products/services. | • Subjective norms influence a person's debt behavior and also spending norms for specific purchases. Tipping behavior. | • Subjective norms influence one's choice of vendors. Government has list of approved vendors. |
| High- and low-involvement | • Users are very involved with some products, exhibiting fanatic consumption. | • Payers differ in their concern about what happens to the money they pay. | • Some buyers are highly involved, and others are not. |

social class shop at. We don't shop around too much if we have a friend along. And government-funded projects specify a list of approved vendors.

Involvement, an attitudinal state of the customer, also is manifested in all three roles. As users, we are highly involved in some products and services, exhibiting fanatic consumption of these—for example, a collection of art works. As payers, we differ in our concern with what happens to the money we give. Some parents, for example, might give their children an allowance and not worry about how they spend it while other parents may want to keep a close eye on how that money is being spent. As donors to charity organizations, we might be uninterested in the exact uses of that money, or we might want to be on the board of directors so that we may influence the distribution of funds. Finally, as buyers, we might shop disinterestedly, or alternately, we might enjoy shopping or take keen interest in making the most judicious purchase. As business customers, we might routinely reorder from the existing vendor, or we might diligently search for new vendors.

These examples cover only the main concepts of attitude. Other concepts discussed in this chapter—the multicomponent model, attribution processes, cognitive dissonance and consistency, and the functional theory of attitude—also are relevant to the three roles. For example, as a payer, we might like and use a particular credit card simply because that card has offered us a higher credit limit, even though we would never even come close to exhausting the much lower limit of a competing card; we may do so because it serves our ego-defense function. Or we might prefer a credit card because of its higher prestige (value-expressive function). We leave it to you to reflect on and tease out the relevance of these and other attitude concepts to the three customer roles.

# Summary

This chapter dealt with the concept of attitude and how it applies to customer behavior. Attitudes were described as customers' likes and dislikes toward various products and services and their predispositions to respond to them (approach or avoid them). These attitudes have three components—cognition (thoughts), affect (feelings), and conation (actions). Customers acquire these three components in a specific sequence, and three such sequences were identified: rational, emotional, and low-involvement. Because the three components usually exist in harmony (i.e., consistency), changing any one of them would usually drive a change in others. Accordingly, we have identified three routes to attitude change: the cognitive, affective, and conative routes. In the conative route, behavior is shaped or encouraged by such means as incentives, information structuring, and regulation. Corresponding thoughts and feelings then follow to become consistent with the shaped behavior.

Various psychological processes underlie attitude change. First, attitudes are changed when we learn something; accordingly, all four methods of learning (classical conditioning, instrumental conditioning, modeling, and cognitive learning) also become methods of attitude change. Attitudes change because humans have an innate need for attribution of causes (i.e., to understand causality) and seek cognitive consistency (e.g., Heider's balance theory, Festinger's dissonance theory). Furthermore, low- and high-involvement learning processes lead to attitude change in very different manners.

Computational models of attitudes seek to capture the arithmetic of how object beliefs (i.e., cognitions) combine to form an overall attitude or evaluation of the object. Two major models have been developed by Rosenberg and Fishbein. Fishbein's model also has an extended form, which adds a normative component to the basic model's cognitive component. Together, these predict a customer's behavioral intention.

Next, we discussed a functional theory of attitude. Advanced by psychologist Daniel Katz, this theory expounds on the motivational reasons why customers hold an attitude at all. They hold it, according to Katz, because these attitudes serve one or more of the four functions: utilitarian, value-expressive, ego-defense, and knowledge. Applications of these functions for customer behavior were discussed.

These attitude concepts have been applied to the task of planned social change. Concerned with changing people's behaviors so that the acquired behaviors are in the interests of the customers themselves or society at large, planned social change can use diverse strategies of social marketing. The appropriateness of these strategies depends on the nature of attitude-behavior gaps.

In the last section, we highlighted the applicability of various attitude concepts covered in the chapter to each of the three customer roles and the market values they seek.

# Key Terms

Affect 203

Attitude Hierarchy 203

Attitude Molding 207

Attitude Persistence 216

Attitude Strength 206

Attitude Valence 206

Attitudes 200

Beliefs 201

Brand Belief 202

Buyers' Remorse 213

Central Processing Route 214

Change Agent 222

Change Targets 222

Cognitive Dissonance 213

Conation 203

Descriptive Beliefs 203

Diagnosticity 220

Door-in-the-Face Strategy 211

Ecological Design 210

Ego-Defense Function 220

Emotional Hierarchy 204

Evaluative Beliefs 203

Festinger's Dissonance Theory 213

Fishbein Model 216

Fishbein's Extended Model 217

**Foot-in-the-Door Strategy** 211

**Heider's Balance Theory** 214

**Inference Making** 212

**Knowledge Function** 220

**Learning Hierarchy** 204

**Low-Involvement Attitude
Hierarchy** 205

**Multiattribute Models of
Attitude** 216

**Norm of Reciprocity** 213

**Normative Beliefs** 203

**Peripheral Processing Route** 214

**Planned Social Change** 222

**Process-Induced Affect** 208

**Rosenberg Model** 216

**Self-Perception Theory** 212

**Social Marketing** 222

**Subjective Norms** 218

**Utilitarian Function** 220

**Value-Expressive Function** 220

# Discussion Questions and Exercises

1. What are consumer attitudes? What are the two primary uses of the concept of consumer attitudes in marketing? How can marketers do a better job of satisfying customer needs by understanding customer attitudes? Since attitudes are learned predispositions to respond (i.e., engage or not engage in a specific behavior), why don't marketers and market researchers simply measure purchase response (i.e., behavior) and forget about attitudes?

2. How does the central mode of attitude processing differ from the peripheral mode? What differences in attitude might accrue as a result of processing in one way or the other? Provide one example of central processing being stressed by a company in its communications and another example of a company where peripheral processing is stressed. Under what conditions should a marketer select one route versus another in attempting to change consumer attitudes?

3. Put the three-component model of attitude to work by providing three measurement statements for each component of the model for the following three objects: (a) Nike running shoes, (b) surfing the World Wide Web, and (c) McDonald's fast-food restaurants.

4. Describe an attitude you recently developed toward a product or service in terms of classical conditioning, instrumental conditioning, modeling, and cognitive learning theory. Give one example of your acquiring an attitude in each of these four learning modes.

5. Assume the role of strategic marketing manager for a new line of South Korean automobiles. You are very familiar with the problems that your predecessors, such as Hyundai and Kia, have had in creating a high-quality automobile image among U.S. customers. In South Asia and Europe, your new line has tested very well, and you are confident that your cars will succeed in the United States given that you can properly shape U.S. attitudes toward Korean auto imports. Given your knowledge about the attitudes of American consumers toward their cars, which of the three alternative routes to attitude molding will you take in your promotional campaign? Why have you chosen this route? Briefly describe the types of attitudes you hope to invoke in your target customers.

6. Despite the raging war against the tobacco industry and the generally negative sentiments toward cigarette smokers, a lot of people continue to smoke. Based on the model of planned social change presented in this chapter, evaluate various strategies and identify the ones you would recommend for an antismoking marketing program of action.

# Notes

1   Sandra Swanson, "More than Technology: User Attitudes Make a Difference," *InformationWeek*, February 26, 2001, p. 48. Reprinted with permission. Permission conveyed through Copyright Clearance Center, Inc.

2   Gordon W. Allport, "Attitudes," in C.A. Murchinson, ed., *A Handbook of Social Psychology* (Worcester, Mass.: Clark University Press, 1935), pp. 798–844.

3   Qimei Chen and William D. Wells, "Attitude Towards the Site," *Journal of Advertising Research*, September–October 1999, pp. 27–38.

4   Neil Whitehead, "Terms of Engagement," *Brand Strategy*, 09/01/2000.

5   Ellen C. Garbarino and Julie A. Edell, "Cognitive Effort, Affect, and Choice," *Journal of Consumer Research*, 24, September 1997, pp. 147–58.

6   See Philip Kotler, "Atmospherics as a Marketing Tool," *Journal of Retailing* 49 (Winter 1973–74), pp. 48–64; Robert Donovan and John Rossiter, "Store Atmosphere: An Environmental Psychology Approach," *Journal of Retailing* 58 (Spring 1982), pp. 34–57.

7   Ronald E. Milliman, "Using Background Music to Affect the Behavior of Supermarket Shoppers," *Journal of Marketing* 46 (Summer 1982), pp. 86–91; "The Influence of Background Music on the Behavior of Restaurant Patrons," *Journal of Consumer Research* 13 (September 1986), pp. 286–89. Also see, Charles S. Areni and David Kim, "The Influence of Background Music on Shopping Behavior: Classical versus Top Forty," in *Advances in Consumer Research*, Leigh McAlister and Michael L. Rothschild, eds., 20 (Provo, Utah: Association for Consumer Research, 1993), pp. 336–40; James J. Kellaris and Robert J. Kent, "The Influence of Music on Consumers' Temporal Perceptions: Does Time Fly When You Are Having Fun?," *Journal of Consumer Psychology* 1, No. 4 (1992), pp. 365–76.

8   Jagdish N. Sheth and Banwari Mittal, "A Framework for Managing Customer Expectations," *Journal of Market-Focused Management* 2 (1996), pp. 137–58.

9   See Robert E. Krapfel, "Marketing by Mandate," *Journal of Marketing* 46 (Summer 1982), pp. 79–85; Jagdish N. Sheth, *Winning Back Your Market: The Inside Stories of the Companies that Did It* (New York: John Wiley, 1985), pp. 59–72.

10  Jagdish N. Sheth and Banwari Mittal, "A Framework for Managing Customer Expectations," *Journal of Market-Focused Management* 2 (1996), pp. 137–58.

11  Sam Albert, "A New, Nimbler IBM?," *Midrange Systems*; Spring House; September 4, 2000, p. 46; Ruth Stevens, "How IBM Made Its Branding Campaign Pay Off," *Business Marketing*, June 1, 1998.

12  John C. Mowen and Robert Cialdini, "On Implementing the Door-in-the-Face Compliance Strategy in a Marketing Context," *Journal of Marketing Research* 17 (May 1980), pp. 253–58.

13  Leon A. Festinger, *A Theory of Cognitive Dissonance* (Evanston, Ill.: Row, Peterson, 1957).

14  Charles A. O'Reilly III and Jeffrey Pfeffer, *Hidden Value: How Great Companies Achieve Extraordinary Results With Ordinary People* (Harvard Business School Press, 2000).

15  Jennifer L. Aaker and Durairaj Maheswaran, "The Effect of Cultural Orientation on Persuasion," *Journal of Consumer Research*, 24, (December 1997), pp. 315–28.

16  Jaideep Sengupta, Ronald C. Goodstein, and David. S. Boninger, "All Cues Are Not Created Equal: Obtaining Attitude Persistence Under Low Involvement Conditions," *Journal of Consumer Research*, 23, March 1997, pp. 351–61.

# CHAPTER 7

## Researching Customer Behavior

## Internet Tracking Helps to Create Value for Customers

Internet portal Yahoo! records every click made by every visitor, accumulating about 400 billion bytes of data per day—the equivalent of 800,000 books. Direct marketing giant Fingerhut has 4 million names of repeat customers and keeps information on 1,000 attributes for each of these customers. As product differentiation blurs in the market, companies are using technology to identify patterns in customer transactions so as to customize products to customer preferences. This technology enables web sites to recognize the customer as he or she revisits the web site, suggest recommendations based on their own previous purchases and purchases by similar customers, and target them with appropriate banner advertising messages and email promotional offers. For example, Clinique.com interviews customers about their natural hair color and their tendency to sunburn among other information collected, and uses this data to recommend the right products to customers. Over half a million users have registered at the Clinique.com site. Marketers are using transaction and click-stream data to build relationships with customers. With competition just a click away, researching customers is helping online businesses create value for the customer and for the business.[1]

In a competitive environment, with mounting pressures on firms to do more with less, the firms that will survive will be those that research and understand their customers well, the values customers are seeking, and how they judge and find those values in the marketplace. Thus, researching customer behavior is critical for marketing success. (See Figure 7.1 for the conceptual framework.)

This chapter introduces the means by which marketers conduct research to understand customer behavior. It begins by describing the many methods available for conducting the two broad categories of research:

1. *Qualitative*—measuring in terms of general descriptions and categories.
2. *Quantitative*—measuring in terms of numbers.

We also describe research methods for investigating the ways people process information and techniques for simulating customer behavior. The chapter then covers secondary research, which uses existing data such as that available in a library or database. We explore some recent innovations in marketing research, specifically applications of virtual reality and the collection of data on the Internet. The Internet is being used for research by marketers and researchers due to increased accessibility (depending on the target segment) via e-mail; speed of communication and convenience of the medium. With the growth in the number of net users, an estimated 30 to 40 percent of marketers are expected to use on-line primary research in 2005, and online methods are projected to generate $3.1 billion (50 percent) of revenue for marketing research firms.[2] Finally, we consider the ways in which customer behavior research can shed light on the three customer roles.

## Conceptual Framework                                         FIGURE 7.1

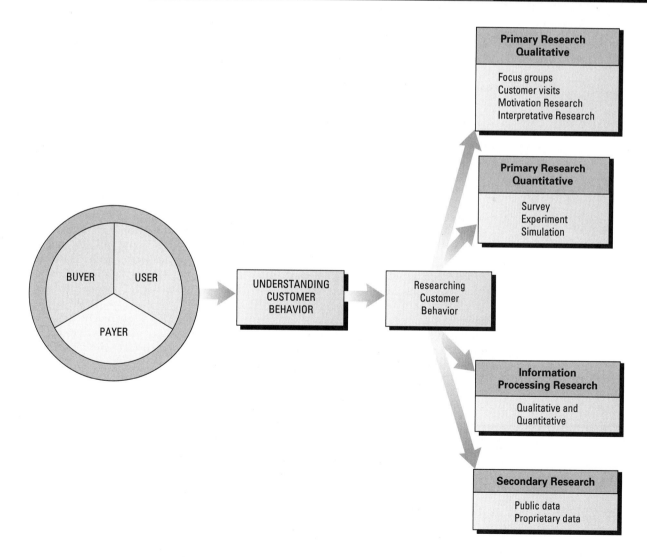

# Qualitative Research

The basic distinction of **qualitative research** is that qualitative methods do not ask the customer to limit his or her answers to preassigned response categories. The answers are verbal rather than numerical, and the respondent is requested to state the answer in his or her own words. As a student, when you answer a true/false or a multiple-choice question, you are providing a quantitative answer. But when you answer an essay question, you are providing a qualitative answer. In fact, the researcher or marketer may not even know what the possible answers might be; and, indeed, that is why the researcher chooses a qualitative research approach. This approach allows researchers to discover consumers' consumption values, motives, attitudes, opinions, perceptions, preferences, experiences, actions, and future intentions.

Several specific methods or techniques are available for implementing qualitative research. These include focus groups, customer visits, motivation research, and interpretative research.

## Focus Groups

With **focus groups**, a small group of customers is assembled in a room, and a moderator steers the group discussion along certain questions of interest to the marketer. The group members can range in number from 6 to 15 and are generally chosen by **convenience sampling** (a method in which respondents are recruited based on convenient availability) but are prescreened to represent the target market. The moderator is a trained marketing research professional, and he or she generally uses a discussion guideline (a list of issues to probe). A good moderator endeavors to avoid biasing the opinions expressed by the group members. He or she also tries to ensure that no one member dominates the discussion, that all group members get a chance to have their say, and that the discussion stays focused on the topic at hand. The discussion room is generally a specially equipped room with a one-way mirror on one of its walls. Behind the mirror, client companies' executives sit and watch the group session. Also, the focus group is generally audio- and/or video-recorded for later review and analysis of data. Focus groups are often used both in business and household markets, to understand customers' worldview about the topic at hand.

Since focus groups are not a statistical sample of the target population, the findings of focus group research are not projectable to the entire population of target customers. Rather, focus groups offer a window into the customer's mind, bringing to surface things the marketer may not have known about the consumer and his or her view of the product. What the marketer discovers through focus groups (and other qualitative research methods) he or she can then use to design specific questions for a subsequent large-scale quantitative research study. Thus, the principal utility of focus group research is to explore the customer behavior about which marketers didn't know much to begin with. In this role, focus groups have several applications:

- Generating ideas for product improvements or new products. A discussion of the problems customers currently face in using the product or of how the product can be made more convenient in use can suggest new directions for product research and development (R&D). Some customers use the product innovatively; conversations with these customers about their use of the product can also suggest new product uses.
- Understanding customer perceptions of competing brands. A firm can display its own brand (keeping the sponsor's identity unrevealed) and competing brands and engage the customer group in comparing these.
- Testing new concepts. New product concepts, packaging prototypes, new distribution channels, new brand names, and, certainly, advertising photo boards or finished commercials can all be presented to focus-group members for their feedback.

"Imagine a focus-group discussion without the participants really present in the same room. This is focus group *online*." The Internet facilitates a virtual meeting of discussion groups in Internet "chat rooms" in real time through services like AOL, EarthLink, MSN, etc. Depending on the topic of the discussion, participants for the focus group are recruited from different usegroups or from specific web sites. The moderator and participants log in at a prespecified time, and the focus group is conducted as it would be in a regular research setting—the only difference being that the participants are in their own homes or workplaces—continents apart from each other.

The advantages of online focus groups compared to its conventional counterpart are time savings, costs savings, and the ability to bring together customers or users from around the world. The focus group can also be made extremely interactive by presenting new product concepts or advertisements, using realistic computer graphics as opposed to a paper-and-pencil concept description. (This feature of computer graphics can be utilized in face-to-face discussion groups as well.) Disadvantages of online focus groups include lack of face-to-face interpersonal dynamic that could sometimes lead to nonresponse. There is also a greater reliance on verbalizable responses, and hence, it is difficult for marketers to get a feel for the emotional responses generated by the product concept or advertisement.[3]

Online focus groups constitute an interesting use of information technology. However, as is true with any new application of a technology, consumer researchers should be aware of some still-unanswered questions about this method. Is an online focus-group moderator able to establish rapport with and communicate trust to the discussion group members? In comparison to face-to-face focus groups, do online respondents assume that they are being exposed to a large number of online users, or do they assume anonymity because no one can identify them? Finally, does such anonymity bring forth more candid or less candid responses? As experience with the method grows, these questions will be answered.

## Customer Visits

Any activity that entails visiting a consumer or a customer, observing him or her, and discussing his or her experience with the product is a kind of customer visit. However, we describe the customer visit in terms of the specific program of research that was designed, implemented, refined, and documented by marketing researcher Edward F. McQuarrie of Santa Clara University.[4]

A typical program involves visiting a dozen or so customer firms to hold interviews with customers and observe each customer's experience with the supplier's product. The visits are made by cross-functional research teams comprising people from design, production, logistics, and marketing. (Thus, the research task is not delegated to the marketing research department.) The visits are closely planned, with a thoughtful selection of the team members, the sample of customer firms, and the personnel to interview. Specific objectives for the visit are developed and communicated to the customer firms ahead of time. The purpose of the visit is solely to learn about the customer's experience with the product and requirements, not to sell anything.

During the visit, the vendor research team holds interviews with design engineers, production engineers, shop floor supervisors, assembly workers, craftspeople, and others who handle the vendor's product, as well as with purchasing managers and others who participate in the selection of suppliers. These interviews are loosely structured dialogues. However, the team uses a discussion guide that identifies areas of questioning. In addition, the vendor research team takes plant tours in order to observe firsthand the vendor's product in use.

## Advantages of Customer Visits

The program offers several advantages. First, it affords a good opportunity to understand customer requirements. Face-to-face interactions between the customer's and vendor's engineers help to develop the specs jointly so that the product may better fit the overall customer requirements and may be easier for the vendor to produce.

A second advantage of a face-to-face visit is that it enables the technical staff of the vendor firm to understand and respond to the customers' thought world. Typically, vendors and customers live in different thought worlds, even if their technical specialty is the same. A face-to-face visit helps to align the thought world of a design-and-production engineer (revolving around bits, bytes, and baud rates in a computer-manufacturing company) to the thought world of a customer engineer that is more end-use or task oriented (for example, the speed of data processing or the format of the printed report).

Furthermore, a customer visit makes the technical personnel more market/customer oriented because they understand customers' needs as well as their psychology firsthand, rather than learn about them indirectly from reading the market research report done by the marketing department or an outside research firm. Here is what an R&D manager had to say about the benefits of customer visits:

> There is a lot I get out of visiting customers. I get unfiltered information. In addition, I have a different set of eyes; I can hear things that are different from what my marketing and sales counterparts hear. The customer is the one who has the information I need to design products.[5]

Certain things can be learned, not by interviews, but only by observing the product as it is handled or used at the customer firm, and, furthermore, only through an observation done by a person directly involved with the design and/or production of a particular aspect of the product. In fact, such potential learning opportunity may be missed not only by a market research specialist but also by the user-customer him- or herself. For example, only a logistics and packaging person from the vendor firm may, while observing how the firm's product is being unloaded and handled by the customer, identify a better way of packaging and/or shipping the product. That is why a program of customer visits includes a plant tour by a cross-functional team from the supplier organization.

Obviously, the utility of a program of customer visits varies from industry to industry, and from one business firm to another. But one of the factors that will determine its usefulness is the skill with which these visits are planned and the investment the supplier makes in establishing mutual *trust* with the customer personnel before and during customer visits.

## Applications of Customer Visits

This type of research program is primarily suited to business-to-business marketers (as opposed to households), and it is especially beneficial to the producers and vendors of high-tech or otherwise complex products (such as computers, communication networks, defense equipment, aircrafts, health insurance, and delivery systems). Currently, it is practiced by such firms as Hewlett Packard, IBM, Sun Microsystems, and CIGNA Insurance.[6]

It should be noted that customer visits are *discovery* research. It is not necessary where customer requirements are quite simple, stable, and well met by current offerings (i.e., where there is not much to be discovered). And, it is not suitable for *confirmatory* research where the objective may be to test the acceptability and profitability of, say, a new product concept.

## Motivation Research

Motivation research (MR) is research directed at discovering the reasons (i.e., motives) for a person's behavior. In customer behavior, motivation research is conducted to find out the conscious or subconscious reasons that motivate people to buy or not to buy a particular product, service, or brand, or to patronize or avoid a store, or to accept or reject a marketing communication. Since most motivation research entails the use of the techniques of clinical psychology, some researchers reserve the term MR only for these techniques. However, MR is defined by the research purpose (namely, to discover customers' reasons for particular marketplace responses), not by the research technique. Accordingly, as shown in Table 7.1, a variety of techniques are useful for MR.

| Techniques for Motivation Research | TABLE 7.1 |

**DISGUISED?**

|  |  | YES | No |
|---|---|---|---|
| **STRUCTURED?** | Yes | Disguised Structured Techniques | Nondisguised Structured Techniques |
|  | No | Disguised Nonstructured Techniques | Nondisguised Nonstructured Techniques |

## Nondisguised-Structured Techniques

The research design may make the research purpose obvious and may seek response along prespecified response categories. Such designs are called nondisguised-structured techniques. To infer someone's reasons for a particular marketplace behavior, consumer researchers often ask for opinions or attitudes on pertinent topics. For example, to understand customers' preferences among various car makes, especially between the domestic and foreign makes, you can simply ask questions concerning people's beliefs about buying American, by using such rating statements as: American goods are of equal or better quality than foreign-made goods; buying foreign automobiles is bad for the American labor force, and so on. The answer categories are prestructured, such as agree/disagree or true/false. Thus, neither is the purpose of the study disguised, nor is anyone looking for unexpected reasons or explanations of behavior. Rather, we simply want to know the proportion of customers to whom a particular (preknown) reason or motive applies. Political polls and referendums are also common examples of this technique.

## Nondisguised-Nonstructured Techniques

With other techniques, called nondisguised-nonstructured techniques, the purpose of the study is not disguised, and the consumer response categories are not predetermined. The questioning is open-ended and broad, encouraging the respondent to supply whatever answer he or she thinks fit. This set of methods is known as unstructured interviews, qualitative interviews, nondirective interviews, and so on. The researcher simply names a broad topic and encourages the respondent to talk about whatever he or she knows, thinks, and feels about the topic. For example, customers may be asked to talk about cars to learn about how individual customers relate to automobiles and what place automobiles occupy in their lives.

## Disguised-Structured Techniques

In disguised-structured techniques, the real intent of the question is disguised, but the response categories are provided. The question is one whose answer is not supposed to be known to the respondent so he or she is supposed to guess the answer. It is in the guessed answer that the respondent unknowingly reveals his or her own biases toward the marketer's product or brand. For example, a researcher might ask, "Of the following, who is most likely to own a motorcycle: (a) a professor, (b) a student, (c) an actor, or (d) a mechanic?" The respondent's answer will reveal the image he or she holds of a motorcycle owner. The Window on Research box describes a classic study that illustrates this method well. In this study, researcher Mason Haire tried to understand consumers' perceptions of instant coffee in the 1940s soon after its introduction. Using projective techniques that allowed respondents to describe the personality of the person using instant coffee, he found that the instant coffee user was considered to be lazy, not fond of cooking, and a poor housewife.

# WINDOW ON RESEARCH

## Why Housewives Didn't Buy Instant Coffee: The Mason Haire Classic Study

When the Nescafé brand of instant coffee was introduced in the 1940s, consumer response was less than enthusiastic. When asked in a conventional questionnaire whether they (the consumers) liked instant coffee, and if not, why not, a typical response was that they did not like its taste. This answer would seem an obvious and logical answer, so it was unclear whether it represented a true answer or whether it was simply a sensible-sounding answer respondents thought appropriate to justify their rejection of the brand. To find out more about customers' real motives behind the rejection of the brand, the firm sought the help of an MIT psychologist, Mason Haire.

Haire prepared two shopping lists that were identical except that one had Nescafé Instant Coffee listed on it and the other had Maxwell House Coffee (drip ground). The researchers showed one list to a random sample of consumers and showed the other list to another, matching sample. Each group was unaware of the existence of the other list. The respondents were asked to guess the type of person whose shopping list it was and describe the personality of that person.

The responses were verbal and elaborate. Here are two of the responses about the woman who bought Maxwell House coffee:

> I'd say she was a practical, frugal woman. She must like to cook and bake. . .
> She is probably quite set in her ways. . .
> [The purchase of Del Monte canned peaches indicates that] she may be anxious to please either herself or members of her family with a treat. She is probably a thrifty, sensible housewife.

Statements describing the woman who bought Nescafé instant coffee included these conclusions:

> This woman appears to be either single or living alone. I would guess that she had an office job. . .
> She seems to be lazy because of her purchases of canned peaches and instant coffee.
> I think the woman is the type who never thinks far ahead. . .
> The girl may be an office girl who is just living from one day to the next in a sort of haphazard sort of life.

## Disguised-Nonstructured Techniques

In the set of techniques called disguised-nonstructured techniques, the research purpose is not apparent to the consumer, nor are the response categories prestructured. The general characteristic of these techniques is that the respondent is given a fairly vague stimulus and is then asked to interpret that stimulus. Since the stimulus is vague, interpreting it requires that the research subject project himself or herself into the stimulus situation. These techniques are, therefore, called projection techniques. From this self-projection, the researcher is able to infer a customer's motives for a particular marketplace behavior. This set of techniques is especially helpful in uncovering motives that respondents would

Note that the inclusion of instant coffee on the list influenced the inferences drawn from other items (e.g., canned peaches) as well. Thus, many of the attributions made to the shoppers with the list were not even acknowledged as coming from the inclusion of instant coffee. Thus, the techniques help surface stereotypes that would otherwise not be acknowledged in a straightforward questionnaire. Haire coded the results of these interviews to indicate whether responses were made by women who had instant coffee in their own homes. The following table summarizes Haire's findings:

| THE WOMAN WHO BUYS NESCAFÉ IS SEEN AS: | BY WOMEN WHO HAD INSTANT COFFEE IN THE HOUSE | BY WOMEN WHO DID NOT HAVE INSTANT COFFEE IN THE HOUSE |
|---|---|---|
| Economical | 70% | 28% |
| Can't cook or does not like to | 16% | 55% |
| Lazy | 19% | 39% |
| Good housewife | 29% | 0% |
| Poor housewife (doesn't care about family) | 16% | 39% |

Consumer researcher Jagdish N. Sheth replicated the study in the late 1960s and found the same negative perceptions about the instant coffee user:

| | DESCRIPTION OF WOMEN WHO WOULD SHOP WITH | |
|---|---|---|
| | INSTANT COFFEE LIST | REGULAR COFFEE LIST |
| Lazy | 12.3% | 3.8% |
| Poor planner | 15.4% | 11.4% |
| Good planner | 1.6% | 6.1% |
| Good wife | 4.8% | 11.4% |
| Doesn't like to cook | 12.3% | 2.3% |
| Busy | 28.7% | 9.2% |

Note that while the negative perceptions persisted (e.g., poor planner, not a good wife, and so on), the gap in the perceptions of the two groups had narrowed. Moreover, respondents tended to excuse the instant coffee user as being disinterested in cooking and busy.

**Source:** Adapted from Mason Haire, "Projective Techniques in Marketing Research," *Journal of Marketing,* April 1950, pp. 649–56.

not knowingly and voluntarily reveal. The specific techniques are word association, sentence completion, and story completion.

**Word Association.**   In the word association technique, the researcher either reads or flashes a set of words before the consumer, who is instructed to respond with whatever word comes to his or her mind. For example, the word or expression "instant coffee" might bring out such associations as *tasteless*, *ordinary*, and *cheap*, revealing the reason this group of customers may not buy instant coffee; another group of respondents might respond with such words as *convenient*, *quick*, and *invigorating*, revealing why this group of customers includes heavy users of instant coffee.

**Sentence Completion.**   The sentence completion techniques are similar to word association. Here, the customer is presented with an incomplete sentence and is asked to fill in the blank. For example, an incomplete sentence like, "I drink instant coffee only when I am. . ." might elicit such responses as *in a hurry* or *in the office*; or alternatively, such responses as *entertaining at home* or *relaxing*. These two sets of responses will reveal two different sets of motives for consuming instant coffee and vastly divergent perceptions about it.

**Story Completion.**   The most common form of story completion is the thematic apperception test (TAT), which consists of a series of ambiguous pictures shown to the customer. The customer is then asked to describe the story of which the picture is a part. To continue with the coffee example, a customer might be shown someone preparing a cup of instant coffee and asked to describe the story surrounding this situation. Someone might say, "The customer shown in the picture is an office secretary preparing coffee for a high-level executive meeting;" or the customer's story might instead be that the person in the picture is a bored housewife, getting ready to watch daytime TV. These two stories illustrate two very different sets of perceptions, attitudes, and motives for or against the consumption of instant coffee. A related use of this technique in marketing would be to show a customer or a group of them in a product-buying or usage situation apparently looking at some product information or talking about the product and ask research respondents to fill in the thoughts of people shown in the picture.

**Hybrid Techniques.**   Customer researchers often experiment with hybrid techniques that are in part disguised and nondisguised and likewise in part structured and nonstructured. Thus, the respondent is told the topic of research, say dieting (nondisguised), but not what specific dieting behaviors or product-use issues are being investigated (disguised); the respondent is guided to some extent, such as, "Think about the people you know who diet and those who don't" (structured), but still is asked a very broad question to elicit the most individualistic responses possible, for example, "How would you describe the dieters as a group?" (nonstructured). One recent innovation in such hybrid techniques is what is called the ZMET method. The Zaltman metaphor elicitation technique (ZMET) is a method of guiding customer respondents to collect and build pictorial images (i.e., metaphors) that capture their thoughts about a product or about shopping, and so forth. The respondents are subsequently questioned by structured techniques such as laddering, a method of asking a series of questions to elicit causal linkages for a specific response: for example, Why did you want that; why is that important to you; and what do you gain by getting this thing that you said is important to you?[7] See the Window on Research box entitled "Seeing the Voice of the Customer: The Zaltman Metaphor Technique."[8]

An example of a hybrid technique in web-based data collection is presented by researchers Englis and Solomon. Most of the data collection on the Web tends to be verbal in nature; however, this technique called "Life/Style Online" is visual in nature and suitable for a variety of consumer research applications. "Life/Style Online" was initially developed to explore how fashion trends take root and diffuse among young female customers. Another important objective was to understand the linkages between the consumers' fashion choices and their other lifestyle choices. In this technique, the respondent is aware of the project objective, but the Web-based data-collection process allows each respondent to express her unique tastes and preferences through a choice of several visual images of

# WINDOW ON RESEARCH

## Seeing the Voice of the Customer: The Zaltman Metaphor Technique

Let us say that you are a customer, and you have agreed to participate in our research project. We make an appointment for you to visit us at our research site 7 to 10 days from now. In this interim time, we ask you to collect a minimum of 12 images representing your thoughts and feelings about the research topic. The topic can be what you think of a particular brand or company, what your experience is when you use a particular product or brand, how you feel about a new product concept, and so on. However, you are to avoid pictures that directly show the product under discussion.

Armed with these images, you come on the appointed day and time. What follows is a two-hour one-on-one interview. During this interview, you will begin by describing each image, telling a story of how each image or picture relates to the topic, any particular image you may have had in mind but were unable to locate, any image that is *not* representative of the topic, and what in each image is most representative of the topic.

The next step uses a technique called Kelly repertory grid. In this technique, you will be asked to select three images at random and then identify how any two are similar and yet different from the third. Suppose you said that the two pictures are similar in showing trust. A technique called laddering is then used to identify the causes of trust. In laddering, you will be asked what leads to trust, then what leads to whatever leads to trust, and so on.

In the next step, you will be asked to create a mind's-eye video incorporating some of the more important ideas you have expressed so far.

In the final step, you will be asked to create a collage summarizing all your thoughts and feelings. This collage is created by digital-imaging techniques, with the help of a computer technician. As input for this step, all your images will have been scanned into the computer, and the technician will help you manipulate these digital images until a composite collage is obtained that captures all your feelings and thoughts on the topic. This concludes your participation in the research.

Sound like fun? It is. Nearly 2,000 diverse customers have gone through this process. This interesting research method, pioneered by Harvard University Marketing Professor Gerald Zaltman working with Professor Robin Higie Coulter of the University of Connecticut, is called the Zaltman Metaphor Elicitation Technique (ZMET). A metaphor is something that stands for something else. Zaltman believes that metaphors not only are ways of hiding or expressing thoughts but they also actively create and shape them. Among his other beliefs that form the foundation of this method are: most social communication is nonverbal; thoughts occur as images; and metaphors can capture these images better than verbal responses most often sought in customer research. Thus, the patented ZMET method is inherently more capable of capturing the rich imagery customers hold and experience in the consumption of a product or service.

*(continued)*

The final research report is equally unusual. The entire data are stored on a digital disk, with commentaries and interpretations by researchers that can be accessed interactively by managers.

Additional information is located at **http://www.hbs.edu/mml/zmet .html**.

**Source:** Adapted from Gerald Zaltman, "Metaphorically Speaking," *Marketing Research* 8, No. 2, (Summer 1996), pp. 13–20.

products. The respondent first selects an "ideal" person image and then navigates through rooms of the person's house, making product selections for every room of the house, associated with different social scenarios. For example, if the respondent's task were to help the "ideal" person prepare for a dinner party for business associates, the respondent would go to the closet and select an outfit, shoes, and other items. Then she would move to the living room and select furnishings, music, artwork, etc. Finally, the respondent would move to the dining room to select table settings, entrees, beverages, and so on. Once the respondent completes this process, she is asked to complete a questionnaire that probes her perceptions of the social category the "ideal person" belongs to, perceptions of the assortments and their constituent elements. This technique is extremely useful for marketers because it allows aggregation of responses from a large number of respondents. This gives the marketer a feel for how a particular concept is perceived by a reasonably large number of respondents in that particular target segment. New product development, packaging design, advertising testing, store layout, and brand equity studies can also be conducted using this methodology.[9] What results from such hybrid methods is a research insight into customers' mindset, comprising both verbal and nonverbal, well-formed and conscious as well as unconscious or vague and undefined ideas, motivations, perceptions, attitudes, and preferences.

## Interpretative Research

With interpretative research, another qualitative method, a researcher observes a customer or a group of customers in their natural setting, and interprets that behavior based on an extensive understanding of the social and cultural characteristics of that setting. The researcher spends extensive time understanding the culture and becomes a participant observer of the scene. These types of studies are also called *ethnographic* studies. The term *ethnographic* means taking the cultural perspective of the population being studied. Thus, the behavior of specific customers is interpreted from the vantage point of the customers themselves. The question the researcher asks is: What meaning does a particular customer behavior have for the customer himself or herself? How does it make sense within the context of the culture that the customer group shares?[10]

Interpretive research is an example of what has been termed *post-modern research*. The focus of the post-modern research is on understanding the meaning of a product or consumption experience in a consumer's life. The purpose here is not limited to the buying decision, but rather it covers the consumer's lifestyle, his or her well-being, satisfaction, and the role that material objects and worldly activities play in his or her life.[11]

## The Consumer Behavior Odyssey

An eminent example of this kind of research is what has come to be known as the Odyssey project. The Consumer Behavior Odyssey was a qualitative research project involving personal visits by an interdisciplinary team of academic customer researchers to a variety of customer sites. The project was undertaken in summer 1986 by a group of leading consumer researchers (trained in such disciplines as sociology, psychology, anthropology, consumer behavior, and marketing research) who traveled in a recreational vehicle (RV) from coast-to-coast on a journey of discovery, so to speak. The data collection methods consisted of taped interviews, still photos, on-site recording of diaries, and day-end writing of reflections in personal journals. Researchers visited department stores and garage sales, county fairs and tourist resorts, opera performances and rock concerts, and picnics and weddings (i.e., virtually any consumption site that came their way). The objective was to observe in a *non*intrusive way the acquisition, consumption, and disposition of products and services wherever these occurred.[12]

Let us cite three examples of the kind of customer knowledge that projects of this nature can yield.

**Motorized versus Nonmotorized Mobile Homes.** The Odyssey researchers visited and observed the owners and renters of motorized and nonmotorized mobile homes. They found notable differences in the consumption experience of mobile home living by these two groups. Nonmotorized mobile homeowners seemed to view their mobile units as much more of a home than did the owners of motorized mobile homes. The former parked their units more permanently, shared community activities with others in the RV park, and externally personalized (e.g., named their units by their last names) and beautified their mobile units. The latter, in contrast, did not engage in any joint activities with their neighbors, were preoccupied more with traveling and reaching their destinations than with relaxing in one spot in their units, and did not attempt any personalization in the external appearance of their mobile units.

This customer perspective could not have been discovered by the more conventional quantitative methods. It can be helpful to marketers of mobile homes, travel accessories, and travel destinations to identify these two different groups of customers.

**The Psychology of Buyers and Sellers at a Swap Meet.** Why do consumers frequent flea markets and garage sales? Who sells at the swap markets and why? And, beyond the commercial exchange of pre-owned and used goods, are there other cultural and community rituals transpiring here that draw participants like a magnet to these events?

These questions, again, warrant a qualitative discovery study, and the Odyssey researchers did just that. Three Odyssey researchers spent a weekend at a swap meet at Red Mesa and reported these findings and observations.

- The swap meet is a forum for the exchange of goods, services, and ideas. In addition to being a site of lateral recycling (i.e., where the product passes on from one consumer to another), retailing, and wholesaling, it is for many sellers a temporary residential area with a feeling of community. And for buyers, it is a festival or a fair.
- Both buyers and sellers feel a special kind of freedom. They enjoy being free from the confining sites of indoor retail stores, from having to pay income tax, and from the formal rules of behavior in regular malls or shopping plazas. Although the swap administration imposes rules (e.g., no dogs allowed, or limitations on the number of lights used), there is deliberate pleasure taken in selectively breaking and flouting rules. The exercise of a strong sense of individual freedom was evidenced, for example, in vendors wearing sidearms or knives to defend themselves and their merchandise.
- Roles of buyers and sellers interchange. Many vendors themselves become buyers of others' merchandise. Some products are being produced on the spot (e.g., the imprinting of logos on T-shirts). Both buyers and sellers enjoy people watching.
- Selling personal possessions amounts, for many sellers, to transforming what was once a sacred object (one's prized possession beyond commercial valuation) into a profane good. While the need to dispossess the object may be strong, there exists a strong desire to resist undervaluing it by selling it at a throwaway price. A low price seems to be interpreted as a detraction from one's personal self, whose part the merchandise once formed. This is in sharp contrast to the absence of any such feeling for those merchants who are selling items not personally pre-owned.

**Cultural Objects.** Based on three years of observations of visitors to the Vancouver Museum of Anthropology (MOA), consumer researcher Robert Kelley found an interesting pattern: Almost one-third of the visitors to the museum who come on a tour bus and pay the admission fee to the museum never visit the exhibits gallery. Instead, they directly go to the museum shop, buy something representative of the museum, and go back to the bus and wait there. Most of them were foreign visitors on their first visit to the museum and came with recommendations from friends to visit the museum.

The researcher identified these as techno-consumers. Techno-consumers are those who derive consumption satisfaction merely from having been to a high-culture place. In contrast, trads (short for traditionals) are educated in high-culture exhibits, have a taste for high culture, spend time visiting the exhibit galleries, and derive their satisfaction from being there.[13]

## Advantages and Disadvantages of Subjective, Interpretative Research

The advantages of interpretive research are manifold. First, the researcher is able to encounter customers and consumption activities in their natural settings, thus eliminating the artificialness of surveys, focus-group rooms, or laboratory settings. Further, one observes a customer for one hour or one day or one week as necessary, rather than for a few minutes. The researcher observes firsthand the customer activity, rather than inquire about it of respondents. Even when the respondent is interviewed, the researcher's own observations supplement the respondent's answers. Besides, the questioning is much more open-ended and qualitative rather than close-ended and quantified. Because of the extended mutual exposure between the researcher and the customer, a greater trust is built, which then leads to customer answers being more sincere. Finally, the customer activity being analyzed and questioned is much more immediate and physically present. For example, a researcher who observes certain possessions in a customer's house can actually point to them rather than ask the question in the abstract.

This method also has some shortcomings. It requires highly skilled and well-trained researchers who are less preoccupied with recording but more directed to constantly interpreting what they are observing. It is obviously very time-consuming and very expensive. In addition, the interpretation of data is too subjective, despite following certain analytic procedures. Finally, the methods are good at generating hypotheses, but not at confirming hypotheses or suggesting generalizable principles.

# Quantitative Research

In **quantitative research**, the consumer's answers are on a numerical scale, such as a scale of 0 to 10. The comparability of numerically scaled answers allows us to research a large number of customers and then pool their answers to come up with an overall measure of whatever aspect of consumer behavior we are researching.

## Quantitative Research Methods

Quantitative research can use either of two broad methods: survey and experiment.

### Survey

In the survey method, respondents are simply asked to respond to a questionnaire. The researcher reads (on the phone or in face-to-face settings) a series of predetermined questions, one at a time, and records the consumer's answers. Alternatively, in a self-administered questionnaire (sent by mail or given in person), respondents write in the answer themselves.

Basically, the method is useful to elicit customers' beliefs, opinions, attitudes, and perceptions. One limitation of this method is that respondents will give the answers they consider safe to give. Thus, information they consider personal will not be given. Also, respondents do not like to appear ignorant and will, therefore, make up an answer even if they have never before thought about the topic. When the topic might be one in which customer motivations might be hidden or where consumers may hesitate to candidly share their opinion, qualitative disguised techniques discussed before are more appropriate.

Surveys typically use prespecified numerical scales for answer categories, so we discuss this method as a quantitative technique. However, surveys can be used just as well for eliciting respondent answers **verbatim** (i.e., in their own words). In many cases, questionnaires contain a few questions that seek open-ended verbatim responses, even though the majority of the questions seek numerical responses.

The basic form of online surveys over the Internet involves sending personalized e-mails to potential respondents with a questionnaire or posting a set of questions on a site that a customer can respond to. Today there are several web sites, such as Inetsurvey.com and zoomerang.com, which offer researchers a hassle-free option to conduct online surveys. For a fee, these sites will provide several options for the different kind of questions that you want to use on the survey—including Likert scales and questions for preferential mapping or cluster analysis. They will host the survey at their web site and also help in the analysis of the responses. Once the questionnaire is ready, the researcher contacts the respondents through e-mails which contain a link to the survey. The respondent clicks on the link and is directed to the survey. All responses are collected in a database that has been designed for the particular questionnaire and the data is collected for analysis.[14] Firms that have conducted both online and traditional surveys find that the cost per respondent of online research is lower than offline research since production and mailing/interviewing costs are reduced, and lower respondent incentives are needed. Online research is faster since responses to surveys can come almost instantaneously or in 24 hours after the survey has been posted. Online surveys also tend to have lesser "yea saying" and the responses are more frank, resulting in lower purchase intent, satisfaction scores, higher price sensitivity, and more "don't know" responses. The Internet does allow the marketer to get responses from a more geographically dispersed sample, but a major disadvantage of the online surveys is that online samples may not be representative of the target population. There is no master list of Internet users and, as mentioned in Chapter 2, Internet users tend to be more educated and from higher income households. However, with higher levels of PC penetration and the increasing diversity of users online (with respect to the different demographic parameters), this problem should get reduced. Marketers are trying to overcome this problem by choosing samples from large representative Internet user panels maintained by research agencies like NFO Interactive, NPD, Greenfield Online, Cyber Dialogue, etc. Other research firms are developing techniques that allow them to adjust results from online surveys for differences between the online sample and the actual target population. Prequalifying respondents through e-mail solicitation, putting links to surveys at popular Internet portals, and offering incentives to participation are some other methods used to get representative online samples. Online surveys are, without a doubt, best for all research related to the Internet, such as the effectiveness of Web advertising, evaluation of a Web site, etc.[15] There are some ethical concerns that surround online survey research. As Fred Bove of Socratic Technologies puts it "Spam is starting to do the same thing to e-mail surveys that telemarketing did to phone surveys in the 1980s." As marketers gather e-mail addresses from newsgroups and purchase data from web sites, sometimes without permission of the customers, privacy has become an extremely important issue. With more and more web sites asking for personal information for customization of offerings of customers, web sites that are able to balance information gathering and personalization, along with privacy concerns of users, stand a much better chance of success in the online marketplace.[16]

## Experiment

One limitation of survey methods is that questionnaires are limited to assessing consumer opinions and thoughts. In respect to *behavior*, survey questionnaires can only measure what respondents say they will do, not what they will actually do. For that purpose, experimental methods are employed. An **experiment** is a method in which the researcher places respondents in a situation that does not normally occur and then observes or records their response.

A prime example of experimental research in marketing is test marketing. **Test marketing** is a method of testing a marketing mix on a limited market as a precursor to deciding whether to implement that mix in the entire market. Suppose, for example, that you wanted to launch a new product. Rather than launch it in the entire nation (and incur huge losses in case the product does not sell), you could launch it in two cities and observe customer response. Or let us say that you simply wanted to test the relative appeal of two types of packages, or two different price levels, or two different advertisements, or any combination of these. You could select two matching cities (i.e., cities similar in their demographic profiles) and place one package, price, or advertisement (called a stimulus) in one city and the second stimulus in the second city, and observe which elicits a more favorable customer response. While a fuller discussion of these methods is beyond the scope of this book, we may note that experiments such as these can be performed also in laboratory settings. Representative customers are invited to come to a research site where they are exposed to alternative stimuli, and their reactions—verbal as well as behavioral—are recorded.[17] We discuss virtual test marketing in the final section on virtual reality techniques in this chapter. In the online world, experiments are possible at very low cost and with instant feedback. For example an e-tailer could vary the prices of products based on the day of the week, the time of day, or the profile of the buyer and could "test" various products, promotions, and prices in real time. The Window on Practice presents the case of Amazon.com that shows how marketers need to be careful not to alienate customers as they dynamically manipulate prices on the Web.

# WINDOW ON PRACTICE

## Amazon.com—Implications of Dynamic Pricing

In October 2000, a group of consumers found that Amazon.com was charging different prices for DVDs for different people on the same day. Consumers reacted angrily. Most consumers on the Web are resigned to the fact that prices are not uniform on the Web and that there is always going to be someone who finds a lower price for the same product with a more careful search. They, however, felt violated in this case because they felt that the company was adjusting prices, on the sly, based on the personal preferences that they had revealed when shopping on the site. Amazon.com officials went on the defensive and attributed the change in prices to a marketing test and issued refunds to people who paid more than others.

As the data trail left by consumers on the Internet is used for efficient segmentation and targeting, this process of dynamic pricing will soon be the defining characteristic of online shopping. Over a period of time, Amazon.com would not only be able to predict the consumer's tastes but also would be able to state exactly how much he or she would be willing to pay for a product. The company is bound to use such information to extract maximum possible profits from each customer. But the key to making dynamic pricing work is in keeping the consumer informed. As long as consumers know how the system works and realize that they have a way to opt out, they will not have any problems with the system.

Amazon.com's mistake was choosing to experiment on customers, not with them.

**Source:** Adapted from Joe Salkowski, "E-Tailers Could Lose Trust of Clients Over Pricing Plan," *Los Angeles Business Journal*, October 9, 2000, Volume 22, issue 41, p. 20. Reprinted with permission from Tribune Media Services.

## Simulation

Simulation is a special form of quantitative, experimental method, in which researchers create real-world conditions in a laboratory to study the behavior of consumers. By observing their behavior in this laboratory setting, marketers are able to forecast how they (the consumers) would behave in the real marketplace. Just as astronauts use a flight simulator to train for the real flight, so too marketers simulate the marketing mix (i.e., create the market mix on a smaller scale in the laboratory) before investing money on the full-fledged marketing program.

     Pretest market lab simulation is a specific procedure for testing new-product concepts and prototypes. In a typical procedure, consumers representative of the target market are recruited by mall interception and invited to view a TV program and look at some product samples. They are also shown a 15-minute program segment, a pretaped TV program with one change: one of the commercials has been substituted by the test commercial. After viewing the program, the consumers are surveyed on the perceptions and persuasive impact of the commercial. Next, they are given some shopping money (say, $3.00) and are requested to examine the mock-up store display that contains the new test brand as well as other brands. Customer purchases are recorded, and later consumers are called to obtain their reactions to the test product. The data can then be analyzed by statistical models to predict the performance of the new product in the real world. For details about an actual simulation model, see the Window on Practice box.

# WINDOW ON PRACTICE

## Assessor: A Simulation Model

A simulation model called ASSESSOR was designed by two marketing professors at MIT, Glen L. Urban and Alvin J. Silk. The ASSESSOR research process consists of the following steps.

1. Respondents are screened and recruited.
2. Respondents' existing attitudes and perceptions about the product category are measured by a self-administered survey questionnaire. This includes finding out what brands respondents consider relevant to their need (i.e., what is their consideration set), what attributes and criteria they use to evaluate various brands in the product category, the relative weight they place on these criteria, and their current brand preferences.
3. Customers are exposed to advertising for existing brands and the new brand, usually in a studio.
4. Customers' reactions to the advertising material are measured by a questionnaire. Questions asked include whether they liked the advertised brand or not and why. This allows the researcher to know not only the effectiveness of the advertisement but also diagnostic information as to which aspects of the advertised brand or of the advertisement itself were viewed favorably or unfavorably.
5. Customers are given shopping money and exposed to a simulated store display of the new brand and its competitors.

*(continued)*

6. An observer records the brands the consumer purchased or the fact that no purchase was made.
7. Respondents not buying the test brand are given a sample of the brand for use at home.
8. Respondents are called back after a few days to survey their experience with the product. At this stage, satisfaction or dissatisfaction with the new brand is measured. Also, customer perceptions of the new brand on its various attributes are obtained. Finally, new preference ratings for the new brand and other established brands are assessed.
9. Data are analyzed via computers using statistical models to forecast repeat buying rates and market share.

**Source:** Alvin J. Silk and Glen L. Urban, "Pre-Test Market Evaluation of New Packaged Goods: A Model and Measurement Methodology," *Journal of Marketing Research* 15 (May 1978), pp. 171–191. Reprinted with permission of American Marketing Association. Additional information is located at http://www.mit.edu.

Advanced computer technology (including graphic ability) is now available to simulate the entire procedure on the computer; that is, computers are used not only for running the data through statistical models but also for information display and for collecting the data. To do this, the real-world store environment is mimicked on the computer. For example, the computer can show store shelves with the test brand and other brands displayed exactly as they would be in the real store. The advertisements, end-of-aisle displays, shelf tags, store specials, point-of-purchase advertisements, manufacturers' coupons, and store coupons are all displayed and made available on the computer. The customer sits at a computer terminal and goes on a weekly shopping trip. His or her purchases are automatically recorded by the computer.

In an interesting simulation experiment, some customer researchers simulated the exact store conditions that had existed in specific stores in a neighborhood over the last seven months. The purpose of the experiment was to investigate the degree to which such simulations correctly predicted the real-world behavior. During the six months preceding the experiment, all shopping receipts were collected from customers. The computer simulated week by week store merchandising programs of the past six months; that is, in the same sitting, consumers went through about 25 weekly shopping trips. The results suggested that in the simulation, consumers tended to buy more quantity of products featured that week than they actually did in the real world under similar circumstances. They also tended to buy store brands to a lesser extent (perhaps due to no real money constraints), and tended to switch brands less often. More important, however, the lab results performed very well in predicting market share. This study, therefore, attested to the utility of simulation tests.[18]

Virtual reality simulations are addressed at the end of the chapter in a separate section.

## Applications of Quantitative Research

Quantitative research on consumer behavior uses a variety of concepts and numerical scales. As shown in Figure 7.2, typical ones include attitude research, image and self-concept measurement, multiattribute attitude models, and perceptual and preference mapping.

### Attitude Research

As described in Chapter 7, attitudes are evaluations of an object, such as a brand or person. It is easy to measure attitudes by various scales. For example, the *semantic differential* scale asks respondents to rate the object in terms of pairs of traits:

## Selected Applications of Quantitative Research     FIGURE 7.2

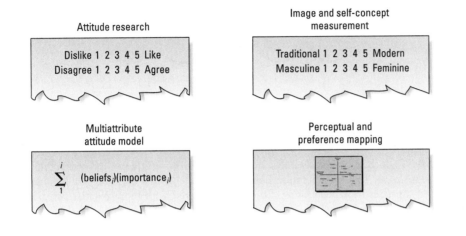

**Brand A office equipment is:**

| Poor | 1 | 2 | 3 | 4 | 5 | Excellent |
|------|---|---|---|---|---|-----------|
| Effective | 1 | 2 | 3 | 4 | 5 | Ineffective |
| Economical | 1 | 2 | 3 | 4 | 5 | Uneconomical |
| Good | 1 | 2 | 3 | 4 | 5 | Bad |
| Low quality | 1 | 2 | 3 | 4 | 5 | High quality |

**My opinion of this brand of office equipment is:**

| Favorable | 1 | 2 | 3 | 4 | 5 | Unfavorable |
|-----------|---|---|---|---|---|-------------|
| Negative | 1 | 2 | 3 | 4 | 5 | Positive |
| I dislike | 1 | 2 | 3 | 4 | 5 | Like this brand very much. |

Similarly, *Likert scales* request a numerical rating, but they ask respondents the degree to which they agree or disagree with statements:

Please express your opinion on the following questions about seatbelts, by circling an appropriate number.

1. Strongly Disagree
2. Disagree
3. Feel Neutral
4. Agree
5. Strongly Agree

| | | | | | |
|---|---|---|---|---|---|
| • Seatbelts prevent injuries. | 1 | 2 | 3 | 4 | 5 |
| • Seatbelts are inconvenient. | 1 | 2 | 3 | 4 | 5 |
| • Seatbelts can trap you in case of an accident. | 1 | 2 | 3 | 4 | 5 |

The attitude scales can also be pictorial, rather than numerical. Such a scale is particularly useful for less literate respondents, or respondents who speak a different language. When the research purpose is to measure the emotions the respondent experiences, pictures of various facial expressions can be used.[19] (See Figure 7.3.)

Pictorial scales are also especially useful for researching children as customers. One particular variety of pictorial scale was developed recently by consumer researchers Yvonne

| FIGURE 7.3 | Pictorial Scales to Measure Customer Attitudes |

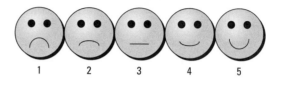

Cariveau Karsten and Deborah Roedder John. This type of scale is called a **behaviorally anchored scale** because these scales are anchored in specific behaviors that children are likely to relate to. The consideration behind these scales is that children will be able to report their attitudes more accurately if they are presented with representations of situations depicting the kind of behaviors they will engage in when they experience those attitudes. Two scales, meant to elicit children's attitudes toward cereals, are shown in Figure 7.4, along with their verbal interpretations in Table 7.2.

| FIGURE 7.4 | Behaviorally Anchored Rating Scales |

A. "Shopping" Scale (BARS1)

B. "Sharing" Scale (BARS2)

**Source:** Yvonne Cariveau Karsten and Deborah Roedder John, "Measuring Young Children's Preferences: The Use of Behaviorally Anchored Rating Scales," Report Number 94-122 (Cambridge, Mass.: Marketing Science Institute), November 1994.

## Image/Self-Concept Measurement

Consumers' own self-image as well as their image of specific products and brands can be measured by using a semantic differential scale, such as the following:

| Modern | ___ | ___ | ___ | Traditional |
| Economic | ___ | ___ | ___ | Uneconomic |
| Pleasant | ___ | ___ | ___ | Unpleasant |
| Feminine | ___ | ___ | ___ | Masculine |

## Description of Behavioral Incidents in Figure 7.4     TABLE 7.2

| Setting | Preference Level | Description |
|---|---|---|
| Shopping | Like a lot | Child asking Mom for cereal<br>Jumping up and down |
| | Like | Child putting cereal box into cart |
| | Neutral | Child looking at cereal box |
| | Dislike | Child looking at cereal gesturing dislike |
| | Dislike a lot | Child throwing cereal box on floor |
| Sharing | Like a lot | Child hugging cereal box, with a full bowl of cereal in front of him or her; other child has empty bowl |
| | Like | Child hugging cereal box, with a moderately full bowl of cereal in front of him or her; other child has a small amount of cereal in bowl |
| | Neutral | Both children have bowls with equal amounts of cereal in them |
| | Dislike | Child pushing cereal box and bowl away; other child has a full bowl of cereal |
| | Dislike a lot | Child pushing cereal box and bowl to the floor; other child has full bowl of cereal |

**Source:** Yvonne Cariveau Karsten and Deborah Roedder John, "Measuring Young Children's Preferences: The Use of Behaviorally Anchored Rating Scales," Report Number 94-122 (Cambridge, Mass.: Marketing Science Institute), November 1994.

As mentioned in Chapter 5, psychographics describes us in terms of lifestyles, or the way we live. To measure psychographics (i.e., values, self-concepts, and lifestyles), researchers present a series of statements about possible activities, interests, and opinions. Respondents indicate their agreement or disagreement with these statements. Some sample activities, interests, and opinions defining a few lifestyle categories are presented below.[20]

CHILD-ORIENTED
When my children are ill in bed, I drop most everything else in order to see to their comfort.
My children are the most important things in my life.
I try to arrange my home for my children's convenience.
I take a lot of time and effort to teach my children good habits.

FINANCIAL OPTIMIST
I will probably have more money to spend next year than I have now.
Five years from now the family income will probably be a lot higher than it is now.

PRICE CONSCIOUS
I shop a lot for specials.
I find myself checking the prices in the grocery store even for small items.
I usually watch the advertisements for announcements of sales.
A person can save a lot of money by shopping around for bargains.

FASHION CONSCIOUS
I usually have one or more outfits that are of the very latest style.
When I must choose between the two, I usually dress for fashion, not for comfort.
An important part of my life and activities is dressing smartly.
I often try the latest hairstyles when they change.

## Multiattribute Attitude Model

According to the multiattribute attitude model, a consumer's attitude toward a product or service is a weighted sum of his or her beliefs about the extent to which the product or service possesses a set of attributes or characteristics. Each belief is weighted to measure the importance of the attribute to the person. Thus, one first needs to measure consumers' perceptions or beliefs about the attributes of the product and then measure the importance consumers assign to these attributes. The following scale is designed to measure perceptions of attributes:

Please rate Brand A long-distance phone company on the following characteristics using a number 1 through 5, where 1 means "very poor," and 5 means "excellent."

| | | | | | |
|---|---|---|---|---|---|
| Sound quality | 1 | 2 | 3 | 4 | 5 |
| Speed of connection | 1 | 2 | 3 | 4 | 5 |
| Operator assistance | 1 | 2 | 3 | 4 | 5 |
| Payment plan | 1 | 2 | 3 | 4 | 5 |

The following question then measures the importance of each attribute:

And how *important* are these attributes to you? Please circle a number 1 through 5, where 1 means "not important" and 5 means "very important."

| | | | | | |
|---|---|---|---|---|---|
| Sound quality | 1 | 2 | 3 | 4 | 5 |
| Speed of connection | 1 | 2 | 3 | 4 | 5 |
| Operator assistance | 1 | 2 | 3 | 4 | 5 |
| Payment plan | 1 | 2 | 3 | 4 | 5 |

## Perceptual and Preference Mapping

To understand what attributes and criteria consumers use to judge and evaluate alternative brands, products, services, retailers, or vendors, researchers can use **perceptual and preference mapping**. These analytical techniques provide a visual map in a multidimensional space that shows how similar or different various brands are considered to be by the consumer. The miracle of these analytical methods (collectively called multidimensional scaling) is that they enable a researcher to plot the alternative brands in a perceptual space without knowing beforehand what the dimensions of this space are; that is, without knowing what dimensions consumers base their judgments on.

Suppose you were to ask consumers how similar or different a number of beverages are, say on such attributes as sweetness, carbonation, pungentness, viscosity, and color. How do we know that consumers use these attributes in beverage evaluation; for example, does viscosity matter to them? And are these the only attributes they use? Could not aroma be one of the attributes, or aftertaste? Finally, are we sure they can judge magnitude differences on individual attributes; for example, is Beverage A sweeter than Beverage B? Multidimensional scaling avoids this problem by requiring consumers to tell the researcher only which of the two brands are more similar than some other pair, without probing the basis of judging such similarity. Alternatively, instead of similarity, we can ask consumers to indicate which of a pair of brands they prefer. Table 7.3 shows the format in which these data may be collected.

A computer program then performs the mapping technique. It locates the alternative brands in a space so that the distances between the brand locations represent brand differences. That is, more similar brands are plotted close to each other.

The computer has to determine how many dimensions this space will have. To do this, it attempts to place the brands in one-dimensional space, then in two, three, and so on, dimensional space. Each time, it indicates the stress each solution represents. To understand this, consider that if three chairs were lying at the same distance from one another, it would be difficult to locate these along a single line; however, it would be easy to plot them perfectly in two dimensions as points of an equilateral triangle. Likewise, four

| Methods of Measuring Customer Perceptions and Preferences | TABLE 7.3 |
| --- | --- |

PERCEPTION MEASUREMENT 1

Brand A of soda is more similar to: ___ Brand B or ___ Brand C
Brand A of soda is more similar to: ___ Brand C or ___ Brand D
Brand B of soda is more similar to: ___ Brand C or ___ Brand D
Brand B of soda is more similar to: ___ Brand A or ___ Brand D

PERCEPTION MEASUREMENT 2

In the following matrix, place 1 in the cell for the pair of brands most similar, 2 for the next most similar, and so on.

A B C D E . . .

A
B
C
D
E

PREFERENCE MEASUREMENT 1

Which brand do you prefer more in each pair (circle one brand in each pair)?
A or B
B or C
A or C
A or D
B or D
C or D

PREFERENCE MEASUREMENT 2

Please rank the following brands from the most preferred (1) to the least preferred (5).
Brand A ___
Brand B ___
Brand C ___
Brand D ___
Brand E ___

objects that are equidistant would require a three-dimensional space. Thus, when a number of brands have been rated as pairs, the relative similarity or dissimilarity creates constraints that make the solution fit better in a space of a particular dimensionality.

After determining the number of dimensions, the computer plots the resulting maps two dimensions at a time. These maps allow us to visually see how a specific brand compares to the others. See Figure 7.5 for a perceptual map (which is based on similarity perception judgments).

Although it is not necessary to know the dimensions of the perceptual space to draw these maps, the researcher does want to know what these dimensions possibly represent. There are two ways of making this inference. First, by looking at the brands clustering together, a marketing manager might be able to infer the identity of the underlying dimensions. For example, if all the soda drinks that were at the high end of an axis were cola drinks, one could label that axis to be cola-ness.

**FIGURE 7.5**          **A Perceptual Map**

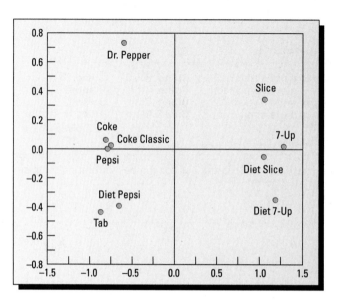

**Source:** From *Marketing Research: An Applied Orientation* by Malhotra, p. 695, ©. Reprinted by permission of Pearson Education, Inc., Upper Saddle River, NJ.

Alternatively, a marketer could also ask the respondents to rate all the drinks on a set of attributes and then superimpose a plot of these attributes on the perceptual map obtained earlier. Figure 7.6 provides an example; the attributes are shown as vectors (arrows indicating magnitude). The attributes are plotted such that the vertical projections of the brands on these attribute vectors represent the relative magnitudes of brand ratings on these attributes. By inspecting which attribute vectors cluster around the axes of the space, the researcher can interpret and identify the perceptual maps' dimensions.

In the preference map, it is possible to locate the ideal point of individual consumers. An ideal point is a brand alternative that, if available, would meet the consumer's requirement perfectly. This is done by locating a point such that, for each pair of brands, the brand more preferred is always closer to this ideal point than is the other brand in the pair. When all the respondents are plotted in this manner (i.e., one ideal point for each consumer), it is then possible to identify segments of consumers with differing preferences (see Figure 7.7).

Perceptual and preference maps are very useful in identifying new-product concepts, in perceptually repositioning a brand, and in identifying market segments best suited to one's own brand.

# Information Processing Research

Rather than asking direct questions about decisions consumers make, information-processing research studies what information consumers are looking for, looking at, paying attention to, considering, and using to make decisions. Ultimately, they hope to discover what information led consumers to choose certain brands or products and services. The advantage of this method is that the researcher comes closer to understanding

## A Perceptual Map with Product Attributes     FIGURE 7.6

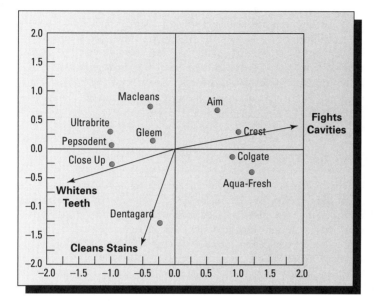

## A Perceptual Map with Ideal Points (I₁ & I₂) Shown     FIGURE 7.7

Sportiness (high)

Corvette

Firebird    I₁

Jaguar    Camaro

Monte Carlo    Capri

High prestige/ expensive ————————————————— Economy

Chevy    Vega

Continental    Buick

Cadillac

I₂    Dart

VW

Mercedes

(low)

what goes on inside the mind of the consumer. It tells the researcher what effect certain information has on the final decision. It offers guidance on how to present product information to consumers. The disadvantage is that it is very time-consuming even though it can offer valuable insight on consumer decisions.

A number of methods are available for conducting such research. We can quietly observe consumers, keeping an eye on the information they are acquiring and evaluating; or we could ask them to share with us their information acquisition and processing behavior. The techniques that have been developed for studying consumers' information-processing activity include information boards; measures of eye movement, galvanic skin response, and brain activity; visual image profiles; and protocols. These methods can be quantitative or qualitative.

## Information Boards

An **information board** is a table of information with brand names in the rows and attribute names in the columns (see Figure 7.8). Cells contain the information about the extent to which the brand specified in the corresponding row contains the attribute specified in the corresponding column. The attribute information could be in the natural units of the attribute (e.g., miles per gallon for car fuel efficiency or 200 calories for a food item) or on a common rating scale (e.g., poor to excellent). Initially, all the cell entries are covered; the customer participating in the research study is asked to make a brand decision by uncovering the cells in whatever order he or she desires, and as many or as few cells as he or she feels necessary to come to a decision. Some brand names may be hypothetical (often designated by letters of the alphabet (e.g., Brand K), or one of the brands may be the sponsor's brand. As the customer uncovers the cells, the sequence of this uncovering is recorded.

---

**FIGURE 7.8**    **Information Board**

● Click the window to see brand information

Later, the researcher analyzes consumers' sequence of information acquisition. Based on the sequence, the researcher draws inferences about the evaluative criteria customers use in appraising alternative brands, the comparison process they employ in making their choice (for example, do they compare two brands on the same attribute, or weigh two or more features for the same brand?), and the judgment model (compensatory or noncompensatory) they utilize to form their final judgment.

This kind of research helps a marketer understand which product features are important to customers and which features should be emphasized in marketing communications. It is possible, for example, that the very last attribute uncovered on the information board was the one on which the marketer's brand was edged out by a competitor's brand, even though the former was superior on all the preceding attributes. The marketer now has the choice of either improving this last-considered feature in his or her brand or educating the consumer about his or her brand's considerable superiority on all the features taken as a group.

An information board *can* be a simple card or wooden board with pegs on the cells for hanging information cards. More often, it is an electronic information board created and displayed on a computer. The research participant simply clicks on the desired cell to reveal the information. The computer automatically records the sequence of uncovering the information cells.

A variation on this is a menu-driven microcomputer-based program for information search experiments, such as the program called Search Monitor. Search Monitor enables the consumer to obtain information on various alternatives by offering a battery of such questions as:

**Q.** What type of __ does brand __ have?
**Q.** What price is brand __ in store __?
**Q.** Does brand __ have a __?

The customer chooses a question from the list and fills in the blanks with the desired brand, store, and feature name. Then the answer appears on the screen. In some applications, the researcher can build in delays in response times in order to make the respondent realize that information search will consume time just as it does in the real world. The program permits the researcher to design the question menu, key in the answers according to the product and brands being studied, and vary the waiting times before the answer will appear on the screen.[21]

## Eye Movement

Another device to capture customers' information processing is an eye camera. The camera records the pupil movement as the customer looks through a piece of information. This method can be used to study customer's information acquisition while reading or viewing an advertisement, looking at aisle displays, and examining package information on products in a supermarket, or participating in an experiment such as an information board.

The researcher uses data gathered by the eye camera to identify the information at which the customer gazed longest. Such data help the researcher pinpoint the selective appeal and use of information by the customer.

## GSR

Galvanic skin response (GSR) measures the amount of skin resistance to electric current between two electrodes. When a customer reacts to any stimuli, her or his sweat glands are activated; this, in turn, reduces the skin resistance. Thus, GSR activity indicates customer response to a stimulus, such as an item of information (e.g., price) or an emotional story line in an advertisement.

## Brain Activity

When customers process any information or react to any marketing stimulus, electric impulses are generated in the brain. These impulses can be measured by sensors attached to the skull, which generate electroencephalographic (EEG) measures.

One of the brain activities measured in this way is called alpha activity. Alpha activity inversely measures the degree of the brain's attentiveness. When we are sleeping, resting, or otherwise inactive, the alpha activity is high; when we are paying attention to a commercial, the alpha activity is low. During the viewing of different ads, viewers' alpha activity levels will vary, and, accordingly, they will serve as indicators of the ad's ability to attract and hold viewer attention.

## Visual Image Profile

Measurement of alpha activity, GSR, and eye movement get at the physical responses to stimuli, and questionnaires asking consumers to describe their reactions address their conscious, cognitive responses. However, much communication is nonverbal, and much of its content is emotional. Respondents may have difficulty describing their visual (nonverbal) and emotional responses to stimuli.

To elicit nonverbal responses, therefore, some firms are using nonverbal methods such as the **visual image profile**. The Foote, Cone, & Belding and BBDO ad agencies use a set of pictures illustrating facial expressions that represent a wide range of human emotions. They ask customers to identify which pictures best reflect how they themselves felt when they were watching the commercial. The cards selected by the customer can be counted and scored to reflect a customer's reaction to the ad.

## Protocol

Information boards indicate to the researcher only what information the customer acquired, not what information was processed, much less *how* it was processed. For example, after uncovering a cell in the information board study, the consumer may simply decide to discard that information from further consideration, but the researcher has no way of knowing this.

The protocol method, in contrast, allows a peep into the customer's mental processing. In the **protocol** method, the consumer is asked to speak his or her thoughts out loud. For example, a customer making a selection in a supermarket aisle would be asked to say what information he or she is looking at, thinking of, deciding about. The researcher who is accompanying the customer and recording the respondent's spoken thoughts would periodically prompt the respondent with questions like "Now what are you thinking?" "Why did you just look at that?" "Why did you put that brand down?" or "Why did you finally select that?" These customer thoughts, spoken aloud and recorded, are called protocols. The protocols are later analyzed to gain insight into customers' decision-making process.

There are two types of protocols: concurrent and retrospective. **Concurrent protocols** are the customer thoughts recorded at the time of decision making, such as in the supermarket aisle when the customer is actually making a brand selection. Concurrent protocols can also be combined with data from information boards so that we gain information on both customers' information *acquisition* and *processing*.

**Retrospective protocols** are customers' reports on the decision *process* for a decision they made in the recent past. For example, a researcher might contact recent car buyers and ask them to describe the process of information search and alternative evaluation they went through in making their car purchase. The researcher would begin by asking such questions as "When did you begin thinking of buying a car?" "What cars did you consider in the very beginning?" and "Then what did you consider about these cars, and how did you narrow down the field?" In effect, the customer is remembering and reconstructing the decision process. Obviously, the less time elapsed since the decision was made, and/or the more significant the decision, the more accurate the protocols would be.

An obvious criticism of concurrent protocols is that they might interfere with the actual information processing; that is, if the customer didn't have to verbalize his or her thoughts, his or her information processing may have been different. Researchers have found, however, that after a few initial minutes of performing the required speak-out task, respondents return to their normal way of making shopping decisions.

# Secondary Research

So far, we have been describing forms of primary research—research to gather data that does not already exist. When the marketer is considering the launch of a new product, for example, the marketer would not know how consumers will react to the particular product without conducting primary research. However, many questions can be answered more efficiently with **secondary research**—an examination of data that already exist (that is, secondary data).[22] A researcher's first attempt should always be to study secondary data since they already exist and can save the expense of collecting primary data. However, often the secondary data are outdated, or information relevant to research issues at hand may simply not exist. In such cases, managers have to resort to primary data.

There are two types of secondary data: public and proprietary. These types refer to the source of the data.

## Public Data

Secondary data in the public domain are those collected mostly by the government and other domestic, foreign, and international public organizations. These reports are available in most public libraries or are obtainable free or at nominal costs from the various organizations that collect them. The U.S. Census Bureau publishes a number of reports on both households and businesses. A prime example of the household census is the Decennial Census of Population report; a prime example of the businesses census is the Census of Manufacturers report. These two reports, along with a few others, are briefly outlined in Table 7.4.

| Selected U.S. Government Publications | TABLE 7.4 |
|---|---|

*Statistical Abstract of the U.S.*, updated annually, provides summary data on demographic, economic, social, and other aspects of the American economy and society.

*County and City Data Book*, updated every three years, presents statistical information for counties, cities, and other geographical units on population, education, employment, aggregate and median income, housing, bank deposits, retail sales, and so on.

*U.S. Industrial Outlook* provides projections of industrial activity by industry and includes data on production, sales, shipments, employment, and so on.

*Marketing Information Guide* provides a monthly annotated bibliography of marketing information.

Other government publications include the *Annual Survey of Manufacturers; Business Statistics; Census of Manufacturers; Census of Population; Census of Retail Trade, Wholesale Trade, and Selected Service Industries; Census of Transportation; Federal Reserve Bulletin; Monthly Labor Review; Survey of Current Business;* and *Vital Statistics Report.*

An important development in data availability is the 2000 census published on CD-ROM, an electronic medium disk readable by personal computers. Also made available is a mapping device, called TIGER (Topographically Integrated Geographic Coding and Referencing) system. TIGER enables a digitized street map of the entire United States along with its demographic information. This system will enable direct marketers to pinpoint addresses of the target markets they are interested in. The census data and the IDB summary demographic data is also available online at **http://www.census.gov**. The U.S Bureau of Labor Statistics (**http://www.bls.gov**) provides the latest statistics on employment. The U.S. Securities and Exchange Commission (**http://www.sec.gov**) provides detailed information on public companies, and the U.S Patent and Trademark Office (**http://www.uspto.gov**) maintains information on all patents and trademarks held by a company.

Other sources of secondary data include public reports by other governmental agencies, including international agencies. If a pharmaceutical company wants, for example, information on the incidence of various diseases in a foreign country, it can find that information in World Health Survey published by the World Health Organization, an agency of the United Nations.

The Internet is a rich source of information for researchers with a variety of web sites that offer information on trends in technological, political, competitive, and economic context. Secondary research is relatively easier on the Internet since the data is indexed and searchable using a variety of general and specialized search engines (Altavista.com, Yahoo.com, Google.com). Several web sites, such as emarketer.com, cyberatlas.com, and digitrends.net, provide access to general statistics relating to Internet usage and commerce on the Internet; and market research companies such as the Gartner Group, Media Metrix, and Forrester Research also offer research reports that may be purchased at their web site. Archives of news groups are also another source of online information for marketers. There are, however, limitations of conducting secondary research on the Internet. Web coverage for specific issues may not be extensive with general purpose search engines, and there is no guarantee of "freshness of links." Secondary research on the Internet also means that the researcher will need to sift through a large amount of information that has no bearing to the actual objective of the research. The researcher also has to be careful about verifying the quality of this information before it is used.[23]

## Proprietary Data

Marketers may also use **proprietary data**, or data collected by private business firms for their own use or by firms that are in the business of collecting and marketing information of interest to a class of clients. A brief description of some important secondary databases is provided in Table 7.5. Proprietary data are of two kinds: syndicated and customized.

### Syndicated Data

The first type, **syndicated data**, are data of interest to a potentially large number of users, collected by standardized procedures, and with regular periodicity. Also the content of information remains the same every survey period. The compiled reports are then sold to whoever may want to buy them without any exclusive right to use the data.

An example of a syndicated report is the Nielsen TV ratings report. The Nielsen Market Research Company monitors people's TV watching behavior via placing an electronic device (called Peoplemeter) in the homes of a sample of U.S. TV households. The recordings of this device (along with certain data collected via diaries that the households will fill in) are then compiled and published as Nielsen TV ratings reports. This report enables advertisers to select programs and media vehicles that would best reach their target audience.

Standard Rates and Data Service (SRDS) Company publishes an annual report titled *Lifestyle Marketing Analyst*. For each of the 212 individual Area-of-Dominant-Influence (ADI) market areas, the report profiles its populations' demographics, lifestyles, and distrib-

| Selected Sources of Commercial Data | TABLE 7.5 |
|---|---|

*A. C. Nielsen Company* provides data on products and brands sold through retail outlets (Retail Index Services), supermarket scanner data (Scantrack), data on television audiences (Media Research Services), magazine circulation data (Neodata Services, Inc.), and others.

*MRCA Information Services* provides data on weekly family purchases of consumer products (National Consumer Panel) and data on home food consumption (National Menu Census).

*Information Resources, Inc.* provides supermarket scanner data (InfoScan) and data on the impact of supermarket promotions (PromotioScan).

*SAMI/Burke* provides reports on warehouse withdrawals to food stores in selected market areas (SAMI reports) and supermarket scanner data (Samscam).

*Simmons Market Research Bureau* (MRB Group) provides annual reports covering television markets, sporting goods, and proprietary drugs, giving demographic data by sex, income, age, and brand preferences (selective markets and media reaching them).

Other commercial research houses selling data to subscribers include the *Audit Bureau of Circulation; Arbitron, Audits and Surveys; Dun and Bradstreet; NFO WorldGroup; Standard Rate & Data Service;* and *Starch.*

**Source:** *MARKETING MANAGEMENT: THE MILLENNIUM EDITION,* 10/e by Kotler, Philip, ©. Reprinted by permission of Pearson Education, Inc., Upper Saddle River, NJ.

ution over 42 market segments. If marketers are interested in reaching particular geographic areas, the profile tells them how best to communicate with them to suit the demographics and the lifestyle of the residents of that area. If marketers instead have a certain prospect profile in mind, the report helps them figure out which ADI markets to their target.

Another example of syndicated data is the PRIZM scheme by the Claritas Co., which consists of 40 demographic and lifestyle clusters. (See Window on Research box.) This database enables marketers to target specific zip codes and also to decide which media to use to reach the selected zip codes.

## Customized Data

The other category of proprietary data is **customized data**. This type of data is collected at the behest of a small group of pre-identified consumers, and their use is generally restricted to the sponsoring companies. Research companies collect customized data to answer specific research questions. Therefore, the collection is done on a project-by-project basis, with both the survey questions and the research method identified individually for each study.

Some of the more prominent suppliers of customized information are research companies with a customer panel. For example, market research firms like Market Facts (CMP—Consumer Mail Panel—**http://www.marketfacts.com**) and NFO WorldGroup (NFO Consumer Panel—**http://www.nfow.com**) have consumer panels of 500,000 to 600,000 U.S. families. The data from these consumer panels is compiled to make reports that are used by companies. Internet Portals like Yahoo.com have developed consumer panels to understand how people use the World Wide Web. This information helps Yahoo! design new content, products, and services to meet customer's needs.

## Tracking Services

Some secondary research supplier firms provide tracking services. They survey customers to track their opinions and attitudes on a longitudinal basis. Four leading tracking studies for consumer markets are the Yankelovich Monitor, the ABC News/Harris survey, the

# WINDOW ON RESEARCH

## PRIZM

The most widely known geodemographic segmentation scheme is PRIZM. Its foundational premise is the maxim "Birds of a feather flock together." Devised by Claritas Corporation of Alexandria, Virginia, the scheme is based on clustering 250,000 neighborhoods into 40 groups based on their zip codes (which number about 36,000). The unit of measurement is a zip code; that is, all the households in a zip code are placed in a cluster as a group. But the basis of clustering is lifestyles, so zip codes with residents manifesting a particular lifestyle are grouped together. People's lifestyles directly influence what they will buy and, thus, the market potential for specific products and services in those clusters of zip codes; hence, the name Prizm (Potential Rating Index by Zip Codes). Claritas also links the zip code information with behavioral purchase data, credit card information, magazine subscriptions, and radio and TV listening/viewing data.

The 40 PRIZM groups are listed in the table below, ranked by relative affluence scale called a Zip Quality (ZQ) scale. ZQ is computed from a number of indicators, such as median income, education, and median home value. Note, for example, that the groups Bohemian Mix and Grain Belt have about equal median income but are far apart on the ZQ scale, numbers 11 and 33 respectively. Of course, they differ vastly on median home value and on education. They also differ on lifestyle and purchase of products and services. Let us examine these groups briefly.

Bohemian Mixers (ZQ 11) are young residents (18–34 years) of urban hodge-podge neighborhoods; the majority never married or are divorced singles, and are predominantly students, artists, writers, actors, and the like, with a U-shaped income distribution concentrated on the high- and low-income groups. They are college graduates, with white-collar jobs, live somewhat adventuresome, funky lives, exercising both their bodies and minds hanging out at sidewalk cafes, public libraries, bookstores, discussion groups, health food stores, social and voluntary organizations, benefit programs, and public demonstrations and protest campaigns on social issues. They shun domestic cars, subscribe to literary magazines (e.g., *Atlantic Monthly*), and buy healthy foods. Sample neighborhoods are Greenwich Village, New York, New York (10014); Dupont Circle, Washington, D.C. (20036); Cambridge, Boston, Massachusetts (02139); Lincoln Park, Chicago, Illinois (60614); Shadyside, Pittsburgh, Pennsylvania (15232); and Haight-Ashbury, San Francisco, California (94117).

In sharp contrast are Grain Belters (ZQ 33), who live in America's most sparsely populated rural communities and small farm towns, now in economic decline. They are older (55+ in age), predominantly white families with high-school educations and in blue collar or farm occupations. Barely solvent on farm income, they are conservative, have faith in God, and are believers in providence (the purchase rate for burglar alarms is zero). They patronize domestic brands of cars, read such magazine as *Hunting*, and spend leisure hours in such activities as watching rodeo and horseback riding. Sample neighborhoods are Early, Iowa (50535); Lehr, North Dakota (58460); Jetmore, Kansas (67854); Butte, Nebraska (68722); Granville, Iowa (51022); and Chokio, Minnesota (56221).

Since Claritas links purchase behaviors with zip code information, PRIZM is very useful for identifying the zip location and lifestyle of customers, product by product or by store category. For example, the top cluster for U.S. retailer Sears is Levittown (ZQ 12), while for U.S. retailer Kmart it is Shotguns & Pickups (ZQ 24). For McDonald's, the top cluster is Rank & File (ZQ 20), and the bottom cluster is Tobacco Roads (ZQ 38).

## 40 PRIZM CLUSTERS OF NEIGHBORHOODS IN AMERICA

| CLUSTER ZQ# | CLUSTER NAME | PERCENT U.S. HOUSEHOLDS | MEDIAN INCOME | PERCENT COLLEGE GRADUATES | THUMBNAIL DESCRIPTION |
|---|---|---|---|---|---|
| 1 | Blue Blood Estates | 1.1 | $70,307 | 50.7 | America's wealthiest neighborhoods, including suburban homes and one in ten millionaires |
| 2 | Money & Brains | 0.9 | 45,798 | 45.5 | Posh big-city enclaves of townhouses, condos, and apartments |
| 3 | Furs & Station Wagons | 3.2 | 50,086 | 38.1 | New money in metropolitan bedroom suburbs |
| 4 | Urban Gold Coast | 0.5 | 36,838 | 50.5 | Upscale urban high-rise districts |
| 5 | Pools & Patios | 3.4 | 35,895 | 28.2 | Older, upper-middle-class, suburban communities |
| 6 | Two More Rungs | 0.7 | 31,263 | 28.3 | Comfortable multi-ethnic suburbs |
| 7 | Young Influentials | 2.9 | 30,398 | 36.0 | Yuppie, fringe-city condo and apartment developments |
| 8 | Young Suburbia | 5.3 | 38,582 | 23.8 | Child-rearing, outlying suburbs |
| 9 | God's Country | 2.7 | 36,728 | 25.8 | Upscale frontier boomtowns |
| 10 | Blue-Chip Blues | 6.0 | 32,218 | 13.1 | The wealthiest blue-collar suburbs |
| 11 | Bohemian Mix | 1.1 | 21,916 | 38.8 | Innercity bohemian enclaves a la Greenwich Village |
| 12 | Levittown, U.S.A. | 3.1 | 28,742 | 15.7 | Aging, post-World War II tract subdivisions |
| 13 | Gray Power | 2.9 | 25,259 | 18.3 | Upper-middle-class retirement communities |
| 14 | Black Enterprise | 0.8 | 33,149 | 16.0 | Predominantly black, middle- and upper-middle-class neighborhoods |
| 15 | New Beginnings | 4.3 | 24,847 | 19.3 | Fringe-city areas of singles complexes, garden apartments, and trim bungalows |
| 16 | Blue-Collar Nursery | 2.2 | 30,077 | 10.2 | Middle-class, child-rearing towns |
| 17 | New Homesteaders | 4.2 | 25,900 | 15.9 | Exurban boom towns of young, midscale families |
| 18 | New Melting Pot | 0.9 | 22,142 | 19.1 | New immigrant neighborhoods, primarily in the nation's port cities |
| 19 | Towns & Gowns | 1.2 | 17,862 | 27.5 | America's college towns |

(continued)

| Cluster ZQ# | Cluster Name | Percent U.S. Households | Median Income | Percent College Graduates | Thumbnail Description |
|---|---|---|---|---|---|
| 20 | Rank & File | 1.4 | 26,283 | 9.2 | Older, blue-collar, industrial suburbs |
| 21 | Middle America | 3.2 | 24,431 | 10.7 | Midscale, midsize towns |
| 22 | Old Yankee Rows | 1.6 | 24,808 | 11.0 | Working-class rowhouse districts |
| 23 | Coalburg & Corntown | 2.0 | 23,994 | 10.4 | Small towns based on light industry and farming |
| 24 | Shotguns & Pickups | 1.9 | 24,291 | 9.1 | Crossroads villages serving the nation's lumber and breadbasket needs |
| 25 | Golden Ponds | 5.2 | 20,140 | 12.8 | Rustic cottage communities located near the coasts, in the mountains or alongside lakes |
| 26 | Agri-Business | 2.1 | 21,363 | 11.5 | Small towns surrounded by large-scale farms and ranches |
| 27 | Emergent Minorities | 1.7 | 22,029 | 10.7 | Predominantly black, working-class, city neighborhoods |
| 28 | Single City Blues | 3.3 | 17,926 | 18.6 | Downscale, urban, singles districts |
| 29 | Mines & Mills | 2.8 | 21,537 | 8.7 | Struggling steeltowns and mining villages |
| 30 | Back-Country Folks | 3.4 | 19,843 | 8.1 | Remote, downscale, farm towns |
| 31 | Norma RaeVille | 2.3 | 18,559 | 9.6 | Lower-middle-class milltowns and industrial suburbs, primarily in the South |
| 32 | Smalltown Downtown | 2.5 | 17,206 | 10.0 | Inner-city districts of small industrial cities |
| 33 | Grain Belt | 1.3 | 21,698 | 8.4 | The nation's most sparsely populated rural communities |
| 34 | Heavy Industry | 2.8 | 18,325 | 6.5 | Lower-working-class districts in the nation's older industrial cities |
| 35 | Share Croppers | 4.0 | 16,854 | 7.1 | Primarily southern hamlets devoted to farming and light industry |
| 36 | Downtown Dixie Style | 3.4 | 15,204 | 10.7 | Aging, predominantly black neighborhoods, typically in southern cities |
| 37 | Hispanic Mix | 1.9 | 16,270 | 6.8 | America's Hispanic barrios |
| 38 | Tobacco Roads | 1.2 | 13,227 | 7.3 | Predominantly black farm communities throughout the South |
| 39 | Hard Scrabble | 1.5 | 12,874 | 6.5 | The nation's poorest rural settlements |
| 40 | Public Assistance | 3.1 | 10,804 | 6.3 | America's inner city ghettos |

**Source:** Adapted from Michael J. Weiss, *Clustering of America* (New York: Harper & Row, 1988) pp. 5, 13.

Gallup poll, and the DDB Needham study. The questions include customer views on domestic, foreign, and international issues, on their economic outlooks, and on their personal interests (e.g., the extent of TV viewing) and marketplace behaviors such as brand loyalty. Figure 7.9 presents selected trends from these studies.

## Selected Trends Measured by Monitoring Services    FIGURE 7.9

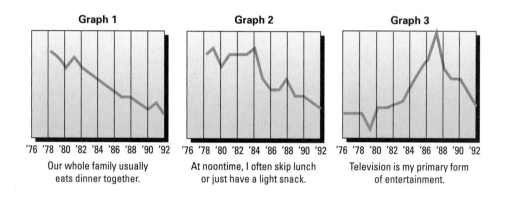

**Source:** *Advertising: Principles & Practice* by Wells/Burnett/Moriarty, p. 191, ©. Reprinted by permission of Pearson Education, Inc., Upper Saddle River, NJ.

## Single-Source Data

A common problem marketers face is having to combine diverse sources for different pieces of the information puzzle. For example, the MRCA household panel report gives the marketer information about what households with different demographic profiles are buying, but not on what media they are viewing or reading. On the other hand, Nielsen TV reports provide data on the audience profile of particular TV programs but not on their buying preferences. This necessitates that marketers match aggregate information from two diverse sources. To overcome this problem, some research suppliers now offer what are known as single-source data. These data directly link customers' exposure to advertising with their purchase response at the individual consumer level.

One of the companies that offers this service is Information Resources Inc., with its behavior-scan system. In the *behavior-scan* system, matched samples of population in the sampled geographic markets are recruited as panel members. The members are given ID cards for shopping at the area's supermarkets. The two samples are fed, via their home cable TVs, TV programs that are identical except for one of the commercials, which is different between the two samples. Since the panel members use their shopping ID at the supermarket where they shop, their purchases can be tied to the viewing of the commercial. The marketer can find out which commercial was more effective. Furthermore, since an individual panel household's demographic profile is prerecorded in the database, the purchase response data can be analyzed by demographics. That is, the marketer knows not only which commercial was more effective but also whether it was more effective for some demographic groups than others. A brief outline of behavior-scan and other single-source systems is presented in Figure 7.10.

Another type of single-source data is the scanner data that links consumer identity with products bought. When you go to a supermarket, the cashier scans the universal price code (UPC) on the package, and the computer automatically identifies the product and supplies the price information. The store can collect this scanner data and use it to track

## FIGURE 7.10 — The Process of Single-Source Data Collection

| | | | |
|---|---|---|---|
| UPC's for each grocery item are scanned at checkout. Information is sent from store to chain and on to IRI via telecommunicationsystems. | Household panel members present an identification card at checkout, which identifies and assigns items purchased to that household. Coupons are collected and matched to the appropriate UPC. Information is electronically communicated to IRI computers. | IRI field personnel visually survey stores and all print media to record retailer's merchandising efforts, displays, and ad features. Field personnel also survey retail stores for a variety of custom applications, e.g., average number of units per display, space allocated to specific sections, and number of facings. Results are electronically communicated to IRI computers. | Household panel members are selected for television monitoring and equipped with meters, which automatically record the set's status every five seconds. Information is relayed back to IRI's computers. |

Information is received at IRI and processed through the Neural Network (Artificial Intelligence) Quality Control System. the system approves the over 35 million records obtained weekly for further data processing and identifies records that require further verification.

Completed databases are converted to the required client format, transferred to appropriate recording mediums . . . hard copy, mag tape, pc diskette, etc . . ., and sent to the subscriber.

**Source:** David A. Aaker, V. Kumar, and George S. Day, *Marketing Research* (John Wiley & Sons, Inc., 1995), p. 152. Reprinted by permission of John Wiley & Sons, Inc.

product sales. Some retailers link this scanner data to household data for its shoppers. To do this, they issue the shopping households a membership card, which would be scanned every time the household made the purchase.

### Database Research

Marketers may also build their own database containing the names and relevant information about their current customers or about prospective customers. This information is obtained by a number of means, such as warranty cards, sweepstake entries, rebate forms, special surveys customers are asked to return for free products, and premiums. The most significant feature of such a database is consumer **addressability**. That is, each customer's address is known. This feature enables a marketer to address marketing communications individually on a one-on-one basis.

Equally important is the potential of this database to do customer research. An analysis can be performed to find out patterns of customer purchases by customer groups, by geography, by demographics, by seasonality, by product clusters, and so forth. For example, a credit card company can identify heavy travelers or heavy users of fine dining; it can analyze the data for whether those who patronize fine dining restaurants are also heavy users of theater performances, beauty parlors, or educational seminars, for example. This type of analysis of customer profiles and clustering of products bought by individuals can be immensely useful to marketers in planning and directing their communications and product offerings to customers.

# Virtual Reality: New Tool of Customer Research

An advanced use of technology is virtual reality simulations. Virtual reality refers to interactive, computer-generated 3D immersive displays and sound. The virtual reality equipment consists of a stereoscopic head-mounted display, body suit, and glove to provide tactile and sensory input. With virtual reality, test environments can be simulated to be indistinguishable from their real (physical) versions.

## Virtual Reality Techniques in Consumer Research

Let us describe two typical applications of virtual reality: virtual shopping and virtual test marketing.

### Virtual Shopping

Using computer technology, a store aisle can be simulated on the computer. Sitting in front of a video game type of screen, customers can walk through the aisle, look at a shelf display, examine a product, read the label, request additional information, learn if a coupon is available, put the item back on the shelf, or place it in a cart (depicted by a visual icon), all with the click of a mouse. The computer displays whatever information the customer wants and, in turn, keeps a record of customer activity. Thus, it is a useful tool to study customers' information-seeking behavior as well as customer responses to alternative shelf displays. A version of this system, called Visionary Shopper, is currently being tested in the United Kingdom. It will cost a fifth of the conventional simulated test-marketing approaches. An example of use of the "Visionary Shopper" to answer a key category management question—namely, shelf layout, is presented. This study conducted in the frozen foods section of a store showed how a simple rearrangement of shelf layouts could be beneficial for customers, manufacturers, and retailers. At the time when the study was conducted, it was common practice to stock frozen food shelf sections by segments—single serve entrees, family style entrees, kids's entrees, pot pies, etc. The manufacturer felt that stocking by brand instead of segment would increase the time that consumers spent at the shelf and make shopping easier for them as well. As a part of the experiment, two layouts were created for the shelf in addition to the existing layout. In the first layout, brands were blocked together and then segments within the brand were blocked. In the second layout, brands were blocked, and key competitive items between the manufacturer and their main competitors were stocked together on the shelf in a "competitive" set. The results of the experiment were extremely positive. The manufacturer's brand dollar sales increased by 16 percent in the "competitive set" layout over the "only brand-blocking" layout (the manufacturer had a price and size advantage over the competitor). Brand blocking also increased retailer's dollar sales by 18 percent and the competitive layout increased sales by 16 percent.[24]

## Virtual Test Marketing

In an actual virtual reality test marketing project, the goal was to evaluate demand for electric cars. Respondents were placed in front of a multimedia display. The screen flashed newspaper stories from an imagined future time. This was done to move respondents *forward in time*. Respondents then interacted with the program and a laser disc full of an array of verbal, pictorial, text, and video material. Respondents could look at the car display, walk around it, talk to salesmen, read press reports, and talk to other customers. After this simulation, they were asked to drive a conventional car with the engine replaced by an electric engine. Following the real-world test drive, they returned to their computers to answer questions on their attitudes and preferences. The proprietary name of this technique is the Information Acceleration, designed by MIT professor Glen Urban and his colleagues.

Harvard University's Business School also operates a Marketing Simulation Lab that is equipped to create virtual shopping environments.

Recently, the technique has been adapted to test new services (as opposed to physical products). Called SERVASSOR, the technique employs simulation of a service on the computer such as telebanking.[25]

## Advantages of Virtual Reality Techniques

Virtual-shopping research has several advantages over other methods. Compared to focus-group and concept-test research, the virtual-shopping method is able to simulate the real-world shopping environment much more realistically. In the virtual-shopping experiment, the customer is exposed to very realistic shelf displays, complete with the clutter of competing brands; even the hustle-bustle and the sight and sound of other shoppers can be simulated. Another advantage is that the computer is able to record much more detailed data about the shopper behavior. These data include the amount of time the shopper took to examine the product and make the decision, the content of information he or she sought and examined, the sequence in which the information was examined, and the sequence in which brands were examined and products chosen.

The method also has advantages over the conventional store-simulation methods. In the conventional method, a small-scale physical model store (or store shelf) is created, without the benefit of electronic display and manipulation of information. The virtual-shopping research tool presents the store information not only more realistically but also more economically. It costs much less to program and create virtual images and also to record customer processing data. Moreover, the computer records the data unobtrusively (i.e., without the consumer being conscious of being observed).[26] The Window on Research box illustrates these advantages.

## Data Trail From Shopping on the Internet

Shopping on the Internet is a new use of technology that is widening its appeal. Customers can access product information on web sites or home pages created by business firms. With electronic commerce (or e-commerce), consumers can use the Internet to pay with their credit cards, and companies can get bank authorization for credit payments, also on the Internet. Among the firms that are trying out this capability is Uncover, Inc., a database company that offers table-of-contents information for thousands of journals. The company has experimented with offering the information on the Internet to preapproved customer accounts.

E-commerce leaves a rich data trail. Since the information about every transaction is tracked by cookies (unique identifiers), it will be possible to analyze this data for customer profiles and patterns of purchasing, including the cluster of products different individuals buy. This enables sites to customize data for the customer when he or she visits the site again and also to send the customer information relating to his or her interests. Thus, Internet-based commerce will make available one more tool of research for insight into customer behavior.

# WINDOW ON RESEARCH

## A Virtual-Reality Consumer Research Project

A snack manufacturer wanted to find out if its line of snacks included items that consumers perceived as close substitutes. If two or more items were perceived as substitutes, then the firm could trim the line without reducing sales (but reducing the costs). On the flip side, the firm wanted to know what snack products of the competition were perceived to be substitutes of the firm's own products. If there was a competitor's snack product against which the firm's product was briefly compared but then rejected as not being a good substitute, this would suggest a gap in the firm's own product line. The firm could fill this hole by bringing out a new product.

To answer these questions, the firm employed a virtual-shopping experiment. Four hundred consumers were recruited from six shopping malls across the United States. They were invited to the local simulation lab repeatedly to buy snack products from a virtual vending machine. Since they were invited for repeated shopping trips, it was possible to first study their preferences and then custom-design the vending machine inventory to force a reconsideration of their choices. For example, in a subsequent shopping trip, the vending machine display was manipulated to show the item of a particular customer's preference as being out of stock. The customer was, thus, forced to consider substitutes (although he or she was free to buy or not buy a substitute). This enabled the researcher to study customer perceptions of what was a close substitute of their favorite brand versus what was not.

This method had three advantages: First, it was much less costly to set up vending machine displays on the computer screens than would have been the case with physically real displays. Second, the out-of-stock manipulation could be custom designed for each consumer based on the knowledge of what his or her current preference was. Finally, the consumer perception and preference data could be collected *unobtrusively*.

For additional information visit Web site **http://www.vendline.com**.

**Source:** Adapted from Raymond R. Burke, "Virtual Shopping," *ORMS Today*, 22, No. 4 (August 1995), pp. 28–34.

# Customer Behavior Research and the Three Customer Roles

Adopting a customer orientation implies that marketers assess the needs and wants of customers in each of their three roles (see Table 7.6). Thus, research concerning customer behavior should cover not only the user role but also the payer and buyer roles. Much of the research in the past has focused on users, such as the research to identify potential needs and wants that new products and services might satisfy. For payers, research is needed to understand the price sensitivity of various customer segments, or their reference prices (i.e., the price they expect to pay and the price they consider fair). Research is also needed to understand customer preferences for alternative financing options (e.g., leasing). Finally,

| TABLE 7.6 | Researching Customer Behavior and the Three Customer Roles |
| --- | --- |

| | **User** | **Payer** | **Buyer** |
| --- | --- | --- | --- |
| Need to Research Customer Behavior | • Researching user needs and wants for new product designs. | • Researching price-sensitivity of customers.<br><br>• Researching customer preferences toward leasing.<br><br>• Researching customers' reference prices. | • Researching customer attitudes toward alternative vendors (e.g., home-shopping network).<br><br>• Researching buyer use of an experience with EDI systems. |
| **Specific Research Methods** | | | |
| Focus groups Customer visits | • To explore user views and to identify unfulfilled needs and wants. | • Perceived value and reference price as discussion topics in focus group and customer visits. | • Perceptions of alternative vendors can be explored. |
| Motivation research | • To identify subconscious motives of users. | | |
| Survey research | • To elicit user's beliefs, attitudes, behaviors, etc. | • Survey of customers for target pricing, price awareness, and so on. | • Survey of buyers to assess vendor attitudes. |
| Experimental research | • Blind taste tests.<br><br>• Product use tests. | | • Test markets. |
| Information processing research | • Research on how viewers process advertising messages. | | • Primarily applicable to study the information processing by buyers. |

research is needed in the attitudes of buyers toward shopping, alternative vendors, and alternative means of doing the marketplace transactions (e.g., home-shopping networks and banking on the ATMs). For business customers, we need to research their attitudes toward and experience with electronic data interchange (EDI) systems used in purchasing.

Different research techniques discussed in this chapter are also applicable to the three roles, although some are more suited to one particular role than others. Qualitative research methods of focus groups and customer visits are useful primarily for user roles to identify unfulfilled needs and wants. But topics explored during focus groups and customer visits can include payer concerns (e.g., perceived value, reference prices, and affordability) and buyer concerns (e.g., perceptions of alternative vendors). Motivation research is likely to be useful primarily for users, to identify their subconscious motives.

The quantitative research technique of survey research has the widest applicability across three roles. The content of the survey can pertain to users (to elicit users' beliefs, attitudes, and behaviors), to payers (questioning them about their desired price in order to determine target pricing), and to buyers (to assess their attitudes about vendors). The experimental method is often used and is very useful for users. Blind taste tests are designed to elicit customer preferences for new products per se and then again for new products under specific brand names. On the other hand, test markets (a form of experimental research) are designed primarily to test buyer response to new products and the related marketing mix.

So far, information-processing research has been used primarily for buyers. For example, it has sought to answer such questions as: Do shoppers pay attention to nutrition information? Do they compare brands by attributes or by overall brand ratings? How many stores and brands do they examine? Recently, advertising research has adopted this method. Typically, customers are shown advertisements and asked what they remember of the message and what impressions they form. This is researching the user since the advertising message has to appeal to the user who has to accept the advertised product or service as meeting his or her needs.

# Summary

The various methods of researching customer behavior are either qualitative or quantitative. Qualitative methods include focus groups, customer visits, motivation research, and interpretative research. Quantitative methods entail surveys or experiments. Surveys find out what customers think, know, or feel already. Experiments, in contrast, present some stimuli and seek customer reactions to these stimuli. Some major topics researched by quantitative methods are customer attitudes, image or self-concept measurement, multiattribute models, and perceptual and preference maps.

Along with these specific quantitative and qualitative methods, there are several special streams of research in the customer behavior field: information-processing research, simulation, secondary research, and research using virtual reality and the Internet. These methods range from qualitative (verbal, unordered responses) to quantitative (numerically scalable responses), exploratory (discovering response possibilities hitherto unknown) to directed (finding out the incidence of previously known responses), secondary (using published data) to primary (collecting new data), low-tech (e.g., face-to-face interview) to high-tech (e.g., using virtual reality), and from objective (e.g., measuring eye movement) to subjective (e.g., interpretive research, such as Consumer Behavior Odyssey).

Although these methods differ in their technique as well as goals, the common purpose is to help marketers understand the customer to get inside customers' minds, to know what concerns them, what market values they are seeking, what they like and dislike, how they perceive various marketing stimuli, how they respond to them, and why they respond that way. In other words, marketers want to know why customers manifest the particular marketplace behaviors that they do. Such an understanding of customers and of the market values they seek is a prerequisite to designing a good marketing program.

# Key Terms

Addressability 264

Behaviorally Anchored Scale 248

Concurrent Protocols 256

Consumer Behavior Odyssey 240

Convenience Sampling 232

Customer Visit 233

Customized Data 259

Disguised-Nonstructured Techniques 237

Disguised-Structured Techniques 235

Experiment 243

Focus Groups 232

Information Board 254

Information Processing Research 252

Interpretive Research 240

Motivation Research (MR) 234

Nondisguised-Nonstructured Techniques 235

Nondisguised-Structured Techniques 235

Perceptual and Preference
  Mapping 250

Proprietary Data 258

Protocol 256

Qualitative Research 232

Quantitative Research 242

Retrospective Protocols 256

Secondary Research 257

Simulation 245

Single-Source Data 263

Syndicated Data 258

Test Marketing 244

Thematic Apperception Test
  (TAT) 238

Verbatim 243

Virtual Reality 265

Visual Image Profile 256

Word Association 238

Zaltman Metaphor Elicitation
  Technique (ZMET) 238

# Discussion Questions and Exercises

1. Recently, companies have been disappointed by the results of traditional quantitative market research data. Many companies like Honda, Mattel, Sony, and Yamaha have adopted "live learning labs," where they can mingle with, talk to, and directly observe consumers using their products and can learn firsthand about these users' likes and dislikes. This approach is called interpretative research. Discuss the advantages and disadvantages of this method of customer inquiry.

2. Assume you are the product manager in charge of launching a new chain of pizza outlets. One of the needs that customers have identified in the past is the desire to "make their own" pizzas in the restaurant when they come in to eat. To gain deeper insight into this customer need, you decide to conduct some consumer research. Develop a list of research questions you would want to have answered and outline appropriate research methods.

3. Recently, companies have been creating huge customer databases as a way of better understanding their customers, to analyze patterns of customer purchases, and to enable marketers to better target their one-on-one communications. What databases are you a part of? How did the company get its information about you? What kinds of communications have you been receiving from it? Have these communications been effective at getting you to buy the company's products or services?

4. Interview ten consumers and for each create a perceptual map for the following products, using two different dimensions to distinguish at least six brands for each product: (a) breakfast foods, (b) pizza, and (c) alcoholic beverages. How do these maps help marketers of these products?.

5. What type of research—qualitative or quantitative—is most appropriate for the following situations and why? What type of sample should be used? What method would you use to contact respondents? Explain each of your answers.
   a. Unilever wants to determine whether a new brand of fabric softener will be accepted by consumers.
   b. Calvin Klein wants to find out what new fashion designs will be most appealing to college students.
   c. R.J. Reynolds wants to gain some insight into the attitudes towards smoking among teenagers and young adults.

6. Using the Internet, access the web site of the U.S. Government Census Bureau: **http://www.census.gov**. Document the kind of information that is available from this resource.

# Notes

1  Thomas H. Davenport, Jeanne G. Harris, and Ajay K. Kohli, "How Do They Know Their Customers So Well?" *Sloan Management Review*, Vol. 42, Issue 2 (2001), pp. 63–73.

2  Dana James, "The Future of Online Research," *Marketing News* (January 3, 2000) pp. 1–11, Quoted by Judy Strauss, Raymond Frost in *E-Marketing*, Upper Saddle River, NJ: Prentice Hall, 2000.

3  Margaret R. Roller, "Virtual Research Exists, But How Real Is It?" *Marketing News* (January 15, 1996), p. 13.

4  Edward F. McQuarrie, *Customer Visits: Building a Better Market Focus* (Newbury Park, Calif.: Sage, 1993).

5  Gary McWilliams, "A Notebook That Puts Users Ahead of Gimmicks," *Business Week*, September 27, 1993, p. 92.

6  For an example of how the Japanese use customer visits as a research tool, see Johnny K. Johansson and Ikujiro Nonaka, "Market Research the Japanese Way," *Harvard Business Review*, May/June 1987, pp. 16–19.

7  Thomas J. Reynolds and Jonathan Gutman, "Laddering Theory, Method, Analysis, and Interpretation," *Journal of Advertising Research* 28, No. 1 (February/March 1988), pp. 11–31.

8  See Gerald Zaltman and Robin A. Higie, "Seeing the Voice of the Customer: The Zaltman Metaphor Elicitation Technique," Report Number 93-114, September 1993, Cambridge, Mass.: Marketing Science Institute; Gerald Zaltman and Robin Higie Coulter, "Seeing the Voice of the Customer: Metaphor-Based Advertising Research," *Journal of Advertising Research*, July/August 1995, pp. 35–49.

9  Basil G. Englis and Michael R. Solomon, "Life/Style Online: A Web-Based Methodology for Visually-Oriented Consumer Research," *Journal of Interactive Marketing*, 14 (1), Winter 2000, pp. 2–14.

10 For further readings, see Bobby J. Calder and Alice M. Tybout, "Interpretive Qualitative, and Traditional Scientific Empirical Consumer Behavior Research," in Elizabeth C. Hirschman, *Interpretive Consumer Research*, 1989, pp. 199–208. Provo, Utah: Association for Consumer Research.

11 Elizabeth C. Hirschman and Morris B. Holbrook, *Postmodern Consumer Research: The Study of Consumption as Text*, (Newbury Park, Calif.: Sage, 1992).

12 Russell W. Belk, Melanie Wallendorf, and John F. Sherry, "The Sacred and the Profane in Consumer Behavior, Theodicy on the Odyssey," *Journal of Consumer Research*, June 1989, 16, pp. 1–38. Russell W. Belk, "The Role of the Odyssey in Consumer Behavior and in Consumer Research," in *Advances in Consumer Research*, ed. by Paul Anderson & Melanie Wallendorf, 1987, Vol. XIV, pp. 357–61, Provo, Utah: Association for Consumer Research. Russell W. Belk, John F. Sherry, and Melanie Wallendorf, "A Naturalistic Inquiry into Buyer and Seller Behavior at a Swap Meet," *Journal of Consumer Research*, March 1988, Vol. 14, pp. 449–70. Harold H. Kassarjian, "How We Spent Our Summer Vacation: A Preliminary Report on the 1986 Consumer Behavior Odyssey," *Advances in Consumer Research* 14, pp. 376–77.

13 Robert F. Kelley, "Culture as Commodity: The Marketing of Cultural Objects and Cultural Experiences," *Advances in Consumer Research* 14, pp. 347–51.

14 Judy Strauss and Raymond Frost, *E-Marketing* (Upper Saddle River, NJ: Prentice Hall 2000).

15 Raymond R. Burke, Arvind Rangaswamy, and Sunil Gupta, "Rethinking Marketing Research in the Digital World," eBRC Research Center Working Paper, January 1999, http://www.ebrc.psu.edu/publications/researchpapers.html.

16 Maryann Jones Thompson "When Market Research Turns into Marketing," *The Industry Standard*, August 23, 1999, pp. 68–70.

17 For further discussion, see Naresh K. Malhotra, *Marketing Research: An Applied Orientation* (Upper Saddle River, NJ: Prentice Hall, 1996); David Aaker, V. Kumar, and George S. Day, *Marketing Research* (New York: John Wiley & Sons, 1995).

18 Raymond Burke, Barbara E. Kahn, Leonard M. Lodish, and Bari A. Harlam, "Comparing Dynamic Consumer Decision Processes and Real and Computer-Simulated Environments," Report Number 91-116, June (Cambridge, Mass.: Marketing Science Institute, 1991).

19 See Gilbert A. Churchill, *Marketing Research: Methodological Foundations*, 6th ed. (Fort Worth, Tex.: Dryden, 1994).

20 Adapted from William D. Wells and Douglas J. Tigert, "Activities, Interests, and Opinions," *Journal of Advertising Research* 11 (August 1971), p. 35. Reprinted from the *Journal of Advertising Research* © 1971, by the Advertising Research Foundation.

21 Merrie Brucks, "Search Monitor: An Approach for Computer-Controlled Experiments Involving Consumer Information Search," *Journal of Consumer Research* 15 (June 1988), pp. 117–21.

22 For more detailed coverage of this topic, see David W. Stewart and Michael A. Kamins, *Secondary Research: Information Sources and Methods* (Newbury Park, Calif.: Sage, 1993).

23 Raymond R. Burke, Arvind Rangaswamy, and Sunil Gupta, "Rethinking Marketing Research in the Digital World," eBRC Research Center Working Paper, January 1999, http://www.ebrc.psu.edu/publications/researchpapers.html.

24 Stephen P. Needel, "Understanding Consumer Response to Category Management Through Virtual Reality," *Journal of Advertising Research*, 38 (4), July/August 1998, pp. 61–67.

25 For further reading, see Philip J. Rosenberger III, and Leslie de Chernatony, "Virtual Reality in NPD Research," *Journal of the Market Research Society*, Vol. 37, No. 4, pp. 345-54. Raymond R. Burke, "Virtual Shopping," *OR/MS Today*, August 1995, pp. 28–34.

26 For further reading, see Raymond R. Burke, "Virtual Shopping," *ORMS Today*, 22(4), August 1995, pp. 28–34.

# PART 3

## Customer Decisions and Relationships

Chapter **8**    *Individual Customer Decision Making*

Chapter **9**    *Institution Customer Decision Making: Household, Business and Government*

Chapter **10**    *Relationship Based Buying*

# CHAPTER 8

## Individual Customer Decision Making

## Cultural Differences in the Buying Process

In a study of Chinese customers in Montreal, interviews were conducted with recent buyers of electronic equipment (e.g., audio systems, VCRs, and televisions). The study found that the most notable cultural characteristic of this group of customers was the high value the group placed on thrift and the habit of saving. Buying by debt financing was generally disapproved in this group, and, consequently, impulse buying of an expensive purchase was rare among the Chinese. Credit cards were used for convenience, not for credit; most Chinese customers paid off their entire balances monthly. This is in sharp contrast to North American customers, who usually finance their major purchases by credit.

This norm of not buying on credit makes every major purchase a three-stage process for Chinese customers: (1) budgeting for the purchase, (2) accumulating the savings, and (3) implementing the purchase. Information search takes on a different character during these stages. In the budgeting and saving stage, the search is lengthy, broad in scope, and leisurely. The customer is broadly scanning the environment rather than focusing on a specific aspect. The purpose of this search is to become familiar with the product or service category and various brands available in the market in order to learn price points, to seek others' general impressions about various brands and features, and to decide on the amount they would like to spend. In the second stage, the search virtually stops, and the customer focuses on saving the amount needed. Finally, in the third, post-saving stage, which begins after the needed budget amount has been saved, the search is intense, short in duration, and directed at specific information about specific brands and models.

The study also observed some differences in the sources of information Chinese customers utilized. They distinguished between factual and evaluative information. They relied on salespersons for the former but not for the latter. Thus, they could ask the salesperson about the product features and other objective features, but for judgments about overall product quality, they sought independent sources like *Consumer Reports* and personal sources like friends and relatives. This general distrust of salespersons also required them to rely much more on their own product inspection even for objective features. Thus, Chinese customers tended to search for product information in stores where they could browse without being approached by salespersons.

Because the implementation of the decision process is influenced by cultural background, it is important that marketers study the decision-making process for customers in different countries and for customers of different cultural backgrounds within the same country. (Kathleen Brewer Doran, ACR 1994)[1]

As a customer, understanding your own decision processes might improve your future decisions (see Figure 8.1 for the conceptual framework). As a marketer, understanding the process helps organize marketing efforts in a fashion that is responsive to the customer's decision-making imperatives.

To lay the foundation for such an understanding, this chapter begins by describing the role of the individual decision maker. It identifies the steps in the decision process, including the types of decisions relevant to customer behavior and the ways in which customers gather information. We present several models for the process of evaluating alternatives, and we identify conditions under which a customer is likely to use each model. Finally, the chapter analyzes purchase and post-purchase behavior as part of the decision process.

## Conceptual Framework                                    FIGURE 8.1

# The Individual Decision Maker

Purchase decisions are sometimes made by individuals in households; at other times, they are made by groups of people such as spouses or by committees in business organizations. The next chapter deals with group decisions; this chapter focuses on *individual* decision makers. This focus includes situations when the individual decision maker is making a decision about any product or service in any context, as long as he or she is making the decision about a product or service for his or her own use. Thus, it includes purchase decisions customers make not only in their personal capacity but also in their capacity as an employee in a firm. Thus, employment-related travel purchases, when made by individual employees (rather than by a corporate travel officer), are considered individual purchase decisions even though they occur in an organizational context, and even though someone else pays for them. Of course individual decisions use somewhat different criteria when someone else is the payer (as in business travel) compared to when the decision maker himself or herself is the payer. In the former case, the decision maker may be less concerned with the economic and financing values compared with the other values. But the decision process remains the same.

## Roles of the Decision Maker

In individual decision making (as opposed to organizational decisions), the three customer roles (payer, user, and buyer) could all be played by a single individual, or each could be played by a different individual. Often, at least two of the roles of a customer—those of buyer and user—come together within a single person. In these cases, the individual decision maker has to be concerned with at least four of the six market values of our framework (i.e., the market values relevant to the user and the buyer roles). In addition, the payer role is often played by the same individual so that all six market values—performance, social/psychological, convenience, service, economic, and financing—come into play in individual decision making. The individual may also be the buyer and payer but not the user in some situations. But even when the same individual plays all three roles, the concerns may differ for each role, creating internal role conflict. This chapter covers the decision processes of all individual customers, whether they are playing one, two, or all three roles.

When we think of an individual making a choice, we tend to limit our attention to the benefits of a product or service (i.e., values it will satisfy), whether these be performance-related or social/emotional outcomes. This is a limited view, confining the decision maker to the user role. In reality, to the individual decision maker, the buyer and payer roles are also pertinent so that the service, convenience, economic, and financing values (i.e., market values relevant to the buyer and payer roles) become equally important. In some situations, some of these values might determine the choice.

## Location and Cost of an Individual's Decision

Individual consumption can occur in three places: (1) at home, (2) in business organizations (e.g., at work or at school), and (3) in public places (e.g., restaurant, airplane, on the road, in the park, or on the beach). For products or services consumed at home, purchase decisions tend to be made in advance, substantially ahead of time. Consumption in organizational settings and in public places is much less separated in time from the purchase decisions. When purchase decisions are made close to the time of consumption (or for immediate consumption), convenience value of the buyer role acquires much more prominence. That is why individual customers readily buy a soda can from a vending machine for one dollar when they are on the road; the same customers might choose their supermarket-of-the-week based on a measly 20-cent deal on a case of Coke or Pepsi for consumption at home.

Likewise, consumption in public places tends to bring into prominence the social values of the user relative to the values of the payer. Price sensitivity is lessened in favor of how good the product will look in public. Purchase of items like a Rolex watch or a Jaguar car reflect these social values. However, the price value for the payer gains prominence while shopping on the Internet since the convenience value for the buyer is taken care of. People are more willing to spend time comparing prices across retailers from the comfort of their home than actually visiting multiple physical locations. The online competition for a consumer's money is just a click away instead of miles away.

When products and services are given away free, whether by government or by organizations, the decision criteria change. Free public roads become quickly congested, whereas toll roads encourage car pooling. At one extreme, customers will willingly accept any type of freebies, such as a free hat or a free coffee mug, disregarding its low quality; while at the other extreme, if they are not the payers (for example, when employees are buying something for self-use), they would want the best quality, making user values most salient.

The more you combine the user, the payer, and the buyer roles, the more conflicting the decision process becomes. It is in individual buying decisions, then, that the values of the three roles interplay, and trade-offs become integral to the decision process, making it an intriguing process to study.

# Customer Decision Process

**Customer decisions** are decisions customers make in the marketplace as buyers, payers, and users. Typically, these decisions include *whether* to purchase, *what* to purchase, *when* to purchase, from *whom* to purchase, and *how* to pay for it. *Whether* to purchase something is the first level of decision that entails weighing alternative uses of money and time resources. Customers have finite amounts of money and time, and they must allocate them judiciously. Alternative demands on time, such as a deadline at work, may constrain a customer to postpone or dismiss a purchase altogether, say a vacation plan. Allocating *money* resources entails weighing alternative needs at the level of the product or service category. For example, a family may have to choose between taking a cruise and investing in remodeling the house. This product/service-level choice is both a *whether* to purchase and a *what* to purchase decision.

An important customer behavior at this category-level decision is **mental budgeting** —how the budget customers set for a product category guides their subsequent behavior as a customer. This concept of mental budgeting is explained in the Window on Research box. The concept of mental budgeting highlights the importance of the payer role. The payer role (regardless of whether it is the customer or someone else in the payer role) imposes relatively inflexible budget limits, and in this way, imposes some self-discipline on the user, whose needs and wants can sometimes be infinitely expandable. Unfortunately, research on mental budgeting is limited, and it is based solely on Western consumers. It is entirely possible that consumers in other cultures, and/or consumers who live from hand to mouth, might not practice the concept of mental budgeting, or might implement it in a flexible way, adjusting the budget at the time of the purchase. This is an issue that needs cross-cultural research.

Nevertheless, the concept of mental budgeting can guide marketers' positioning efforts; a product or service may be positioned in one category rather than the other to take advantage of the budget earmarked for each category. For example, a frozen dinner of lobster may be viewed by the customer as an expensive food item; the marketer might, in contrast, present it as a relatively economical entertainment (compared to going out to eat at a restaurant).

Following the choice at the product/service level, the customer makes another "what to purchase" decision—a choice among brands. Thus, illustratively, if a product category-level decision is made—namely, "take the cruise"—the next decision is which brand to purchase (e.g., which travel destination to select and which cruise line to purchase tickets on).

These decisions at various levels of hierarchy can all be framed in a general way: these are all *alternatives*, and the customer task is to decide among alternatives. Thus, this section uses the term *alternatives* generically to refer to product and service categories, brands, stores, suppliers, and so on, and deals with customer choice decisions among alternatives.

The process of customer decision making consists of the steps shown in Figure 8.1.

# WINDOW ON RESEARCH

## Mental Budgeting and Customer Behavior

Do people set a budget for different categories of consumption, such as entertainment, clothing, food, and investment? And what happens if the money budgeted turns out to be too much or too little? Do these budgets become limiting? Do they result in underconsumption of one product category and overconsumption of another? Interestingly, the answer to all these questions from recent research is yes.

Consider two consumers, A and B. Consumer A has put aside some money for clothing to purchase a pair of slacks. After finding no acceptable slacks, he can easily put that money into another product category; instead, he just goes ahead and purchases a sweater that he had no prior intention of buying. Consumer B has allocated some money for entertainment. She receives an invitation to join a dinner group but discovers that the money she has allocated to the entertainment category is not adequate to cover the cost of dinner with the group. So she declines, even though she could have easily moved some money out of allocation to another consumption category. For Consumer A to buy a sweater just to utilize the budget for clothing is an example of overconsumption. For Consumer B to decline the dinner invitation even though she knew she would have enjoyed the event is an example of underconsumption.

Consumer researchers Chip Heath and Jack B. Soll studied this topic recently. They asked a group of consumers a set of questions about how much they had set aside to spend and how much they would spend if certain hypothetical incidents had occurred. Their questions and respondents' answers are best illustrated by this example. Suppose a respondent said at the outset that she had set aside $100 for entertainment this week; now suppose she had already spent $30 on a dinner, how much did she expect to spend on entertainment for the rest of the week? The answer, as expected, was about $70. Now, what if the dinner was paid for by a friend; the respondent still wanted to spend about $100 rather than about $70. What if the respondent had to unexpectedly buy a birthday gift for someone costing $30? She still expected to spend $100 for entertainment. This pattern of response demonstrates the mental budgeting effects. Heath and Soll obtained this pattern of responses from a majority of their research respondents.

Additional information available at **http://www.journals.uchicago.edu/ JCR.**

**Source:** Adapted from Chip Heath and Jack B. Soll, "Mental Budgeting and Consumer Decisions," *Journal of Consumer Research* 23, 1 (June 1996), pp. 40–52. Reprinted with permission of the University of Chicago Press.

## Step 1: Problem Recognition

The decision process begins with a customer recognizing a problem to be solved or a need to be satisfied. The customer notices, for example, that he or she is hungry and needs to get some food, that the light bulb has blown out and needs to be replaced, that the roof has begun to leak and needs to be repaired, or that the office copier has run out of paper and needs to be refilled.

As these examples illustrate, a customer problem is not necessarily a physical problem, such as a hungry stomach or dirty laundry. Rather a **customer problem** is any state of deprivation, discomfort, or wanting (whether physical or psychological) felt by a person. **Problem recognition** is a realization by the customer that he or she needs to buy something to get back to the normal state of comfort physically and psychologically.

## Stimuli for Problem Recognition

Problem recognition can occur in two ways: due to an internal stimulus or an external stimulus. **Internal stimuli** are perceived states of discomfort and can be physical or psychological (e.g., hunger or boredom, respectively). **External stimuli** are marketplace information items that lead the customer to realize the problem. Thus, an advertisement about multivitamins or the sight of a Pizza Hut can serve as external stimuli to arouse the recognition of a need. The Window on Practice box provides examples of how banks have attempted to use such stimuli.

The terms *external* and *internal stimuli* are commonly used in psychology; however, more apt terms would be problem-stimuli and solution-stimuli. A problem-stimulus is one in which the problem itself is the source of information. This source could lie *within* the customer (as in hunger pangs) or outside the customer (as in dirty laundry). The solution-stimulus is the information emanating from a solution itself; exposure to a potential solution arouses the recognition of the need or the problem. For example, the smell of fresh-baked cinnamon rolls from a bakery might arouse your desire for cinnamon rolls. Marketing communications, product or service samples, window shopping, and so on, have their utility precisely because they serve as problem-recognition stimuli. On the Internet, broadband providers (cable and DSL) use banner advertising with messages like "You are wasting your time" and "Your Internet connection is too slow" to try to make people aware of faster alternatives to their current dial-up ISP.

As customers, you can expect to encounter solution-stimuli in three states of mind:

1. When you have already recognized the problem and are looking for a solution; for example, suppose you have dandruff and are looking for a more effective shampoo than the one you are using currently; or you find your current food service contractor for the company cafeteria unsatisfactory and are planning to find a new contractor.
2. When the problem had been recognized in the past, but it was just not salient (i.e., not in the top-of-the-mind awareness) at the moment of the exposure to the solution. An example would be that you had thought of buying some exercise equipment, but you never pursued the thought actively; an infomercial or a product display or the fact that a friend bought exercise equipment rekindles the need you had previously recognized.
3. When you never recognized the need in the past, but exposure to the solution-product makes you realize that the product or service would solve a condition now perceived as a problem. Thus, a display of a caller-ID device in a store and the salesperson's explanation of its use might make you realize that not knowing who is calling had been a frustrating experience all along, even though until now you never viewed it as a problem. For a health-conscious customer, information on dietary requirements obtained during exploratory browsing of the Internet could act as problem-recognition stimuli. The consumer might now perceive a problem in his or her eating habits and change them accordingly.

Life situations that cause inconvenience but have no solutions are generally not viewed as problems; they are simply viewed as life conditions, taken for granted. Only when a solution appears on the horizon does the life condition become a problem. For example, before the invention of the microwave ovens, the slow process of conventional ovens was not perceived as a problem. Or before the home delivery of pizza, going to the pizzeria was not perceived as a problem. Before e-mail and fax, the effort, cost, and delay in getting messages from one person to another was not perceived as a problem.

# WINDOW ON PRACTICE

## Problem Recognition: A Key to Selling Bank Loans

Often the trickiest part of generating a demand for a firm and satisfying customer needs is helping customers make the connection between a firm's product or service offering and the customers' needs. This connection is not always obvious to the customer, and marketers sometimes miss this opportunity. Take, for example, bank loans. Most banks market them predominantly by advertising the interest rate and other terms of financing. That works if consumers are already looking for a loan. But looking for a loan and having the need for a loan are not the same thing. Customers may want to do things for which they need money, but if those things have not been associated in the customer's mind as legitimate purposes for a bank loan, then the idea of getting a bank loan for that purpose would not occur to them. So there may be a customer need (i.e., a problem), and there may be a solution available. But the customer problem and the marketplace solution remain disconnected in the customer's mind. To establish that connection is to facilitate problem recognition. And recently, some banks have done just that.

One category of bank loans is the home equity loan—money banks loan using the borrower's house as the collateral. It is a desirable type of loan for the bank because the collateral makes the loan less risky. And it appeals to the customer because the rate is generally lower than other types of loans, and the interest is tax-deductible. Yet most customers inadvertently think that a home equity loan is for financing the purchase of a home, or at most, for financing a home improvement project, and for no other purpose. That is, home equity loans are perceived the same as mortgage loans.

A number of leading banks realized this quirk in the customer assumption recently. They realized why rate advertising was not creating new demand for loans. People's Heritage Bank of Portland, Maine is a case in point. The bank ran an advertising campaign that educated the customer about the various uses for which a home equity loan could be obtained. The bank developed three advertisements that featured people who achieved their dreams with the help of a home equity loan. In one advertisement, a veterinarian opened her practice with the home equity loan. In another advertisement, a customer bought the guitar he had always wanted. In a third advertisement, a teenager and her dad were featured with the computer they bought with the home equity loan so they could explore Europe on the Internet. By the end of the advertising campaign, which involved print and radio as well as more targeted direct mail, the bank had tripled the average number of home equity loan sales each month.

Reflecting on the situation, a senior product manager commented: There was a lot of rate advertising in the market when we introduced this product. We were offering a good competitive rate, yet we wanted to offer customers something more. We wanted to show them that our product had value. In other words, the bank needed to make a connection between the things customers valued and the product the firm offered.

**Source:** Adapted from Katherine Morrall, "Marketing Loans that Make Consumers' Dreams Come True," *Bank Marketing*, April 1996, pp. 19–24.

This distinction is important for two reasons. First, it underscores the role of what is known as educational or pioneering marketing. Pioneering marketing and communications promote a new product or a new service by educating the customer about what the product or service will do and how it can solve a hitherto unsolved or unrecognized problem. Some of these marketing efforts are intended to create primary demand rather than secondary demand. **Primary demand** is demand for the product or service category itself, seeking to convert nonbuyers of the product/service category into buyers. **Secondary demand** (also known as **selective demand**), in contrast, is simply to deflect demand from one brand to the other. There is a noteworthy controversy on this issue in cigarette advertising today. The government and anti-tobacco groups claim that cigarette advertising is targeted at the youth, promoting the primary demand for smoking among new customers. If this is true, then cigarette advertising is a solution-stimulus arousing a problem recognition among youth by presenting the product as a solution to their enduring need to be perceived by their peers as being cool. The tobacco industry, on the other hand, argues that it is merely creating secondary demand for specific brands, rather than enticing and recruiting new smokers. Advertising on comparison sites like MySimon.com, Dealtime.com and Bizrate.com are attempts by advertisers to switch demand from another brand to theirs (secondary demand). To reduce the risk involved in shopping from "unknown" vendors, MySimon, Dealtime and Bizrate rate the sellers to give buyers a degree of confidence. The distinction between primary and secondary demand for products is visible in emerging versus mature markets as well. Several products like automobiles, cellphones, and video cameras already have a secondary demand in the mature Western markets, while marketers are still trying to create primary demand for these products in the emerging markets in Asia.

The second implication of solution- versus problem-stimulus goes to the heart of a basic controversy in marketing. An often-asked and hotly debated question is, "Does marketing create a need or merely satisfy one?" In arguing that it indeed *creates* needs, critics note that no one needed a VCR, a video camera, a cellular phone, a $150 pair of Nike shoes, or an overnight document delivery service until advertising came along, parading these products and services in an enticing way. Our view is that a need ought to be defined in terms of the function the product or service serves, rather than in terms of the product or service itself (as in "no one needed a VCR"). When needs are properly defined in terms of the function, it is easy to see that the only products or services that would be successful in the marketplace are those that serve some function. Thus, a VCR serves the function of enabling time-shifted viewing, and the need to be able to watch a program at your convenience was always a need, albeit unrecognized as a problem and, as such, relegated from consciousness simply as a life condition. The invention of the VCR, like all other inventions, helped surface that latent need. Likewise, in the world of business, there is a product to which every executive and every staff member is addicted— Post-it® notes. Yet before their invention, no one even sensed the problem now addressed by this innovative product.

## Problem Recognition by Each Customer Role

Problem recognition can occur for each customer role and for each of the six values customers seek. The VCR and Post-it® examples illustrate the latent needs of the user role. For business consumers, 3M has a Post-it® easel pad which can be stuck on the wall like a white board, used, and peeled off without any paint peeling off the walls. This is clearly fulfilling a latent need of the business customer. For the buyer role, the example of problem recognition is the home delivery of pizza, which offers convenience value. Similarly online shopping offers the convenience of searching for information and completing the purchase from the confines of one's home. For the payer, the availability of leasing automobiles to individual customers or for a corporate fleet has improved affordability. Also, availability of credit makes many customers realize the need to buy a *new* car or furniture. A parallel in business markets is vendor financing.

## A Typology of Problems

To see the variety of problems customers recognize, we can classify them along two dimensions: familiar versus novel and vivid versus latent (see Table 8.1). Familiar problems generally occur due to what is commonly called stock depletion; for example, a hungry stomach or a worn-out tire. Novel problems arise generally with life events that mark passage from one stage to another, as discussed in Chapter 4. Examples include a new job, a marriage, or international relocation, or for business customers, the life-stage changes occur when firms go public, change ownership, or form alliances.

| **TABLE 8.1** | **Four Situations for Problem Recognition** |
| --- | --- |

|  | VIVID | LATENT |
| --- | --- | --- |
| FAMILIAR | Stock depletion | Educational marketing |
| NOVEL | Life-stage change | New product technology |

Vivid problem situations are immediately obvious and recognized, as in a just-emptied cereal box, the arrival of the back-to-school month, power outages in California, or network traffic on web pages on the Internet causing the web server to shut down. A latent problem is not immediately obvious and needs shaping, either by self-reflection or more likely by an external agent such as a salesperson. Examples of a latent problem are regular car tune-ups, preventive maintenance and scheduled repairs and replacements for machines, or the ability to know who is calling you on the phone (a novel-latent problem). Availability of the caller ID service from the local phone company makes the novel-latent need salient (i.e., recognized). Thus, recognition of novel-latent problems is stimulated by solution-stimuli, generally in the form of new technologies and new products/services. In addition, however, the recognition of latent problems (whether familiar or novel) generally requires educational marketing efforts (e.g., counseling by a salesperson about the need for a life-insurance policy).[2]

## Step 2: Information Search

Once the need has been recognized, customers search for information about various alternative ways of solving the problem. That search rarely includes every brand in existence. Rather, as shown in Figure 8.2, customers consider only a select subset of brands/suppliers, organized as follows:

- The **awareness set** consists of brands/suppliers a customer is aware of.
- An **evoked set** consists of the brands/suppliers in a product or service category that the customer remembers at the time of decision making.
- The **consideration set** consists of the brands/suppliers from the evoked set that a customer will consider buying after the brands/suppliers that are considered unfit have been eliminated.

Initially, customers seek information about the consideration set of brands which is a subset of the evoked set. New information can bring in additional brands/suppliers into

# Awareness, Evoked, and Consideration Sets      FIGURE 8.2

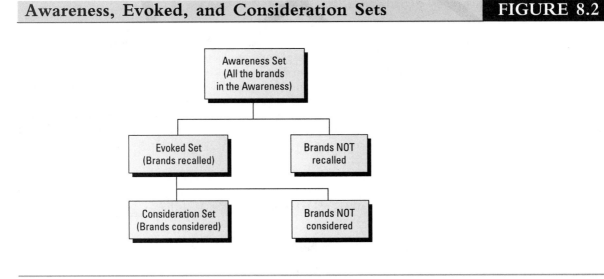

the awareness, evoked, and consideration set. It should be the minimum objective of all marketing communications to place the brand in the consideration set (rather than merely in the awareness or evoked set) of its target customers. Consideration sets will include alternatives from different categories when the consumer experiences goal conflict (a single category cannot deliver on all salient and conflicting goals) or goal ambiguity (a lack of salient goals). For example, when the salient goals for a car are maximum fuel efficiency and capability of driving off-road, the consumer may find that one category does not satisfy all salient goals. Subcompacts may offer fuel efficiency but not off-road driving, and four-wheel-drive trucks would do the opposite. Similarly there is goal ambiguity when the consumer has a fuzzy goal like appeasing hunger or a need for personal transportation. Products from several categories could be used to form a consideration set to satisfy these goals.[3]

One of the most significant outcomes of the Internet revolution is the "democratization of information" across the vast customer population. Information search is one of the first uses of the Internet. A vast number of alternatives are available to the customer, and it is common to find most consumer decisions being researched on the Internet before the products or services are bought offline or online. Thus, the fundamental benefit of "Interactive Home Shopping" (IHS—shopping electronically from home, that is, via the Internet) is the low cost of information search. Yet, researchers Alba, et al. state that the growth of IHS is dependent on several other factors:

1. *Selection:* Customers should be able to access a large set of items fairly quickly.
2. *Screening:* Consumers should be able to screen the available options effectively. If they are not able to do this, then the benefits of a vast selection will be offset by the high costs of search.
3. *Reliability:* The customer should be able to comprehend the benefits from products/services reliably in the IHS shopping format. If experiential information available from stores is better than the information from IHS, and the consumer is not comfortable enough with the information available through IHS to make a purchase decision, the IHS format will lose the customer to the store.
4. *Product comparison:* The IHS format should provide the consumer with superior methods for comparing between alternatives in order to make the purchase decision.[4]

Three elements characterize the information-search phase of the decision process: (1) sources of information, (2) search strategies, and (3) amount of search.

## Sources of Information

Sources of information may be categorized into marketer or nonmarketer. (See Table 8.2.) Marketer sources are those that come from the marketer of the product or service itself. These consist of advertising, salespersons, product/service literature and brochures, and in-store displays. One of the latest marketer sources is the Internet. More and more companies have opened a home page on the Internet, a site customers can visit at their convenience. Since these sources have a vested interest in providing favorable information, these are also referred to as advocate sources (i.e., sources that have a vested point-of-view to advocate or promote). As such, these sources have lower credibility compared with nonmarketer sources.

| TABLE 8.2 | Sources of Information for Customers |
|---|---|

| Marketer Sources | Nonmarketer Sources |
|---|---|
| Advertising | PERSONAL |
| Salespersons | Friends and other acquaintances |
| Product/service brochures | Past experience |
| Store displays | |
| Company web sites | |
| | INDEPENDENT SOURCES |
| | Public information (e.g., *Consumer Reports*, Better Business Bureau, news reports in media, government publications such as *The Census of Manufacturers*) |
| | Product or service experts: (e.g., auto critic, home appraiser, pharmacist) Internet (bulletin boards) |

Nonmarketer sources are those that are independent of the marketer's control. Nonmarketer sources include personal sources and independent sources. Since these have no vested interest in biasing the information, they are viewed as nonadvocate sources and are deemed more credible. Friends and other acquaintances with past experience and the customers' own past experience with the product or service are credible sources of information. Independent sources are usually publications and organizations with relevant expertise. For example, *Consumer Reports*, published in the United States, provides performance data based on product trials by independent judges and based on systematically collected reports of other past users' experiences. Online sites like **http://www.epinions.com** attempt to recreate the informal social information-gathering experience by using their Web of Trust. Online sites are willing to pay independent rating sites like Bizrate (**http://www.bizrate.com**) and Gomez (**http://www.gomez.com**) to get reviewed. Professional appraisers/advisors are sometimes used for very large purchases. Thus, home appraisers are used by home buyers, and car mechanics are used to appraise used cars. In business-to-business buying, such as for plant and equipment, engineering consultants are utilized as sources of information.

There are marketer and nonmarketer sources for every conceivable topic on the Internet from businesses to alternative medicine. For example, there are hundreds of sites, sponsored by auto manufacturers, dealerships, government agencies, insurance industry groups, consumer and car-buff magazines, newspapers, financial institutions and an assortment of new and used-car price information services for prospective car buyers. Table 8.3 gives a list of a few sites that prospective car buyers can visit.

| Sources of Information on the Internet for Prospective Car Buyers | TABLE 8.3 |
|---|---|

1. **http://www.kbb.com**—Kelley Blue Book, new- and used-car prices and dealer costs, evaluations, links to manufacturers' sites, others offering financing and insurance.
2. **http://www.edmunds.com**—Edmunds Publications, broad guide to new- and used-car buying, with suggested retail prices and dealer costs for new cars and options, used-car values, evaluations, links to related sites for financing and insurance.
3. **http://www.nhtsa.dot.gov**—Federal government's auto safety agency posts recall information and comparative crash test results for cars and trucks.
4. **http://www.carsafety.org.**—Insurance industry ratings of cars for safety equipment, loss experience, and crash-test performance.
5. **http://www.jdpower.com**—Summaries of the market research firm's surveys of car quality and dealer performance.
6. **http://www.nada.com**—National Automobile Dealers Association's used-car shopping guide, values, lists of local dealerships.
7. **http://www.consumerreports.org.**—Evaluations, comparisons, detailed pricing printouts from the consumer magazine.
8. **http://autos.yahoo.com**—General information, car and dealer locator, links to numerous related sites.
9. **http://www.hotbot.com/cars**—Used-car locator, links to numerous web sites useful in car shopping.
10. **http://www.cars.com**—General buying information, reviews, used-car locator, run by eight major newspaper groups.
11. **http://www.autoweb.com**—Shopping service links buyers with dealers pledged to offer discounts on new and used cars; also general information, links to finance and insurance retailers.
12. **http://www.carpoint.msn.com**—Microsoft shopping service, links buyers and dealers pledged to offer discounts on new cars; general information; used-car values.
13. **http://www.autobytel.com**—New- and used-car shopping service, links buyers and dealers pledged to offer discounts; general information, links to finance and insurance vendors.
14. **http://www.autoconnect.com**—Used-car shopping guide and car locator.
15. **http://www.dealernet.com**—New- and used-car locator, used-car values, guide to local dealerships.
16. **http://www.bankrate.com**—Bank Rate Monitor's guide to best financing deals.

**Source:** List taken from Tom Incantalupo, "Car Shopping? Just Click Here/Web Sites Let Buyers Find Dream Ride, Haggle-free," *Newsday*, April 11, 1999. © 1991 Newsday, Inc. Reprinted with permission.

## Search Strategies

The choice of information sources depends partly on the customer's search strategy. A **search strategy** is the pattern of information acquisition customers utilize to solve their decision problems. Since information acquisition has costs in terms of time, physical effort, and mental effort, customers weigh the costs against the likely gains from information acquisition. That comparison helps them decide how much information they will acquire and from what sources.

**Routine, Extended, and Limited Problem Solving.** Based on the amount of search deemed necessary, customer decision strategies may be routine, limited, or extended problem-solving strategies. **Routine problem solving** is a strategy in which no new information is considered. This strategy is utilized for purchase problems that have occurred and have been solved previously. Consequently, when these problems recur, these are solved simply by repeating the past choice, as in purchasing the brand bought in the past. Information search is minimal. This is common in business because search costs are enormous. Sometimes, nonstrategic supplies are outsourced. **Extended problem solving** occurs when the search is extensive and deliberation prolonged. This strategy becomes necessary for purchases never made before or made long ago, or where risks of wrong choice are high.

Examples are purchase of a new home or building a new factory in a business context. Finally, **limited problem solving** is a strategy wherein the customer invests some limited amount of time and energy in searching and evaluating alternative solutions. Customers adopt this strategy when purchases are nontrivial, the risk is limited, and the product or service is not complex or technical in terms of its features. There is some familiarity with the product/service class, but a desire for variety (e.g., buying a new dress) or unavailability of previous solutions (e.g., stockout of your usual brand) necessitates some amount of search. In the business context, users might request a change in the products offered in the vending machine placed in the office cafeteria. The company would have to undertake limited problem solving to look for vendors who can accomdate the choices requested. Textbook adoption by professors in the business school would also involve limited problem solving.

These three strategies are related to the problem typology discussed earlier. Generally, familiar-vivid problems are likely to be solved with routine problem solving. Novel-latent problems would tend to be solved with extended problem solving. Familiar-latent problems (e.g., starting to get your car regularly tuned) may entail routine (go to your regular mechanic) or limited problem solving (comparison shopping with coupons). Finally, novel-vivid problems may entail limited or extended problem solving, depending on the risk involved and/or prior familiarity. Note that the familiar-novel/vivid-latent typology has to do with the genesis of problem *recognition*, whereas the routine/extended/limited continuum has to do with search efforts.

**Systematic versus Heuristic Search.**    So far, the description of search strategies may seem to suggest that customers prefer systematic strategies. **Systematic search** consists of a comprehensive search and evaluation of alternatives. Systematic searchers have been found to search information extensively, consult with a variety of sources, shop with others, take a long time, and deliberate a lot, and they are especially price-comparison shoppers. However, customers also use a contrasting search strategy, termed heuristics. **Heuristics** are quick rules of thumb and shortcuts used to make decisions.[5]

Heuristics can be implemented in a variety of ways:

- Broad inferences are quickly drawn from partial information (e.g., price may be used to judge quality). Technical-sounding terms may be used to infer overall brand superiority (e.g., many customers may not know what Dolby sound in stereos or even pH-balanced in shampoos means, but they would conveniently infer that these imply advanced products). Another trademark that is used to infer quality of products is "UL Listed," and the phrase "Intel Inside" for computers instills confidence in the purchase.
- Past experiences are considered adequate.
- Others' judgments are sought and summarily adopted as final choice. In business, companies benchmark against competitors or seek consultants to give them advice.
- Brand names/suppliers are heavily relied on to the exclusion of seeking further attribute information.

Although these strategies are not systematic, they are also not irrational. They are rational to their users in terms of the cost versus benefit trade-offs they perceive.

Consider inferences, for example. Customers often have to make their decisions on partial information about various product or service alternatives. In these situations, customers make product or service assessments by supplying the missing information in the form of inferences. Scholars have identified various strategies customers use for handling missing information:

- **Interattribute inference**—The value of one attribute is inferred based on another attribute. For example, thickness of the fabric in an item of clothing might be used to infer crease-resistance (whether correctly or incorrectly). Refinement of chemicals may infer purity.
- **Evaluative consistency**—The missing attribute is assumed to conform to the overall evaluation of the brand/supplier. Thus, if a brand is positively evaluated in overall terms, the brand is assumed to be good on the missing attribute as well.

- **Other-brand averaging**—The missing attribute value may be assumed to be an average of its values across all other brands. This is likely to occur, however, only if the variance in the values of this attribute for other brands is low.
- **Negative Cue**—The customer may simply treat the missing information as a negative cue and then use one of the two substrategies: avoid altogether the option with the missing information, or assume a low or poor value on this attribute. A customer may look for the ISO 9000 certification in a supplier and consider the absence of the certification as a negative cue.

The Window on Research box discusses the application of intuitive theories to these strategies.

The extent and type of inference making will depend on several factors. One is the need for inference; that is, how critical is the attribute considered for product or service assessment? Another factor is customer involvement in the purchase; that is, how critical is it to make the right choice? Finally, the use of inferences will depend on the customer's product or service category knowledge. More knowledgeable customers are more likely to infer the missing information.

## Determinants of the Amount of Search

Imagine that you are in the market for a CD player, or a pair of shoes, or a greeting card, or a catering service for an office party, or business consulting services or training. How much information will you seek? How much effort will you put into processing this information? Actually, this depends on several factors. These factors include perceived risk, involvement, familiarity, expertise, time pressure, the functional versus expressive nature of the product or service, information overload, and relative brand uncertainty.

**Perceived Risk.** The **perceived risk** is the degree of loss (i.e., amount at stake) in the event that a wrong choice is made.

There are five types of risks:

1. *Performance risk*—The product or service may not perform well or not as well as some other alternatives. Examples are plastic surgery undertaken to improve one's looks or software bought for a specific purpose.
2. *Social risk*—Reference group members and significant others may not like it. Clothing and country club memberships may be subject to social risk.
3. *Psychological risk*—The product or service may not reflect oneself. A foreign product purchase may not reflect yourself as well as American-made products.
4. *Financial risk*—The alternative may be overpriced; there may exist a better purchase. There may be some alternative that you did not consider from competitors that you are not aware of, which may be cheaper than what you paid for the product.
5. *Obsolescence risk*—The alternative may be replaced by newer substitutes. Fashion and software are subject to obsolescence risk.

The financial risk is of most concern to the payer, whereas other risks are of concern to the user.

The greater the perceived risk, the more extensive the search and deliberation. Marketers, therefore, attempt to overcome these risks by various strategies—performance warranties to overcome performance risks, price guarantees (matching a competitor's price or refunding the difference) to overcome price risks, and product upgrades and trade-in of old models to overcome obsolescence risk. Social and psychological risks are addressed by liberal return, exchange, or refund policies. Consumers that are contemplating buying products through the Internet face the added risk of not seeing and touching a physical product before making the purchase. This presents a bigger challenge for marketers on the Internet compared to the "brick and mortar" ones. Similarly, for business customers, marketers attempt to free customers from various perceived risks by assuming the risks themselves. For office machines, for example, performance risk is minimized by offering a lifetime

# WINDOW ON RESEARCH

## Intuitive Theories in Customer Inference Making

An important research issue concerning inferences is the extent to which customers' intuitive theories play a role in inference making. For example, people generally expect the length of warranties to be positively related to a product's reliability (i.e., the longer and better the warranty, the more reliable the product or service is likely to be). But what if we did not find this to be true in a specific case? For example, suppose you were shopping for a camera and you found that across different brands of cameras there was no correspondence between reliability and warranty. Brands that had poor warranties had just as good or poor a reliability record as brands with exceptional warranties. However, another attribute, say shutter speed, was perfectly correlated with reliability record; that is, the model that had a high shutter speed also had more reliability. Note that there is no logical connection between shutter speed and reliability. It just so happens that for all the models you examined, the reliability record happens to be uncorrelated with warranties but related to shutter speed. Now, suppose you encounter another brand and find reliability information missing. How are you going to infer its value? Is your inference going to be based more on data (i.e., in the models examined, reliability related with shutter speed was a mere coincidence) or is it going to be based more on your general intuitive theory, which tells you that, logically, reliability should be related to warranty?

This important question was examined by customer researchers Susan M. Broniarczyk and Joseph W. Alba. These researchers presented customers information about alternative brands of cameras to choose from. After they made the choice, customers were presented with information about a new set of brands, except that the information on their reliability record was missing. In choosing from these new, incompletely described brands, customers could rely for inference about the missing attribute either on their knowledge of the value of the missing attribute on an otherwise identical brand in the previous set (which would be in conflict with intuitive theory), or they could base such an inference on intuitive theory. The experimental subjects' choices revealed that in inferring the missing information, customers drew on their intuitive theory, even when the previously exposed data were in conflict with the logical theory.

Of course, further research is needed on this topic; but this important finding of research done thus far implies that marketers should understand their customers' intuitive theories about the relationships among diverse brand attributes in particular, and about various marketplace phenomena in general.

**Source:** Adapted from Susan M. Broniarczyk and Joseph W. Alba, "The Role of Consumers' Intuitions in Inference Making," *Journal of Consumer Research* 21 (December 1994), pp. 393–407. Additional information available at http://www.ConsumerReports.org. Reprinted with permission of the University of Chicago Press.

repair maintenance contract. Financial and obsolescence risks are minimized by offering the product on lease. Many consulting firms and advertising agencies guarantee certain results for the client, and some even make their fees contingent on the degree to which intended results are achieved.

**Involvement.**   On the positive side of the equation, involvement is defined as the perceived importance of the product or service. There are some products and services that we just purchase routinely while there are some others that we consider important, which we purchase with great care. In business, there are strategic and nonstrategic decisions.

Consumer researchers have distinguished between two types of involvement: purchase decision involvement and enduring involvement. **Purchase-decision involvement** is the degree of concern and caring that customers bring to bear on the purchase decision. Purchase decision involvement is high for most of the high-ticket items, but price and involvement do not have one-to-one correspondence. What brings in purchase involvement is the degree of risk, whether performance, financial, or social. For most products and services, customers' involvement ends when the purchase is made. After buying an appliance, for example, most customers just use it without deliberation. For some products or services, however, the involvement continues well beyond the purchase, into the product or service use. This is termed **enduring involvement**, ongoing interest in the product or service. Customer researchers refer to this state of enduring involvement as deep involvement. In the business context, service contracts and single sourcing are examples of enduring involvement with suppliers. Consider this quote from Morris Holbrook, professor at Columbia University; here he speaks as a consumer himself, specifically as a fanatic consumer of jazz music:

> I just want to hear the music. What I do need is music in every location where I might spend any appreciable amount of time (say five minutes). This includes the living room, my study, Christopher's room, Sally's office, Sally's desk, the Oldsmobile, and [my other] house in Pennsylvania. For other locations and for traveling, I also keep a backup collection of portable radios and tape players.[6]

Table 8.4 illustrates measures of these two forms of involvement.

The relationship between purchase involvement and enduring product involvement is that enduring product involvement will create high purchase involvement, but high purchase involvement does not necessarily involve enduring product involvement. For example, purchases like a washer-dryer could be highly involving without the product or service itself eliciting any long-term enduring involvement. In contrast, a music lover wants to buy a stereo sound system. His enduring interest in music raises his purchase involvement, and his involvement in the product continues beyond the purchase occasion.

Purchase decision involvement directly affects the extent of information search and processing. Enduring product involvement, on the other hand, leads customers to develop expertise on the product or service category, to search information on an ongoing basis, to take interest in product care, and to augment and upgrade it. Marketers expect these people to become opinion leaders and advocates for the brand, to purchase add-on options, to build a bonding relationship with the company, and to participate in new-product or service idea generation. Nintendo and KOOL-AID® coordinate membership clubs to channel product fans' enthusiasm.

**Familiarity and Expertise.**   Customers have familiarity and expertise as a result of prior information acquisition and prior personal experience. The relationship between prior experience and external information search is generally inverse; with increasing prior experience, less external search occurs.

Prior experience also implies that the purchase problem is solved in the routine problem-solving mode, as happens with most of the day-to-day purchases of staple items. However, even with high prior experience, routine problem solving may not be considered a desirable strategy under these conditions:

- If the experience with the prior purchase was not positive (e.g., last year's lawn maintenance service was unsatisfactory or the past training or consulting was not up to the mark).
- If the technology has changed substantially since the last purchase, thus rendering prior experience obsolete (e.g., newer generation of computers and servers).

## TABLE 8.4    Illustrative Measures of Consumer Involvement

PRODUCT INVOLVEMENT OR IMPORTANCE:

This product is

| Unimportant | _____ | Important |
| Means a lot to me | _____ | Means nothing to me* |
| Unappealing | _____ | Appealing |
| Valuable | _____ | Worthless* |
| Unexciting | _____ | Exciting |

ENDURING PRODUCT INVOLVEMENT:

(Example: consumer involvement with cars)

- Cars offer me relaxation and fun when life's pressures build up.
- I prefer to drive a car with a strong personality of its own.
- To me, a car is nothing more than an appliance.*
- I enjoy conversations about cars.

PURCHASE INVOLVEMENT:

- In choosing this product, I would not care at all/would care a lot about which brand, make, or model I buy.
- How important would it be for you to make a right choice of this product?

    Not at all/Extremely important
- It is not/it is a big deal if I make a mistake in choosing (the product name).*

*Reverse scored.

Compiled from: Peter H. Bloch (1981), "An Exploration into the Scaling of Consumers' Involvement in Product Class," in K. Monroe (ed.), *Advances in Consumer Research*, Vol. VIII, pp. 61–65; Judith Lynne Zaichkowsky (1985), "Measuring the Involvement Construct," *Journal of Consumer Research*, 12 (December), pp. 341–352; Banwari Mittal, "Measuring Purchase Decision Involvement," *Psychology and Marketing*, 6, 1988, pp. 147–62.

- If the goal is to build an assortment rather than replace the older or prior purchase (e.g., the purchase of clothes or music CD collection).
- If the purchase is infrequent and long after the last purchase so that there is natural desire to explore what is new (e.g., an automobile, factory equipment, business consultants).
- If the product or service is a high-risk purchase so that there is a need to optimize the purchase anew; last time's optimal choice may not be the optimal choice now (e.g., investment portfolios, new generation equipment).
- If the product or service is one of high-interest/high-enduring involvement, so it is inherently enjoyable to search information about the alternatives in the product or service class (e.g., antiques). In these instances, information search is likely to occur despite prior experience.

It is useful to distinguish between prior experience and expertise. Prior experience refers simply to the history of purchase and consumption and information obtained with respect to that product or service. In contrast, expertise refers to the *understanding* of the attributes in a product or service class and knowledge about how various alternatives stack up on these attributes.

Once a customer judges prior experience to be inadequate for the impending purchase and decides that a new information search will be useful, expertise comes into play in determining how much search will be undertaken. Interestingly, the role of prior expertise is counterintuitive. At first, marketers thought customers with low prior expertise would seek more information to overcome their knowledge deficit (the deficit hypothesis). However, it turns out that customers with prior expertise seek even more information about the impending purchase than do those less knowledgeable.[7] For example, in one recent study of 1,400 car buyers, it was found that the amount of prior experience was negatively correlated with the amount of search effort customers undertook prior to making their choice. However, customers' general interest in cars was positively correlated with their product knowledge (i.e., expertise), and both interest and expertise were *positively* correlated with the amount of search effort.[8] We term this tendency of less knowledgeable customers to seek less information rather than more as the **ignorance paradox**! The ignorance paradox occurs in that those who do not know also do not know that they do not know.

A survey of 3,000 online shoppers by ebates.com/Harris Interactive in December 1999 shows that buying behavior on the Internet reflects this trend. Table 8.5 presents a classification of shoppers on the Internet based on their shopping behavior. The Newbies are the smallest group online and are most apprehensive about shopping on the Internet due to lack of familiarity and prior experience. However, as consumers gather experience, they gravitate toward different modes of shopping on the Internet—the Time-sensitive Materialists look for fast checkouts and one-stop shopping, while the Brand Loyalists visit the site of their choice, and the Hunter-Gatherers undertake comparison shopping for the best deals for a family.[9]

## A Classification of Shopping Types on the Internet    TABLE 8.5

| Harris Interactive Shopping Type | Description | % of Total Online Shoppers |
| --- | --- | --- |
| 1. eBivalent Newbies | Newest to the Internet; does not spend a lot online and likes online shopping the least | 5% |
| 2. Hooked, Online and Single | Likely to be young males; has been online the longest; banks, invests, and shops online the most often | 16% |
| 3. Time-Sensitive Materialists | Most interested in convenience and saving time; want fast check-out and one-stop shopping | 17% |
| 4. Brand Loyalists | Go directly to the site of the merchant they know; spend the most online | 19% |
| 5. Hunter-Gatherers | Ages 30–49 with two children; utilize sites that compare and provide analysis | 20% |
| 6. Clicks-and-Mortar Group | Shops online but prefers to buy offline; concerned with online privacy and security; visits shopping malls the most | 23% |

**Source:** http://www.emarketer.com/estats/dailyestats/b2c/20001101_shoptypes.html.

**Time Pressure.** One of the most conspicuous characteristics of the customer in the twenty-first century is time pressure. Time has become and is becoming more and more scarce, due to (a) both spouses working, (b) many customers being employed in more than one job, (c) many customers re-enrolling in school to acquire new skills necessary for a more complex employment market, and (d) new leisure activities enabled by technology. Some have called *the always on the go customer* the harassed decision maker. Time pressure is making customers look for more convenient outlets of shopping (e.g., home-shopping networks, catalog shopping, and the Internet). In addition, time-pressed customers are likely to cut short their information search, comparison shopping, and decision-making time.[10] Services like Peapod (online purchase of groceries) aim to create more free time for busy individuals and families by striking at one of the important home tasks—grocery shopping. By setting up regular shopping lists that users can update on a weekly/regular basis through the Web, they make it easier to shop, saving time and effort in the process.

**Relative Brand Uncertainty.** Researchers Moorthy, Ratchford, and Talukdar propose that relative brand uncertainty is also an important factor determining the amount of search undertaken by a consumer. They state that "Relative brand uncertainty is the uncertainty about which brand is best among a set of brands, while individual brand uncertainty is the uncertainty about what each brand offers." Consumers feel the need to search for information only when they experience relative brand uncertainty. A consumer has a utility distribution for every brand. When the consumer perceives the brands in his consideration set to be completely differentiated, he or she can clearly identify the best brand, implying that the consumer does not experience any relative brand uncertainty. Hence, there is no search. Similarly, when the top two brands in the consideration set are perceived to be identical, the consumer has to search for information on only one brand. This search gives him information about all other brands since the brands are homogenous. Thus, there is no relative brand uncertainty, and hence, no search. The authors show that relative brand uncertainty is non-zero only when the consumers perceive brands to be partially differentiated or when the top two brands are perceived to have homogenous utilities, but are not considered identical. In both these cases, the consumer has to search between brands to select—the best brand among the set.[11]

## Functional versus Expressive Nature of Products and Services

In Chapter 1, we distinguished between performance value and social and psychological value. This distinction highlights the fact that people buy some products and services primarily for their physical performance, whereas others are bought primarily or significantly for their social image or for their hedonic (sensory enjoyment) utilities. These two end goals in product or service purchases have implications for evaluation criteria.

Specifically, only performance value products and services (detergents, appliances, and financial investments, for example) lend themselves to choice by information processing. In the **information processing mode (IPM)**, the customer is thought to acquire information about brand/supplier attributes, form evaluative criteria, judge the levels of these attributes in various brands/suppliers, and combine these attribute-levels for overall brand/supplier evaluation.[12] Sites like **http://www.cellmania.com** help users navigate through the many choices of cellphones and plans by asking ten simple questions about intended use. Based on the user responses, it returns a list of plans that meets the user's requirements. Users can then compare and contrast these plans and features side by side to make an informed decision. Products and services sought for social and psychological values (for example, perfumes, clothing, jewelry, country clubs, and trade shows) are chosen in contrast by an affective choice mode. In the **affective choice mode (ACM)**, affect or liking for the brand ensues based not on attribute information, but based on judgments that are holistic, self-implicative, and difficult to articulate. That is, the overall style and appearance matters (holistic); the product or service is judged in relation to oneself, as in "How will I look in this dress?" (self-implicative); and the decision cannot be verbalized since it is the nonverbal cues and emotional experience (vicarious at the time of choosing) that lead to choice. For business customers, the purchase of raw materials, components, and equipment utilizes IPM while the purchase of a corporate jet, office furniture, and even an office location, say with a prestigious street address, are driven to a large extent by ACM. It will be interesting to see whether sites like **http://www.bluenile.com** (sells diamonds and fine jewelry) will be able to persuade people to part with significant amounts of money (usually more than $1,000) for a decision that often follows ACM.

The implication of this distinction is two-fold. First, for social/psychological value-fulfilling products and services, customers would not seek much feature information, though the deliberation time may still be just as much as in the IPM strategy. Second, marketers should not burden the customer with a lot of attribute information; instead they should emphasize showing the product or service in its entirety (i.e., holistically), stress on supplier reputation which is holistic in nature, and create social/psychological symbolism via nonverbal communication and via association with positive role models.

**Information Overload.** Information overload is the condition of being exposed to too much information—so much so that you are unable to process it to make a decision.

To illustrate this phenomenon, let us review how researchers study it. Typically, some customers are asked to participate in a research study. They are provided information about a number of attributes of various brands/suppliers and are asked to make a brand/supplier selection. Some customers are provided more information; others not as much. Researchers then analyze these customer decisions in terms of their accuracy. Although results of various studies are not conclusive, the findings tend to show that as the number of attributes or alternatives were increased, customers experienced information overload and made suboptimal decisions.

A general principle of the customer information search is that customers are *selective* in their acquisition of information, and because of this selectivity, they may not always make the best decisions. An important lesson from this to marketers is that they should carefully consider what information they should provide. Marketers should not overload the customer with information, should organize the information so that it is easy to process, and should ensure that the subset of information presented is still adequate for the customer to make an informed choice.[13] Advertising, catalogs, and in-store displays aid exploratory visual information search. Here, attention for the focal object is a function of the competition for attention created by the nonfocal information. Hence, in a catalog for instance, marketers can draw attention to focal items by not just increasing the size of the focal object or removing other items from the page, but by rearranging items on the page in such a way that the entire display is not visually competitive.[14]

A study shows that factual information about products has higher impact on choices online than in traditional supermarkets. Brand names are found to be important in online decision making when information on other attributes in not available.[15] As consumers face an information overload on the web, the type of information provided for decision making will decide whether the customer will buy from a web site or leave the site. In fact, a specialized discipline called "Human Computer Interaction" has come into place, and courses are offered on the subject at several universities so that web developers and companies interface better with the customer.

## Step 3: Alternative Evaluation

Now that the customer has all the information, how does he or she use that information to arrive at the choice? In this section, we discuss the specific manner in which customers select one of the several alternatives (e.g., brands or suppliers) available to them. These specific processes and steps are referred to by researchers as choice *models*. There are two broad categories of choice models: compensatory and noncompensatory.[16] Consumers also use affect to evaluate a target object by asking themselves "How do I feel about it?" This mode of evaluation is particularly used by consumers for consumption behaviors that are "intrinsically rewarding" compared to consumption behaviors that are undertaken to achieve goals (reading a book for pleasure versus reading a book to pass an exam). When consumers are faced with noncomparable alternatives and when they believe that their feelings are representative of the target object and are not attributable to any external reasons such as the background music in the store or a pleasant salesperson or store atmosphere, positive feelings toward the target object lead to a favorable evaluation of the object.[17]

## The Compensatory Model

In the compensatory model, the customer arrives at a choice by considering *all* of the attributes and benefits of a product or service and mentally trading off the alternative's perceived weakness on one or more attributes for its perceived strength on other attributes. A customer may go about making this calculation in two ways. One method of arriving at a choice is simply to add the number of positive attributes and subtract the number of negative attributes each alternative has, and then choose the one that has the most positive and fewest negative attributes. However, often, the individual does not consider each plus or a minus equally significant. Some considerations are clearly more important than others, and every minus may or may not cancel a plus on some other feature. A second and more systematic approach is to weigh every attribute for each alternative in terms of its relative importance. To implement this approach, the decision maker also estimates the degree to which the alternative possesses each positive or negative attribute. This can be done either on a numerical scale of, say, 0 to 10 where 10 means a perfect performance on that attribute, or in verbal rating categories such as poor, average, excellent, and so forth. The latter ratings are then multiplied by the relative weight of the attribute. The sum of these products for each alternative provides a total score for that alternative. The alternative with the highest score is then chosen. Table 8.6 provides an example of how business customers could use the compensatory model for vendor selection (use of a vendor score card). In this example, Vendor 2 has the greatest total score, so the business customer would choose Vendor 2.

## TABLE 8.6 — Use of the Compensatory Choice Model by a Business Customer

| Attribute | Weight | Supplier 1 | Supplier 2 | Supplier 3 |
|---|---|---|---|---|
| | | **Supplier Ratings** | | |
| Quality | 4 | Average (2) | Excellent (4) | Poor (1) |
| Fit with desired performance standards | 3 | Good (3) | Poor (1) | Good (3) |
| Customer support | 1 | Poor(1) | Good (3) | Excellent (4) |
| Price | 2 | Good (3) | Average (2) | Poor (1) |
| Total | | 4(2) + 3(3) + 1(1) + 2(3) = 24 | 4(4) + 3(1) + 1(3) + 2(2) = 26 | 4(1) + 3(3) + 1(4) + 2(1) = 19 |

This model is called compensatory because a shortfall on one attribute may be compensated by a good rating on another attribute. Illustratively, a vacation spot that has less learning opportunity but more activities for fun for the whole family might receive the same overall rating as another destination with few family fun activities but more learning opportunities.

### Noncompensatory Models

While there are several noncompensatory models identified in the literature, four are most common and useful. These are called conjunctive, disjunctive, lexicographic, and elimination by aspects.[18]

**The Conjunctive Model.** In the conjunctive model, the customer begins by *setting the minimum cutoffs on all salient attributes*. Each alternative is then examined on each attribute, and any alternative that meets the minimum cut-offs on all attributes can potentially be chosen. If an alternative fails the cut-off, even on one attribute, it is dropped from further consideration. If all alternatives fail to meet the cut-off levels, then the customer may revise his or her minimum cut-off levels or use another decision model. On the other hand, if more than one alternative meets all the minimum cut-off levels, the customer might resort to another decision model to further eliminate alternatives until only one survives the process.

Consider a customer buying a car. He or she might want a car that is priced below $20,000, gets at least 30 miles per gallon, has at least an average reliability and repair record, and has at least a good safety rating (these latter two ratings can be read from *Consumer Reports*, for example). The customer eliminates cars that fall below these cut-off levels. If more than one car satisfies all these cut-offs, the customer may next decide on the basis of style, or may simply raise the desired cut-offs on one or more attributes. Online resources like MSN'S Carpoint (**http://www.carpoint.com**) and Autotrader (**http://www.auto trader.com**) allow consumers to specify the minimum features/criteria that they want in an automobile and then provides a list of products that meet these criteria, thus helping the customer with his or her conjunctive model in decision making.

The conjunctive model can be used by both household and business customers. Since businesses often buy components and raw materials that have to fit into finished products and production processes, meeting the minimum specifications becomes a necessity. For example, in the chemical industry, required chemicals have to meet certain minimums on such attributes as purity, side-effects, and disposability. Business-to-Business exchanges like ChemConnect (**http://www.chemconnect.com**) allow businesses to specify their minimum criteria and generate efficiencies and cost savings through the Internet. Such indispensable minimums serve as cut-offs in the conjunctive model. The conjunctive model is, therefore, especially important in business-to-business markets.

**The Disjunctive Model.** The **disjunctive model** entails *trade-offs between aspects of choice alternatives*. Sometimes the customer is willing to trade off one feature for another. For example, a home buyer might say that the house he or she would be willing to consider buying should have either five bedrooms or, if it has only four bedrooms, it should have a finished basement. A business customer buying a copy machine might be willing to trade off copying speed if the machine has dual-side copying capability because, in a sense, automatic dual copying saves time and inconvenience.

Although these trade-offs are made also in the compensatory model, there are important differences. First, the disjunctive model considers the sheer presence or absence of attributes, rather than the degree or amount in which these attributes are present. Thus, the attributes tend to be those that do not vary on a graduated scale. For example, gas mileage rating tends to be used in a compensatory fashion, whereas the presence or absence of a finished basement tends to be traded off in a disjunctive model. This categorical (Is it present or not?) rather than graduated (How much of it is there?) appraisal of an attribute makes the disjunctive model simpler to execute than the other models. Customers could use attributes such as country of origin as a required attribute and drop all alternatives that are foreign made. Similarly, when customers came to know that Nike shoes and the "Kathie Lee" line of clothing were manufactured by underpaid and underage workers, the presence of this information was enough to drop these products from their choice set.

Second, in the compensatory model, the attributes traded off need not serve the same purpose while in the disjunctive model they tend to. Thus, in the compensatory model, lower gas mileage of a car can be compensated by superior rating on a totally unrelated attribute, such as safety. In the disjunctive model, on the other hand, gas mileage could be traded off only with other cost-saving features, such as low-maintenance costs. Or for copiers, the high speed and the dual-copying capability address the same time and convenience utility.

**The Lexicographic Model.** Another model customers use to make a choice is termed the **lexicographic model**. In this model, *attributes of alternatives are rank-ordered in terms of importance*. Customers examine all alternatives on the most important criterion and identify the one with the highest level on that criterion. If more than one alternative remains in the choice set, then they consider the second most important criterion and examine the remaining alternatives with respect to that criterion. The process continues until only one alternative remains.

For an example of business-to-business service, consider a business traveler (a salesperson, say) deciding on a hotel for an out-of-town trip. His most important criterion might be the hotel location within the downtown business district (rather than in the outlying areas of the city); therefore, he does not even bother looking at the listing of the outlying area hotels (in the AAA guide books, hotels are listed in separate sections for downtown and outlying areas). Since there are several hotels in the business district listing, he next considers the second most important criterion, availability of office and business services (fax, copying, a VCR-equipped TV monitor in the room, and so on). Suppose only four hotels in the AAA listing meet this criterion. He next considers the third most important criterion, say price. He then chooses the one with the lowest price, and the decision is made. But if two (or more) hotels had the same low price, the customer would have to go through the next round of processing the alternatives on the criterion next in importance, such as the availability of a health spa on the hotel property. The process stops when one alternative is identified.

**Elimination by Aspects.**  The **elimination by aspects (EBA)** model, first proposed by psychologist Amos Tversky, is similar to the lexicographic model but with one important difference. The customer rates the attributes in the order of importance and, in addition, defines cut-off values. He or she then examines all alternatives first on the most important attribute, admitting for further consideration only those that satisfy the minimum cut-off level on this most important attribute. If more than one alternative meets this requirement, then the customer goes to the next step, appraising the remaining alternatives on the second attribute, delineating those that meet the minimum cut-off level on this attribute, and so on.[19]

## How and When the Models Are Used

Several concepts shed light on how and when various choice models are used. These are processing by brand/supplier or by attribute, comparative features of various choice models, the two-stage choice process, rapid heuristics, and satisficing.

**Processing by Brand or by Attribute.**  Customers making choice decisions employ various models according to the choice situation facing them. An important characteristic of these models is the manner in which the evaluation proceeds: one brand/supplier at a time or one attribute at a time (i.e., in Table 8.6 by rows or by columns). Conjunctive models entail considering one brand at a time with respect to all the attributes. The process of assessing one brand/supplier entirely before moving on to the second brand is called **processing by brands**. Note that the term *brand* is being used here to connote any alternative from which the choice must be made. Thus, the model is applicable to supplier choice as well as to choice of products and services.

In contrast to conjunctive models, the lexicographic and EBA processes entail **processing by attributes** (i.e., processing all the brands simultaneously on one attribute at a time). This is simpler to execute than processing by brands. However, processing by brands allows a more thorough evaluation of brands than does processing by attributes. Furthermore, the lexicographic model is simpler to execute than the EBA, but the lexicographic loses the opportunity to purchase a brand that may be superior on the next set of attributes.

In processing by attributes, brands are also subject to a "direction-of-comparison effect." When two brands are compared, one brand becomes the focal subject of comparison, while the other brand is the less focal referent of comparison. This process of comparison naturally leads to an elicitation of more thoughts about the focal brand compared to the referent brand. As a result of this process, the unique attributes of the focal brand gain prominence in the comparison, and if these attributes are positive, they gain more weightage in the evaluation of the two brands. The attributes of the referent brand are compared against these attributes of the focal brand, and given that the referent brand does not have the unique attributes of the focal brand, it is more likely that the focal brand is preferred over the referent brand. In the same way, when the unique attributes of the focal brand are negative, they work against the focal brand's favor, and the referent brand is preferred. The direction-of-comparison effect is marked in judgments made by people who have a high need for cognition because they are more likely to use an attribute-based processing strategy. This effect is least when consumers use an attitude-based processing strategy that involves the use of general attitudes, summary impressions, intuitions, or heuristics to make judgments.[20]

**Comparative Features of Various Choice Models.** The conjunctive, disjunctive, lexicographic, and EBA models are all *non*compensatory models, since the deficiency on one attribute is not allowed to be made up for by excess on another. An alternative may be eliminated in the first step for being only marginally inferior to an otherwise substantially better alternative on the second most important attribute; it doesn't matter that the eliminated alternative is much superior on all other attributes. The compensatory model eliminates the possibility of making such suboptimal choices.

The compensatory model is more burdensome to execute, however, because the customer has to consider several dimensions or attributes at the same time and somehow weigh them in his or her mind. Typically, therefore, the compensatory model is used sparingly and only for important decisions.[21] Most low-ticket items are likely to be chosen with the help of noncompensatory models. Thus, a customer may buy table salt based simply on a single criterion, such as familiarity with the brand or whether or not it is iodized, or perhaps on price alone. Another customer buying an entree might use fat content as the important criterion and then either choose the one with the lowest fat content (thus employing a lexicographic model) or consider all entrees with fat content not exceeding 15 percent of total calories (thus employing EBA). Calories per serving might then be used as the second criterion, and, if need be, price as the third.

In terms of the three routine/limited/extended problem-solving strategies, the compensatory model is likely to be used generally for extended problem solving. Noncompensatory models are likely used for limited and routine problem-solving situations. Furthermore, noncompensatory models may also be used in the initial stage of an extended problem-solving decision situation, as explained next.

**Two-Stage Choice Process.** For the more important decisions, a customer might first use a noncompensatory model and then, to further identify the choice, use a compensatory model. Customer researchers Bettman and Park have described customer decision process as a two-stage process, termed phased decision strategy.[22] In the first stage, termed alternative-elimination stage, customers narrow the set of alternatives for closer comparisons. In the second stage, termed alternative-selection stage, the smaller set of alternatives is further examined. The objective of the first stage is to identify the *acceptable* alternatives, whereas the second stage is meant to identify *the best*.

Since noncompensatory models are easier to execute, a large number of alternatives can be examined relatively quickly, particularly if processing is done by attributes rather than by brands. In the second stage, when only three or four alternatives remain, customers can more efficiently employ the compensatory model. Even here, if one or more attributes are matching across the alternatives, one simply ignores this attribute and applies the compensatory model on the smaller set of attributes. In this way customers can take advantage of the compensatory model to make an optimal decision without incurring the information-overload cost that would have accrued if all of the initially available large number of alternatives were to be processed by the compensatory model throughout.

**Rapid Heuristics.** For a common, repeat purchase of low-risk, low-ticket items such as shampoo, snacks, cereals, or office supplies in the business context, customers are unlikely to spend much time or effort. These purchases are perceived to be low-risk, low-involvement decisions. As such, hardly any information is examined, and brand choice is made by using a heuristic (simple rule of thumb). Examples of heuristics used for such repeat purchase items are: "Purchase the known brand only;" "Purchase whichever brand is on sale;" and "I saw my friend using this brand, so I too will purchase this one."

A study illustrating this was done by professor Wayne D. Hoyer of the University of Texas at Austin on U.S. customers; the study was later replicated on Chinese customers by the National University of Singapore's professor Siew Meng Leong.[23] In these studies, customers were observed in a supermarket selecting a common, repeat purchase item (namely, detergent and shampoo) and later approached and asked the basis of their decision. In a subsequent experimental study, customers were given a product that could be examined by taste (namely, peanut butter in one study and cheese in another). Of the three brands presented to research customers, one was a well-known brand.

The researchers found that customers in the supermarket study spent very little time (less than 15 seconds) to complete their in-store decision, examined a small number of packages (about 1.5 on an average), made few brand comparisons, and looked at only a few shelf tags. In response to the question as to why they chose the brand they did, an overwhelming majority (approximately 95 percent) mentioned a single reason. This single reason, for the largest majority, was, "It worked better."

In the experimental study where customers were making a choice anew (since none of their usual brands were in the choice set), and where one of the three brands was known but the other two were not, customers overwhelmingly (97 percent) chose the known brand. Thus, "purchase the known brand" is a choice heuristic customers use most often, especially in a new choice task of a low-ticket, common, repeat-purchase item. Not in vain, then, do advertisers spend considerable monies keeping their brands in the top-of-the-mind awareness of their target customers.

**Satisficing.**  No matter what decision model they use, customers as decision makers can never consider and appraise all of the alternatives exhaustively. Indeed, customers *do not* typically make the most optimal choice. As already pointed out, the use of lexicographic or EBA or other noncompensatory model might eliminate a brand from further consideration based on the first attribute even though the brand's other features could have made the brand more attractive overall. Yet customers are perfectly happy making a choice by noncompensatory models. This is a concept that Nobel Prize-winning psychologist Herbert Simon calls satisficing.[24] Satisficing refers to customer's (or decision maker's) acceptance of an alternative that he or she finds satisfying, rather than pursuing the arduous search for the most optimal alternative there might be. Thus, even the ardent comparison shoppers finally give up and buy the product or service they find most acceptable from among those they have considered so far, even though they recognize that there might well be a slightly or even substantially better product or service or deal at the next store. In the business context, cost of searching for information for a myriad of alternatives and then evaluating them is enormous. Hence, satisficing is common even in the business context.

## Step 4: Purchase

Once the customer has evaluated the alternatives, he or she makes the purchase. This at first appears a straightforward step, but even here customer behavior at times becomes intriguing. In fact, this behavior can be broken down into three substeps. The first substep occurs when the customer identifies the most preferred alternative, based on the alternative evaluation process just described. The next substep is to form a purchase intent—a determination that one will buy that product or service. The final substep is implementing the purchase. This entails arranging the terms of the transaction, seeking and obtaining the transfer of the title or ownership from the seller, paying for the product or service, and receiving possession of the product or the service commitment from the seller.

The first substep (choice identification) is the conclusion of a process where the customer's user role and his or her needs and wants as user become most salient. Although the payer's concern (e.g., whether it is affordable) and buyer's concern (e.g., where to get it) may also be taken into account, the emphasis is likely to have remained on the fit between the product/service and the performance and social/psychological values the customer seeks in the user role. In the second substep (purchase intent), the payer's concerns become most salient. If the payer is different from the user, a formal budget approval may be needed. The payer may have to assess whether the product or service is overpriced, whether the required cash or credit is available at this time, whether it sits well with established guidelines for allocating the budget over different categories of products or services, or whether it offers equity to other users (e.g., other members of the household or other employees in the organization) who may have claims on the budget pool. Finally, the purchase implementation substep activates the buyer role and is influenced most by the concerns of the buyer. The buyer's market values (convenience and service values) become the determining forces. This may influence the store or supplier from whom the preferred item is bought, the day and time it is bought, how soon or late it is bought, and whether it is even bought. For example, a 13-year-old boy we know wanted to attend a space camp run by NASA. He called the camp organizers, got the brochures, identified the specific program he wanted to attend, and got his parents to agree to pay for the trip. The final task of putting together and sending the application was left to the older brother, who procrastinated until the deadline expired. Even when the same person plays the payer, user, and buyer roles, the buyer role may hinder the implementation of the choice identified and approved by the other two roles. Thus, as the above example shows, the customer journey from choice identification to purchase implementation does not always proceed in predictable ways. Sometimes, the purchase intention may not be implemented, as, for example, when a customer almost decides to join a particular weight-reduction program but somehow never gets around to actually doing it. But even if the purchase implementation eventually occurs, the customer journey may take a different route. Two factors can potentially derail the journey: postponement or delay in implementation and deviation from the identified choice. The business procurement process is discussed in detail in Chapter 9.

## Delay in Implementation

Causes of delays in implementation occur throughout the customer decision process, from problem recognition through alternative evaluation to purchase. We discuss these here for convenience and because it is the purchase step that they ultimately delay. A recent consumer study by consumer researchers Eric A. Greenleaf and Donald R. Lehmann identified the reasons consumers give for delay in their purchase decisions. The study interviewed recent buyers of such products as home appliances, electronics, personal computers, clothing, furniture, sports equipment, and automobiles. The consumers were asked to describe the reasons that caused them to delay the decision in buying these products, and also the reasons or factors that subsequently caused them to close the decision. These factors, along with their importance ratings in this study, are described in Table 8.7. The top three reasons for delay in buying the products was time pressure, need for more information, and inability to afford the product at the time. Top reasons for closure are deciding on another alternative and finding the time to make the decision.

Delays in purchase implementations occur among business customers as well. One reason for such delay is a change in management: the new management may want to review all capital equipment procurement plans and/or redesign the procurement policies. Another possible reason is declining financial performance; if sales and profits fall below projected levels, then some capital equipment purchase plans may be put on hold. Decisions may be delayed because of fourth-quarter syndrome: businesses typically postpone making major purchases until the last quarter of the accounting year; thus, purchase decision making may be delayed until the fourth quarter, either to avoid committing money early in the year or because time pressure did not permit decision making earlier. Interest rates and the economic situation—domestic or global—may also cause delay in purchase implementations.

An ATKearney report states that four out of five shoppers abandon their shopping carts on the Internet. Customers stated that the top reason for not completing the purchase was that the site required too much personal information before making the purchase. This shows that customers are not very comfortable sharing a large amount of personal information at their first visit to a site. They are willing to part with more information only when they trust the retailer and believe that providing more information will lead to increased benefits. Reluctance to give credit card details, Web site malfunction and an inability to find the desired products are other reasons stated by customers for incompletion of a purchase.[25]

| TABLE 8.7 | Reasons for Delay and Delay Closure |
|-----------|--------------------------------------|

| Reason | Mean Importance | Customer Role |
|--------|-----------------|---------------|
| REASONS FOR DELAY | | |
| Time Pressure; too busy to devote the time | 3.91 | User, payer, buyer |
| Needed more information | 3.43 | User |
| Couldn't afford at the time | 3.19 | Payer |
| Not sure if needed the item | 2.75 | User |
| Social and psychological risk if a wrong choice is made | 2.70 | User |
| Felt another product at home would do | 2.70 | User |
| Performance and financial risk if a wrong choice is made | 2.65 | User, payer |
| Expected price reduction or product modification in the near future | 2.52 | User, payer |
| Needed others' consent | 2.41 | User, payer |
| Find shopping unpleasant | 2.34 | Buyer |
| | | |
| REASONS FOR DELAY CLOSURE | | |
| Decided on another alternative | 3.84 | User |
| Found the time | 3.62 | User, buyer |
| Need had become passing | 3.51 | User |
| Lower price became available | 3.10 | Payer |
| Tired of shopping further | 2.70 | Buyer |
| Found a good store | 2.41 | Buyer |
| Was able to justify the expense | 2.32 | Payer |
| Obtained the advice and consent I needed | 2.14 | User, payer |
| Due to good word-of-mouth | 2.01 | User |

**Source:** Reasons and means are from Eric A. Greenleaf and Donald R. Lehmann, "Reasons for Substantial Delay in Consumer Decision Making," *Journal of Consumer Research*, 22(2), 1996, pp. 186–199.

Understanding these reasons is important for marketers because it helps them facilitate the customer journey from problem recognition to purchase. By identifying the particular reason and the step where it has a delaying effect, marketers can work to overcome that barrier. Furthermore, marketers can implement separate actions directed individually toward the three roles of the user, payer, and buyer.

## Deviation From the Identified Choice

The second factor that may derail the customer purchase implementation is deviation from the identified choice. Several conditions may account for this. First, the preferred brand may be out of stock, thus forcing the customer to buy a brand different from the one identified, especially if one needs the product immediately. Second, new in-store information may reopen the evaluation process. Third, financing terms may render a purchase infeasible, forcing the customer either to abandon the purchase altogether or to substitute the purchase with a lower-level model or another brand available on preferred terms. In the business context, stock-outs at the regular supplier may force a change to another supplier. Financing of the project, say from World Bank or the Import-Export bank, may change the options considered. These conditions may also shift the relative impact of the customer roles. While the values of the user are most influential in the alternative evaluation phase, the values of the buyer (e.g., convenience of buying) or of the payer (e.g., the financing available) become influential at the purchase stage.

# Step 5: Postpurchase Experience

The customer's decision process does not end with the purchase. Rather, the experience of buying and using the product provides information that the customer will use in future decision making. In some cases, the customer will be pleased with the experience and will buy the same product from the same supplier again. In other cases, the customer will be disappointed and may even return or exchange the product. The consumer may also experience *regret* as a result of comparing one's outcome with a better outcome that would have occurred had a different alternative been selected. Regret has a negative influence on satisfaction with the chosen alternative and on repurchase intentions for the chosen alternative.[26] In general, the post-purchase process includes four steps: decision confirmation, experience evaluation, satisfaction or dissatisfaction, and future response (exit, voice, or loyalty) in that order.

## Decision Confirmation

After a customer makes an important choice decision, he or she experiences an intense need to confirm the wisdom of that decision. The flip side is that he or she wants to avoid the disconfirmation. One of the processes that occurs at this stage is *cognitive dissonance*, discussed in Chapter 6, which is a postpurchase doubt the buyer experiences about the wisdom of the choice.

Methods of reducing dissonance and confirming the soundness of one's decision are seeking further positive information about the chosen alternative and avoiding negative information about the chosen alternative. Thus, customers reread product literature reviewing the brand's positive features, and avoid competitors' advertisements or negative information from others. They seek out friends to tell them about their purchase, hoping that their friends will validate their decision by praising the selected brand. Marketers can put this principle to use: After the purchase (say, during product or service delivery), salespeople can review with customers all the features of the product or service, and this review during the postpurchase phase is likely to bring to customer attention a few positive features previously ignored, thus improving the perceived attractiveness of the product. In the business context, the company could arrange for a formal celebration with customers or could provide customer testimonials in its advertisements to reassure prospective customers.

## Experience Evaluation

Following purchase, the product or service is actually consumed. Marketers need to know whether customers consume it routinely or while consciously evaluating it. This depends on the level of enduring involvement in the product or service and the finality of the preference that caused this purchase.

Earlier in this chapter, enduring involvement was defined as the interest customers take in the consumption of the product or service on an *ongoing basis*. We use most products and services routinely and notice them only if something does not work as expected. On the other hand, we are very enthusiastic about some products or services. In consuming these, we are conscious of the consumption experience, appraising and relishing it continually (e.g., wine drinking by wine connoisseurs). These, then, are the products and services that undergo conscious evaluation during use. In the business context, companies would be enduringly involved in a service contract or a single-source supplier, but the appraisal and evaluation would be more formal than in the case of an individual customer's evaluation of a product in which he is enduringly involved.

Secondly, customers buy some products and services on a trial basis, without making their preference final yet. These products, even if not of enduring involvement, are the ones that the customer is likely to use with an eye to appraisal. Free samples received are usually used routinely without conscious appraisal of the performance of the product.

Sampling is productive when the product's or service's superiority is substantial and would be conspicuous in consumption, and when the samples are targeted at customers who are not satisfied with the current solutions. Because of their dissatisfaction, they would be actively appraising the sampled product or service. Airbus is using this strategy and offering its airplanes to several U.S. airlines on a trial basis to break into the market.

## Satisfaction/Dissatisfaction

Whether or not they actively evaluate a product or service during product use or consumption, users do experience the usage outcome. This outcome is characterized as satisfaction or dissatisfaction. Measuring overall satisfaction/dissatisfaction is easy. Customer researchers can simply ask, "How satisfied or dissatisfied are you with___(the product or service name)?"

What is more challenging is to understand *why* customers feel the way they do. There are two approaches to this challenge. One is to get the customer to rate a product or service on its various attributes, such as handling, gas mileage, acceleration, and braking for a car, and satisfaction or dissatisfaction with these product attributes can then be used to explain the customer's *overall* satisfaction or dissatisfaction with the product.

But this approach raises another question: What causes satisfaction or dissatisfaction with individual attributes? This question is successfully addressed by a theoretical approach to understanding satisfaction. Customer behavior scholars have proposed that satisfaction depends not on the absolute levels of performance on various attributes but rather on how the actual performance compares with the *expected* performance. Thus, if the product or service experience fulfills prepurchase expectations, then satisfaction results, and if doesn't, dissatisfaction results. Therefore, satisfaction or dissatisfaction stems respectively from the confirmation or disconfirmation of our expectations. The theory makes intuitive sense in our everyday experience. For example, we may find a particular level of cleanliness unsatisfactory in a Marriott hotel but quite satisfactory in, say, an economy motel. This is because our expectations about the Marriott are quite high compared to those we hold for the economy motel.

A new type of market-based performance measure for firms, industries, economic sectors, and national economies, named the American Customer Satisfaction Index (ACSI), was first introduced in the fall of 1994, with information on 40 industries and seven major sectors of the U.S. economy.

The index is produced through a partnership among the University of Michigan Business School, the American Society for Quality, and the CFI Group. It is a national economic indicator of customer satisfaction with the quality of goods and services available to household consumers in the United States.

"An individual firm's ACSI represents its customers' overall evaluation of total purchase and consumption experience, both actual and anticipated." An industry ACSI represents an industry's customers' overall evaluation of its market offering; a sector ACSI is an overall evaluation of that sector, and the national ACSI gauges the nation's total consumption experience. Hence, ACSI represents "a cumulative evaluation of a firm's market offering, rather than a person's evaluation of a specific transaction." The American Customer Satisfaction Index uses a 100-point scale and presently measures satisfaction with 164 companies and 30 government agencies. The score fell from the baseline level of 74.2 in 1994 to a low of 72.6 in the fourth quarter of 2000. The value of the index has increased every year since 1997, but remained flat in 2000. The flat index could be a result of low customer service levels and low productivity improvements in this period.[27]

In the online context, a study of "e-satisfaction"—customers' satisfaction with e-retailing—by researchers Szymanski and Hise shows that shopping convenience (represented by total shopping time, convenience, ease of browsing), site design (represented by uncluttered screens, easy search paths, and fast presentations) and financial security of online transactions are the three most important drivers of e-satisfaction. Surprisingly, product information (quantity and quality of information) had a very small impact on e-satisfaction, and product offerings (number and variety of offerings) had no impact at all.[28] The cost and effort of voicing dissatisfaction online with products and services is also rapidly declining for customers. With services like PlanetFeedback (**http://www.planetfeedback. com**) and the Better Business Bureau (**http://www.bbbonline.org**), it is much easier for customers to voice their grievances addressed. This puts added pressure on marketers since the impact of dissatisfied customers is also magnified through the medium of the Internet (higher reach).

The theory of satisfaction has important implications for shaping expectations.[29] If marketing communications and other elements of the marketing mix (e.g., advertising, salespersons, price, appearance of the store) promise too much, they may create expectations that the product or service would almost surely fail to fulfill, thus risking customer dissatisfaction. Of course, if the expectations are too low, the sale may not result. The right strategy, therefore, ought to be to create realistic expectations, implying a performance level that the target market finds attractive enough to select the brand. To assess whether they are on target, marketers may use a measure of satisfaction such as the one illustrated in Table 8.8.

| Measuring Satisfaction in Terms of Expectations | | | TABLE 8.8 |
|---|---|---|---|

How did we do? How was our:

|  | **Fell Below Expectations** | **Met Expectations** | **Exceeded Expectations** |
|---|---|---|---|
| Room appearance | O | O | O |
| Room cleanliness | O | O | O |
| Registration speed | O | O | O |
| Friendliness of staff | O | O | O |
| Room service promptness | O | O | O |

## Future Response: Exit, Voice, or Loyalty

Following the experience of satisfaction or dissatisfaction, customers have three possible responses: exit, voice, or loyalty.

**Exit.** If customers are dissatisfied with their experience with a brand, they may decide never again to buy the brand. This places them back to the start of the decision process the next time the problem recognition arises. They have to go through the arduous process of information search, alternative evaluation, and so on, all over again. This "churn" in customers is very common in credit-card services, and long-distance carriers as customers tend to switch from suppliers when they are dissatisfied.

**Voice.** Dissatisfied customers may complain and then decide either to give the brand or marketer another chance or simply to exit.

What accounts for customers' tendency to complain or not complain? A customer's likelihood of complaining depends on three factors: dissatisfaction salience, attributions to the marketer, and customers' personality traits (see Figure 8.3).

- *Dissatisfaction salience*—Not all dissatisfaction is salient (i.e., bothersome to customers). Generally small gaps between performance and expectations are ignored; moreover, even substantial gaps are not likely to be noticed if the product or service is trivial. Thus, importance of the product or service and the degree of performance-expectations gap determine dissatisfaction salience, which, in turn, determines the likelihood of customer complaints. Malfunction of the vending

# FIGURE 8.3     Determinants of Complaining

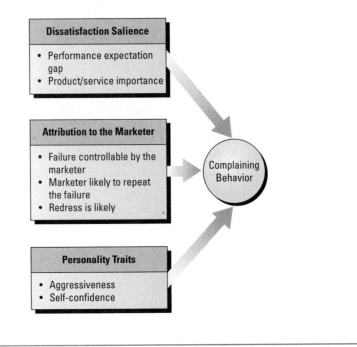

machine at a supermarket or the nonavailability of the desired product in the vending machine is a matter that causes dissatisfaction, but not enough for it to be salient.

- *Attributions to the marketer*—Customers make attributions about who is to blame for poor product or service performance. For example, in the case of airlines, delays are more often than not attributed to the marketer, even though the actual delay may have been caused by weather problems. If customers blame themselves or circumstances, then complaining would not occur; on the other hand, if they attribute failure to the marketer, then they are likely to complain. Furthermore, if customers thought that the failure was not likely to be repeated, they would be less motivated to complain. Finally, customers must also believe that the marketer is likely to take the corrective action; if they think that redress from the marketer is unlikely, they may consider complaining a waste of effort.
- *Customers' personality traits*—Customers' personality traits play an important role in complaining. Customers differ in self-confidence and in their degree of aggressiveness/submissiveness. Complaining requires self-confidence, and aggressiveness drives customers to assert themselves. These traits, therefore, lead customers to complain rather than meekly accept poor marketer performance.

Following the complaint, negative word-of-mouth is less likely and repatronage more likely if the complaint is successfully redressed. An important concept here is perceived justice. **Perceived justice** is customers' perceptions that they were treated with respect during the conflict resolution process, the policy and procedures followed were fair, and the decision outcome itself was fair.[30] When perceived justice seems not to have occurred, then hostility increases.

Research has found that customer complaint is actually good for the marketer. According to one research study, about 19 percent of dissatisfied customers complain; of the complaining customers, a significant majority continue to buy the product or service, compared to those who are dissatisfied but do not bother to complain. Thus, complainers care enough to complain. Noncomplainers simply walk out, taking their patronage to a competitor.

**Loyalty.** The third response is, of course, loyalty. Customer loyalty means the customer buys the same brand repeatedly. The concept of loyalty has been debated in the literature in various definitions of *brand loyalty*. First, brand loyalty can be defined simply as the consistent repurchase of the same brand. This definition has two problems. First, in many product or service categories, customers buy an assortment of brands to satisfy their need for variety in the consumption experience. For example, eating the same cereal every day or eating lunch every day in the office cafeteria would not be satisfying. This problem of variety can be handled by asking customers if the focal brand is consistently at least a part of the assortment the customer buys, if not an exclusive purchase. In the business context, companies are loyal to multiple vendors.

The second problem with defining and measuring brand loyalty as a consistent repurchase is that one does not know if the consistent repurchase is merely due to convenience, is a routinization of the purchase decision, or reflects genuine preference for the brand. To overcome this uncertainty, some researchers have defined brand loyalty in attitudinal terms: the brand attitude underlying the repurchase. Only if a favorable brand attitude underlies repurchase is brand loyalty thought to exist. This topic is discussed more fully in Chapter 11.

At first thought, one would think that if customers are satisfied, they would not switch brands. Thus, a satisfaction rating may be deemed to ensure loyalty. Recent customer research has shown, however, that while customers are less likely to switch when they are satisfied than when they are not, being satisfied does not guarantee loyalty. One study showed that despite satisfaction, as many as 30 percent of customers were likely to switch suppliers.[31] Several potential reasons explain why satisfied customers may still switch. First, customers report being satisfied with a brand, but they may also be satisfied with some other brands. The implication of this is that one should measure customer satisfaction with a brand *relative* to competitors' brands. The second reason is that the marginal utility of a repeated use may decline simply due to familiarity, and need for variety can drive brand switching. Research shows that increasing the variety in the context—that is, providing variety in a different product category that is purchased simultaneously with the focal category—may reduce variety seeking in the focal category. This happens because consumers try to achieve an optimal level of stimulation by balancing the stimulation that comes from variety seeking and the stimulation available from the context.[32] Finally, customers may switch brands because they expect to receive even greater value or satisfaction from some other brand.

# Individual Customer Decision Making and the Three Customer Roles

In this section, we pull together various concepts covered in the chapter and illustrate their relevance to the three customer roles (see Table 8.9). First, we talked about the setting of individual decision making. By definition, the user and buyer roles, and often the payer role as well, are played by the same individual. Since buyer and user roles are combined in the same individual, the user has more control over what to buy and where. At the same time, the convergence of buyer and user role may also cause some sacrifice in weak user values. For example, if the individual feels too lazy to go out (a buyer role) to eat (a user role), he or she has to make do with a home-delivered pizza that may not be as good in quality and taste. Sometimes the payer role is separated, as in the consumption of free public services; with someone else as payer (government or employers), the users tend to consume more as well as evaluate the product less stringently.

| TABLE 8.9 | Individual Customer Decision Making and the Three Customer Roles |
|-----------|------------------------------------------------------------------|

| Concepts | User | Payer | Buyer |
|----------|------|-------|-------|
| **INDIVIDUAL DECISION MAKER** | • User in control of buying role as well; strong user values rule over payer/buyer values. | • With someone else as payer, users tend to consume more; also user evaluation is less stringent. | • Role convergence sometimes causes sacrifice in weak user values. |
| **DECISION PROCESS** | | | |
| Problem recognition | • Users are the most frequent problem recognizers. | • Buyer dissatisfaction with service, convenience, and personalization values can cause problem recognition.<br>• New delivery channels serve as solution stimuli to cause problem recognition by buyers. | • Awareness of better price value from competitors causes payer role problem recognition. |
| Information search | • Information pertaining to user values is sought. | • Payer role seeks information about competitors' prices. | • Inadequate buyer motivation to expend search efforts constrains user's and payer's desire for more information. |
| Search determinants:<br>Perceived risk | • User-felt risk causes more information search. | • Payers willing to pay more to avoid user risks. | • Buyers lean on trustworthy sources. |
| Involvement | • User involvement may demand sacrifice in buyer/payer values. | | • Involved buyers do extensive information search. |
| Familiarity | • User familiarity enables greater use of available information. | | • Familiarity lulls buyers into less search effort. |
| Time pressure | • Users seek time-saving features in products/services. | | • Time pressure affects buyers the most who seek efficient exchanges. |
| Alternative evaluation | • Users' values are most important evaluation criteria. | • For parity products (i.e., with user indifference), payers seek to maximize price value. | • For parity products, buyer values become important criteria. |
| Decision models:<br>Compensatory | • Users participate actively. | | |
| Noncompensatory | • One or the other role may play a major role. | • Payer value may be exercised through use of some noncompensatory model. | • To minimize cognitive effort, buyers like to use noncompensatory model. |
| Functional/expressive Product | • For expressive products, users must participate in evaluation. | | |
| Purchase | | • Lack of agreement on financing may hinder purchase. | • This stage is most relevant to the buyer role.<br>• Buyer role subject to remorse; seeks more favorable information to ward decision confirmation. |
| Post-choice processes:<br>Buyer's remorse/<br>decision confirmation | | | |

*(continued)*

| Individual Customer Decision Making and the Three Customer Roles (Concluded) | | | TABLE 8.9 |

| Concepts | User | Payer | Buyer |
|---|---|---|---|
| Post-choice processes: | | | |
| Experience evaluation | • Product use experienced by the user role. | | |
| Satisfaction | • Determined largely by satisfaction of user values. | | |
| Exit, voice, loyalty | • User satisfaction leads to loyalty. | | • Loyalty simplifies buyer's task. |
| | • Users spread word-of-mouth. | | |
| Complaint | • User dissatisfaction motivates complaints. | | • Buyer aggressiveness determines if complaint will be made. |

The three roles also come into play in the decision-making process stages: problem recognition, information search, alternative evaluation, choice or purchase, and postchoice experience. Although most products or services are bought in response to the problem recognition by the user role, the other two roles can also be the source of problem recognition. When the buyer values are violated (for example, lack of prepurchase assistance or rude store employees) or if a new means of obtaining the product or service becomes available (such as home delivery of groceries), the buyer's problem recognition is triggered. Payers recognize the problem when a competitor brings home the point that they are paying too much for their current product or service.

In the information-search stage, information is sought relevant to user and payer values. While some information is received without the buyer effort (e.g., information through advertisements), the information that requires visits to the store or going to the library, and so on, depends on the buyer motivation to undertake the effort. The buyer's values (i.e., his or her desire to limit the search effort) then constrain user and payer roles' desire to maximize its values. Buyers who enjoy browsing help the user role identify new solutions. Buyers who are comparison shoppers help the payer find the best price value. Various determinants of search (namely, perceived risk, involvement, familiarity, and time pressure) also implicate the three roles differently.

Perceived risk generally necessitates search on brand features, the concern of the user role. To ensure risk-free product or service for the user, payers may be willing to sacrifice on payer value. Buyers may want to limit consideration to suppliers they have come to trust in their interaction with them. Involvement with the product again emphasizes the user role, whose concern with getting the best product or service (in the case of high involvement) demands sacrifice in payer and buyer values, if necessary. High involvement, again, leads to extensive search. Buyers' roles can also vary in involvement. Some customers simply dislike shopping while others enjoy it, reading product labels in the store and comparing products on features. Involved shoppers, thus, end up doing extensive information search. Uninvolved shoppers (i.e., buyers) would lead users to make do with less information. Familiarity with the product enables the user to more easily absorb the current information that the user comes across, such as in advertising, but the buyer may feel less need to make the effort to search for new information. Time pressure is most relevant to the buyer role in the information-search stage and also in the purchase stage as the buyer would seek time-saving means of acquiring the product. Time pressure on users also is a factor, and it will affect the performance criteria inasmuch as the users will seek time-saving features in products, such as ready-to-eat meals or faster cycle machines.

In the alternative evaluation stage, since the buyer is the same as the user, the market values the user seeks become the overriding criteria. Only in the case of parity products do the buyer's market values (e.g., convenience) become determinant so that the buyer buys whatever is convenient to buy. Furthermore, given user indifference to alternatives (which happens with parity products), the payer's concern with obtaining the best price value also becomes a prominent decision criterion. Decision models also implicate the roles differently. Compensatory models require simultaneous consideration of various criteria, mostly comprising user values; therefore, users participate actively in the decision. Noncompensatory models generally emphasize one or the other of the three roles; for example, in seeking the lowest price as the sole factor (lexicographic model), the payer role is being given prominence. Buying whatever is available (another lexicographic rule) makes the buyer role the determinant. Functional versus expressive products also influence the interplay of the three roles. Expressive products can be evaluated only by the user, much more than is the case for functional products. For functional products, the user can specify the performance criteria, and then let the buyer role match the product or service against those criteria; in contrast, for expressive products, product evaluation against the desired social/emotional values can be done only by the user role, not the buyer role. Of course, users can subsequently routinize their choice by brand name for functional and expressive products alike and let the buyer simply execute it.

In the next stage, purchase, the values of the buyer and the payer become most important. Sometimes when the decision is made outside the store, or if the purchase cannot be executed as soon as the user decision is made, the buyer may delay buying the product or may fail to implement the decision, sometimes foregoing the purchase altogether. The payer value of best price and good financing or credit may sometimes hinder the purchase of the user's choice; for example, when price negotiations fail. Clearly, the buyer skills in negotiating price, payment, and delivery terms and the payer's ability to receive credit or meet the payment terms block the purchase.

In the postpurchase stage, dissonance (or buyer's remorse) and the consequent decision confirmation are processes experienced by the buyer role. Experience evaluation is done by the user. Buyer and payer values received in the transaction are soon forgotten, but the user values persist. Satisfaction is largely determined by the extent to which the user gets the expected value during the product's use. Satisfactory user experience simplifies the buyer's task for the future; he or she can now simply execute the future purchases in the routine problem-solving mode. Favorable or unfavorable word-of-mouth ensues from satisfied or dissatisfied customers in their user role. Satisfied users display loyalty behavior; dissatisfied users seek exit from their current supplier and trigger the buyer role of finding a new source. If dissatisfied, the user role can feel enough anger to motivate a complaint, but the aggressiveness of the buyer role will determine whether or not the complaint is actually made.

The Elimination by Aspects (EBA) model is most sensitive to the user, payer, and buyer roles. Whichever role has the opportunity to influence the decision uses EBA to emphasize its own value. If the customer is most concerned with user values, then the user role's market values become the first EBA criterion. On the other hand, if the customer's constraints as a payer or the buyer are insurmountable, then those roles' market values become the first EBA criterion. Thus, if the user value is most important, then the customer gets to buy his or her favorite brand, say of clothing or computers. Thus, a popular or reputed brand name becomes the first EBA criterion. On the other hand, if the payer constraints are strong, then budget constraints or economic value (good value for the money) become the first EBA criterion. Finally, if the buyer role's constraint become the key decision influencer, then convenience or service values become the first EBA criterion.

# Summary

In this chapter, we studied customer decision making as a five-step process: problem recognition, information search, alternative evaluation, choice, and postchoice. The customer decision problem begins with problem recognition. The problem recognition occurs due to an internal cue which comes from one's motives being in a state of unfulfillment, or from external stimuli evoking these motives. A typology of problems was suggested—namely, familiar-latent, familiar-vivid, novel-latent, and novel-vivid—and its marketing implications were discussed. Once problem recognition occurs, the customer (a) either relies on prior knowledge and previously learned solutions or (b) searches for new solutions through new information acquisition and its evaluation and integration. In the information-search stage, there are several determinants of information search, such as perceived risk, involvement, familiarity and expertise, and the functional versus expressive nature of products.

Evaluation of alternatives entails use of compensatory and noncompensatory decision models. The latter include conjunctive, disjunctive, lexicographic, and elimination-by-aspects models. The outcome of these evaluation processes is the identification of a preferred brand and the formation of a purchase intent. Such purchase intent is then implemented by the actual purchase act, but it was suggested that the purchase act does not always occur as planned. Sometimes, substantial delays occur in purchase implementation, and at other times, the brand actually bought is different from the one planned because of stock outs or new information at the time of purchase. In the post-choice phase, the processes of decision confirmation, satisfaction/dissatisfaction, exit, voice (complaining), and loyalty responses were discussed.

The individual purchasing behavior is determined by a person's individual characteristics, such as demographics, personality, and motives (all discussed in previous chapters). This chapter focused on the process itself—how the individual buying behavior unfolds. Understanding this process should help you be aware of your own marketplace behavior in the future. And understanding the individual buying behavior is helpful to marketing managers, as reflected in the many applications and implications we outlined throughout the chapter. Ultimately, it behooves marketers to structure their offerings and their communications in a fashion that responds to and resonates with customers' decision processes.

# Key Terms

Advocate Sources 284

Affective Choice Mode (ACM) 292

Awareness Set 282

Compensatory Models 293

Conjunctive Model 294

Consideration Set 282

Customer Decisions 277

Customer Problem 279

Disjunctive Model 295

Elimination by Aspects (EBA) 296

Enduring Involvement 289

Evaluative Consistency 286

Evoked Set 282

Extended Problem Solving 285

External Stimuli 279

Heuristics 286

Ignorance paradox 291

Information Overload 292

Information Processing Mode (IPM) 292

Interattribute Inference 286

Internal Stimuli 279

Lexicographic Model 295

Limited Problem Solving 286

Marketer Sources 284

Mental Budgeting 277

Negative Cue 287

Nonmarketer Sources 284

Other-Brand Averaging 287

Perceived Justice 304

Perceived Risk 287

Phased Decision Strategy 297

Primary Demand 281

Problem Recognition 279

Processing by Attributes 296

Processing by Brands 296

Purchase-Decision Involvement 289

Routine Problem Solving 285

Satisficing 298

Search Strategy 285

Secondary (Selective) Demand 281

Systematic Search 286

# Discussion Questions and Exercises

1. Reflect on your customer behavior, drawing on examples from each consumption location where individual decision making can occur—at home, at work, and in public places. Discuss which of the three customer roles and six customer values become more influential in different situations.

2. Reflect on how you might choose each of the following products or services:
   a. Graduate business schools
   b. Restaurant for dinner with your spouse on your anniversary
   c. Hotel for a business trip to Eastern Europe
   d. Toothpaste during a business trip to an Asian country where none of your usual brands are available
   e. A fax for your home office.
   For each, please indicate whether you will use:
   (i)    a two-phase or a single-phase decision strategy
   (ii)   a compensatory or a noncompensatory model, or both
   (iii)  a heuristic, and what this heuristic might be.

3. Assume that you recently made these three customer decisions: (1) after evaluating three lawn-maintenance service companies, you just gave the contract to one of them; (2) you wanted to watch a movie on your hotel room TV and rented one from the choice of two; and (3) at the restaurant, you debated briefly between iced tea and Coca-Cola and ordered iced tea. For which of these decisions are you likely to have experienced cognitive dissonance? Why or why not? What actions are you likely to have taken to reduce that dissonance? What can a marketer do, in each case, to help you overcome that dissonance?

4. You are intrigued by the concept of mental budgeting that you read about in this chapter. One issue that is nagging you is that the concept has been studied only in a Western country. You wonder if customers in other cultures set mental budgets and whether their mental budgets are as inflexible as those reported here. To find out, you want to interview five customers from a different country (say China) living in your country; for example, foreign students or employees. Prepare a discussion guideline for such interviews. Pay special attention to what happens for those instances of mental budgeting where the payer is a different member of the household than the user and/or buyer. Are mental budgets in such instances more or less flexible? Then, conduct the interviews and write your report, summarizing your findings. If you do not have access to foreign customers, then interview any five customers to find out to what extent they engage in mental budgeting

**5.** Interview two customers on each of the following: (a) a recent major appliance purchase and (b) a recent supermarket product that was purchased for the first time. Query them on how they went about making their brand selection. Then identify for each the decision model they used, contrasting the two customers as well as contrasting the two types of purchases for each customer.

**6.** Interview five customers about their most recent complaint (every consumer has complained at one time or another). Identify what led them to complain in terms of the model of complaining presented in the chapter. Then try to assess how they felt after the complaint and whether it depended on how the complaint was resolved.

# Notes

1   Adapted from Kathleen Brewer Doran, "Exploring Cultural Differences in Consumer Decision Making: Chinese Consumers in Montreal," *Advances in Consumer Research*, Chris Allen and D. John, ed. 21 (1994), pp. 318–22.

2   Banwari Mittal, "Problem Recognition in Consumer Decision Making: How Marketing Can Help It," Unpublished Manuscript, 1996.

3   S. Ratneshwar, Cornelia Pechmann, and Allan D. Shocker, "Goal-Derived Categories and the Antecedents of Across-Category Consideration," *Journal of Consumer Research*, 23, December 1996, pp. 240–50.

4   Joseph Alba, John Lynch, Barton Weitz, Chris Janiszewski, Richard Lutz, Alan Sawyer, and Stacy Wood, "Interactive Home Shopping: Consumer, Retailer and Manufacturer Incentives to Participate in Electronic Marketplaces," *Journal of Marketing*, 6, July 1997, pp. 38–53.

5   See Shelley Chaiken (1980) for a technical discussion of the terms *heuristic* versus *systematic*; and Furse, Punj, and Stewart (1984) for discussion of their use by consumers in one study; Shelly Chaiken, "Heuristic Versus Systematic Information Processing and the Use of Source Versus Message Cues in Persuasion," *Journal of Personality and Social Psychology* 39 (November 1980), pp. 752–66; David H. Furse, Girish N. Punj, and David W. Stewart, "A Typology of Individual Search Strategies among Purchasers of New Automobiles," *Journal of Consumer Research* 10, No. 4 (March 1984), pp. 417–31.

6   Morris D. Holbrook, "An Audiovisual Inventory of Some Fanatic Consumer Behavior: The 25-Cents Tour of a Jazz Collector's Home," in *ACR* 14 (1987), Wallendorf and Anderson, pp. 144–49.

7   C. Whan Park and V. Parker Lessig, "Familiarity and Its Impact on Consumer Decision Biases and Heuristics," *Journal of Consumer Research* 8 (September 1981), pp. 223–30; James R. Bettman and C. W. Park, "Effects of Prior Knowledge and Experience and Phase of Choice Process on Consumer Decision Processes: A Protocol Analysis," *Journal of Consumer Research* 7 (December 1980), pp. 234–48.

8   Narasimhan Srinivasan and Brian T. Ratchford, "An Empirical Test of a Model of External Search for Automobiles," *Journal of Consumer Research* 18 (September 1991), pp. 233–42; also see Rajan Sambandam and Kenneth R. Lord, "Switching Behavior in Automobile Markets: A Consideration-Sets Model," *Journal of the Academy of Marketing Science* 23, No. 1 (1995), pp. 57–65.

9   http://www.emarketer.com/estats/dailystats/b2c/20001101_shoptypes.html.

10  Peter L. Wright, "The Harassed Decision Maker: Time Pressure, Distractions, and the Use of Evidence," *Journal of Applied Psychology* 59 (October), pp. 555–61; C. Whan Park, Easwar Iyer, and Daniel C. Smith, "The Effects of Situational Factors

on In-Store Grocery Shopping Behavior: The Role of Store Environment and Time Available for Shopping," *Journal of Consumer Research* 15 (March 1989), pp. 422–33.

11  Sridhar Moorthy, Brian T. Ratchford, and Debabrata Talukdar, "Consumer Information Search Revisited: Theory and Empirical Analysis," *Journal of Consumer Research* 23 (March 1997), 263–78.

12  Banwari Mittal, "The Role of Affective Choice Mode in the Consumer Purchase of Expressive Products," *Journal of Economic Psychology* 9 (1988), pp. 499–524.

13  Jacob Jacoby (1984), "Perspectives on Information Overload," *Journal of Consumer Research* 4 (March 1982), pp. 432–35; Naresh K. Malhotra, "Information Load and Consumer Decision Making," *Journal of Consumer Research* 9 (March 1982), pp. 419–30; Naresh K. Malhotra, Arun K. Jain, and Stephen Lagakos (1982), "The Information Overload Controversy: An Alternative Viewpoint," *Journal of Marketing* (Spring 46) pp. 27–37; Naresh K. Malhotra, "Reflections on the Information Overload Paradigm in Consumer Decision Making," *Journal of Consumer Research* 10, No. 4 (March 1984), pp. 436–40.

14  Chris Janiszewski, "The Influence of Display Characteristics on Visual Exploratory Search Behavior," *Journal of Consumer Research* 25 (December 1998), pp. 290–301.

15  Alexandru M. Degeratu, Arvind Rangaswamy, and Jianan Wu, "Consumer Choice Behavior in Online and Traditional Supermarkets: The Effects of Brand Name, Price, and Other Search Attributes," *International Journal of Research in Marketing* 17 (March 2000), pp. 55–78.

16  For a fuller discussion of these and other models, see James R. Bettman, *An Information Processing Theory of Consumer Choice* (Reading, Mass.: Addison-Wesley, 1979), pp. 173–228.

17  Michael Tuan Pham, "Representativeness, Relevance and the Use of Feelings in Decision Making," *Journal of Consumer Research* 25 (September 1998), pp. 144–59.

18  See Hillel J. Einhorn (1970), "Use of Nonlinear, Noncompensatory Models in Decision Making," *Psychological Bulletin* 73, pp. 221–30.

19  Amos Tversky, "Elimination by Aspects: A Theory of Choice," *Psychological Review* 79 (July 1972), pp. 281–99.

20  Susan Powell Mantel and Frank R. Kardes, "The Role of Direction of Comparison, Attribute-based Processing and Attitude-based Processing in Consumer Preference," *Journal of Consumer Research* 25 (March 1999), pp. 335–52.

21  See Peter L. Wright, "Consumer Judgment Strategies: Beyond the Compensatory Assumption," in M. Venkatesan, ed., *Proceedings of the Third Annual Conference* (Chicago: Association for Consumer Research, 1972), pp. 316–24.

22  See James R. Bettman and Michael A. Zins, "Constructive Processes in Consumer Choice," *Journal of Consumer Research* 4 (September 1977), pp. 75–85; James R. Bettman and C. Whan Park, "Effects of Prior Knowledge and Experience and Phase of Choice Process on Consumer Decision Processes: A Protocol Analysis," *Journal of Consumer Research* 7 (December 1980), pp. 234–48; Denis A. Lussier and Richard W. Olshavsky, "Task Complexity and Contingent Processing in Brand Choice," *Journal of Consumer Research* 6 (1979), pp. 154–65.

23  See Wayne D. Hoyer and Siew Meng Leong, "Consumer Decision Making for Common, Repeat-Purchase Products: A Dual Replication," *Journal of Consumer Psychology* 2, No. 2 (1995), pp. 193–208.

24  Herbert A. Simon, *Models of Man* (New York: John Wiley & Sons, 1957); also see Peter L. Wright, "Consumer Choice Strategies: Simplifying Versus Optimizing," *Journal of Marketing Research* 11 (1975), pp. 60–67.

25 Blake Rohrbacher, "Top Reasons for Abandoned Online Purchases," 01/17/2001, http://www.clickz.com/article/cz.3178.html.

26 Michael Tsiros and Vikas Mittal, "Regret: A Model of its Antecedents and Consequences in Consumer Decision Making," *Journal of Consumer Research* 26 (March 2000), pp. 401–17.

27 Claes Fornell, Michael D. Johnson, Eugene W. Anderson, Jaesung Cha, and Barbara Everitt Bryant, "The American Customer Satisfaction Index: Nature, Purpose and Findings," *Journal of Marketing* 60 (October 1996), pp. 7–18, http://www.bus.umich.edu/research/nqrc/acsi.html.

28 David M. Symanski and Richard T. Hise, "e-Satisfaction: An Initial Examination," *Journal of Retailing*, Vol. 76 (3) 2000, pp. 309–22.

29 Jagdish N. Sheth and Banwari Mittal, "A Framework for Managing Customer Expectations," *Journal of Market-Focused Management*, 1, (1996), pp. 137–58.

30 C. Goodwin and I. Ross, "Salient Dimensions of Perceived Fairness in Resolution of Service Complaints," *Journal of Satisfaction, Dissatisfaction, and Complaining Behavior* 2 (1989), pp. 87–92.

31 See Bradley T. Gale, *Managing Customer Value* (Free Press, 1994).

32 Satya Menon and Barbara E. Kahn, "The Impact of Context on Variety Seeking in Product Choices," *Journal of Consumer Research* 22 (December 1995), pp. 285–95.

# CHAPTER 9

## Institution Customer Decision Making: Household, Business, and Government

## Football Players for Sale

Buying a football player at any of England and Scotland's 134 soccer league clubs is very similar to buying other goods and services. The buying and selling prices of football players fluctuates from month to month, depending on whether they are scoring 30 goals in the season or giving up goals or are sidelined with injuries. What are the steps involved in purchasing a football player?

1. Identify the type of player you need: defender, midfielder, striker?
2. Source the players from professional talent scouts, clubs-transfer lists, Internet sites, or specialist recruitment companies.
3. Choose players using assessments that cover character, physical fitness, pace, mobility, technical skills, footballing intelligence, etc. The player could even come for a trial.
4. Begin negotiations with the club, agent, and player over the transfer fee, length of contract, salary package, and other incentives including bonuses, relocation packages, insurance and agent's fees. Lack of face-to-face negotiations and language difficulties can compound the difficulties of this process.
5. The player arrives at the club and you find out if your money has been well spent.

The process involved in purchasing a player is very time consuming and costly and involves interaction with several stakeholders. Player relocation costs one of the clubs—Aberdeen, 50,000 pounds a year and player write-off, when a player fails to perform, can cost 15,000 pounds annually. Players' wages account for 85 percent of Aberdeen's 7 million annual turnover. In the near future, the purchase process for a football player is likely to become more difficult as the EC proposes new regulations on the transfer of players. Finally, if the players do not perform as expected, can the club send them back? This is usually not possible and there is no guarantee on the price if the club tries to sell the player to recoup costs. Few purchases are risky as players in the football industry—buying the wrong one can end a soccer buyer's career for good. (Cathy Hayward, 2001)[1]

The purchase of a football player in a soccer league club involves several stakeholders—the club, the player, the player's agent, and the professional talent scout agency, to name a few—and each of these stakeholders influences the purchase. This decision-making process is different from the individual decision-making process that we studied in Chapter 8. The decision-making process is formalized, different members in the club play separate roles of payers and buyers, and these club members are not only directly accountable to the club owners for their decision but also indirectly accountable to the thousands of people who pay to see the player win for their favorite soccer club. The buying process is further complicated by the fact that the player and his agent can negotiate a deal with the club, and there are also government regulations that have a bearing on the final decision. This is an example of institution customer decision making.

Our focus in this chapter is on group customer decision making in households, in business, and in the government (see Figure 9.1 for conceptual framework). The chapter first explains the roles husbands and wives, mothers and daughters, fathers and sons, and boyfriends and girlfriends play in influencing each other's marketplace choices. It discusses the various methods people use to resolve their differences over what to buy and explains how families and households buy.

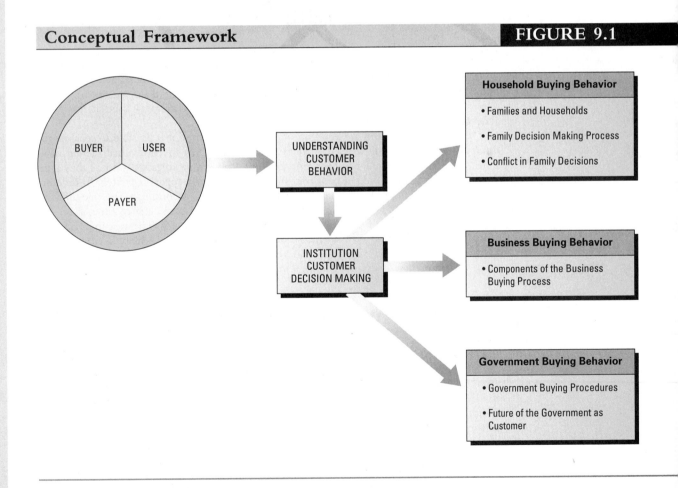

**Conceptual Framework**                    **FIGURE 9.1**

We then examine the decision processes of business and government customers. The challenge of marketing to organizational customers is to understand the decision-making process of organizational customers as end users, payers, and buyers. These customers include business and government customers, as well as institutions (both private and public) such as universities, hospitals, religious groups, and charitable organizations, which purchase products and services for use by their employees, members, or clients. The chapter discusses the components of the business buying process, including the steps in, influences on, and participants in the process and their conflict resolution techniques.

The next part of the chapter covers the buying behavior of government. It explores ways in which business buying behavior and government buying behavior differ from and resemble one another. It describes procedures and regulations that characterize government buying, as well as challenges and rewards of doing business with the government. Finally, we explore developments in government buying.

# Household Buying Behavior

Households are the basic unit of buying and consumption in a society. A **household** is a consumption unit of one or more persons identified by a common location with an address, such as the Rodrigues residence. While a number of customer decisions are, no doubt, made by individuals for their personal consumption, their decisions as members of a household are more complex, since these decisions must accommodate the diverse needs and wants of various household members.

Household decisions are also important to study because it is possible to separate the three customer roles: the user, the payer, and the buyer. In the individual buying decisions, all three roles often merge in one person. When these roles separate, as they generally do in household buying behavior, the marketer has to appeal separately to different members of the households, differentiating the selling appeal according to the role the family member plays. These role allocations are dynamic, vary from time to time, from one product to another, and from one family type to another. That is why it is important for a marketer to understand how an individual family changes over its lifetime, how households are changing in the aggregate, and how different members of these changing households make purchase decisions.

# Families and Households

There are two types of households: family and nonfamily. A **family** is a group of persons related by blood and/or marriage. Among the family households, four types are most common: (1) married couples alone, (2) married couples with children, (3) a single parent with children, and (4) extended family, which may include parents, children's spouses, and/or grandchildren, and occasionally cousins. A **nonfamily household** is a household that contains people who are not at all related. Examples of nonfamily households are (1) a single person living alone in a dwelling unit, (2) roommates, two persons living in the same dwelling unit, including persons of the opposite sex sharing living quarters (POSSLQ), a category used by the U.S. census, and (3) boarding houses (three or more unrelated persons living in the same dwelling unit). We focus on decision making in family-type households since decision making in a family household is influenced by several members and it is different from individual decision making.

# The Family Decision-Making Process

Family decisions differ from individual decisions in two ways. First, the payer, buyer, and user roles are distributed across family members (the same family member may not have all three roles). In addition, these roles are shared by various family members (a single role may be jointly held by more than one individual). Given the distribution and sharing of the three roles among family members, how is the purchase decision process implemented? Specifically, who decides what to buy, when to buy, which brand to buy, and so on?

## Steps in Family Buying Decisions

If you think back to a recent marketplace decision made in your household, you might recall that various members undertook various activities en route to the final decision. Based on research and observations, several consumer-behavior and marketing scholars have identified and described the family buying process as consisting of the following steps.[2]

1. Initiation of the purchase decision
2. Gathering and sharing of information
3. Evaluating and deciding
4. Shopping and buying
5. Conflict management

The first four steps are self-explanatory and are similar in interpretation to those described in the previous chapter. Therefore, these will be discussed here only briefly. The fifth step is particularly salient in all group decision making (and the family is a group). Therefore, that step will be discussed in detail in a later section.

Regarding the first four steps, although their meaning is self-evident and their basic operation is similar to that in individual decision making, the actual dynamics are more involved. Different members of the family play different roles in the decision process. Thus, one member might initiate the purchase decision by making a product request. Another member of the family might collect information. A third member might evaluate and decide. Yet another member might make the actual product purchase. Finally, someone might take the responsibility of resolving any differences of preference and conflicts that may arise. One solution to avoiding conflict is to find a product or service brand that satisfies every family member's unique preferences.

Throughout this process, different family members may influence the decision to varying degrees. Of particular interest to marketers is the influence of spouses and children.[3]

## Husband-Wife Decision Roles

With regard to the roles of husband and wife, five patterns of relative influence are possible: (1) autonomous decision by the husband, (2) husband-dominated decision, (3) syncratic decisions (equal role by both), (4) wife-dominated decision, and (5) autonomous decision by the wife. Autonomous decisions are decisions made independently by the decision maker. Syncratic decisions are decisions in which all play an equal role in making the decision.

In a study of 200 households, reported in 1979, for the purchase of three products (laundry washer, carpeting, and television), the wife's influence was stronger for washers and carpeting while the husband's was greater for televisions. But even for TVs, husbands reported more self-influence compared to wives, who reported more *joint* decision making. For each product, however, more families use joint decision making than autonomic decisions. The relative influence shifts during the decision stages. Generally, one spouse initiates the purchase consideration, but the process becomes more joint as the decision moves to advanced stages, such as information gathering. Although the study is two decades old, it provides a point of comparison. Has the pattern of relative influence between the spouses changed since then? In what manner?

## Joint Decision Process

**Joint decisions** are those in which more than one decision participant made the decision. When couples report they made joint decisions for a specific purchase, it is not easy to visualize exactly how each member participated to make it a joint decision. In fact, noted consumer researcher C. W. Park has termed joint decisions as a muddling-through process. His study of home buying by couples revealed very interesting patterns of interpersonal dynamics among the spouses. Park studied the decision-making process for 45 couples soon after they had bought a home.[4] Among his findings:

- The similarity between the decision plans of the spouses is relatively low.
- When spouses agree on features that the product must have, this agreement on must-have features leads them to perceive that their decision plans are similar (even when they disagree on other optional features). Contrarily, when there is disagreement on must-have features, spouses perceive conflict.
- Individual spouses are more satisfied with some features of the product purchased than with others, and the features with which the spouses are satisfied differ between the spouses. Each spouse feels greater satisfaction with the feature whose inclusion was influenced more by that spouse.
- Spouses agree more with each other on salient objective dimensions (e.g., number of bedrooms, presence of a swimming pool) than on subjective dimensions (e.g., interior design, amount of insulation).
- Spouses grant each other certain role specialization with respect to the feature they are expert at or they should have a say about. Thus, a husband might be viewed by both spouses as an expert on insulation, but the wife is considered to be the expert on interior design. On these role-specialized features, spouses acknowledge the partner's relative influence. On other features, each believes he or she influenced the decision more than the other partner did.

To understand a couple's joint decision process, Park constructed a decision plan net as shown in Figure 9.2. A decision plan net is a tree diagram of the criteria that the decision maker will use and the sequence and manner in which he or she will use them.

## Factors Influencing Interspousal Influence

Several factors affect the pattern of decision sharing among spouses. Factors that have been identified include gender-role orientation, wife's employment status, family life-cycle stages, time pressure, purchase importance, and socioeconomic development level of the population group.

**Gender-Role Orientation.**  Gender roles among spouses can be placed on a continuum of traditional to modern. The degree to which specific behaviors and norms are linked to a person's gender, rather than being shared across genders, is called **gender-role orientation**. The traditional view is one of sharply dichotomous roles for the husband and wife, while the modern view is one of more sharing of responsibilities among the two sexes.[5] In the United States, there is a trend toward merging of buyer, payer, and user role in the same person and sharing of a single role (e.g., payer) by both the spouses. Even in traditional households, Asian or Middle Eastern, purchase decisions are domain specific—cooking-related materials are the domain of women though bought from the market by men.

**Wife's Employment Status.**  The wife's employment status significantly influences gender-role orientation. In families where a wife is employed outside of the home, there is greater acceptance of her role in important family decisions. She makes autonomous decisions, and she is consulted on others because she contributes to family finances and because she is knowledgeable from her exposure to the world outside.

## Decision Plan Nets for a Husband and Wife        FIGURE 9.2

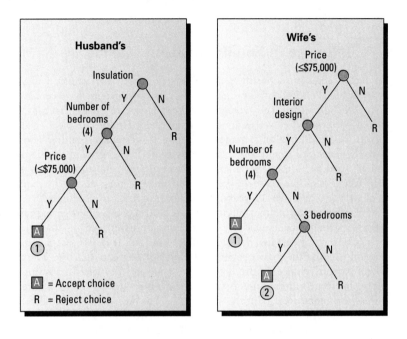

**Source:** C. Whan Park, "Joint Decisions in Home Purchasing: A Muddling-Through Process," *Journal of Consumer Research,* 9, September 1982, pp. 151–162. Reprinted with permission of the University of Chicago Press.

**Stage in Family Life Cycle.** Family life cycle has also been found to influence decision making in the families. Recently married couples tend to make more joint decisions; as the marriage ages, the chores become allocated along with the purchases that accompany those chores (e.g., grocery supplies for cooking, car wax for car washing) and get to be decided autonomously. However, the age of the marriage is not likely to affect decision making for important purchases.

**Time Pressure.** Families with high time pressure tend to rely less on joint decision making since autonomous or one-member-dominated decision processes are generally perceived to be more time-efficient. However, such decisions may sacrifice effectiveness; the decision may not be optimal.

**Importance of Purchase.** Purchase importance refers to how important the family perceives the product to be. The importance of the purchase may stem from the financial outlay or from the centrality of the product to the individual's life. The more important the purchase, the more the decision making is going to be a joint one because it involves using common family resources, and it is a decision that family members will have to live with for a long time.

**Socioeconomic Development of the Population.** Gender roles and role specializations vary from one culture and country to another. Specifically, the culture of a country is related to the stage of socioeconomic development of the population. Thus, underdeveloped countries have more traditional gender roles than do more developed countries. With development and the resulting modernization, urbanization, and concomitant increasing employment of women outside of the home, women's influence on marketplace decision making increases. Marketers need to be cognizant of these cultural differences in their marketing communications.

## Children's Influence in Family Decision Making

Children as family members constitute an important target market for marketers of all household products. Research on teenagers of different age groups by Teenage Research Unlimited in 1999 shows that the average weekly spending of 12-to-15-year-olds is $53, of which $27 is spent on themselves and $26 is spent for family purchases. Teenagers 16 to 17 years old spend $103 in an average week, $65 on themselves and $38 for the family, and 18-to-19-year-olds spend $125 weekly, with $105 being spent on themselves and $20 on family.[6] Children's influence increases with age. In one study, it was found that 21 percent of mothers of five-to-seven-year-olds yielded to their children's requests while 57 percent of mothers of 11-to-12-year-olds yielded to children's requests.[7]

Children influence household buying in three ways. First, children express individualistic preferences for products paid for and bought by parents (e.g., small children demanding particular toys or cereals). Second, children in their teen years begin to have their own money and become their own payers and buyers of items of self-use. Third, children influence their parents' choice of products that are meant for shared consumption (e.g., family vacation or home entertainment system) or even products used by a parent, by exerting expertise influence (e.g., clothes, perfumes). The Window on Research box describes summary findings of a research study on children's influence.

Nickelodeon Online/Harris Interactive KidPulse and MTV/Harris Interactive Youth-Pulse conducted 3,878 interviews in July 2000, and found that online U.S. kids, teenagers, and young adults, aged 8 to 24, are spending at a projected rate of $164 billion per year. 8 to 24 year olds account for 24 percent of the total U.S. population (65.4 million) and have a high influence on family purchases. 75 percent of online 8 to 12 year olds influence the groceries bought by the family and about 49 percent influence their parents clothing choices. 7 in 10 said they have a major influence on where the family decides to go on vacation. As mentioned in Chapter 2, lack of credit cards is restricting online purchase by kids, but companies like Rocketcash, Cybermoola.com, and Icanbuy.com offer methods by which kids can shop online without credit cards. These e-tailers are providing services that try and bridge the role of payer and buyer to enable children to make purchases.[8]

George P. Moschis, a marketing professor at Georgia State University, has studied the role that children play in family decision making. One of his insights is that children's influence in the family decisions depends on whether the family has a social or concept orientation. **Social orientation families** are the ones more concerned with maintaining discipline among children, whereas **concept-oriented families** are those that are concerned with growth of independent thinking and individuality in children. Children from families with social orientation are less likely to make independent decisions and less likely to be involved in family decisions. Those with concept orientation are likely to have greater product knowledge, have a higher regard for their parents' opinion, and a preference for objective sources of information such as *Consumer Reports*.[9]

Another way of classifying families is by how authority is exercised in the family. On this basis, families worldwide can be classified into four types:[10]

1. **Authoritarian families**—The head of the household (mother in matriarchal societies and father in patriarchal societies) exercises strict authority on children, and children learn to obey their elders in all matters. Although a culture of obedience to elders is considered to be a virtue, especially in Asian cultures, it does curb individuality among children and, consequently, their influence on family buying decisions.

2. **Neglectful families**—Parents are distant from their children, who are neglected in these families because the parent(s) place more priority on their individual affairs. Single-parent families risk this behavior most, some due to time pressure,

# WINDOW ON RESEARCH

## Children's Influence on Family Decisions

Consumer researchers Ellen Foxman, Patria Tanshuhaj, and Karin Ekstrom studied the role of adolescent children and found the following:

- Children (adolescents) had more influence on products for their own use.
- The greater the teenager's financial resources, the greater the influence he or she exercised.
- The greater the perceived knowledge, the greater the perceived influence.
- The greater the importance to the teenager of the product category, the higher the teenager influence.
- Teenager influence was higher in dual-income families.
- Teenagers exercised more influence at the initiation stage than at the search and decision stages.
- Mothers attributed less influence to their children than did children themselves. This discrepancy was less between mothers and their daughters than between mothers and their sons.

In an extension of this research, consumer researchers Sharon E. Beatty and Salil Talpade collected new data and analyzed purchases of durables (TV, stereo, phone, and furniture) made for family use versus made primarily for use by the teenager. Some of their findings were as follows:

- Financial resources of teenagers influenced only those durable purchases that were for the teenager's own use (as opposed to family use) and only in the purchase initiation stage, not in the search and decision stages.
- Children's product knowledge was influential only in the initiation of purchase consideration and only for products intended for teenager use. For family purchases, teenager influence was significantly enhanced with product knowledge but only in the search and decision stages and only for stereos (not for the other products investigated).
- Importance of purchase to teenagers affected their influence for both for-family and for-teenager purchases, and in both initiation and search and decision stages.
- When teenagers were the major users of for-family durables, they exercised more influence (than if they were not going to be the major user) in both initiation and search and decision stages.
- Children had greater influence in dual-income families than in single-income families; however, this influence was significant only for purchases made for shared family consumption. For purchases for their own use, children had influence alike in both single- and dual-income families.

Additional information located at **http://www.aafcs.org**.

**Source:** Adapted from Ellen R. Foxman, Patria S. Tanshuhaj, and Karin M. Ekstrom, "Family Members' Perceptions of Adolescents' Influence in Family Decision Making," *Journal of Consumer Research* 15 (March 1989), pp. 482–91; and "Adolescents' Influence in Family Purchase Decisions: A Socialization Perspective," *Journal of Business Research* 18 (March 1989), pp. 159–72; also see George E. Belch, M. A. Belch, and G. Ceresino, "Parental and Teenage Child Influences in Family Decision Making," *Journal of Business Research* 13 (1985), pp. 163–76.

and others due to the undisciplined lifestyle of the single parent. Of course, not all single parents neglect their children. Children exercise no influence on their parents' purchases in such families and are able to exercise relative autonomy for their purchases, if they have the resources.

3. **Democratic families**—Every member is given equal voice. Most family matters are discussed among family members, especially those who would be affected by the decisions. The final decision could be a joint one, or it could be exercised by the family head(s). Self-expression, autonomy, and mature behavior are encouraged among children. Children share influence with other members in democratic families.

4. **Permissive families**—Children are given relative independence in conducting their own affairs, especially in their adolescent years. Unlike parents in the neglectful families, however, permissive parents closely watch children's interests and exercise of freedom.

The relative prevalence of these types differs across different countries, and their proportions would change in the same country over time. Also, families could have partial tendencies of more than one type. Depending on whether the product is for the children's own use or for shared use in the family, the degree of influence children will have in each of the four types of families is shown in Table 9.1. Marketers can use this classification as a tool to understand family decision making in different countries. However, the classification has been studied in relation to family buying decisions only in one study, limited to preschoolers in one U.S. city.[11] The foregoing relationships between the four family types and children's relative influence are our intuitive judgments.

## TABLE 9.1    Children's Role by Family Type

| | Children's Role | | | |
|---|---|---|---|---|
| | For Own-Use Products | | For Family-Use Products | |
| FAMILY TYPE | DIRECT CONTROL | SHARED INFLUENCE | DIRECT CONTROL | SHARED INFLUENCE |
| Authoritarian | Low | Low | Low | Low |
| Neglectful | High | High | Low | Low |
| Democratic | Moderate | Moderate | Moderate | Moderate |
| Permissive | High | Moderate | Moderate | Moderate |

# Learning the Customer Roles

Families, especially parents and respected elders, are the first source of information about how to carry out the three customer roles. Even as we become adults, we often seek the influence of family members with greater experience or expertise. Primary modes of learning customer roles are, therefore, consumer socialization and intergenerational influence.

## Consumer Socialization

How do children learn to become consumers and become socialized to engage in marketplace exchanges? And they do become socialized to an amazing degree. In one study, children 7 to 12 years old were found to possess strong brand preferences. And children who cannot yet read have been found to be able to recognize brand symbols, such as McDonald's golden arches and Tony the Tiger, mascot for Kellogg's Frosted Flakes.[12]

**Consumer socialization** refers to the acquisition of knowledge, preferences, and skills to function in the marketplace.[13] That is, consumer socialization occurs when one or more of the following are learned or acquired by children:

- preferences among alternative brands and products;
- knowledge about product features and the functioning of the marketplace; and
- skills in making smart decisions, such as making price and product comparisons, discounting advertising and salespersons' claims, and evaluating trade-offs across options (including the option to buy or not to buy).

Researcher Deborah Roedder John suggests that "consumer socialization can be viewed as a developmental process that proceeds through a series of stages as children mature into adult consumers." She identifies three stages of consumer socialization—perceptual, analytic and reflective. In the perceptual stage (age 3-7 years), children tend to emphasize perceptual compared to abstract or symbolic thought. Their consumer knowledge is characterized by perceptual features and distinctions, usually based on a single dimension or attribute. They can recognize brands and retail stores in the market, but do not have any in-depth understanding about them. In terms of influence strategies and decision making, children in the perceptual stage are able to look at things only from their own perspective. They may be aware that others do not share the same perspective, but they are not able to incorporate their views into their decision-making process. In the analytical stage (age 7-11 years), children are able to approach situations in a more detailed and analytical manner. An increase in information processing abilities and better understanding of the marketplace in terms of product categories, prices, advertising, and brands mark this stage. Children are able to use more than one dimension or attribute in their evaluations and their decision-making approach is more adaptive and flexible as they weave perspectives of family and friends into the process. Finally, in the reflective stage (age 11-16 years), children focus on understanding the social meanings that exemplify the marketplace. Their information processing and social skills are well developed and they have a clear understanding of brands, prices, advertising, and promotions. There is complete awareness of other people's perspectives and consumer decisions are made adaptively, depending on situation and task. Their influence strategies are also strategic based on what they think will be best received by the person being influenced.[14]

Thus, we can conclude that two types of factors play a role in consumer socialization of children: cognitive and environmental. Cognitive factors are age-related mental abilities. Cognitive development proceeds with age, and so does children's consumer socialization. Environmental factors are socialization agents (sources of information and influence): mass media, peers, and family. Family has been the strongest influence on children's socialization in general, not just on their socialization as consumers.[15] As the child becomes older, peer influence and media influence grows, and the influence of family likely declines. In our experience, the weakening of family influence with advancing years is less prevalent in Asian and traditional countries than in the more industrialized Western countries. The Window on Research reflects on the consumer socialization of children in China.

## Learning Mechanisms

The socialization influence from parents to children occurs basically through the learning mechanisms described in Chapter 4: instrumental conditioning, modeling, and cognitive learning. These three mechanisms correspond to the three bases of reference-group influence (a topic covered in Chapter 2): utilitarian, value-expressive, and informational, respectively.

Instrumental conditioning refers to learning to do those things that are rewarded. Children learn those behaviors and the underlying values that receive rewards from their

# WINDOW ON RESEARCH

## Socialization of Chinese Children as Consumers

China adopted the one-child policy in 1979. As only children, Chinese children exert great influence on the spending of their families and spend a considerable amount of their own money in the marketplace. It has been found that Chinese children's overall index of influence on family spending of 25 items is around 68 percent. Socialization of children as consumers involves gaining an understanding of the marketplace, one aspect of which is knowledge of sources of information about products. Researchers James McNeal and Mindy Ji conducted a study of 460 children between the ages of 8 and 13 years in the Beijing area to understand Chinese children's utilization of new product information sources and their perceptions of the relative importance of each of the information sources. The children were provided with a list of products and asked where they learned about each product. Children were also asked to rank their most important sources of information from a predefined list of sources and data on their media use was collected from parents.

Children identified television to be the most important source of information for products. Parents and stores were also identified as information sources, but they were not relied upon as much as television. It is believed that "the family in the Chinese culture would be the most instrumental in introducing children to products new to them due to the fact that in China the family is the basic social unit." But this finding shows that television, though a relatively new medium is powerful in its influence in China (see box on Symbolic consumption of products: Television in China on pg. 22). Penetration of television is very high in China, and children spent 17.2 hours each week watching television, compared to 2.7 hours reading newspapers, 2.6 hours reading magazines, and 6.3 hours listening to the radio. With its potent combination of entertainment and information value—termed "infotainment," the television is the most valued source for new product information for children in China. The researchers state that two models of two-step flow of communication exist in Chinese families: "media to children and children to parents," and "media to parents and parents to children."

Marketers need to set aside their stereotypes and focus on the new influences on the emerging consumer generation in China. These influences are more commercial than interpersonal and they are affecting consumer socialization.

**Source:** Adapted from James U. McNeal and Mindy F. Ji (1999), "Chinese Children as Consumers: An Analysis of Their New Product Information Sources," *Journal of Consumer Marketing*, Vol. 16, Issue 4, http://www.emerald-library.com.

parents. The second mechanism is modeling. Here children look up to their parents as role models and try to internalize and adopt their values, roles, and aptitudes. The cognitive mechanism of learning toward socialization can occur at two levels: low involvement and high involvement. In the low-involvement mode, there could be undeliberated adoption of product choices because of familiarity or because these products were used by one's parents. At the high-involvement level, socialization influence can occur due to communication and education by parents about various brands or buying strategies. Learning from the media can occur through cognitive (communication and education) and/or modeling (identification with models) processes. Learning from peers occurs predominantly via modeling, but occasionally it can be through cognitive means (information) or through instrumental conditioning (reward of approval).

## Socialization Outcomes

Whether the socialization agents are the family, peers, or the media, there are several possible socialization outcomes. First, children can adopt certain products and brands simply by noticing them in use in the house or seeing them in advertisements and can firm up preferences based on satisfactory use experience. Children also can learn about desirable product features, alternative products, brands, suppliers, stores, and other market options, and can make this information a part of their stock of marketplace knowledge. Finally, children can learn the knowledge and skills to make smart choices. They can learn to clip coupons, do comparison shopping, and select items from mail catalogs.

## Intergenerational Influence

The **intergenerational influence (IGI)** of family members refers to the transmission of values, attitudes, and behaviors from one generation to another.[16] In studies done in the early 1970s as well as more recently in the late 1980s, transfer of market values in terms of product and service preferences has been found for a range of products and services, including banks, auto insurance, grooming products, and supermarket items.[17] See Window on Research box.

IGI can take place in two directions: forward (from parents to children) and reverse (from children to parents). Forward IGI occurs both when the child is young and lives with parents and during adult years when the parents and grown children live in separate households. Typically, researchers have studied forward IGI during early childhood (that is, during consumer socialization). In contrast, forward and reverse IGI during the adult years of sons and daughters has not been studied much.

## Reverse Influence

The *reverse influence* begins to occur as children grow up and are exposed to new knowledge and to new role models. Consequently, they begin to depend less on parents as role models or for guidance and begin to carve out their individual identity.

This influence can occur for two reasons. First, the offsprings begin to influence their parents' preferences and marketplace choices because on certain products children acquire greater knowledge and expertise than their parents, which their parents acknowledge. The second mechanism of children-to-parent influence occurs due to what can be called democratic justice. **Democratic justice** refers to a family norm in which each family member is given a voice in family decisions. Thus, in the purchase of common assets (e.g., car, furniture), and for products consumed exclusively by children, many families may consider it legitimate to give youngsters a voice and, thus, to allow them to influence parents' preferences. However democratic justice as a mechanism of offspring-to-parent influence can cause tensions in a family when the offsprings' preferences become incongruent with their parents' values. For example, when offsprings want to get a punk-style haircut or turn a room into a discotheque, or when offsprings' preferences make excessive demands on parents' resources, then it is likely to violate parents' sense of propriety and, thus, cause conflict. Both these sources of conflict are mediated, of course, by who controls the resources. If offsprings depend entirely on parents for financial support, then the rejection of the former's preferences is more likely. On the other hand, if they contribute to the family's financial resources, or at least earn part of their living, then parents are likely to allow more leeway. But the value incongruence does not disappear with resource sharing.

# WINDOW ON RESEARCH

## Research Findings on Intergenerational Influence

*Bank preference.* A study from the 1970s found that 93 percent of college freshmen patronize the same bank as their parents do.

*Financial planning.* The extent to which families preplan their financial goals and then act to fulfill those goals was found to be consistent over three generations studied.

*Auto insurance.* In one study, 40 percent of married couples had automobile insurance from the same company as the husband's parents. In another, 32 percent of adult men had the same auto insurance agency as did their fathers. This influence decreased with the age of adult children: 62 percent among men in their 20s and 19 percent among men 50 years of age or older.

*Grocery items.* In a study of 49 female college students and their mothers, brand preferences between mothers and their grown daughters were found to be more similar for grocery items with high brand-name visibility (e.g., toothpaste, facial tissues, pain reliever, and peanut butter) than for products with low brand-name visibility (spaghetti sauce, canned vegetables, coffee, and frozen juices). For high-visibility brands, 49 percent of mothers and daughters agreed on their brand preference, compared to only 31 percent agreement for low-visibility brands. There was also similarity on such choice rules (i.e., the rules of thumb consumers employ to make their buying more efficient) as buying items on sale, brand loyalty, relying on others for advice or information, and prepurchase planning. Moreover, there was similarity in mothers' and their daughters' marketplace beliefs, such as beliefs that there is positive price-quality relationship, marketer-given information is useful, advertising has positive value, and private brands and sale merchandise are good value.

Additional information located at **http://www.usadata.com.**

**Sources:** Adapted from Elizabeth S. Moore-Shay and R. J. Lutz, "Intergenerational Influences in the Formation of Consumer Attitudes and Beliefs about the Marketplace: Mothers and Daughters," *Advances in Consumer Research*, M. Houston, ed., 15 (Ann Arbor, Mich.: Association for Consumer Research, 1988), pp. 461–67; J. Fry, D. C. Shaw, C. H. von Lanzenauer, and C. R. Dipchard, "Customer Loyalty to Banks: A Longitudinal Study," *Journal of Business* 46, pp. 517–25; Hill, 1970; L. G. Woodson, T. L. Childers, and P. R. Winn, "Intergenerational Influences in the Purchase of Auto Insurance," in W. Locander, ed., *Marketing Looking Outward: Business Proceedings*, (Chicago: American Marketing Association, 1976), pp. 43–49.

## Family Characteristics That Influence IGI

Forward and reverse IGI are both influenced by family relationship and relative expertise across generations. Family relationship refers to the degree of mutual respect and trust between parents and their adult offsprings, and the harmony of relations and communication among them, in all areas of life (not just about products and shopping activities). *Relative expertise* is the acknowledgement by the offsprings that parents possess expertise about a product (or, for reverse IGI, that parents acknowledge their offsprings to be experts).

Based on these two characteristics, four IGI states can occur (see Table 9.2).[18] When perceived expertise is high but the family relationship is negative, there will be disaffected IGI. This means the person acknowledges the soundness of the expert advice in principle but does not act upon the advice because he or she psychologically rejects the adviser. When perceived expertise is high and the family relationship is positive, there will be high

| Intergenerational Influences (IGI) | | | TABLE 9.2 |

| | | **Family Relationship** | |
|---|---|---|---|
| | | **Negative** | **Positive** |
| **Perceived Expertise** | **High** | Disaffected IGI | High IGI |
| | **Low** | No IGI | Discounted IGI |

IGI. Children and their parents will seek out and act on one another's advice. In contrast, when perceived expertise is low and family relationship negative, there will be no IGI. Finally, when perceived expertise is low and family relationship is positive, there will be discounted IGI, meaning the person receives the advice politely but discounts it as not being credible.

**IGI Across Households.** A special case of IGI occurs when offsprings have formed their own households separate from parents. This can be termed IGI across households.[19] IGI occurs across households mainly because of *expertise*. If grown offsprings still consider their parents experts on the purchase of a specific product (e.g., a house, life insurance, stocks, or traditional rituals), they would turn to them for advice, despite household separation. Conversely, on matters where adult offsprings are perceived to possess expertise (e.g., computers, CD players, or even cars), parents will seek the former's advice. Another reason for IGI across households is *lifestyle similarity* between the generations. Illustratively, a mother returning to the workforce might appreciate her successful daughter's insights on what chic people wear to work. Yet another factor, *resource control*, refers to who finances the expense for the purchase under control. When parents finance the purchase, they would exercise IGI. On the other hand, if retired parents depend on their grown offsprings, then reverse IGI occurs.

These three factors correspond closely with the three types of reference group influences we studied in Chapter 2: informational, identificational, and normative or instrumental. Informational influence occurs when the influencing agent provides useful information that guides, facilitates, or alters the choices the influence recipient makes. Identificational influence occurs when the influenced identifies with the influencer, viewing the latter as the role model and emulating his or her behavior. Finally, instrumental influence occurs due to the ability of influence agents to reward or punish the influence target. This also includes what has been called normative influence: the expectations of significant others. As mentioned earlier, for any of these influences to operate, there must also be a positive family relationship. It is a necessary condition, and the others are sufficient conditions.

# Conflict in Family Decisions

Family decision making may give rise to conflict, whether the customer roles are distributed among family members or shared by family members. Conflict among *distributed roles* arises when the user, payer, and buyer roles are played by different family members, and alternatives (such as brands/suppliers) do not satisfy the goals (market values) of each.

Conflict due to *shared roles* arises when a single role is shared by multiple family members and their goals (market values) diverge. For example, when both husband and wife play the payer role as they draw on common family funds, they may experience conflict on how much can be spent on home refurnishing.

## Types of Conflict

The conflicts that are inevitable if the family decision process entails joint decision making will arise if there is disagreement between family members either on goals (market values) or on perceptions (evaluation of alternatives). The nature of the conflict will differ according to whether there is disagreement in one or both of these areas (see Table 9.3). When goals are in agreement but alternative evaluations differ, there is solution conflict. When both goals and perceptions diverge, conflict is *compounded*. This would happen in buying a condominium when spouses may desire different goals (e.g., the husband may want a city view, and the wife may prefer a view of the lake) and also perceive two condominiums differently on a common goal (e.g., they may differ on which of the two condominiums they examined is more aesthetic).[20] When both values and evaluations converge across family members, there is no conflict; choice of many daily consumption items exemplify this setting. When goals diverge but perceptions of solutions are in agreement, there is goal conflict. This occurs when the husband may want a stylish, youthful car but the wife wants a large, safe car.

## TABLE 9.3        Types of Conflict

|  |  | Goals/Values | |
|---|---|---|---|
|  |  | **Convergent** | **Divergent** |
| **Perceptions/ Evaluations** | **Divergent** | Solution conflict (family vacation) | Compounded Complex, important Purchases (home buying) |
|  | **Convergent** | No Conflict (daily consumption items) | Goal conflict (What to buy) (Product-level conflict) |

## Conflict Resolution

Four strategies of conflict resolution have been suggested by scholars: problem solving, persuasion, bargaining, and politicking (see Table 9.4). Problem solving entails members trying to gather more information or to add new alternatives. When motives/goals are congruent and only perceptions differ, obtaining and sharing information (i.e., problem solving) often suffices to resolve conflicts. Persuasion requires educating about the goal hierarchy; the wife might argue how a safe and large car is in the best interest of the whole family since the car is needed to transport children. Bargaining entails trading favors (husband gets to buy a house with a den and the finished basement provided the car he buys is one of his wife's preference). When goals and evaluations are so divergent that even bargaining is infeasible, politicking is resorted to. Here, members form coalitions and subgroups within the family and by so doing simply impose their will on the minority coalition.[21] Marketers can help household members resolve a conflict by aiding the problem-solving mode; they can provide additional information about alternatives, especially in interpersonal selling situations.[22] Recent research has further focused on the interpersonal dynamics of how household members such as spouses influence each other in joint decisions. See the Window on Research box.

## Conflict Resolution Techniques

TABLE 9.4

|  | Goals/Values | |
|---|---|---|
|  | **Convergent** | **Divergent** |
| **Evaluations** Divergent | Problem solving | Politicking Bargaining |
| Convergent | No conflict | Persuasion |

# WINDOW ON RESEARCH

## How Spouses Influence Each Other's Decisions

In one study of married spouses' influence strategies, consumer researcher Margaret C. Nelson identified the following repertoire of influence strategies spouses used.

1. Punishments, threats, authority, and negative emotions
   - Refuses to do chores
   - Threatens punishment
   - Becomes angry
   - Questions spouse's right to disagree
2. Positive emotion and subtle manipulation
   - Puts the spouse in a receptive mood
   - Appeals to spouse's love and affection
   - Promises to do something nice in return
   - Acknowledges that it would be a favor
3. Withdrawal and egocentrism
   - Denies affection, acts cold
   - Clams up
   - Looks hurt, sulks
4. Persuasion and reason
   - Uses logic
   - Persists in arguing and requesting compliance
5. Miscellaneous others
   - Simply gives in
   - Argues that he or she knows more
   - Compromises; meets in the middle
   - Pleads or begs
   - Comes up with a new solution acceptable to both

Additional information is available at **http://acr.webpage.com**.

**Source:** Adapted from Margaret C. Nelson, "The Resolution of Conflict in Joint Purchase Decisions by Husbands and Wives: A Review and Empirical Test," in *Advances in Consumer Research*, Michael J Houston, ed., 15 (1988), pp. 436–41.

# A General Framework for Understanding Family Buying Decisions

It is useful to bring together the major topics covered in this chapter in an organizing framework. Figure 9.3 presents such a framework. Since we have already discussed most of the variables contained in this figure, we describe the model only briefly here.

## Decision Process

The linchpin of the model is the decision process, which can be either autonomous (i.e., decision made by a single family member), or joint decision making. It is the joint decision making that distinguishes household buying from individual buying. The decision is joint if family members exercise any degree of influence during any of the stages of the decision process. These decision-process stages (not shown in Figure 9.3) are initiation, information gathering, evaluation and decision, shopping and buying, and conflict resolution. Conflict occurrence is a significant component of the decision process. The conflict may arise either because the family members do not agree on purchase goals and criteria or because they disagree on their perceptions as to which alternatives would best meet these goals and criteria. Its resolution would typically follow one of the four strategies discussed earlier: problem solving, persuasion, bargaining, or politicking.

## Influences on the Decision Process

The extent to which a decision process will be autonomous rather than joint, or vice versa, will depend on the nature of the purchase, separation of the buyer, payer, and user roles, individual member characteristics, and family characteristics. And, of course, sources of information will influence the decision process. Different members may be exposed differently to different sources of information, and their individual perspectives and perceptual distortions make the decision process less or more involving and conflicting.

### Nature of the Purchase

**Consider the Nature of the Purchase.** If the purchase is important and if there is high perceived risk associated with the purchase, then the decision will more likely be a joint decision. If the product or service is required urgently, then the time-consuming process of joint decision will be avoided in favor of autonomous decisions. Finally, if the product to be bought is for shared consumption among the family members, then the process is likely to be a joint one.

**Separation of the Three Roles.** The extent to which the three customer roles are separated in a household will influence the customer decision. In some households, one spouse assumes all three roles, while in others spouses divide the role responsibility or jointly share each role. Likewise, the influence of children varies from household to household. Where the three roles do not converge in the same person, or where household members do not delegate their roles to others, joint rather than autonomous decisions are more likely, and, consequently, conflicts too are more likely.

### Individual Characteristics

Among the individual characteristics, the first factor is whether any given individual in the family carries all three role responsibilities: buyer, payer, and user. If these roles converge

## A Framework for Understanding Family Buying Decisions

FIGURE 9.3

in the same individual, then the decision making is likely to be autonomous. The more these roles are distributed across the family members, the more the decision process is likely to be a joint one.

Other characteristics of the individual are personality and lifestyle, time pressure, product expertise, and education. These influence both the extent of joint decision making and the way in which the conflicts are resolved. Time pressure on one or more members will lead to less joint decision making. If individual members have a lifestyle and personality that is individualistic rather than sharing and inclusive (i.e., a "me" rather than "us" personality), then autonomous decisions are more likely. Of course, product expertise of individuals will bring them more into family decisions. Finally, education will closely influence the interaction and the conflict management. Spouses and parents with more education will likely keep the conflicts manageable and solve them via rational arguments and persuasion, rather than by politicking.

## Family Characteristics

One set of family characteristics that would impact the decision process includes family life cycle (FLC), socioeconomic status, and dual versus single career. Consider FLC: Newly marrieds have generally been found to use the joint process to a much greater extent than couples with aging marriages. Adolescent children begin to make more autonomous decisions for products for which they are the primary users. Socioeconomic status (SES) influences the extent of joint process and also how the conflicts may be resolved. Although there is no conclusive research evidence on this, for products meant exclusively for an individual member's use, the decision is more likely to be an autonomous one for both upper-class and lower-class (compared to the middle-class) households—the upper class because they can afford it, and the lower-class because funds are controlled by the head of the household.

A second set of family characteristics is the gender-role orientations and role specialization. In families where gender roles are traditionally oriented, there will be many more autonomous decisions. Also, with role specialization, purchases will tend to be assigned for autonomous decisions by those perceived to possess the most specialized knowledge of the topic. A related variable is dual versus single career in the family. In dual-career families, gender-role orientation is less likely to be traditional, making the decision process a joint one between spouses.

The last set of family characteristics comprises the communication and interaction patterns. Does the nominal head of the household govern and manage the family in an authoritarian or a democratic way? The decisions would be much more joint in the latter than in the former type of households. Furthermore, are day-to-day communications among the family members marked with harmony or discord? The answer to this would affect whether influence attempts by one member will be accepted by other members, as we stated in discussing the intergenerational influence (IGI). Also, conflict resolution would be closely influenced by democratic versus authoritarian management style and harmony versus discord in everyday communications within the family. Finally, the more family members share time and lifestyle, the more they are likely to engage in a joint decision process.

However, our description in this chapter of the family's customer behavior is founded on research in North America. Students of customer behavior need to deliberate over how the concepts described in this chapter would be adapted for families in other nations and in other cultures.

# Business Buying Behavior

A business is a licensed entity engaged in the activity of making, buying, or selling products and services for profit or nonprofit objectives. This definition considers any organization that makes and sells something to be a business. As customers, businesses buy products or services (raw materials, components, supplies, support services, and machinery) to provide value for their customers, end users, resellers, value-added resellers, employees, or owners (i.e., the key stakeholders).

Business buying typically differs from household buying in several key ways: greater specialization of roles, more formalization of the buying process, more formal accountability for decisions, greater internal capabilities, and more complex requirements (see Table 9.5).

**Specialization of Customer Roles.** As we explained in Chapter 8 and earlier in this chapter, individual buying requires that the three customer roles—payer, buyer, and user—be combined in a single individual, whereas in household buying decisions, these roles may be held by a single person or distributed among various family members. Such role specialization is even more marked in business buying. An exception to this pattern is a one-person entrepreneur, who makes decisions equivalent to individual decision making.

| Comparison of Household and Business Buying | | TABLE 9.5 |

| Characteristic | Household Buying | Business Buying |
| --- | --- | --- |
| Specialization of customer roles | Combined or slightly specialized | Moderately to very specialized |
| Formalization of the buying process | Informal | Slightly formal (small businesses) to formal (large businesses) |
| Accountability for decisions | Usually not formally measured | Strict measures |
| Internal capabilities | Weak | Weak (small businesses) to very strong (large businesses) |
| Complexity of requirements | Little complexity | Operational and strategic complexity |

**Formalization of the Buying Process.**  Business buying is formalized with respect to policy, procedures, and paperwork. Generally, businesses have written policies and rules to guide the solicitation of price quotes, preferential treatment to a certain class of vendors (e.g., minority businesses), and the way the decisions are to be made in the buying firm. This degree of formalization is rare in family buying behavior.[23] The degree of formalization may vary from business to business—slightly formal in small businesses to very formal in regulated industries and in the government. Large businesses tend to be somewhere in the middle.

**Accountability for Decisions.**  Unlike household buying, business buying holds accountable those who are in charge of paying and buying. This results in more formal evaluation of and feedback on these purchase decisions. This greater accountability in business arises because ownership is divorced from management, and buying is divorced from usage. Therefore, business buying encourages formal supplier ratings and scorecards as well as constant feedback and communication to its suppliers.

**Internal Capabilities.**  More often than households, business customers are capable of producing certain items in-house rather than buying them from others. This capability requires business customers to analyze the economics of the make-versus-buy options.

**Complexity of Requirements.**  Business customers have both operational and strategic complexity of buying behavior. Operationally, complexity results from the number of employees participating in the buying process, from the need to adhere to government rules and regulations, and because decisions involve multiple authority and expertise levels. Additionally, procurement is often a strategic function since it is the single largest cost center to a business organization. It is also strategic because it is responsible for buying both capital goods and materials, so the risks associated with failure are enormous.

# Components of the Business Buying Process

With purchasing being such a significant and complex function, all but the smallest organizations have formal systems for carrying it out. These systems, called procurement systems, have several components—nature of the purchase, organizational characteristics, buying center, rules and procedures, and a decision process. These components also exist in small businesses, but tend to be simpler and less rigidly defined. By determining the way the components fit together in a particular business, marketers can describe the business's customer behavior.

## Nature of the Purchase

The way an organization makes a purchase decision depends to a large degree on the nature of the purchase. This nature is defined by the buyclass (type of purchase need); the significance of the decision in terms of perceived risk, importance, and product complexity; and the time pressure faced by the decision makers.

### Buyclass

For an individual, purchase needs may require routine problem solving, limited problem solving, or extended problem solving. Similarly, businesses have three types of procurement needs, or buyclasses: straight rebuy, modified rebuy, and new task.

A **straight rebuy** is a need that has been processed and fulfilled before. It is for an item that is needed repeatedly and has been bought before. Examples include shop supplies (e.g., lubricants), worker uniforms, and office stationery. If the outcomes of prior purchase have been satisfactory, the business simply places the order with one of the past suppliers because the gains in savings from a new search of suppliers is unlikely to outweigh the costs of the effort. Thus, businesses often negotiate an annual purchasing agreement for these items with automatic reordering.

There are tremendous efficiencies that can be realized by automating straight rebuys. Most companies use the airline web sites for direct corporate travel bookings. Firms like Wal-Mart and Procter & Gamble collaborate so that inventory can be restocked as it falls below predetermined levels. In order to maintain a reliable connection to its thousands of suppliers, Wal-Mart transformed Retail Link, its traditional dial-in supplier network, into an Internet application. Wal-Mart's suppliers now have quick and easy access to inventory systems, resulting in faster replenishment, a product mix attuned to customer needs, and lower inventory costs. The network also helps keep prices low and maintains inventory on the shelves. Ingram has also set up an online procurement platform called Rosetta to make the procurement process faster and more streamlined and to lower transaction costs. Similarly, specialized business-to-business exchanges like Foodservice.com and Restaurantpro.com for the restaurant industry aim to do the same thing.

A **modified rebuy** represents a need that is similar in broad nature to the previously fulfilled needs, but it entails some changes either in design/performance specifications or in the supply environment. For example, the firm wants to buy more desk-top computers; although the firm has bought these before, it wants to re-examine the latest technology available or the firm wants to evaluate a new supplier of higher reputation who has entered the market. Made-to-order online purchases allow the business customer with this ability to execute modified rebuys without expending a lot of time and effort. For example, with more and more companies offering online ordering for off-the-shelf products, customers can register with several suppliers and be provided with a password-protected page at these supplier's sites where they can create purchase orders and buy products. The product images and technical specifications are given on the web site, and it becomes a matter of sifting through the required set of products at different sites to change from one supplier to another in a modified rebuy.

**New task** purchases pertain to those needs that are new to the organization. A purchase of this item has never been made, and, indeed, the need has never before been experienced. Therefore, there is considerable uncertainty about the design/performance requirements, which are still being assessed. Also, suppliers may not already be on the company list, and, at any rate, new suppliers may need to be added and all suppliers may have to be appraised anew. Deciding on new technology for a process or a new design would be examples of new task purchases.

The concept of buyclass is important because the purchase process is different across the three buyclasses (see Table 9.6). On a continuum of straight rebuy to modified rebuy to new task, the more the purchase is of the new task type, the more the buying group:

- Perceives the need for information.
- Is large.
- Is deliberative and patient.
- Is concerned with finding a good solution.
- Underplays low price and assured supply as evaluation criteria.
- Will consider new suppliers.
- Will value the influence of technical persons, relative to the influence of buying agents.[24]

| Buying Behavior Associated With Buyclasses | | | TABLE 9.6 |
|---|---|---|---|
| **Buyclass** | **Description of Need** | **Buying Center Size** | **Information Search** |
| Straight rebuy | Item is frequently needed and has been satisfactorily bought before | Very small; ordering may even be automated | Brief or nonexistent; new suppliers rarely considered; technical expertise rarely sought |
| Modified rebuy | Need is broadly similar to one that has been fulfilled before but requires some change in specifications or the supply environment | Moderate | Some information is gathered; new suppliers may be considered; technical experts may have input into decision |
| New task | Need is completely new to the organization | Large | Extensive; new suppliers, often considered experts, usually have major input into decision |

## Perceived Risk, Importance, and Complexity

Each type of purchase involves a different level of perceived risk, importance, and complexity for the decision maker.

**Perceived risk** refers to the expected probability that the purchase may not produce a satisfactory outcome. It is a product of two factors: (1) the degree of uncertainty that a choice may be wrong, and (2) the amount at stake should a wrong choice occur.

Uncertainty stems from the absence of prior design/performance specifications and from lack of experience with potential suppliers. Thus, new tasks have the most uncertainty, and straight rebuys have the least. Amount at stake is the financial loss or performance loss from a suboptimal choice. Financial loss depends on the purchase price in absolute terms (the more expensive the purchase, the greater the financial loss) as well as from a less advantageous price (the supplier chosen may not be the best-priced supplier). Performance loss comes from the product not performing to standards, which may, in fact, cause systemwide damage (e.g., a chemical ingredient of lesser purity than required might damage the processing equipment).

The **importance of purchase** is a combination of the amount at stake and the extent to which the product plays a strategic role in the organization. The higher the amount at stake, and the more strategic the product's role, the more important the purchase. Thus, a large fleet of transportation vehicles might cost more than a communication network; yet the latter might be viewed as a more important purchase due to its strategic role in equipping the customer firm for the information age.

Complexity refers to the extensiveness of effort it takes to comprehend and manage the product during its acquisition. Complexity has two dimensions: (1) the number of performance dimensions and (2) the technical and specialist knowledge required to understand those dimensions. Thus, a single-dimensional product like a chemical is simpler than a multidimensional item like a personal computer (even though the risk might be greater with the purchase of a chemical than with that of a computer). Office furniture is less technical than surgical sutures. The latter require more specialist knowledge to understand the design/performance characteristics and the supplier information.

As the foregoing examples suggest, importance, complexity, and perceived risk are often but not always, related. Together, these influence how extensive and involved the purchase decision process will be. See the Window on Research box, which summarizes the findings of 25 years of research on perceived risk and organizational buying.

## Time Pressure

Customers behave differently when they are under time pressure. Time pressure refers simply to how urgently the item is needed. When the item is needed urgently, the purchase decision will tend to short-circuit the usual process, make the process less deliberative, and give more direct role to the user/requisitioner.

## Organizational Characteristics

Four organizational characteristics of the customer firm affect buying behavior: (1) size, (2) structure, (3) purchase resources, and (4) purchase orientation.

## Size

The size of the business determines not only the customer's potential dollar volume, but also the sophistication of its buying process. Small business organizations behave more like a family in their buying behavior; entrepreneurial firms usually consist of a one-person purchasing group and, thus, resemble an individual buying decision. Large organizations, in contrast, have larger buying groups and more formalized procedures.

## Structure

A business's structure refers to the number of departmental units, geographical locations over which the units are spread out, and its degree of centralization. The more departments a business has, the larger the buying group and the more prolonged the buying process is likely to be. Multilocation buying firms create more complexity for the seller than single-locale firms. For example, a firm selling construction equipment may have to visit the administrative headquarters of a construction firm as well as its construction site managers.

## Purchase Resources

Purchase resources refer to the availability of professional buyers and the extent to which the purchase office is staffed with the required type and number of experts as well as equipment (e.g., computerized supplier information system). Generally, large and professionally managed (as opposed to owner-managed) firms would have better resourced purchasing departments leading to well-evaluated decisions and formal and rigorous vendor evaluation.

# WINDOW ON RESEARCH

## What Perceived Risk Does to Business Buying Behavior

Over the past quarter-century, researchers have studied extensively the impact of perceived risk on buying behavior. Their findings have supported the view that when business customers perceive high risk, they adjust their buying behavior to protect themselves and their organizations.

For example, with higher perceived risk, the buying group (center) becomes more complex. That is, more people are involved in the purchase decision throughout the purchase process, and they are drawn from a greater variety of departmental and/or organizational interests. Additionally, buying-center participants will generally be of higher organizational status and authority; if not, the buying center will not have authority to make the final purchase decision. Instead, its function will be (1) to gather and evaluate relevant information and (2) to make recommendations to upper-level management.

Participants in a high-risk purchase decision process are more educated and experienced in their area of expertise. Also, since the purchase decision is important, participants are motivated to expend greater effort and deliberate more carefully throughout the purchase process.

High-risk decisions favor sellers who offer proven products and solutions. Product quality and post-sale service will be of the utmost importance. Price will be considered only after product and service criteria have been fully met. If (after careful scrutiny) two or more sellers appear equally capable of satisfying purchase requirements, price will play a dominant role in the purchase decision.

Information search is active, and a wide variety of information sources are used to guide and support the purchase decision. Buying-center participants may rely more heavily on impersonal, commercial information sources (e.g., trade publications, sales literature) during the earlier stages of the decision process. As the procurement decision progresses, personal, noncommercial information sources (e.g., consultants, other organizations that have already made similar purchases) may become more important.

Within the buying firm, conflict between buying-center participants increases. One reason is that more departments (through their representatives) are involved in the purchase decision. Also, since the purchase outcome is important, buying-center participants will be reluctant to make concessions without some form of reciprocal reward. Therefore, buying-center participants will most likely use a bargaining negotiation strategy.

Role stress among decision makers increases. One cause is the size and complexity of the buying center, resulting in greater conflict among participants with differing perspectives and motivations. Also, in a highly visible (important) purchase where the outcome is uncertain, the chances of making a wrong decision and the associated consequences of a wrong decision intensify participant stress.

**Source:** Adapted from Wesley J. Johnston and Jeffrey E. Lewin, "Organizational Buying Behavior: Toward an Integrative Framework," *Journal of Business Research* 35 (January 1996), pp. 1–15. Additional information is available at http://www.mcb.co.uk/cgibin/journal1/jbim.

## Purchase Orientation

The organization's purchase orientation refers to its purchasing philosophy along a continuum from viewing purchasing simply as an administrative function that finds the most economical sources of materials needed when they are needed to viewing it as a strategic, managerial function whose goal is to add value to the organization's ability, in turn, to offer better value to its customers. As a strategic function, purchasing is engaged in several key activities:

- Scrutinizing make-versus-buy decisions. It questions the very need to buy something, or even whether it may not be better to buy the whole thing, rather than buying an intermediate product and then converting it into a final marketable product.
- Continually finding better products, materials, and technology.
- Developing long-term sources of supply and building relationships with the suppliers.

## The Buying Center

In all but the smallest organizations, purchase decisions are handled by a formal or informal buying center—a multifunction, multilevel internal organization that is responsible for the centralized purchasing function. The buying center represents a subset of *roles* within the organization, which participate in the buying process. Several roles have been identified:

- *User*—This is the user department that would use the product to be purchased by an organization.
- *Buyer*—The buyer, alternatively called purchasing manager or purchasing executive, has the formal authority to execute the purchase contract and place a purchase order.
- *Analyzer*—One who performs technical analysis of suppliers by using such tools as cost analysis and value analysis.
- *Influencer*—By their expert advice, these role holders influence the evaluative criteria and supplier ratings and/or the final decision itself. Typically, these are design engineers and external consultants.
- *Gatekeepers*—They regulate the flow of information from suppliers to the other members of the buying center. They permit or deny salespersons access to design and user departments or to other executives. Sometimes, the legal department in an organization is a gatekeeper.
- *Decider*—The deciders make the final decision. This role may be played by a formal buying committee, or by the CEO, CFO, or purchasing executive alone. Sometimes, the user and engineering departments short list and rank the suppliers, and then a high-level executive who may or may not be a member of any buying committee makes the final decision.

The buying center roles (e.g., user, influencer) are roles, not titles or persons, and an individual may play multiple roles, such as influencer and gatekeeper. Although various executives may play a crucial role in the buying decision, personnel from three departments are typically involved more extensively: purchasing, manufacturing, and quality control. The buying center is a concept and should not be confused with buying committees that many organizations may have. When buying committees exist, persons other than those on the formal committee may influence the decision and are, therefore, deemed to be a part of the buying center concept. When buying committees do not exist, buying centers still exist as virtual groups.

Firms that decide to target large companies as customers have to deploy more resources to go through the decision process. This process is typically longer, but it results in larger dollar value sales. For example, ICG Commerce, an e-procurement company that targets Global 1000 companies, would have longer sales cycles than companies that target small and medium companies.

## Rules and Procedures

Businesses generally set up elaborate policies (e.g., favor a minority supplier), rules (e.g., purchase needs must be consolidated for the entire organization), and procedures (e.g., minimum number of bids required). The degree of formalization and decision freedom varies from buyer to buyer. If the buying firm is less obligated to adhere to prescribed rules and procedures, a business marketer has a lot more freedom to innovate and add value to offerings and educate the buyer about them.

## Decision Process

Like individual and household buying decisions, organizational buying decisions entail a multistage process. Business buying decisions comprise the following stages:

- Need assessment—Deciding the technical and performance specifications for the needed item.
- Development of choice criteria—Identifying supplier selection criteria.
- Request for proposals (RFPs)—Calling for proposals by publishing requests for quotes (RFQs) and inviting suppliers to submit bids. Additional suppliers are actively solicited if adequate suppliers are not already on the list. For suppliers who submit proposals, additional information is collected about their capabilities and past performance. This information comes from suppliers themselves and, more important, from other independent sources such as consultants, trade associations, word-of-mouth, and formal rating reports from independent sources. E-procurement service providers like ICG Commerce offer eRFPs and eRFQs. Such firms also allow forward and reverse auctions. These allow qualified bidders to compete on price in an anonymous online auction. These services drastically reduce the time for the process as well as the prices the company can get from suppliers.
- Supplier evaluation—Rank-ordering vendors. Some negotiations may occur toward reconciling differences both on technical aspects and on price variations among various bidders or suppliers.
- Supplier selection—Awarding the contract or placing an order.
- Fulfillment and monitoring—Monitoring for smooth fulfillment in a timely fashion and to the satisfaction of the buyers and users.

These steps are similar to individual decision making except that there is a lot more formal analysis as well as use of more structured procedures. The Window on Research box describes the buying process customer researchers found in their study of business purchases of items purchased on a long-term contract and on a repeat purchase basis.

# WINDOW ON RESEARCH

## How Businesses Award Long-Term Contracts for Repeat-Purchase Items

To study the process of selecting a vendor for long-term contracts, customer researchers Niren Vyas and Arch Woodside interviewed managers in six buying firms. Among the 18 products included in the study were corrugated boxes, metal bars, rubber gaskets, fuel oil, and electric cables—a sample of all three buyclasses.

*(continued)*

Based on their study, the researchers described the vendor selection decision as comprising five steps:

1. *Identifying the suppliers:* For straight rebuy and modified rebuy items, the buyer firm already had a list of potential suppliers. For new task items, potential suppliers were identified from prior experience, advice from design engineers, and trade journals.

2. *Qualifying the suppliers:* Buyers assessed suppliers on such factors as capacity, location, manufacturing facility, and financial resources judged from brochures, salespeople-supplied information, and plant visits. To qualify suppliers, buyers applied conjunctive decision rules (a list of required minimums). Some buyers had a policy of including minority suppliers in the list even if this necessitated relaxing some criteria.

3. *Inviting bids:* The buyers issued RFQs (requests for quotations), which detail the design specifications and product performance criteria. The specifications are generated by design and production engineers, based on their technical need and their knowledge of what is available. Buyers preferred to have at least three bidders. If the list of qualified suppliers was long, the conjunctive decision rule was made more demanding (i.e., the required minimums were raised). If this step left more than three bidders, buyers tried to eliminate other suppliers with a lexicographic rule (i.e., eliminate the supplier with the least-attractive value on the most desirable criteria).

4. *Bid evaluation:* Bids were evaluated on both technical and commercial criteria. Commercial evaluation, done by the purchasing department, entailed checking items such as payment terms, price escalation, labor contracts expiration dates, and shipping terms. Technical evaluation was done by user departments and design engineers, generally without the price information so that the technical evaluation was unbiased. A chief goal was to determine the amount of price premium to allow suppliers for superior quality and service. None of the firms used a formal evaluation system, so the price premium decision was simply an intuitive judgment by the buying center.

5. *Bid selection:* If only one bid was received, buyers started immediate negotiations with the bidder on price and delivery schedule. With multiple bids, the first decision was whether to patronize more than one supplier. Buyers often preferred the bargaining advantage of two (or more) suppliers. Factors that affected the final selection were successful experience with a bidder, supplier reputation, and location of the service organization. These factors were weighed against the quoted price in a compensatory decision rule (i.e., the lack of one factor is compensated by superiority on others). The lowest bidder was often selected, but bidders with as much as 6 percent price premium over the lowest bidder were sometimes awarded the contract. When multiple suppliers were selected, the current supplier was given more than 50 percent of the annual order.

**Source:** Adapted from Niren Vyas and Arch G. Woodside, "An Inductive Model of Industrial Supplier Choice Process," *Journal of Marketing* 48 (Winter 1984), pp. 30–45. Additional information is available at http://www.ama.org/pubs/jm.

Various roles in the buying center participate more in some stages than others (see Table 9.7). Generally, users exercise more influence at the need assessment and choice criteria stages; buyers shoulder the major responsibility at the RFP, supplier search, and fulfillment stages; analyzers help most at the supplier evaluation stage; influencers, at supplier evaluation and selection stages; and decision makers, at the vender selection stages. Gatekeepers, of course, would be active throughout, depending on the inflow of information, influence, and salesperson communications, all vying for the decision makers' attention. However, the exact pattern of influence each member exercises at each decision stage varies from case to case.

## Varying Influence of Buying Center Roles    TABLE 9.7

| | Buying Center Roles | | | | | |
| | User | Buyer | Decider | Analyzer | Influencer | Gatekeeper |
|---|---|---|---|---|---|---|
| Need assessment | XX | | X | | X | |
| Vendor search | | XX | XX | | XX | XX |
| Choice criteria | X | X | | X | XX | |
| RFP | | XX | | | | |
| Supplier evaluation | | | | XX | XX | |
| Selection | X | X | XX | X | X | XX |
| Fulfillment/monitoring | XX | XX | | | | |

X Influence, XX Strong Influence

It is the task of a business-to-business salesperson and marketer to identify and map this pattern for each business client individually. According to a recent survey reported in *Purchasing* magazine, engineering and technical staff participate more during the need identification and specification generation stages, whereas purchasing agents/managers participate more in the later stages of identifying the sources of supply and evaluating and choosing them.[25]

## Procurement Costs

In business buying, when decision makers weigh costs, they consider the total costs of a purchase. These costs consists of acquisition costs, possession costs, and usage costs. These three component costs consist of the items listed in Table 9.8.

## Components of a Business Customer's Total Costs    TABLE 9.8

| Acquisition Costs | Possession Costs | Usage Costs |
|---|---|---|
| Price | Interest cost | Field defects |
| Paperwork cost | Storage cost | Training cost |
| Shopping time | Quality control | User labor cost |
| Expediting cost | Taxes and insurance | Product longevity |
| Cost of mistakes in order | Shrinkage and obsolescence | Replacement costs |
| Prepurchase product evaluation costs | General internal handling costs | Disposal costs |

As a business-to-business supplier, a firm should understand and know these costs for a specific customer, then design market offerings in a way that reduces the customer's total costs, rather than just the selling price.

## Psychology of Decision Makers

The decision-making process is primarily driven by two psychological processes occurring in the decision makers: (1) their expectations and (2) their perceptual distortions.

**Expectations.**  One factor that sets organizational decision making apart from individual and household decision making is that the various members of the buying center tend to have a set of differential expectations. Their expectations are influenced by their background and their satisfaction or dissatisfaction with past purchases.[26]

The background that shapes expectations comprises educational and work experiences. Persons with different technical backgrounds emphasize different decision criteria (e.g., engineers focus on technical factors, and buyers focus on price factors). Expectations are created also by role orientations; for example, expectations of a proactive buying agent would differ vastly from that of an agent playing a reactive role. The second source of individual expectations, satisfaction with prior buying experiences with suppliers, focuses on the price and quality of previously purchased products.

**Perceptual Distortions.**  Business customers, like individual consumers, encode incoming information selectively (attending to some and ignoring other information) and in a biased manner. This tendency is called *selective perceptual distortion*. Expectations play a major role in selective perceptions. Thus, some buying center members might expect that only engineers are able to understand product specifications; they might then discount as unreliable any information that salespeople provide, assuming they do not have an engineering background.

## Conflict and Its Resolution

When expectations of various members in the buying center differ, conflicts arise. These may concern either the relative weight of the evaluative criteria or the rating of different suppliers on these criteria.

When conflicts arise, they may be resolved in the four different ways introduced in the section on household decision making: problem solving, persuasion, bargaining, and politicking.[27]

**Problem solving** is a rational approach to conflict resolution. It entails a search for more information, further deliberation on the new information, and possibly consideration of new suppliers. If the conflict is due to disagreements on what is to be expected from the suppliers and their products, then the conflict will likely be resolved in the problem-solving manner.

**Persuasion**, also a rational method of conflict resolution, is used when there is a disagreement on specific criteria for supplier evaluation (but overall agreement on what is to be expected of them). In this method, additional information is not gathered, but further deliberation among existing parties continues and may even proceed to the inclusion of an outside party to resolve the conflict.

When the difference between the buying parties centers on basic goals and objectives, the conflict resolution method shifts from a rational orientation to **bargaining**, which hinges on distributive justice for all. This method is quite common in the case of a new task purchase. Resolution begins by a recognition and acceptance of differences in goals of dissenting members who negotiate for a give and take.

In **politicking**, resolution comes through back-stabbing techniques and centers on the use of an efficient, nonrational approach to dealing with conflicts. Members form partisan coalitions and then manage the decision with behind-the-scenes maneuvering. The organization suffers when this method is used, as decisions either get delayed or are resolved in a manner not consistent with the overall goals and objectives of the organization.

# A Comprehensive Model of Organizational Customer Behavior

To bring together the individual components of the business procurement system, we can diagram a comprehensive model of organizational buyer behavior, such as the one in Figure 9.4.

As Figure 9.4 shows, the nature of purchase and organizational characteristics (including rules and procedures) influence the structure of the buying center, such as whether

## A Comprehensive Model of Organizational Customer Behavior

**FIGURE 9.4**

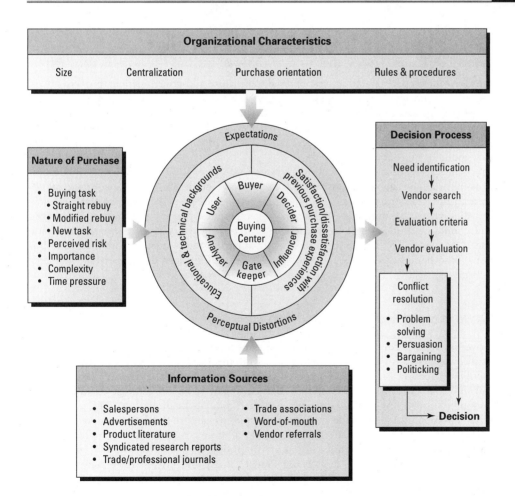

a formal buying center exists, how many members it has, who its members are, and what its charge may be. The buying center is constituted within the framework of buying policies, rules, and procedures (which are determined by the organizational characteristics), and the buying center, in turn, influences these by interpreting, implementing, and/or deviating from them. The decision process is influenced by the buying center as well as by the policies, rules, and procedures. Sources of information form an input at the supplier search stage of the decision process. This input is routed, of course, via the gatekeeper and is filtered through the perceptual distortion processes of the buying-center members. Conflicts may occur at the supplier evaluation and selection stage, and if they do, they are resolved by one of the four methods described earlier.

One factor not shown in the figure is the macroenvironment. It consists of the economic, political, legal, cultural, technological, and marketplace environment (i.e., suppliers and competitors). These envelop the entire buying system. For example, legal restrictions might exist against seeking foreign sources of supply. Economic uncertainty might engender shortage or surplus of certain products. Technology that suppliers use to offer product information (e.g., Internet) or that buyers require (e.g., electronic ordering) might render some suppliers or buyers unsuitable for each other. And certain suppliers or supplier cultures (especially involving cross-national dealings) might mandate certain styles of negotiations (e.g., misrepresenting information) unacceptable. Thus, the entire procurement system is facilitated and constrained within the framework of the macroenvironment surrounding it.

# Government Buying Behavior

Governments are legal entities empowered to organize and govern people, processes (e.g., free trade), and infrastructures (e.g., highways) by the resources and compliance mechanisms they possess as kings and monarchs, dictators and elected presidents, prime ministers, and governors, the military and the civil service, along with the many democratically elected or administratively appointed bodies (e.g., parliament, congress, assembly, or the city council).

In every country, the government buys a lot of products and services; sometimes it is likely to be the single biggest buyer. It buys heavy equipment, appliances, jets, road vehicles, ships, telecommunication equipment, food grain, prepared food, clothes and uniforms, scientific equipment, maintenance parts, supplies, paper, furniture, transportation, and communication services, to name a few. It buys at every level: national, state, city, and village level. The U.S. government's annual purchasing budget is more than $200 billion; some bodies are the Department of Defense (DOD) and the General Service Administration (GSA).

## Government Buying Procedures

Governments typically follow well-specified and rule-driven buying procedures. As an example, we describe the procurement process for the U.S. federal government. Government buys in two basic ways: direct purchase and competitive procurement.[28] In the **direct purchase** method, usually adopted for orders costing up to $25,000, the government buyer may simply call a few suppliers or send a written request for quotation (RFQ), and then place an order with one of the firms so contacted, usually on the lowest-quote basis.

In the **competitive procurement** method, there are, in turn, two approaches: invitation for bid (IFB) and request for proposal (RFP). In an **invitation for bid (IFB)**, the government specifies the item being sought exactly and invites sealed bids. The bidders, who are called offerers, must supply exactly the same item (with no modifications or substitutions) and quote a price. The bids must be received by the deadline, and then they are opened in public at a pre-announced time and place. The lowest bidder that meets the requirements of the IFB is awarded the contract. To get an invitation to bid, you must register yourself by filing a form called a *Solicitation Mailing List Application*.

The government uses the **request for proposal (RFP)** method when it doesn't exactly know what it wants or what might become available, and/or when it wants to negotiate a contract (hence, it is also called a negotiated bid). An RFP is likely to be issued when the product or service is new, complex, and/or entails large sums of money. RFPs are reviewed and evaluated by a team of experts behind closed doors, and the decision is communicated to individual submitters. Quoted price is important but is not the only determining factor, and the final specifications and price are arrived at only after a series of consultations and negotiations with individual offerers.

## Federal Acquisition Regulations (FARs)

Whether by bid or by RFPs, all government procurement has to comply with **Federal Acquisition Regulations (FARs)**, procurement regulations that all agencies of the government have to follow. In addition, the Department of Defense has its own regulations, called **Defense Acquisition Regulations (DARs)**. The bid document will refer to particular FAR or DAR numbers, and the bidder has to become aware of what these specific regulations are. Upon request, the contracting office will make a full text of the relevant FARs available to the bidders.

## Invitation For Bid Procedure

All bid opportunities, along with the name of the contracting officer, are published in *Commerce Business Daily* (CBD). Suppliers on the government's mailing list receive a bid document in the mail, but others may request it upon learning about the opportunity in CBD. The cover letter on the bid document spells out whether it is an open bid or is restricted to a certain category of bidders, such as those set aside for small businesses.

Government is obligated to offer equal access to all potential sellers for its purchase needs. To achieve this goal, government maintains a computerized list of potential vendors and contractors; to get on the list, vendors must register by filing a form that elicits some basic information about the firm. The applicant firm's goods and services are then keyed into a computer file for easy retrieval.[29] Some city governments have also put the complete details of the bidding procedure on their web pages on the Internet. The city of Tallahassee, Florida, has a "Procurement Services" link on its web site, wherein their current procurement list is available with full details that can be downloaded as a pdf document, or it can be ordered by mail. The due dates for the bid, the dates of a pre-bid conference, and the bid status report are also listed here (**http://www.ci.tallahassee.fl.us/citytlh/dma/bids/index.html**). The city of Chattanooga also has the purchasing department home page with the bid opportunities on its web site.

## Bid Specifications

Government entities attempt to develop clearly written specifications. When something is needed, broad range specifications are developed based on the user's requirements.

For products and services that are needed repeatedly, the government has established standard specifications. These are available in the following forms:

- *Federal specifications*—For such routine products as paper clips, motor oil, or janitorial services, the government has established standard specifications that define physical or performance technical requirements. It is available from the General Services Administration (GSA), and all federal government agencies are mandated to follow it.
- *Commercial item descriptions (CIDs)*—These are used to describe the specifications for a commercially available item. The government may sometimes simply refer

to the item by its make and model number, such as Acme Model 1000 yard blower and vacuum. Bidders are expected to provide an equivalent product.

- *Military specifications*—Items required by the Department of Defense are described in military specifications (Mil-Spec). There is also a military specification that specifies what a military specification should look like! Numbered as MIL-STD-490, it is of benefit to bidders because it tells where to find each element of specifications.

For nonroutine items for which no standard specification already exist, the government specifies the item in purchase descriptions or a statement of work. The purchase description identifies the physical and performance characteristics the item must meet. The statement of work tells how the government wants a particular work performed.

## Contents of the Bid Document

Because FARs govern the content and preparation of the bid document, all bid documents are structured according to the Uniform Contract Format (UCF). It is useful for us to peruse this format (in Table 9.9) because it highlights the government's decision considerations.

## TABLE 9.9    Uniform Contract Format

| Section | Title |
|---|---|
| | *Part I—The Schedule* |
| A | Solicitation/Contract Form |
| B | Supplies or Services and Price/Costs |
| C | Description/Specifications/Statement of Work |
| D | Packaging and Marking |
| E | Inspection and Acceptance |
| F | Deliveries or Performance |
| G | Contract Administration Data |
| H | Special Contract Requirements |
| | |
| | *Part II—Contract Clauses* |
| I | Contract Clauses |
| | |
| | *Part III—List of Documents, Exhibits, and Other Attachments* |
| J | List of Attachments |
| | |
| | *Part IV—Representations and Instructions* |
| K | Representations, Certifications, and Other Statements of Offerors or Quoters |
| L | Instructions, Conditions, and Notices to Offerors or Quoters |
| M | Evaluation Factors for Award |

The Uniform Contract Code, as stipulated in the Federal Acquisition Regulations, governs the structure of most bids.
**Source:** Clinton L. Crownover and Mark Henricks, *Selling to Uncle Sam: How to Win Choice Government Contracts for Your Business* (New York: McGraw Hill, 1993), p. 56. Reprinted with permission of the McGraw Hill Companies.

The form consists of four parts:

- *Part I The Schedule.* Section A, Solicitation/Contract Form, seeks basic information about the bidder. Section B describes the item and seeks a price quote from the bidder. Section C describes in detail the work the bidder is required to perform (for example, how the item should be painted). Section D provides detailed instructions on how the items should be packaged and marked to prevent damage in shipping and handling. Section E specifies the level of quality the government wants, the quality inspection system the offerer must maintain, and how the government itself plans to inspect quality. Section F tells when you will have to deliver the goods. Section G, Contract Administration, gives the contracting officer's name and address. Section H outlines special requirements, such as an insurance requirement, information on any parts that may be allowed duty-free entry, or any parts the government will supply.

- *Part II Contract Clauses.* This is a list of all the FARs that apply to the specific bid. These clauses may pertain to prohibition against kickbacks, equal opportunity, affirmative action or small business concerns, drug-free workplace, or Buy American Act. The bidder is supposed to read the FAR in its entirety (not provided with the bid document) and ensure compliance.
- *Part III List of Documents.* Basically, it is a list of all the documents attached to the bid.
- *Part IV Representations and Instructions.* Section K requires the bidder to certify such things as (a) the bid price has been determined independently without conferring with other bidders, (b) whether an outside consultant was retained for bid preparation, (c) the bidder has not violated the Federal Procurement Policy Act, and the bidder's (d) federal tax identification number. Section L gives specific directions on filing the bid; its purpose is to ensure that all essential information is included and, at the same time, to prevent unnecessary details. Section M details the evaluation criteria, which signal what the government thinks is important. Generally, the ultimate judgment the government makes is summed up in a phrase the government often uses, namely, lowest responsive, responsible bidder.

## The Acquisition Team

Generally, the government sets up an acquisition team, drawing individuals from various departments, such as engineering, contract administration, supply support, training, human factors, and quality assurance. They prepare the bid document, and there is a designated contact person to clarify any queries the bidder may have.

## Preproposal Conference

On some occasions, the government holds a preproposal conference after the solicitation has been issued but prior to the bid submission due date. Bidders are asked to submit the questions in writing before the date of the conference; this helps to clarify both bidders' and team members' concerns.

## The Proposal

The proposal has two parts: technical and price. Technical proposals contain all the technical details of the offer. The government requires the technical proposal to be structured according to strict guidelines, set forth in section L of the bid document.

The government prohibits any reference to price in the technical proposal because the technical and price proposals are evaluated by two entirely independent committees. Strict guidelines also include such mechanical requirements as the number of copies to be submitted, the type font to be used, the page size, and the type of binder.

The proposal document itself can run into more than a hundred pages. Organized in different sections, it seeks complete details on all aspects of the company's proposed effort: history of past government contracts, quality program, reliability and maintainability documentation, engineering details, manufacturing details, management organization and personnel, logistics, and cost data along with supporting rationale.

The **pricing proposal**, which is also made using a specific government form, contains the cost data and the offered price. The proposal entails certifying current cost and pricing data for each line item. The bidder must also provide supporting documents for each cost component, such as labor estimates and subcontractor quotations. Certain conditions, detailed in relevant FAR, may allow the bidder an exemption from submitting certified cost or price data.

## Awarding the Contract

Contracts are awarded in two forms:

1. **Annual purchasing agreements** (also called blanket purchase agreements) are agreements established with specific suppliers that allow the governmental entity to purchase small items covered under the agreement throughout the year without having to follow the normal purchase procedure every time. Typical items covered are office supplies, fuel for vehicles, maintenance supplies for equipment and buildings, janitorial supplies, and employee uniforms. These agreements can be made with a single vendor or with multiple vendors. In the multivendor agreement, the government entity needing to purchase an item contracts the primary vendor first and contacts the second vendor only if the primary vendor is unable to supply. Vendors who agree to participate in this program are required to maintain a certain level of stock.
2. **Maintenance/labor agreements** are signed to obtain a maintenance service throughout the year on an as-needed basis. Generally, only the hourly rate is determined, not the total job cost. The number of hours required for job completion is left undetermined; for this reason, the government entity keeps a close eye on the project so that the contractor does not stretch the hours spent on the job.

Generally, the vendor with the lowest cost whose product would meet the agency's need is awarded the contract. The costs are computed by including both the initial purchase price and the maintenance costs.

## Procurement by State Governments

State governments are, collectively, responsible for a huge procurement budget. Each state has its own guidelines for doing business. Many states now have vendor information available on their Internet web site. For example, the State of Kentucky has a web site that allows vendors to view and download current bidding opportunities, view the directory of buyers in the Division of Purchases by commodity type, and view a listing of all of the state agency price contracts. The State of Wisconsin has a web site, called VendorNet, which even allows vendors to register online.

## Similarities between Government and Business Procurement[30]

Government spending, especially at the federal level, involves large amounts of money, complex procedures, and red tape in even the smallest purchase. However, there are some parallels between business buying and government buying—buyclass parallel, buying steps parallel, and procurement management goals parallel.

In business buying, the purchase task was classified as straight rebuy, modified rebuy, and new task. In government, the buying tasks can be viewed as nondevelopmental, modified nondevelopmental, and developmental. These classifications are based on the level of analysis and the degree of buyer attention they require. Generally speaking, buying decisions for both business and government buyers involve either repetition of a previous purchase, some variation of a previous purchase, or a new purchase situation.

The steps in the buying process for business and government buying are similar except for some differences in nomenclature. Both processes begin with the definition of a need and must make those needs known to interested suppliers and invite them to develop offers and bids. Next, a selection process takes place, with some kind of follow-up after the order is placed.

Both business and government buyers pursue the same objectives in managing their procurement responsibilities and in reaching their supplier decisions. Both exist to fulfill the material needs of their user departments, seek to develop competent and reliable sources, must procure at prices most advantageous to the buying organization, must minimize inventory costs, and encourage competition for their business.

## How Government Customers Differ from Business Customers

While there is similarity on the goals and the overall nature of the procurement task between the business and government sectors, there are also a number of differences. These differences arise mainly in how the tasks are *procedurally* implemented.

### Size of the Average Purchase and Standardization

The size of the average purchase by the U.S government is huge, even for simple supplies such as stationery. Because large quantities are needed at various locations by various agencies, centralized purchasing is used wherever possible. The GSA has issued standard specification for a large number of commercial-type items, and there is stricter adherence to them in government than in the private sector. The size of business that the government can provide has brought the dot-coms to the C2G (consumer-to-government) business sector as well. New York-based Govworks.com (**http://www.govworks.com**) offers an array of services, ranging from local government job listings and chat rooms to online government auctions, and it facilitates payment nationwide for parking tickets, utility bills, and real estate taxes.[31]

### Legal Restrictions and Compliance Reviews

Laws regulate government procurement procedures in areas such as competitive bidding, budgetary limitations, auditing of accounts, and the use of standard specifications. See Table 9.10 for examples. Along with the regulations come extensive compliance reviews. Any government procurement contract involves numerous specialists and inspectors who monitor and audit records as well as contractor operations. The audits are intended to uncover any irregularities the government procurement agency may have committed in the awarding of the contract as well as any deviations in compliance by a supplier. The government even has the legal authority to regulate contractors' hiring practices and how they do business with their subcontractors. Such legal jurisdiction over contractor operations is unheard of and unthinkable in private-sector procurement.

### Solicitation of Sellers

Government buyers are obligated to seek suppliers widely and extensively. For example, the Armed Services Procurement Act requires all government procurement (with some exceptions) to be made by a formal advertising process. All RFPs are published in *Commerce Business Daily*, and small business seminars are conducted to expressly encourage small businesses to join the list of government contractors. Although business buyers also engage in soliciting competitive bidders, nothing in the business sector is comparable to the active solicitation of potential suppliers in government procurement.

### Open-Access Information

Unlike what occurs in the business sector, government purchases in the United States take place in a goldfish bowl. In fact, the government publishes in the *Commerce Business Daily*

| TABLE 9.10 | Major U.S. Laws Governing Procurement in Government |
|---|---|
| The Walsh-Healey Act | Requires federal contractors to comply with (1) the wage and hours requirements for its workers on the contract and (2) the health and safety regulations of the state. |
| The Davis-Bacon Act | Establishes labor standards (wages and hours) for labor working on federal construction projects. |
| Equal Employment Opportunity Act | Forbids discrimination in employment and requires affirmative hiring practices. |
| Buy American Act | Requires that preference be given to domestic suppliers. |
| Small Business Act | Promotes contracting with small businesses, and stipulates that solicitation be set aside for small businesses if adequate competition can still be expected. |
| Federal Acquisition Streamlining Act of 1994 | Loosens restrictions on acquisition of more items available commercially and simplifies acquisition procedures through electronic commerce, reporting of contract awards and amounts to unsuccessful bidders, and loosening certified cost and pricing data thresholds. |
| Procurement Integrity Act | Restricts present and former officials of the United States and anyone who has been involved with federal procurement in some way from disclosing and obtaining contractor bid or proposal information or source-selection information. |

the names of contractors and the contract prices after a contract has been awarded. Moreover, under the Freedom of Information Act, abstracts of all bids, including the price information, are available to all competitors as well as customers of the supplying firms.

## Diffusion of Authority

There is much greater diffusion of authority in government than in most private-sector procurement. One reason is that government procurement uses input from multiple users and advisors. In addition, authority for subtasks is separated. If the purchase task is a modified nondevelopmental task, and certainly if it is a developmental task, the government seeks input and assistance from a number of expert groups—accountants, engineers, lawyers, and other high-level officials. In comparison, in the business setting, technical, engineering, and production staff who generate specifications often serve on the *buying center* and actively participate in joint decision making, and the purchasing manager or the user department who may jointly make the supplier selection also authorizes payments. Thus, in the private sector, there is much less diffusion of authority, perhaps because there is less need for checks and balances.

## Procedural Detail and Paperwork

Finally, there is the inevitable paperwork, substantially more voluminous in government than in business procurement. The U.S. government's invitation-for-bids form consists of 13 administrative sections, with typically more than 100 pages. Then there is need for strict adherence and legendary red tape. The product specifications tend to be exhaustive. For example, the description of oatmeal chocolate chip cookies procured by the defense department runs 15 pages! These detailed specifications give the government ample ground to reject suppliers found unqualified.[32]

## The Travails and Rewards of Selling to the Government

When faced with all the rules, regulations, and mountains of paperwork required in government contract bidding, it is easy to be discouraged. However, many of the quirks and nuances in government procurement stem from the responsibilities and obligations of public policy and public expenditures. Public projects of the developmental tasks type are still in the evolutionary phase of planning, and, thus, the process of need identification is prolonged. Public procurement is funded by taxpayers' money, and the government has an obligation to spend it wisely. Most important, government has the responsibility to implement its procurement function in a socially responsible way. Finally, the rules require detailed paperwork so that everything is in writing; this helps to protect the government as well as the bidder.

Although there is room for reform in government procurement, consider some of the unique benefits of doing business with government:

- *Stability*—The economy affects private businesses much more than government. Government buys in bad as well as good economic times. Thus, doing business with the government gives a contractor stability.
- *Security*—As a customer, government has the best credit in the world. Suppliers to a stable government, such as the United States, don't even have to ask for credit references. Sometimes, the government will even pay part of the costs in advance as progressive payments.
- *Size*—Government buys a lot of things and buys them in large quantities. Hundreds of businesses, including some of the biggest, such as General Dynamics, McDonnell Douglas, IBM, and Exxon, came into existence and continue to be supported by government contracts.
- *Breakthrough R&D Work*—Some government contracts entail funding the development of new technology and new applications, which can later be utilized for wider commercial applications. Teflon nonstick cooking surfaces and Tang instant breakfast drink were developed for the U.S. government's space program.
- *Challenge*—The government is a stickler for cost efficiency and performance specifications. (The story about the $600 toilet seat bought by the Department of Defense is often told only because it is rare.) Satisfying the government requires total quality management, mastery of details, an ability to plan long term, and perseverance to do the job (including the daunting paperwork) right. There can be no better training ground than this. If a business firm can successfully do business with the government, it can compete anywhere else.

# Future of the Government as Customer

Just as corporate America is going through changes in its purchasing function, so too government procurement is experiencing pressures to change. The resulting changes include downsizing and restructuring, globalization, and economic pragmatism.

## Downsizing and Restructuring the Government

As businesses have improved efficiency through downsizing and restructuring, people are demanding that their governments do the same. As a payer, the government is becoming more cost-conscious and is more concerned about fraud, waste, and mismanagement. Downsizing is one of the most basic tactics used as the Department of Defense, the Pentagon, and NASA scale down their budgets. Cutbacks are not limited to defense but extend to health care, education, human services, and scientific and regulatory agencies.

One way governments are getting by on reduced funding is through combinations of privatization and outsourcing. Privatization involves converting government operations, such as telecommunications, railroads, airlines, television, and postal services, into private businesses. In the United States, privatization is extending to primary and secondary education, prison systems, military bases, highways, transit systems, museums, and parks and recreation bureaus. Outsourcing, in contrast, involves contracting with private businesses (with relevant expertise) for the handling of certain tasks. Government agencies have outsourced functions such as cafeteria operations and barber shops, and even such critical operations as research and spacecraft.

Along with saving money, restructuring is aimed at reducing suppliers' frustration with government red tape. This program of restructuring includes the goal of saving $22.5 billion by simplifying the procurement process.

## Globalization

The government sector enterprises are becoming global. For example, the Army and Air Force Services or PX stores are worldwide in scope. The services are among the top 10 retailers in the United States and are more global than other retailers, such as Sears and Wal-Mart. Similarly, the Internet is a government network operated by the Advanced Research Programs Agency (ARPA), and the Weather Satellite is operated by the government.

## Economic Pragmatism

Governments are reducing their emphasis on social objectives as a component of procurement. Buying decisions are governed less by concern for affirmative action, minority enterprises, subsidized education, fellowships, U.S. aid programs, foreign aid, and investment in world agencies, such as the United Nations, IMF, and the World Bank. Rather, governments are becoming rigorous in ensuring that procurement decisions are economically sound. We have already seen a trend of some of the large industry players forming online procurement consortia: Covisint (between General Motors, Ford, and Daimler-Chrysler); Avendra (between Marriott International, Inc., Hyatt Hotels Corporation, ClubCorp USA, Inc., and Bass), and Aerospan (American Airlines, All Nippon Airways, Air France, British Airways, Continental, Delta, United, Northwest, Airbus, and Boeing). With this trend and the bargaining power they command, it is not hard to imagine the power that government agencies can command if they centralize their purchasing power. Suppliers need to be cognizant of this.

# Household, Business, and Government Decision Making and the Three Customer Roles

## Household Buying Behavior

Nearly all of the concepts discussed in this chapter have relevance to the three customer roles. Some apply to all three roles; others acquire more or less salience depending on the role. These are outlined in Table 9.11.

Households are classified into *family* and *nonfamily* types. In nonfamily households, payer and user roles are more likely to reside within the same individual, while in family households earning members support nonearning members. The separation of user and payer roles often found in family households brings forth a need for users to persuade

| Household, Business, and Government Decision Making and the Three Customer Roles | | | TABLE 9.11 |
|---|---|---|---|

| Concepts | User | Payer | Buyer |
|---|---|---|---|
| **Household Customers Decisions: Unique Aspects** | | | |
| Family and nonfamily households | • In nonfamily households, user and payer roles reside more likely in the same individual.<br><br>• User values are normatively influenced by nonuser family members. | • In families where user and payer roles often separate, users need to persuade payers. | • In nonfamily households, members may alternate buyer role across situations, but users may not surrender their choice-decision responsibility. |
| Family decisions | • Users initiate and gather information about desirable alternatives. | • Payers approve or disapprove category purchase. | • Buyers often influence brand choices. |
| Children's influence | • Very young children as users depend on parents as payers and buyers.<br><br>• Adolescent children influence user decisions on products for common use. | • Children on allowances look for price and value. | • Teenagers assume purchase task, including brand decisions, for routine shopping and seek convenience value the most. |
| Consumer socialization of children | • Observation of adults and mass media socialize children into becoming users. | • Payer role socialization is the hardest to achieve.<br><br>• Debt accumulation on credit cards is a major concern of parents. | • Accompanying parents on shopping trips socializes children into buying roles. |
| Intergenerational influence | • Users values considerably influenced by and between the generations.<br><br>• Influence based on product expertise or taste. | • Financial resources enable payers to influence user choices across generations. | • Types of stores one shops at can be influenced by intergenerational influence. |
| Conflict resolution | • User-user conflict on items for common use.<br><br>• Usually resolved by problem solving (e.g., finding an acceptable alternative). | • User-payer role separation is principal source of conflict, often resolved by bargaining. | • Buyers imposing their own user values can cause conflict. |
| **Business Customers Decisions: Unique Aspects** | | | |
| Role specialization | • Users focus on performance value evaluation. | • Payers focus on budget allocations. | • Buyers, often separate from users and payers, specialize in buying task. |
| Formalized process | • Users submit a formal requisition and technical specifications. | • Payers use sound budgeting practices. | • Buyers follow well-laid-out policies and processes. |
| Accountability | • Users are accountable for correct specifications. | | • Buyers are accountable for professional buying. |
| Internal capabilities | • User capabilities may lead to in-house production. | • Strong financial position can gain favorable terms for suppliers. | • Buyers with low skills may draw on external advice. |
| Complexity | • Need identification may be an extended process. | | • Buyers may need to coordinate with multiple suppliers. |

*(continued)*

| TABLE 9.11 | Household, Business, and Government Decision Making and the Three Customer Roles (Concluded) | | |
|---|---|---|---|

| Concepts | User | Payer | Buyer |
|---|---|---|---|
| **Business Customers Decisions: Unique Aspects** | | | |
| Buyclass | • Users may automate the requisition for rebuys. | • For new task buys, payers may have to juggle money. | • Rebuys may be routinized and automated. New task buys would require professional talents of buyers. |
| Buying center | • Buying center brings all roles together. | • Payers often are the deciders in the buying center. | • Buyers bring vendors and users together. |
| Decision process | • Users are most active at the specification and vendor screening stage. | • Payers are most active at the decision stage. | • Buyers are active throughout the decision process. |
| Conflict resolution | • Three roles are often in conflict. | • Payers are often overly concerned with cost minimization. | |
| **Government Customers Decisions: Unique Aspects** | | | |
| RFPs | • User specifications are extensive in RFPs. | | • Buyers act as gatekeepers. |
| Bid evaluation | • Users conduct technical evaluation. | • Payers engage in cost evaluation of the bid. | • Buyers coordinate and intensely participate in price evaluation. |
| Acquisition teams | • Users play important role on acquisition teams. | | • Buyers handle principal responsibility for acquisition. |
| Acquisition reforms | • Greater authority to users for direct purchase. | • With rising concern with waste, payers would have to do budget allocations more conscientiously. | • Buyers' job is made more more efficient. |

payers, and the marketer needs to appeal to them by offering good price and credit and financing values. Regarding the buyer role, in family households, there are joint buying trips or role specialization by product categories. In nonfamily households, in contrast, role specialization is less likely, and, instead, each member may take turns performing the buyer role.

In *family decision making*, different family members contribute to the decision differently, according to the role they shoulder, based on their skills and resources. Individuals playing the user roles generally initiate the purchase request or need recognition and also gather information about available alternatives. Payers approve or disapprove the very idea of buying a specific product category. Finally, buyers influence brand choices. *Children influence* family purchases, not only for products for which they themselves are users but also for products meant for common use in the family. In contrast to the user values, the payer values are not much influenced by children except when children spend their own money. Finally, children definitely influence the buyer values as teenagers increasingly assume the payer role for family groceries, making brand decisions and seeking convenience value.

*Socialization* of children as consumers is easy and natural in respect to the user role; children learn both by observation of consumption by parents in the household and also from mass media and peers. It is the payer role that is hard to socialize the children into and takes some judicious shaping (such as asking children to pay rent). Finally, buyer-role socialization also occurs relatively easily as children accompany parents on their shopping trips.

With regard to *intergenerational influence*, parents influence grown sons' and daughters' user values (and vice versa) on products that they have expertise on. Furthermore, in their payer roles, members of one generation influence the choices of other generations, in either direction, by controlling financial resources. Finally, buyer roles are also influenced in terms of selection of outlets.

*Conflicts* among family members are common even where the same member discharges all three roles and when multiple family members share the user role for the same product. User-user conflicts are typically resolved by problem solving (e.g., by identifying alternatives that are acceptable to all members). Next, user-payer role separation is the principal source of conflict, wherein payers exercise their power by ruling whether or not a particular product category will be bought. This conflict is often resolved by bargaining. Finally, buyers are often in a position to control the brand choice since they are the ones to implement the acquisition transaction or their own user values, which can also cause conflict. Such conflicts are generally resolved by persuasion.

## Business Buying Behavior

*Role specialization* is more pronounced for business customers than for household customers because business buying requires specialist knowledge to evaluate each of the six market values. Users focus on technical performance evaluations; payers focus on organization-wide budget allocations; and buyers specialize in buying tasks, especially finding and appraising alternative sources. To ensure that maximum user values are obtained at lowest total costs, organizations lay down a *formalized process* that each role holder has to follow. Users have to seek budget approval from payers and submit a formal requisition, payers use sound budgeting practices, and buyers ensure that vendor selection follows the stipulated process. Each role holder is *accountable* for his or her part in the job—users for ensuring correct specifications for maximum performance value, payers for not overspending, and buyers for making the procurement more efficient and effective. *Internal capabilities* are relevant for all three roles. Users may produce the item in-house, and payers with deep pockets can gain more favorable terms from suppliers. As to the buyer role, if the buyer is not adequately skilled, the procurement itself may be outsourced. *Complexity* makes both user and buyer tasks more demanding as ensuring the fit with requirement becomes crucial. For complex purchases, buyers may need to coordinate with multiple suppliers for complementary portions of the job.

*Buyclass* affects all three roles. Users may automate the requisition process for straight rebuys, but for new tasks, they would need to generate product specifications, perhaps for the first time. For straight rebuy, the budget is easily approved or earmarked; but for new tasks, payers may have to juggle money, including raising new capital. For rebuys, buyers rely on current suppliers; for new tasks, buyers need to go through an extensive process of identifying and evaluating all qualified vendors, bringing professional buying skills and talents to bear on the process.

The *buying center* is a concept unique to business buying, and it is founded on the very idea that the three roles may be, as they often are, separated and allocated among different personnel. Payers (such as senior management) often play the decider role, while buyers bring vendors and users together for exploring technical fit. In the *decision process*, users are most active at the need-specification and vendor-screening stages, payers at the decision stage, and buyers throughout for coordinating the entire process. *Conflicts* may arise among users or among buyers or among payers, if each of these roles is itself shared among more than one individual. Conflicts may also arise among the three roles. Buyers may want to keep certain vendors out of the process; for example, while users may insist on certain preferred vendors. Payers may be driven unduly by price considerations, constraining optimal choices for users.

## Government Buying Behavior

In government procurement, user specifications are extensive in seeking RFPs. Bid evaluation is handled in two independent parts: technical evaluation and price evaluation. Users play a dominant role in the former while costing experts in the buyer department handle the second part. Each is accountable for his or her part, and, thus, each task is handled more rigorously. The acquisition team itself comes from different departments and, thus, from all three roles. Acquisition reform in the U.S. government will simplify the buying process, raising the dollar threshold for adopting routinized buying procedure, and giving greater authority to user departments for direct purchase. This will simplify the buyer task and also give more flexibility to users who will need less lead time to order. As public concern with government waste rises, payers would have to become more cautious in ensuring judicious use of available budgets.

# Summary

We began this chapter with a discussion of the importance and challenge of studying household buying decisions. Principally, these decisions are complex because the user, payer, and buyer roles are shared among different household members. We then defined various types of family and nonfamily households.

The family buying process was described as one in which different members of the family influence various stages of the decision process. Particularly, the relative influence of spouses in joint decision making was described as a muddling-through process. The exact influence of either spouse was determined by such factors as gender roles, wife's employment status, family life cycle, time pressure, importance of purchase, and the socioeconomic development of the relevant population. Children influence parental choices of products and services, as well as receive influence from parents in their own marketplace preferences. The latter process is captured in the concept of consumer socialization of children.

After childhood, the mutual influence of parents and children on each other continues into adult years of youngsters. This influence in either direction is termed intergenerational influence (IGI). IGI occurs because one generation (whether living in the same or a separate household) controls resources for another, has greater expertise than another, or offers a power of identification over the other. Since family buying decisions are shared decisions with different members vying for influence and control, inevitably conflicts occur. We discussed various types of conflicts among the user, payer, and buyer roles. We also discussed four strategies of resolving these conflicts: problem solving, bargaining, persuasion, and politicking.

We then described a general framework for understanding family buying decisions. It views the choice as an outcome of autonomous or joint decision process with or without a conflict occurrence, which is then resolved by one of the four strategies. The decision process is affected by family characteristics, individual characteristics of various family members, the nature of purchase, and sources of information utilized.

In contrast to household buying, the customer behavior of a business involves greater specialization of customer roles, a more formalized buying process, greater accountability for decisions, more sophisticated internal capabilities, and more complex requirements.

The business buying process has several components: the nature of the purchase, organizational characteristics, a buying center, rules and procedures, and a decision process. The nature of the purchase is defined by the buyclass (straight rebuy, modified rebuy, or new task), perceived risk, importance, and product complexity, and the time pressure faced by the decision makers. A business customer spends the most time and effort investigating a new task purchase, and/or purchase that involves relatively great perceived risk, importance, and complexity. In contrast, time pressure will shorten the decision process and increase the impact of the user's input.

Buying behavior is also affected by four organizational characteristics of the customer: size, structure, purchase resources, and purchase orientation. Small organizations behave more like individuals or households, whereas large organizations use more formalized buying procedures. Structure refers to the number of departments in the organization, where they are located, and how centralized they are. Organizations with many departments in multiple locations engage in more complex buying behavior. Purchase resources are the organization's professional buyers and ordering equipment. Purchase orientation is the organization's purchasing philosophy, ranging along a continuum from viewing purchasing as an administrative function to viewing it as a strategic function. A purchasing department with a strategic role is more active in the decision-making process.

The buying center is a multifunction, multilevel internal organization responsible for the centralized purchasing function. Rather than a department or committee, it is a concept, defining the variety of roles involved in a purchase: user, buyer, analyzer, influencer, gatekeeper, and decider. Most businesses set up policies, rules, and procedures that limit the decision criteria and decision process.

Business buying decisions take place in several stages: need assessment, development of choice criteria, request for proposals (RFPs), supplier evaluation, supplier selection, and fulfillment and monitoring. These steps involve more formal analysis than in the typical household buying decision. Total procurement costs, rather than price alone, are an important factor in most business buying decisions. The decision process is primarily driven by buyers' expectations and perceptual distortions. Conflicts are resolved through some combination of problem solving, persuasion, bargaining, and politicking.

Government is a major customer in every country. Governments are powerful customers because their orders are large and their power to make and enforce laws gives them substantial control over the buying process. In the United States, the federal government buys through two highly structured processes: the direct purchase method and competitive procurement. Marketers to the federal government must operate within the strict guidelines of these procedures. State governments are also sizable customers. Each state has its own guidelines for marketers to learn and follow.

Government procurement and business procurement resemble each other in terms of buyclasses, buying steps, and procurement management goals. However, government buyclasses are called nondevelopmental, modified nondevelopmental, and developmental. Also, the government process may be more formal. In other ways, government procurement and business procurement differ. Government purchases tend to be larger and more standardized. They involve more legal restrictions and compliance reviews. Unlike businesses, governments must solicit suppliers widely. Government purchases also involve open access to information, greater diffusion of authority, and more paperwork. Nevertheless, selling to the government offers the advantages of stability, security, size, access to breakthrough R&D work, and a quality-inspiring challenge.

The government's role as customer is undergoing change. Governments are increasingly engaged in downsizing and restructuring, which may include privatization, outsourcing, and acquisition reform. Government buying behavior increasingly takes place on a global scale. Finally, governments are placing more weight on the goal of economic pragmatism.

# Key Terms

**Annual Purchasing Agreements 348**

**Authoritarian Families 320**

**Autonomous Decisions 317**

**Bargaining 342**

**Business 332**

**Buyclass 334**

**Buying Center 338**

**Competitive Procurement 344**

Complexity 336

Concept-Oriented Families 320

Consumer Socialization 323

Defense Acquisition Regulations
   (DARs) 345

Democratic Families 322

Democratic Justice 325

Direct Purchase 344

Family 316

Family Relationship 326

Federal Acquisition Regulations
   (FARs) 345

Gender-Role Orientation 318

Governments 344

Household 316

Importance of Purchase 335

Intergenerational Influence (IGI)
   325

Invitation for Bid (IFB) 344

Joint Decisions 318

Maintenance/Labor Agreements
   348

Modified Rebuy 334

Neglectful Families 320

New Task 334

Nonfamily Household 316

Perceived Risk 335

Permissive Families 322

Persuasion 342

Politicking 342

Pricing Proposal 348

Problem Solving 342

Request for Proposal (RFP) 345

Social Orientation Families 320

Straight Rebuy 334

Syncratic Decisions 317

Technical Proposals 347

# Discussion Questions and Exercises

1. As demographic changes occur throughout the world, particularly as customer roles within the family change, marketers must keep abreast of these changes and alter their marketing strategies accordingly. Identify two or three changing customer roles within the family in your own country and give an example of what marketers ought to do in response to these changes.

2. Conduct an interview with children of the following age groups: (1) 7 years old and younger, (2) between 8 and 12 years old, and (3) between 13 and 17 years old. Ask them how they developed their preferences for their favorite brands of the following products and services:
   a. Breakfast cereal
   b. Sneakers
   c. Clothing
   d. Restaurants (fast food).

3. Contact a manager at any one of the following product-marketing companies: breakfast cereals, toys, personal care, home appliances, cooking products, athletic performance products, (e.g., sports goods) and clothing. Determine whether these companies utilize the concept of IGI and how they do it. If they do not currently utilize IGI, make a case for whether they should begin to utilize the concept and how.

4. When people immigrate into a new country, one of the first things they have to learn is how to go about acquiring the goods and services they need in the unfamiliar, new marketplace. Find three families who have come to your country from another country and one family from your home country. Ask them how they made their decisions about which products and brands to buy. Ask whether or not they were influenced by their parents' earlier education and socialization

in terms of specific customer values. Finally, ask them whether they were influenced by any other agents (e.g., peers, the media) in their choice of certain types of products and specific brands. What differences exist across immigrant families from different countries? What differences exist between immigrant families and native-born families in terms of buying behaviors acquired from parents and from countries of past residence versus behaviors adopted anew in the new country?

5. Assume you are senior vice president of procurement for a large multinational consumer products company. In your attempt to influence others in senior management that your department managers should be given more authority and resources, you bring up the recent notions of "procurement as a core competency" and "global sourcing." What exactly do you discuss with your colleagues?

6. You have recently been hired by the U.S. government to be in charge of procurement for all U.S. embassies abroad. Although you have had enormous experience with procurement in general, your work experience has always been in the business sector, not the government sector. What are some of your concerns about the differences regarding the procurement task in these two contexts? What will you have to keep in mind in terms of the procedural implementation of the tasks in your new job?

# Notes

1  Cathy Hayward, "Finding the Perfect Match," *Supply Management*; March 1, 2001, pp. 20–23.

2  Jagdish N. Sheth, "Models of Buyer Behavior: Conceptual, Quantitative, and Empirical," in *A Theory of Family Buying Decisions* (New York: Harper & Row), pp. 17–33.

3  Ibid.; Harry L. Davis, "Decision Making Within the Household," *Journal of Consumer Research* 2 (March 1976), pp. 241–60.

4  C. Whan Park, "Joint Decisions in Home Purchasing: A Muddling-Through Process," *Journal of Consumer Research* 9 (September 1982), pp. 151–61.

5  Dennis L. Rosen and Donald H. Granbois, "Determinants of Role Structure in Family Financial Management," *Journal of Consumer Research* 10 (September 1983), pp. 253–58; Charles Schaninger and Chris T. Allen, "Wife's Occupational Status as a Consumer Behavior Construct," *Journal of Consumer Research* 8 (September 1981), pp. 189–96; Mary Lou Roberts and Lawrence H. Wortzel, "Role Transferral in the Household: A Conceptual Model and Partial Test," *Advances in Consumer Research* 9 (1982), pp. 261–66.

6  Peter Zollo, "Teen Consumer Brand Loyalty Varies According To Product Category," 07/01/1999. Article adapted from book, *Wise Up To Teens*, 2nd edition, by Peter Zollo, New Strategist Publications, Ithaca, NY.

7  Pierre Filiatrault and J. R. Ritchie, "Joint Purchasing Decisions: A Comparison of Influence Structure in Family and Couple Decision Making," *Journal of Consumer Research* 7 (September 1980), pp. 131–40.

8  Greg Sandoval, "E-tailers Scramble to Win Teen Buyers", December 1, 1999, CNET news.com, http://www.canada.cnet.com/news/0-1007-200-1475177.html; "US Online Youth Spend $164 billion Annually," September 11, 2000, http://www.harris interactive.com/news/index.asp?NewsID=143&HI_election=Other.

9  George P. Moschis, "The Role of Family Communication in Consumer Socialization of Children and Adolescents," *Journal of Consumer Research* 11 (1985), pp. 898–913; George P. Moschis and Gilbert A. Churchill, "Consumer Socialization: A

Theoretical and Empirical Analysis," *Journal of Marketing Research* 15 (1978), pp. 599–609; George P. Moschis and R. L. Moore, "Family Communication and Consumer Socialization," in W. L. Wilkie, ed., *Advances in Consumer Research* 6 (Ann Arbor, Mich.: Association for Consumer Research (1979), pp. 757–59; George P. Moschis and L. G. Mitchell, "Television Advertising and Interpersonal Influences on Teenagers' Participation in Family Consumer Decisions," in R. J. Lutz, ed., *Advances in Consumer Research* 13 (Provo, Utah: Association for Consumer Research, 1986) pp. 181–86; George P. Moschis, A. E. Prahasto, and L. G. Mitchell, "Family Communication Influences on the Development of Consumer Behavior: Some Additional Findings," in R. J. Lutz, ed., *Advances in Consumer Research* 13 (Provo, Utah: Association for Consumer Research, 1986), pp. 365–69.

10 Adapted from Conway Lackman and John M. Lanasa, "Family Decision Making: An Overview and Assessment," *Psychology and Marketing* 12 No. 2 (March–April 1993), pp. 81–93; and from Les Carlson and Sanford Grossbart, "Parental Style and Consumer Socialization of Children," *Journal of Consumer Research* 15, No. 1 (June 1988), pp. 77–94.

11 Les Carlson and Sanford Grossbart.

12 Moschis and Moore (1982), Bahn (1986), and James U. McNeal, "The Littlest Shoppers," *American Demographics*, Vol. 14, No. 2 (February 1992), pp. 48–53.

13 Moschis and Churchill (1978), Ibid.

14 Deborah Roedder John, "Consumer Socialization of Children: A Retrospective Look at Twenty-five Years of Research," *Journal of Consumer Research* 26, December 1999, pp. 183–213.

15 Moschis and Moore; Scott Ward and Daniel Wackman, "Children's Purchase Influence Attempts and Parental Yielding," *Journal of Marketing Research* 9 (August 1972), pp. 316–19; G. W. Peterson and B. C. Rollins, "Parent Child Socialization," in M. B. Sussman and S. K. Steinmetz, eds., *Handbook of Marriage and Family* (New York: Plenum Press), pp. 471–507; Jan Møller Jensen, "Children's Purchase Requests and Parental Responses: Results from an Exploratory Study in Denmark," in Flemming Hansen, *European Advances in Consumer Behavior*, Vol. 2 (Provo, Utah: Association for Consumer Research, 1995), pp. 61–68. Sanford Grossbart, Les Carlson, and Ann Walsh, "Consumer Socialization Motive for Shopping with Children," *AMA Educator's Proceedings* (1988); Bonnie B. Reece, Sevgin Eroglu, and Nora J. Rifon, "Parents Teaching Children to Shop: How, What, and Who?" *AMA Educators' Proceedings* (1988) pp. 274–78; Les Carlson and Sanford Grossbart, "Parental Style and Consumer Socialization of Children," *Journal of Consumer Research* 15 (1988), pp. 77–94.

16 For an exhaustive annotated review of the literature in this area, see Reshma H. Shah, "Toward a Theory of Intergenerational Influence: A Framework for Assessing the Differential Impact of Varying Sources of Influence on the Preferences and Consumption Values of Adult Children," Unpublished working paper, University of Pittsburgh, 1992.

17 Ruby Roy Dholkia, "Intergenerational Differences in Consumer Behavior: Some Evidence from a Developing Country," *Journal of Business Research* 12, No. 1 (1984), pp. 19–34; Patricia Sorce, Philip R. Tyler, and Lynette Loomis, "Inter-generational Influence on Consumer Decision Making," *Advances in Consumer Research* 16 (1989), pp. 271–75.

18 See Shah (1992) for an annotated review of the literature covering the origins of IGI's from parent to child; D. Riesman and H. Roseborough, "Careers and Consumer Behavior," in *Consumer Behavior, Vol. 2: The Life Cycle and Consumer Behavior*, in L. H. Clark (Ed.), New York, NY: New York University Press, 1995.

19 This section is adapted from Reshma H. Shah and Banwari Mittal, "The Role of Intergenerational Influence in Consumer Choice: Toward an Exploratory Theory," eds. Merrie Brucks and Debbie MacInnis, *Advances in Consumer Research* (Provo, Utah: Association for Consumer Research, 1997), pp. 55–60.

20 An interesting conceptual framework with a description of group decision-making processes in conflict situations is found in Kim P. Corfman and Donald R. Lehmann, "Models of Cooperative Group Decision-Making and Relative Influence: An Experimental Investigation of Family Purchase Decisions." *Journal of Consumer Research* 14 (June 1987), pp. 1–13, also see Rosann L. Spiro, "Persuasion in Family Decision Making," *Journal of Consumer Research* 10 (March 1983), pp. 393–402; and Daniel Seymour and Greg Lessne, "Spousal Conflict Arousal: Scale Development," *Journal of Consumer Research* 11 (December 1984), pp. 810–21.

21 James G. March and Herbert A. Simon, *Organizations* (New York: Wiley, 1958).

22 "A Theory of Family Buying Decisions" in Paul Pellemans ed. *Insights in Consumer and Market Research*, Namon University Press, 1971, pp. 32–48.

23 Philip Kotler, *Marketing Management: Analysis, Planning, Implementation, and Control* (Englewood Cliffs, NJ: Prentice-Hall, 1991), p. 247.

24 Based on research by Erin Anderson, Wujin Chu, and Barton Weitz, "Industrial Purchasing: An Empirical Exploration of the Buyclass Framework," *Journal of Marketing* 51 (July 1987), pp. 71–86.

25 "Purchasing Pros Do Select Suppliers Really," *Purchasing*, April 3, 1997, p. 22.

26 For a fuller discussion, see Jagdish N. Sheth, "A Model of Industrial Buyer Behavior," *Journal of Marketing* 37 (October 1973), pp. 50–56.

27 Jagdish N. Sheth, "A Model of Industrial Buyer Behavior" in *Marketing Theory: Classic and Contemporary Readings*, Jagdish N. Sheth and Dennis E. P. Garrett, eds. (Cincinnati: South-Western Publishing Co., 1986), pp. 539–50.

28 A rich and illuminating source on this topic is in Clinton L. Crownover and Mark Henricks, *Selling to Uncle Sam: How to Win Choice Government Contracts for Your Business* (New York: McGraw Hill, Inc., 1993). The material presented here is adapted from various chapters of this book and is intended merely to arouse the appetite for a fuller reading of the book.

29 This section is adapted from Stephen Cole, "Improving the Purchasing Function," *Government Finance Review* (February 1996) pp. 23–27.

30 This section is adapted from Jagdish N. Sheth, Robert F. Williams, and Richard M. Hill, "Government and Business Purchasing: How Similar Are They?" *Journal of Purchasing and Materials Management* (Winter 1983), pp. 7–13.

31 http://www.wired.com, July 2000.

32 Pat Towell, "Pentagon Banking on Plans to Reinvent Procurement," *Congressional Quarterly* (April 16, 1994), pp. 899–901; Ruby Roy Dholakia, Jean L. Johnson, Albert J. Della Bitta, and Nikhilesh Dholakia, "Decision-Making Time in Organizational Buying Behavior: An Investigation of Its Antecedents," *Journal of the Academy of Marketing Science* 21, No. 4 (Fall 1993) pp. 281–92; W. E. Patton III, "Individual and Joint Decision Making in Industrial Vendor Selection," *Journal of Business Research* 38 (1997), pp. 115–22.

# CHAPTER 10

## Relationship Based Buying

## It's More than Just a "Sale"

The philosophy of sheet steel buying is changing at Ford Motor Co. The company is focusing on building relationships with a small set of sheet steel suppliers worldwide who will be partners with Ford in initiatives such as continuous improvement programs and e-procurement. To this end, Ford is trying to improve internal organizational processes that help to identify world-class suppliers, order and distribute metal to fabrication sites, and streamline its supply chain.

Ford has regional operations in North America, South America, Europe and Asia—with different material requirements and buying varies by region. Sheet steel is a key commodity, costing the company almost $3 billion annually, and accounting for 90 percent of the total steel buy at Ford.

Ford's Total Cost Management (TCM) Center already helps sheet steel suppliers adjust to the lean manufacturing systems at Ford, and the Supplier Technical Assistance (STA) personnel provide guidance on product quality issues. In addition to this, Ford buyers are also advising sheet steel suppliers on new levels of expected technical services, product transportation, delivery services, and inventory control. Cost-cutting is the main goal at Ford, and suppliers who will work with Ford on cost-cutting measures through various initiatives will survive with Ford as partners. Hence, Ford sets quality and productivity targets for suppliers in negotiations to improve efficiency and reduce costs. Ford's online information portal—the Ford Supplier Network (FSN)—sends updates to suppliers on company efforts such as quality, cost avoidance, new-technology implementation, and supplier development. Suppliers can log into the portal using a pre-specified ID and password and access key, purchasing related data and information relevant to their business needs. The site also provides a link to Ford's Lean Resource Center, a comprehensive library and resource service for suppliers. In a few years, the Ford Supplier Network Online site is expected to have 100,000 to 200,000 supplier users from 1,100 production and 500 non-production supplier companies. The online Ford Supplier Network has also helped in developing a global virtual training institute for suppliers called the Ford Supplier Learning Institute (FSLI). Ford is now a part of the Covisint—the automotive industry's Internet based e-procurement marketplace and the FSN site has a hot link for suppliers to access Covisint.

Ford has been working to link steel suppliers and buyers online even before it starts buying through Covisint. It is working with e-Steel (now Newview), an online steel business-to-business exchange, to streamline its purchase of steel products, and e-steel will oversee Ford's order fulfillment, claims, financial controls, and audit reporting across its manufacturing and assembly operations.

Bob Mateer, the global manager of raw materials purchasing for Ford, says "teaching, communicating, and sharing are fundamental principles of supplier relationships at Ford." And that fits with the company's online supplier's guide, which says "Collaboration, not confrontation; teamwork, not make-work; cooperation, not competition—those ideas characterize our guidelines for working with suppliers. Ford firmly believes that these principles form the foundation that will deliver dividends for our suppliers and us." (Tom Stundza, 2001)[1]

Seeking and winning long-term patronage—satisfying a customer rather than merely making a sale—is the objective of relationship marketing as in the Ford example above. In a way, this has always been the goal of marketing *per se*. Relationship marketing has rekindled an awareness of this basic purpose of marketing. Increasingly, marketers are pursuing relationship marketing practices. To do so, however, they must understand relationship marketing from the customers' point of view. That is, why would customers want to engage in relationship-based buying?

In this chapter we examine customers' relationship-based buying behavior (see Figure 10.1 for framework). We begin by outlining the value to businesses of relationship-based buying. Next, a model of customers' relationship-based buying behavior is presented. We discuss certain special determinants of trust and commitment applicable specifically in business markets. We also discuss the practice of nurturing suppliers and its place in relationship buying.

## Conceptual Framework     FIGURE 10.1

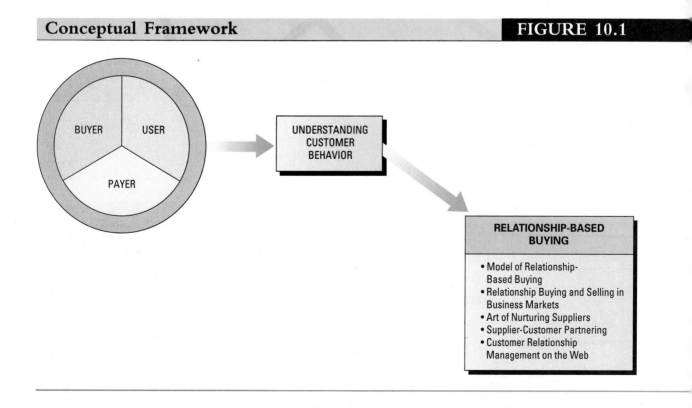

# A Model of Relationship-Based Buying

Customers who engage in the practice of **relationship-based buying** limit their choice to a single supplier and depend on this supplier to handle their needs for a product or service. Why would customers limit choices and not take advantage of a competitive marketplace with multiple suppliers, attempting to gain the best product at the lowest price? The reason is that exercising choices can be wasteful—it costs time, money, and energy; and there is no guarantee that the alternative supplier is better than the old supplier. As a result, customers have powerful motivations to voluntarily limit their choice of suppliers.

The model of relationship buying shown in Figure 10.2 summarizes these motivations and the resulting customer behavior. The model has three sections: (1) antecedents, or the motivations that drive relationship-based buying; (2) the concept of relationships; and (3) the outcomes of the relationship. The two categories of antecedents (cost-benefit factors and sociocultural factors) influence people's decisions about whether to enter into a buying relationship. If such a relationship is characterized by mutual trust and commitment and leads to positive outcomes, the customer may have such postpurchase attitudes and behaviors as increased buying, loyalty to the supplier, and even willingness to pay more for the supplier's offerings.

## Customer Motivations for Relationship-Based Buying

The antecedents in the model are customer motivations for engaging in relationship-based buying. These motivations can be grouped into two broad categories: cost-benefit factors and sociocultural factors.

### Cost-Benefit Factors

When customers make buying decisions, including whether to enter an ongoing relationship with a supplier, they weigh the potential costs and benefits. Marketing professors Jagdish N. Sheth and Atul Parvatiyar have proposed that many of these decisions are driven by the desire to reduce choices.

---

**FIGURE 10.2**     **A Model of Relationship–Based Buying**

**Cost-Benefit Factors**

Search costs
Risk reduction
Switching costs
Value-added benefits

**Socio-Cultural Factors**

Early socialization
Reciprocity
Keiretsu
Friendships

**Relationship-Based Buying**
• Trust
• Commitment

• Supplier loyalty
• Increased buying
• Willingness to pay-more
• Proactive word-of-mouth
• Goodwill (customer equity)

☐ Antecedents (Motivators)     ☐ Relationships     ☐ Outcomes

- Customers favor relationship buying when it saves time, effort, and inconvenience, and they avoid considering new choices if doing so will entail extensive search and information processing. Similarly, if a new supplier makes switching easy (as when a credit card company offers to transfer balances), consumers may consider making a change.
- Customers favor relationship buying if they expect positive reinforcement from it.
- Customers favor relationship buying if they perceive that it will help them avoid risk.
- Customers maintain buying relationships if a change involves costs, such as legal penalties or loss of peer-group approval.
- People tend to resist change because change involves effort. Consequently, they maintain buying relationships out of inertia.

In the model in Figure 10.2, the cost-benefit factors that drive decisions about relationship-based buying include the search costs, the potential for risk reduction, the switching costs, and the value-added benefits of the relationship.[2]

**Search Costs.** The principal cost of breaking free from a relationship with a marketer is the cost of *finding* a new product, service, or supplier. Purchasing is problem solving; customers buy a product or service to solve a problem. Initially, to find a solution, customers expend the necessary effort. Once they find an acceptable solution, they don't want to exert the effort anew to solve the same problem again and again. As discussed in Chapter 5, problem simplification by routinization of the problem-solving task is a basic consumer motive. Thus, once they identify a product or service that meets their needs, customers don't want to exert any unnecessary effort.

**Perceived Risk.** A basic factor in all decisions is the perceived risk, the possibility that the decision may not yield the expected outcomes or may result in negative consequences. Whenever a choice is to be made among alternatives, the magnitude of negative or suboptimal outcomes and uncertainty as to its likelihood constitute risk. Among the various types of risks (discussed earlier in Chapters 8 and 9), several are particularly relevant:

- *Performance risk*—The product may not do the job it is supposed to do. For example, when buying communications networks, a business customer would worry that the new system may not interface well with the existing system or may not accommodate future expansion needs.
- *Financial risk*—The chosen alternative may not be the best-priced alternative.
- *Social risk*—The firm's reputation may be at risk if it chooses a substandard supplier, especially if the supplier's product is used in the finished product sold, in turn, to the buying firm's end-user customers.

Perceived risk is a factor with both business customers and household customers. For example, as household customers or individual consumers, we don't want to change our physician or insurance firm if there is no guarantee that the alternative physician or agency is going to be any better, or if there is some risk that the alternative doctor or agency might be worse.

When a customer does business with the same firm, risk is minimized since the alternative has been tried and tested. But if a customer chooses to do business with new suppliers, then risks are likely. These perceived risks serve as motivations for customers to stay with the current supplier.

**Switching Costs.** Along with search costs for future suppliers, changing suppliers may generate switching costs, costs directly related to switching suppliers. For example, the purchase contract may stipulate termination penalties. In addition, the buyer may not have fully recovered its sunk costs, meaning some costs of writing off investments are not recovered yet. Partner-specific investments, discussed near the end of the chapter, constitute such costs. Finally, getting set up for the new supplier may generate new costs. For example, a change in supplier may entail some retooling of the production process, some retraining of workers, some new software to run the automatic reordering process, and so on. Knowledge of these potential switching costs, therefore, serves as a second motivation for staying with the current supplier.

Switching costs may be combined with perceived risk to shed light on patterns of relationship-based customer behaviors (see the matrix in Figure 10.3). In each quadrant, the customer purchasing strategies are different, so marketer strategies also ought to be different in order to retain the customer's repatronage.

## FIGURE 10.3    Combinations of Perceived Risk and Switching Costs

When both switching costs and perceived risk are low, the customer prefers transactional exchange. As in the case of most supermarket items, switching to a different brand does not entail any extensive information search, and the investment is low. The customer is mainly interested in lower prices, tends to engage in opportunistic buying, and has no stake in continued repatronage. Indeed, his or her preference may be for a *transactional exchange.* To increase the risk of switching, the marketer could offer some extra value (for example, via better service), thus differentiating his or her offering from competitors. A supermarket could differentiate itself, for example, by offering delivery to a customer's car.

The combination of high risk and low switching costs exists for buying a cruise tour. There is a high risk that the chosen cruise may be unsatisfactory, but switching to a new cruise company has no costs. Because the untried alternatives are deemed to be risky, the customer is motivated to maintain continued patronage; at the same time, however, he or she is open to switching (since there are no switching costs) if a reputable competitor offers substantial cost savings. Thus, the customer is in a *vulnerable relationship* with the current supplier. To increase loyalty, the marketer (current seller) should reinforce the product's proven quality and performance.

High switching costs plus no perceived risk combine in the case of airlines that offer frequent-flyer benefits. You can buy your travel on any airline (they are about equal in safety and other features, so there is no risk); but you may not be able to cash in mileage awards unless you accumulate enough of them. In this case, the customer is constrained in the present relationship. Current sellers must ensure continued customer satisfaction. They may also strive to further deepen the customer's investments or stakes in the present relationship, for example, by increasing the rewards for continued patronage.

The strongest barriers to customers switching their patronage arise when switching costs and perceived risk are both high. Here the customer is in relational buying. This situation is exemplified by private medical insurance. To switch from a current provider and enroll with a new provider, you typically have to undergo extensive physical exams and resupply extensive information to the new provider about your medical history. At the same time, there is uncertainty about the skills of the new doctor/provider. Customers are so strongly motivated to maintain a relationship with the present supplier that they may wish to iron out problems rather than drop present suppliers, unless the present suppliers ignore their satisfaction and remain unresponsive to changing customer needs or to complaints about product or service failures. Marketer strategies should focus on continued quality maintenance and on a positive complaint-response system.

**Value-Added Benefits.**    When you buy repeatedly from a supplier or marketer, you treat that supplier as a preferred supplier. In turn, to retain you as a customer, the supplier tends to treat you as a preferred customer. For example, many hotels and car rental agencies have instituted a frequent-guest program. When you become a member of these programs, the hotel or car rental agency is happy to upgrade you to a better room or a bigger car without any extra charge.

For business customers, firms differentiate themselves on the basis of added benefits, especially when the core product remains the same. For example, all suppliers may offer the same product at the same price; however, a firm may customize a financing plan for you, or it may customize the way it does business with you. These added benefits, obtainable from a firm only if there is assurance of repeat business, serve as a motivation for customers to engage in relationship-based buying.

## Sociocultural Factors

As you already know from previous chapters, buying decisions are not purely rational economic decisions based on objective data. For example, a person's culture, business, and personal relationships influence buying decisions. For example, in some cultures such as Latin America, Asia, and Eastern Europe, establishing a personal relationship is often a prelude and a prerequisite to doing business with anyone (see Window on Practice box about building relationships in Russia). With regard to relationship-based buying, the sociocultural factors that influence the formation of a customer relationship include socialization, reciprocity, networks, and friendships.

**Early Socialization.**    One reason why customers choose to engage in relationship-based buying is that they get socialized into it from the time they first begin to use that product or service. As individual customers, we learn many choices from childhood socialization, which we described in Chapter 9 as the learning of behavioral patterns from other social role models, such as parents and other family members. Many of our choices of brands, products, and suppliers are based on our observation in the family.

As a business customer, too, we learn our choices early from what the organization and other role models in it are using. We learn from our supervisor, as he or she grooms us into our job, which document delivery service to use; which restaurants to use to entertain a specific category of customers; and which attorneys, auditors, and consultants to hire when the need for their services arises. These socialization-based choices have an implicit validation of their quality and risk-free character from these role models. Hence, continuing with these choices appears to be a safe practice.

**Reciprocity.**    In some cases, a customer buys from a particular supplier because the supplier in turn buys something from the customer. This practice is called reciprocity—the basis of barter trade in the old days. Even in modern times, a number of market exchanges occur on this basis. For example, employees patronize the company they work for, such as General Electric (GE) employees buying GE appliances or airline employees buying air travel on the carriers for which they work. Among business-to-business customers, reciprocal buying is equally prevalent.

**Networks.**    Networks are a group of firms that deal with each other on a preferential basis. The firms are linked into the network either by common ownership (such as Mitsubishi Industries) or by contractual arrangement. *Keiretsu* is a Japanese term for such

# WINDOW ON PRACTICE

## Getting to Know You: Building Relationships in Russia

International business consultants H. Ned Seelye and Alan Seelye-James narrate this case story about the importance of relationships:

In the aftermath of perestroika, a British engineering firm struck a deal with the Russians to support them in a plant start-up. To staff this project, the firm appointed two Britons, Diana and Horace, who would use interpreters. In the remaining slot of a site consulting engineer's position, Nigel Johnson was appointed. Johnson was a brilliant engineer, plus he spoke Russian fluently. His only drawback was that he was dark, short, and young. This conflicted with Russians' expectations that consultants are tall, light-skinned, and have grey hair and wrinkled faces, reflecting years of experience and wisdom. A middle-aged British colleague had warned him that there may be a problem.

When Johnson arrived at the plant, he gathered plant managers and supervisors and spent the whole morning talking to them, not at all about engineering and the plant, but rather about himself and his family, asking his audience about their families and answering their questions about life in England and other matters, related or not to the business at hand. This perplexed Johnson's own supervisor, who admonished Johnson not to waste any more time in nonbusiness talk. Johnson paid no heed and continued with the relaxed pace and informal conversations during the next few days. A few days later, Johnson was asked into a meeting with the Russian managers and supervisors, and his advice was sought on a particular problem. Although the plant director did not agree with all of his advice, the director let it be known that he was happy to have Johnson to help them.

What to Johnson's supervisor was a waste of time was, in fact, time well invested in establishing relationships. In countries and cultures such as Russia, relationships are a prelude to doing any business at all. Business customers in such relationship-oriented cultures want to spend time with you in social and informal situations to assess your character in order to judge your trustworthiness. Without trustworthiness, they will do no business with you. In such customer cultures, a seller who gets right down to business would likely scare off more than a few customers.

**Source:** Adapted from H. Ned Seelye and Alan Seelye-James, *Culture Clash: Managing in a Multicultural World* (Lincolnwood, Illinois: NTC Business Books, 1995).

networks, and this is a prevalent business practice in Japan. The firms in keiretsu enjoy a lifetime of relationships when there is a mutual understanding that each will give to the other business for its lifetime. For example, in a study of suppliers of U.S. and Japanese automakers, Japanese suppliers reported that they had a 92 percent chance of rewinning the business at model change; in contrast, U.S. automakers' suppliers believed that their chance of rewinning was only 69 percent. In this climate of close-knit supplier-customer networks, it is very difficult for outside suppliers to break in, as has been the experience of many American and European companies trying to get a foothold in Japan.

Similar networks are being established in other business markets. The very idea of supplier partnership is one of building keiretsu-style arrangements. For example, in North

America, the ChryslerDaimler Corporation has entered into agreements with its suppliers. Chrysler now gives most of its suppliers business for the life of the car model. That way, instead of worrying about bidding and winning on the next year's business, suppliers can work toward cost reduction and can share in the resulting savings. This pattern of relationships and the benefits that accrue from it is another strong motivation for customers to engage in relationship-based buying.[3]

**Buying Based on Friendship.**   Many purchases are made on the basis of friendship. Thus, if your neighbor or friend is an insurance agent, you are likely to buy your insurance from him or her. If your friend is an Avon salesperson, you are going to patronize her for all your cosmetics. Similarly, in business markets, many customers are obtained by referral from friends. Lunch meetings of professional associations are primarily intended to expand a person's network of prospective customers. In many cultures, business is done strictly on the basis of friendship. In Chapter 2, we discussed the role of friendship as a cultural factor.

Marketing professors Ingmar Bjorkman and Soren Kock of the Swedish School of Economics in Finland, have studied business buying practices in China. Much of business buying, especially of large contracts with foreign firms, occurs within the friendship and social networks called *guanxi*. These differ from business networks in that the latter are concerned with relationships between organizations. Guanxi, the networks of individuals based on social exchange, are key to gaining access to both initial information about a prospective buyer's needs and also to subsequent decision-making units (DMUs) and their influencers. Buying decisions based on friendships and social networks are instances literally of relationship-based buying.[4] The Window on Research provides more information on guanxi.

# WINDOW ON RESEARCH

## Mapping Relationships: Guanxi in China

Guanxi defines the concept of "relationship" in China. It is defined as "preexisting relationships of classmates, people from the same native-place, relatives, superior and subordinate in the same workplace, and so forth." It involves a hierarchically structured network of relationships embedded with mutual obligations through a self-conscious manipulation of "face", "renqing (favor) and related symbols." The basis of guanxi is in the concept of "obligation." One is expected to oblige friends, relatives, and people from the same native-place, and failure to oblige brings shame on the person and his family. The concept of "face" is defined as "the process by which one gains and maintains status and moral reputation." If you do not fulfill your obligations you "get dirt on your face," while if you meet your obligations, you "put gold on your face." The word "renqing" means "a resource allocated to another person as a gift and also connotes a set of social norms to guide an individual to get along well with other people."

Business alliances in China are structured as guanxi networks. Organizations that are part of a guanxi network cooperate with each other on different areas, are very close to each other, and defend the members of the

*(continued)*

network. Marketers need to be cognizant of the fact that business alliances in China are driven by personal relationships.

Research shows that guanxi can be represented as a set of four insider-outsider psychological processes namely testing, trial, teaming, and trust. In the testing quadrant, each party considers the other party an outsider and tests the other parties' intentions or reactions. In the trial quadrant, each party evaluates its position in terms of its dependence on the other party and the degree of trust in the other party and bargains from this position of power. When a strong guanxi relationship exists between parties, these two initial quadrants are skipped and parties directly work from the teaming quadrant and then move to the trust quadrant. In dealing with Chinese business partners, time taken to build relationships will be directly proportional to the time taken to traverse through these quadrants. If you begin the relationship as an outsider, you will need to go through the four quadrants, but if you are considered an insider, it is relatively easier to build relationships. The implementation and effectiveness of guanxi can also be explained through six dimensions involving a harmonious combination of "mind" and "heart" (the yin-yang harmony). Contact, conflict, and compromise are the three dimensions of the "mind" approach. Contact to build relationships requires time, conflict avoidance is by means of renqing (favor), and compromise is a mutual adaptive behavior. Centrality, convergence, and creativity are the three dimensions of the "heart" approach. Centrality in relationships makes Chinese treat foreigners as outsiders, convergence of yin and yang thinking is necessary to understand Chinese business people, and creativity is to know the best time to deal with aggressors in a relationship.

Guanxi is a manifestation of Chinese culture, traditions and social organization, and doing business in China requires an understanding of guanxi. It is evident that building relationships in China takes time, but the concept of guanxi ensures that they will be long-lasting.

**Source:** Adapted from Y. H. Wong and Jackie L. M. Tam (2000), "Mapping Relationships in China: Guanxi Dynamic Approach," *Journal of Business and Industrial Marketing*, Vol. 15, Issue 1, http://www.emerald-library.com; and Lee C. Simmons (1996), "Is Relationship Marketing Culturally Bound: A Look at Guanxi in China," *Advances in Consumer Research*, Vol. 23, pp. 92–96, http://www.acrweb.org.

## The Supplier-Customer Relationship

Trust and commitment are the twin legs of relationship-based buying. For a customer to be engaged in relationship-based buying at all, the customer has to trust the marketer and then make a commitment to the marketer.

### Trust

The most essential ingredient in any relationship, whether a business or a social relationship, is trust. It is also a key arbitrator of commitment. If there is no trust, there will be no commitment.

Marketing scholars have recognized trust to be so important a building block that they have attempted to define and describe it. (For various definitions by marketing scholars, see Table 10.1). We extract and adapt from these a common-denominator definition: Trust is a willingness to rely on the ability, integrity, and motivation of the other party

| Trust and Commitment: Various Scholars' Definitions | TABLE 10.1 |
| --- | --- |

**TRUST**

We conceptualize trust as existing when one party has confidence in an exchange partner's reliability and integrity. Morgan and Hunt, 1994

Trust is defined as a willingness to rely on an exchange partner in whom one has confidence. Moorman, Deshpande, Zaltman, 1993

[Trust is] a generalized expectancy held by an individual that the word of another can be relied on. Rotter, 1980

The firm's belief that another company will perform actions that will result in positive outcomes for the firm as well as not take unexpected actions that result in negative outcomes. Anderson and Narus, 1990

**COMMITMENT**

Exchange partner's believing that an ongoing relationship with another is so important as to warrant maximum effort at maintaining it. That is, the committed party believes that the relationship is worth working on to ensure that it endures indefinitely. Morgan and Hunt, 1994

Enduring desire to maintain a valued relationship. Moorman, Zaltman, and Deshpande, 1992

**Sources:** Robert M. Morgan and Shelby D. Hunt, "The Commitment-Trust Theory of Relationship Marketing," *Journal of Marketing* 58, July 1994, pp. 20–38; Christine Moorman, Gerald Zaltman, and Rohit Deshpande, "Relationships Between Providers and Users of Market Research: The Dynamics of Trust Within and Between Organizations," *Journal of Marketing Research* 29 (August 1992), pp. 314–38; Christine Moorman, Rohit Deshpande, and Gerald Zaltman, "Factors Affecting Trust in Market Research Relationships," *Journal of Marketing* 57 (January 1993), pp. 81–101; James C. Anderson and James A. Narus, "A Model of Distributor Firm and Manufacturer Firm Working Partnership," *Journal of Marketing* 54 (Spring 1990), pp. 42–58; J. B. Rotter, "Interpersonal Trust, Trustworthiness, and Gullibility," *American Psychologist* 35 (1980) pp. 1–7.

to act to serve my needs and interests as agreed upon implicitly or explicitly. Several elements of this definition are noteworthy:

- The person with trust has confidence that he or she is willing to rely on, willing to act upon.
- Trust concerns all three aspects of a partner's characteristics: ability, integrity, and motivation. Thus, you judge the partner to be competent to carry out his or her obligations and to serve you. Second, you judge the partner to have integrity; you can believe in the partner's word. Finally, you believe the partner has the motivation not to act against your interests; the partner appreciates the stake the relationship requires and will behave rationally.
- The trusted person will look after both parties' needs and interests, not his or her needs and interests alone.
- The partner's behaviors will comply with mutual expectations, both explicit (as stipulated in a contract, for example) and implicit. That is, the partner's behaviors will go beyond the mere letter of the contract; he or she will also honor the spirit of the agreement.[5]

## Commitment

Long-term customer relationships are also characterized by **commitment**, that is, *an enduring desire to continue the relationship and to work to ensure its continuance.*[6] In household markets, for example, a customer who is committed to his or her long-distance phone service supplier would not switch suppliers just to gain a temporary price deal. In business markets, commitment is not merely the carrying out of certain contractual obligations (such as a reseller displaying the product according to the manufacturer's written requirements); rather, it requires making every effort to promote the partner's business. The commitment manifests in cooperative behaviors, but it goes beyond individual acts of cooperation. It refers to a mind-set of pledging to do nothing that would harm the relationship and doing everything needed to nurture it.

## Outcomes of Relationship-Based Buying

As Figure 10.2 shows, the outcomes of successful relationship-based buying are supplier loyalty, increased buying, willingness to pay more, proactive word-of-mouth, and customer equity or goodwill. The most direct outcome of relationship-based buying is supplier loyalty—customers prefer this supplier and consistently buy from the same supplier.

Initially, customers may engage in relational buying with a particular supplier for a specific product or service; with the relationship well founded, however, customers may progress to buying more of the same product from the supplier, and then to buying other products from the supplier as well. Cross-selling is a practice wherein salespeople try to sell other lines of the company's products to the customers of a specific product. For example, an advertising agency that has been developing creative work for a business client may, after a few years, also solicit and obtain media buying work from the client.

Moreover, preference for the relational supplier grows so that customers begin to perceive substantial superiority in this supplier's offering. Eventually, many customers become willing to pay a premium price for the supplier's products.

Proactive word-of-mouth also increases. Word-of-mouth is an outcome when customers are satisfied. But, with relational buying, such positive word-of-mouth acquires a more proactive character because the positive supplier experience is repeated often in frequent repurchase encounters.

Finally, suppliers that keep a customer satisfied enough to receive his or her relational buying acquire customer equity or goodwill, customer support for the supplier's well-being. These are the positive outcomes that flow to the firm from relational buying by its customers.

# Relationship Buying and Selling in Business Markets

Business customers tend to place larger orders than individual consumers do. This makes customer relationships especially important in business markets. However, the historical model of purchasing by business organizations has been transaction-oriented with each purchase being a disjointed transaction without regard to those that preceded it or those that would follow it, and the goal of buyers has been merely to ensure that a source of supply will be available. Now this buying practice is changing in many forward-looking organizations toward relationship-based buying.

The model of buyer behavior we described in Chapter 9 focuses on a *discrete* purchase. That model helps us understand things like how buying centers choose suppliers, what information they process, and how their members interact and make joint decisions. Because that model focuses on the decision-making processes that lead up to a single purchase event, it needs to be supplemented by an understanding of the *long-term relationships* that develop between buyers and sellers.

It is not unusual for a business buyer to purchase from the same supplier firm for 5 or 10 years. When this happens, a relationship develops. The dynamics of relationship building and maintenance brings into the picture certain other variables and factors that marketers need to understand.

# Process of Relationship Buying: The IMP Model

A few years ago, a group of business researchers in Europe studied the buying process in business organizations. The group, called the Industrial Marketing and Purchasing (IMP) group, used case studies of business buying. On the basis of case studies of some 300 companies in five European countries, the IMP group established that *long-term* patronage is quite common in business buying. Organizational buying entails interactions at the individual, departmental, and company levels. They sought to study, therefore, a relational model of buying—a model that describes the processes or steps in the development of relationships in a series of interactions.[7]

## Characteristics of Relational Buying

The IMP model has identified three key factors that characterize all relational buying by business customers:

1. **Transaction-specific investments/adaptations**—These investments are any special equipment, technology, or human resources that need to be obtained and dedicated or set aside only for meeting the needs of a particular customer/supplier partner. Similarly, adaptations mean any specific changes a firm needs to make to accommodate the other partner.
2. **Power dependence**—This term refers to the relative dependence of one party on the other because of the resources the other party possesses. If the customer is going to finance the suppliers' production equipment or R&D work, for example, then the supplier develops a dependency relationship with the customer. On the other hand, if the supplier is going to provide training and technical assistance, then the supplier has the power, and the customer becomes dependent. Often the power between the two parties is balanced, in that each has a resource the other values. However, when one party depends more on the other than the converse (such as when there is a monopolistic supplier), the power dependence is **asymmetrical**.
3. **Role formalness**—This variable defines whether the interactions between the supplier and customer are close and personal or, instead, limited to the formal roles of the parties.

These three variables define the character of supplier-customer relationships. Thus, a relationship may be marked by few or extensive dedicated investments, symmetrical or asymmetrical power dependence, and close-personal or role-formal interactions.

## Steps in Relationship Development

Based on the case studies of business buyers and sellers, the IMP group also identified the steps that companies go through in building a relationship. These comprise need complementarity, interactions/exchanges, outcomes, satisfaction, investment, and commitment.

1. *Needs Complementarity*—First, the parties mutually recognize that each depends on the other for resources it does not have.
2. *Interactions*—Repeated personal contacts or repeated interactions/exchanges serve to build and further the relationship.
3. *Outcomes and Satisfaction*—These interactions result in business and social outcomes. If these outcomes generate satisfaction, then the parties choose to make transaction-specific investments.
4. *Investments*—When dedicated to the other party, investments signify faith that the other party will reciprocate.
5. *Commitment*—With investments, especially when they are reciprocal, commitment to the other partner deepens, and, consequently, the relationship-buying process is perpetuated.

Among business firms, the relationship progresses from initial trial exchange to commitment. The buyer realizes that the vendor has the unique skills and capability to produce the product or service it needs, and the seller realizes that the buyer assures a market for its special skills. With the trial purchase, both are satisfied. To produce the product or service in quantities required by the buyer, the seller would need to invest in additional equipment; and the buyer would have to place an engineer at the seller's factory to assist in the setup of quality control processes. Each decides to invest, and with this dedicated investment, the commitment of each deepens the relationship.

## Reasons for Relationship Development in Business Buying

In addition to the motivations for relationship-based buying described earlier, business customers may also have a few special reasons for relationship-based buying. First, businesses may need a long-term exchange contract to assure long-term supply, and this implies relationship buying. This is helpful generally when the product is a crucial input in a customer's production processes or other operations, and an ongoing supply is critical.

Business customers also want to reduce the cost of buying transactions, particularly such activities as inventory monitoring and order placement, so they transfer this task to the seller organization. This requires the two parties to invest in automated ordering and order-fulfilling systems and to link each others' computers and information systems. Assumption of such responsibility requires a long-term commitment to the relationship.

Buyers and sellers may also have quality and cost goals that require collaboration. The buyers and suppliers can pursue these goals jointly much more effectively than each party acting alone. Such joint pursuit requires relationship buying.

A related factor is the need to form an alliance, or pool resources, to jointly develop the future product to nurture the supplier. Sometimes, customers desire more than improved quality and cost reduction; they desire new-product development and innovation. Suppliers would be unwilling to invest in R&D work unless assured of a long-term buying commitment. See the Window on Practice box for details on how the auto industry has been applying these principles.

## Determinants of Trust and Commitment from Business Customers

Some factors that cause and sustain relationship commitment and trust are specific to business markets. These factors, listed in the left column of Table 10.2, are switching costs, partner-specific investments, mutually shared goals, communication and product support, and avoidance of opportunistic behavior. Of these, switching costs have already been discussed. The remaining factors are described below.[8]

---

**TABLE 10.2** — **Determinants of Trust and Commitment in Business Relationships**

### Determinants for the Customer
Switching costs
Partner-specific investments
Mutually shared goals
Communication and product support
Supplier avoidance of opportunistic behavior

### Determinants for the Supplier
Supplier-specific investments
Customer avoidance of opportunistic behavior
Single-source policy
Data sharing and nurturance

# WINDOW ON PRACTICE

## Relationship Buying by Automobile Makers

Outsourcing is increasing in the automobile industry. Rather than make all the parts themselves, carmakers increasingly buy parts from outside suppliers. In 1994, Chrysler outsourced 66 percent of its parts, Ford 62 percent, and GM 53 percent. Japan's Toyota topped the list by outsourcing 75 percent of its parts.

Not only is the use of external suppliers increasing in a number of companies, but the reliance on outside suppliers is expanding in scope as well. In the past, automakers would actually provide the blueprint of the part; now they simply tell the supplier the outside body dimensions and performance target and delegate the design task to the supplier.

Even more important, the dependence on suppliers is changing qualitatively from transaction-oriented buying; automakers are now seeking long-term relationships. Indeed, suppliers are being invited to be part of the concept/design team for the car. For example, at Honda's R&D center in Ohio, 24 guest engineers (who are the employees of suppliers) were recently reported to be working side-by-side with Honda engineers.

Such relationship buying necessarily requires trimming the number of suppliers. In 1994, Ford Motor Co. used 700-plus suppliers for its Tempo model; in 1995, it relied only on 227 suppliers for its Mercury Mystique.

Relationship buying also involves trusting and nurturing suppliers. This is what one observer wrote of the old approach:

> For years, suppliers were treated as mushrooms proverbially are: kept in the dark and covered with manure. Automakers drew up part specifications, circulated them to a dozen potential bidders, and asked for a price quote down to a thousandth of a cent. Distrust verged on paranoia. Even now, some manufacturers pay for suppliers' equipment so that if production falters, they can yank it out and install it in somebody else's factory.

The new model is illustrated by Chrysler's supplier-building program. "We are willing to cede much of our historical control to suppliers," said Thomas T. Steelkamp, then head of purchasing at Chrysler. Chrysler invited supplier engineers to become charter members on its cross-functional platform teams charged with designing new car models. Suppliers are chosen based on reputation, not price. Chrysler also runs a supplier cost-reduction effort. In the first years of this program, suppliers suggested more than 2,000 cost-saving ideas, which have saved the company more than $600 million annually.

**Source:** Adapted from Alex Taylor III, "The Auto Industry Meets the New Economy," *Fortune*, September 5, 1995, pp. 52–60. Reprinted with permission. Additional information is available at http://www.aiag.com, http://www.honda.co.jp, http://www.americanautoparts.com.

## Partner-Specific Investments

The parties build and sustain relationships when they make **partner-specific investments**, that is, investments that one party makes in processes dedicated to the other party. Suppose that the use of a new material requires some investment in R&D and/or in process equipment; that investment may be made by the supplier or jointly by the two partners. The developmental outcome will be useful only for the customer involved, thus making it a partner-specific investment. Even if the supplier alone shoulders the investment, this exhibits the supplier's commitment, which, in turn, will bring forth the customer's commitment.

In many cases, however, the customer bears the capital costs in equipment dedicated to doing business with the particular supplier. For example, Wal-Mart installed computer systems networked to Procter & Gamble's order receiving and delivery system. These investments build customer trust in suppliers and their commitment to the relationship.

## Mutual Goals

Long-term relationships are also strengthened by **mutual goals**, or goals that require each exchange partner's cooperation and through whose achievement each partner profits. For example, if a supplier succeeds in developing a new material that would improve the customer's end-product, it may increase the customer's market share in the end-user market. If the customer's sales increase, the supplier's sales will increase in turn. This then is a mutual goal that will profit both the partners. Consequently, both the partners should be committed to working toward the accomplishment of that goal.

## Communication and Product Support

If there is open communication, then the customer acquires more knowledge about the supplier activities and knows that the supplier is not secretive. In communicating openly, the supplier confides in the customer. The customer responds by extending the same confidence and trust. In the same vein, the more product and service support the supplier offers, the more the customer sees supplier behavior that is helpful to the customer. This too strengthens the customer's trust.

## Avoidance of Opportunistic Behavior

To cultivate an ongoing relationship, the supplier must avoid engaging in opportunistic behavior. Opportunistic behavior concerns unilateral acts of profiting from opportunities that may arise and that were not stipulated in the contract. Suppose, for example, in developing a particular new material for the customer (with customer-financed R&D work), the supplier's R&D personnel come across a spin-off by-product that will be independently commercially profitable. If the supplier were to transfer some of the customer-financed R&D resources to getting this spin-off by-product market-ready, and if the supplier were not to discuss this with the customer, this would constitute opportunistic behavior. Trust and relationships require that the plans for profiting from opportunities be shared. Worse will be the case when one partner takes the opportunity to profit at another's cost (i.e., even when the act would harm the partner's interests).

## Determinants of Supplier Trust in Customers

Suppliers also need to trust their customers. If they believe that their customers have no commitment to them and that they (the customers) would themselves engage in opportunistic buying, then suppliers would not have any trust in customers. Consequently, suppliers will not be committed to the relationship.

The factors for supplier trust in the customer are similar to the factors for customer trust in the supplier. Some of these factors are the same; others are somewhat different. These are listed in the right column of Table 10.2. Two of the factors have already been discussed; these are supplier-specific investments and nonopportunistic behavior. The other two are single-source policies and data sharing and nurturance.

Perhaps the most important factor is *single-source policy*. If the customer is constantly looking for new suppliers, then the supplier would not trust the customer, especially if the supplier needs to make investments to offer better value to the customer. To engender supplier trust, the customer should seek to rationalize the procurement policies, realizing the benefits of dealing with fewer, rather than more, suppliers.

Relying on a single supplier often necessitates mutual nurturance. Particularly if the customer is more resourceful than the supplier, the customer may have to provide developmental support to the supplier. Or if no one can meet the customer's requirement at present, the customer may have to induce and assist a potential supplier to become one. (This is an instance of "nurturing suppliers" discussed in the next section.)

Along with providing general nurturance, customers need to share their internal data with suppliers in order for suppliers to make long-term plans. For example, customers need to involve suppliers in their own long-term plans so that suppliers can, in turn, adjust their own production capabilities to meet the future needs of customers. If customers are secretive about their long-term plans, then the suppliers would suspect that the customer is planning to switch suppliers or developing other suppliers.

Thus, trust is a two-way street. Trust begets trust. In relationship buying, each party has to engage in trust-building behaviors, and each has to seek and motivate similar behaviors in the other. Each has to make investments specific to the other partner. The roles of mutual trust, investment, and interdependence have been highlighted in a number of studies, as the Window on Research box shows.

## Relationship-Based Buying: The Art of Nurturing Suppliers

The mutuality of goals and behaviors makes a long-term exchange relationship more bidirectional. Often the distinction between who is the buyer and who is the supplier blurs. One party may have to market itself more than the other. Sometimes the marketer may be the customer, marketing itself to the supplier.

One of the key resources that a firm's profitability depends on is how well the firm is able to procure its inputs. In *Competitive Strategy*, professor Michael Porter has suggested that a firm's bargaining power with its suppliers is one of the four forces that determine the firm's profitability and performance. (The other forces are threat of new entrants, rivalry among the existing firms, and threat of substitute products.) Thus, organizations that can establish and maintain mutually cooperative relationships with suppliers are better positioned in a competitive marketplace.

To have good suppliers is to be blessed with good resources. A firm needs suppliers that can produce the product to the high-quality requirements that its own internal standards require. It needs suppliers that can constantly bring down costs, will continuously innovate, will grow as the customer firm's needs grow, and will be ready to change when the customer's needs change.

When a high-caliber supplier does not exist, the customer firm must develop, maintain, and motivate suppliers, current or prospective ones, to get set up to become a long-term supplier.

Imagine yourself to be the purchasing manager of a large chemical company (say Chem-X, Inc.), located in New York, that buys $40 million worth of anhydrous ammonia as a raw material. You become aware of a large foreign producer of fertilizer (say Chem-Y, International) setting up a plant near Boston. One of the ingredients needed to produce fertilizer is ammonia; in turn, ammonia needs hydrogen, and Chem-Y plans to produce this hydrogen by burning residual oil, an expensive process that will contribute to the high cost of ammonia. You know that it is much cheaper to produce hydrogen by

# WINDOW ON RESEARCH

## Nutrients for a Buyer-Seller Relationship

Many marketing scholars have studied the factors that help the nurturance of relationships between buyers and sellers. A recent research study was conducted by marketing professor Shankar Ganesan. He surveyed 124 retail buyers responsible for buying the merchandise for their stores, ranging from men's and women's clothing, to jewelry, silverware, and perfumes. He also surveyed 52 vendors from whom the surveyed retail-store buyers bought the merchandise. The purpose of the study was to verify whether certain factors hypothesized in the relationship-marketing literature were or were not helpful in the development of buyer-seller relationships. Of the 124 retailer buyers, 76 (61 percent) were asked to answer questions with respect to a vendor with which they had a long-term relationship, and 48 (39 percent) with respect to vendors with which they had a short-term relationship. All respondents were questioned on such factors as the buyer firm's trust in the vendor, its dependence on the vendor, its perception of the vendor's dependence on the retailer, transaction-specific investments (TSIs) by the retailer, perception of vendor TSIs, reputation of the vendor, and satisfaction with the past outcomes.

The survey data showed that the retailer's long-term orientation in its dealings with the vendor were positively influenced by the vendor's credibility and trustworthiness and by the extent to which the retailer was dependent on the vendor; however, if the vendor firm itself was perceived to be dependent on the retailer, then the retailer tended to adopt a short-term orientation. These factors were, in turn, affected by TSIs by both parties. Specifically, trustworthiness was positively influenced by the vendor's reputation and the TSIs made by the vendor. And, the retailer's dependence on the vendor was positively influenced both by the TSIs made by the retailer firm itself and by the vendor. Many of these same results were mirrored in the survey data from vendors. For example, in order to adopt a long-term orientation in their dealings with the retailer firm, vendors needed to perceive the retailer to be trustworthy, and also perceive each party to be dependent on the other. Moreover, the retailer was seen to be dependent on the vendor if it (the vendor) had made some TSIs. Vendors were also likely to trust the retailers more if they (the retailers) made some TSIs.

The TSIs by the retailer included investments in displays, salesperson training, and the time and effort in learning about the vendor's method of operation. Correspondingly, TSIs by the vendor included support to the retailer in display materials, salesperson training, and in acquiring the knowledge about the retailer's operations.

**Source:** Adapted from Shankar Ganesan, "Determinants of Long-Term Orientation in Buyer-Seller Relationships," *Journal of Marketing* 58, No. 2, pp. 1–19. Additional information is available at http://www.ama.org/pubs/jml.

burning natural gas. A few years earlier, you negotiated a long-term contract (with provision for substantial growth in supply to meet possible future need) to buy natural gas at very attractive prices.

What if you can persuade Chem-Y to use natural gas (which you will help it obtain from the same source as yours at the same attractive prices) to produce hydrogen, and then to sell ammonia to you? You will, thus, be able to obtain ammonia at a much lower rate, and Chem-Y will get a substantial customer. The only snag is that Chem-Y has already made plans for an oil-based hydrogen extraction plant.

You put together a small team of engineers and planners to do a feasibility study of setting up an ammonia plant next to your own plant. It turns out to be economically viable, provided you are willing to get into the fertilizer business. You aren't, but the proposal makes sense for Chem-Y since fertilizer is what it is setting up the new plant for anyway.

Armed with this feasibility study, you fly out to the Swiss headquarters of Chem-Y to meet with a very suspicious executive team. You lay out your plans. You tell them about the superior economics of using natural gas as a source of hydrogen. You guarantee them the supply source for it. You share your worksheets showing how the added freight costs (due to locating the plant in New York rather than near Boston) as well as the cost of land already bought near Boston, would be easily offset by savings in hydrogen production. You assure them a base price for hydrogen you will buy from them and guarantee an annual demand rate for the next 10 years.

After nine months of deliberations and, no doubt, their own independent feasibility study to corroborate your study, the top management of Chem-Y finally agrees to set up their plant near your factory and become your supplier for hydrogen gas. Your new cost of hydrogen gas will be reduced from $40 million to $30 million annually.

This is a real story. The New York firm is Clair Chemical Corporation (CCC); the foreign firm is Bernier, a Swiss multinational firm. The purchasing executive is John Beck, vice-president of procurement at CCC. Delegating the day-to-day purchasing responsibility to others in the department, John concentrates on aggressively seeking new sources of supply, finding and persuading firms large and small to become its suppliers, on terms that are favorable to CCC. To accomplish this, he puts himself in the shoes of the supplier firm and analyzes why it would be advantageous for the supplier firm to do business with CCC.

In each case, the supplier firm must buy the idea and accept John's proposal. For that proposal, John is the seller, and the future supplier firm is the customer. For John Beck, it is the crucial procurement tool that supports future corporate success.[9]

This art of nurturing suppliers is clearly needed when the existing suppliers cannot meet the required quality, quantity, price, service, and delivery objectives. Rather than select from the slate of existing suppliers, the purchaser task is then to *create* suppliers. Thus, this process is an aggressive and imaginative approach to achieving supply objectives. The purchaser takes the initiative in making the proposal. It is the purchaser's proposal (rather than the seller's) that becomes the agenda for discussion and negotiation.[10]

Creating new sources of supply and persuading current suppliers to build new capabilities to fulfill the customer's objectives is not limited to industrial suppliers. It is feasible for business services as well. For example, convention and meeting organizers do not have to accept standard hotel packages. Once they know what facilities and services will suit them best, they can look for suppliers willing to adapt their standard services to meet specific customers' needs.

## Reasons for Nurturing Suppliers

Businesses engage in the process of nurturing suppliers for several reasons. These include future needs, compliance with government policies, good citizenship, promoting environmental policies, ensuring quality, and cost reduction.

**Meeting Future Needs.** When the existing suppliers are unable to meet future needs, a firm may have to develop specific suppliers by helping them to acquire the capability. This is exactly what Clair Chemical Corporation (CCC), in the example above, did. Another situation occurs when a customer firm is planning an expansion of its operations and wants to assure an increased supply of raw materials and parts. If the current vendor would need to invest significantly to expand its own capacity, then the customer firm would engage in motivating, and, in fact, helping the vendor set up for the expanded capacity.

**Government Policy Compliance.** Federal and state governments may require the development and patronage of local, minority, or domestic suppliers. Yet these suppliers may not be good enough to meet a customer firm's needs and supplier criteria. The customer firm would then develop the capabilities of the local, domestic, or minority vendor firm. Sometimes a condition of doing business with the government, as we saw in Chapter 9, is to hire minority subcontractors. In the event that available minority suppliers lack the capability, the firm would invest in the minority supplier to enable it to do business with the customer firm.

**Good Citizenship.** Often, business firms want to do the right thing even without the government edict: they want to engage in socially responsible or helpful corporate behavior and, thus, show good citizenship. Raytheon Corporation offers an example.

> The Raytheon Corporation adopted a program of nurturing minority business suppliers in 1971, even before Public Law 95-507 was passed requiring support of minority businesses. Raytheon uses a set-aside program for buying a number of its needs from minority businesses. It provides consulting help to vendors to help them become better suppliers. It will even help them find additional buyers.

**Promoting Environmental Policies.** This reason is similar to the foregoing two reasons except that attention is now focused on the supplier firm's environmental record. The buyer firm must motivate and educate the potential supplier firms to adopt environmentally friendly policies as a condition of doing business.

**Quality Assurance.** For more than two decades now, business firms around the globe have been pursuing very high-quality standards in the products and services they produce. A critical requirement of quality output products is that the input materials and parts themselves be of high quality. While the large manufacturing firms have the resources to upgrade their equipment and processes for high-quality output, often small vendors of input materials and parts do not have such resources. Therefore, the customer firm with greater resources and with greater motivation to obtain the quality input materials undertakes to develop the quality capability in the supplier. This may entail supporting the supplier firm with financial resources, managerial skills, technical training, and development resources. The supplier firm needs to be persuaded (i.e., sold on the idea) to invest its own time and effort to meet the quality needs of the customer firm.

**Cost Reduction.** The final reason for nurturing suppliers is the pursuit of cost reductions. The buyer may analyze the supplier's production costs and identify ways the supplier can save enough on production costs that it can charge less yet maintain or improve its own profit margins. But for the supplier firm to engage in the activities necessary to reduce costs may require some persuasion.

An example of a customer firm seeking cost containment via the art of nurturing suppliers is this statement by Texas Instruments:

> We are a company in a highly competitive environment. For us to survive and prosper we need to be able to bring our long-term costs down significantly as fast as we can. To the best of our knowledge, in view of increasing volume and technological and other improvements, it should be possible for you to achieve the following targets for the next three years. Should you agree, we are counting on you to achieve these targets. We are willing to assist you in a variety of ways to make sure you will achieve this. However, if you do not believe you can meet our future objectives, there is no point in making a deal with us now, even though you may be fully competitive now.[11]

## Advantages of Nurturing Suppliers

Since this process begins with the customer's rather than the supplier's proposal, the customer may seek whatever advantages are important to its strategy. Typically, companies nurture suppliers to obtain some combination of substantially improved quality, substantially improved performance, lower costs, better delivery schedule, and extended service support.

## Supplier-Customer Partnering

**Supplier-customer partnering** is establishing a partnership-like relationship with one's supplier or with one's customer. The supplier and customer firm would not merge ownership. Rather, they come together and agree to collaborate so that each partner works to the advantage of the other (which, in turn, helps each partner itself). The principal focus of the process of nurturing suppliers was to motivate the supplier to do business with you, even when the supplier was not in that kind of business. In supplier-customer partnering, the focus is on redefining the way two parties deal with each other.

The traditional model of dealing with the suppliers is for the customer to focus on his or her own efficiency and cost minimization. In contrast, in supplier-partnership arrangements, the focus is on optimizing the efficiency of the entire value chain (i.e., the entire system from the supplier to the end user). In the traditional arm's-length dealings model, the customer firm's focus is on minimizing the price it pays; in the partnering model, the emphasis is on reducing the total system cost and, at the same time, improving quality. In supplier partnering, there is a joint effort to define needs and solutions, and information is freely shared between the partners about cost and demand and capacity data. In partnering, partners make customized investments in each other (what were earlier called transaction-specific investments), and contracts are more flexible, signifying that the parties trust each other and are willing to commit to working toward common goals. Such supplier partnering had its beginning in the Japanese auto industry, whereas traditionally the U.S. auto industry has followed the model of arm's-length dealings with the suppliers, although this practice is now changing. Even though U.S. companies are now increasingly following the supplier-partnering model, for illustrative purposes, the traditional U.S. model of arm's-length dealings with suppliers and the Japanese model of supplier partnering are worth comparing. This comparison is presented in Table 10.3.

Whether or not the parties are already in business with each other, and whether or not they already have a long-term buying contract, the goal of supplier-customer partnering is to broaden the scope of interactions between the two firms at all levels and across all functions.

In arm's-length transactional dealings, the supplier and customer firms' contact point is limited to the supplier's sales staff interacting with the buyer's purchasing department and the buying firm's users seeking the supplier's service personnel. In the partnering model, the two organizations' interactions are broad-based with each function dealing with its counterpart in the partnering firm. In the partnerships, buyers and the buying firm's engineers get involved in the design and development of the seller's product. Conversely, suppliers want to be in on the ground floor when an end product is being designed so that they may suggest changes that would help them more economically produce the component part for the customer. Other departments interface with their counterparts in the customer firm. Thus, engineering and production personnel interface with their counterparts to identify next-generation product and process improvements. Warehousing and materials management personnel deal with the manufacturing and shipping personnel to explore the most efficient logistics. Information-system designers work to interlock their firms' computer systems. Even credit and accounting managers team up with the accounting people from the customer's firm to identify methods of automating the invoice and payment system.[12]

Either party can take the initiative. Either a customer may initiate and spearhead the drive to partner with the supplier, or a supplier may initiate the partnering effort. Illustratively, a customer might invite supplier engineers to be on its design team, or the supplier

| TABLE 10.3 | Vendor Relations in Japan and the United States |
|------------|--------------------------------------------------|

| Traditional U.S. Model | Japanese Partnering Model |
|------------------------|----------------------------|
| Department or firm focus, optimize firm efficiency. | Business system focus (include supplier/customer economics), optimize value chain efficiency. |
| Emphasis on unit cost/price (minimum quality standards). | Emphasis on full value chain (systems) costs as well as on improving quality. |
| Manufacturer defines needs; specialization of activities; sequential planning. | Joint efforts to define needs and problem solve; highly integrated operations and planning. |
| Communication is sporadic, problem driven; little sharing of information or assistance. | Communication is frequent and planned; continuous sharing of information and assistance. |
| General investments; uniform approach. | Customized investments to meet unique customer or supplier needs (e.g., in information systems, people, manufacturing equipment). |
| Precise contracts that split economic benefits beforehand. | Flexible contracts that adjust to split economic gains fully as market conditions change. |

**Source:** Reprinted from "Japanese-Style Partnerhips: Giving Companies a Competitive Edge," by Jeffery H. Dyer and William G. Ouchi, *Sloan Management Review*, Fall 1993, p. 54, by permission of the publisher. Copyright 1993 by Massachusetts Institute of Technology. All rights reserved.

may seek such an invitation. Likewise, a customer may offer to collaborate on the supplier's product design, or the supplier may motivate the customer to contribute to the supplier firm's product design efforts.

## Factors for the Growth of Supplier Partnering

Four factors would influence customers to seek supplier partnering:

1. *Competitive intensity*—Business in the established product categories is going to become more competitive. Competitive intensity would increase due to market saturation, deregulation, privatization of more and more sectors of the economy, and globalization (firms selling and competing worldwide).
2. *Pressure on market prices*—As competitive intensity increases, businesses want to be able to compete on prices. They, therefore, want to reduce the total cost of inputs (i.e., raw materials, parts, components, and manufacturing supplies). Target costing (designing products and making them to meet certain cost goals or targets) would be on the rise, which would further put pressure on costs of inputs. To reduce purchasing costs, centralized buying will be adopted increasingly. This will make buying more of a corporate and strategic function, concertedly pursuing cost-reduction goals.
3. *Concern with quality*—Competitive intensity will also necessitate that firms differentiate themselves on quality. To build quality in the finished products, firms would need an assurance of quality in the input materials and components. To enable consistently high quality, buyers would need to guide and assist suppliers on an ongoing basis.
4. *Enabling technology*—The foregoing three factors offer a reason for businesses to buy more efficiently and more effectively, and supplier partnering is an avenue for it. Yet supplier partnering would remain an elusive goal were it not for modern enabling technology. In particular, customers and suppliers can link computer networks and communications technology to their databases and processes.

Future business buying will be increasingly relational and based on a strategic plan for supplier development. It will entail motivating the supplier to do business with you in a way that produces greater value for both the partners. In the future model of business buying, the customer seeks to link all of his or her firm's business processes to the supplier's identical business processes. In such relational and partnering exchanges, customers and suppliers collaborate to explore avenues of greater profitability for both.

# Customer Relationship Management and the Three Customer Roles

In this section, we bring together various concepts of the chapter and relate them to the three customer roles. Illustrative relevance of selected concepts is shown in Table 10.4. Traditional marketplace transactions have considered the sale to be the end point of all marketing actions. The true contribution of relationship marketing is that it goes beyond the consummation of the sale per se. In so doing, it brings the user role again into focus following the sale. The goal of relationship marketing is to satisfy the user.

    The central concept in the chapter is the model of relationship-based buying, which comprises customer motivations for and outcomes of relationship-based buying. Among

| Customer Relationship Management and the Three Customer Roles | | | TABLE 10.4 |
|---|---|---|---|
| **Concepts** | **User** | **Payer** | **Buyer** |
| General concept of relationship marketing | • Marketer refocuses on the user after the sale. | | |
| A model of relationship-based buying | | | |
| Motivations | | | |
| Search costs | | | • Search entails time and effort of the buyer role. |
| Risk reduction | • Performance risk to user is reduced. | | |
| Switching costs | • Usage learning of product from new supplier. | • Retooling costs. | • Effort to learn to deal with the new supplier. |
| Value-added benefits | • Add-on benefits for the user. | • Better financing plan may benefit the payer. | |
| Early socialization | • User socialization. | | • Buyer socialization. |
| Reciprocity | | • Payment through reciprocal exchange assured. | • Source availability assured. |
| Networks | • Suppliers in network more trustworthy with product/ service quality. | • Firms in network are accommodating in financial exigencies. | • Easier to do business with. |
| Friendships | • Friendly supplier assures quality product/service. | | • Friendly vendors give friendly service. |
| Nurturing suppliers | • Better performance value. | • Lower costs over the long run. | |
| Supplier partnering | • Better performance value; data sharing; joint planning helpful to user. | • Total cost reduction. | • Buying function becomes more efficient. |

the motivations are cost-benefit factors (search costs, risk reduction, switching costs, and value-added benefits) and sociocultural factors (early socialization, reciprocity, networks, and friendships). Search costs occur in terms of the time and effort of the buyer role. Risk reduction is a benefit to the user in that the current product or service from the current supplier, tried and tested, is devoid of uncertainty as to its performance. Switching costs can relate to each of the three roles. Penalties for breaking the contract, if any, and costs of new investments, such as retooling to become compatible with the new supplier, are costs to the payer. Time and effort expended to learn to do business with the new supplier are costs to the buyer. Learning to use the new supplier's product is a cost to the user. Finally, value-added benefits offer an advantage generally to the user, but if these relate to, say, an improved financing plan or terms of payment, then the payer role is benefited as well.

Among the sociocultural factors, early socialization is the learned behavior both of using a product or service and of buying from a particular source (i.e., it is a socialization of both the user and buyer roles). Reciprocity affects at least two of the three roles, the buyer and the payer. The buyer is assured of a source and its commitment since the latter (i.e., the supplier) depends on the buyer for receiving the product or service it (the supplier) in turn needs. The payer is certain to be able to pay since it has the resource the other party values, its own product or service. Networks affect all three roles. Buyers find it easy to do business with other firms in the network due to a history of interaction. Users gain by being assured of performance, and social values suppliers in the network are accountable to one another for delivering the quality product or service, and they command the social approval as a source. Payers are affected by getting an improved price value over time, by being assured of getting credit terms favorably altered in case of future financial exigencies, and by knowing that firms in the network will not abandon the customer in times of financial hardship. Finally, friendship helps all three roles in the same way as do networks. The user can trust the friend for product or service performance, the buyer gets friendly service, and the payer might get a better price and better credit terms.

The process of nurturing suppliers is driven by the buyer search for both user and payer values. We enumerated the benefits of this process as substantially improved quality, substantially improved performance, better delivery schedule, extended service support, and lower costs over the long run. Of these, the first four are benefits to the user role, and the fifth is a benefit to the payer role.

These same benefits occur from supplier partnering. Because suppliers are on board from the design stage, better performance value results from customized design of components and parts or service. Mutual data sharing improves joint production planning for the user role. The payer role benefits from the joint pursuit of long-term total-cost reduction goals. And since the users interface closely with suppliers on a continual basis, the buyer role becomes more efficient; ordering and delivery transactions can also become automated.

# Summary

In this chapter, we have examined the customer's motivation to patronize the same marketer repeatedly, on an enduring basis. To view the consumer as someone always looking for a better deal, always open to competing suppliers' pitches and, always eager to do business with a new marketer makes the marketer resort to a wheeling-and-dealing strategy of marketing. This view is not entirely inaccurate (and for this reason, the marketer should always strive to offer better value to its current customers); however, it is only half of the story. There are powerful forces that make a customer want to patronize the same marketer repeatedly. It is possible and fruitful for marketers, therefore, to learn to keep customers returning for business again and again (i.e., to build long-term relationships with their customers).

This requires understanding about what motivates customers to engage in relationship-based buying. We integrated these motivations in a model of relationship-based buying. In this model, two groups of factors constitute the motivations: (1) cost-benefit factors that comprise search costs, risk reduction, switching costs, and value-added benefits, and (2) sociocultural factors that comprise early socialization, reciprocity, networks, and friend-ships. These antecedent factors result in supplier-customer relationships that are character-ized by commitment and trust. The outcome of these relationships is customer loyalty to the supplier, increased buying, willingness to pay more, favorable word-of-mouth, and customer equity or goodwill.

Next we discussed relationship buying and selling in business markets. The process of relationship buying in business markets was captured by the Industrial Marketing and Purchasing (IMP) group (a group of business researchers in Europe). In the IMP model, three key factors are recognized, namely, transaction-specific investments/adaptations made to meet the need of a specific customer, power dependence that reflects the dependence of one partner on the other, and role formalness that indicates how personal or impersonal the interactions between the partners are.

Following this, we identified a set of reasons for relationship development in busi-ness buying. These reasons include business customers' need to assure long-term supply, to reduce the cost of transactions, and to pursue quality and cost-reduction goals.

Next we described the determinants of trust and commitment, identified earlier as key elements of business relationships. Business customers trust their suppliers when sup-pliers make partner-specific investments, strive for mutual goals, offer open communica-tions and product support, and avoid opportunistic behaviors. Conversely, suppliers also need to trust their customers, and this trust depends on customers adopting a single-source policy and engaging in data sharing and nurturance.

We also discussed the process of developing and nurturing suppliers. This is needed when future needs would not be met by existing suppliers, when specific but unprepared suppliers need to be patronized, when certain environmental policies need to be promoted, when vendors need quality assurance support, or when a program of cost reduction is needed.

We elaborated on the topic of supplier-customer partnering—the establishment of partnership-like relations with one's customers or one's suppliers. Four sets of factors en-courage business firms to engage in supplier partnering: competitive intensity, pressure on market prices, high concern with quality, and the availability of enabling technology. Re-viewing the emerging trends, we suggested that future business buying will increasingly be relational and based on a strategic plan for supplier development.

# Key Terms

Asymmetrical 373

Commitment 371

Customer Equity or Goodwill 372

Mutual Goals 376

Networks 367

Partner-Specific Investments 376

Perceived Risk 365

Power Dependence 373

Reciprocity 367

Relationship-Based Buying 364

Role Formalness 373

Supplier-Customer Partnering 381

Switching Costs 365

Transaction-Specific Investments/Adaptations 373

Trust 370

# Discussion Questions and Exercises

1. The chapter describes the perceived risk/switching costs model of relationship buying. Based on this model, identify for each of the following businesses what a company can do to encourage relationship-based buying by its current customers: (a) a credit card company, (b) a long-distance phone company, (c) a supermarket, (d) a package-delivery company, such as FedEx for its business customers, and (e) a health insurance company dealing with employers as customers.

2. Trust and commitment are advanced as two essential ingredients in relationship-based buying. Write your boss a memo outlining all the actions your company can take to improve its trust and commitment scores with its major customers.

3. Think about your own experiences as a customer, or the experiences of your company as a customer. Think of five or six companies that you (or your company) do business with as a customer. What does the company do or not do to encourage or discourage you regarding relationship-based buying from it? Make a list, and compare it across the companies you have considered.

4. Contact the purchasing director of a company, and interview him or her to identify if the firm engages in any one of the following: (a) supplier partnering, (b) reverse marketing or supplier development, or (c) long-term contract buying. Query him or her about (1) the advantages and disadvantages of this manner of dealing with its suppliers, (2) how the firm goes about establishing this relationship, and (3) what each partner does to satisfy and maintain the commitment of the other.

5. A friend has just graduated from college in liberal arts; a company has offered him a job as an assistant to the director of purchasing. He is wondering how it relates to marketing, his main interest. Unlike him, you took a class in customer behavior where the strategic role of procurement was emphasized and such developments as supplier partnering and reverse marketing were discussed. Would you advise your friend whether or not the job he is offered is a marketing job? How would you explain to him the significance of his job to a career in marketing?

# Notes

1 Adapted from Tom Stundza, "Ford Shakes Up Its Steel Buy," *Purchasing*, March 8, 2001, pp. 27–32.

2 Adapted from, Jagdish N. Sheth and Atul Paravatiyar, "Relationship Marketing in Consumer Markets: Antecedents and Consequences," *Journal of the Academy of Marketing Science* 23, No. 4 (Fall 1995), pp. 255–71.

3 James C. Anderson, Hakan Hakansson, and Lars Johanson, "Dyadic Business Relationships Within a Business Network Context," *Journal of Marketing* 58 (October 1994), pp. 1–15.

4 Ingmar Bjorkman and Soren Kock, "Social Relationships and Business Networks: The Case of Western Companies in China," *International Business Review* 4, No. 4 (1995), pp. 519–35.

5 For further discussion, see Banwari Mittal, "Trust and Relationship Quality: A Conceptual Excursion," in Atul Parvatiyar and Jagdish N. Sheth (eds.), *The Contemporary Knowledge of Relationship Marketing* (Atlanta, GA: Emory University, Center for Relationship Marketing, 1996), pp. 230–40. Also see Jagdish N. Sheth and Banwari Mittal, "A Framework for Managing Customer Expectations," *Journal of Market-Focused Management* 1, No. 2 (1996), pp. 137–58.

6  See Wilson 1995; Dwyer, Schurr, and Oh 1987; Moorman, Zaltman, and Deshpande, 1992.

7  IMP Group, 1982, "An Interaction Approach," in H. Hakansson, ed., *International Marketing and Purchasing of Industrial Goods* (John Wiley & Sons, Chichester).

8  For additional perspectives, see Neeli Bendapudi and Leonard Berry, "Customers' Motivations for Relationships with Service Providers," *Journal of Retailing* 73, No. 1 (1997), pp. 15–37.

9  Adapted from Michael R. Leenders and David L. Blenkhorn, *Reverse Marketing: The New Buyer-Supplier Relationship* (Free Press, 1996), pp. 164–70.

10  Ibid., p. 2. See Alan J. Magrath and Kenneth G. Hardy (1994), "Building Customer Partnering," *Business Horizons*, January–February, pp. 24–28.

11  Ibid., pp. 136–37.

12  See Alan J. Magrath and Kenneth G. Hardy, "Building Customer Partnering," *Business Horizons*, January–February 1994, pp. 24–28.

# PART 4

## Building Loyalty and Customer Value

Chapter **11** *Customer Loyalty to Products, Brands and Stores*

Chapter **12** *Online Customer Buying*

Chapter **13** *Creating Market Values for the Customer*

# CHAPTER 11

## Customer Loyalty to Products, Brands, and Stores

## Are You True to Your Brand?

As the sun beams down the tiny glen in Pennsylvania's Pocono Mountains, an outdoor wedding is in progress. In a mass ceremony, Reverend James S. Massie Jr. reads out the vows to over 250 love-struck people. He takes a deep breath and leans toward the microphone and says "By the power vested in me, I pronounce that you are . . . car and driver." 250 people have just married their Mazda Miatas.

The MacWorld Expo, an annual four-day event at San Francisco's Moscone Center is akin to a pilgrimage to 85,000 Apple Computer fans—a chance not only to experience the latest that Apple has to offer, but also to hear Steve Jobs—"the man who democratized technology by putting computing power in the hands of ordinary people." Job's speech is the highlight of the event, and musicians and artists hang on to his every word.

A study conducted by the International Mass Retail Association showed that consumers shopping for a power screwdriver were more concerned about the product having a national brand name than its price. Contractors and professional tradesmen have always been fiercely loyal to their power tool brands, and now the same kind of loyalty is being seen in the consumer market as well. Doug Bieberich, retail product manager of power and hand tools for Do it Best Corp. says "Consumers see professionals using a particular power tool, and when it comes time for them to purchase a tool, they identify whatever brand the contractor was using with quality and added value."

Customer loyalty towards products is manifest in the loyalty that groups of customers are known to exhibit towards the diet foods product category, the caffeine free product category, or the organic foods category. Businesses also show such exceptional product loyalty when it comes to computer systems, machinery (analog vs. digital), and software.

"Watch for an opening of a new Krispy Kreme store—and the throngs of people, some camping out overnight, queuing up for that first bite of a soft, sugary doughnut." Krispy Kreme spends less than 1 percent of revenues on advertising and yet, sales more than doubled between 1997 and 2001. (Tratensek, 1999, and Wells, 2001).[1]

Stories of such fierce customer loyalty show up in the media from time to time. Less visible, but no less commanding of their owners' and customers' strong loyalty, are such products and services as Macintosh, Nintendo, Nike, Tylenol, Singapore Airlines, and Club Med. Likewise, retail stores such as Sears, Nordstrom, Gap, Limited, and the Body Shop also have their loyal following.

On the flip side of the coin, not all customers are loyal to any one product or store, nor is any one customer loyal to everything he or she buys and uses. For packaged goods, for example, loyalty among U.S. consumers to manufacturers' brands ranges from only 10 to 40 percent. According to a survey by the authors, for a broad range of services, as many as half the customers are willing to switch their current service providers. In Europe, customer purchase of private labels or store brands (which is an indicator of lack of loyalty to manufacturers' brands), is remarkably high, as much as 50 to 60 percent for such supermarkets as Sainsbury's.[2]

Why such variation in customer loyalty? Why are customers loyal to some brands and stores and not to others? What can marketers do to win their customers' loyalty? These questions are the subject matter of this chapter (see Figure 11.1 for the conceptual framework).

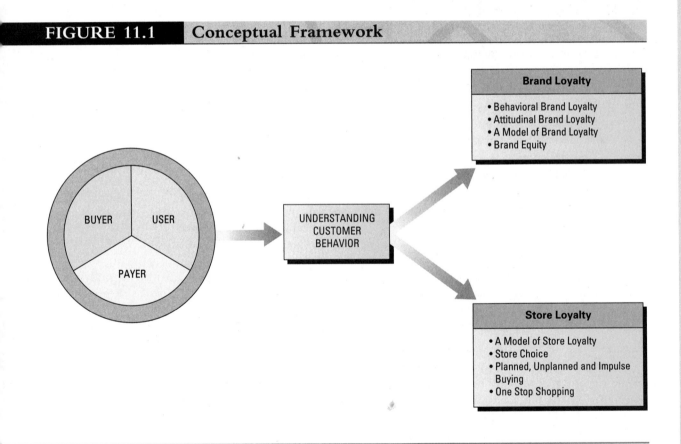

**FIGURE 11.1      Conceptual Framework**

We begin by defining brand loyalty and describing ways to measure it. Next, we introduce a model of brand loyalty that brings together its diverse determinants. In business markets, the brand name is equivalent to the supplier, and supplier loyalty would involve considerations similar to brand loyalty in the consumer markets. We then describe the concept of brand equity and discuss its significance for marketers. Next, we present a model of customers' store loyalty, describing the underlying factors. We also consider customers' shopping behavior in terms of the decision process for choosing which stores to shop, a discussion of diverse shopping motives, as well as a specific customer behavior, namely one-stop shopping.

# Definition and Measurement of Brand Loyalty

There are two ways to think of brand loyalty: brand loyalty as a behavior and brand loyalty as an attitude. That is, marketers define brand loyalty in terms of what brands people buy and how they feel about brands.

## Behavioral Brand Loyalty

In behavioral terms, brand loyalty is simply a customer's consistent repurchase of a brand. Every time a customer repurchases a product (shampoo, cologne, wine, jeans, shoes, frozen pizza, motor oil, automotive tools, computers, mail delivery service, cable company, plumbing service, or car insurance), if the customer buys the same brand of that product, we can consider that customer a brand-loyal customer for that product category. This consistent repurchase of the same brand is called behavioral brand loyalty.

Completely consistent repurchase of the same brand would show perfect behavioral brand loyalty, but in practice even brand-loyal customers may deviate from their regular brand by occasionally buying an alternative brand. To allow for imperfect consistency, marketers have measured behavioral brand loyalty in several ways: proportion of purchase, sequence of purchase, and probability of purchase.

### Proportion of Purchase

Marketers sometimes measure loyalty as a percentage: the number of times the most frequently purchased brand is purchased divided by the total purchases. Thus, if the most frequently purchased brand is purchased 7 out of 10 times, then brand loyalty is 70 percent.

### Sequence of Purchase

Another measure is based on the consistency with which the consumer switches between brands. Consider the following sequences between two brands, A and B: AAABAAAABBB and ABABABABABA. Both are patterns of divided loyalty between the two brands, with 60 percent loyalty toward brand A; however, the first pattern shows more consistent sequence than the second pattern. Accordingly, the customer exhibiting the first pattern would be deemed to be more brand loyal than the customer exhibiting the second pattern.

Jacob Jacoby, marketing professor at New York University, designed a more elaborate measure of loyalty using panel data, where he looked at both the sequence and frequency of purchases as a measure of loyalty. For example, Jacoby defined undivided loyalty as six purchases of the same brand in a row. However, if the consumer made six purchases that switched back and forth between two brand names, then the consumer had divided loyalty. If the consumer made three purchases and switched to something else, the consumer had what Jacoby called unstable loyalty. He referred to any other pattern as nonloyalty.

## Probability of Purchase

Marketers also may combine proportion and sequence measures to compute the probability of purchase based on the customer's long-term purchase history. First, the marketer computes a proportion of purchase for the long-term history. Then, at any point in time, the proportion is adjusted to reflect the most recent purchase. Every time the customer purchases a specific brand, the purchase increases the statistical probability of repurchasing that brand on the next occasion.

## Attitudinal Brand Loyalty

The problem with behavioral brand loyalty is that it simply shows that customers repurchase the same brand, not whether they actually like the brand more than other brands. A customer could buy the same brand simply out of habit or convenience, without thinking much about it. This kind of loyalty cannot be stable; if a competing brand offers a price deal, the customer would readily buy the other brand. On the flip side, on a particular occasion, if we notice a customer buying a brand different from his or her regular brand, we would interpret it as a lack of brand loyalty. However, the customer may, in fact, have been forced to switch brands, for example, due to a stockout of his or her regular brand.

For these reasons, marketing scholars have argued that in measuring brand loyalty, we should assess customers' attitude toward the brand. Only if the customer attitude for a brand is more favorable than for the competing brands should that customer be considered brand loyal to that brand. This way of looking at brand loyalty—that is, a greater liking for the brand—can be termed attitudinal brand loyalty. This can be measured by asking customers to rank various brands in terms of how much they like a brand or which brand they prefer the most.

## Brand Loyalty as Attitude-Based Behavior

Soon, marketing scholars who had earlier proposed behavioral measures of loyalty began to view loyalty jointly in behavioral and attitudinal terms. Jacoby himself proposed a new definition of brand loyalty: Brand loyalty is the biased (i.e., nonrandom) behavioral response (i.e., purchase), expressed over time by some decision-making unit, with respect to one or more alternative brands out of a set of such brands, and is a function of psychological (decision-making, evaluative) processes.[3] George S. Day, currently a professor at the Wharton School, defined brand loyalty as consisting of repeated purchases prompted by a strong internal disposition. The phrase *internal disposition* refers to a favorable attitude. Thus, true loyalty incorporates both a behavior and an attitude.[4] Note that here we employ the term *attitude* to refer to the overall liking and predisposition rather than the three-component view discussed in Chapter 6.

Based on this definition, some measures of brand loyalty are shown in Table 11.1. In that table, the first two statements capture attitudinal bias toward the brand, the next two statements reflect consistent behavior, and the last statement taps commitment. Marketing scholar Susan Fournier refers to a construct similar in spirit to brand loyalty—"*brand relationship quality*." It can be defined as "relationship oriented view of customer-brand interactions which are positively held, voluntarily engaged, long-term, and affectively intense (in short, brand-loyal relations) in nature." The "brand relationship quality" construct has six facets:

1. *Love/Passion*—Strong affective ties with the brand.
2. *Self-Connection*—Degree to which the brand delivers on important identity concerns, tasks, or themes expressing a significant aspect of the self.

| Illustrative Measures of Brand Loyalty | TABLE 11.1 |
|---|---|

These statements may be rated on a five-point scale (from 1 – Strongly Disagree to 5 – Strongly Agree); stronger agreement shows higher loyalty.

1. I like this brand very much.
2. In this product category, I have a favorite brand.
3. When buying _____, I always buy my favorite brand no matter what.
4. In the past, almost all of my purchases of _____ have been this brand.
5. If my favorite brand of _____ is not available in the store, I would go to another store rather than buy a substitute brand.

3. *Commitment*—High commitment in terms of an intention to behave in a manner supportive of the relationship longevity.
4. *Interdependence*—High degree of interdependence between brand and consumer involving frequent brand interactions (using a brand many times in the day), increased scope and diversity of brand-related activities (e.g., purchasing extensions of the brand), and heightened intensity of individual interaction events (e.g., considering the use of the brand to be an occasion in itself).
5. *Intimacy*—Brand relationship memory of personal associations and experiences and the intimacy that comes from these elaborate meanings.
6. *Brand Partner Quality*—Consumers' evaluation of the brand's performance in the partnership role. (As discussed by Fournier, 1998—pages 363–365.)[5]

# A Model of Brand Loyalty

What makes a customer brand-loyal? Several factors induce brand loyalty; others work against it. The degree of brand loyalty is the net outcome of these positive and negative factors (see Figure 11.2).

## Contributors to Brand Loyalty

As shown in Figure 11.2, several factors contribute to brand loyalty. The three major contributors are the perceived brand-performance fit, social and emotional identification with the brand, and habit combined with a long history of using the brand.

Thus, favorable brand attitude and brand loyalty result primarily from the satisfaction of user values, namely, (1) performance and (2) social and emotional identification. Some insights on customer satisfaction and loyalty to brands in several international markets is presented in the appendix.

### Perceived Brand-Performance Fit

Basically, customers like brands that meet their needs and wants well. If they have a positive usage experience, customers want to seek that reward again.

Brands differ not only in the quality of their performance (e.g., how well a shampoo cleans hair or the reliability of a network communication system) but also on specific performance dimensions (e.g., shampoo that gives hair body versus one that eliminates dandruff; or a network's data capacity, transmission speed, and portability). Furthermore, customers have different needs for specific performance features (e.g., shampoo for oily,

## FIGURE 11.2     A Model of Customers' Brand Loyalty

dry, or thick or thin hair; speed versus data volume in a network). Consequently, brand loyalty depends not merely on whether a brand does what it is intended to do but also on the degree of fit between the customer's specific performance requirements and the brand's performance capability.

Brands targeted at specific customer segments are likely to fit better than those mass-marketed to the public at large. That is why customer loyalty is generally higher in niche markets compared with mass markets.

Another measure of a brand's performance is its overall quality (e.g., workmanship, durability, reliability). Perceived brand quality is a very important factor in a person's preference and loyal patronage of the brand. Motorola, AT&T, Xerox, Mobil, and Marriott are examples of brands well known for their quality. Once customers experience the quality of these brands, they become loyal users. For an example of how customers measure quality in healthcare services, see the Window on Research box.

### Social and Emotional Identification With the Brand

The second category of user values is social and emotional identification with the brand. Brands come to acquire certain social images through marketing communications and/or by real-world observations of who is buying what brands. Such associations are particularly inevitable and, indeed, quite strong for conspicuous products such as clothing, cars, office furniture, and places of leisure and recreation. Brands that reflect social self-concept—the kind of person you like to be seen as—win over the user-customer's loyalty.

Emotional identification with the brand is related. User-customers enjoy some brands so much that psychologically they begin to see those brands as part of themselves. They identify themselves with the brands. The classic case of old Coke's brief withdrawal from the marketplace resulted in a groundswell of public protests from the brand's loyal fans who believed that the brand's absence had created a void in their personal lives! Brand communities on the Web also help foster social and emotional identification with the brand. For example, Heineken (**http://www.heineken.com**) allows individuals to establish their own virtual bars where they can chat with visitors and friends as a bartender,

# WINDOW ON RESEARCH

## In Healthcare Services, Caring Matters More Than Cure

Recently, we surveyed a national consumers panel in the United States to assess their commitment to their health-care providers—specifically, three categories of health-care professionals (physicians, dentists, and pharmacists) and three health-care institutions (public hospitals, private hospitals, and hospitals with religious affiliations). In the survey, we asked consumers, "Would you switch providers to get better products and services?"

Based on this question, we computed the percentage of respondents who said that they would switch. Potential switching rates ranged from 18 to 24 percent for health-care professionals, with dentists receiving the lowest switching rate of 18 percent. Among the hospitals, the switching rate was higher for public (34 percent) than for private (30.2 percent) and religious (28.3 percent) hospitals.

Consumers also answered two questions relating to their perceptions of quality: (1) the rating of the quality of service these professionals and institutions provided, and (2) the rating of the way they provided the service, each rated on a 0-to-10 scale where 10 meant excellent. We termed these ratings the quality of cure and the quality of caring, respectively.

What did we find? First, potential switching rates were strongly correlated inversely with the perceived quality for all six services. For example, among those who rated the quality of physician service as low, 84.8 percent were willing to switch physicians. As quality levels rose, this percentage fell, dropping to only 3.6 percent for physicians. The response patterns for the other five services were similar.

To identify what mattered more, the cure quality or the caring quality, we divided the entire sample into four groups, based on whether their rating of each measure was high or low. As Figure 11.3 shows, for each health-care provider, when both dimensions of quality were scored low, the switching propensity was high. And, not surprisingly, the switching propensity was much lower when both measures of quality were scored high. But what happens if both measures of quality are adequate, and only one is then improved? Which measure of quality will have the larger impact? According to our results, improving the caring dimension did more to reduce the propensity to switch than did improving the cure dimension.

These results imply important lessons for health-care professionals and marketers. To satisfy and retain clients, the service quality has to be in the top two boxes (i.e., 9 or 10 on a 0-to-10 scale). This is where the loyalty rates of 80 percent or higher are seen. Furthermore, although quality of cure and caring both matter, quality of caring pays off immensely in winning customer loyalty.

**Source:** Adapted from Jagdish N. Sheth and Banwari Mittal, "The Health of the Health–Care Industry: A Report Card from American Consumers," *Marketing Healthcare Services*, Winter 1997, pp. 29–35.

and Nescafé (**http://connect.nescafe.com**) has its own virtual café. By creating online communities on the Web relating to their brands, companies are forging stronger relationships with their customers.

| FIGURE 11.3 | The Role of Cure Quality versus Caring Quality in Retaining Customers |
|---|---|

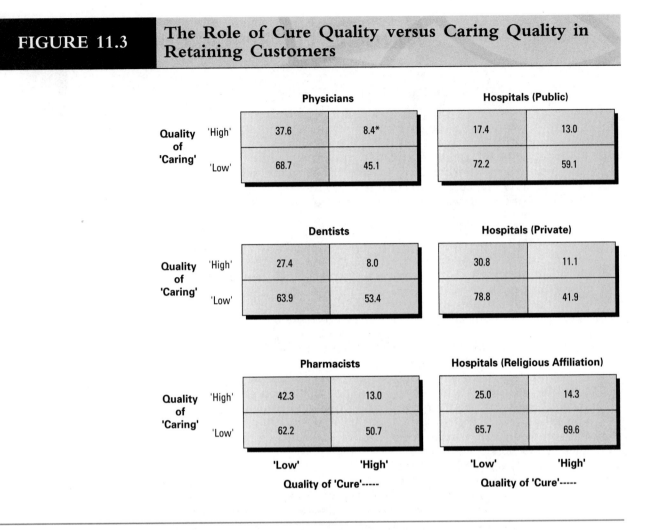

*For physicians, read: Of those who rated both the cure and caring quality high (i.e., 0.7), 8.4 percent showed willingness to switch.

**Source:** Jagdish N. Sheth and Banwari Mittal, "The Health of the Health Care Industry: A Report Card from American Consumers," *Marketing Healthcare Services*, Winter 1997, pp. 29–35.

## Habit and History

Finally, brand loyalty arises from habit and a long history of brand usage. Customers acquire some of their preferences simply by repeated use. This can happen for three reasons. First, we become familiar with the brand, and we feel comfortable with it. As in the case of services, we like to stick to the same doctor, the same accounting firm, the same restaurant, and even the same hair salon.

We also develop a taste for the brand by conditioning. For example, initially we may not like Mexican or Chinese food, but upon repeated consumption, we may learn not only to like it but, in fact, to crave it. Likewise, for certain brands of wine, certain food items, certain perfumes and colognes, certain music styles, or even certain artists. This acquired taste is the reason why many brands try to catch user-customers young. If an individual uses a brand while growing up, he or she is likely to remain loyal to it lifelong, such as to Colgate toothpaste or Life cereal.

Finally, if customers saw a brand being used in their parental home as they were growing up, they are likely to view this long history of use by parents as testimony to the brand's goodness. Intergenerational influence by family members, a topic we discussed in Chapter 9, is an important determinant of acquired brand loyalty.

## Detractors from Loyalty: Attraction of Alternatives

While performance fit, social and emotional identification, and history of use engender and contribute to brand loyalty, a set of factors detracts from it. This group of factors is called **attraction of alternatives**—that is, how attractive a customer finds alternative brands to be. Attraction of alternatives depends on factors relating to the market environment and others pertaining to the customer personally.

### Market Factors

The market influences attraction of alternatives through brand parity and competitive promotional activity. **Brand parity** refers to how similar and mutually substitutable the brands are. The more alike the brands in a product category are, the less motivation there is for a customer to stick with a particular brand. Of course, the parity matters, not in its absolute form, but rather as perceived by the customer, and customers may evaluate parity in terms of performance utility or their social and emotional identities. Credit cards are a good example of a product category with very similar and mutually substitutable brands.

    **Competitive promotional activity** refers to the special price deals available on competing brands. These price deals provide the motivation to switch from a favorite brand to a featured brand. Generally, this switching is limited to brands that the customer perceives to be comparable to his or her chosen brand. Of course, customer response to promotional activity depends on the customers' price sensitivity. Long-distance telephone services and beer are examples of categories that have constant promotional activity prompting customers to switch between brands.

### Customer Factors

The second group of detractors is customer factors: variety seeking, product involvement, price sensitivity, multi-brand loyalty, withdrawal from the product category, and change in needs. As noted in Chapter 4, some customers like to seek variety in their experience because they are bored with the same product or life experience; they may not be dissatisfied with the first brand's performance and other values. The more variety-seeking a customer is, the less brand loyal he or she is likely to be.

    Product involvement defines how central to a customer's life the customer considers a product to be. Many products, such as light bulbs, salt, sugar, and cotton swabs, are considered trivial while others like clothing, hairstyles, cars, and movies, are deemed to be central in our life. For these products, the customer would like to obtain the most value repeatedly, so he or she is likely to develop a favorite brand and, accordingly, show brand loyalty. For products of low importance and involvement, there is no reason to favor a brand, so brand loyalty will be low. Marketing professors Sharon Beatty and Lynn Kahle have shown in their study that customer involvement in a product is a direct determinant of brand commitment (i.e., brand loyalty).[6]

    Customers also differ in their price sensitivity. Some customers check the prices even on small items and notice even small price differences. A number of marketing studies have found consumers' price sensitivity to be negatively related to brand loyalty and positively related to coupon use.[7] Of course, not all consumers are equally price sensitive. Accordingly, they differ in their brand-loyalty behavior and in their response to competitor's promotional activities. For more on the link between price sensitivity and customer loyalty, see the Window on Practice box.

# WINDOW ON PRACTICE

## Customer Segments by Loyalty

A. C. Nielsen Company recently did a study of British supermarket shoppers and, based on their attitude toward price and promotions, identified the following five groups of customers:

1. *Branded EDLP Seekers (19 percent)*—Strapped for cash due to restricted income, they shop around to get the best price on their favorite brands, generally seeking everyday low prices (EDLP) rather than promotions that require them to alter their buying patterns (e.g., bulk buying). Thus, they are low on store loyalty but high on brand loyalty.
2. *Low-Price Fixture Ferrets (23 percent)*—These are young families with financial resources strained due to growing expenses (e.g., mortgage). Very budget-conscious, they use coupons and seek price deals (but dislike bulk buys). They respond well to store-loyalty schemes and are store loyal, tend to switch brands, and spend a lot on store brands.
3. *Promotion Junkies (18.4 percent)*—These customers will do anything to get the lowest shopping bill. They switch back and forth between national and store brands and have loyalty to neither stores nor brands. They experience a thrill in finding a bargain and pride in telling others where the bargains are. Nielsen describes them as a peril to retailer and manufacturer alike, as there is no long-term gain from them.
4. *Stockpilers (21 percent)*—These shoppers are affluent and are unconcerned about the size of their bill. Their store selection is driven by location, product assortment, and product quality rather than by price or promotions. They tend not to switch brands due to promotions; however, they will take advantage of promotions on their favorite brands, happily buying in bulk to stockpile and save money. Nielsen describes them as a retailer and manufacturer Nirvana due to their loyalty to both brands and stores.
5. *Promotionally Oblivious (18.3 percent)*—This group is basically driven by habit, settled on brands and stores, and not interested in exploring better deals. Promotions and special deals just pass them by, and while they might occasionally indulge in soft deals such as a free item or coupons, they dislike aggressive promotions and deals. They are not a source of growth for manufacturers or stores, but they are reliable and, as Nielsen puts it, the bedrock of their franchises.

**Source:** Adapted from Rachel Miller, "Does Everyone Have a Price? Consumer Types and Their Attitudes to Promotion," *Marketing*, April 24, 1997, p. 30. Additional information is available at: http://www.sainsburys.co.uk, http://www.safeway.co.uk.

Finally, the customer may purchase more than one brand in the same category regularly and, thus, not be completely loyal to either. The customer may also withdraw from a category—stop smoking, for instance—and, thus, his or her loyalty to a brand of cigarettes may cease. Also, as the customer moves from one stage of the life cycle to another, his or her needs may change and loyalty to brands may also change.

# Brand Equity

A few years ago, when Marriott Hotels built a new chain of mid-priced inns, they tested two alternative names for the property: Fairfield Inn and Fairfield Inn by Marriott. Survey respondents who saw the property under the second name estimated a reasonable price that was 35 percent more than that estimated by the other group of respondents, who were shown the same property but under the first name. This power of the brand name is referred to as brand equity.

## Two Views of Brand Equity

Brand equity can be considered from two points of view: investors' and customers'. David Aaker, a marketing professor at the University of California at Berkley and a leading expert on brand equity, offers a definition that encompasses both points of view. According to Aaker, brand equity is a set of brand assets and liabilities linked to a brand, its name, and symbol, that add to or subtract from the value provided by a product or service to a firm and/or to that firm's customers.[8] Let us look at the value to the firm (or its stockholder investors) and the value to its customers separately.

From the investors' standpoint, brand equity is called **brand valuation** and is measured as the financial worth of a brand name. If we take a new soft drink, for example, and stick the brand name Coca-Cola on it, then over the new soft drink's lifetime how much additional earnings will the brand name Coca-Cola generate over and above the earnings from the same soft drink if sold as a no-name brand? This is brand valuation. Indeed, according to a recent study, the Coca-Cola brand name was valued at the top, at $35 billion. Among the other top 10 brands were Marlboro ($33 billion), Nescafé ($11 billion), Kodak ($10 billion), Microsoft ($9.8 billion), Budweiser ($9.7 billion), Kellogg's ($9.4 billion), Motorola ($9.3 billion), Gillette ($8.2 billion), and Bacardi ($7.2 billion).[9]

From the customers' point of view, brand equity is the value of that brand to the customer compared to other brands. More formally, **brand equity** may be defined as the enhancement in the perceived utility and desirability that a brand name confers on a product. It is the customer's perception of the overall superiority of a product carrying that brand name compared with other brands. Customer perceptions of a brand's superiority are based on the brand associations that the customer makes (for example, that Head & Shoulders shampoo is very effective in eliminating dandruff; that Xerox copiers will work reliably; that Tommy Hilfiger clothing is for very contemporary, self-confident young adults; or that Mercedes is the subtle statement of success). These associations are at the heart of brand equity, and these are the outcomes of a long history of brand communications and the image projected in these communications, as well as from personal usage experience.[10]

Brand equity reflects the greater confidence that customers place in the brand than they do in the competing brands. This confidence then translates into customer preference for the brand, brand loyalty, and even a willingness to pay a premium price for the brand. For example, a study by McKinsey & Company and Intelliquest Inc. found that consumers tend to buy brands with low brand equity, like Packard Bell, only at a price discount compared to such brands as Compaq or IBM. The resulting market share and profit potential translate into financial gains, so much so that the holding company's net worth is raised. For example, when Cadbury-Schweppes bought the Hires and Crush brands of soft drinks from Procter & Gamble, it paid a total price of $220 million; of this amount, 90 percent is said to be due to the brand equity itself.

## Brand Equity versus Brand Loyalty

The concepts of brand equity and brand loyalty are related but also distinct. Brand loyalty is a consistent repurchase of the brand accompanied by a favorable brand attitude. Brand equity itself does not include brand purchase, although customers who perceive a higher brand equity in a brand should obviously buy that brand. Rather, brand equity is a mental concept of a brand's superiority. Brand attitude, a component of brand loyalty, is also a mental concept, but because it is an attitude, by definition it is a general evaluation of the brand and predisposition to buy it. In comparison, brand equity is based more on specific brand associations and a consideration of the value those associations represent. Thus, the emphasis in studying brand equity is on the brand associations and value.

## Components of Brand Equity

What considerations underlie customer perceptions of brand equity? This question was answered recently in a study by marketing professors Walfried Lassar, Banwari Mittal, and Arun Sharma.[11] They identified five dimensions of brand equity:

1. *Performance*—a customer's judgment about a brand's fault-free and long-lasting physical operation and flawlessness in the product's physical construction.
2. *Social image*—the consumer's perception of the esteem in which the consumer's social or reference groups hold the brand.
3. *Value*—the brand's perceived utility relative to its costs, based on a comparison of what is received with what is given up.
4. *Trustworthiness*—the customer's trust the brand has won—trust that the brand will maintain its strengths, and that it will not compromise its quality or otherwise take advantage of its customers. An example of a trust-failure is the press story a few years ago about Sears automotive shops doing unneeded repairs on cars; this story detracted from Sears' brand equity.
5. *Identification*—the degree to which customers identify themselves with the brand or feel some attachment to it. In effect, consumers would say that it is their brand; it is the kind of brand they would be happy to be associated with. Often, identification occurs because the brand is associated with things, persons, ideas, or symbols we find engaging. In particular, celebrities and role models are often used to develop identification.

In many cases, brand identification springs from the social policy the brand's makers promote (e.g., diversity in hiring, environmental friendliness). Benetton has long employed shocking images of social issues (e.g., AIDS research, racial harmony); it hopes to generate bonds of identification among its core customers in whom such images strike an emotional chord. Identification suffers when the brand marketer adopts some policy that goes against the value system of its customers. Currently, the Denny's Restaurant chain has come under fire for discriminating against minority customers in some of its restaurants; while these are isolated incidents by independent restaurant franchisees, the costs in customer goodwill are substantial. Denny's stands to lose patronage not only from minority customers but also from other customers who abhor discriminatory practices.[12]

Marketers can measure the components of brand equity by seeking customer ratings of brands on these aspects. Table 11.2 shows a sample measurement scale. Brand equity will be highest when the brand scores well on all five components. Managers can identify which components are weak and can work to improve those aspects of the brand. Thus, measurement of these components helps managers to map their own brands vis-a-vis competitors, then take action to improve the deficient component.[13]

## Customer Loyalty

The concept of loyalty that marketers have developed for brands applies equally well to stores, service suppliers, and other vendors. To refer to all these targets of loyalty, we can use the general term *customer loyalty*. Thus, **customer loyalty** is a customer's commitment to a brand, store, or supplier based on a strong favorable attitude and manifested in con-

## Illustrative Measures of Components of Brand Equity    TABLE 11.2

State your opinion on the following statements by rating them 1 through 5, where 1 means strong disagreement and 5 means strong agreement:

**Performance**
P1  From this brand of television, I can expect superior performance.
P2  During use, this brand of television is highly unlikely to be defective.
P3  This brand of television is made so as to work trouble-free.
P4  This brand will work very well.

**Social image**
SI1  This brand of television fits my personality.
SI2  I would be proud to own a television of this brand.
SI3  This brand of television will be well regarded by my friends.
SI4  In its status and style, this brand matches my personality.

**Value**
V1  This brand is well priced.
V2  Considering what I would pay for this brand of television, I will get much more than my money's worth.
V3  I consider this brand of television to be a bargain because of the benefits I receive.

**Trustworthiness**
T1  I consider the company and people who stand behind these televisions to be very trustworthy.
T2  In regard to consumer interests, this company seems to be very caring.
T3  I believe that this company does not take advantage of consumers.

**Attachment**
A1  After watching this brand of television, I am very likely to grow fond of it.
A2  For this brand of television, I have positive personal feelings.
A3  With time, I will develop a warm feeling toward this brand of television.

**Source:** Walfried Lassar, Banwari Mittal, and Arun Sharma, "Measuring Customer-Based Brand Equity," *Journal of Consumer Marketing* 12, No. 4 (1995), pp. 11–19.

sistent repatronage. The Window on Research presents some insights on customer loyalty online.

This definition of loyalty includes both behavior and attitude. These two components define four possible situations, as shown in Figure 11.4 on page 404. When both attitude and behaviors are weak, no loyalty exists. Weak attitude means the customer does not have any liking or preference for the brand. Weak behavior means purchase of the brand is sporadic (i.e., the same brand is not purchased consistently). When both are strong (i.e., attitude is very favorable and the same brand is purchased consistently), strong loyalty exists. The remaining two cases are more interesting.

When behavior is high but attitude is low, the customer has spurious loyalty—loyalty that is incidental and not well founded. The customer buys the same brand again and again or shops at the same store regularly, but he or she feels no preferential attitude toward it. Thus, the choice of the brand or store is due to reasons of convenience or mere inertia since the customer perceives all brands to be more or less the same. In such a case, given more choice or a price deal on competitive brands, the consumer might switch. To move this customer into the loyalty quadrant, the marketer would have to strengthen the customer's perception of the brand's image.

# WINDOW ON RESEARCH

## How Important Is Customer Loyalty Online?

In a series of joint studies in online retailing by Bain & Company/Mainspring, it was found that customer loyalty, measured as repeat purchases and referrals, is the key to profitability for online businesses. The studies covered three categories—apparel, groceries, and electronics—with over 2,000 online customers. Customers were found to be profitable for online retailers only if the retailer could retain the customer for a minimum of 12 months, with at least four visits from the customer to the site in this 12 month time period. The study showed that the behavior of loyal online customers is very similar to that of loyal offline customers. Online customers who are loyal spend more, refer more people and also make purchases in more categories from the same retailer. For example, by the third year of their relationship with an online apparel retailer, repeat customers spent 67 percent more than they did in the first six months. Over three years, referrals from online grocery customers purchased an additional 75 percent of the original shopper's purchase value. Specific findings from the Bain & Company/Mainspring research include:

1. Online retailers lose money on one-time shoppers—online grocers can break even only if they retain a customer for 18 months.
2. Repeat purchasers spend more over time—customers spent 23 percent more in months 31–36 of their relationship than in the first six months at online grocers.
3. Referrals obtained through positive word-of-mouth is the best way for online retailers to get new customers—after the first purchase, an apparel shopper had referred three people to the site, and after 10 purchases, the shopper had referred at least seven people. For consumer electronics, the average customer had referred 13 people after 10 purchases.
4. Retailers need to treat customers as "assets," not "transactions"— Online retailers can expect loyalty from customers only if they make efforts to provide value and convenience to customers and earn their trust.
5. Finally, as in the offline world, it is extremely important for online retailers to measure customer satisfaction and retention parameters on a regular basis. This will help the online retailer segment customers according to their shopping habits, identify the factors that are important to each segment, and develop strategies that cater uniquely to each segment.

Reichheld and Schefter from Bain & Company state that "Price does not rule the web, trust does." When customers trust an online vendor, they are willing to share personal information in return for customized advertising, promotions, products, and services from the retailer. This, in turn, increases trust and strengthens loyalty. Having surveyed repurchase patterns at leading web sites, they found that the five primary determinants of loyalty are quality customer support, on-time delivery, compelling product presentations, convenient and reasonably priced shipping and handling, and clear and trustworthy privacy policies.

Researchers Venkatesh Shankar, Amy K. Smith, and Arvind Rangaswamy compare customer satisfaction and loyalty in online and offline environments. They focus on attitudinal loyalty since it signifies repurchase based on commitment and an internal predisposition to the brand/organization. With the travel industry as the context (lodging sector—data on customers who used online and offline mediums to make hotel reservations), they show that levels of customer satisfaction for a service chosen online is the same as when it is chosen online. However, loyalty to a service provider is higher when the service is chosen offline. They propose that characteristics of the online medium may be responsible for this difference in loyalty. As the customer considers fewer options from a smaller consideration set, through regular use of bookmarks, information on these options is more frequently reinforced than in the offline context. Online chat groups and communities can also create an "envelope" (as discussed earlier in this chapter) that restricts the influence of competitive brands. As the customer's online experience becomes more and more positive, some of this positive feeling rubs off to the online medium itself and this strengthens the medium's role in loyalty creation. It follows from the study that online service providers need to improve their service quality, offer a good online experience, and invest in loyalty building initiatives to keep customers loyal.

Several e-merchants are trying to lure new customers through online e-coupons (some examples of coupon web sites are Kwik coupons—**http://www.kwikkoupon.com**, E-coupons—**http://www.e-coupon.com**). An e-coupon reduces search costs for consumers in terms of sifting through newspapers and other print media. Since the customer goes through an active process of identifying and printing the e-coupon, it is also more likely that he or she will redeem this coupon, as against other coupons that are usually available to the customer. It has been found that e-coupons are most popular among grocery shoppers. Other categories that show a high redemption of e-coupons are toys, books, and music. The NPD Group found that 59 percent of grocery shoppers use online coupons, and nearly half as much redeem online coupons for books and health-related products. Yet, a survey of 1,200 online customers by Jupiter communications found that only 22 percent of online customers considered loyalty programs as an incentive to buy online. It follows that retailers cannot rely on coupons and points as the only form of online loyalty programs. The online retailer must reward customer loyalty with improved service such as priority service, personalized offers, and e-mail updates.

**Source:** Adapted from Michael Pastore "Customer Loyalty: Key To E-commerce Profitability," March 30, 2000, http://cyberatlas.internet.com/markets/retailing/article/0,,6061_331431,00.html. Frederick F. Reichheld and Phil Schefter, "E-Loyalty: Your Secret Weapon on the Web," *Harvard Business Review*, July–August 2000, pp. 105–113. Venkatesh Shankar, Amy K. Smith, and Arvind Rangaswamy, "Customer Satisfaction and Loyalty in Online and Offline Environments," eBRC Working paper, October 2000, http://www.ebrc.psu.edu/pubs.html; Darren Allen, "Earning Customer Loyalty," November 22, 2000, *eMarketer*, http://www.emarketer.com/etopics/articles/20001122_ loyalty.html; David R. Fortin, "Clipping Coupons in Cyberspace: A Proposed Model of Behavior for Deal-Prone Consumers," *Psychology & Marketing*, 17(6), June 2000, pp. 515–534.

## FIGURE 11.4 — Loyalty Needs Both Attitude and Behavior

Source: Adapted from Alan S. Dick and Kunal Basu, "Customer Loyalty: Toward an Integrated Conceptual Framework," *Journal of the Academy of Marketing Science*, 22 (2), 1994, p. 101.

Finally, in the quadrant with high attitude and low behavior, the customer has latent loyalty. He or she likes the brand but has been unable to buy it; perhaps the price is too high or the customer lacks access to the brand or the store. Here, the marketer needs to tap into this hidden potential market by lowering whatever barriers prevent customers from buying this desired brand.

Well-known researcher Richard Oliver has developed a framework (Figure 11.5) to specify four different levels of customer loyalty. The vertical dimension in the framework reflects the "degree of individual fortitude"—the degree to which the customer is able to resist offers/advances from competition, a result of the customer's own commitment to the brand. On the "individual fortitude" continuum, at the low end, the customer only has brand-related information, while at the high end, the customer builds a defensive shield against competition.

## FIGURE 11.5 — A Framework for Brand Loyalty

**COMMUNITY AND SOCIAL SUPPORT**

| INDIVIDUAL FORTITUDE | HIGH | LOW |
|---|---|---|
| HIGH | Immersed Self Identity | Determined Self-Isolation |
| LOW | Village Envelopment | Basic Product Superiority |

Source: Richard L. Oliver, "Whence Consumer Loyalty," *Journal of Marketing*, Vol. 63, Special Issue, 1999, pp. 33–44. Reprinted with permission of American Marketing Association.

The horizontal dimension refers to low and high phases of community and social support. At the low end, the community and social support is persuasive but passive in nature, while at the high end, it serves to proactively promote loyalty. Thus a 2 × 2 grid is formed across the two dimensions as shown in Figure 11.5. At high levels of individual fortitude and community and social support, customer loyalty is highest. Conversely at the low levels of both dimensions, customer loyalty is weakest since its stems only from product superiority. This is the traditional view of loyalty.

As the customer moves from low to high fortitude (and low social support), the customer becomes more committed to the brand and brand, repurchase is based on his or her own "determined self-isolation." In terms of relationships, this state is equivalent to "love for the brand." The low fortitude, high social support cell, is labeled "village envelopment," where the customer is nurtured and proactively encouraged to use selected brands without his or her own active commitment to the brand. Some examples of villages or communities are web site chat rooms, senior citizen organizations, card clubs, etc., where attention from group members makes the customer want to be a part of the community. The customer experiences a state of "immersed self-identity" at high levels of individual fortitude and social support—the highest form of loyalty in the framework. Here, the customer proactively seeks the social environment for the brand, since it not only supports the customer's self-concept, but also reinforces it through the social system. Some examples of this highest state of loyalty are found in religious institutions, fan clubs, alumni organizations, the Harley Davidson H.O.G (Harley Owners Group) club, where the customer associates with the product/service and affiliates with the social setting, since it is highly reinforcing and supportive of the same.[14]

# Customer Loyalty to Stores

The concept of store loyalty is analogous to that of brand loyalty. Following the definition of customer loyalty presented earlier, **store loyalty** is a customer's predominant patronage of a store, based on a favorable attitude. That is, the customer shops at the store more than at any other store for a type of merchandise and has a more favorable attitude toward that store. Like brand loyalty, store loyalty can be measured by customer agreement with pertinent statements, such as those shown in Table 11.3.

| Illustrative Measures of Store Loyalty | TABLE 11.3 |
| --- | --- |

These statements may be rated on a five-point scale (1 - Strongly Disagree to 5 - Strongly Agree); stronger agreement shows higher loyalty.

1. I like this store very much.
2. For this group of products, I have a favorite store.
3. When buying _____, I always shop this store first.
4. In the past 3 months, a majority of my shopping trips have been to this store.
5. I prefer to shop at this store even if another store advertises some deal.
6. I usually divide my shopping among two or three stores.

Note: Item 6 needs to be reverse-scored so that strong disagreement indicates store loyalty.

## A Model of Store Loyalty

Marketers want customers not only to visit their store but also to visit it again and again. They want to earn their customers' loyalty. Therefore, they want to know what makes a customer loyal to a store. Customers' store loyalty depends on two sets of factors—the what factor and the how factor. The what factor refers to what products and services the customer gets at the store—these are what he or she goes to the store for in the first place, and these are what he or she walks out with when leaving the store. The how factor refers to the process that is entailed in customers' acquisition of those products and services.

## The What Factor

What a customer goes into a store for includes some mix of merchandise quality, assortment, price value, and store brands.

**Merchandise Quality.** By merchandise quality, we mean the quality of the products or services the store carries and offers. Stores differ vastly on this element, with merchandise ranging from shoddy to medium to premium quality. The merchandise quality is generally controlled by the brand names the store decides to carry. The store could carry well-reputed, high-quality brands, or it could carry lower-quality brands. It is intuitively obvious that the better the merchandise quality of a store, the more likely the customers are to develop store loyalty toward that store.

**Assortment.** A store's assortment is the number of different items the store carries. This includes the number of diverse product categories (e.g., appliances versus food), product varieties (e.g., in the produce section, whether or not the store carries products like tropical fruits and exotic vegetables), and the number of brands for the same product categories (e.g., for photo films, Kodak, Fuji, and so on), and the size and color varieties.

Although assortment will influence a customer's patronage, customers do not necessarily want an unlimited, vast assortment that could create shopper confusion. Instead, they want the store to carry their preferred brand and a few other related major brands in order to be able to compare both initially when their brand preference is still fluid, and later from time to time when they want to compare leading brands. For example, a regular buyer of Kodak photo film may see an advertisement for Fuji film and may want to check it out in the store. If the regularly visited store did not carry Fuji film, this is likely to negatively affect the customer's perception of the store as an adequate store.

Within the preferred brand, customers also want availability of different sizes and colors. For example, customers would want to be able to buy, on different occasions, a Kodak film with 12, 24, or 36 exposures without having to visit another store.

In many product categories, such as in clothing, cosmetics, perfumes, jewelry, music CDs, and books, customers intrinsically desire variety. For these product categories, they value a large assortment of styles or content.

For services, too, the concept of assortment applies. Service providers who offer a bundle of related, rather than limited, services are likely to be preferred by customers. For example, in business services, an accounting firm that provides account audit services, cost-containment consulting, and tax advice is likely to be preferred over the one that offers audit services only.

Both in business and household customer markets, customers like to do **one-stop shopping**, buying all of their requirements of related products in one place or from one source. Stores like Meijer, Sam's Club, and Wal-Mart in the United States and Food Giant and ASDA in the United Kingdom attract customers by offering an assortment of product categories far greater than a typical supermarket (such as Kroger in the United States or Tesco or Sainsbury's in the United Kingdom) and yet at lower prices. For business products, OfficeMax and Staples offer one-stop shopping for such wide-ranging items as paper supplies, fax and phone machines, and furniture. For business services, Kinko's offers a complete range of document-preparation services.

**Price Value.** Customers seek low prices for the merchandise they buy. This is the appeal of all deep discounters, such as Costco (United States), Kwik Save (United Kingdom), Aldo (Netherlands), Dia/Dirsa (Spain), or Netto (Denmark).

However, customers do not always, or even often, seek low-price merchandise; rather, for the quality of merchandise they desire, they seek the lowest or near lowest price. In addition, customers do not always bother to ensure that the price they are getting is the lowest possible; they want to feel confident only that the price is comparably low, and that if there is a lower price elsewhere, it is negligibly lower. The important point to note is that customers seek a generally low price for a given quality of merchandise. Wal-Mart is a good example of offering customers a low price.

**Store Brands.** Yet another attraction for the customer is store brands, the brands that carry a store label and are available exclusively in that store chain. Store brands add to the assortment the store presents the customer for comparison. One of these comparisons is, of course, on price vis-a-vis the national brands. Since store brands are considerably lower in price, the availability of store brands becomes one avenue for customers to maximize their price value from the store. In addition, store brands could be unique either in value or in performance or features, available, by definition, only at the specific store chain. This exclusive availability is yet another source of customers' loyal patronage. (For more on the role of store brands, see the Window on Research box.)

## The How Factor

Store loyalty also depends on how favorable the shopping experience is in a particular store. This how factor includes ease of merchandise selection, in-store information and assistance, convenience, problem resolution, and personalization.

**Ease of Merchandise Selection.** A store's merchandise selection ease refers to how easily and effortlessly customers of the store select products. This depends on several features: layout of aisles and shelf displays, shelf tags, product information cards, and signage. Merchandise should be arranged for easy access and for easy interbrand comparisons. According to some reports, until recently, customers complained about the tall shelves in Toys R' Us stores; customers, especially short and elderly customers, found it difficult to reach the merchandise for inspection. Similarly, correct price and brand shelf tags should allow easy evaluation, and comparable size and quality brands (including store brands) should be placed side by side for easy comparison. Store signage should be visible from throughout the store to locate the aisles and shelf facings. Finally, items should not be out of stock.

These actions make it easy for the customer to make his or her product selection efficiently and effortlessly. This ease, in turn, positively influences a customer's decision to patronize the store regularly.

**In-Store Information and Assistance.** By in-store information and assistance, we mean the availability of credible information about the merchandise and salesperson assistance in shopping. Merchandise selection ease provides efficiency in the self-selection of items, and most stores in the Western world are organized for self-selection. But beyond self-selection, customers sometimes need information and assistance from salespersons (for example, to see a product demonstration). If customers find that salespersons are not easily available, or if they are not knowledgeable or fair and impartial in their advice, then it detracts from customers' buying efficiency or effectiveness. On the other hand, the availability of salespersons who are knowledgeable, credible, and trustworthy makes the store attractive for customers to patronize it.

**Convenience.** Customers also want convenience, or ease in getting to the store and getting out of it once the merchandise selection is completed. This translates into ease of reaching the store location, parking availability, and quick checkouts.

Location has always been a critical variable in a store's success. Generally, a supermarket attracts customers from up to a five-mile radius, and a department store or a mall from up to a 15-mile radius. The location, therefore, basically determines who will choose to shop there regularly. Convenient parking is also a consideration in store preference, particularly for older consumers.

Once a customer has completed his or her product selection, nothing is more important to the customer than to be able to check out and go home as soon as possible. Quick checkouts, therefore, become another important component of convenience. All else being equal, customers like to patronize stores that are convenient to access.

**Problem Resolution.** When they need problem resolution, or remedy for mistakes or oversights, customers want this service to be easy and hassle-free. The most typical

# WINDOW ON RESEARCH

## Determinants of Store Brand Acceptance

What leads customers to buy store brands? This important question was investigated in a study of supermarket shoppers by marketing professors Paul S. Richardson, Arun K. Jain, and Alan Dick. They surveyed a sample of 582 grocery shoppers about their acceptance and purchase of store brands in 28 product categories (e.g., bacon, soups, juices, frozen vegetables, paper towels, and laundry detergents). Their findings were the following:

- Among the demographic characteristics, family size and income were correlated with store (private) brand buying behavior, but education level and age were *not* related. Larger households were more likely to buy private brands, as were lower-income households.
- Among beliefs and psychological variables, shoppers' familiarity with store brands, perceived value for money, perceived quality differential between national and store brands, and perceived risk affected store-brand buying. Shoppers familiar with store brands and believing that store brands give you good value for the money were more likely to buy store brands, but if they perceived risk of poor quality (a perception that was aided by lack of familiarity), then they were less likely to buy store brands.
- The personal trait of intolerance for ambiguity (i.e., discomfort in uncertain situations) acted against private-brand acceptance.

Another recent study of 1,000 grocery shoppers in the United Kingdom, by professor Ogenyi Ejye Omar of the School of Retail Studies, The London Institute, has shed some light on this question.

Generally, national food brands were perceived as superior to store brands in terms of quality, packaging, consistency, and image, but were perceived as lower on good value for money.

The store-brand shopper had slightly less formal education, was young, likely to be a female between 18 and 24 years of age, had at least one or two children living at home, had a larger family, had lower socioeconomic status, lived mainly in rented accommodations, and tended to be thrifty and more adventurous.

The store-brand shopper shops frequently and longer, ostensibly striving for the best price and value for money. In contrast, national-brand shoppers prided themselves on shopping for food quality, good product packaging, and good product design and appearance.

**Sources:** Adapted from Paul S. Richardson, Arun K. Jain, and Alan Dick, "Household Store Brand Proneness: A Framework," *Journal of Retailing* 72, No. 2, 1996, pp. 159–85; Ogenyi Ejye Omar, "Grocery Purchase Behavior for National and Own-Label Brands," *Service Industries Journal* (January 1996), 16 No. 1, pp. 58–66. Additional information is available at http://www.luc.edu and at http://www.buffalo.edu.

problems are the need to return or exchange the merchandise. Stores that have a liberal return policy that allows customers to return unused merchandise within a reasonable time, or that will repair or replace the faulty merchandise within a reasonable time, even beyond the warranty period, are likely to earn customers' repeat patronage.

**Personalization.** By personalization, we mean positive employee behavior toward customers. Customers expect store employees to be pleasant and courteous in their interaction and eager to help customers during their shopping. Stores differ greatly on this dimension. Stores that hire employees with poor interpersonal skills and low aptitude for socialization with customers are likely to earn less loyalty from their customers.

# Store Choice

In the above section, we discussed the factors that contribute to store loyalty. But how do customers decide which grocery store to shop at? Do they shop there regularly or occasionally? Do they shop there exclusively, or is it just one of the several grocery stores that they shop at? Why do they shop there rather than at other stores? Are there other stores in the area? Are they less convenient? More expensive? Less friendly? Or what? And what about the clothing store, the hardware store, or the appliance store? Do they have a favorite store in each of these categories?

These questions are important to any store owner. Owners want to get you to shop at their stores, again and again in preference over other competing stores—become their loyal customers. Therefore, they need to understand customers' shopping behavior, how customers decide where to shop, as well as factors that influence customers' store loyalty.

## How Customers Shop

A typical customer generally has the option of three or four general merchandise stores to shop at; for supermarket items, the choice may even extend to ten stores. How does the customer choose the store to shop at? The number one factor in store choice is location; this was also the conclusion of a survey of about 10,000 supermarket shoppers conducted by *Consumer Reports*.

But location is a relative criterion, not an absolute one. That is, customers do not always go to the nearest store, even though they want to minimize the travel distance. Sometimes, they will go to a distant store if they get better quality or selection or price. Merchandise quality and price were the second and third criteria in the *Consumer Reports* study. In actuality, customers do not choose a store on the basis of a single factor, or they do not always value various factors in a specific priority order. Rather, a dynamic *interplay* of factors influences their choice.[15]

To understand this dynamic interplay, let us consider the supermarket-shopping behavior of a family we shall call the Brown family. The Browns live in a suburb of a U.S. metropolis, near two supermarkets—Kroger, two miles to the south, and Thriftway, one and a half miles to the north (both are big supermarket chains with stores in a number of U.S. cities). The nearest convenience stores are a Speedway gas station at a main-road crossing about half a mile to the northeast and an Ameristop at about the same distance but slightly off the main road.

The Browns rarely shop at the convenience store except for gas. Their most frequent gas station is Speedway, where they occasionally buy milk when they run out of it and it is not convenient to visit the supermarket. They never shop at Ameristop. They divide their main food shopping between Thriftway and Kroger, shopping more often at Kroger because it is on Mrs. Brown's way to work. Also, it offers a double-coupon feature. They shop Thriftway every week or so to take advantage of price specials. They visit Kroger about once a week for a major shopping trip when they buy the bulk of the weekly requirements, and once a week for a filler trip to buy only a few items. In some weeks, they split the major shopping between Kroger and Thriftway to take advantage of price deals at each store.

The Browns also shop for food at a few other stores. About one and one-half miles beyond Thriftway is a new store, Meijer, which is a *supercenter*, a store that sells food as well as apparel and hard goods (e.g., small appliances, electronics). Although it is farther, the Browns shop there once every two to three weeks; this would be their major shopping trip, and they typically spend substantially more than at Kroger. There is also a Sam's Club (about five miles west) and Bigg's, a warehouse store about eight miles west, but the Browns never shop at either. Even though the Browns visit the nearby mall (about a half-mile from the Bigg's store), they never consider food shopping and mall shopping as a single trip. Finally, about ten miles to the northeast, there is Jungle Jim, a store that features exotic vegetables and international food items. The Browns shop there about every two months because they enjoy the merchandise variety. They consider the trip an excursion, a combination of purchasing and the excitement of browsing through the exotic products.

## The Interplay of Decision Criteria

Although no two families are alike in their food shopping (and shopping for other products), the Brown family illustrates the sort of interplay of factors that influences a customer's store choice:

- Distance is an important consideration, but it is not always measured from home or in kilometers/miles; rather, it is measured by convenience, such as whether it is on the way to work and on or off the main road or main commuting route. Moreover, small differences in distances are ignored so that a slightly farther store may be chosen on occasion even without any other advantage. In fact, Weber's Law and the related concept of just noticeable difference (JND), which we discussed in Chapter 4 in respect to customers' price perceptions, apply to store distances as well: some stores that are only slightly farther than the nearest may not even be perceived as being farther (particularly if they are not on the same linear path). Moreover, even among the distance differences that are perceived, some small differences might be considered negligible as trade-offs with other store features.
- If two or more stores are equally convenient from a distance standpoint, then other factors (quality, assortment, and price) influence the store choice. If these other factors are significantly inferior at the nearest store, then a distant, less convenient store is likely to be chosen for regular shopping. The most convenient store may continue to be chosen, however, for filler trips.
- A typical customer does not limit food shopping to just one store. Rather, customers have a repertoire of stores, with one store shopped most frequently and regularly. For example, an average American household makes an average of 2.2 visits per week to a supermarket. However, for a majority of households (more than 80 percent), only one visit is made to their most preferred supermarket. Thus, a majority of American households rely on more than one food store for their food needs.[16]
- If there are stores that specialize in quality, assortment, or price deals, these stores are likely to be included in the repertoire of stores. They will be visited despite the locational disadvantage, but on a special occasion rather than a regular basis.

The most important point is that customers have a repertoire (i.e., assortment) of stores. This concept is analogous to the consideration set, or preference set, discussed in Chapter 8. Customers have consideration sets and preference sets not only for brands but also for stores. They limit their shopping to these stores. The choice of a specific store from the repertoire is based on the exigencies of the specific situation. For example, is this an emergency, a major shopping trip, or a filler trip? Is one of the stores in the repertoire running a price special?

As shown in the flow chart of the decision process in Figure 11.6, a store decision begins, but often does not end, with distance considerations. (The flow chart is an attempt to assemble a reasonable description of the process as inferred from a number of unrelated studies, existing marketing literature, and the authors' own customer observations and intuitive reflections.[17] To understand the store choice process for a particular clientele, marketers and researchers must conduct specific studies in their trading area).

## A Flow Chart of Customers' Store Choice Decision Process

FIGURE 11.6

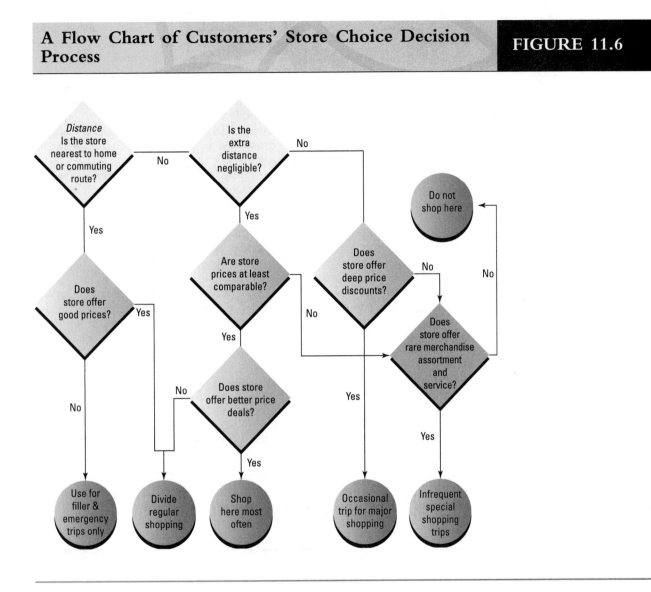

Yet another way of looking at the store choice decision is in terms of the total costs of shopping, both fixed and variable. A shopper is likely to visit the store with the lowest total shopping costs. The fixed costs for the customer are travel distance, shopper's inherent preference for a store, and historic store loyalty, and the variable cost is dependent on the customer's shopping list—the products and the respective quantities to be purchased. Researchers Bell, Ho, and Tang suggest that the concept of "basket-size threshold" can be used to measure the relative competitiveness of a given pair of stores. Depending on the level of fixed and variable costs associated with a store, a threshold level for the customer's basket size can be determined, which can help him or her decide which store is best to shop. For large basket sizes, stores with high fixed costs and low variable costs would be preferrable since the fixed costs are distributed among large number of items.[18]

### Choices Based on Nonlocational Criteria

The previous description mainly contrasts location and nonlocation as choice criteria. How do customers choose among the other factors—namely, quality, assortment, and price? The answer is twofold.

First, as we saw in the case of the Brown family, if the store offers a substantial advantage on any one of these factors, it may be included in the repertoire. If different stores offer one each of these advantages, they all may be included in the repertoire although for occasional shopping only.

Second, if all the stores offering price or quality or assortment were conveniently located, convenient enough for the customer to make each a regularly shopped store, customers might select the store with the advantage they value the most. While some customers may patronize each type of these stores to regularly take advantage of each of these three factors, most customers would value one advantage more than others and choose the store with that advantage as their regular store.

This last point is important in understanding how stores differentiate themselves. They differentiate themselves first on price, assortment, or merchandise quality. These serve as the basis of the first tier of store classification: Supermarkets tend to offer medium levels of merchandise and assortment at moderate prices, at levels considered acceptable by the mass market. Some supermarkets, such as Food Lion and supercenters such as Meijer, feature low prices more than do other supermarkets. Warehouse stores offer limited selection but very attractive prices. Specialty stores, such as Jungle Jim or H-E-B Marketplace in San Antonio, Texas, focus on merchandise selection and assortment.

Some supermarkets, such as Harris Teeter, make fresh produce their stores' special focus. Such differentiation strategies work by a process of customer self-selection—customers self-select themselves to be the customers of the store that offers the advantage they seek.[19]

Three other factors also play a role: (1) service—the courtesy and helpfulness of store personnel; (2) in-store display—the ease of finding the merchandise; and (3) atmospherics—the pleasantness of the ambiance (e.g., the lighting, the appearance, the music, and in general, the cheeriness or the gloominess of the store). These factors are generally used, however, as second-tier factors; that is, they help in choosing the store from among those that offer similar price, assortment, and quality. When these first-tier factors are equalized, customers are likely then to choose a store that offers one or all three of the second-tier advantages.

# Planned, Unplanned, and Impulse Buying

Once a customer selects and visits a store, the marketer's next concerns are whether he or she buys something and what he or she buys.

All products that customers buy in the store can be classified as planned or unplanned purchases. Planned purchases are those that the customer had planned to buy before entering the store. Unplanned purchases are those the customer did not intend to buy before entering the store. The customer need not have specifically decided not to buy those products; the customer may have simply not thought about those products.

Unplanned purchases can be of three types:

1. Restocking unplanned purchases are items the shopper had not thought about buying at the time but has been using regularly. He or she buys it due to an in-store display or special deal, knowing that the item will be needed in the future.

2. Evaluated new unplanned purchases are those the customer needs but which had not been recognized prior to this purchase occasion. These may either be products not already in use by the customer (e.g., a cellular phone) or products in use already and not in need of a replacement yet. The customer simply decides to buy additional units to expand the collection (e.g., wardrobe, one more TV set in the house) or to get extra features in newer units (high-definition television).

3. **Impulse purchases** are the extreme kind of unplanned purchases—items bought spontaneously and completely unpremeditated. The customer buys in response to feeling a sudden urge to buy something. These purchases are made quickly and without an evaluation of need.[20]

The best way to study planned buying is to observe the use of shopping lists. According to a recent Gallup study, about 55 percent of supermarket shoppers use a shopping list. However, the use of shopping lists does not rule out unplanned buying. One reason is that the use of unplanned buying depends on how exactly an item is written down on the shopping list. A person may write only the general item type (e.g., entree), a specific product category (frozen pasta), or a specific brand (Sara Lee). Thus, there can be degrees of unplanned buying. Second, even when the product or brand is specified, customers may deviate from the shopping list, buying a brand or product different from the one on the shopping list. Finally, customers may buy additional items not on the shopping list. For example, the same Gallup study found that an average shopping list user had planned to buy 10.5 items, on the average, but ended up buying 16.

Unplanned purchases can occur for several reasons. The planned item may be out of stock and may be substituted by another item. Or a substitute item may be on sale. In addition, the store may be featuring an item not on the list, and the customer may realize he or she had forgotten to write it down, or may judge it as being needed in the future. Thus, a good price deal might induce customers to **forward buy** an item for future consumption.

Customers may make mental rather than physical paper lists; a researcher might count these customers as list nonusers making nonplanned purchases, whereas, in fact, they are merely buying items on their mental lists. Still, the use of a shopping list does signify greater use of planned compared to unplanned purchases. A study in New Zealand found that grocery shoppers who had come to the store with a shopping list bought seven fewer items and spent $13.13 less than other shoppers who did not bring a list.[21]

## In-Store Factors

Whether the purchase is planned or not, several in-store factors influence exactly what is bought or not bought. In-store factors refer to those characteristics of the store, customer, or situation that surround the customer's decision process inside the store. These include knowledge of the store, time pressure, purchase companion, special store promotions, atmospherics, and customer mood.

Generally, customers shop at stores about which they are knowledgeable in terms of merchandise display and store procedures. Customers like to shop at stores where they feel in control; familiarity with the store gives them a feeling of control. This encourages **exploratory shopping**, just browsing around after collecting the planned items in contrast with unfamiliar stores where they would feel disoriented about where items are.

Time pressure is the second in-store factor. Customers hassled with time pressure tend to limit their purchases to preplanned items. The effect is compounded if the customer is under time pressure and is shopping in a new store where prior store knowledge is absent.[22]

Purchase companions also influence the purchases. More than half of customers shop with a companion.[23] Often children accompany parents on shopping trips, and they make new requests inside the store, many of which parents will accede to. Other companions, such as a friend, limit exploratory shopping and, consequently, unplanned purchasing if they themselves are under time pressure.

Special store promotions play a significant role in inducing unplanned purchases. Some customers find special promotions simply irresistible and take advantage of the special deal either for forward buying or for making an impulse purchase of a new item.

**Atmospherics**, the physical setting of the store, can make a store a pleasure to linger in or a drag that one wants to be done with quickly. Atmospherics include colors, lighting, cleanliness, even fragrances or smell, and, of course, the background music. One study showed that when the background music tempo was slow, customers spent more time in the store and, on an average, spent more money.[24]

A customer's pleasant mood induces some exploratory shopping and a desire to reward oneself by buying unplanned items. Unpleasant moods limit customer attention to the task at hand, namely buying the planned items. Customers bring moods into the store, but moods are also created or altered by store atmospherics.[25]

## Nonfood Store Shopping

While many factors described above apply to nonfood shopping as well, the selection process for a nonfood store is somewhat different because of the infrequent nature of purchase. While a customer shops in a food store almost weekly or more often, the shopping for nonfood items may be once every few months (clothing), once a year, or even less often (e.g., appliances).

Since nonfood shopping is generally more high-involvement shopping and consumers take interest in it, distance and convenience take a back seat, up to a limit. Suppose you wanted to buy some furniture (say a sofa). You are likely to be willing to drive 5 to 10 miles, and even 20 miles if you thought the store might offer something of great value. Significant factors in deciding on the store are expected merchandise and price levels, customer service, store image, and special advertised promotions.

By merchandise (quality and assortment) and price levels and by customer service, nonfood stores differentiate themselves (just as food stores do) from their competitors, and customers decide which stores meet their level of needs. For example, among furniture stores, some sell country-style furniture, some colonial style, and some contemporary American or contemporary European; customers would readily eliminate some stores on that basis. Regarding price levels, some stores are priced very upscale, and they would intimidate customers seeking economy-priced furniture. On the other hand, low-priced furniture stores would not interest upscale clientele.

**Store image**, the sum total of perceptions customers have about the store, is determined by these merchandise, service, and price factors; it is also determined by atmospherics, advertising, and store personnel. Store image determines the kind of clientele a store will attract, but the clientele also feed back into store image.

Finally, the sale promotions of the day exert a major influence in the store's inclusion in the customer's list of stores to shop.

## Shopping Motives

So far we have described shopping purely as a purchasing activity. That is, we shop so we can buy what we want; if we did not want to buy anything, we would not go shopping. But from personal experience, we know that is not always true. We often go shopping even when we don't really have anything particular in mind to buy. In common parlance, this activity is called window shopping. A more accurate term would be **store visiting**— the practice of visiting various stores and shopping centers without necessarily having plans to buy anything.

If customers don't necessarily have any plans to buy, why would they visit the stores? What, in other words, are customers' **shopping motives** or reasons to visit the stores? When not expressly shopping to buy something, customers may be motivated to visit stores for one or more of the following reasons:[26]

- *Recreation*—Visiting stores can be fun. Many stores are set up to provide a sensory experience. The colorful display of clothing in specialty clothing stores such as Benneton, the rock video blasting in Merry Go Round, the strong aromas in the coffee store, and even the hustle and bustle of people walking, chatting, browsing all of these can be very stimulating for the senses. Many customers, therefore, visit stores as a means of recreation when they have nothing better to do at home.[27]
- *Socialization*—Visiting stores also offers opportunity for social interaction with other people, both acquaintances and strangers, and with store personnel them-

selves. Some stores even become the hangouts for singles who want to meet others with similar tastes, such as customers with literary interests at Barnes and Nobles bookstore.

- *Seeking Status*—Store employees often attend to customers with great politeness and courtesy, address them with terms of respect, and respond to their information and assistance needs, thus providing a good source of getting some sense of social status.
- *Self-gratification*—In contrast to all other motives, this one does require some actual purchasing. But the goal of purchasing is not as much the utility of the product or service purchased, but rather the sense of rewarding oneself by spending money. This can occur both when a person is feeling depressed, or alternatively, when the person feels he or she deserves a reward.
- *Information*—Visiting stores is a good source of information about what is new in the market and what is fashionable. Some customers have a strong interest in particular product categories, and they like to stay well informed about these. Market mavens, described in Chapter 5, often visit stores to satisfy this motive.

Shopping motives can also be classified as utilitarian and hedonic in nature. As discussed above, the customer experiences utilitarian shopping value when he or she gets the desired product on a shopping trip with the least effort, while hedonic value is obtained from fun and pleasure associated with the buying process. In a comparison of overall shopping value (utilitarian and hedonic) of a typical American and Russian shopping experience, researchers Griffin, Babin, and Modianos found that American shoppers report higher levels of utilitarian shopping value compared to Russian shoppers. However, Russian and American shoppers report comparable levels of hedonic value. They found that Russian shoppers report comparable levels of hedonic value even in the face of poor service and unpleasant shopping experiences because they make relative judgements based on their own shopping experiences and expectations, and not based on absolute information about the shopping experiences in external environments like the U.S.[28]

# One-Stop Shopping

Suppliers that offer a variety of products or services may want their customers to engage in one-stop shopping (OSS), the practice of acquiring all related products from one supplier. This supplier may be a manufacturer, a service company, or a reseller. The phrase "related products" refers obviously to an arbitrary set of products. To some customers, it may mean all products of a particular type (e.g., all appliances or all clothing); to others, these product categories may be more broad (e.g., all household durable goods). Customers may also construe related products to mean products pertaining to a category of needs: for example, all of one's health-care needs or all of the financial products, such as checking account, savings account, credit card, debit card, mortgage, and investments. Often, the customer's view of what are related products is shaped by an observed instance of one-stop availability. For example, until banking became available inside supermarkets, customers may not have thought of banking services as belonging to the basket of supermarket goods.

However one delineates related products to be included in one-stop shopping, the issue is important for marketers. Currently, telecommunications companies are facing OSS decisions that can mean grand success or utter failure for them. The U.S. Federal Communications Commission is progressively lifting regulatory restrictions on local and long-distance phone companies, making it possible for each to enter the other's business domain. Each, therefore, faces the choice of what services to offer, ranging from dial-tone to long-distance to cellular to cable (which will bring into the home video signal both to the TV and to the video phone). What will constitute, from the customers' point of view, OSS in communications services?

## Customer Motivations for Seeking OSS

Customers seek one-stop shopping because of its potential to provide convenience, cost savings, and integrated products. Customers today are experiencing increased time pressure. They value OSS because it saves time by not having to acquire related products from different suppliers or stores.

Buying related products from different suppliers will also add to the cost of buying. For household customers, it may be the cost of transportation to different stores and the cost of baby-sitting services if adults like to leave their children home when shopping. For business customers, the increased employee time needed for multiple-stop shopping translates directly into labor costs. Secondly, suppliers of OSS save on costs of doing business (just as customers do), and they might be able to pass on a part of these cost savings to customers.

The third benefit of OSS to customers is that it becomes possible to obtain better-integrated product groups. For example, when customers obtain all of their financial services from an OSS supplier, there is better coordination between various financial products, and the customer can move funds from one portfolio to another. Business customers of computer software can be offered more integrated software suites if they buy them from the same supplier.

A superb example of one-stop shopping is Wal-Mart, which carries apparel, general merchandise, and packaged food products. Even though food is less profitable than general merchandise or apparel, Wal-Mart carries it because it offers customers one-stop shopping convenience. In its supercenters, Wal-Mart's big pull for customers is that it carries approximately 6,000 different items, from food (produce, bakery, deli, frozen foods, meat) to toothpaste to treadmills under one very big roof. Wal-Mart's experience demonstrates that the lure of one-stop shopping brings in new customers, or it brings in current customers more often.[29]

## Risks of OSS

On the flip side, one-stop shopping has some potential perceived risks. Customers may not want to put all their eggs into one basket. Customers may believe, rightly, that they can lower the risk by diversifying the suppliers. For example, in financial services, apportioning one's investments among two or three brokers may seem to offer better protection against bad investment decisions. Or customers may perceive that physicians of different specialties employed by the same health maintenance organizations may follow a uniform cost-minimizing treatment strategy, and may, therefore, be riskier than if the specialists were independent. Business customers of advertising agencies might perceive the risk that the creative work will not be creative enough if handled by a single agency; hiring multiple agencies for portions of work will diffuse this risk.

A second risk is that the customer's fate is tied to a single supplier. If the supplier goes out of business, for example, the customer's business could suffer.

## Implications For Marketers

For marketers, OSS gives rise to some imperatives. First, due to increasing customer demand for time and cost savings, customer preference for OSS is going to increase. Marketers who don't constantly expand the product and service portfolio to offer OSS are at risk. What is critical is to find out, by constant customer research, just what products or services are considered appropriate candidates for OSS.

Another implication is that OSS offerings should be value-based. In other words, OSS should offer better value to customers, in time and/or cost savings, than what the customer can obtain from buying the bundled products or services individually.

Finally, OSS suppliers should study the risks customers perceive in OSS buying and should endeavor to reduce these risk perceptions. They should design OSS bundles with reduced risks (for example, by dealing in diversified financial portfolios, or by hiring diverse creative talent in advertising). Then they should communicate how the company minimizes potential risks.

# Customer Loyalty to Products and Stores and the Three Customer Roles

In this section, we discuss the relevance of various concepts covered in the chapter to the three customer roles: user, payer, and buyer. Some concepts are relevant to the market value that users seek; others are relevant to payers; and still others capture the buyer role. Table 11.4 presents an overview.

The first concept is brand loyalty. We defined it in two ways: behavioral and attitudinal. The former relates to the buyer role, as it stems from the buyer's consistent purchase of the same brand. The latter, the attitudinal brand loyalty, reflects the user's preference for the brand based on a favorable attitude. Next, we presented a model of brand loyalty, describing factors that promote or, alternatively, detract from brand loyalty. Of the factors that promote loyalty, brand-performance fit, as well as social and emotional identification, is a user value. When users find a brand to offer these values, they want the reinforcement of rewards these values reflect. Habit and history are relevant to both user and buyer roles. Users get conditioned to the brand and its specific features and seek it as a conditioned response. Buyers want to routinize their purchases, and buying based on history or habit helps achieve this routinization. The factors that act against brand loyalty are the attraction of alternatives, which comprises brand parity, competitors' promotional activities, and the customer's variety-seeking drive, product involvement, and price sensitivity. Brand parity reflects user indifference to brand choice. Competitors' promotional activity is directed the most at the payer role. Variety seeking is primarily the user desire to interject some variety in use experience, but buyers too may tire of dealing with the same brand seller and may, therefore, seek an alternative. Product involvement means that users care about what they use. Finally, price sensitivity is most relevant to the payer role; when customers are price sensitive, the payer role dominates in brand decision.

The next concept is brand equity, which has five components: performance, social image, value, trustworthiness, and identification. The first two components are most relevant to the user role. If a brand scores well on these two components, the user is pleased; accordingly, the payer is willing to pay for these superior user values. The third component, value, as defined here, refers to the ratio of outcome to input (i.e., how much reward the customer gets at what cost). Therefore, in the computation of value, the user value and the payer value are both taken into account. With trustworthiness, users can use and enjoy a product without fear of failed performance. It also gives buyers relief from the fear of being taken advantage of. Finally, identification is a user value. When products and services give superior scores on all five components, they satisfy the needs and desires of all three roles. Accordingly, then, that brand's equity is high.

We then discussed a model of store loyalty. Here, the "what" factors of merchandise quality and assortment appeal to the user role; users want to maximize these factors. Price value appeals most to payers. And store brands also appeal to payers as a means of cost reduction; for users, they imply a burden to evaluate the store brand and ensure that it has good quality. The "how" factors (merchandise selection ease, in-store assistance, convenience, problem resolution, and personalization) all appeal to the buyer role. It is as buyers that customers often seek these factors in the store to which they choose to be loyal.

In explaining how customers make their store choice, we described three decision criteria: distance/convenience of location, price, and merchandise quality and assortment. These three criteria are of relevance, respectively, to the buyer, payer, and user roles. When a store is chosen despite the greater distance, the buyer is giving up his or her convenience for the sake of either the payer (i.e., to get better prices) or the user (i.e., to get better merchandise) or both.

Finally we discussed unplanned and impulse buying and six factors that encourage or suppress it: namely, exploratory shopping, in-store promotions, atmospherics, knowledge of the store, time pressure, and purchase companion. Exploratory shopping may be driven by the user role in that the user may be trying to explore what else might be worth having. The buyer may also be trying to explore what else is in the store so that, by buying

## TABLE 11.4 — Customer Loyalty to Products and Stores and the Three Customer Roles

| Concept | User | Payer | Buyer |
|---|---|---|---|
| **Brand Loyalty** | | | |
| Behavioral | | | • Reflects buyer's sale consistent behavior. |
| Attitudinal | • Reflects user preference. | | |
| **A Model of Brand Loyalty Determinants** | | | |
| Brand-performance fit | • User value. | | |
| Social/emotional identification | • User value. | | |
| Habit and history | • User conditioning to product/source. | | • Buyer routinizes brand decision. |
| Attraction of alternatives | | | |
|   Brand parity | • Reflects user indifference. | | |
|   Competitor promotions | | • Most appealing to payer. | • Buyers may desire variety in sellers they deal with. |
|   Variety seeking | • Users may seek variety in product/use. | | |
|   Product involvement | • Users care about the brand. | | |
|   Price sensibility | | • Payer role dominates when customers are price sensitive. | |
| **Brand Equity** | | | |
| Performance | • Most relevant to user roles. | • Payers willing to pay for these superior user values. | |
| Social image | | | |
| Value | • User values are compared with payer value. | | |
| Trustworthiness | • Users can enjoy the product/service with assurance. | | • Trust of brand maker most valuable to buyers who may be accountable for this decision. |
| Identification | • Users feel an attachment to the brand. | | |
| **Store Loyalty** | | | |
| "What" factors | • Users want to maximize these factors. | | |
|   Merchandise quality | | | |
|   Assortment | | | |
|   Price value | | • Payers most interested. | |
|   Store brands | • Users want to ensure quality. | • Payers want to minimize costs. | |
| "How" factors | | | • Buyers seek these benefits in a store. |
|   Merchandise selection ease | | | |
|   In-store assistance | | | |
|   Convenience | | | |
|   Problem-resolution | | | |
|   Personalization | | | |
| **Store Choice** | | | |
| Distance/convenience | | | • Of concern to buyer. |
| Price | | • Of concern to payer. | |
| Merchandise quality and assortment | • User influence. | | |
| **Unplanned and Impulse Purchases** | | | |
| Exploratory shopping | • Can be driven by user role seeking new items. | | • Buyers may try to minimize future task. |
| In-store promotions | | • Most relevant to payer role. | |
| Atmospherics | | | • Buyer is influenced the most by these factors. |
| Knowledge of the store | | | |
| Time pressure | | | |
| Purchase companion | | | |

it now, he or she may minimize the future buying task. In-store promotions are targeted to the payer role. Finally, the last four factors influence the buyer role. Thus, any of the three roles may drive a particular unplanned or impulse buying act.

# Summary

We began this chapter with a description of brand loyalty. We defined behavioral brand loyalty as consistent purchase of the same brand and attitudinal brand loyalty as high liking for the brand. Combining these two concepts, brand loyalty is the consistent repurchase of the same brand based on favorable attitude toward it.

We then presented a model of brand loyalty, accounting for factors that induce and promote a customer to become brand loyal as well as those that detract from it. Among the former are three factors—perceived brand performance, social and emotional identification with the brand, and habit and history of brand usage. The detracting factor is the attraction of the alternative brands, which, in turn, consists of market factors, such as brand parity and competitive promotions, and customer factors, such as variety seeking, price/promotion sensitivity, and low product involvement.

Following this, we presented a related concept, namely brand equity and its two views. From the investors' viewpoint, it is a brand's financial worth; from the customers' point of view, it is the perceived relative superiority of a brand name. The rest of the discussion focused on the customer-based brand equity, which was described as having five components—performance, social image, value, trustworthiness, and identification. Brand equity is highest when the brand scores well on all five components.

In the second part of the chapter, we discussed customers' store choice and loyalty behavior. We described the concept of store loyalty, which refers to a customer's predominant patronage of a store based on a favorable attitude. We presented a model of store loyalty that comprises what factors and how factors. The former refer to the products and services the customer gets at the store, whereas the latter comprise the processes entailed in shopping at that store. The what factors include merchandise quality, assortment, price value, and availability of store brands. The how factors include the ease of finding the merchandise; availability of in-store information and assistance; convenience of location, parking, and checkout procedures; the quality of problem resolution (e.g., ease of refunds and exchanges); and personalization (i.e., the employee behavior).

We then discussed the fact that customers choose stores based on location and distance as their first criterion, but this criterion is tempered by a consideration of other factors: quality, assortment, and price. These factors lead customers to form a repertoire of stores at which they usually shop. We presented a flow-chart model of how customers form this repertoire and then distribute their shopping over this repertoire.

Once the store is chosen, product choice begins. Customers do not always buy just what they had planned to buy. Rather, unplanned and impulse purchases also occur. We described these types of purchases. Several in-store factors play a role in a customer's shopping experience and the extent to which unplanned and impulse purchases would occur; these factors include knowledge of the store, time pressure, special store promotions, store atmospherics, customer mood, and whether there is a purchase companion.

Customers generally shop to make a purchase. Often, however, other motives also exist. These include recreation, socialization, status seeking, self-gratification (i.e., rewarding oneself by spending some money), and acquiring information.

An important development in customers' shopping behavior is the concept of one-stop shopping (OSS). This refers to the practice of acquiring all related products from the same supplier or store. Customer motivations for seeking OSS include convenience, cost savings, and integrated products, a range of products or services that coordinated well (e.g., buying all the computer network components from the same supplier). These benefits are balanced by consideration of risks in OSS, which is dependence on a single source. We suggested OSS to be an important opportunity for marketers. Marketers need to find out, through constant customer research, just what products customers consider appropriate for OSS. And then marketers should develop OSS offerings that give customers some added value over the alternative of customers buying those products from individual sources.

In the final section, we revisited the various concepts described in the chapter, identifying their relevance to the three customer roles. We pointed out that consideration of the three customer roles helps a marketer identify the link between specific product and store loyalty-building tools and role-specific market values that customer seek.

# Key Terms

Assortment 406

Atmospherics 413

Attitudinal Brand Loyalty 392

Attraction of Alternatives 397

Behavioral Brand Loyalty 391

Brand Equity 399

Brand Loyalty 392

Brand Parity 397

Brand Valuation 399

Competitive Promotional Activity 397

Customer Loyalty 400

Evaluated New Unplanned Purchases 412

Exploratory Shopping 413

Forward Buy 413

Impulse Purchases 413

One-Stop Shopping (OSS) 406

Planned Purchases 412

Restocking Unplanned Purchases 412

Self-Selection 412

Shopping Motives 414

Store Image 414

Store Loyalty 405

Store Visiting 414

Unplanned Purchases 412

# Discussion Questions and Exercises

1. Identify any five brands to which you are loyal. Discuss why you are loyal to those brands, using the explanation offered in this chapter.
2. As a store manager, you just read the model of store loyalty described in this chapter. You are excited because you believe you have found the key to making your customers loyal to your store. Briefly outline your action plan.
3. You just read the section on brand equity discussed in this chapter. As a brand manager of (1) a consumer packaged-goods company or (2) an automobile insurance company, you make it your goal to strengthen your customer-based brand equity considerably over the next five years. Outline your plan of action.
4. Interview five household customers to understand their store-choice process for supermarkets. Create a flow chart of their store-selection process similar to the flow chart shown in the chapter. Identify how different customers differ in their store choice and discern if there might also be a common underlying overall pattern.
5. Interview two customers who do not buy store brands and two who do. Synthesize your interviews to describe customers, perceptions of store brands, and what explains whether or not customers would consider any store brands. Relate the underlying reasons for both types of customers to components of brand equity (treating store as a brand).

# Appendix

## Customer Satisfaction and Loyalty to Brands—Insights from International Markets

### Europe

A survey of English adults by BMRB International shows that 61 percent of the UK's most affluent shoppers agree to a philosophy of brand loyalty: "when they find a brand they like, they stay with it." However, an alarming finding is that 50 percent of the respondents do not believe that brands are better than own-label. Own-label brands have claimed 31 percent of the UK's grocery sales according to Datamonitor. The trend in the UK is to create brand loyalty through coupons, and the overall UK market grew by 5.15 percent in 1995 due to retailer-funded coupons. In March 1996, NatWest became the first UK bank to issue promotional vouchers to its customers via 1,000 cash machines, and research shows that 67 percent of bank customers were likely to use these promotional vouchers dispensed from the ATM machines.

### Japan

The Japanese are strong brand loyals. The older Japanese customers' reliance on brand names dates to their formative years during the Second World War and the years of post-war poverty when goods were scarce and brand names provided the customers with safety and dependability in a product. The younger Japanese customer is status- and fashion-conscious, and brand names cater to this consciousness. The Japanese consumer's hierarchical concern with brands can be seen in the way the various Suntory brands have occupied different positions in society. In the early 1960s, the best-selling Suntory was a light whiskey called Red; a few years later, Kaku was priced higher. The most premium brand was called Old. Later on, priced even higher for senior executives, came Suntory Reserve. When a Japanese salaryman selects a Suntory brand, he does so solely according to his position in the

company. Suntory Old dominates the Japanese market in the middle level, and Reserve is what you drink when you reach high management.

### Mexico

NAFTA (the North American Free Trade Agreement), enacted in January 1994, has created a regional trading block within North America, and it has benefited U.S. firms by fostering rapid growth in the Mexican market. The very first year after NAFTA's adoption saw an increase of more than 22 percent in total merchandise traded to Mexico by the United States. NAFTA is slowly reshaping Mexico's infrastructure and economic environment, yet the United States has to tackle several brand-management issues to succeed in the Mexican market. Given the low purchasing power of the consumer and the peso devaluation, price is more important to the Mexican consumer than quality. Yet quality considerations are not completely discarded. The Mexican consumer favors generic products to branded products in canned foods due to the price advantage, but not in categories like personal care. This is because the consumer lacks the confidence in the performance of generic personal care items compared to the branded products. Thus, private labels or generic brands could be used to penetrate the mass market in some categories. Small pack sizes, persuasive advertising, focus on warranty, value, and country-of-origin could help reduce price-sensitivity. U.S. firms must understand and follow Mexican labeling requirements to sell in Mexico. They are continually changing, and the ambiguity in law makes compliance difficult. Distribution in Mexico is dominated by family-owned and-operated stores, and U.S. firms need to understand the importance of personal relationships and trust in Mexican business. Finally, distribution pattern and consumer behavior seem to differ considerably across the country, and regional variations of strategies would be essential to succeed in the Mexican market.

### China

A survey of Chinese consumers in 20 cities shows a preference for well-known brands in the food and beverage categories. Seventy-eight percent of consumers continually purchase the top three brands of instant noodles, while 57 percent of consumers buy the leading three brands of MSG. The top three brands of toilet bowl cleaner and washing machine detergent are continually purchased by 75 percent and 65 percent of consumers. However, for certain foods and daily products, such as soy sauce and some detergents, brands are almost all local, with few major national brands. Professor Zhang Zhongliang, general-secretary of the China Economic Prediction Center, predicts that renovated household appliances such as DVDs; convenience foods such as instant noodles and prepared frozen foods; IT products that facilitate communication, including PCs, pagers, and mobile phones; relaxation and recreation products that improve health; educational products; and consumer products associated with home remodeling are the hot products for consumer purchase in the coming years.

## Russia

Results of the first Russian survey on customer satisfaction conducted by the Stockholm School of Economics provide information on consumer loyalty patterns in several sectors, such as food, clothes, and telecommunications. The European Customer Satisfaction Index (ECSI) was calculated for brands in the different categories. The food market survey included commonly used products, such as beer, sausage, and yogurt. Consumers indicate high satisfaction levels with imported products in each of these categories, sometimes more than the local brands, yet loyalty is more toward the local brands, primarily because they are cheaper than the imported

brands. The researchers divided the clothes sector on the basis of producers and found that among central department stores, local markets, local supermarkets, boutiques, and other stores, consumers are least satisfied with the local markets, but are most loyal to them, primarily because of the price factor. Boutiques are highest on satisfaction ratings and follow second on loyalty. The telecommunications market was divided into two kinds of providers: wire communications providers and mobile telecommunications providers, and it was found that sub-sector local providers have room for improvement in their services as they are at a much lower level of satisfaction than foreign ones.

## Other Countries

In Cambodia, beer drinkers display little brand loyalty, and this has led beer manufacturers to different tactics to reduce brand switching among consumers, such as give-aways, ring pull or bottle top competitions, point-of-purchase promotions, and billboards. Name changes are not necessarily voluntary; in India, because of a ban on the use of foreign brand names, hybrid brand names are the norm: Maruti-Suzuki, Dcm-Toyota, Kinetic-Honda, and Lehar-Pepsi.

**Source:** Adapted from Fred Palumbo and Paul Herbig (2000), "The Multicultural Context of Brand Loyalty," *European Journal of Innovation Management*, Vol 3, Issue 3, http://www.emerald-library.com; Amit K. Ghosh (2000), "Brand Management in Post-NAFTA Mexico," *Journal of Product & Brand Management*, Vol. 7, Issue 2, http://www.emerald-library.com; Rama Yelkur (2000), "Consumer Perceptions of Generic Products: A Mexican Study," *The Journal of Product & Brand Management*, Vol. 9 Issue 7, http://www. emerald-library.com; "Survey Of Consumer Behavior In China" (1999), http://www.chinaonline.com/industry/consumer/ NewsArchive/Secure/1999/november/B9111715-SS.asp; Janna Agasieva (1999), "Statistical Research on Consumer Behavior in the Northwest Region of Russia." http://www.bisnis.doc.gov/ bisnis/country/.

# Notes

1   Dan M. Tratensek, "Hand and Power Tools: Consumers, Professionals Show Increasing Brand Loyalty," *Do-It-Yourself Retailing*, June 1, 1999; Melanie Wells, "Cult Brands," *Forbes*, April 16, 2001.

2   Reported in John A. Quelch and David Harding, "Brand versus Private Labels: Fighting to Win," *Harvard Business Review*, January–February 1996, pp. 99–109. For classical literature on brand loyalty, where these measures are developed, see R. M. Cunningham, "Measurement of Brand Loyalty," *The Marketing Revolution*, Proceedings of the Thirty-Seventh Conference of the American Marketing Association, Chicago: American Marketing Association, 1956, pp. 39–45.

3   Jacob Jacoby and Robert W. Chestnut, *Brand Loyalty Measurement and Management* (New York: John Wiley & Sons, 1978), p. 2.

4   See Alan S. Dick and Kunal Basu, "Customer Loyalty: Toward an Integrated Conceptual Framework," *Journal of the Academy of Marketing Science* 22, No. 2 (1994), p. 101.

5   Susan Fournier, "Consumers and Their Brands: Developing Relationship Theory in Consumer Research," *Journal of Consumer Research*, Vol. 24, March 1998, pp. 343–74.

6   See Sharon Beatty and Lynn Kahle, "The Involvement-Commitment Model: Theory and Implications," *Journal of Business Research*, Vol. 6 (30), 149–68.

7   See Banwari Mittal, "An Integrated Framework for Relating Diverse Consumer Characteristics to Supermarket Coupon Redemption," *Journal of Marketing Research* 31, November 1994, pp. 533–44.

8   David A. Aaker, *Managing Brand Equity* (New York: The Free Press, 1991).

9   Reported in Synn B. Upshaw, *Building Brand Equity: A Strategy for Success in a Hostile Marketplace* (New York: John Wiley & Sons, Inc. 1995), p. 16.

10  See Kevin L. Keller, "Conceptualizing, Measuring, and Managing Customer-Based Brand Equity," *Journal of Marketing* 57 (January 1993), pp. 1–22.

11  Walfried Lassar, Banwari Mittal, and Arun Sharma, "Measuring Customer-Based Brand Equity," *Journal of Consumer Marketing* 12, No. 4, (1995), pp. 11–19.

12  For further reading on bonds of identification, see C. B. Bhattacharya, Hayagreeva Rao, and Mary Ann Glynn, "Understanding the Bond of Identification: An Investigation of Its Correlates Among Art Museum Members," *Journal of Marketing*, October 1995, Vol. 59, No. 4, pp. 46–57.

13  For further reading, see Kevin L. Keller, Wagner A. Kamakura, and G. J. Russell, "Measuring Customer Perceptions of Brand Quality with Scanner Data: Implications for Brand Equity," *Report Number 91-122* (Cambridge, Mass.: Marketing Science Institute). Pierre Francois and Douglas MacLachlan, "Ecological Validation of Alternative Customer-Based Brand Strength Measures," *International Journal of Research in Marketing* 12 (1995) p. 322; R. Kenneth Teas and Terry H. Grapentine, "Demystifying Brand Equity," *Marketing Research* 8, No. 2 (Summer 1996), pp. 25–29.

14  Richard L. Oliver, "Whence Consumer Loyalty," *Journal of Marketing*, Vol. 63, Special Issue, 1999, pp. 33–44.

15  An excellent reader on American consumers' supermarket shopping behavior, a source that has richly informed our own description here is by Barbara E. Kahn and Leigh McAlister, *Grocery Revolution: The New Focus on the Consumer* (Reading, Mass.: Addison-Wesley, 1996).

16 Ibid., p. 96.

17 For further reading, see Dennis W. Rook, "The Buying Impulse," *Journal of Consumer Research* (September 1987), pp. 189–99; Easwer S. Iyer, "Unplanned Purchasing: Knowledge of Shopping Environment and Time Pressure," *Journal of Retailing* 65 (Spring 1989), pp. 40–57.

18 David R. Bell, Teck-Hua Ho, and Christopher S. Tang, "Determining Where to Shop: Fixed and Variable Costs of Shopping," *Journal of Marketing Research*, Vol. 25, August 1998, pp. 352–69.

19 Art Thomas and Ron Gardland, "Supermarket Shopping Lists," *International Journal of Retail and Distribution Management* 21, No. 2 (1993), pp. 8–14; Also see Susan Spiggle, "Grocery Shopping Lists: What Do Consumers Write?" in Melanie Wallendorf and Paul F. Anderson eds., *Advances in Consumer Research* 14, (Provo, Utah: Association for Consumer Research, 1987), pp. 241–45.

20 Rook, "The Buying Impulse."

21 Thomas and Gardland, "Supermarket Shopping Lists."

22 See, C. Whan Park, Easwer S. Iyer, and Daniel C. Smith, "The Effects of Situational Factors on In-Store Grocery Behavior: The Role of Store Environment and Time Available for Shopping," *Journal of Consumer Research* 15 (March 1989), pp. 422–33.

23 Quoted in Kahn and McAlister, p. 123.

24 Ronald E. Milliman, "Using Background Music to Affect the Behavior of Supermarket Shoppers," *Journal of Marketing* 46, No. 3 (1982), pp. 86–91.

25 For further reading on the effect of store atmospherics on customer shopping behavior, see Robert J. Donovan, John R. Rossiter, Gilian Marcoolyn, and Andrew Nesdale, "Store Atmosphere and Purchasing Behavior," *Journal of Retailing*, 70 (3), pp. 283–94, 1994.

26 For some research literature on this topic, see Edward M. Tauber, "Why Do People Shop?" *Journal of Marketing* 36 (October), 1972, pp. 47–8. Danny Bellenger and Pradeep K. Korgaonkar, "Profiling the Recreational Shopper," *Journal of Retailing* 56, 3, 1980, pp. 77–92; and Barry J. Babin, William R. Darden, and Mitch Griffin, "Work and/or Fun: Measuring Hedonic and Utilitarian Shopping Value," *Journal of Consumer Research* 20 (March 1994), pp. 644–56.

27 See Peter N. Bloch, Nancy M. Ridgway, and Scott A. Dawson, "Shopping Mall as a Consumer Habitat," *Journal of Retailing* 70, No. 1 (1994), pp. 23–42.

28 Mitch Griffin, Barry J. Babin, and Doan Modianos, "Shopping Values of Russian Consumers: The Impact of Habituation in a Developing Economy," *Journal of Retailing* 76 (1), 2000, pp. 33–52.

29 Based on a report in *Chicago Tribune*, June 23, 1996, Business Section, p. 1.

# CHAPTER 12

## Online Customer Behavior

## Creating an "Amazon" Online Shopping Experience

If there is a company synonymous with the Internet, it is Amazon.com. Over the last few years, this Seattle, Washington, based company has diversified from selling books to a large selection of other products such as music CDs, cookware, toys and games, and tools and hardware. Its revenues have also grown from $147 million in 1997 to $2.8 billion in 2000. When Jeff Bezos, founder of Amazon.com, was vice president at D.E. Shaw, a Wall Street investment bank, he read a statistic that the Internet was growing at the rate of 2,300 percent. This encouraged him to enter the unchartered territories of e-commerce.

Bezos' vision comprised primarily two elements—"He wanted to build the world's most customer-centric company and he wanted to establish a place where customers could buy anything." To this end, he first tried to understand how the medium of the Internet could be used best to develop a customer-centric company. Early on, he realized the potential of the Internet in developing relationships with customers through an understanding of customer preferences and their actual purchase behavior. Amazon used this feature of the medium to its best advantage to provide customers with personalized recommendations, thus building loyalty for the Amazon brand. Its main aim was to deliver values of convenience, large selection, reliable service and delivery, and low prices to customers, all at one place. In line with his vision, Bezos also wanted Amazon to move from being the "world's biggest online bookstore to becoming the world's biggest store," a place where a customer could buy anything. Amazon's vision struck a chord with customers, visible in the growth of its customer base from 1.5 million in December 1997 to 2.3 million in December 2001. The store also had an enviable repeat purchase rate of 78 percent in 2000, up from 64 percent in 1998.

Why did Amazon get into the books business online? Books represent one of the few product categories suitable for online selling. First, it has a large number of items— there are more than 3 million different titles available and active in print worldwide. Second, a book is informational in nature and, therefore, can be featured online with sample chapters, table of contents, editorial reviews, and customer reviews. Third, it is a low-value and, hence, a low-risk item; and finally, it is easy to ship. With this clear value proposition,

Amazon has dominated the book market. Amazon is best known for the compelling shopping experience it provides to its customers. Some of the innovations that it has pioneered are:

1. One-click shopping—Amazon realized that customers want an ordering process that is simple and wherein each new transaction with the retailer would not require them to enter personal information again and again. Hence, the company introduced one-click shopping. It retains in its database all relevant customer information, thereby speeding up the ordering process.
2. Product reviews—Customers can read product reviews on the Amazon Web site and can also see other customers' ratings of these reviews.
3. Purchase circles—The company groups items sent to particular zip and postal codes and items ordered from each domain name. This data is aggregated, and bestseller lists of items popular with specific customer groups are generated, called Purchase Circle lists, and posted online.
4. E-mail alerts—Amazon sends e-mails to customers about products available from their favorite author or musician.
5. Recommendations—Amazon uses different personalization techniques, including "collaborative filtering" (explained later in the chapter) to suggest different products to its customers. It greets customers by name every time they log in and recommends books based on their earlier purchases, their preferences, and the preferences of other customers who have bought items similar to the customer's purchase.
6. Wish list—Every customer can create a wish list of items on the site, and friends and acquaintances can view the wish list to order gifts.
7. The page you made—Amazon found that customers often want to revisit a portion of the site that they visited a moment ago, and there is no way to do this except using the "back" button on the browser. Hence, they create a special page for each customer with those portions of the site that the customer has recently viewed. Now all the customer needs to do is visit this page to learn immediately what he or she viewed a few clicks ago.

Yet, in its attempt to get a greater share of the customer's overall shopping basket, Amazon made forays into several other categories, namely, music, DVD/video, toys and electronics, home improvement, software and video games. The diversification has brought its share of problems. Amazon had a relationship with the customer as the "Earth's largest book store." Customers have not been too keen on extending this relationship to other product categories. Most of these added product categories are also non-informational in nature. Hence, the advantage that established Amazon's dominance in the books category is missing in these categories. Amazon also has well-entrenched competitors in each of these categories, and that makes selling more difficult.

Where does that leave Amazon today? Its sales grew from $147 million in 1997 to about $2.8 billion in 2000. This represents an average growth rate of 183.32 percent, which in 2000 slowed to approximately 68 percent and actually dropped by 3 percent in 2001. However, the company has posted its first profits in early 2002. Amazon represents the face of e-commerce. It has brought the best of the Internet to customers, for which it has been amply rewarded with a large customer base and loyalty. At the same time, it also has experienced withdrawal from customers when it deviated from what made it successful in the first place. Most retailers on the Internet, including Amazon, now realize that the Internet is a tough place to survive, and the savvy customer who buys on the Internet is even tougher to please. (Krishnamurthy, 2001)[1]

In every chapter of this book, we have addressed issues related to online customer behavior. This chapter focuses specifically on emerging buying behavior, both of individual and institutional customers, in the online world (see Figure 12.1 for conceptual framework). The chapter begins with a brief history of the Internet and e-commerce and then elaborates on the activities in the three main stages of online customer behavior—pre-purchase, purchase, and post-purchase. A section on business-to-business (B2B) business models and e-procurement is presented next, and the chapter closes with a harbinger on the trends in online customer behavior.

## Conceptual Framework                                    FIGURE 12.1

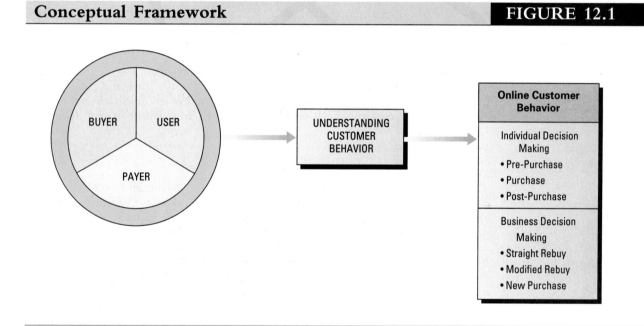

# The Internet and E-commerce:
# A Brief History

## History of the Internet and the World Wide Web

Let us briefly visit where it all started—the history of the development of the Internet and the World Wide Web. The Internet is a large system of interconnected networks. It originated in the 1960s when the U.S. Department of Defense, in preparing for the possible effects of a nuclear attack, commissioned the development of networks that could operate independently without central control. The network model was used to connect four computers in 1969—one each at the University of California at Los Angeles, SRI International, the University of California at Santa Barbara, and the University of Utah—laying the foundation for the first network, called the ARPANET. Many computers were connected to this network over the years, and several applications, like e-mail, FTP (file transfer protocol), and Telnet, were developed to send and receive messages and files across computers on the network. Several other networks, such as the BITNET, CSNET, and USENET, came into existence in the later years. The early 80s saw an explosion in personal computer use with powerful and affordable computers in the market. Soon there was a need for a public network across which businesses could interact with each other for commercial transactions. In 1986, the NSFNET was developed with funding from the National Science Foundation (NSF), and it functions as the backbone communication service for the Internet even today. By 1995, the Internet was substantially privatized and the operation of main Internet connections was taken over by a group of privately owned companies. Since then, the Internet has been opened to business activity, and this has fueled its growth.

The World Wide Web, according to Tim Berners-Lee, the inventor of the hypertext system, is an "abstract space of information." The Web exists because of programs that communicate between computers on the Internet. The Web made the Internet useful for commercial use by making it simple to organize and retrieve information.[2] According to Nielsen/Net Ratings, Internet use in United States grew 15 percent in October 2001 to about 115.2 million people, up from 100.3 million in October 2000. Approximately, 60 percent of U.S. residents have access to the Internet at home, and the average user spent 19 hours online in October 2001.

The Appendix in Chapter 3 also detailed the status of the Internet information infrastructure in different regions of the world such as Europe, Asia, and countries like India, China, Hungary and Russia in specific. The Window on Practice box shows the impact of the Internet and the World Wide Web in a small village in rural India.

## Projections for E-commerce

Today, e-commerce is taken for granted. Despite the dot-com bust in 2000, there is no denying the fact that e-commerce is big and is here to stay. Online research firm eMarketer estimates that U.S. business-to-consumer (B2C) e-commerce revenues will quadruple from $38.3 billion in 2000 to $156 billion by 2005. It also predicts that the number of people, ages 14 and over, who have purchased something online will grow from 64.1 million in 2000 to more than 130 million by 2005. eMarketer estimates that the online customer conversion ratio (proportion of web site visitors who end up making a purchase), which was 1.9 percent in 1999, will more than double by 2003 as e-tailers attract and win new customers with more targeted, customized marketing campaigns.

In the United States business-to-business (B2B) commerce sector, revenues are expected to grow from $336 billion in 2000 to $747 billion in 2003 and are projected to touch $6.3 trillion in 2005. Online B2B activity currently represents 3 percent of the B2B market, but it will represent 42 percent by 2005. By 2003, 80 to 90 percent of firms will be buying via the Internet and 30 to 40 percent will be selling online.

In fact, even as budgets are being slashed in a weak economy, statistics show that companies are spending roughly 10 to 20 percent of their IT budgets on e-business initiatives and that they plan to hold the same or increase this outlay in the coming years. There is a growing realization that the Internet is no longer a channel that it is "cool to be on"; the Internet is the channel that it is "essential to be on" for long-term survival.

## Characteristics of the Internet that Aid E-commerce

The launch of the Netscape browser in 1994 kick-started the e-commerce revolution. The technology barrier was broken, and anyone could get on to the Internet and use it for commerce without being a technology geek. The Internet was also amenable to commerce

# WINDOW ON PRACTICE

## Impact of Internet in Rural India

Rosy opens her PC, logs on to Yahoo chat and types out a message. "Madhu, are you there?" Comes the reply "Yes, what's the matter?" "Can you tell me where I can find information on colleges which offer diploma courses in automobile engineering?" "Give me a few minutes. I'll find out and send you an e-mail." Five minutes later she opens her e-mail and finds a few URLs relevant to her query. Common enough scenario, right? Happens between friends all the time. Easiest way to get information using the Internet and a little help from your friends. Except that Rosy lives in a small village in the state of Tamil Nadu in India called Padinettamkudi, about 22 miles from the nearest big city, Madurai. Padinettamkudi has about 1000 people, does not have any public telephones, does not have a road leading to the village and the local school offers classes only up to the eighth grade. A few months ago, most people in Padinettamkudi had not even seen a PC, much less used one. And today, in this little village, Rosy is one of the many stakeholders in a mission to make Internet a part of the reality of every individual in rural India. She is a Village Internet Kiosk Operator, managing a kiosk in her village, set up for her with the assistance of n-Logue, a Rural Internet Service Provider, incubated by the TeNeT Group of IIT—Madras, a premier educational institution in Chennai. Using the services n-Logue enables for her, she is able to bring the benefits of the Internet to the people of Padinettamkudi. The Kiosk equipment cost Rs. 51,500 (about $1,075) and was bought by a local retailer with a loan from a bank. He appointed Rosy to run the kiosk for him for a fixed salary and a percentage of the profits.

Through Rosy's help, people in the village of Padinettamkudi are using the Internet to connect to the outside world for a variety of their needs. They are contacting the government for birth certificates, income, community and pension certificates, and to send complaints about various problems in the village. They are contacting hospitals requesting information on symptoms of cataract and sending them pictures of the affected eye so that doctors may suggest the next course of action for the patients. Rosy has been trained to take pictures of the cataract-affected eye by personnel from the Aravind Eye Hospital. She can also conduct a similar preliminary test for myopia in young children and then set up appointments for them at the eye hospital to correct the problem. Experts at the Tamil Nadu Agricultural College and Research Institute answer queries from farmers on crops, and livestock related queries are sent to the Tamil Nadu Association for Veterinary and Animal Sciences. A local software company has provided the kiosk with software—free of cost, to promote adult literacy and Rosy helps adults learn how to read and write. The common uses of the Internet also abound—looking up horoscopes, sending e-mails to children abroad, watching movies, booking bus and train tickets, online job search, and so on.

Rosy has announced a movie show for 7 p.m. and rented a DVD from a video library. A couple of kids and women await the show eagerly. Soon, it's show time! As Rosy presses the "Play" button, the little room is filled with the sounds of a popular Tamil movie song. "Gemini, Gemini, Gemini, Gemini . . ." and the audience watches the small screen with rapt attention!

**Source:** Adapted from Elizabeth Alexander, "A Day in the Life of a Village Kiosk Operator," 2002, n-Logue, Chennai. Reprinted with permission of the author.

because of a few very salient characteristics. Researchers Peterson, Balasubramanian, and Bronnenberg list the special characteristics of the Internet as follows:

1. The ability to inexpensively store vast amounts of information at different virtual locations
2. The availability of powerful and inexpensive means of searching, organizing, and disseminating such information
3. Interactivity and ability to provide information on demand
4. The ability to provide perceptual experiences that are far superior to a printed catalog, although not as rich as personal inspection
5. The ability to serve as a transaction medium
6. The ability to serve as a physical distribution medium for certain goods (e.g., software)
7. Relatively low entry and establishment costs for retailers. (Peterson, Balasubramanian, and Bronnenberg, 2001)[3]

These characteristics of the Internet as a marketing channel have changed the way customers shop for products and services. The Internet has eased the time and place constraints that are imposed by traditional retailing. Further, the vast availability of information, the ease with which it can be searched, and the comparison aids available to evaluate the information have resulted in an informed consumer. Armed with such information, the customer is able to exercise a lot more power in a buying decision today, both offline and online. For example, today there are few consumers who purchase a car without obtaining information on the invoice price of the car on the Web. Knowing the invoice price makes it easy for the customer to bargain for prices with the dealer.

At the same time, the Internet is also increasing revenues for marketers by allowing them to personalize their products or services and marketing communications for customers. It is also driving down costs for marketers through the use of web self-service channels at the consumer end, and through e-procurement and market research at the supplier end. Dupont cut procurement costs by $200 million in 2001 with a $15-million e-procurement initiative. P&G is already reaping the benefits of online market research. The company spends $150 million for about 6,000 surveys annually, and it devoted around 20 percent of its budget to online research in 1999. While a traditional survey takes 3 to 4 weeks and costs $50,000, an Internet survey can be completed in 10 days at one-fifth the cost—$10,000. For the year 2001, P&G has allocated 50 percent of its market-research budget to be used on the Web. It definitely makes economic sense to be part of the Internet revolution.

Today's World Wide Web is still an approximation of the capabilities and functionality that can be expected in the next five to ten years. As communication bandwidths rise with the increase of broadband connections, and as customer terminals (i.e., Internet access devices) becomes more powerful, sophisticated, easier to use, affordable, and portable, it will be possible to exchange an enormous range of services on the Web at nominal cost.[4]

## Who Is the Online B2C Customer in the United States?

Jupiter Media Metrix presents a breakdown of the Internet's demographics based on sample traffic patterns of a sample group of Web users in the United States in August 2001.[5] It found that 50.3 percent of the online population is female, and 49.7 percent is male (Table 12.1 presents a gender breakup of the Internet population until 2003). This trend is also being seen in other markets worldwide, but most rapidly in Asia-Pacific, where in Australia women now make up 48 percent of the Internet population, followed by New Zealand (46 percent), South Korea (45 percent), Hong Kong (44 percent), Singapore (42 percent), and Taiwan (41 percent).[6] However, as mentioned in Chapter 2, women are "seekers" online, meaning they go online for a specific reason, while men tend to be "surfers" or "browsers." It follows that women spend relatively less time on the Internet compared to men and are light users. However, women have been found to be loyal to the sites they visit.

| Total Online Population by Gender 1999–2003 (Millions and Percentage of Females Online) | | | TABLE 12.1 |
|---|---|---|---|

| Year | Total online population in the United States | Male online population | Female online population |
|---|---|---|---|
| 1999 | 80.4 | 42.5 | 37.9 (47%) |
| 2000 | 102.4 | 52.2 | 50.2 (49%) |
| 2001 | 140.2 | 58.3 | 60.7 (51%) |
| 2002 | 136.4 | 67.4 | 69.1 (51%) |
| 2003 | 153.9 | 75.0 | 78.8 (51%) |

**Source:** eDemographic & Usage Patterns Report, 2000, eMarketer. Reprinted with permission.

The largest age group on the Internet is the 35–49 age group, comprising 29.9 percent of the total online population, followed by the 25–34 and 2–17 age groups with 19.2 percent each. And while 17.3 percent of the population online is in the 50+ age group, 14.4 percent falls in the 18–24 age group. A Gartner Research report states that U.S. consumers over age 35 accounted for nearly two-thirds of all online spending in the first quarter of 2001. Average online spend in this quarter for seniors was $92, while that for Generation Y was $40. The report also states that "Buy to Browse" ratios in the U.S. are close to saturation and 60–65 percent of the online population will buy on the Internet in the next five years. Comparatively, buying levels in Europe are lower—only half of all Europeans (with three years' Internet experience) are expected to buy online.[7]

Adults 55 and older represent the fastest growing group of U.S. Internet users, according to International Data Corp. (IDC). It is expected that the number of seniors will more than triple from 11.1 million in 1999 to 34.1 million in 2004, and they will account for 20 percent of all new users.[8] Given that the population in the Western countries is growing older and given that they have the purchasing power, it makes sense for web sites to target older consumers and pay special attention to customer service as a differentiator. As it becomes difficult for seniors to engage in recreational and social activities outside of home, they are looking to the Internet as a substitute outlet. Marketers need to understand this motivation of seniors when they are online and provide them with a compelling retail experience.[9]

In terms of income, the largest income group on the Internet is the $60,000-to-$100,000 bracket comprising about 28.4 percent of the population online. Compared to the situation from 1995 to 1996, the population distribution of the Internet population is divided almost equally among the income classes with about 27.8 percent of the Internet population having an annual income of under $40,000, 25.8 percent having an income between $40,000 and $60,000, and about 18.1 percent having an income above $100,000. Thus, the Internet is no longer the bastion of the economically privileged class. Even in terms of the time spent online, these four income groups are quite similar. Thus, the Internet population is fast becoming representative of the general population of the United States.

However, the U.S. Department of Commerce has found that a child in a low-income white family is three times more likely to have Web access than a low-income African-American child and is four times more likely than a low-income Hispanic child. African Americans are the smallest group online (32 percent) compared to whites (45 percent).[10] Apart from income and education differences that lead to the small online population, African-American users may not find general-purpose search engines very useful in locating content that suits their requirements.[11] Forrester Research estimates show that about 74 percent of Asian Americans were online by the end of the year 2000. Asians are wealthier and better educated than any other ethnic group in the United States, and this is one of the reasons why they lead the digital revolution.[12]

Finally, Ernst & Young has charted the psychographic profile of the online customer in its second annual Internet Shopping Study in 1999. It found that leisure-time activities of the study's online buyers were not much different from the average household. Some differences were visible in movie attendance (37 percent of online shoppers go to movies frequently or regularly compared to 26 percent of the average household), recreational travel (42 percent versus 32 percent), performing arts attendance (25 percent versus 17 percent), and family-time pursuits (57 percent versus 50 percent). A smaller percentage of online shoppers watched television (61 percent) compared to 65 percent of average households. Online shoppers are, however, similar to all households in volunteer activities, gardening, gourmet cooking, photography, and attending sporting events.[13]

## Products and Services Customers Buy Online

In order to understand the buying behavior of Internet customers, it is first necessary to understand what products and services are suitable or not suitable for e-commerce. One factor that makes products and services more or less suitable for online commerce is what researcher Rashi Glazer has called "an 'information intensiveness continuum,'" signifying the levels of various types of information associated with products." At one end are traditional products and services that are information-independent, and at the other end information about the products/services is itself extremely important (see Table 12.2). Products and services become more and more amenable to e-commerce as their information intensiveness increases.[14]

Another factor is in terms of search goods versus experience goods. Search goods are products whose features can be objectively assessed before the purchase; in contrast,

## TABLE 12.2          The Information Intensiveness Continuum

| Information Intensiveness Continuum | Details | Examples |
| --- | --- | --- |
| Information Independent | Information exchanged by firm with customers in transactions has no bearing on product features. | Traditional products, standardized services |
| Information is critical to marketing effort. | Information is not part of the product itself, but is critical in providing a solution to the customer's problem. | Information associated with selling effort in industrial buying situations |
| Information helps provide customized offerings. | Information collected through customer feedback and other sources is processed to develop customized products and services at individual or segment level. | "Custom built" computers, bicycles, and products in high-technology industries |
| Information is part of the offering, but is secondary to the main product. | Information is collected for the secondary product in the bundle and it is of help to market the primary product, but the secondary product is not marketable by itself. | Electronic inventory system to sell hospital supplies |
| Information about the product is a marketable product itself. | Information is used to "initially" market the product/service, but later becomes an independently marketable product that adds to company revenues and profits. | FedEx tracking services, airline reservation systems |

**Source:** Adapted from Rashi Glazer, "Marketing in an Information-Intensive Environment: Strategic Implications of Knowledge as an Asset," (pp. 37–39) in Sheth, Eshghi, and Krishnan eds. *Internet Marketing*, Orlando, Florida: Harcourt Inc, pp. 31–61.

experience goods need to be personally experienced to judge their quality. Accordingly, the Internet makes it easier for customers to engage in an online transaction for search goods. However, for experience goods, information alone may not be sufficient for the consumer to purchase it on the Internet unless the customer has already experienced the product or service before. Peterson, Balasubramanian, and Bronnenberg suggest three additional factors—cost and frequency of purchase, value proposition, and degree of differentiation. On the first dimension, goods vary from low-cost, frequently purchased goods to high-cost, infrequently purchased goods. The more frequently purchased and low cost the product is, the less suitable it is for Internet-related marketing. On the second dimension, products and services vary according to their value proposition—that is, whether they are tangible and physical or intangible and service-related. Intangible and service-related goods, especially if they are digital in nature, have an advantage on the Internet. The third dimension defines the degree to which a product or service is differentiable. The higher the degree of differentiation possible for a product or service, the more suitable it is for the Internet. This is because the vast amount of information available on the Internet makes it very easy for consumers to compare prices, leading to extreme price competition for goods and services that are not differentiable from their competitors.[15]

# Online Decision Making— Pre-Purchase Stage

The Internet affects customer decision-making behavior in all three stages: pre-purchase, purchase, and post-purchase. Let us discuss each in turn. Marketers have always been interested in the way customers search for information, the sources they use, and the mental processes that aid and detract from their search process. They also have studied how customers evaluate the information collected to make a decision on the product to purchase among competing alternatives. The task of deciding from among alternatives is vastly complicated by the options that are available to the online shopper.

## Problem Recognition

Customer problem recognition is triggered by internal or external stimuli. Its occurrence due to internal stimuli is similar for an online and offline customer. The occurrence due to external stimuli may, however, differ. For instance, the sight of a computer may itself act as a stimulus to go online and browse the Internet. The customer could also be motivated to go online by offline advertising, on television, for example, where an Internet company could advertise an online product or service offering. The Internet itself may also serve as an external stimulus for problem recognition, primarily through banner advertising while the customer is browsing the Internet. The customer may not have recognized a need in the past, but exposure to the solution-product would make the customer realize a latent deprivation. For a health conscious customer, for example, information on dietary requirements obtained during exploratory browsing of the Internet could act as problem recognition stimuli.

Advertising on the Internet is used to generate primary as well as secondary demand. The customer becomes educated about what a new product or service will do and how it can solve a problem. It is hoped that this will then generate secondary demand. For instance, a banner advertisement could urge the customer to click on it to find out how to lose weight and manage a diet. When the customer clicks on the banner, they are taken to a generic web site where marketers of exercising equipment, diet foods, and nutritional supplements have pop-up advertising. This is an example of how the Internet can generate primary and then secondary demand. Comparison sites are another source of secondary demand generation. Comparison sites not only give the customer increased confidence by reducing the risk of purchasing from unknown web sites, but they also offer the customer the opportunity to switch brands.

## Information Search

Once the need has been recognized, customers search for information about various alternative ways of solving the problem. Although traditionally, the customers have been restricted to a fairly narrow evoked set of brands, this has now expanded greatly due to the easy availability of information on the Internet.

As discussed in earlier chapters, the most conspicuous characteristic of the 21st-century customer is time pressure. The advent of technology, including mobile computing devices, permits the "always-on-the-go" customer to make well-informed purchase decisions via the Internet. As a result, consumers are using the Internet in large numbers and in almost all categories for information search. The Multi-Channel Retail Report 2001 conducted by J.C. Williams Group and Bizrate.com found that the Internet is the most effective pre-purchase influencer among all channels—store, catalog, and online channels.[16]

According to J.D. Power and Associates, more than half of all new-car buyers and a third of used-car buyers do research on the Internet by looking at reviews, feature lists, and invoice prices before making a purchase. This market-research firm found that people who use the Internet for buying the car or for price research pay an average $400 less than people who buy the same car from a dealership without going on the Internet. Yet J.D. Power estimates that only a miniscule 5 percent of car sales actually come directly from web car-shopping services. Customers are, thus, still not comfortable about making a complex decision such as the purchase of the car directly on the Internet.

In the real-estate category, it is a little more difficult to complete every aspect of the transaction online as compared to the purchase of a car. The closing and the attendant paperwork cannot be done online yet. Most people end up using a broker online as well but pay lower commissions. However, sites like ziprealty.com and eRealty.com can provide customers with the data available in the Multiple Listing Services, the huge proprietary databases available only to real-estate agents. Jupiter Media Metrix Inc. states that the number of unique visitors to real estate web sites increased from 9 million in September 2000 to about 14 million in September 2001.[17]

Apart from the web site itself, an important source of information for customers on the Internet is word-of-mouth communication. The online equivalent of word-of-mouth communication is visible in online discussions, chat rooms, and community discussions. Sites like epinions.com consolidate buyer feedback and provide customer reviews for products to aid others in making a purchase decision. The reviewers are actually compensated based on how useful their reviews are rated by readers. A study by Bickart and Schindler shows that consumers who gathered information from online discussions (Internet forums or bulletin boards) reported greater interest in the product topic than did those consumers who acquired information from the marketer-generated sources (such as corporate web pages).[18]

In some areas, online groups have gone beyond influencing other customers. For example, health is an area that is widely researched on the Internet. Studies show that more than 100 million people logged on to the Internet in the year 2000 to seek health-related or medical information, and online patient groups are becoming a big force in the health sector. Take, for example the clinical trials by Novartis AG in 2000 for a new drug called Gleevec for leukemia patients. Patients who were on the first trials for the drug used their own Internet support groups to lobby with Novartis to speed up production of the drug and expedite approval from the Food and Drug Administration.[19]

**Recommendation systems** exert another type of interpersonal influence and mass customization on the Internet. Currently these systems fall into two classes that use different types of information sources to provide recommendations. The first system is collaborative filtering—"prediction of a person's preferences as a weighted sum of other people's preferences." Correlations are calculated between common sets of products bought by groups of people over a period of time, and these correlations are used to calculate weights. Amazon.com uses this process of collaborative filtering to recommend new books to customers. However, when the site does not have enough customers, these recommendations are made based on common products bought by few customers that may not be representative of the group. In order to overcome this problem, researchers suggest that web sites could create "pseudo-users" or "bots" and combine them with real customers in a collaborative filtering system. The other drawback of the system is that it does not incorporate the customer's own preferences with regard to product attributes to make the recommendation. The second system used by web sites for recommendations is content-based filtering. Here, the recommendations are based on consumer preferences for product attributes. It follows that when customers do not provide a reasonable amount of information with regard to their preferences, the content-based filtering system will not be able to make relevant recommendations. Ideally, recommendation systems should incorporate five different kinds of information, namely, a person's expressed preferences, preferences of other customers, expert evaluations, item characteristics, and individual characteristics to provide exact recommendations.[20]

From the above discussion, it is evident that democratization of information leading to low costs of information search is one of the most significant outcomes of the Internet revolution, and information search is one of the first uses that is put to the Internet.

Finally, research shows that customers are more likely to express search and purchase intentions via the Internet when they have a positive attitude towards Internet shopping in general. A greater number of purchasing experiences on the Internet also resulted in higher search and purchase intentions via the Internet. Perceived behavioral control in terms of access to the Internet, skills to navigate the Internet, time, and so forth, was also significantly related to intention to search on the Internet. Marketers can draw from these results to encourage people to search on the Internet, specifically by creating an image of risk-free shopping on the Internet, providing rewarding Internet shopping experiences, and offering easy-to-navigate sites on the Web. The study also found that intention to search via the Internet was the strongest predictor leading to purchase intent in an online pre-purchase intentions model. This shows that search and purchase may not be independent processes, especially for search goods, and it is important for online retailers to make it extremely simple and pleasurable for customers to use the Internet and their web sites for search so that search may lead to purchase via the Web.[21]

## Evaluation of Alternatives

As is evident from the above section, the Internet has paved the way for a very informed customer. But it is said that the customer is also a "cognitive miser." It is difficult for customers to make decisions when they are inundated with information. Given that the Internet has increased the amount of information available to customers, it has also developed methods for customers to make the best use of the information available to them.

Electronic recommendation agents called "smart bots" or "shopbots" make it easier for consumers to reduce their search costs and also improve the quality of their shopping decisions. Researchers Häubl and Trifts define an electronic recommendation agent as "a software tool that (1) calibrates a model of the preference of a consumer based on his or her input information and (2) uses this model to make personalized product recommendations (in the form of a sorted list) in a decision task based on its understanding of the consumer's preference structure."[22] Shopbots allow comparison by price and product features and across retailers. Some examples of shopbots are mySimon.com, Deal-Time.com, and Shopper.com, which compare products, prices, and stores across several categories such as books, clothing, electronics, software, jewelry, and health and beauty. Analyzing customer behavior with shopbots, researchers Brynjolfsson and Smith show that, although price is an important determinant in the purchase decision of shopbot customers, retailer brand name is also considered an important dimension in the decision-making process. Customers are found to use the brand name to make judgments about the retailer on issues like delivery time. Hence, to ensure a positive brand image, web sites should endeavor to provide customers a positive online retail experience in terms of ease of use, delivery services, privacy policies, and return policies. However, shopbot customers are very sensitive to how price is allocated among item cost, shipping costs, and tax, hence, retailers may need to find innovative ways to reduce shipping costs for shopbot customers.[23]

In Chapter 8, we explained that customers use two broad categories of choice models, compensatory and noncompensatory, to select one of the several alternatives available to them. In a compensatory model, the customer arrives at a choice by considering all of the attributes of a product or service and mentally trading off the perceived weaknesses of one alternative for its perceived strengths. Given the large amount of information available on the web on an equally large number of alternatives, it is difficult for customers to evaluate the alternatives using a compensatory model. Even at the shopbots discussed above, the customer is more than likely to use a noncompensatory model to deal with the information deluge.

As discussed in Chapter 8, there are several noncompensatory models: conjunctive, disjunctive, lexicographic and elimination by aspects. The customer can use any of these models to select an alternative. The conjunctive and disjunctive models seem best suited for the choice process on the Internet. In the conjunctive model, the customer sets a minimum cut-off on all salient attributes and examines only those alternatives that meet the minimum cut-off on each attribute. For example, customers can compare different brands of digital cameras at sites like dpreview.com by specifying their preferences on different criteria such as price, resolution, digital zoom, manual focus, and built-in-flash. The site then gives you a table with different brands of cameras compared side by side that meet the criteria that the customer has specified. This table makes it easy for the customer to evaluate the alternatives and make a choice. Customers can also use the disjunctive noncompensatory model to make a choice. This model entails a trade-off between aspects of choice alternatives to arrive at the chosen brand/product.

In the B2B sector, the Internet can provide tremendous cost savings in searching for buyers and suppliers, and making price and product comparisons. Especially with regard to small purchases, search costs can be high relative to the value of the product. Alf Sherk, the founder of e-chemicals, claims: "When you are dealing with one- or two-drum quantities, the cost of comparison shopping can be more than the cost of the product."[24] Shopbots are already in use in B2B commerce for purchase of nonstrategic items. For example, NexTag is a hybrid search agent that uses a combination of shopbot and web auction and allows users to negotiate directly with merchants over product prices, configurations, and options. NexTag's Business eXchange also provides companies with a forum to reach a deal on a wide range of products.[25]

As the Internet grows into a medium that is widely used for commerce, there is one difference that marketers can envisage between the online and the offline medium. They realize that the information that they provide to customers at the web site and the information that they collect about the customers shopping at the web site is as valuable as, or is even more valuable than, the products and services that they sell online. Marketers find that information given to customers online keeps them coming back to the site, thereby building interest and loyalty in the brand. The Window on Practice example of King Arthur Flour shows how a company has used the online medium to develop and sustain loyalty for a product as generic as flour. Further, the information collected at the site on each customer visit makes it easy for the marketer to personalize its marketing pitches, promotions, and products to the customer.

# WINDOW ON PRACTICE

## King Arthur Flour

Flour may be one of those products that really cannot be imagined sold or bought online. Most people consider it a commodity, available in stores across the country and relatively cheap—clearly, a "low-involvement" product. The King Arthur brand of flour, more than 100 years old, has a history dating back to the late eighteenth century. The King Arthur Brand is not a commodity for its loyal following—the company's portfolio comprises more than 50 different flours, nine different kinds of yeast, and eight different kinds of salt. The product is available only at select shops in many states, but the brand's loyal customers have no problems buying it from these specialty stores. Using this loyal consumer community as the basis, King Arthur flours designed its web site in 1996 as a place to get recipes and to track down stores selling King Arthur products. The map for finding stores that sell the flour is the third most popular part of the site, after recipes and requests for a catalog. The primary objective for the web site is definitely not "sales" of flour. The web site is designed to provide visitors with all possible information about the product and what they can accomplish with it. Then, if they decide they want the product, the site tells them where they can buy it. To this effect, the Web site has online baking classes—recipes with pictures and detailed baking instructions. There is a list of frequently asked questions and links to a schedule of in-person classes. They have also recently launched a new bulletin board feature called the "Baking Circle" where Web visitors can write in to pose questions, answer questions, and share recipes and tips. In the first two weeks of putting up the bulletin board, about 5,000 new visitors signed up and more than 1,500 messages were posted. The online business accounted for about $3 million of the company's total $25 million in sales last year. It is difficult for the company to pinpoint exactly the actual sales at its stores that come from people who have been to the site, but it would definitely be safe to say that "the information keeps the customers coming."

**Source:** Adapted from Michael Totty, "Information Please—The Rise of I-commerce," *The Wall Street Journal*, October 29, 2001. Reprinted with permission of The Wall Street Journal, © 2001 Dow Jones & Company, Inc. Permission conveyed through Copyright Clearance Center, Inc.

# Online Decision Making— Purchase Stage

Once customers have evaluated the alternatives available for purchase, they are faced with two options. Using the information garnered from the Internet, they can visit a brick-and-mortar store and buy the product, or they can make the purchase on the Internet itself. The online marketer is trying to make the purchase process more attractive to customers through personalization. The customers are, however, plagued by concerns of privacy of information submitted to retailers and security of credit-card transactions on the Net.

## Personalization

Online retailer Lands' End found personalization to be the answer for customer returns caused by the problem of "poor fitting clothes." To tackle one of the top reasons for returns on its site, it set up a utility on its web site that allows customers to order custom-made chinos. A general description of the customer's hip shape, thigh shape, and some specific measurements are sent to a joint creator software company called Archetype Solutions. This company uses algorithms to create an appropriate clothing pattern based on the measurements, which is electronically transmitted to the custom manufacturer. Thus, both the customer and the Lands' End site benefit from personalization—the customer gets clothes to size and the site has low returns.[26] Likewise, coffee manufacturer Millstone asks new customers about their preferences with respect to salad dressings and chocolate, among other questions, to decide on the blend of coffee that would best suit the customer's taste.

As described in Chapter 2, it is now possible for marketers to mass-customize products because of flexible manufacturing technology in the production stage and computer capabilities in managing customer-specific preferences. Customers will, thus, be able to routinely offer direct input into the making of the product, a process called co-production. Also, by linking directly into production systems, customers will engage in self-service, self-design, and self-ordering and provisioning.

This concept of mass-customization and personalization is not just restricted to tailoring the product. In the online marketplace, personalization in the decision-making process begins with recognizing the customer by name when he or she visits the web site. This can be followed by a personalized page for the customer, presenting only products and services of interest to the customer (developed through an analysis of preferences stated by the customer). Customers can be apprised of promotions and deals for products of their choice and interest using data from their previous purchases and their stated preferences as a guide. Amazon.com, discussed at the beginning of the chapter, is a case in point. The possibilities are endless, and web sites are doing all they can to ensure customer loyalty.

As marketing consultants Don Peppers and Martha Rogers put it, the key is to "identify" your customers, "differentiate" between customers on their needs and their value to the firm, "interact" with your customers, and finally, "customize" your company's response to the customer based on his or her needs. Personalization is "customizing some feature of a product or service so that the customer enjoys more convenience, lower cost, or some other benefit."[27] Researchers Wind and Rangaswamy define another concept called "customerization," which they propose to be an improvement over one-to-one marketing and personalization. They state that customerization is a strategy that is under the "control of customers" as opposed to personalization and one-to-one marketing, which are usually under the "control of the marketer." Under the customerization strategy, the customer is involved in designing the product and supplies, with just a reasonable amount of prior information needed for a "build-to-order" production process designed to develop a product to best fit his or her needs. B2B customers also get a higher advantage of direct links to the production and supply systems of their suppliers. For example, design engineers can use the information and tools available at the Marshall Industries site (**http://www.marshall.com**) to design new products. The same trend towards customerization is seen in all B2B markets and exchanges on the Internet, such as Chemdex, e-Steel, etc.[28]

At the next level, companies also can use the data available to tailor prices for different customer segments in the online world, as is the case in the offline world. Dell has implemented a successful customized pricing mechanism through its premier-pages program. Dell has developed customized web sites for each of its corporate customers with the models that have been approved by the customer purchase department. The site is also customized with the price that has been negotiated for each corporate customer depending on the volumes bought by the customer. The system also takes into account the purchasing process and billing procedures specific to each customer. Buy.com has incorporated a semblance of dynamic pricing (a pricing system of nonfixed pricing that varies the price in real time across customers) on its web site. It uses dynamic pricing software that has bots, which search for price changes that have occurred at competitor sites and recommend changes in prices of products at Buy.com. This is verified by a person at Buy.com, and this pricing process ensures that the web site has the lowest prices for consumer electronics and computer hardware and software on the Web. However, the company's ability to tailor prices is tempered by customer acceptance. As mentioned in the Window on Practice in Chapter 7, Amazon faced irate customers when it instituted a dynamic pricing strategy on its site without informing its customers.

Over a period of time, it is also important to note that customers are not going to take the trouble of switching from site to site for a few dollars. In a Columbia/Wharton School study conducted between July 1997 and February 1999, researchers, led by Dr. Eric Johnson from Columbia Business School, found that just 10 percent of the households that shopped for a book online visited more than one site during a shopping trip, and just 20 percent of such households looking for compact disks shopped around. However, 80 percent of airline ticket shoppers visited at least two sites. Customers tend to stay with sites that they are already familiar with—in terms of navigation and purchase experiences. For most customers, it seems a waste of time to go through this whole process at another site just for a few dollars. In a 1999 study, Professor Johnson and others found that on an average, the customer spent 400 seconds at the Amazon site on his or her first visit, which dropped to less than 200 seconds on his or her fifth visit to the site. If the median income for Web users is estimated at $53,000, the study states that the customer saves $1.44 for the 200 seconds saved in time that comes from site familiarity. In fact, Dr. Erik Brynjolfsson from MIT found that online shoppers who use shopbots to compare prices also tend to patronize sites they are familiar with, although the items are available a few dollars cheaper on another site. He calculated the price advantage of an already-visited retailer over a new retailer at $2.49 for the same item.[30]

## Privacy Concerns in Online Purchase

There is a growing concern among customers about the amount of personal information collected on the Internet and how it is used. Results from a survey of 1,503 customers by Forrester Research, Inc. shows that only 6 percent of those surveyed have a high level of trust in how web sites handle their personally identifiable information. Forty-seven percent think that it is very likely that their personal information will end up in the wrong hands if they respond to an advertisement on a banner ad or in a pop-up window. For those customers who read a privacy policy before they shop online, concerns about privacy reduce to 50 percent. Up to 72 percent of customers surveyed felt that it is an extreme violation of their privacy for businesses to collect data about customers and then supply it to other companies. A large percentage of customers (70 percent) feel that Congress should pass legislation to protect their privacy on the Internet.[31]

Apart from the overt method of collecting data on customers through forms at the web site, online businesses also constantly plant electronic "cookies" onto the customer's computer that enable them to get different kinds of data about the customer. The World Wide Web Consortium has developed a standard called the "Platform for Privacy Preferences Project" (P3P) over the last several years, and Microsoft's newest version of Internet Explorer browser, 6.0, comes equipped with P3P. This standard makes it possible for the customer to find out which web site is sending cookies, what kind of information the cookie gathers, and who is going to see this information. The P3P also has an automatic blocking device with which the customer can prevent "cookies" from residing on the hard drives of their computers. P3P allows the customer to decide which cookies to block and which ones to allow access to. This allows them to keep those cookies that help sites recognize the customer, remember passwords, and store other preferences about the site. At the same time, the customer can block those cookies that collect personal information to transmit to their respective Web sites.[32]

Companies are using authentication technology, filters, audit controls, custom-tailored software, professional consulting services, and permission-based content technology to ensure privacy of customer data. As mentioned in Chapter 2, the FTC endorses industry self-regulation in the context of consumer privacy in the online environment. It has developed five fair information practice principles to protect consumers in the collection, use, and dissemination of their information. Privacy is even more important in the case of children wherein the information posted by them on sites can be used to identify them by name, e-mail, or postal address. Such information can be misused by predators and by companies for marketing purposes. To address this concern, The Children's Online Privacy Protection Act (COPPA) and its implementing Rule went into effect on April 21, 2000. Third-party entities also have emerged online to provide legitimacy and trustworthiness to web sites with their seals of approval that confirm adequate privacy compliance. TRUSTe, Council for Better Business Bureaus (BBBonline), and Alliance for Privacy are three such organizations.

As privacy concerns increase, customers are more likely to a) provide incomplete information to web sites, b) notify ISPs about unsolicited mail, c) request removal from mailing lists, and d) "flame" online entities sending unsolicited e-mail. They are also unlikely to register at web sites that request information and decrease purchase behavior.[33] An interesting finding is that consumers' attitudes toward direct marketing indirectly affect purchase decisions on the Internet through their level of concern for privacy. When consumers have a positive attitude toward direct marketing, their concern for privacy is lower, and the lower the concern for privacy, the higher is their catalog shopping experience. The study showed that the greater the consumer's catalog shopping experience, the greater is his or her purchase intention for products on the Internet. Consumers' privacy concerns are also lower when they have more control over the personal information they provide to web sites.[34]

## Security Concerns in Online Purchase

After privacy, the second most important reason that customers do not complete a purchase online is online credit card payment security. After surveying 8,500 adults, ages 18 and over, in 16 different countries, research firm Ipsos-Reid reports that potential online credit-card fraud was cited as a "major" concern by 46 percent of adults and a "moderate" concern by 26 percent. This concern with security was found to vary by country: In France, 63 percent of respondents considered security a major concern, while only 15 percent of respondents cited it as a major concern in China. About 47 percent of people in the United States considered online credit fraud as a "major" concern.[35]

There are also gender-based differences in the perceptions of risk related to credit-card misuse, fraudulent sites, and loss of privacy associated with online purchasing. Research shows that women perceive a higher level of risk in online purchasing than men, even after controlling for differences in their Internet usage. Yet, women are more willing to buy online when a site is recommended by a friend, compared to men.[36]

One of the methods by which web sites tackle security is to force customers to log in with a username and password. Technology is making it easy for customers to keep track of passwords at several sites. Customers can take advantage of a new device called U.are.U Personal to recognize their fingerprint and then can set it up for several of their frequently visited web sites. Once it is set up, a touch of the finger can log you into the site, and there is no way anyone else can hack this information. Apart from this, companies also rely on encryption of data, such as credit-card information, to ensure transaction security. The Secure Sockets Layer (SSL) and Secure HyperText Transfer Protocol (S-HTTP) are two protocols used by companies to provide secure information transfer through the Internet.

## Trust in Online Purchase

The final solution to security and privacy problems for online retailers would be to engender trust in their brands. A study of 299 consumers across 12 countries in three broad regions of the world (North America, Western Europe, and Latin and South America) showed that the three important factors that affect customers' online purchase intention and loyalty are site quality, affect, and trust. The trustworthiness of the site has a positive impact on both purchase intention and loyalty. It follows that web sites need to engender trust by providing such things as service guarantees, privacy policies, third-party credentials of credibility, and customer testimonials.[37]

Researchers Urban, Sultan, and Qualls state that "Web trust is built in a three-stage cumulative process that establishes (1) trust in the Internet and the specific web site, (2) trust in the information displayed, and (3) trust in delivery fulfillment and service." They suggest that web sites could use software-enabled virtual advisors in the form of personal shopping consultants. These virtual advisors could interact with customers to understand their needs and could provide customers with suggestions to fulfill those needs. They developed a site called Truck Town for truck and sport-utility vehicle buyers featuring a virtual auto mechanic, and they asked 280 Boston-area respondents who had purchased a truck within the previous 18 months to evaluate the site. They found that more than 75 percent of Truck Town's visitors said that they trusted these virtual advisors more than the dealer from whom they last purchased a vehicle. They conclude that "trust will soon be the currency of the Internet," and virtual advisors can be a cost-effective method to build trust in web sites.[38]

In the area of delivery fulfillment, shoppers mention shipping or delivery charges as one of the important reasons for abandoning a virtual shopping cart, according to research firm Jupiter Media Metrix. Since shipping charges are a crucial element of the cost for an online retailer, Jupiter suggests that retailers should give related shipping charges information to customers much before they reach the last stage of their purchasing process. Standardizing shipping rates according to weight (as the U.S. Postal Service) would also make customers more comfortable about the charges since they are familiar with the system. After e-tailer 1-800-flowers.com allowed customers to preview potential shipping charges along with shipping charge options, the number of delivery related calls dropped from 100 a day to nearly zero. Other retailers like Sears and Best Buy are allowing customers to purchase online and then pick up the item at the nearest Sears or Best Buy brick-and-mortar outlet, eliminating shipping charges altogether.[39]

## Turning Browsers into Buyers

Last but not least, a challenge for online retailers is to devise strategies to convert online browsers to buyers. Researchers Wendy W. Moe and Peter S. Fader have built an online buyer-conversion model to determine when browsers will turn into buyers. They state that a customer might require a number of visits to the web site before deciding to purchase from the site. They classify the visits as

1. Directed purchase visits—Customer visits the site to purchase a product or service.
2. Search-and-Deliberation visits—Customer is searching for information, is considering different options, and intends to purchase in the future.
3. Hedonic-browsing visits—The customer is browsing on the Net for pleasure and recreation.
4. Knowledge-building visits—The customer is scanning the market, and any information gathered in this process could impact future purchases.

Moe and Fader's model analyzes visit and purchase data for a customer to predict the exact visit that will lead to a purchase. Web sites can use these models to provide customers with the right cues to induce purchase. For example, when the web site knows that a particular customer is going to purchase on his third visit to the site, he can be routed to a faster server on that visit so that his purchase experience is quick and convenient. On the other hand, customers who need an incentive to purchase can be targeted with promotions. Several e-tailers have already started directing frequent buyers to faster servers to enhance their experience on the site. Online retailers need to track customer response to these tactics to help customers convert from browsers to purchasers.[40]

# Online Decision Making—
# Post-Purchase Stage

## Satisfaction and Loyalty

A report from Boston Consulting Group (BCG) states that the most satisfied online consumer spent an average of $673 online in 2000 while the least satisfied spent $428 on average. It follows that customers who have had a satisfying first purchase experience online are likely to spend more time and money online. Some of the problems that consumers encounter with retail web sites are long upload sessions, difficulty accepting credit cards, never receiving an item that was paid for, no phone number listed for contact, slow response time, and lack of coordination between different parts of the company.[41] Yet, according to a survey conducted by Knowledge Systems & Research, sponsored by Andersen, 58 percent of online consumers in the United States are either very or somewhat satisfied with the customer service they receive on the Internet. Knowledge Systems surveyed 1,149 Internet users in the United States in early March 2001 and found that 46 percent say the act of shopping for or buying products online is better than it was in 2000 (see Table 12.3). The cost and effort of voicing dissatisfaction online with products and services is also rapidly declining for customers. With services like PlanetFeedback (**http://www.planetfeedback. com**) and the Better Business Bureau (**http://www.bbbonline.org**), it is much easier for customers to get their grievances addressed. This puts added pressure on marketers since the impact of dissatisfied customers is also magnified through the medium of the Internet (higher reach).

| **TABLE 12.3** | **Online Satisfaction** |
| --- | --- |

**Online Experience in the United States That Is Better in 2001 Than It Was in 2000 (as a % of online users who think that it is "somewhat" or "much" better)**

| | |
| --- | --- |
| Shopping for or buying products | 46% |
| Conducting financial transactions | 37% |
| Obtaining customer service/support | 35% |
| Obtaining online statements/billing | 33% |
| Making travel arrangements | 24% |

**Source:** Knowledge Systems & Research, 2001. Reprinted with permission.
010462 ©2001 eMarketer, Inc. www.eMarketer.com.

Customer service has received a major boost after the widespread adoption of the Internet. In fact, Web-based, self-service is a boon to customers and companies alike. Customers are able to take care of minor repetitive issues such as address changes, tracking a package, or looking at the status of a submitted application, without having to call the company and waste time. At the same time, companies realize that allowing customers to handle these issues by themselves not only saves them a packet, but also helps them keep a customer better satisfied. This feeling comes from the control that the customer feels over the whole process. Web self-service can be primarily segmented into content based and transaction based services.

1. Content-based services—Most of these customer inquiries are general in nature and require static information. Site FAQs are a great way to handle these queries.
2. Transaction-based services—These services require dynamic information. Customers want to place orders, fill out applications, make payments, keep track of their purchases, etc. Each of these transactions requires individualized information to be retrieved from back-end databases and supplied to the customer when there is a specific request.[42]

Yet, it is important that companies not assume that the Internet is a self-service channel. All customers do not have the same level of comfort with the Internet, and even if they are extremely Internet-savvy, they are not always willing to do most of the job when it comes to purchasing a computer or buying airline tickets. "Co-production" is a good alternative since it focuses on "customer service" and not "self-service." In this model, customers state their preferences once, and the company helps reduce the customer's consideration set by generating a set of alternatives that closely match the customer's preferences. The focus is on providing the customer with the right choice, as opposed to many choices or not enough choices. Companies like Dell are already using the model. Dell completes all the back-end processes such as grouping products by customer segments and displaying in-stock items, while allowing customers to configure their own PCs and check their order status online. It has also developed custom web pages for all its corporate customers that display only those configurations that have been preapproved by the company and the negotiated prices for the configurations.[43]

Finally, as mentioned in the Window on Research box in Chapter 11, customer loyalty is the key driver of profitability for online businesses.

Loyalty by customers is manifest in two ways—by repeat purchases at a site and by referring customers to the site. Research shows that a web site cannot expect to break even without at least four repeat visits from a customer in a period of twelve months. Further, referrals represent the best form of new customers since the site does not have to spend a single penny to get them to the site and they provide revenues and refer more people if they have a satisfying shopping experience. Hence, the key to success in online retailing is to foster loyalty among its customers.

## Tackling Returns

One of the most annoying parts of the online purchase process is tackling returns. Customers appreciate the convenience of purchasing online, but they also hate the thought of having to ship the product back to the company if it is not to their satisfaction. Some companies like Best Buy have found a solution to this problem by integrating the brick-and-mortar operations of the company with the online arm. Customers who have purchased online and are not satisfied with their purchase can return the product at the nearest brick-and-mortar outlet.

# Customer Behavior in Business-to-Business (B2B) Commerce

B2B commerce is much larger than B2C. EMarketer expects that worldwide B2B revenues will grow from $185 billion in 2000 to $1.26 trillion in 2003. U.S. B2B will reach $747 billion in 2003, accounting for 59 percent of worldwide B2B e-commerce. Europe will follow the United States at $365.6 billion in B2B e-commerce. Asia's B2B revenues in 2003 will hit $76.6 billion, up from $12.2 billion in 2000. We believe that the purchasing function will see two strategic shifts in the future, and these strategic shifts underlie the basis of B2B commerce.

*Global sourcing*—The Internet is the answer to global sourcing that businesses have been waiting for. It overcomes the limitations of geography and provides the key catalyst required for B2B commerce, bringing together suppliers and buyers on a common platform across the world with a transparency on price (Does price vary by geographic region or by size of customer and am I getting the market price?), availability (Where can I find the product I need?), suppliers (Are there suppliers of the same product?), and products (Is there a substitute or alternate product available in the market?).

*Relationship orientation*—Business buying behavior is both operationally and strategically complex. Suppliers and buyers would like to tap into the "self-help" model associated with the Internet to make business-to-business transactions transparent and efficient, but simple buy-sell transactions will not be the end goal. Suppliers would like to learn of their buyers' demand function so that they can adjust their production schedules and inventory holdings and lower their order-processing costs. In turn, buyers would be interested in uniform pricing, finding alternative sources of supply, and better control over their procurement processes. These preferences will lead both buyers and sellers to seek a relationship orientation.

# Value Creation in B2B Marketplaces[44]

B2B marketplaces create customer value in at least four ways. First, they expand everyone's market reach. Half of the U.S. gross domestic product comes from fragmented industries such as electronic components, health care, and life sciences. B2B marketplaces help buyers and suppliers in these industries meet at a common platform. Chemdex maintains a register of 2,200 suppliers and more than 26,000 users of life sciences materials.

Second, B2B marketplaces generate lower prices for buyers. In a survey of companies using B2B marketplaces for procurement, half reported paying lower prices after they used the B2B marketplace. FreeMarkets (a B2B exchange company) says that its customers have experienced savings of 7 to 10 percent for commodities and 7 to 25 percent for custom purchases. Buyers are able to get lower prices because they reach more suppliers through the marketplace or, sometimes, more efficient suppliers. Other elements working to their advantage are price competition among suppliers and access to excess-inventory stocks at really low prices.

Third, B2B marketplaces cut the cost of the buyers' operations. Most B2B marketplaces are trying to provide value-added services to their customers that usually need to be taken care of at the buyer end. The e-Steel B2B exchange, with more than 2,200 buyers and sellers, automates the entire transaction process and takes care of order tracking, inventory management, and reordering processes that generate significant cost savings for buyers. Among companies that have begun online procurement, 56 percent cited greater efficiency and improved speed and accuracy in procurement as a result of B2B exchanges.

Finally, these marketplaces identify industry best practices. Some e-marketplaces have developed distinctive, high-value-added content. For example, SiteStuff is a property maintenance exchange that monitors materials, repair, and operations spending per building and compares these costs with those of average and best-run buildings of the same type and size. Neoforma.com singles out and profiles hospital medical departments with the best floor plans, equipment, and stock of materials.

# B2B Business Operating Models[45]

How do B2B customers find suppliers and vice versa? This depends on how B2B exchange operations are set up. They can be classified into four types: (1) sell-side models, (2) buy-side models, (3) marketplaces and exchanges, and (4) auctions and reverse auctions. The sell-side business models are "online exchange sites run by a single supplier or distributor seeking buyers." Companies like Cisco and Dell are the best examples of this model; they have set up personalized web pages for their business customers. The buy-side business models involve a "buying organization using Internet-based technologies to buy from contracted suppliers." This process is called e-procurement. For example, General Electric uses a buy-side web site for its procurement function. The third form of B2B models are the neutral marketplaces and exchanges, "web sites run by a third party to bring buyers and sellers together vertically within an industry sector or horizontally across industry sectors." Chemconnect is an example of a vertical exchange for the chemical industry. Finally, the last B2B business model is auctions and reverse auctions which involve "a structured electronic market for bidding for products by buyers (auctions) or sellers (reverse auctions)." Autodaq and FreeMarkets Online are examples of auctions and reverse auctions, respectively.

Which B2B business model would a B2B customer use? That depends on the type of purchase need or buyclass. The buyclass could be straight rebuy, a modified rebuy, or a new task procurement need.

## Straight Rebuy

A B2B Internet-based business model is most beneficial in a straight rebuy purchase occasion for several reasons. First, decision making is generally autonomous for straight rebuys. Second, transaction costs of procurement are high, particularly in view of a low value of each transaction; third, product requirements are clear and prespecified. Since competitive brands are relatively undifferentiated, the buyers of straight rebuys have tremendous power over sellers, and if the prices are non-standardized, the Internet helps in driving down prices. Typically, the buyers have the option of following types of B2B marketplaces: the catalog hub, buyer aggregator, market exchange, and liquid exchange.

*Catalog Hub*—This is a sell-side web site featuring an online catalog, encompassing a large number of product manufacturers/suppliers, and guaranteeing that a listed product is available at a fixed price. For example, Cambridgesoft's site ChemACX.com is an online catalog site featuring more than 200,000 products from over 210 chemical suppliers. This model is best suited when the search costs for buyers are high, time is critical in purchasing, and price volatility is relatively low. Sciquest.com and PlasticsNet.com are some other catalog hubs.

*Buyer Aggregator*—This is a buy-side online site that combines demand within and across buying enterprises to transact as a buyer group. Because it represents a large demand aggregated from a multitude of buyers, it is able to gain an advantageous low price from suppliers, thus benefiting the buyers. This model was pioneered by Accompany.com. In the UK, demand aggregators like Purchase Pooling Solutions, Inc. (**http://www.transitpool.com**) provide procurement savings for public-sector customer entities.

*Market Exchange*—Online market exchange sites bring together buyers and sellers, such as MetalSite or ChemConnect's World Chemical Exchange, and New View Technologies™ (**http://newview.com**). The pricing mechanism can be a simple offer/buy, offer/negotiated buy, or an auction offer/bid approach. Some major companies like General Electric, Siemens, and Shell are now using for their entire straight rebuy procurement private exchanges that link the company and its chosen suppliers. Dupont recently invested in a $15 million e-procurement initiative that streamlined its entire purchasing, from software to sulphur dioxide. Dupont has cut procurement costs by $200 million this year, a 5 percent reduction, and expects another $200 million in annual savings by 2003.[46]

*Liquid Exchange*—Finally, straight rebuy customers in some product categories can also use the liquid exchange model—"a model where buyers and sellers bid and ask for the products and services in real time, and prices are transparent and purchases are guaranteed via a constant supply that generates the market's liquidity." For example, HoustonStreet.com is a liquid exchange for physical crude oil and refined products, and Gofish is a spot market for fish.

## Modified Rebuy

In case of a modified rebuy, the complexity is increased by the new specifications that are introduced. There is a higher degree of interaction between the three roles. Therefore the seller will have to be capable of managing increasingly complex conflict resolution issues. This is obviously far more challenging to manage via the Internet. Typically, reverse auctions are the B2B model adopted under the modified rebuy purchase occasion.

*Reverse Auctions*—A reverse auction involves one buyer (usually large) and multiple sellers. In a reverse auction format, the buyer presents his need and multiple sellers bid prices to meet this need. The seller who quotes the lowest price at closing is offered the bid. The best example of a reverse auction market is FreeMarkets™ (**http://www. freemarkets.com**), which helps large buyers like GM, Quaker Oats, and Deere & Co. drive down their procurement costs. Eastman Kodak Co. has recently added reverse auctions to its e-procurement platform. Kodak spends more than $6 billion every year for goods and services, and it wants 20 percent of this amount to be met by reverse auctions. Using the reverse auction format on a pilot basis, the company has already been able to slash up to 20 percent off the prices of the goods it purchases, and in some cases, savings are as high as 40 percent.[47]

## New Purchase

When the customer is considering a new purchase situation, there is extensive interaction between the three roles. Payers have to juggle money, including raiding new capital, while buyers may need to go through an extensive process of identifying new suppliers. There is considerable uncertainty about the design/performance requirements of the product. Hence, the buyer seeks information extensively, is far more concerned with finding the right solution, and relies on the technical expertise of the seller. In this scenario, it is extremely difficult to market or sell on the Internet. The challenge of satisfying all three parties becomes considerably greater over such an impersonal medium where the level of human interaction is low. A business trading community B2B model provides the specialized information that the buyer will need; auctions are more often used for one-time and unique purchases.

*Business Trading Community*—A concept pioneered by VerticalNet.com, a business trading community is a site that acts as an "essential, comprehensive source of information and dialogue for a particular vertical market." VerticalNet's communities contain product information and enable B2B exchanges of information, supplementing existing trade shows and trade association activities. Another web site, Buzzsaw.com, in the building design and construction industry allows building owners, architects, engineers, contractors, suppliers, and manufacturers to share information and manage building projects more efficiently.

*Auction*—In this model, the price of an item is determined dynamically by bids submitted for the item over a period of time. This model is based solely on price and is best used when the items being traded are unique in nature, there is high price volatility, buyers and/or sellers are fragmented, and time is less critical in purchasing. Autodaq.com, which conducts B2B auctions of used cars, and Liquidation.com are auction models.

## Learning New Behaviors in the B2B Marketplace

According to a report from Sterling Commerce, 28 percent of global companies are already participating in at least one online marketplace, with an additional 25 percent planning participation within one year. Both buyers and sellers have to adapt to a new set of marketplace rules to obtain the highest efficiency from online exchanges.

Buyers need to realize that B2B exchanges are more than just "simple order matching." In order to reap significant benefits from B2B exchanges, they will need to adopt a "relationship approach" and invest time and effort in acquiring/building capabilities, implementing new technologies, and changing the organization.

Firms participating in exchanges also need to realize that their nature of participation in exchanges is dependent not just on their IT capabilities but also on their own motivations to join the exchange. They should join a marketplace exchange not just to establish an image of being technologically savvy in the market but also to achieve specific goals of efficiency. The firm will need to reengineer its business processes to participate in the exchange, and this will require building IT capabilities.[48]

Sellers will have to focus on specialization as they search for comparative advantage in the B2B commerce arena. As of spring 2000, the *Economist* estimated that there were about 750 online marketplaces in the United States, and most analysts estimate that the number of online marketplaces in the United States will continue to rise. But they also predict that three companies in each segment will end up with 70 percent of the market share in technology markets, and, hence, the market will consolidate at around 2,000 to 3,000 exchanges in total. The ones that will remain will be the ones that have focused on specialization and that offer the customer end-to-end solutions, beginning with deep information content for (and related to) the transaction, facilitation of the transaction, and, finally, providing all the support services for the transaction by connecting not only with buyers and sellers but also with different entities at every step of the supply chain.

Private exchanges are also becoming popular because public market exchanges have not been able to live up to their expectations. Fifteen percent of the world's largest companies already have private exchanges according to Jupiter Research, mainly because they provide the ability to centrally manage procurement across many business units; integrate with back-end systems; link production, inventory, warehouse, and order-management systems; are more secure; and can limit participants to suppliers whom the company knows and trusts. Companies like Volkswagen have bought close to $5.2 billion in goods on their private exchange in 15 months, slashing procurement costs by 40 to 50%.

# Future Technology and the Internet Customer

Two developments in technology will offer new opportunities for the Internet customer: **mobile commerce** and **telematics**.

## Mobile Commerce

An aid to the anytime/anywhere purchasing and consumption need is the mobile phone, and a new study from Strategy Analytics shows that the mobile e-commerce market could be worth $200 million by 2004. Furthermore, transactions made using mobile phones could generate $14 billion per annum in four years' time, marking a fundamental change in consumer behavior dynamics. The report predicts that people will be able to use their mobile phones to purchase goods from vending machines, buy cinema and train tickets, and shop on the Internet. Take, for example, Unilever's mobile recipe book concept that is to be available to digital phone users in Europe. The customer would use the mobile recipe book while shopping, and use the tool to consider recipes that will then be broken down into ingredients, wherever possible with their Unilever brand name. Based upon the customer's identity and location, Unilever could also issue mobile coupons for these ingredients at the time of purchase to provide incentives.

More than 300 million people around the world, already own mobile phones and this figure is expected to reach one billion by 2003. As handset penetration increases, Nokia predicts that, consumers will begin to use their phone to connect to the Internet more than personal computers. Wireless Internet services can be made more personalized for customers compared to any other means of communication. First, mobile telephones are usually with customers and are switched on most of the time. Second, wireless network operators using a GSM (global system for mobile communication) standard would be able to uniquely identify a user and be able to send him or her personalized communication. Finally, the operator is able to pinpoint the user's location exactly, thus presenting the user with an array of new applications.

## Telematics

In the next ten years, customers can expect the car, the refrigerator, the television, and the medicine cabinet in their bathroom to be Internet-ready, thus presenting thousands of opportunities for service from marketers. The car could keep track of the date when it is to be serviced next, and the refrigerator could automatically order items that fall below a particular stock level. Interactive television could make it easy for customers to order through the television, and the medicine cabinet could supplement discussions with the pharmacist and the doctor. As an example, the ubiquitous Internet could help GM convert its car into a "communications intermediary." The gas companies would be interested in knowing how much gas is left in the tank, mechanics would want to know when the car is due for its next service, and restaurants and retailers would be interested in knowing the area in which the car is cruising.

The concept of the ubiquitous Internet could apply to any other place where the customer is physically present—shopping malls, airport lounges, parking garages, and so on. At all these locations, marketers can provide customers with mobile devices that help the customer by providing him or her with information relevant to their needs, and at the same time, capture information for marketers. For example, Simon Properties, the largest retail mall developer in the United States, allows shoppers to generate electronic wish lists and order products for home delivery using mobile devices. It is expected that in the future, these devices will be able to track customers as they navigate the mall so that they can be provided timely incentives to visit certain stores in the mall as they are passing by.[49]

# Online Customer Behavior and the Three Customer Roles

In this section, we pull together all the various concepts covered in the chapter and illustrate their relevance to the three customer roles, with emphasis on what marketers can do to influence and manage online customer behavior (see Table 12.4). In the case of individual decision-making, by definition, the user and buyer roles are combined in the same person. Often the same individual also plays the payer role. Therefore, the customer has more control over what to buy and is less likely to indulge in impulse purchases. The three roles come into play in the online decision making process: problem recognition, information search, alternative evaluation, choice or purchase, and the post-choice experience.

Recognizing a problem or deprivation through internal stimuli is similar for an online and offline customer. Although problem recognition has been considered the domain of the user role, the other two roles can also be the source of problem recognition. For instance, from the payer perspective, the perception that online purchases may cost less than offline purchases, may act as an impetus to browse the Internet for bargains. The key issue is how to demonstrate price value for online products. For example, airlines suggest a 10 percent reduction in tickets if you buy online as opposed to purchasing tickets through travel agents or call centers. Likewise, buyers, when exposed to banner ads on the Internet, may feel that current vendors do not provide convenient or satisfactory service.

In the information search stage, ample product information is readily available, enabling users to evaluate a product's benefits more thoroughly. The payer can compare prices across a wide variety of vendors, and the buyer finds it easy to collect all the information. Buyers who enjoy browsing help the user role identify new solutions, whereas those who are comparison shoppers help the payer find the best value. Although traditionally the customers have been restricted to a fairly narrow evoked set of brands, this has

## Individual and Business Online Decision Making and the Three Customer Roles

**TABLE 12.4**

| Concepts | User | Payer | Buyer |
|---|---|---|---|
| | Individual Customer Online Decisions: Unique Aspects | | |
| Problem Recognition | • Users are most frequent problem recognizers.<br>• Offline advertising media creates pull demand for web site. | • Realization that online prices are more competitive than offline can act as a stimuli for problem recognition. | • Buyer dissatisfaction with current options and well-targeted banner advertising can provide an impetus to seek change. |
| Information search | • Users can seek pertinent information from other users via Internet forums; managing word-of-mouth is therefore critical. | • Payer seeks price comparisons, which is extensively available on the Internet.<br>• Marketers should also promote economics of online shopping. | • This is critical to the buyer.<br>• Information is extensively available on the Internet.<br>• Marketers must ensure that the web site is easy to navigate with neither too much or too little information.<br>• The low switching costs enable buyers to move to another web site quickly. |
| Evaluation of Alternatives | • User values are most important.<br>• Marketers should try to understand the online profile of the customer and provide products and services accordingly. | • Payers will seek to maximize price value through comparison.<br>• Transparency of all costs will be beneficial to the marketer and the payer. | • A compensatory choice model to aid selection is generally not suitable in an Internet environment. Instead web pages provide the option for the buyer to use a conjunctive or disjunctive model. |
| Purchase | • The user role is less important in this aspect. | • The key issue is how to demonstrate price value for online products.<br>• Prior experiences and comparable prices are key.<br>• Marketers should make price simple and transparent and state all additional charges upfront. | • Marketers should address buyer concerns about trust, security and privacy when purchasing over the Internet.<br>• The buyer is also concerned about the ease of use of the web site. |
| Post-Purchase | • Experience is determined largely by user role.<br>• Similar to the offline market, marketers can provide stimuli to convince the customers that they have made the right choice, thereby increasing satisfaction and developing loyalty. | | • The Internet largely facilitates dissemination of word-of-mouth.<br>• The promise of anonymity ensures that a nonaggressive buyer can also express opinions freely.<br>• The extent of salience in the dissatisfaction and the degree of attribution to the marketer may, however, impact the tendency for the buyer to complain. |

*(continued)*

| TABLE 12.4 | Individual and Business Online Decision Making and the Three Customer Roles (Concluded) |
|---|---|

| Concepts | User | Payer | Buyer |
|---|---|---|---|
| | Business Customer Online Decisions: Unique Aspects | | |
| Straight rebuy buyclass | • User role is limited due to the standard product specifications. | • Payer is seeking price advantages via the Internet.<br><br>• Reduction in transaction costs is an incentive to use catalog hub, buyer aggregator, market exchange or liquid exchange models. | • The buyer is seeking to routinize and automate the process as much as possible and therefore prefers to use Internet exchanges as much as possible. |
| Modified rebuy class | • User is more involved as new specifications have to be defined. | • Payer involvement also increases as an acceptable price level has to be determined. | • Buyer role interacts to a great extent with user and payer; increased supplier involvement is also sought. |
| New risk buyclass | • User is very involved in the process as a completely new set of specifications is defined.<br>• Supplier input is key. | • Extensive pricing search is undertaken by the payer role to understand and determine an acceptable price level. | • Buyer role is very complex as there is extensive interaction with user and payer departments as well as with suppliers who are also seen as playing consultant roles.<br><br>• Selling over the Internet is very challenging in this scenario. |

now expanded greatly due to the ease of accessing information on the Internet. Even an uninvolved buyer can provide extensive information to the user role, due to the minimal search effort required.

In the alternative evaluation stage, the user values are the overriding criteria. Marketers find that information given to customers online keeps them coming back to the site, thereby building interest and loyalty toward the brand and increasing the probability of positive user evaluation. Given the large number of options available to the buyer, a compensatory choice model to aid selection is generally not suitable in an Internet environment. Instead, web pages provide the customer with the option of using a conjunctive or a disjunctive model.

In the purchase stage, the buyer and payer values become the most important. The payer needs to know what the additional charges are (shipping, tax etc.). Often, high shipping costs are a deterrent to purchase. Fortunately, online purchase is sales tax free and there is an economic incentive to buy if the local sales taxes are high. The buyer seeks ease of use and navigation when looking at a web site. If a web site is difficult to navigate and there is either inadequate information or an overload of it, the switching costs are low enough to make the buyer move to another web site immediately.

In the post-purchase stage, the buyer may experience buyer's remorse, while the user evaluates the usage experience. The Internet has opened forums to disseminate positive or negative word-of-mouth by the buyer, even for a less aggressive buyer role.

In the business-buying scenario, role specialization is far more pronounced than it is for household customers, which increases the complexity of online business-to-business marketing, depending on the buy class occasion. The buyclass affects all three roles.

In a straight rebuy situation, a B2B Internet-based business model is most beneficial. Decision making is more autonomous when compared to other models and the web site does not have appeal to all three roles; typically, the buyer will be the only point of interaction. In this scenario, the buyer has tremendous power and if prices are nonstandardized, the Internet helps to drive down prices. Typically, the catalog hub, buyer aggregator, market exchange, and liquid auction models are used to satisfy this procurement need.

In the case of a modified rebuy situation, the complexity is increased by the new specifications that are introduced. There is a higher degree of interaction between the three roles, and reverse auction is a suitable B2B model for the modified rebuy purchase occasion.

When the customer organization is attempting to undertake a new purchase occasion, there is extensive interaction between the three roles. Payers have to raise new capital, and buyers seek information extensively from suppliers to meet the new design/performance requirements. A business trading community B2B model provides the specialized information that the buyer will need, while auctions are more often used for one-time and unique purchases.

# Summary

We began this chapter by discussing the Internet's potential. Predictions for e-commerce revenues as well as for the number of people going online indicate that e-commerce is big and is here to stay. Furthermore, the Internet has certain characteristics, including the ability to inexpensively store vast amounts of information at different virtual locations; the availability of powerful and inexpensive means of searching, organizing and disseminating such information; interactivity; the ability to provide information on demand; the ability to provide perceptual experiences that are far superior to a printed catalog, although not as rich as personal inspection; and the ability to serve as a transaction medium and serve as a physical distribution medium for certain goods (example, software). From a retailer's perspective, the relatively low entry and establishment costs make this an attractive marketing and sales medium.

We then described the individual customer's decision-making process online. In the problem recognition phase, the Internet is used as an external stimulus. Advertising on the Internet is used to generate primary as well as secondary demand. When the customer moves to the information search stage, the easy availability of information on the Internet has greatly expanded the customer's traditionally narrow evoked set of brands. As a result of this accessible information and increasing time pressures, consumers are using the Internet in large numbers and in almost all categories of information search. When the individual moves into the evaluation of alternatives phase, while the Internet has increased the amount of information available to customers, it has also developed methods for customers to best make use of the information available to them. In this context, electronic recommendation agents called "smart bots" or "shop bots" make it easier for consumers to reduce their search costs and also improve the quality of their shopping decisions. In the choice stage, we discussed personalization as well as the challenges of privacy and security concerns that customers have while transacting over the Internet. Finally, under post-purchase behavior, we discussed ways that the Internet can be used to increase satisfaction and develop loyalty after purchase of the product or service.

We then discussed the implications of conducting B2B transactions over the Internet. We stated our belief that the purchasing function will see two strategic shifts in the future, global sourcing and relationship orientation, which underlie the basis of B2B commerce, directly impacting the business decision-making process. We then discussed how B2B marketplaces create value by expanding everyone's market reach; generating lower prices for buyers; cutting the cost of the buyer's process; and identifying and disseminating industry-wide best practices.

B2B e-commerce business models are very simply listed in four categories as sell-side models, buy-side models, marketplaces and exchanges, and auctions and reverse auctions.

The sell-side business models usually pertain to a single supplier or distributor, seeking buyers using the Internet. The buy-side business models involve a buying organization using Internet-based technologies to buy from contracted suppliers. This process is called e-procurement.

The B2B business model that is typically selected will vary, depending upon the type of purchase need or buyclass. The buyclass could be a straight rebuy, a modified rebuy, or a new task procurement need. A straight rebuy occasion utilizes the catalog hub, buyer aggregator, market exchange or liquid exchange models, while a modified rebuy occasion demands the use of reverse auctions. A new task purchase occasion uses a business trading community or an auction model.

To best derive value from the Internet, buyers have to develop a relationship approach to doing business, and focus on partnering with supplies. Sellers have to focus on specialization as they search for comparative advantages in the B2B commerce arena. Finally, firms participating in exchanges must realize that their nature of participation in exchanges is not just dependent on their IT capabilities, but also on their own motivations to join the exchange, which in turn impacts their degree of efficiency in operations.

# Key Terms

Buy-Side Business Models 445

Buy-to–Browse Ratios 431

Collaborative Filtering 434

Content-Based Filtering 435

Co-production 438

Customer Conversion Ratio 428

Customerization 438

E-Procurement 445

Exchanges 445

Experience Goods 432

Global Sourcing 444

Information Intensiveness Continuum 432

Mobile Commerce 447

Neutral Marketplaces 445

Recommendation Systems 434

Search Goods 432

Sell-Side Business Models 445

Shopbots 435

Smart Bots 435

Straight Rebuy 445

Telematics 447

# Discussion Questions and Exercises

1. The chapter outlines the characteristics of products that better lend themselves to being sold on the Internet. Interview three consumers regarding whether or not they would feel comfortable buying each of the following products and compare and analyze their reasons vis-à-vis the product characteristics:

   a. Online advice on personal health issues.

   b. A private-brand pasta sauce from your grandmother.

   c. Milk from your local grocer delivered within one hour of ordering online under a one-year binding contract at a price current in that store on the day of ordering with two gallons minimum and 50 cents per-delivery charge.

   Also comment on what kinds of consumers might find these online product offerings to be attractive.

2. The chapter discusses various steps in consumer decision making and the Internet's ability and limitations in taking the consumer through these steps. Discuss these for the following situations:

   **a.** A consumer deciding which anti-virus program to buy online

   **b.** A consumer choosing an MBA program to enroll in

   **c.** A consumer unfamiliar with Europe leasing an apartment in Paris for one year

3. You market one of the following products to business customers: (a) office furniture, (b) lubricating oil for machine tools, or (c) scrap leather collected from shoe factories. Review all online alternatives described in the book and identify which options the prospective customers of each of these products are most likely to use. Explain your answer.

4. Select two companies—a consumer-goods company and an industrial-goods company—that have in place an e-procurement program, and interview the director of each program. Identify the hurdles in bringing more of their procurement online, i.e., expanding the scope of e-procurement.

5. You are the marketing director of a Fortune 500 company with both online and offline presence. A renowned consumer advocate (who is also the president of a consumer privacy group) has written a letter to your president, expressing concern about the tracking of web site visitors using cookies and other tools. The writer acknowledges that this practice is common to all web sites, but still asks that you stop this practice altogether. Write a letter to the consumer advocate outlining the advantages of such consumer online-behavior tracking to consumers themselves and how your company utilizes that information to deliver these advantages while at the same time ensuring no negative effects on the consumers who visits your web site.

# Notes

1　Adapted from Sandeep Krishnamurthy (2002), "The Amazon.com Case," published in *E-Commerce Management: Text and Cases*, South-Western College Publishing, http://krishnamurthy.swcollege.com, ISBN: 0324152523.

2　"A Brief History of the Internet and Related Networks," http://www.isoc.org/internet/history/cerf.html; Gary P. Schneider and James T. Perry, *Electronic Commerce*, Canada: Thomson Learning, pp. 14–20.

3　Robert A. Peterson, Sridhar Balasubramanian, and Bart J.Bronnenberg, "Exploring the Implications of the Internet for Consumer Marketing" in Sheth, Eshghi, and Krishnan eds. *Internet Marketing*, Orlando, Fla.: Harcourt Inc., pp. 120–47.

4　Jagdish N. Sheth and Rajendra S. Sisodia, "Consumer Behavior in the Future," in Sheth, Eshghi, and Krishnan eds. *Internet Marketing*, Orlando, Fla.: Harcourt Inc., pp. 72–90.

5　"The Rise of I-Commerce," Supplement to *The Wall Street Journal*, October 29, 2001.

6　Michael Pastore, "Online Consumers Now the Average Consumer," July 12, 2001, http://cyberatlas.internet.com/big_picture/demographics/article/0,,5901_800201,00.html#table.

7　David Schehr, Sample Research Summary, Gartner Group, *BusinessWeek*, October 15, 2001.

8　"Demographics of the Net Getting Older," August 29, 2000, http://cyberatlas.internet.com/big_picture/demographics/article/0,1323,5901_448131,00.html.

9　"Seniors Use Internet for Shopping," August 31, 1999, http://cyberatlas.internet.com/big_picture/demographics/article/0,,5901_192461,00.html.

10  e-Demographics Report, http://www.emarketer.com, 2000.

11  Donna Hoffman, Tom Novak, and Ann E. Schlosser, "The Evolution of the Digital
    Divide: How Gaps in Internet Access May Impact Electronic Commerce," *Journal of
    Computer Mediated Communication*, Vol. 5 (3), March 2000, http://www.ascusc.org/
    jcmc/vol5/issue3/hoffman.html.

12  e-Demographics Report, http://www.emarketer.com, 2000.

13  The Second Annual Ernst & Young Internet Shopping Study, 1999, p. 9.

14  Rashi Glazer, "Marketing in an Information-Intensive Environment: Strategic Im-
    plications of Knowledge as an Asset," in Sheth, Eshghi, and Krishnan eds. *Internet
    Marketing*, Orlando, Fla.: Harcourt Inc., pp. 31–61.

15  Robert A. Peterson, Sridhar Balasubramanian, and Bart J. Bronnenberg, "Exploring
    the Implications of the Internet for Consumer Marketing," in Sheth, Eshghi, and
    Krishnan eds. *Internet Marketing*, Orlando, Fla.: Harcourt Inc., pp. 120–47.

16  Michael Pastore, "Multichannel Shoppers Key to Retail Success," October 11, 2001,
    http://ecommerce.internet.com/news/insights/trends/article/0,3371,10417_902101,00.
    html.

17  Nick Wingfield, "The Best Way to Buy a Car"; Patrick Barta, "The Best Way to
    Buy a House," *The Wall Street Journal*, November 12, 2001.

18  Barbara Bickart and Robert Schindler, "Internet Forums as Influential Sources of
    Consumer Information," *ACR* Vol. 28, 2001, p. 135, http://www.vancouver.wsu.edu/
    acr/home.htm.

19  Laura Landro, "The Best Way to Get Reliable Health Information," *The Wall Street
    Journal*, November 12, 2001.

20  Asim Ansari, Skander Essegaier, and Rajeev Kohli, "Internet Recommendation Sys-
    tems," *Journal of Marketing Research*, 37 (August 2000), pp. 363–75; Mary Kwak, "Web
    Sites Learn to Make Smarter Suggestions," *Sloan Management Review*, 42(4), Summer
    2001, p. 17.

21  Soyeon Shim, Mary Ann Eastlick, Sherry L. Lotz, and Patricia Warrington, "An On-
    line Prepurchase Intentions Model," *Journal of Retailing*, 77(3), Fall 2001, pp. 397–416.

22  Gerald Häubl and Valerie Trifts, "Consumer Decision Making in Online Shopping
    Environments: The Effects of Interactive Decision Aids," *Marketing Science*, 19 (1),
    2000, pp. 4–21.

23  Eric Brynjolfsson and Michael D. Smith, "The Great Equalizer? Consumer Choice
    Behavior at Internet Shopbots," *MIT Sloan School of Management*, July 2000, http://
    ebusiness.mit.edu/papers/tge.

24  Kevin Jones, "Ecommerce Liposuction: Key to Stealth Strategy," *Forbes ASAP*,
    June 4, 1999.

25  John Edwards, "Is That Your Best Offer?" November 1, 2000, http://www.cio.com/
    archive/110100_et.html.

26  "Front End," *Information Week*, November 12, 2001, p. 17.

27  Don Peppers and Martha Rogers, *The One-to-One Manager*, 1999, New York: Dou-
    bleday, Random House Inc.

28  Jerry Wind and Arvind Rangaswamy, "Customerization: The Next Revolution in
    Mass Customization," *Journal of Interactive Marketing*, 15(1), Winter 2001, pp. 13–32.

29  Eric J. Johnson, Steven Bellman, and Gerald L. Lohse, "Cognitive Lock-In and the
    Power Law of Practice," March 12, 2002, http://www.cebiz.org/downloads/power_

law_lockin.pdf; Eric J. Johnson, Wendy W. Moe, Peter S. Fader, Steven Bellman, and Gerald L. Lohse, "On the Depth and Dynamics of Online Search Behavior," July 2002, http://www.cebiz.org/downloads/power_law_lockin.pdf.

30 Erik Brynjolfsson and Michael D. Smith, The Great Equalizer? Consumer Choice at Internet Shopbots, MIT Working paper, July 2000, http://ebusiness.mit.edu/papers/tge.

31 Johanna Bennett, "It's My Life," Supplement to *The Wall Street Journal*, October 29, 2001.

32 Bill Richards, "Following the Crumbs—The Rise of I-Commerce," Supplement to *The Wall Street Journal*, October 29, 2001.

33 K. B. Sheehan and M. G. Hoy, "Flaming, Complaining, Abstaining: How Online Users Respond to Privacy Concerns," *Journal of Advertising*, 28(3), pp. 37–52.

34 Joseph E. Phelps, Giles D'Souza, and Glen J. Nowak, "Antecedents and Consequences of Consumer Privacy Concerns: An Empirical Investigation," *Journal of Interactive Marketing*, 15(4), Autumn 2001, pp. 2–17.

35 "Online Fraud: Though Victim Percentage is Low, Fear is High," *Estats-Enews*, http://www.emarketer.com—June 29, 2001.

36 Ellen Garbarino and Michal Strahilevitz, "Gender Differences in the Risk Perceptions and Effectiveness of Risk Reducers in Online Purchasing," *Advances in Consumer Research*, Volume 28, 2001, p. 99.

37 Patrick D. Lynch, Robert J. Kent, and Srini S. Srinivasan, "The Global Internet Shopper: Evidence from Shopping Tasks in Twelve Countries," *Journal of Advertising Research*, May–June 2001, pp. 15–23.

38 Glen L. Urban, Fareena Sultan, and William J. Qualls, "Placing Trust at the Center of Your Internet Strategy," *Sloan Management Review*, 42(1), Fall 2000, pp. 39–48.

39 Ellen Neuborne, "Break It to Them Quickly," *Business Week e.biz*, October 29, 2001, p. Eb10.

40 Wendy W. Moe and Peter S. Fader, "Which Visits Lead to Purchases? Dynamic Conversion Behavior at E-commerce Sites," Working paper discussed in Mitch Betts, "Turning Browsers to Buyers," *Sloan Management Review*, 42(2), Winter 2001, pp. 8–9.

41 Michael Silverstein, Nina Abdelmessih, and Peter Stanger, Winning the Online Consumer 2.0—Converting Traffic into Profitable Relationships, BCG Report, 2/25/2001, http://www.bcg.com/publications/files/022101_Winning_online_consumer_report_summary.

42 Bill Chambers, Gail Donnelly, and Joshua Shehab, "Web Self-Service: A Good Buy," *Information Week*, August 13, 2001, pp. 39–42.

43 Youngme Moon and Frances X. Frei, "Exploding the Self-Service Myth," *Harvard Business Review*, May–June 2000, pp. 26–27.

44 Ryan Kerrigan, Eric V. Roegner, Dennis D. Swinford, and Craig C. Zawada, B2-Basics, The McKinsey Quarterly, 2001 Number 1, http://www.mckinseyquarterly.com.

45 The entire section on B2B commerce has been adapted from several research reports—E-commerce B2B report, 2000, http://www.emarketer.com; Andy Blackburn, Hal Sirkin, and Jim Andrew, The B2B Opportunity: Creating Advantage through E-Marketplaces, October 2000, http://www.bcg.com/publications—browse by E-commerce; Coming into Focus: Using the Lens of Economic Value to clarify the Impact of B2B e-Marketplaces, CAPS Research and Mckinsey and Company, September

2000, http://www.mckinsey.com/features/caps_white_paper/featured%20paper.html; Charles Phillips and Mary Meeker, The B2B Internet Report—Collaborative Commerce, Morgan Stanley Dean Witter, April 2000; Building the B2B Foundation—Positioning Net Market Makers for Success, ATKearney 2000, http://www.atkearney.com/main.taf?site=1&a=5&b=3&c=1&d=4.

46 David Rocks, "The Net as a Lifeline," *BusinessWeek e.biz*, October 29, 2001, pp. Eb16–eb23.

47 Chuck Moozakis, "Reverse Auctions Pictured," *InternetWeek*, October 29, 2001, p. 17.

48 Rajdeep Grewal, James M. Corner, and Raj Mehta, "An Investigation into the Antecedents of Organizational Participation in Business-to-Business Electronic Markets," *Journal of Marketing* 65 (July 2001), pp. 17–33.

49 David Kenny and John F. Marshall, "Contextual Marketing: The Real Business of the Internet," *Harvard Business Review*, November–December 2000, pp. 119–25.

# CHAPTER 13

## Creating Market Values for the Customer

## Wanted: VALUE

> Value, not money, is the basic currency of all human interaction. When we meet someone, we try to quickly assess how long it would be worth our while to talk to that person. If an incoming phone call shows up on our caller ID, we promptly decide if we would gain anything by taking the call at that time. If we get 10 letters in the mail, we look through them and then choose to open only those that we expect to contain some information of value to us. This is even truer for marketplace exchanges. The only reason the customers are even in the marketplace is that they are looking for something of value. The business that can deliver them that value, and deliver more of it than its competitors, gains the customer's patronage.
>
> (*ValueSpace*, 2001, pages 3–4)[1]

What underlies some companies' ability to offer outstanding value? How can other marketers create market values for their customers? Examples of value innovation abound: Barnes and Nobles bookstores are large theaters, complete with coffee shop and music room; British Airways offers showers in the arrival lounge; Nordstrom's salespeople keep an eye out for merchandise that may be of interest to specific customers; L.L. Bean will gladly refund merchandise returned anytime during its lifetime, no questions asked; and Southwest Airlines' cabin crew will announce a garage sale in the destination city.

We begin this chapter by discussing the two dimensions of value delivery—effectiveness and efficiency. Following that, we present specific management tools that would enable firms to deliver market values to customers. These tools are specific to individual values that the firm might wish to pursue. We also discuss the ethical issues specific to each of these values from a consumer's standpoint. The next section deals with a measurement strategy. Our discussion dwells first on a method of determining customer values; it then suggests measurement statements to assess how well various value-delivery tools are doing their job, from the customers' viewpoint. In the final section, we return to the opening theme of the book, namely, customer orientation and the firm's ultimate goal of keeping customers happy. We conclude by suggesting a measurement tool that tells the firm just how happy its customers are.

# Value Delivery

As defined in Chapter 1, value is what customers seek in products, services, and suppliers.[2] It stems from a product's potential to satisfy a need or want of the customer. The fulfillment of a customer's need or want is called value delivery.

## Dimensions of Value Delivery

Value delivery has two dimensions, effectiveness and efficiency. Effectiveness is the ability of the product or service to meet the customer's needs and wants. Efficiency is minimal cost to the customer, measured in money, time, and physical effort, to receive that value. The less a product or service costs, the more efficient it is from the customer's point of view.

If a marketer's offering fulfills a customer's needs and wants very well, and if in obtaining and using that offering, the customer has to expend as few resources (time, money, and physical effort) as possible, then both efficiency and effectiveness are being simultaneously harnessed to achieve the *best value* for the customer (see Figure 13.1). There are many examples of companies offering both effectiveness and efficiency in delivering customer value. For example, the Toyota Camry is a high-quality car sold at a relatively low price. Mass merchandise catalog companies, such as L.L. Bean or J. Crew, offer customers better-known, branded products (effectiveness) with the convenience of shopping from home (efficiency).

---

**FIGURE 13.1**     **Dimensions of Value Delivery**

|  |  | Efficiency (Resource conservation) | |
|---|---|---|---|
|  |  | Poor | Good |
| **Effectiveness** (Need/want fulfillment) | Good | Effectiveness value | Best value |
|  | Poor | Poor value | Efficiency value |

---

In the business-to-business service markets, Federal Express offers a value via both effectiveness and efficiency. It offers effectiveness by satisfying customer need for on-time, guaranteed delivery of time-sensitive documents and packages. On the efficiency side, it conserves the customer's time and effort resources via its pickup service and via giving customers computer software so they may process the shipping themselves. However, its price value is no better than its competitors'. Business firms also offer efficiency value to customers by providing access via the Internet so that customer effort in interacting with the firm is minimized.

Firms that offer electronic document delivery, such as a database or an article from a journal, offer both effectiveness and efficiency; having the information on an electronic medium allows customers to use that information more effectively, for example, via word search, cutting and pasting, moving the text around, or enhancing the graphs and photos. Also the customer effort is minimized (saves the effort to get it by mail or to go to the library).

## Tools for Creating Customer Values

To offer various values to the customer, marketers need to incorporate certain attributes and elements in their offerings. For example, to offer convenience as a value, marketers have to incorporate certain time- and effort-saving mechanisms in the product or in the manner in which customers can purchase that product or service. As described in Chapter 1, different types of value are sought by the user, payer, and buyer roles. Users seek performance value and social and emotional values. Payers want price value and credit and financing values. Buyers desire service value and convenience and personalization values. Offering each of these market values requires certain marketing tools, summarized in Table 13.1 and described in the following sections.

## Tools for Creating Market Values              TABLE 13.1

| User Values | **Performance** | **Social** | **Emotional** |
|---|---|---|---|
| | • Quality improvement.<br>• Innovations.<br>• Mass customization.<br>• Warranties and guarantees. | • Price exclusivity.<br>• Limited availability.<br>• Social image ads.<br>• Exclusive offerings. | • Emotional communications. |
| **Payer Values** | **Price** | **Credit** | **Financing** |
| | • Low price from lower margins.<br><br>• Low price from increased productivity (achieved through economies of scale, modernized plant, automation, business process reengineering). | • Acceptance of credit cards.<br><br>• Offering of own credit card.<br>• Deferred payment. | • Leasing.<br><br>• Customized financing. |
| **Buyer Values** | **Service** | **Convenience** | **Personalization** |
| | • Product display and demonstration.<br><br>• Knowledgeable salespersons.<br><br>• Responsiveness.<br>• User support and maintenance service. | • Convenient point-of-access.<br><br>• Automated transaction recording. | • Personal attention and courtesy.<br><br>• Interpersonal relationships. |

# Creating Market Values for Users

The user is primarily concerned that the product or service performs as desired and that its use delivers social and emotional benefits.

## Performance Value

The user obtains the universal value of performance when the product or service delivers its physical performance better than competing alternatives do and when the product performs that way consistently without failure. A vivid example of what's meant by performance value is 3M Worldwide's double-coated tape, used to bond two surfaces. As reported in *ValueSpace*, one application of this tape is sheet metal bonding in the body of a truck. The current methods for bonding are riveting or welding. 3M is working toward replacing the rivets with double-coated tapes. The adhesive tape will eliminate any air gaps that inevitably remain between any two riveted surfaces and will give a seamless joint. This would mean a good moisture seal and no vibration noise. And, of course, the bonding is as strong as possible. Moreover, using adhesive tape instead of rivets or welding will save on production costs as it takes much less time and skill to apply a bonding tape than to apply rivets or welds.

Physical performance stems from the physical composition of the product. As such, it is directly linked to product attributes and to product quality. More specifically, firms can offer superior performance value by adopting four tools: quality improvement, product innovations, mass customization, and warranties and guarantees.

## Quality Improvement

Companies can offer better performance value by building quality into their products. Many firms aim for zero defects, eliminating product failures completely. The automobile industry is an illustrative case. As late as the early 1980s, the U.S. automobile industry offered cars that, with few exceptions, broke down frequently. Japanese cars became the choice of many consumers simply because they were more reliable. In the late 1980s to early 1990s, the U.S. car industry turned to building quality into their cars and, consequently, regained some of the lost market share. In fact, Saturn was created by General Motors simply to build a quality car company from scratch—free from the legacy of poor quality with which its parent company, in the eyes of many consumers, has been afflicted.

In the services industry, firms can improve the quality of their offering by hiring well-qualified service staff and then by continually training and retraining them. An example of consumer service in which quality is very critical to the customer is surgical procedures. The patient wants to be absolutely sure that the procedure will be carried out with expertise and dependability. Hospitals can offer the desired performance value by hiring qualified and skilled surgeons and nursing staff, and by acquiring high-quality equipment and keeping the operating room meticulously sterilized.[3] For an example of a service firm committed to zero defects, see the Window on Practice box.

An absence of quality in products can be a major ethical concern, in both the consumer and business markets. Take the case of the tread separation in the Firestone/Bridgestone ATX tires on the Ford Explorer in late 2001 that resulted in several hundred injuries including the deaths of at least 46 people in the United States. Most troubling in this case is the fact both Ford and Firestone may have known of these quality defects since 1993, but they remained quiet about it, until they finally had no choice but to recall millions of these tires. Similarly, in the case of machinery, it is important that the machines are absolutely safe to use; otherwise, they endanger the lives of several people working on them in factories.

## Innovation

Firms can also increase the performance value of their offerings by designing new features in products and/or services. Consider VCRs that enable slow-motion viewing, cassette recorders that feature voice-activated recording, automobiles equipped with antilock braking devices, aqua-tread tires that do not slip on wet pavement, detergents that clean in cold water, and hotels that offer in-room fax service. Today we take them for granted, but when they first appeared, each added to the performance value derived by the user. Current examples of innovations are automobiles equipped with navigation devices (an electronic map that shows where you are and gives directions to the desired destinations), a great value to rental-car customers driving in unfamiliar cities; computers that convert

# WINDOW ON PRACTICE

## FedEx Quality Improvement Program

Quality has been a top priority at Federal Express right from the outset. It achieved, for example, 99 percent levels of reliability on its on-time delivery. Yet FedEx was not satisfied, for it realized that a 99 percent on-time delivery would still leave a lot of customers (those affected by the 1 percent error rate) irate. So it began a program of zero failures, counting errors in absolute numbers rather than as percentages.

The company developed a Service Quality Index (SQI), computed daily, based on errors in 12 different delivery events weighed by the seriousness of the error that was reflective of the amount of aggravation caused to customers. For example, missing a promised delivery date generated five points, compared to one point when a customer requested that an invoice be adjusted. If *everything* went wrong, the SQI daily score would be 40 million.

In 1988, when the program was established, the estimated SQI score was 152,000 points per day. The company set its first goal at holding this level (which actually implied a 20 percent improvement, given forecasted growth in package volume of 20 percent). FedEx's employees surpassed this goal, with the actual 1989 SQI score at 133,000 points. Accordingly, the company's profit goals were reached too. This level of attention to detail in its quality program has enabled FedEx to offer its customers unparalleled performance value.

**Source:** Adapted from Christopher H. Lovelock, "Federal Express Quality Improvement Program," Case 44, in Christopher H. Lovelock and Charles B. Weinberg, *Marketing Challenges: Cases & Exercises* (New York: McGraw Hill, 3rd ed., 1993), pp. 545–558. Additional information available at http://www.federalexpress.com.

voice into written text; software that allows manipulation of photographic images; many Internet-based information sources; and new antidepressant medications.

Companies that focus on innovation have a culture of innovation. One of the most innovative companies in America is 3M. To foster its climate of innovation, 3M is reported to have the following work rules: (1) twenty-five percent of each division's revenue should come from products that did not exist five years ago; and (2) researchers are encouraged to spend up to 15 percent of their resources on unassigned projects of personal interest. Other innovative companies are Microsoft and Intel, where products are being constantly upgraded by their newer versions every 18 months or so.

Innovative companies also spend more on R&D. PIMS (Profit Impact of Marketing Strategies) is a program of data gathering and analysis that analyzes about 3,800 business units on about 200 pieces of data to identify strategy factors that determine business profitability. An analysis of firms in the PIMS database found that R&D investment leads to more sales from new products (see Figure 13.2). Furthermore, the proportion of sales from new products was positively correlated with the gains in market share.[4] See Figure 13.3.

Innovations are the lifeline of a company, yet innovations that result in unneccessary obsolescence, are nonmigratory in nature, and do not create value for the customer are really not innovations in an ethical sense. Another ethical issue with regard to innovations arises when certain products are introduced in developing countries as innovations. Nestlé came under fire for its aggressive marketing of powdered baby formula in developing countries. Its marketing messages suggested that the powdered baby formula was better for the baby compared to mother's milk. Nestlé has also launched a brand of

**FIGURE 13.2**      **R & D Leads to More Sales from New Products**

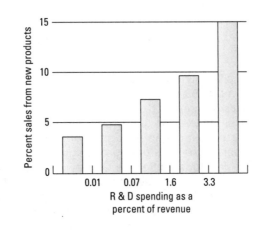

**FIGURE 13.3**      **New Product Activity Leads to Gains in Market Share**

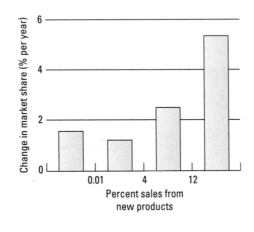

bottled water called "Pure Life" in Pakistan and Brazil which is raising ethical issues of selling water in countries where an estimated one billion people lack access to basic water services.[5] Product innovations in certain categories, like alcoholic beverages, can also be risky. In a test marketing exercise of St. Ides Freeze & Squeeze, a Slurpee-style "Special Brew" with 6 percent alcohol, the product was placed alongside children's frozen snacks and Italian ices in the stores. This prompted children to ask for the product and parents purchased it for them assuming that the product was good for children since it was in the aisle for child products. The test marketing created a stir against marketers who are trying to use such products to train children to be future drinkers.[6]

## Mass Customization

The third tool for improved performance value is **mass customization**, the offer of customized products to individual customers without raising the price due to customization.[7] Motorola, for example, offers 20 million varieties of pagers and assembles them after it receives the customer order from one of its salespersons in the field who transmits the order from a laptop. Similarly Hewlett-Packard offers customized products to its business customers. This is made possible mainly by producing the product in modules and then assembling the product from these modules at the last step in the supply chain, such as at the distributor warehouse.

  The first customers to benefit from mass customization were organizations because their orders tend to be relatively large. However, advances in automation and information processing have enabled mass customization to meet the needs of consumers. As detailed in the Window on Practice box, Levi Strauss will even customize a single pair of jeans.

  The ethical question in the case of mass customization concerns whether too much variety is good or bad for the consumer. And is lack of standardization necessarily a bad thing?

## Warranties and Guarantees

To alleviate customer apprehensions of possible product failures, companies also offer warranties or guarantees. Whereas warranties offer certain insurance by the manufacturer that specific product features will perform as promised, guarantees are offered by the stores that sell the product. Sears, for example, offers a satisfaction guarantee that gives customers the opportunity to return a product if they are not satisfied with it. L.L. Bean offers a lifetime warranty that you can return its merchandise if it proves unsatisfactory, no matter how

# WINDOW ON PRACTICE

## Blue Jeans for You Alone

If you walk into the Original Levi's Store in Cincinnati, Ohio, you will be greeted by a sales clerk with a measuring tape in hand and a personal computer (PC) on a nearby desk. He will take your measurements, feed the data into a computer, make final adjustments to the blueprint of a pair of jeans that pops up on the PC screen, push the transmit key, give you a receipt for the $40 you paid, and send you home. Forty-eight hours later, the jeans arrive at your home, delivered by FedEx! The jeans must fit you like a glove or you can return them for a full refund.

  This is how it works: The PC in the retail store transmits the data to the Levi's factory in Tennessee. There, the computer data are received directly by a robotic tailor who cuts a bolt of denim precisely to the customer's measurements. Usually, the jeans are shipped back to the store in three weeks, but for a slight extra charge, customers have the option of receiving them within 48 hours. The service is a blessing to women, many of whom have difficulty finding jeans that fit them. When the service for women's jeans was introduced in the Cincinnati store, sales went up by 300 percent compared with the same period the previous year.

**Source:** Adapted from Glenn Rifkin, "Digital Blue Jeans Pour Data and Legs into Customized Fit," *New York Times*, November 8, 1994, pp. A1, D8. Additional information available at http://www.levi.com.

long ago you bought it. In business-to-business markets, companies like Caterpillar and Boeing are well known for offering outstanding warranties.

One service company that offers unmatched performance value is the Miami-based Bugs Burger Bug Killer (BBBK), which provides a zero-defect exterminating service. This zero-defect performance is backed by, and is reflected in, its extraordinary performance guarantee. Customers don't pay a dime unless they are satisfied that the company has successfully destroyed all pests and breeding and nesting places. Should defects be found later, the company refunds the last 12 months' service fee and pays for service by a competing firm for one year. Should a guest in a hotel or restaurant serviced by BBBK find a bug, the company would pay for the guest's meal or room and offer a free gift for a future meal or room. The company charges about four times the market rate, and customers who value performance and quality happily pay it.[8]

Sometimes, warranties and guarantees from manufacturers provide customers with immeasurable security; however, when there is a problem, the manufacturer gets out of its commitments using the fine print on the warrantee or guarantee—a cause of ethical concern.

## Social and Emotional Values

The personal values that satisfy customers' wants are the social and emotional values. These are neither engineered in the product nor delivered via better service. Rather, they are created by association with other desirable objects, persons, situations, or symbols.

Social values are derived from the association of a product with one or more social groups in society. These groups may be defined on the basis of demographic, socioeconomic, or cultural-ethnic characteristics and tend to be defined in the customer's mind as either a positive or negative stereotype. For example, the stereotype of a rich person driving a Cadillac may be perceived to be a positive stereotype by some and a negative stereotype by others.

Marketers offer social and emotional value through prestige pricing, limited availability, social-image-based marketing communications that focus on association with desired persons or objects or symbols, and new exclusive offerings. Emotional value is also deliverable through emotional advertising.

### Prestige Pricing

Pricing a product high enough so that only a few customers can afford it ensures that the product will be sold in limited target markets. Ubiquitous availability and universal use of a product detract from its exclusivity. High price itself leads to prestige, which is further fueled by limited penetration in the mass market. Marketers seeking to offer customers this value would not then seek to simultaneously offer price value. High-priced cars such as Lotus, Rolls Royce, and Lamborghini; watches such as Rolex and Concorde; and pens such as Mont Blanc all give their owners social prestige.

At the same time, when price is used as an indication of quality, it sometimes leads to irrational buying and conspicuous consumption. Sometimes children and consumers who really cannot afford prestige prices become targets of prestige pricing. Children are driven by peer group pressure to purchase high-priced products, and the poor use prestige pricing as their insurance against the risk of product failure.

### Limited Availability

Related to exclusive pricing is the strategy of limited availability. Many products are offered in limited editions and quantities and, for this reason, acquire social value for their owners. Examples include the Cobra limited edition of Ford Mustang; or First Day postage stamps, which are bought by customers on the first day of issue; and rare pieces of art, such as original Rembrandt or Van Gogh paintings.

Limited editions of products are sought by customers not just for their real value but also for their possession value, and this is a cause of ethical concern. It creates extra transaction costs for the customers as they search harder for the product, and it also creates artificial demand and inflated prices. Web sites like eBay thrive in the trade of such collectibles.

## Social-Image-Based Marketing Communications

Much of the social and emotional value stems from marketing communications that associate the product or service with certain social symbols and feelings. Thus, Nike athletic shoes are depicted as suited to the serious athlete while Air Walk is for the young and trendy. Elizabeth Taylor's Passion perfume is for the successful, mature woman while Tommy Boy or Tommy Girl colognes are for teenagers and adolescents.

These communications stem not just from advertising but also from other elements of the marketing mix. Thus, a product design could convey a sleek, modern image or traditionalism; it could be gaudy or subtle, signifying poor or refined taste. Price also communicates social exclusivity. Place has social image associated with it, such as a location in a business district or in a run-down strip mall. Moreover, social observations on the street about who is using a product or service also communicate its social value. Loss-leader pricing is one specific approach within the lower-margin strategy category. Stores typically offer a few selected items at a very low price, sometimes below cost, to attract customers. They take a loss on these items in the hope of making more profit on other items that the customers buy.

The most important drawback of social image-based marketing communications is that it leads to consumerism and materialism. It is manifested in the chronic purchasing of new goods and services without a thought for whether these products are actually needed or not. Such marketing communication in the fashion and beauty industry for its products has also created the image of the "perfect woman." Millions of women around the world go on diets to conform to this image, leading to eating disorders like anorexia and bulimia. A report in *The Wall Street Journal* also states that over 1.5 million Americans have nose jobs, tummy tucks, and breast enhancements every year to achieve this ever-elusive image. In fact, children's toys, such as the Barbie and Ken dolls, have also been criticized for beginning the indoctrination for such images in childhood itself.

## New Exclusive Offerings

The fourth avenue to delivering social and emotional value is expanded product offerings that already possess social or emotional value for a segment of customers. For example, Budget Rental Car Company was the first one to recognize the opportunity and to offer luxury cars, like the Lincoln. Today, Budget is the only company that offers Jaguars, a car that connotes a great social value to many consumers.

## Emotional Communications

Many of the tools that create social value also create emotional value. The feeling of exclusivity of ownership, for example, gives some people an emotional uplift. But a more direct route to engendering emotional value is the use of **emotional communications**— communications that evoke some emotional experience in the viewer or reader. Valentine's Day gifts like flowers, candy, and diamond jewelry are sold as symbols of love, and much of the emotional symbolism is communicated to customers by marketing communications. **Social cause marketing** programs that promote social causes, such as race unity, arouse strong emotional bonds of identification among many viewers. For example, Benetton uses very vivid images of social causes, such as race harmony and AIDS research, to establish such an emotional bond with its target customers, who generally can be characterized as global youth—broad-minded youth with awareness of global issues. A car dealer of U.S. cars in Michigan gives out American flags on the Fourth of July and urges people to buy American.

One legendary commercial that is the epitome of emotional advertising is by the Coca-Cola Company. In the ad, a child offers a bottle of Coke to Mean Joe Greene, a football star. After initially declining, the football player finally accepts the Coke at the child's insistence. The child watches his hero gulping the beverage; and the football star is so moved by the child's gesture, and perhaps so delighted by the thirst-quenching beverage, that he tosses his jersey to the grateful child. This advertisement was so successful in generating the desired emotions in viewers that it was used worldwide.

Use of children in emotional communication to sell products has long been criticized as unhealthy. Another example of emotional advertising that seems really opportunistic is advertising the "hope," "wish," and "longing" for babies to the vulnerable group of infertile or desperate couples. As Dr. Kathleen Nolan, a bioethicist at the Hastings Institute, says cautiously, "It seems wrong to play upon the pain of infertility in order to sell fertility services."[9]

# Creating Market Values for Payers

The types of value most important to payers involve low cost and ease of making payments. Thus, marketers' tools to create value for payers include keeping the cost of purchasing and using the product low and offering services that are helpful to payers.

## Price Value

The price value represents the relative affordability of the product or service to the customer. It is the degree of economic sacrifice the customer has to make to purchase the product or service.

As discussed in Chapter 1, affordability is a function of buying power and prices. Buying power depends on the buyer's disposable income. Price comprises both the initial purchase price and the cost of maintaining the product usage-ready or the cost of using the product. The concept of lifetime cost or life-cycle costing is supposed to capture these two components. Marketers of initially high-price items need to draw customer attention to the life-cycle cost of their offerings.

Take a refrigerator, for example. The cost of electricity and maintenance over the 12 years it is likely to last is estimated to be as much as 65 to 70 percent of the total cost of using the product. In other words, the initial cost is only approximately 30 percent of the total cost. With such a product, affordability goes beyond the initial cost and must include the cost of upkeep and maintenance over the product's life. One way in which companies are sensitizing customers to this notion of life-cycle costing is by attaching energy guide tags to the front of appliances in stores.

While affordability is a characteristic of the customer (which the marketer cannot alter), price is an element of the marketing mix, and the marketer can do something about it. Companies that want to differentiate themselves on this value are constantly striving to offer the product or service at a lower price. To reduce price, companies can opt for two approaches: (1) accept lower margins, and/or (2) reduce costs of production by improving productivity.

The AMA Code of Ethics recognizes that the ethical issues in pricing arise from marketers engaging in price fixing, practicing predatory pricing, and not disclosing the full price associated with any purchase.

### Low Price from Lower Margins

The **lower-margin approach** consists of selling at a low-profit margin to attract customers. Many firms use this approach, cutting their prices below the competitors' price to attract the competitors' customers. Long-distance phone companies that are not the market-share leaders (e.g., MCI and Sprint) have used price as a competitive weapon to take share away from the market leader. Similarly, smaller airlines, such as the now defunct People's Express and currently successful Southwest Airlines, offer extremely low fares. These companies offer limited schedules; the national airlines attempt to match fares on the routes these smaller airlines operate.

The lower-margin approach is often the outcome of a *strategic insight*. That is, some companies simply figure out the right formula that enables them to offer the required price value. Budget Rental Car Company performed an analysis of its costs and car-usage pattern and figured out that it can profitably offer unlimited mileage, a practice the company then pioneered. Likewise, Texas Instruments decided to sell its electronic calculators with a low-price strategy because it foresaw the potential drop in production costs that would result from the experience learning curve.[10]

Some companies, such as Hanna Andersson Corp., a Portland, Oregon, mail-order business selling children's clothing, use tactics that not only appeal to the payer but also encourage repeat business for the firm while reinforcing the company's image as an ethical firm. Customers can return clothes back to the company when their children have outgrown them. If the returns are in good condition, customers can get up to 20 percent of the original price of the clothes as credit towards their next purchase. This strategy does lead to reduced margins for the business, but it has also generated good publicity and loyalty from its customers. The used clothes are donated to local charities, disaster relief organizations, and orphanages. Since 1984, more than 750,000 articles of clothing have been donated to charity. Customers feel good about being part of this effort and the strategy is bound to be beneficial for the business in the long run.[11]

## Low Price from Increased Productivity

The second enabler of lower price is the **increased-productivity approach**, in which a firm strives for a lower cost of production. Higher productivity makes individual firms or whole industries more competitive by enabling them to offer better economic value to the customer. A case in point is Compaq, which had been losing in sales and market share for years. In 1992, following a major restructuring effort designed to sharply hike productivity, it was able to cut prices, offering customers good economic value on its computer products, which were already known to be high in performance value. By 1994, the company's revenues had doubled, making it Number 1 in the PC business with a 12-percent market share. More important, despite a price cut, its profits increased fourfold.[12] More recently, both Dell and Gateway computers have successfully expanded the consumer PC market with very clever commercials and lower prices through economies of scale.

To lower production costs, companies can choose from among several strategies. They can develop economies of scale, use modernized plants that operate more efficiently, automate processes, and use business process reengineering.

**Economies of Scale.** Economies of scale occur when larger volume leads to lower per-unit costs. This happens both because larger production units may run more efficiently and because they distribute fixed-cost overheads over a larger number of product units. High-volume firms can also negotiate more favorable prices from their suppliers, which then reduces their cost of production or of acquisition of resalable items. Wal-Mart, for example, is able to negotiate long-term contracts with its suppliers on favorable terms because of the size of its purchases.

One of the key findings of the PIMS study referred to earlier also confirms the role of the economies of scale. The PIMS study found that market share and profitability are strongly related. The reason, as the authors explain, is that the larger shareholders produce and operate on a larger scale and, thus, obtain a lower cost due to economies of scale. This reduced cost allows them both a higher margin and a capability to offer better price value to customers.[13]

**Modernized Plant.** Outdated plant and equipment run inefficiently, and any modernization of plant reduces production costs. The casebook *Marketing Challenges* describes a company in Vancouver that produced skylights, whose modernized plant gave it a 20 percent cost advantage over Columbia Plastics, a manufacturer of skylights in Seattle. This cost advantage gave the Vancouver firm the ability to offer better economic value to Columbia's customers, stealing substantial business from the latter.[14]

Furthermore, the adoption of better substitute technologies may enable better cost structures. Thus, use of plastic and fiberglass as a substitute for metal components in such wide-ranging products as automobiles, chemical tanks, plumbing piping, boats, and rocket combustion chambers has enabled various pioneering companies to differentiate themselves by offering their customers better price value.

**Automation.**  Many companies have reduced costs through automation—the use of technology and machines to substitute, partly or wholly, for human labor that would otherwise be required to perform a task. Automation may simply make an employee's work more efficient, or it may remove the need for an employee to personally attend to the customer.

As an example, consider a warehouse automation program at Kinney Drugs, a drug retail chain store headquartered in New York. The overall warehousing process under the newly automated system uses bar codes to track all inventory from the time it arrives to outgoing shipment. Radio frequency (RF) computer terminals match the purchase order upon inventory arrival and assign a unique bar-coded number, which is then easily tracked and managed so that arrivals are available immediately for outshipping without first going to a central inventory area (i.e., arrivals can be cross-docked immediately). The outgoing shipment order is itself automated by an EDI (electronic data interchange) system that links the warehouse to retail drug stores, where the inventory-movement data are generated and fed back to the warehouse. Such automations not only increase productivity but also reduce errors.[15]

Examples of the automation of the encounter with the customer include the use of ATM banking machines, voice mail in companies, or automatic checkout on the TV screen in many hotels. Also, electronic commerce is the latest in business's attempt to automate customer information services and sales transactions. Business web sites offer information, searchable by the user, based on his or her specific information needs. Because users self-navigate, it saves company costs over a human agent providing information. Not only do these procedures reduce a company's cost of serving its customers, but sometimes they also save customers time and hassle and, thus, offer convenience value.

A recent report shows that there are some banks that charge a customer for the automated ATM services without being completely transparent about the issue. This results in small charges on customers' accounts, which may or may not come to their notice. Similarly, customers are quite happy about the e-ticketing option offered by airlines, but they are not too happy about the fact that most airlines are going to charge them a $10 fee if they ask for a paper ticket. It feels like automation is leading to a charge for the basic services that a customer takes for granted.

**Business Process Reengineering.**  The objective of business process reengineering is to design entire business processes (e.g., order-fulfillment process, equipment-installation process, new-product-development process) to make them more efficient. Reengineering differs from simple quality upgrade or continuous improvement. Rather than merely improving it, **reengineering** redesigns a process starting from a blank slate. The objective is to reduce the **cycle time** (the total time it takes for the entire production and/or delivery task to be completed), the amount of labor input, and the component and processing costs.[16]

For example, McDonnell Douglas Corp., bought by Boeing, Inc., in 1997, undertook a program of reengineering for the assembly of the C-17 military cargo plane. The C-17 plane was a new type of airlifter to support the military's Rapid Deployment Force and was initially ordered in 1980. Subsequent funding was erratic, and changing military goals made timely and efficient development and production difficult. The company managed to meet the required delivery schedule but only at substantial cost overruns. Under the U.S. Air Force's contract, however, its price was firm, so McDonnell Douglas had to reexamine and reengineer its processes. Two years into reengineering, the Drivematics team (the unit assigned to explore reengineering first) had produced dramatic results. It had cut work time on assembly of the wing skin on a pair of wings by 75 percent, and the time spent in correcting mistakes on this part of the job had plunged from 8,625 hours to 611 hours. The company estimates that reengineering this procedure alone saved $1 million per plane.[17] To learn how another firm (Taco Bell) used reengineering to help it offer more value to payers, see the Window on Practice box.

# WINDOW ON PRACTICE

## Reengineering at Taco Bell

In the late 1980s, Taco Bell embarked on a major reengineering effort. In many fast-food restaurants, the cost of food that a customer gets is about 25 cents of every dollar the customer spends; the rest goes into operations and marketing. Taco Bell turned this around. It did some customer research and found that what customers wanted was good food, served in a clean environment and at an affordable price. To increase the value customers get for every dollar they spend, Taco Bell cut down costs by simplifying both the management process and the operations. The company eliminated entire layers of management and gave restaurant managers more responsibility. To reduce operations costs, the company redesigned the restaurant building. It reduced the kitchen area from 70 percent to 30 percent and increased the customer area to 70 percent, doubling the seating capacity. To accomplish this, the company implemented the concept of K-minus (i.e., kitchenless restaurant). Now all cooking is done in central commissaries, from which food is delivered to individual restaurants that now focus on serving the customer rather than cooking the food ingredients.

The gains from this effort are best described in the words of John E. Martin, the company's CEO, who led the effort:

> "This has also doubled our productivity. Today, our peak capacity is $1,000 per hour (compared to $400 per hour before the reengineering effort), and our average customer pricing has gone down by about 25 percent!"

**Source:** Adapted from Michael Hammer and James Champy, *One Company's Experience: Taco Bell, Reengineering the Corporation* (New York: Harper Collins, 1993), pp. 171–181. Additional information available at http://www.tacobell.com.

## Credit and Financing Values

Payers seek credit and financing values because they improve affordability by creating deferred payments or providing credit. Specifically, credit value is delivered in several ways:

- Sellers may accept credit cards issued by third parties or banks.
- Sellers may issue their own credit cards or give credit by other instruments (e.g., a small store might give a credit voucher that the customer signs as proof of having received credit).
- Sellers may allow a delayed or deferred payment, such as in 90-days-same-as-cash options utilized by many vendors.

Offering credit was a pioneering strategy adopted by Sears, which, on top of its promise of satisfaction guaranteed, always offered financing arrangements enabling customers to charge their purchases. Sears had credit cards available to customers long before any other major retailer did, reaching almost 40 million households.

Financing goes beyond simple credit and involves specific payment schedules designed for a customer or for a group of customers. Leasing is one such system of financing. Another means is customized financing offered by many companies especially to business customers of capital equipment. Lucent Technologies, formerly AT&T Network Systems, which manufactures telephone equipment such as switches, cable, and transmission equipment, has created a financing feature that enables customers without the necessary capital to quickly modernize their telephone networks.

Leasing not only helps as a mechanism to defer large cash outlay but also may offer tax advantages to both individuals and companies. Some companies have leasing subsidiaries or divisions. One of these, GE Capital, offers customers affordable options to finance their purchases. GM has reaped great benefits from its leasing program on the Cadillac Seville. Even though a Seville may cost close to $55,000, it can be leased for approximately $500 per month. After 24 months, the user walks away with the automobile at a price that may even be lower than the depreciated value of the car. Business customers of manufacturing equipment also find leasing to be an attractive option. Currently, the equipment leasing business is estimated to be about $150 billion. In addition to the financing value received from leasing, customers also receive enhanced performance value: leasing avoids technological obsolescence, which is an important concern in purchases of computers and telecommunications equipment.[18]

Financing is possible for both services and products and for consumables and durables. For example, dental-care costs may add up to thousands of dollars, which becomes a significant burden on customers lacking dental insurance. Recognizing an opportunity, some dentists have begun to accept credit cards or installment payments from patients. By doing this, dentists provide a financing value and make themselves more attractive than their fellow dentists who do not offer financing.

Ethical issues abound in credit and financing. Customers are lured by the "no annual fee," "pre-approved" credit cards and then are charged massive interest for the balances they run up on the card. One wonders whether it is ethical for financial institutions to lure a minimum-wage earner or a college student in this manner. In the lending sector, the Home Ownership and Equity Protection Act came into place to guard homeowners against unscrupulous lenders. These lenders targeted elderly homeowners with lending schemes that involved giving them home secured loans with high interest rates or high closing fees and impossible repayment terms. More often than not, these homeowners would not be able to meet the repayment terms and the lenders were able to foreclose on the house. Customers need to be wary of scams in credit and financing as they look to satisfying these values from marketers.

# Creating Market Values for Buyers

In general, buyers are looking for good service before and after they make their selections. In addition, they want their purchases to be convenient, not too time-consuming, and in a time and place that fits their schedule.

## Service Value

Whereas the performance value is built into the product or service by the manufacturer or the service designer (economists call this **form utility**), the service value is created by the distribution system. Customers receive service value during pre-purchase and post-purchase phases of product or service acquisition.

# Prepurchase Service

During prepurchase, a buyer needs product information and help in assessing the fit between customer needs/wants and what the product/service delivers. Marketers in general, but retailers in particular, are generally expected to offer these values, and retailers who offer them in a superior way can differentiate themselves from their competitors. Marketers can offer this value by having the product on display or ready for demonstration and/or for trial use and by hiring knowledgeable and responsive salespersons who can answer customer questions.

**Product on Display or Demonstration.** Although a number of alternative forms of *non*store retailing (e.g., telemarketing) have come into existence, retail stores continue to have their appeal, foremost because of their merchandise-on-display utility. For some customers, there is nothing like being able to walk into a store and see, touch, and feel the merchandise. Stores that showcase their wares better (for example, with life-size models, reality-enhancing props, and attractive lighting) would have an edge, other things being equal, over their poorly merchandised competitors. Industrial distributors offer similar value by offering the product for demonstration. Trade shows are an effective means of displaying product developments, as are fashion shows for clothing. Even catalog marketers recognize the service value of product displays, so they use high-resolution photographs of goods in their catalogs.

Another tool marketers can use to offer service value is having the product available in trial sizes. In supermarkets, new food items are offered as taste samples. A test drive of a car offers similar service value. Various kinds of subscriptions and memberships, offered free for the first month, are instances of service value to the purchase decision maker. Similarly, shoe stores offer the customer an opportunity to take the shoes home, try them for a week or a month indoors, and return them if they do not fit; this offers service value to the customer. This service value in product trial is unavailable to you when you are a tourist; as a tourist you will generally not consider buying products that you want to have the option of returning later if they do not fit.

Several of these free subscriptions and memberships play on the premise that once the customer tries the product, he may not take the trouble to return it after 30 days or cancel the membership afterward. Sometimes, even when the customer wants to cancel the same, the marketer makes it very difficult for the customer to quit, causing dissatisfaction for the buyer.

**Knowledgeable Salespersons.** The second resource that marketers can use and offer to customers is product knowledge. Retail store salespersons and other salespersons vary greatly in the degree of competence and product knowledge they possess. Salespersons at a discount store tend to be substantially less knowledgeable about their products than those at a specialty store. Professional photographers, for example, would prefer to patronize specialty camera shops than discount stores; likewise, those who play any game seriously (rather than leisurely) would prefer to shop at specialty sporting-goods stores.

Professional, knowledgeable salespersons help not only by offering better product knowledge but also by assisting the customer in choosing a product that would better fit the customer's needs and wants. Clothiers with personal service, for example, would help the customer choose the right suit; such personalized advice is simply unavailable at large department stores. Likewise, a computer company's salesperson helps the customer figure out which equipment and options would meet his or her needs better. Insurance salespersons can distinguish themselves by taking the time to assess a customer's needs and recommending an insurance product accordingly. Financial asset managers, stock brokers, and other bank officers can likewise distinguish themselves from their competitors by offering up-to-date information and advice about their products and services.

Yet, there are salespeople who provide the customer with selective information and betray the buyer's confidence in this resource. Such tactics might help the marketer sell the product the first time, but when the buyer realizes the fraud, he or she boycotts the marketer for good.

### Service in the Post-Purchase Phase

Generally known as after-sales service or after-sales product support, service in the post-purchase phase refers to all the assistance a marketer can provide to maintain the product use-ready. This service value accrues inasmuch as it enables the user to derive the maximum utility from the product or service. Two specific avenues are available to marketers for this service: product-use advice and product maintenance. The Window on Research describes the process of "aftermarketing"—marketing efforts directed at the customer after he or she has made the purchase.

**Product-Use Advice and Support.**  Consumers often need assistance in using the product, and marketers who offer this assistance differentiate themselves from their competitors.

# WINDOW ON RESEARCH

## Aftermarketing

Whether or not customers are satisfied with the outcome of a purchase decision, the customer relationship can benefit from aftermarketing. Aftermarketing refers to the marketing efforts directed at the customer after he or she has made the purchase. The goals of aftermarketing are to ensure customer satisfaction and to maintain the relationship. Marketing professor Terry Vavra coined the term *aftermarketing* in the book of the same title. In it, he defines aftermarketing as the process of providing continued satisfaction and reinforcement to individuals or organizations that are past or current customers. Customers must be identified, acknowledged, communicated with, audited for satisfaction, and responded to. The goal of aftermarketing is to build lasting relationships with all customers.

Relationship marketing or retaining customers becomes important in markets that are saturated (i.e., demand is not growing) and where major competitors have achieved parity on the core product. According to one study, some 65 percent of the average company's business comes from current satisfied customers. Says marketing scholar Philip Kotler, "Smart marketers try to build long-term, trusting, 'win-win' relationships with customers, distributors, dealers, and suppliers."

Retaining customers requires marketers to exhibit care and concern for them after they've made a purchase. It includes:

- Promoting activities and efforts to keep customers satisfied, even after the purchase.
- Doing everything possible to ensure repurchase.
- Constant measurement of sustained customer satisfaction.
- Letting customers know they are cared for.

The first step in the aftermarketing process is maintaining a customer information file. Without customer records containing the customer's contact address as well as a history of previous interactions and transactions, it is not possible to engage the customer in an aftermarketing program, much less build a relationship. For example, a car dealer who sells the customer a car would need to save the customer information from the sales docu-

Thus, companies have toll-free technical assistance lines, especially for technical products like personal computers. In 1993, General Electric Co. commissioned a state-of-the-art customer advice facility it calls the Customer Answer Center. The service representatives who answer customer questions on its toll-free phone lines are equipped with online product information as well as an instant display of customer records. This helps them resolve customer problems efficiently and efficaciously. The center receives about two million calls a year, and the company has experienced a significant increase in customer satisfaction since the center began.

Note that the quality of user advice is a user value, but ease of obtaining it is a buyer value. For example, if user support is not part of the original seller's offering, then the buyer has to procure it from elsewhere. Thus, service value for the buyer is obtained when user support and maintenance support are available to the buyer along with the original item's purchase.

---

ments; moreover, it would help if the information is stored on an electronic medium so that it is accessible to the car service personnel who are responsible for aftermarketing.

The second step is the identification of possible customer contact points and specifying them on a time line that also spells out the purpose and content of each contact (i.e., the firm prepares a blueprint of customer contact points). In the automobile dealer example, the service shop would prepare a blueprint for each recent car buyer, identifying when the dealer service should contact the customer and for what purpose. The next step is the analysis of informal customer feedback. Customers would, from time to time, offer comments on their experience with the product and advise on what the company might do differently. It is very important for a marketer to analyze and use this feedback. However, rather than just depend on informal feedback, the firm should conduct satisfaction surveys from time to time. The firm should respond to specific customer concerns voiced in formal surveys or informal feedback. The firm should also have in place a program of periodic communication with its customers. This can be in the form of a periodic mailing, such as a newsletter, or a periodic callback just to inquire if the product is performing to the customer's satisfaction. Beyond such communications, the marketer should consider hosting special events that will bring the customer closer to the marketer and give an opportunity for the marketer to listen to the customer. Some customers will inevitably switch to an alternative marketer/supplier; the marketer should learn from a lost customer. This can be done by an exit interview (i.e., asking the customer to share his or her reasons for switching to a competitor).

Additionally, the marketer may examine customer records to identify, for the switching customers as a group, any special characteristics or circumstances that motivate switching customers to change their suppliers. These steps will bolster a marketer's aftermarketing efforts, whose goal is to bring customers into a long-term relationship with the firm.

**Source:** Adapted from Terry G. Vavra, *Aftermarketing: How to Keep Customers for Life through Relationship Marketing,* 2nd ed. (Chicago: Irwin Professional Publishers, 1996); Philip Kotler, *Marketing Management,* (Upper Saddle River, NJ: Prentice Hall, 1997), p. 12.

**Product Maintenance.** Perhaps the most significant service value accrues from the product maintenance service the marketer offers a customer. If a car breaks down, the customer wants it repaired quickly and without any inconvenience. It is for this reason that Lexus gives the customer a loaner car during the repair period.

Product downtime can be immensely consequential in business products, such as computers, copiers, and communication networks. Xerox realized the importance of minimizing the downtime on its office equipment and set up an infrastructure—an army of 12,000 service reps—so that its service reps could reach any customer's location within the whole United States within 30 minutes. This outstanding service value (along with the performance value of its improved equipment) made Xerox the preferred supplier for many new customers. The company experienced the greatest growth rate of the past ten years.

In the service industries, the core product itself is service (e.g., haircutting for a hair salon, access to special channel broadcasts for cable TV companies). How good this core product is constitutes the performance value. The manner in which this core product is delivered constitutes service value in our values framework. The cable TV industry was the subject of very high consumer complaints during the late 1980s to early 1990s. These complaints focused not only on the poor quality of signals (i.e., poor performance value) and the service being overpriced (i.e., poor economic value), but most important on the poor responsiveness to consumer complaints (i.e., poor service value). The cable industry had ignored consumer concern for a long time, but from 1993 to 1995, it faced the prospect of losing its monopoly (regulators were increasingly permitting a second cable operator to start operating in what previously had been an exclusively licensed territory); consequently, it turned to repairing its poor image with consumers. It worked to improve its servicing of a customer's request and began to offer service guarantees.

Gearing a firm to deliver superior service value to customers is actually what differentiates a manufacturing-driven company from a marketing-driven company. Generally, manufacturers are concerned with producing the right products in the right quantities at the right time and at the right cost. They see marketers as having little understanding of their role in the corporation. In a manufacturing-driven company, everything is done to ensure low costs and a smooth production process. Simple products, narrow product lines, and high-volume production are the goals of a manufacturing-driven firm. In contrast, a marketing-driven firm will be more concerned with satisfying customers' needs.[19] The importance placed on service value forces companies to move from a manufacturing-driven to a marketing-driven mentality.

## Convenience Value and Personalization Value

As described in Chapter 1, convenience and personalization values accrue from being able to obtain a product or service in a hassle-free and socially pleasant exchange with delivery personnel. Similar to the social and emotional values, it represents an influence on the customer's wants. It is something that is preferred, not needed.

## Convenient Point of Access

To deliver convenience value, firms can provide convenient points of access. They can locate the distribution and retail facilities conveniently and keep them open 24 hours. Banks now have branch locations inside supermarkets, and many banks offer Saturday and Sunday banking services. Domino's distinguished itself by offering convenience value through home delivery of pizzas, a pioneering practice that made a significant dent in market leader Pizza Hut's market share. Ultimately, to remain competitive, Pizza Hut had to offer home delivery as well. Supermarkets offer this value by ensuring short checkout lines and by delivering the groceries to a customer's car. Some clothiers will alter a suit, press it, and deliver it to a customer's home. Companies like Office Depot will deliver office products over a minimum purchase price to a customer's home. Many fast-food restaurant chains, such as Taco Bell, McDonald's, and Burger King, have increased their sales by going beyond their free-standing traditional store design and opening small-scale service counters at such diverse locations as schools, corporate cafeterias, shopping malls, and airports, and, for Taco Bell, even within gas stations.

Some companies sell in the customer's home or office. Banking by phone, computer, and Internet is an example of such a convenience. This service is valued so much by a segment of British customers that a British bank works exclusively as a banking-by-phone bank.

## Automated Transaction Recording

Automation is a significant means of offering convenience. Automation, such as at ATMs for banking, and telephone-based automated response systems, such as the ones used by banks, document shipping companies such as FedEx, and customer service departments of many companies, offer convenient access. They also offer convenience by automating the transaction so it is not held up by the unavailability of service employees. Selected supermarkets are testing a device that the customer uses to scan each item as he or she places it in the shopping cart; this would eliminate altogether the need for checkout lines. Similarly, many gas stations are equipped with a credit card reader right at the pump. This pay-at-the-pump feature is a source of great convenience value, especially to customers with small children in the car, who may be apprehensive about leaving the car unattended.

The advantage for marketers in e-commerce is the fact that there is an automated recording of all the data at the site that is visited by the consumer. This data relates both to personal information with regard to the consumer and to transaction information. The data is of great value to the marketer, but the use of the information to send unsolicited offers to customers, spamming their mail, and selling the data to other parties who also then target these consumers is an ethical concern.

## Interpersonal Relationship

As explained in Chapter 1, personalization value accrues from sales and service employees treating customers with personal attention and courtesy. This avenue of offering service value is especially important in service businesses. A car rental agent, hotel registration clerk, airline ticket agent, or a waiter or waitress who shows courtesy in dealing with the customer is offering a service value, and this can be an important differential advantage for service firms. Likewise, insurance agents, doctors, and even hairstylists should get to know their clients personally. And if customers communicate with the company via e-mails, the company response should not look like a form letter; rather, it should show caring for the customer as an individual. In business markets, interpersonal relationships matter even more. To deliver personalization value, companies need to engage in frequent, personalized communications. And, designated account reps as well as senior executives should make frequent client visits. The purpose of these visits should be not only to discuss task related issues but also to build a personal relationship with clients.

Window on Practice presents examples of customer value drivers employed by some of *Fortune* magazine's Most Admired Companies.

# Measuring Value Delivery

With so many tools available for delivering customer values, marketers must make sure their organization is delivering the values their target markets most desire and that customers are aware it is doing so. The effective way of ensuring this is with the basics of marketing management: (1) find out what customers want, (2) organize to deliver those values, and (3) measure how well, in customer perceptions, those values have been delivered.

# WINDOW ON PRACTICE

## Customer Value Delivery Excellence of the World's Most Admired Companies

### Performance Value from Quality Obsession at Caterpiller

Caterpillar measures its product quality by defect rate, which is any failure in machine operations. It tracks these defects by the age of the machine in three brackets—VEHR—very early hour failure, registered within the first 21 hours of operation; DRF1—Dealer Repair Frequency One, registered during 22 to 200 hours of operations; and DRF2, registered during 201 to 1,000 hours of operations. Such close tracking is part of its vigorous Continuous Quality Improvement (CQI) programs.

For a glimpse of the vigor and power of its CQI programs, let us briefly look at its CQI project for the paint job on its tractors. While some might think of paint on a heavy machine as mere cosmetic feature, Cat recognized that the quality of the paint job (good or poor) is the first thing a customer notices. And, indeed, customers noted and complained about such paint defects as poor coverage, runs and sags, embedded dirt, and uneven gloss and finish. So the paint line team in the Track-Type Tractor (TTT) division set up a CQI project. The team identified and implemented improvements in equipment, processes, and worker tasks. The result? Within 20 months after the project started, the CQI team virtually eliminated all paint defects. And Cat counts, mind you, any slight unevenness in finish on any square inch of the tractor surface as a defect. And customer response? Customer complaints about paint on the machines had declined from 113 in 1990 to 7 in June 1995, and to zero since then!

### Performance Value Theory from Innovation at 3M

Is there room for product innovations in such basic products as roof granules? It would be unlike 3M if it did not innovate, no matter how established the product category. So the company's roofing granules division has developed a very innovative type of granule for special applications. It is the algae block copper roofing granule system. If you drive in Florida, you will notice a black streak on the rooftops there. For a long time it was believed to be fungi that possibly develops in humid climates. 3M researched this problem and found that it is not fungi; rather, it is an organism which, to protect itself from the sunrays, secretes a black-brown-reddish pigment. It is this pigment that gives the roof shingles their undesirable streak. So, 3M set out to find a solution. With experimentation, its scientists discovered that copper is toxic to the organism. The new granule system, therefore, first coats the granules with a layer of soluble copper (cuprous oxide) prior to applying the ceramic and color layers. This is done with a highly sophisticated proprietary process—the expensive process raises the cost of these granules to about $800 per ton (as compared to $80 per ton for ordinary granules). Fortunately, copper-granules need be used only in a 10 percent mix with regular granules, thus bringing this delightful innovation within affordable price range.

### Performance Value for Product Customization at UPS

A second avenue is custom-designing a shipping service specific to a client. Yes, indeed, the company has the capability to put into place a custom-designed package-movement operation either as a one-time or ongoing operation. Case in point: A few years ago, a music company was launching a new CD featuring a Beatles' anthology of songs never before published. The company's plan was to introduce the CD on Sunday Night Network TV and have the CDs in the stores on Monday morning. Secrecy was the company's top concern—and for fear of leaks, it would not even deliver the product to UPS before that Friday. UPS agreed to take on this special task. The client delivered the packages on Friday evening in armored vehicles. From that point, UPS assumed control and "staged" the product movement to meet both security and on-time delivery requirements to music stores all over the country. The special network UPS put together for this music company is testimony to the company's customization capability.

## Performance Value from Warranties at AutoNation

As proof, AutoNation has some of the most customer-value-centered guarantees in the industry. As one poster at its dealership reads: "AutoNation uses only OEM parts and guarantees the repair work for 12 months or 12,000 miles whichever comes last." Last? No, it is not a typo! AutoNation is explicit: "whichever comes last, not first," its brochure states loud and clear.

As to timely completion of work, the company guarantees the speed (and costs) for 13 of its routine maintenance services. Some examples: oil and filter change: $19.95 and within 30 minutes; automatic transmission service: $69.95 and within 60 minutes; air filter replacement: $10.95 and within 20 minutes. "If we don't finish the work within the specified time, you will receive the service for free," a brochure declares.

## Price Value Through Increased Productivity at Rosenbluth

Rosenbluth International (RI) has also constantly sought to reduce its operational costs. It has done it by two means: automation of the reservation processes and low cost location of its centralized services. One clear example of automation is its E-Res® system; E-Res® is an agentless system useable by clients themselves on their desktop/laptop computer; it includes and automatically applies the client's travel policy constraints. U.S. giant retailer Wal-Mart is a recent RI client, where travelers use the E-Res® system when they can, and the company estimates that it will save 10 percent of its $30 million air travel budget!

To reduce its operating costs, RI was the first travel agency to create a centralized reservation center in 1980—called IntelliCenters. Where would you think these centers are located? At its headquarters in Philadelphia? In some other metropolis? Near its major client clusters? No. In rural North Dakota, Delaware, and Allentown, Pennsylvania because the labor costs are low there. If clients use these centers rather than customer service centers (CSC) or dedicated offices, they can save 30 to 40 percent per ticket in booking costs. That is a tremendous value price.

## Service Value Through User Support at Fossil

What value retailers seek most is good profit margins on a product with good performance. Fossil's scientific inventory management at the retail level is a source of higher margin for the retailer since his or her inventory costs are significantly reduced. Fossil acts almost like a partner in managing the retailer's inventory. The average watch inventory turnover in department stores is 4 percent; that is, 4 percent of the inventory moves every

*(continued)*

week. Fossil make its inventory move 5 percent so that the retailer has to carry only 20 weeks' inventory instead of the usual 25 weeks. And the company aims to make 65 percent of the watch lines move at this speed. The other 35 percent are newer styles, not yet established. Recall that five times a year, the company introduces new styles. Fossil claims that, by its initial margin and by enabling lower inventory costs, its watches are the one of the most profitable product lines for its department store merchants.

## Personalization Value at XBS

A manufacturing company makes sewing machines, and the machines come packed with an owner's manual. The current practice is to print it in bulk and enclose it with the product being shipped to retailers. This practice is slated to change for many of the businesses. In the digital age, the manual can be stored and distributed digitally, and then printed by the dealer at the time of the product sale. The manual can even be customized for a specific model and/or for a specific customer. Now, as a supplier of this out-sourced service, XBS can simply take over the current (traditional) manual printing service and run it more efficiently, or, it can print more model-specific manuals in smaller quantities, or, better still, it can distribute the manual to the retailer in a digital form for the retailer to customize it, incorporating value-added aftermarket services the dealership might offer, and print it on a "just in time" basis. This is, in fact, what it does for a number of clients.

Suppose XBS runs your company's mailroom services, and you want a certain category of mail distributed much earlier than currently delivered or even feasible. XBS can do it. One of its financial services clients, for example, wanted the mortgage applications distributed by 9 a.m. instead of the current delivery by 11 a.m. (Doing so would shorten the entire loan-approval cycle by one full day.) So XBS redesigned the whole document process for mortgage applications. It created a special return envelope that could be identified by sight, contracted with FedEx Corporation for a special 8:30 a.m. delivery of that envelope, and assigned an associate to deliver the envelope to the designated mortgage processing officer by 9 a.m.

Thus, from initial service configuration for a new customer site to sub-process redesign on an ongoing site, XBS offers customization to enhance its total performance valuespace for its clients.

**Source:** Banwari Mittal and Jagdish N. Sheth, *Valuespace: Winning the Battle for Market Leadership, Lessons From the World's Most Admired Companies* (McGraw Hill, 2001).

To identify the specific benefits and processes customers want on each of the six values, the marketer would conduct customer research. A blueprint for conducting this research is presented in the Window on Research box.

That model focuses on value assessment related to product use. We can also apply this type of evaluation to the purchase and payment situations. In keeping with the three customer roles, a complete assessment should include customer values in using, paying for, and buying the product.

Once the values are identified, an organization has to organize efforts and strategies to deliver these values. This may require substantial investments in equipment, technology, and human resources. The principal action strategies have been described in the chapter.

As these strategies are implemented, they need to be appraised to determine whether implementation is progressing as planned and whether the strategies are effective. One means of appraisal is internal audits, in which a cross-functional team of managers could

# WINDOW ON RESEARCH

## Process for Determining Customer Value

Robert B. Woodruff, marketing professor at the University of Tennessee, has done research with a number of firms, helping them identify a process for determining exactly what value means to customers of a specific product or service. As a basis for this process, he defines *customer value* as a customer's perceived preference for and evaluation of those product attributes, attribute performances, and consequences arising from uses that facilitate (or block) achieving the customer's goals and purposes in use situations. Thus, customer value includes customer perceptions at three levels:

1. *Attribute performance* whether the product has the desired attributes and attribute performances.
2. *Attribute consequences* whether using the product has the desired consequences.
3. *Goals pertinent to attribute consequences* whether the consequences of using the product help the customer meet his or her goals.

If using the product meets each of these desires, the result is satisfaction in that area.

To measure a customer's overall satisfaction with the received value, the marketer would assess satisfaction at all three levels. For example, for Healthy Choice frozen entrees, attribute performance might be that fat content is low; a related consequence could be that it will keep blood-cholesterol level low. Customer goals would be staying healthy. To assess customer value for Healthy Choice, then, marketers would have to assess how well the brand meets the performance, consequences, and goals levels.

How can managers use this process to form a strategy to enhance customer value? As shown in Figure 13.4, the marketer begins by conducting research to learn which values at the three levels (performance, consequence, and goals) customers desire. Further research, combining customer interviews with management intuition, would then narrow the list to the most important of those values. Further surveys would assess the firm's delivery of those important values—how well the firm is satisfying those values. The final step is not a measurement but a diagnostic analysis; managers must identify causes of the value-delivery gap and possible corrective actions. All these steps should be informed by a futuristic perspective: what are the customers likely to value in the future?

Additional information available at **http://www.healthychoice.com**.

**Source:** Adapted from Robert B. Woodruff, "Customer Value: The Next Source for Competitive Advantage," *Journal of the Academy of Marketing Science* 25, No. 2 (1997), pp. 139–153.

rate the various processes. For example, for reengineering the process (which helps deliver price value), managers should assess the degree to which the reengineering project has been implemented as well as the extent to which reengineering has improved productivity and lowered costs.

Some of these processes are not visible to customers, so customer input cannot be used to assess progress; for example, the reengineering process itself is not visible to customers, nor are customers concerned about *how* a firm manages to deliver specific values.

**FIGURE 13.4     A Process for Determining Customer Value**

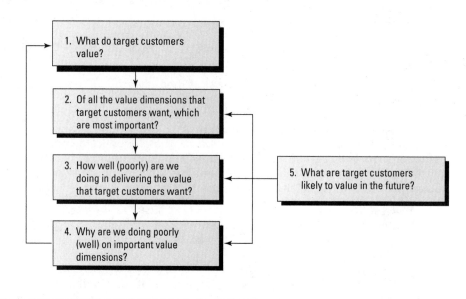

For these internal processes, management's own assessment is the only option. However, the outcome of these processes, as delivered to customers, is visible to customers and, indeed, experienced by them as six market values. Therefore, marketers should solicit customer appraisal of these experiences.

To do this, marketers should assess the firm's success, both in satisfying the six values and in using value-creation tools in a way that customers experience and appreciate. They can make both assessments by asking customers to rate statements about the product and the firm. Thus, to measure success in satisfying the six values, the marketer can use statements such as the ones given in Chapter 1. For example, to measure the performance value of a Saab automobile, customers can be asked to rate their degree of agreement with the statement "My Saab gives me good gas mileage"; to measure the price value, they can rate the statement "This brand at this price is a good bargain."

Marketers can also measure how well the various tools are delivering specific values they were purported to deliver, and whether the firm has been able to improve value delivery over the years. Marketers can do this by having customers rate statements such as those in Figure 13.5. These statements are illustrative and may not all apply to every company. Some are especially suitable for business-to-business customers, and others are general but may still need adaptation to specific product or service situations. As a marketer, you would use them as a basis for thinking about how they apply to individual situations, and for researching their utility in improving your firm's ability to deliver customer values.

# Fulfilling the Business Purpose by Delivering Customer Value

Research into value-delivery processes helps marketers focus on what should be their fundamental business purpose: to make the customer happy.

| Sample Questions for Measuring Customer Perceptions of Value Delivery Processes | FIGURE 13.5 |

### User Values

| | Disagree Strongly | Disagree | Agree | Agree Strongly | Don't Know |
|---|:---:|:---:|:---:|:---:|:---:|
| | 1 | 2 | 3 | 4 | DK |

**PERFORMANCE VALUE PROCESSES**

**Quality improvement**

| | 1 | 2 | 3 | 4 | DK |
|---|:---:|:---:|:---:|:---:|:---:|
| The quality of this firm's products and services is superb. | ☐ | ☐ | ☐ | ☐ | ☐ |
| The quality of this firm's products and services has been improving continuously over the last several years. | ☐ | ☐ | ☐ | ☐ | ☐ |

**Innovation**

| | 1 | 2 | 3 | 4 | DK |
|---|:---:|:---:|:---:|:---:|:---:|
| The firm has consistently introduced breakthrough designs and new technologies in its products/services. | ☐ | ☐ | ☐ | ☐ | ☐ |
| The firm's current products represent significant advances over its earlier versions of a few years ago. | ☐ | ☐ | ☐ | ☐ | ☐ |
| The firm's products/services are one step ahead of what the competition offers. | ☐ | ☐ | ☐ | ☐ | ☐ |

**Customization**

| | 1 | 2 | 3 | 4 | DK |
|---|:---:|:---:|:---:|:---:|:---:|
| The firm is able to offer me individually customized products and services. | ☐ | ☐ | ☐ | ☐ | ☐ |
| The firm's products and services are available in a large variety and with options so that I can have the kind of product/service I like. | ☐ | ☐ | ☐ | ☐ | ☐ |
| I can purchase a custom-made product from this firm without sacrificing timeliness. | ☐ | ☐ | ☐ | ☐ | ☐ |

**Warranties and guarantees**

| | 1 | 2 | 3 | 4 | DK |
|---|:---:|:---:|:---:|:---:|:---:|
| The firm offers one of the best warranties in the industry. | ☐ | ☐ | ☐ | ☐ | ☐ |
| The firm truly follows a no-questions-asked full-refund policy. | ☐ | ☐ | ☐ | ☐ | ☐ |

**SOCIAL VALUE**

**Price exclusivity**

| | 1 | 2 | 3 | 4 | DK |
|---|:---:|:---:|:---:|:---:|:---:|
| The firm prices the product/service high enough to maintain its exclusivity. | ☐ | ☐ | ☐ | ☐ | ☐ |
| The product's/service's price gives me a special satisfaction of possessing an exclusive, not-too-common product/service. | ☐ | ☐ | ☐ | ☐ | ☐ |

**Limit availability**

| | 1 | 2 | 3 | 4 | DK |
|---|:---:|:---:|:---:|:---:|:---:|
| The firm makes its products/services available too widely.* | ☐ | ☐ | ☐ | ☐ | ☐ |
| I like the fact that the product's/service's distribution is restricted. | ☐ | ☐ | ☐ | ☐ | ☐ |

**Social image ads**

| | 1 | 2 | 3 | 4 | DK |
|---|:---:|:---:|:---:|:---:|:---:|
| Advertisements for the product/service show the product in association with people and images that I find appealing. | ☐ | ☐ | ☐ | ☐ | ☐ |

**Exclusive offerings**

| | 1 | 2 | 3 | 4 | DK |
|---|:---:|:---:|:---:|:---:|:---:|
| Over time, the firm has extended its product line to include other prestigious brands. | ☐ | ☐ | ☐ | ☐ | ☐ |

**EMOTIONAL VALUE**

**Emotional communications**

| | 1 | 2 | 3 | 4 | DK |
|---|:---:|:---:|:---:|:---:|:---:|
| I can personally identify with the social causes that the firm promotes in its communications. | ☐ | ☐ | ☐ | ☐ | ☐ |
| When I view the firm's advertisements, I can visualize the wonderful emotional experience I will have using the product. | ☐ | ☐ | ☐ | ☐ | ☐ |

*The item should be reverse scored so that disagreement is given the higher value on the scale.

*(continued)*

| FIGURE 13.5 | **Sample Questions for Measuring Customer Perceptions of Value Delivery Processes (Continued)** |
| --- | --- |

|  | Disagree Strongly | Disagree | Agree | Agree Strongly | Don't Know |
| --- | :---: | :---: | :---: | :---: | :---: |
| **Payer Values** |  |  |  |  |  |
| **Price value** | 1 | 2 | 3 | 4 | DK |
| Over time, this firm has consistently offered me better price value for its products/services. | ☐ | ☐ | ☐ | ☐ | ☐ |
| Compared with three years ago, the firm is offering me better products without raising the prices. | ☐ | ☐ | ☐ | ☐ | ☐ |
| I think that the firm cares about reducing my costs without sacrificing what I get from its products/services.** | ☐ | ☐ | ☐ | ☐ | ☐ |
| **Credit** |  |  |  |  |  |
| The firm offers liberal credit terms. | ☐ | ☐ | ☐ | ☐ | ☐ |
| The firm offers interest-free deferred-payment plans. | ☐ | ☐ | ☐ | ☐ | ☐ |
| **Financing** |  |  |  |  |  |
| The special financing plan the firm offers suits my needs very well. | ☐ | ☐ | ☐ | ☐ | ☐ |
| Over the years, the firm has customized its financing options for my needs.* | ☐ | ☐ | ☐ | ☐ | ☐ |
| **Buyer Values** |  |  |  |  |  |
| SERVICE VALUE |  |  |  |  |  |
| **General** |  |  |  |  |  |
| Over time, the firm has made it increasingly easy for me to do business with it. | ☐ | ☐ | ☐ | ☐ | ☐ |
| **Product display** |  |  |  |  |  |
| The firm makes it easy for me to inspect the product and see it working before deciding to buy it. | ☐ | ☐ | ☐ | ☐ | ☐ |
| **Knowledgeable salespersons** |  |  |  |  |  |
| This firm's employees seem to have been well screened and trained for their jobs, and I find them very knowledgeable about their products/services. | ☐ | ☐ | ☐ | ☐ | ☐ |
| **User support** |  |  |  |  |  |
| If users of this product need help in operating or using the product, they can easily receive advice from the firm. | ☐ | ☐ | ☐ | ☐ | ☐ |
| **Maintenance support** |  |  |  |  |  |
| It is easy to obtain the required maintenance to keep the product always ready for use. | ☐ | ☐ | ☐ | ☐ | ☐ |
| **Responsiveness** |  |  |  |  |  |
| The firm welcomes complaints and tries to do whatever it takes to win a customer over. | ☐ | ☐ | ☐ | ☐ | ☐ |
| CONVENIENCE |  |  |  |  |  |
| **Points of access** |  |  |  |  |  |
| I find the firm's products and services conveniently located. | ☐ | ☐ | ☐ | ☐ | ☐ |
| I can access the firm anytime from anywhere I like. | ☐ | ☐ | ☐ | ☐ | ☐ |
| Over past few years, the firm has considerably expanded the ways I can obtain its products/services. | ☐ | ☐ | ☐ | ☐ | ☐ |

*The item should be reverse scored so that disagreement is given the higher value on the scale.
**These items may be especially useful for business customers.

| Sample Questions for Measuring Customer Perceptions of Value Delivery Processes (Concluded) | FIGURE 13.5 |
| --- | --- |

| Buyer Values *(continued)* | Disagree Strongly | Disagree | Agree | Agree Strongly | Don't Know |
| --- | :---: | :---: | :---: | :---: | :---: |
| | 1 | 2 | 3 | 4 | DK |
| **Automated transaction recording** | | | | | |
| Employees who record the transaction seem to be well equipped with technology to complete my transaction efficiently. | ☐ | ☐ | ☐ | ☐ | ☐ |
| The firm has the system and technology in place that makes it very easy for me to obtain its products/services. | ☐ | ☐ | ☐ | ☐ | ☐ |
| This firm seems to have organized its various departments, operations, and procedures to maximize customer convenience.* | ☐ | ☐ | ☐ | ☐ | ☐ |
| I find it very convenient to complete the transactions with this firm using its self-service technology. | ☐ | ☐ | ☐ | ☐ | ☐ |
| PERSONALIZATION | | | | | |
| **Personal attention** | | | | | |
| The firm's employees are very polite, courteous, and pleasant. | ☐ | ☐ | ☐ | ☐ | ☐ |
| The firm's employees and managers consider no other activity more important than to attend to a customer like myself. | ☐ | ☐ | ☐ | ☐ | ☐ |
| The firm's employees seem to show an understanding of my perspective and treat me as a person so that I feel very happy dealing with them. | ☐ | ☐ | ☐ | ☐ | ☐ |

*The item should be reverse scored so that disagreement is given the higher value on the scale.

Addressing that issue returns us to the theme with which we started the book. Most marketers don't have the luxury of being customers for the products that they market. Hence, by applying the concepts in this book, managers learn about customers and their behavior with respect to the various market values they seek. The tools we presented in this chapter are supposed to deliver those values. The ultimate goal of implementing these value-delivery tools is to make the customer happy.

As we proposed in Chapter 1, the purpose of the business is to satisfy a customer. In this context, General Electric Company's vision of itself, is worth reading.

> Customers are . . . the lifeblood of a company. Customers' vision of their needs and the company's view become identical, and every effort of every man and woman in the company is focused on satisfying those needs.[20]

We would paraphrase GE's assertion slightly: *Happy* customers are the lifeblood of a company. Therefore, a firm must do everything feasible to make and keep its customers happy—so happy, in fact, that customers delight in doing business with the firm.[21] They take pride in the company's existence and in its actions; rather than just draw on its resources, they are eager to support it. Establishing such relationships of mutual support and nurturance is the ultimate goal of customer orientation.

That customers would support such a relationship for a long time in the future is the *final customer judgment* for which companies should strive. Figure 13.6 presents an instrument to assess this final judgment by asking customers to rate a set of statements. The total of each customer's ratings is his or her judgment, conveniently scored as an index anchored at zero and 100, with 100 being the perfect score. Companies falling below this score should strive to bridge the gap.

Companies and organizations must never underestimate the mandate to become customer oriented. As authors argue in *ValueSpace*, companies that invent new customer value possess certain traits. They observe customers real close. They dig customer need to its essential core. And they keep their eyes on a singular target: creating far fetched new ValueSpace for the customer. These traits indeed lead a business to mold its own self-concept in the customer's image. . . .

This reinvention of oneself as a corporate being, this customer-centered adoption of a new self-identity, the constant contemplation of the customer desires—this is what it takes to invent unparalleled ValueSpace for the customer. This is what it takes to win the battle for market leadership. This is what it takes to thrive.

—*ValueSpace, 2001, page 250*[22]

The customer behavior concepts and applications presented in this book can help solicit important customer-value orientation.

**FIGURE 13.6    Assessment of the Customer's Final Judgment**

Please rate the following statements on a 0–10 scale where 0 means you disagree entirely, and 10 means you agree wholeheartedly.

- The firm understands my needs and preferences well.
- I can trust the firm not to take advantage of me as a customer.
- The firm values and shows its appreciation for my business.
- The firm takes specific actions to keep me as a customer.
- I can identify myself with the firm's products and its actions.
- The firm can count on me as its supporter.
- I enjoy dealing with the employees of this firm.
- I love this firm's products.
- I love to do business with this firm.
- I expect to continue my relationship with this firm for a long time.

# Summary

In this chapter we presented various strategies and tools that businesses can employ to offer each of the six values to customers. For the universal, performance value, companies need to focus on programs of quality improvement, R&D to create innovations in products and services, mass customization, and warranties and guarantees. To differentiate themselves on service value, firms need to become more responsive in their dealings with customers. They need to offer better service during prepurchase as well as post-purchase phases. Superior service value depends on employee competence, knowledgeability, courtesy, and responsiveness. These employee traits can be managed by careful selection and training and retraining. Service value also requires an infrastructure capable of handling product repair or maintenance service without much downtime. Finally, price value can be offered by lower-margin or higher-productivity strategies. Firms can improve productivity by automation and process reengineering.

The three personal values, too, require certain strategies and tools. For social and emotional values, a marketer needs to manage its marketing communications. All of its communications need to be strategically directed to create a focused social image and associations. Quality, price, and distribution exclusivity can be harnessed to give a product a social image of prestige. Situations and settings (i.e., ambiance) can be used to create mood and emotional association. The convenience value can be enhanced by increasing the points of access (e.g., by strategic location of product delivery and by 24-hour easy access by customers to a firm's employees). Another avenue of offering convenience value is by automating the recording of the transaction. Finally, firms can differentiate themselves on financing value by offering easy payment terms, low financing rates, and leasing arrangements.

Firms should attempt to differentiate themselves by exceeding on more than one type of customer value. Of course, what exactly will constitute value to a specific customer in a specific product or market situation needs to be constantly researched. Customer-driven companies are constantly listening to the voice of the customer and are continually striving to offer better value to their customers.

# Key Terms

| | |
|---|---|
| Cycle Time 468 | Lower-Margin Approach 466 |
| Effectiveness 458 | Mass Customization 463 |
| Efficiency 458 | Reengineering 468 |
| Emotional Communications 465 | Social Cause Marketing 465 |
| Form Utility 470 | Value Delivery 458 |
| Increased-Productivity Approach 467 | |

# Discussion Questions and Exercises

1. Consider your own role as a customer of the following companies: (a) your supermarket, (b) your post office, (c) your physician and health-care facility, and (d) the mail catalog company you occasionally buy clothing from. For each of the company's products/services, reflect on your own needs, wants, and preferences for doing business. Identify what each company could do to offer you better marketing values, illustrating your answer for each specific market value you might desire.

2. Assume that you are the marketing director for a large chain of hotels. How will you ensure that you are delivering superior market values to your customers? Write your company president a memo outlining your plan of action to substantially enhance the market values your hotel chain is currently delivering to its customers. Now do the same exercise assuming that you are a health insurance agency. Consider all three.

3. Review Figure 13.5, Sample Questions for Measuring Customer Perceptions of Value Delivery Processes. The measures in the questionnaire are generic, and they may need adaptation (and wording change) for specific companies or product/service categories. Adapt these measures and design a questionnaire for use by a (a) bank, (b) supermarket, and (c) company selling office furniture and supplies to small home offices. *Note:* To make sure that the questionnaire makes sense, answer it yourself as a customer of these companies.

**4.** Is it possible to measure the usefulness of a company's various actions in delivering value to customers? What approaches are there for this purpose? Briefly explain each approach relating it to specific values.

# Notes

1 Banwari Mittal and Jagdish N. Sheth, *ValueSpace, Winning the Battle for the Market Leadership, Lesson from the World's Most Admired Companies* (McGraw Hill, 2001).

2 For theoretical essays on customer value, see Robert B. Woodruff, "Customer Value: The Next Source of Competitive Advantage," *Journal of the Academy of Marketing Science* 25, No. 2 (Spring 1997), pp. 139–53; A. Parasuraman, "Reflections on Gaining Competitive Advantage through Customer Value," *Journal of the Academy of Marketing Science* No. 2 (Spring 1997), 25 pp. 154–61; Stanley F. Slater, "Developing a Customer Value-Based Theory of the Firm," *Journal of the Academy of Marketing Science* 25, No. 2 (Spring 1997), pp. 162–67, for a practitioner's essay on the topic, see Bradley T. Gale, *Managing Customer Value* (New York, NY: The Free Press, 1994).

3 For further reading, see Robert Jacobson and David A. Aaker, "The Strategic Role of Product Quality," *Journal of Marketing* 51 (October 1987), pp. 31–44.

4 Michael Schrage, "Few Try to Imitate 3M's Successes," *Boston Globe*, October 11, 1992, p. B2; also see, "Competing on Science: The Agenda for Senior Management," *Harvard Business Review*, November–December 1989.

5 Ernest Beck, "Populist Perrier? Nestle Pitches Bottled Water To World's Poor," *The Wall Street Journal*, June 18, 1999.

6 http://web4.insite2.gale.com/insite2/session/122/987/14641402w4/InSite2?Cmd= top&Code=&Dbav=CCDB_CHLT_CMGZ_CPNL _CBF_CBF_PRM,1997.

7 B. Joseph Pine II, Bart Victor, and Andrew C. Boynton, "Making Mass Customization Work," *Harvest Business Review*, September/October 1993.

8 Tom Richman, "Getting the Bugs Out," *Inc.* (June 1984), pp. 61–64; also see, Christopher W.L. Hart, "The Power of Unconditional Service Guarantees," *Harvard Business Review* (July–August 1988), pp. 54–62.

9 Ellen Goodman, "The Ethics of Marketing Babies," *The Boston Globe*, April 13, 1989.

10 George S. Day and David B. Montgomery, "Diagnosing the Experience Curve," *Journal of Marketing* (Spring 1983), pp. 44–83.

11 "Give More, Get More, 301 Great Customer Service Ideas" (details), January 1, 1997, http://www.inc.com/articles/details/1,,CID10403_REG6,00.html.

12 "Productivity to the Rescue," *Business Week*, October 5, 1995, pp. 134–36.

13 Robert D. Buzzell and Robert T. Gale, *The PIMS Principle Linking Strategy to Performance* (New York: The Free Press, 1987); R.G. Wakerly, "PIMS: A Tool for Developing Strategy," *Long-Range Planning*, June 1984, pp. 92–97.

14 Christopher H. Lovelock and Charles B. Weinberg, "Columbia Plastics Division of Fraser Industries, Inc.," in *Marketing Challenges: Cases and Exercises* (McGraw Hill, 1993).

15 Nick Adams, "New Warehouse Automation Improves Customer Service at Kinney Drugs," *Industrial Engineering*, October 1993, pp. 21–23.

16 William Wrennall, "Productivity: Reengineering for Competitiveness," *Industrial Engineering* 26, No. 12 (December 1994) p. 12 (3).

17 John McCloud, "McDonnell Douglas Saves Over $1 Million per Plane with Reengineering Effort," *Industrial Engineering* 25, No. 10 (October 1993), pp. 27–30.

18 "Equipment Leasing Is a Wise Investment," *The Office* 118 No. 2 (August 1993), p. 18 (3).

19 Philip Kotler, *Marketing Management: Analysis, Planning, Implementation, and Control,* 7e, (New York: Prentice-Hall, 1991), p. 701.

20 General Electric, *1990 Annual Report.*

21 For a research report on the conceptual distinction between customer satisfaction and customer delight, see Richard L. Oliver, Roland T. Rust, and Sajeev Varki, "Customer Delight: Foundations, Findings, and Managerial Insight," *Journal of Retailing* 73, No. 3, (1997), pp. 311–36.

22 Banwari Mittal and Jagdish N. Sheth, *ValueSpace, Winning the Battle for the Market Leadership, Lesson from the World's Most Admired Companies* (McGraw Hill, 2001).

# Glossary

## A

**Acculturation** The process of learning a new culture.

**Actual self** A person's self-image of who he or she is.

**Addressability** A feature of a database wherein each customer's address is known in order to enable a marketer to address marketing communications individually on a one-on-one basis.

**Adoption (of an innovation)** Customer acceptance of an innovation for continued use.

**Advocate sources** Communication sources that have a vested point of view to advocate or promote.

**Affect** The feelings a person has toward an object or the emotions that object evokes for the person.

**Affective choice mode (ACM)** A decision mode wherein affect or liking for the brand ensues a choice based not on attribute information, but based on holistic judgments.

**Affordability** The possession of adequate economic resources needed to buy and use a product or service.

**Aggressive personality** A person who values personal accomplishment over friendship and seeks power and admiration from others.

**Annual purchasing agreements** Agreements made by government agencies with specific suppliers, which allow the governmental entity to purchase small items routinely.

**Approach/avoidance motivation** The human desire to attain a goal-object and desire to avoid an object of negative outcomes.

**Arousal-seeking motive** The drive to maintain the organism's stimulation at an optimal level.

**Assimilation and contrast** Information within the acceptance range is assimilated and accepted; information outside of this range is contrasted and rejected.

**Assortment** The number of different items a store carries.

**Asymmetrical power** One party has more power over the other.

**Atmospherics** The physical setting of the store that influences customer behavior.

**Atomistic family unit** A person living alone.

**Attitude hierarchy** The sequence in which the three components of attitude—cognition, affect, conation—occur.

**Attitude** Learned predisposition to respond to an object or class of objects in a consistently favorable or unfavorable way.

**Attitude molding** Forming a new attitude or changing a preexisting attitude.

**Attitude persistence** After initial attitudes are formed through exposure to ads, the extent to which these attitudes persist over time until the actual purchase decision is made.

**Attitude strength** The degree of commitment one feels toward a cognition, feeling, or action.

**Attitude valance** The favorableness and unfavorableness of attitudes, i.e., of thoughts, feelings, and actions about an object.

**Attitudinal brand loyalty** A customer's consistent repurchase of a brand due to his or her preference for it.

**Attraction of alternatives** How attractive a customer finds alternative brands to be.

**Attribution motivation** Humans' innate need to assign causes to events and behaviors.

**Attributions** Inferences that people draw about the causes of events and behaviors.

**Authoritarian families** Families where parents exercise strict authority over children; children learn to obey their elders in all matters.

**Autonomous decisions** Decisions that are made independently by the decision maker.

**Autonomy** One's power to control his or her own life.

**Awareness set** Brands a customer is aware of.

## B

**Bargaining** A method of conflict resolution, based on distributive justice for all, wherein the dissenting members negotiate a give and take.

**Behavioral brand loyalty** A customer's consistent repurchase of a brand.

**Behavioral compatibility** The degree to which an innovation requires no change in existing behavior.

**Behaviorally anchored scales** Measurement scales that utilize descriptions of specific behaviors to which the respondents express their reactions.

**Behaviorism theory** The theory that a person develops a pattern of behavioral responses because of the rewards and punishments offered by his or her environment.

**Beliefs** Expectations that connect an object to an attribute or quality.

**Biological determinism** The belief that human behavior is determined by biological factors such as genetics and DNA.

**Borrowing power** The anticipated level of income of a person (lifetime disposable income and asset accumulated through savings); a primary indicator, in addition to income and wealth, of a customer's economic condition.

**Brand belief** A thought about a specific property or quality associated with a brand.

**Brand equity** The enhancement in the perceived utility and desirability that a brand name confers on a product.

**Brand loyalty** A customer's commitment to buy and use a given brand repeatedly.

**Brand parity** The concept of how similar and mutually substitutable the brands are.

**Brand valuation** The financial worth of a brand name.

**Business** A licensed entity engaged in the business of making, buying or selling products and services for profit or nonprofit objectives.

**Business cycle** A cycle of boom and recession experienced by the business world and caused by fluctuations in the economic environment.

**Business markets** Customers who buy products for use of the organizations they work for.

**Buyclass** Type of purchase need in terms of its newness.

**Buyer** A person who participates in the procurement of the product.

**Buyers' remorse** The regret customers feel after buying a product or service because they are unsure if buying it was wise.

**Buying center** All the members of a customer firm who play some role in the purchase decision.

**Buy-side business models** A buying organization using Internet-based technologies to buy from contracted suppliers.

**Buy-to-browse ratios** The proportion of customers who come to browse on the internet concluding the browsing by buying.

# C

**Central processing route** Message content is attended to and scrutinized actively and thoughtfully.

**Change agent** A person or organization that brings about a planned social change.

**Change targets** People whose behavior is sought to be altered by change agents.

**Changing demographics** Change in characteristics such as age, income, and geographic location of customers in a given market.

**Classical conditioning** The process in which a person learns an association between two stimuli due to their constant appearance as a pair.

**Climate** A component of the geophysical market environment, consisting of temperature, wind, humidity, and rainfall in an area that affects consumers' needs for food, clothing, and shelter.

**Cocooning** The habit of staying at home rather than going out.

**Cognition** A thought about an object.

**Cognitive consistency** The principle that a person desires consistency among all his or her beliefs or thoughts.

**Cognitive dissonance** A tension between two opposite thoughts, typically manifested after a customer has bought something but is uncertain whether a correct choice was made.

**Cognitive learning** The acquisition of new information from written or oral communication.

**Collaborative filtering** A computer program that allows the prediction of a person's preferences as a weighted sum of similar other people's preferences.

**Commitment** An enduring desire to continue the relationship and to work to ensure its continuance.

**Communicability** The extent to which an innovation is socially visible or easy to communicate about in social groups.

**Compensatory model** A decision rule and process where a customer arrives at a choice by considering all of the attributes and benefits of a product or service and mentally trading off the alternative's perceived weakness on one or more attributes for its perceived strength on other attributes.

**Competitive procurement** A government buying procedure whereby there are two approaches: invitation for bid (IFB) and request for proposal (RFP).

**Competitive promotional activity** Special price deals available on competing brands.

**Complexity** Extensiveness of effort it takes to comprehend and manage the product during its acquisition.

**Complexity of an innovation** The difficulty in comprehending an innovation.

**Compliance** Steering customer behavior by government regulation.

**Compliant** A personality trait where a person acts in an agreeable manner to earn others' acceptance and friendship.

**Compulsive buying** A chronic tendency to purchase products far in excess of one's needs and resources.

**Compulsive consumption** An uncontrolled and obsessive consumption of a product or service, likely to ultimately cause harm to the consumer or others.

**Conation** The action a person wants to take toward an object.

**Concept-oriented families** Families that are concerned with the growth of independent thinking and individuality in children.

**Concurrent protocols** A record of respondent thoughts at the time of decision making.

**Conditioned stimulus (CS)** A stimulus to which a new response needs to be conditioned.

**Conjunctive model** A decision-making procedure wherein the customer examines all alternatives on a set of attributes or evaluative criteria in order to identify an alternative that would meet minimum cut-off levels on each attribute.

**Consideration set** All the brands in a product category that a customer will consider assessing for purchase.

**Consumer** Another term for customer but in a household market.

**Consumer behavior odyssey** A qualitative research project undertaken in the late 1980s in the U.S. that involved personal visits by an interdisciplinary team of academic consumer researchers to a variety of consumer sites.

**Consumer socialization** The acquisition of knowledge, preferences, and skills to function in the marketplace.

**Content-based filtering** A recommendation for web sites based on consumer preferences for product attributes.

**Convenience sampling** A method wherein a group of customers are recruited based on convenient availability.

**Convenience value** Saving in time and effort needed to acquire the product.

**Co-production** A situation wherein customers routinely provide direct input into the making of a product or service.

**Corporate image** The public perception of a corporation as a whole.

**Corrective advertising** Advertising whose message includes a correction of a previous deception.

**Country-of-origin effects** Bias in customer perceptions of products and services due to the country in which they are made.

**Credit value** Freedom from having to exchange cash at the time of purchase or from becoming liable for immediate payment.

**Culture** Everything a person learns and shares with members of a society, including ideas, norms, morals, values, knowledge, skills, technology, tools, material objects, and behavior.

**Customer** A person or an organizational unit that plays a role in the consummation of a transaction with an organization.

**Customer behavior** Mental and physical activities undertaken by customers that result in decisions and actions to pay for, buy, and use products and services.

**Customer conversion ratio** Proportion of web site visitors who end up making a purchase.

**Customer culture** A culture that incorporates customer satisfaction as an integral part of corporate mission and plans.

**Customer decisions** Decisions customers make in the marketplace as buyers, payers, and users.

**Customer equity (goodwill)** Customer support for a supplier's well-being.

**Customer expectations** Customers' economic outlook about the near future that shapes their spending.

**Customer loyalty** A customer's commitment to a brand or a store or a supplier, based on a strong favorable attitude, and manifested in consistent repatronage.

**Customer militancy** The behavior of frustrated and dissatisfied customers entailing the taking of the law into their own hands.

**Customer orientation** Gaining a thorough understanding of customers' needs and wants, and utilizing them as the basis for all of the firm's plans and actions in order to create satisfied customers.

**Customer problem** Any state of deprivation or discomfort or wanting (whether physical or psychological) felt by a person.

**Customer satisfaction** A positive feeling ensuing from a successful outcome of a market transaction.

**Customer visits** A research program wherein a marketing firm's managers visit customer firms to interview buyers as well as users of their product and to observe their product in-use.

**Customerization** An improvement over one-to-one marketing and personalization.

**Customization** Receiving the product or service in a manner tailor-made to an individual customer's circumstances.

**Customized data** Data that are collected at the behest of a small group of pre-identified customers, and made available only to sponsoring companies.

**Cycle time** The total time it takes for the entire production and/or delivery task to be completed.

## D

**Deceptive advertising** Advertising that has the capacity to deceive a considerable segment of the public.

**Deep involvement** A customer's extreme interest in a product or service on an ongoing basis.

**Defense Acquisition** Regulations (DARs) Procurement regulations that apply to the Department of Defense.

**Democratic justice** A family norm in which each family member is given a voice in family decisions.

**Democratic families** Families where every family member has an equal voice and who encourage self-expression, autonomy, and mature behavior among children.

**Demographics** Easily verified, objective characteristics of a group of customers.

**Descriptive beliefs** An association in the customer mind that links an object or person to a quality or outcome.

**Detached personality** A person who is independent minded, entertains no obligations, and admits little social influence on personal choices.

**Diagnosticity** The ability to diagnose why certain attitudes are the way they are.

**Diffusion process** The spreading of an innovation's acceptance and use through a population.

**Direct purchase method** A method usually adopted by the U.S. government for orders costing up to $25,000, which entails directly contacting a few suppliers and placing an order with one of them, usually on the lowest quote basis.

**Discretionary expenditures** The purchase of goods and services to make life physically or psychologically more comfortable beyond sustenance.

**Disguised-nonstructured technique** A questionnaire design wherein the research purpose is not apparent to the consumer nor are the response categories provided.

**Disguised-structured technique** A questionnaire design wherein the real intent of the question is disguised, but the response categories are provided.

**Disintermediation** A practice in which the customer is enabled to transact directly with a firm without any intermediaries.

**Disjunctive model** A decision-making procedure that entails trade-offs between aspects of choice alternatives.

**Door-in-the-face strategy** A strategy of eliciting a behavior by first making a large request whose refusal is followed by a small request.

**Drive** An internal state of tension that produces actions purported to reduce that tension.

## E

**Ecological design** A strategy of influencing behavior by the design elements of the physical facility surrounding the customer.

**Ecology** Natural resources and the balance and interdependence among vegetation, animals, and humans.

**Economy** The state of a nation with respect to levels of employment, wages, inflation, interest rates, currency exchange rates, and aggregate household savings and disposable income.

**Effectiveness** How well a product or service meets the customer's needs and wants.

**Efficiency** How little it costs the customer in money, time, and physical effort to receive the value he or she seeks.

**Ego** The conscious mediator between the Id and the super-ego.

**Ego-defense function** An attitude that is held to protect a person's ego.

**Electronic data interchange (EDI)** A computer-based link between a supplier and its business customer that transmits customer inventory data to the supplier and automates reordering and shipping of the depleted product.

**Elimination by aspects (EBA)** A decision-making procedure wherein the customer examines all alternatives one attribute at a time in the ranked-order sequence with minimum cut-off attribute values.

**Emotional communications** Communications that evoke some emotional experience in the viewer or reader.

**Emotional hierarchy of attitude** A sequence of attitude components in which a person first feels an emotion toward an object, then acts on it, and then becomes knowledgeable about it.

**Emotional value** The enjoyment and emotional satisfaction users obtain from products and services.

**Emotions** The consciousness of the occurrence of some physiological arousal followed by a behavioral response along with the appraised meaning of both.

**Enculturation** The process of learning one's own culture.

**Enduring involvement** The degree of interest a customer feels in a product or service on an ongoing basis.

**Environmental marketing** Marketing of products and services in a manner that attempts to minimize the damage to the environment.

**Environmentally conscious** A customer who actively seeks out products with minimal impact on the environment.

**E-procurement** A buying organization uses Internet-based technologies to buy from contracted suppliers.

**Evaluated new unplanned purchases** Purchases for which the need had not been recognized prior to the purchase occasion.

**Evaluative beliefs** An association in the customer mind that links an object to personal likes or dislikes, preferences, and perceptions.

**Evaluative consistency** A process wherein the missing attribute is assumed in order to conform to the overall evaluation of the brand.

**Evoked set** Brands in a product or service category that the customer remembers at the time of decision making.

**Exchanges** Web sites run by a third party to bring buyers and sellers together vertically within an industry sector or horizontally across industry sectors.

**Expectations** Prior beliefs about what something will possess or offer.

**Experience goods** Products that need to be personally experienced to judge their quality.

**Experiential consumption** The use of a product or service in which the process of use itself offers value.

**Experiment** A research method in which respondents are placed in a controlled situation, and then their response is observed or recorded.

**Expertise** Possessing knowledge about the innovation that is not yet common knowledge.

**Exploratory shopping** Just browsing around after collecting the planned items.

**Extended problem solving (EPS)** A product or service selection strategy wherein the customer engages in an extensive information search and prolonged deliberation in order to minimize the risk of a wrong choice.

**External attributions** Assigning the cause to situational demands or environmental constraints that were beyond the control of the individual.

**External stimuli** Marketplace information that causes problem recognition.

# F

**Family** A group of persons related by blood and/or marriage.

**Family life cycle concept** The different stages a family goes through—starting from the time a person is young and single to the time when he or she becomes a single solitary survivor.

**Family relationship** The degree of mutual respect and trust between parents and adult offsprings, and the harmony of relations and communication among them.

**Federal Acquisition Regulations (FARs)** Procurement regulations that all agencies of the government have to follow.

**Festinger's Dissonance Theory** Theory that two cognitions are in dissonance (i.e., in conflict): the cognition that the decision has been made and the cognition that the decision may not have been the best choice.

**Financial well-being** Financial products and services such as financial planning, wills and trusts, mutual funds and stocks, and so on acquire new significance in aging customers' lives.

**Financing value** Offering the terms of payment more affordable by distributing the liability over an extended period of time.

**Fishbein model** Psychologist Martin Fishbein's formulation that attitude toward an object is the sum of the consequences of that object weighted by the evaluation of those consequences.

**Fishbein's extended model of behavioral intention** Psychologist Martin Fishbein's formulation that a person's intent to engage in a behavior is the weighted sum of his or her own attitude toward that behavior and others' expectations about his or her performing that behavior.

**Focus groups** A research method wherein a small group of customers participate in a group discussion steered by a moderator on specified issues.

**Foot-in-the-door strategy** A strategy of eliciting a behavior by first asking for a small favor whose acceptance is followed by a larger request.

**Forced irrelevance** An external environmental factor that renders prior solutions irrelevant.

**Form utility** Whereby performance value is built into the product or service by the manufacturer or the service designer.

**Forward buying** A practice wherein customers buy an item for future consumption.

# G

**Gender-role orientation** The degree to which specific behaviors and norms are linked to a person's gender rather than being shared across genders.

**Generation 'X'** Persons born in the United States between 1965 and 1975.

**Geographic redistribution** Refers to the shift in population density from one region of a nation or world to another.

**Geographical variation** Different patterns of consumption in different regions.

**Global sourcing** A purchasing function that overcomes the limitations of geography and seeks suppliers all over.

**Global warming** Earth's climate becoming warmer due to an increase in hydrocarbons in the atmosphere resulting from increased industrialization.

**Goal-object** Something in the external world whose acquisition will reduce the tension experienced by an organism.

**Government** Legal entities empowered to organize and govern a city, state, or nation.

**Government policy** A market context factor comprising monetary/fiscal policy and public policy.

**Green consumer** A customer concerned about the deteriorating environment and willing to modify his or her customer behavior to save the environment.

**Group traits** Common biogenic categories such as race, gender, and age.

**Groups** Two or more persons sharing a common purpose.

# H

**Habit** A learned sequence of responses to a previously encountered stimulus.

**Habitual purchasing** Simply repeating previous purchases.

**Hedonic consumption** The use of products/services for the sake of intrinsic enjoyment rather than to solve some problem in the physical environment.

**Heider's balance theory** The principle that a person will modify some of his beliefs to make them balanced or congruent with the rest of his or her beliefs.

**Heuristics** Quick rules of thumb and shortcuts used to make decisions.

**Household** A consumption unit of one or more persons identified by a common location with an address.

**Household markets** Customers who buy products for their personal use.

# I

**Id** A division of the human psyche that refers to the basic source of inner energy directed at avoiding pain and obtaining pleasure; it represents the unconscious drives and urges.

**Ideal self** A person's self-image of who he or she would like to be.

**Ignorance paradox** The tendency of less knowledgeable customers to seek less information rather than more.

**Imitative behavior** Adopting the behavior of those whom a person admires or considers successful.

**Imitators** Those who adopt an innovation after observing others who have it.

**Importance of purchase** How important a purchase is in the customer's life.

**Impulse purchase** The implementation of previously unplanned purchases, with purchase decisions made on the spur of the moment.

**Increased productivity approach** An approach in which a firm strives for a lower cost of production by raising productivity.

**Index of consumer sentiment** A nationally tracked measure of economic pessimism/optimism felt by customers in the United States.

**Individual traits** Unique biogenic and psychogenic aspects of the individual customer.

**Inference making** Reaching a judgment about an object based on incomplete information.

**Information board** A table of information in which the cells contain the information about the extent to which the brand specified in the corresponding row contains the attribute specified in the corresponding column.

**Information content** The information contained in the stimulus that moves the perceptual process beyond sensation or stimulus selection toward organization and interpretation.

**Information intensiveness continuum** Signifies the levels of various types of information associated with products, with traditional products and services that are information-independent at one end and information-dependent products/services at the other end.

**Information overload** Customers are exposed to so much information that they are unable to process it to make a decision.

**Information processing mode (IPM)** A decision mode wherein the customer acquires, evaluates, and integrates information about brand attributes to arrive at an overall brand evaluation.

**Information processing research** A class of research whose focus is on studying the information customers process for reaching a decision.

**Innovation** A product, service, or an idea that a customer perceives as new.

**Innovators** Customers who are the first ones to adopt an innovation.

**Instant gratification** The desire for an immediate satisfaction of a need or want.

**Instant marketing** Being ready to offer without delay a product or service when the customer wants it.

**Institutions** Relatively permanent groups with a pervasive and universal presence in a society, such as schools, religions, and the family.

**Instrumental conditioning** The learning of a response because it is instrumental to obtaining some reward.

**Instrumentality of market values** Products and services being instrumental in fulfilling needs or wants of customers.

**Interattribute inference** A process wherein the customer infers the value of one attribute based on another attribute.

**Intergenerational influence (IGI)** Influence of family members and the transmission of values, attitudes, and behaviors from one generation to the other.

**Internal attributions** Ascribing the cause of someone's behavior to personal dispositions, traits, abilities, or motivations and feelings.

**Internal stimuli** Perceived states of physical or psychological discomfort that cause problem recognition.

**Interpretation** A step in the perception process in which meaning is attached to the stimulus.

**Interpretative research** A method of research in which a researcher observes a group of consumers in their natural setting and interprets their behavior based on an extensive understanding of the social and cultural characteristics of that setting.

**Invitation for bid (IFB)** A method of government procurement wherein the government specifies the item being sought exactly and invites sealed bids.

**Involvement** The degree of personal relevance of an object or product or service to a customer.

### J

**Joint decisions** Decisions wherein more than one decision maker participates.

**Just noticeable difference (j.n.d.)** The magnitude of change necessary for the change to be noticed.

### K

**Knowledge function** Related to whether the object adds to a person's knowledge.

### L

**Laddering** A research technique to identify means-end linkages.

**Lead users** Innovative users of a product who use it in ways that suggest how the product should be modified for better utility.

**Learning** Any change in the content of long-term memory.

**Learning hierarchy** A sequence of attitude components wherein a person thinks first, feels next, and acts last.

**Level of adaptation** A person developing adequate familiarity with a stimulus so that the stimulation is perceived as normal or average.

**Lexicographic model** A decision model wherein the available alternatives are compared in sequence by the rank-ordered attributes.

**Life status change** Major events in a customer's life that change his or her status or personal context.

**Lifestyle retail brands** Brands sold in retail stores that are sought by customers principally for symbolic value and meaning for their lifestyles.

**Lifestyles** The way a person lives.

**Lifetime revenues** The cumulative revenues a firm can obtain from a customer over his or her lifetime.

**Limited problem solving (LPS)** A product or service selection strategy wherein the customer invests some limited amount of time and energy in searching and evaluating alternative solutions.

**Lower-margin approach** Selling at a low-profit margin in order to attract customers.

**Low-involvement attitude hierarchy** A sequence of attitude components in a person's acquisition of attitude toward objects that are of low salience or importance.

### M

**Maintenance/labor agreements** Agreements made by a business firm or government for obtaining a maintenance service throughout the year on an as needed basis.

**Market mavens** Individuals who possess information about markets and disseminate it to other customers.

**Market orientation** *See* Customer orientation.

**Market values** The benefits (tangible or intangible) a customer receives from a product or service.

**Marketer sources** Communication sources that act on behalf of the marketer of the product or service itself.

**Marketing concept** A firm focuses on making what the customer wants.

**Marketing myopia** A narrow vision wherein a firm views itself in limited, product- or service-centered ways—as makers and sellers of products and services they produce and sell.

**Maslow's hierarchy of needs** Psychologist Abraham Maslow's theory that human needs and wants exist in a hierarchy so that higher level needs are dormant until lower level needs are satisfied.

**Mass customization** Tailoring the product to the customer's specific needs, without sacrificing the speed or cost efficiencies of conventional mass production methods.

**Materialism** The importance a consumer attaches to material possessions.

**Maturation** A self-perceived obsolescence of prior preferences.

**Means-end chains** Linkages between the product's physical features and customers' fundamental needs and values.

**Mental budgeting** The idea that customers mentally set aside budgets for product categories.

**Mobile commerce** The buying and selling of products and services with the aid of mobile phones.

**Modeling** The learning of a response by observing others.

**Modified rebuy** A purchase item that is similar to the previously purchased item, but entails some changes either in design/performance specifications or in the supply environment.

**Moods** Short-lived and less intensely felt emotions.

**Motivation research (MR)** A research method directed at discovering the conscious or subconscious reasons that motivate a person's behavior.

**Motivation** The state of drive or arousal that impels behavior toward a goal-object.

**Multiattribute models of attitude** A rule that suggests that overall attitude is formed on the basis of component beliefs about the object weighted by the evaluation of those beliefs.

**Mutual goals** Those goals that require each exchange partner's cooperation and by whose achievement each partner profits.

## N

**National culture** The culture prevalent in a nation.

**Nature** Biological factors; premise that a person's genetic makeup determines human behavior, such as our emotions, sexual preference, tribalism, love of status, notions of beauty, sociability, creativity, and morality.

**Necessary expenditures** The purchase of products and services needed for minimal sustenance.

**Need** An unsatisfactory physical condition of the customer that leads him or her to an action that will remedy that condition.

**Need for cognition** Humans' need for information and for understanding the world around us.

**Negative cue** An inference-making strategy wherein the customer simply treats the missing information as a negative cue, which then affects the overall judgment negatively.

**Neglectful families** Families having parents who remain distant from their children and neglect them.

**Negligent consumer behavior** Customer behavior that puts oneself or others at risk, or that would, in the long run, impose heavy costs on society.

**Neo rich** Persons who have recently become affluent.

**Networks** A group of firms that deal with each other on a preferential basis.

**Neutral marketplaces** *See* Exchanges.

**New task** A purchase item new to the buying organization.

**Nondisguised-nonstructured technique** A technique in which the purpose of the study is not disguised; however, the consumer response categories are not predetermined.

**Nondisguised-structured technique** A technique that makes the research purpose obvious and seeks responses along prespecified response categories.

**Nonfamily household** A household that does not contain a family.

**Nonmarketer sources** Communication sources that are independent of marketer influence.

**Norm of reciprocity** An expectation that an act of favor or concession toward someone must be returned by a comparable act of favor.

**Nuclear family unit** A family comprising a married couple with children.

**Nurture** The familial and social environment; premise that behavior is determined by a person's upbringing, family life, parental values, peer group influences, school, and church groups.

## O

**Odd pricing** The setting of prices just below the next round number.

**One-stop shopping (OSS)** The practice of acquiring all related products from one supplier.

**Opinion leadership** The giving of information and advice, with acceptance of the advocated position by the opinion recipient.

**Optimal level of stimulation** A level at which balance is reached so that the person is neither bored nor overwhelmed by new experience.

**Organization** A process of stimulus categorization in which the sensed stimulus is matched with similar object categories in one's memory.

**Other-brand averaging** A process wherein the missing attribute value is assumed to be an average of its values across all other brands.

**Outsourcing** Procuring products and services that were once produced by the customer him/herself.

## P

**Partner-specific investments** Investments that one party makes on processes dedicated to the other party.

**Passive consumers** Persons who are not consuming the product themselves but who, as bystanders, are being negatively affected by the consumption of others.

**Payer** A person who pays or finances the purchase.

**Perceived justice** Customers' perception that they were treated fairly during the conflict resolution process and that the decision outcome itself was fair.

**Perceived risk of an innovation** The uncertainty that the innovation might cause an unanticipated harm.

**Perceived risk** The degree of loss (i.e., amount at stake) in the event that a wrong choice is made.

**Perception** The process by which an individual selects, organizes, and interprets the information received from the environment.

**Perceptual and preference mapping** An analytical technique of obtaining a visual map in a multi-dimensional space that shows consumer perceptions of similarity among and preference for various product or service alternatives.

**Perceptual distortion** In interpreting a stimulus, a person's prior beliefs interfere and distort the meaning to conform to those beliefs.

**Perceptual threshold** The minimum level or magnitude at which a stimulus begins to be sensed.

**Performance risk** The probability that the product may not perform as expected or desired, or that there may be physical side effects or unwanted consequences.

**Performance value** The quality of physical outcome of using a product or service.

**Peripheral processing route** A message is interpreted cursorily by attending to its form rather than its content.

**Permissive families** Families wherein children are given relative independence in conducting their own affairs, especially in their adolescent years.

**Personal safety** The safety of one's own person from crime or harmful consumption.

**Personality trait** A consistent, characteristic way of behaving.

**Persuasion** A rational method of conflict resolution wherein some members persuade others by demonstrating how the other person's position will lead to a suboptimal outcome.

**Phased decision strategy** A two-stage decision procedure wherein the alternatives are first eliminated, and then the remaining alternatives are compared for a final choice.

**Planned purchases** The purchases that a customer had planned to buy before entering the store.

**Planned social change** Active intervention by an agency with a conscious policy objective to bring about a change in some social or consumption behavior among the members of a population.

**Politicking** A conflict resolution method wherein members form partisan coalitions and then "manage" the decision with behind-the-scenes maneuvering.

**Popular culture** The culture of the masses in a nation, with norms, rituals, and values that have a mass appeal.

**Power dependence** The relative dependence of one party on the other because of the resources the other party possesses.

**Price value** A fair price and other financial costs incurred in acquiring the product.

**Pricing proposal** A proposal made by a supplier to government, using a specific government form, certifying current cost and pricing data for each line item.

**Primary demand** Demand for the product or service category itself.

**Primary emotions** Basic human emotions that humans have acquired based on the evolutionary process.

**Problem recognition** A realization by the customer that he or she needs to purchase something to get back to the normal state of comfort—physically and psychologically.

**Problem routinization** Defining a decision problem so that no new decisions need to be made.

**Problem solving** A rational approach to conflict resolution wherein participants search for more information, and deliberate on the new information.

**Process-induced affect** Affect (i.e., feelings) that is generated when a customer processes information about a product.

**Processing by attributes (PBA)** The process of assessing brands wherein all the available brands are compared simultaneously on one attribute at a time.

**Processing by brands (PBB)** The process of assessing one brand entirely before moving on to the second brand.

**Proprietary data** Data collected by private business firms that are in the business of collecting and marketing information of interest to a class of clients.

**Protocols** Customers' verbatim responses to certain information-processing tasks, often elicited by asking the respondent to speak out his or her task-related thoughts aloud.

**Psychographics** Characteristics of individuals that describe them in terms of their psychological and behavioral makeup.

**Psychology of complication** The customer desire to redefine a problem so that decisions have to be made anew.

**Purchase-decision involvement** The degree of concern and caring that customers feel in a purchase decision.

**Purposive behavior** When a person expends energy to attain some goal-object.

# Q

**Qualitative research** A method of gathering data wherein the respondent states the answer in his or her own words rather than being limited to preassigned response categories.

**Quality cue** A piece of information that can be used for making inferences about the quality of a product or service.

**Quality of life** Living condition measured by the absence of crime, traffic congestion, and pollution, and the opportunity for education, recreation, and general well-being.

**Quantitative research** A research method wherein a person's answers are obtained on a numerical scale.

# R

**Reciprocity** The customer practice of buying from a supplier because he or she (the supplier) in turn buys something else from the customer.

**Recreational needs** A person's need for entertainment and recreation.

**Reengineering** The redesign of business processes to make them more efficient.

**Reference groups** Persons, groups, and institutions that we look up to for guidance for our own behavior and values.

**Reference price** The price customers expect to pay.

**Regional economic integration** The realignment of nations into region-based economic blocs, such as the European Free Trade Association (EFTA).

**Regional marketing** The practice of adapting the marketing program according to customer diversity from one region to another.

**Relationship-based buying** The customer practice of limiting his or her choice to a single supplier.

**Relative advantage** The superiority of an innovation compared to the current product it will substitute.

**Request for proposal (RFP)** A method of government procurement adopted for products or services that are new, complex, or entail large sums of money, and where negotiations are deemed necessary.

**Restocking unplanned purchases** Purchase of items that the shopper had not thought about buying at the time but had been using regularly.

**Retrospective protocols** Respondents' reports of their thought processes about a decision made in the past.

**Role formalness** The degree to which interactions between the supplier and customer are limited to the formal roles of the parties.

**Role specialization** Dividing the customer roles (user, payer, and buyer) among individuals or groups.

**Roommate families** Families whose members structure their time, location, and activities independently of one another and with minimal sharing.

**Rosenberg model** Psychologist Milton Rosenberg's formulation that attitude toward an object is a function of the extent to which the object is instrumental in obtaining various values, weighted by the relative importance of those values.

**Rote memorization** The rehearsal of information until it gets firmly lodged in the long-term memory.

**Routine problem solving (RPS)** A product or service selection strategy wherein the customer considers no new information, and instead simply repeats previously made choices.

# S

**Satisficing** Customer (or decision maker's) acceptance of an alternative that he or she finds satisfying, rather than an arduous search for the most optimal alternative.

**Schachter's two-factor theory** Psychologist Stanley Schachter's theory that the experience of emotion depends on two factors: autonomic arousal and its cognitive interpretation.

**Search goods** Products whose features can be objectively assessed before the purchase.

**Search strategy** The pattern of information acquisition by customers to solve their decision problems.

**Secondary demand** Demand for a specific brand of product or service.

**Secondary research** An examination of secondary data to answer the questions of interest to the marketer.

**Selective demand** Demand for a specific brand of product or service.

**Self-concept** A person's image of oneself—who he or she is.

**Self-perception theory** The idea that people often infer their attitude by observing their own behavior—thus making attitude an inference from behavior rather than a cause of it.

**Self-selection** The idea that customers self-select themselves to be the customers of the firm that offers the advantage they seek.

**Selling concept** The firm focuses on persuading the customer to buy what it makes and offers.

Sell-side business models (p. 445)

**Sensation** A step in the perception process in which the person attends to an object or an event in the environment with one or more of the five senses.

**Sensory** A stimulus characteristic that stimulates any of the five senses.

**Service value** The assistance customers seek in buying a product or service.

**Shopbots** Internet tools that allow comparison by price and product features and across retailers.

**Shopping motives** The reasons customers have for visiting stores.

**Simulation** A research method wherein real-world conditions are created in a laboratory to study the behavior of customers.

**Single-source data** Organization of both purchase incidence and consumer characteristics data collection in a single integrated record.

**Situational involvement** The degree of a person's interest in a specific situation or on a specific occasion.

**Smart Bots** *See* Shopbots.

**Smart products** Products that can communicate their "functioning status" to an outside agent or receive communication from an outside agent to adapt their function within predefined limits.

**Social class** The relative standing of members of a society reflecting a status hierarchy.

**Social marketing** The application of the principles and tools of marketing for planned social change.

**Social risk** The probability that significant others may not approve of the innovation adoption.

**Social value** The benefit of a product or service directed at satisfying a person's want for gaining social approval or admiration.

**Social cause marketing** Marketing programs that promote social causes.

**Social orientation families** Families that are more concerned with maintaining discipline among children than promoting independent thinking.

**Stimulus** Any object or event in the environment that a person perceives.

**Store image** The sum total of perceptions customers have about a store.

**Store loyalty** A customer's predominant patronage of a store, based on a favorable attitude.

**Store visiting** The practice of visiting various stores and shopping centers without necessarily having any plans to buy anything.

**Straight rebuy** A product and service that has been purchased before and needs to be repurchased without any modifications.

**Straight rebuy** A product and service that has been purchased before and needs to be repurchased without any modifications. Telematics The wave of the future whereby one's car, refrigerator, television, and medicine cabinets would be Internet-ready.

**Subculture** The culture of a group within the larger society.

**Subjective norms** A person's perception about what others expect from him or her.

**Superego** The moral side of the psyche, which reflects societal ideals.

**Supplier-customer partnering** Establishing a partnership-like relationship with one's supplier or with one's customer.

**Switching costs** Costs a customer would have to incur if he or she switched suppliers.

**Syncratic decisions** Decisions in which all family members play an equal role.

**Syndicated data** Data that are of interest to a potentially large number of users, regularly collected by standardized procedures and made commercially available to all interested marketers.

**Systematic search** A comprehensive search and evaluation of alternatives.

## T

**Technical proposal** A proposal required by the government as part of the bid document submitted by commercial firms.

**Technology** Use of machines and devices to facilitate a practical task.

**Technophiles** Customers who are deeply interested in technology.

**Technophobes** Customers who fear new technology.

**Telematics** The wave of the future whereby one's car, refrigerator, television, and medicine cabinets would be Internet-ready.

**Test marketing** A research method of testing a marketing mix on a limited market as a precursor to deciding whether to implement that mix in the entire market.

**Thematic apperception test (TAT)** A series of ambiguous pictures shown to respondents who are then asked to describe the story of which the picture is a part.

**Time shift** A period when nonwork related activities may be pursued.

**Time shortage** The lack of free time.

**Tolerance for ambiguity** The degree to which a person remains free from anxiety in the face of uncertainty and lack of complete information.

**Topography** The terrain, altitude, and soil conditions of a location on Earth where customers buy and use the product or service.

**Trait theory of personality** The view of a person as a composite of several personality traits.

**Transaction-specific investments (TSIs)** Any special equipment or technology or human resources that need to be dedicated for meeting the needs of a particular customer/supplier partner.

**Trialability** The extent to which it is possible to try out the innovation on a smaller scale.

**Trust** A willingness to rely on the ability, integrity, and motivation of the other party to act in the best interests of the trusting party.

**Trustworthiness** The perceived benevolence and dependability of the opinion giver.

## U

**Unconditioned stimulus (UCS)** A stimulus toward which a person already has a pre-existing specific response.

**Universal values** Product or service benefits that satisfy the needs of the customer.

**Unplanned purchases** Purchases that a customer did not intend to buy before entering the store.

**Usage segmentation** Segmenting the market based on the brand, product, and quantity customers use.

**User** A person who actually consumes or uses the product or receives the benefits of the service.

**Utilitarian function** Related to whether the object serves some utility.

## V

**Value compatibility** The degree to which an innovation is free from contradicting a person's deeply held values.

**Value delivery** A firm fulfills a customer's need or want.

**Value synergy** Each value enhances the utility of another value.

**Value-expressed function** Related to whether the object helps express a customers' personal values and tastes.

**Values** The end states of life; the goals one lives for.

**Values and lifestyles (VALS)** A well-known psychographic segmentation scheme, widely in use, based on customer responses to a set of questions on their values and lifestyles.

**Verbatim** The recording of respondent answers exactly in their own words.

**Verifiable benefit** An advertising claim that can be verified by independent scientific tests.

**Virtual reality** An interactive, computer-generated 3D immersive visual and sound display of stimuli and situations representative of their real (physical) versions.

**Visual image profile** A research technique to elicit the nonverbal response of customers by presenting them with visual images of human emotions to identify their own emotional experiences.

**Voluntary simplicity** A tendency to simplify life and adopt economic behaviors of low consumption and ecological responsibility.

## W

**Want** An unsatisfactory psychological/social condition of the customer that leads him or her to an action that will remedy that condition.

**Weber's Law** Named after the German Scientist Earnst Weber, the law states that the larger the base quantity, the larger the magnitude of change needed for being noticed.

**Word association** A research technique wherein the respondent is asked to state whatever association the presentation of each word in a set evokes.

## Z

**Zaltman metaphor elicitation technique (ZMET)** Consumer researcher Gerald Zaltman's patented research technique to help respondents identify and report the rich imagery they hold as a result of their experience in the consumption of a product or service.

# Company Index

1-800-flowers.com, 441
3M, 10, 165, 281, 461, 476

A. C. Nielsen Company, 398
A. M. Best Company, 67
AARP, 96
Access Markets International (AMI) Partners, 16
Air Canada, 198
Air France, 352
Airborne, 9
Airbus, 302, 352
Aldo, 406
All Nippon Airways, 352
Amazon.com, 25, 27, 244, 425, 435
America Online, 32, 77, 98, 217, 220, 233
American Airlines, 136, 352
Ameristop, 409
Amway, 112
Andersen Consulting, 180
Apple Computers, 6, 34, 61, 130, 176, 389
ASDA, 406
AT&T, 9, 11, 24, 77, 217, 220, 394
AT&T Network Systems, 470
AutoNation, 29–30, 477

Bacardi, 399
Backer, Spielvogel, and Bates (BSB) Research Company, 79, 184
Bain & Company, 9, 402
Barnes and Noble, 415, 457
Bass, 352
Bell System, 11
Ben & Jerry's, 165
Benetton, 136, 165, 180, 400, 414
Best Buy, 441, 443
Better Business Bureau, 222
Bigg's, 410
BMRB International, 421
Body Shop, 390
Boeing, Inc., 10, 352, 464, 468
Boston Consulting Group (BCG), 4
BP, 73
Bristol-Myers Squibb, 159
British Airways, 352, 457
Brittain Associates, 25
Budget Rental Car Company, 465, 467
Budweiser, 399
Bugs Burger Bug Killer (BBBK), 464
Burger King, 474
Business Women's Network (BWN), 98

Cadbury-Schweppes, 399
Cadillac, 464
Campbell's Soup, 71, 143
Caterpillar, 28, 129, 464, 476
Centers for Disease Control (CDC), 159
Charolais Coal, 28
Chevy, 58
Chrysler Credit Corporation, 24
ChryslerDaimler Corporation, 369, 352, 375
CIGNA Insurance, 234
Circuit City, 34
Cisco, 445
Citigroup, 5
Claritas Corporation, 260
Clinique.com, 230
Clorox, 159
Club Med, 389
Club-Corp USA, Inc., 352
CNN, 169
Coca-Cola Company, 10, 130, 139, 210, 276, 394, 399, 466
Colgate-Palmolive Co., 159
Columbia Plastics, 468
Compaq, 34, 399, 467
Compuserve, 6, 32, 96
Computerland, 34
Concorde, 464
Consulting Resources Corporation, 46
Continental, 352
Costco, 406
C-Span, 169
Cyber Dialogue, 131

Dekalb Farmers Market, 113
Dell, 34, 438, 443, 445, 467
Delta Airlines, 11, 136, 137, 352
Denny's Restaurant, 400
Dia/Dirsa, 406
Dial Corp., 159
Do It Best Corp., 389
Domino's, 474
Donnelley Marketing Information Services (DMIS), 49
DuPont, 73, 430, 445

EarthLink, 233
Eastern Airlines, 11
Eastman Kodak, 80, 399, 446
Professional & Printing Image Division, 80
Elderhostel, 53
Emery, 9
Ernst & Young, 51, 149, 180, 432
Exxon, 351

Federal Express Corporation (FedEx), 9, 31, 106, 107, 210, 458, 461, 463, 475
Fingerhut, 230
Firestone, 460
First USA, 5
Food Giant, 406
Food Lion, 412
Ford Motor Co., 58, 61, 352, 362, 375, 460
Forrester Research, Inc., 49, 439
Fortino Group, 54
Fossil, 477

Gap, 180, 390
Gartner Research, 431
Gateway, 467
GE Capital, 24, 470
General Dynamics, 351
General Electric (GE), 61, 367, 445, 473
General Foods, 67
General Motors, 352, 375, 446, 448, 460
Gillette, 399
GMAC Financial Services, 24

Hallmark, 79
Hanna Andersson Corp., 467
Harley-Davidson, 6, 176
Harris Teeter, 412
H-E-B Marketplace, 412
Heineken (http://www.heineken.com), 394
Hewlett Packard, 234, 463
Hitachi, 136
Home Shopping Network, 113
Honda, 375
Hyatt Hotels Corporation, 352
Hyundai, 135

IBM, 10, 27, 34, 61, 176, 180, 208, 212, 234, 351, 399
IMIXrecords (http://www.imixrecords.com), 79
*Inc. Magazine*, 16
Intel, 461
International Data Corp. (IDC), 95, 431
IT, 212

J. Crew, 458
Jaguar, 276
John Deere & Co., 129, 198, 446
John Deere Harvester Works, 79
John Lewis department stores, 201
Jungle Jim, 410, 412
Jupiter Communications, 52
Jupiter Media Metrix, 430, 434, 441
Jupiter Research, 447

Kellogg's, 3, 323, 399
Kimberly-Clark, 53
Kinko's, 406
Kinney Drugs, 468
Kmart, 260
Kodak, *see* Eastman Kodak
Krispy Kreme, 389
Kroger, 406, 409, 410
Kwik Save, 406

L. L. Bean, 457, 458, 463
Lamborghini, 464
Lands' End, 4, 438
Levi Strauss, 165, 463
Lexus, 17
Limited, 390
Lincoln, 465
Los Angeles Century Plaza Hotel, 93
Lotus, 464
Louis Harris & Associates, 27
Lucent Technologies, 24, 470
Lysol, 159

M&M/Mars, 134
Macintosh, 389
Mainspring, 9, 402
Maritz Marketing Research, 43
Maroone-Toyota, 29
Marriott Hotels International, Inc., 10, 302, 352, 394, 399
Marshall Industries (http://www.marshall.com), 438
Maxwell House Coffee, 67, 236
Mazda, 389
McDonald's, 10, 11, 117, 260, 323, 474
McDonnell Douglas Corp., 351, 468
MCI, 9, 467
Media Matrix and AdRelevane, 133
Meijer, 406, 409, 412
Mercedes, 17, 105, 399
Merrill Lynch, 27, 131
Merry Go Round, 414
Microsoft, 399, 439, 461
Millstone, 438
Mobil, 394
Mont Blanc, 464
Motorola, 105, 394, 399, 463
MSN, 233
MTV, 113

National Association of Automobile Dealers (NADA), 153
National Science Foundation (NSF), 428
Neiman Marcus, 151
Nescafe (http://www.Nescafe.com), 395
Nestle, 461
Netscape, 77, 94, 428

Netto, 406
New View Technologies (http://newview.com), 445
NFO Research, Inc., 74
Nielsen Market Research Company, 258
Nike, 281, 295, 389, 465
Nintendo, 6, 289, 389
Nokia, 447
Nordstrom, 10, 198, 390, 457
Northwest Airlines, 352

Office Depot, 26, 474
OfficeMax, 406
Oldsmobile, 289
Opinion Research for Privacy and American Business, 27
Oracle, 77

Parmalat, 128
People's Express, 467
Pepsi, 139, 210, 276
Pier 1 Imports, 113
Pizza Hut, 279, 474
Playskool, 159
Polo, 136, 167, 180
Porsche, 17
PPG Industries, 30
Procter & Gamble, 10, 79, 200, 334, 376, 399, 430

Prodigy, 32
Purchase Pooling Solutions, Inc. (http://www.transitpool.com), 445

Quaker Oats, 446

Raytheon Corporation, 380
Rolex, 276, 464
Rolls Royce, 464
Rosenbluth International, 31, 477
Royal Crown (RC) cola, 139
Royal Dutch/Shell, 73

Saab, 35, 480
Saatchi & Saatchi, 55
Sainsbury's, 390, 406
Sam's Club, 16, 406, 410
Sanka, 67
Saturn, 460
Sears, Roebuck and Co., 11, 260, 352, 390, 441, 470
Service Merchandise, 136
Shell, 445
Shiseido, 6
Siemens, 445
Simmons Market Research, 52
Simon Properties, 448

Singapore Airlines, 10, 389
Sony, 94
Southwest Airlines, 61, 457, 467
Speedway, 409
Sprint, 467
SRI Consulting Business Intelligence (SRIC-BI), 184
SRI International, Inc., 180, 185, 427
Standard & Poor's, 67
Standard Rates and Data Service (SRDS) Company, 258
Staples, 406
State Farm, 54
Sterling Commerce, 446
Stratcom, 55
Sun Microsystems, 224, 234
SYSCO, 28

T. J. Maxx, 151
Taco Bell, 469, 474
Tandem Computers, 77
Techtronics, 129
Tesco, 406
Texas Instruments, 380, 467
Thriftway, 409
Thrifty Car Rental Co., 53
Tommy Hilfiger, 399

Toyota, 224, 375
Toys R' Us, 407
Tracom Corporation, 59
Traveler's Insurance Company, 131
Tupperware, 112
Tylenol, 10, 389

U.S. Sprint, 9
Uncover, Inc., 260
Unilever, 447
United Airlines, 11, 352
UPS, 10, 210, 476

Value City, 151
Virginia Atlantic, 61
Volkswagen, 447

Walgreen Pharmacies, 96
Wal-Mart, 79, 198, 334, 352, 376, 406, 416, 467, 477
Warner-Lambert, 76
Wired, 77

XBS, 31, 478
Xerox, 394, 474
Xerox Global Services, 31

Yahoo.com, 27, 149, 258
Yuban, 67

# Name Index

3M Worldwide double-coated tape, 460

Aaker, J. L., 214
Aaker, Jennifer, 62
ABC News/Harris survey, 259
Accompany.com, 445
Achrol, Ravi S., 5
Advanced Research Programs Agency (ARPA), 352
Aerospan, 352
African American web sites, http://netnoir.com, http://www.everythingblack.com, 48
Ahtola, Olli T., 166
Air Walk, 465
Alba, Joseph W., 288
*Allhealth.com*, 50
Alliance for Privacy, 440
*Alloy*, 52
Allport, Gordon, 200
Almash, John, 55
Altavista.com, 258
AMA Code of Ethics, 466
American Assembly of Colleges and Schools in Business (AACSB), 165
American Automobile Association (AAA), 296
American Customer Satisfaction Index (ACSI), 302
American Express card, 24
American Marketing Association (AMA), 65
American Society for Quality, 302
Andersen, 442
Annual Internet Shopper Study, 51
AOL/Roper Start Cyberstudy, 78
Application Service Providers (ASPs), 163
Armani, 191
Armstrong, Arthur, 6
ARPANET, 428
AskJeeves.com, 16
AskMe.com, 16, 167
ASSESSOR, 245
ATKearny report, 299
Autodaq.com, 445, 446
Autotrader (http://www.autotrader.com), 295
Avendra, 352

Baldrige, Malcolm, 165
Barone, Miniard, and Romeo (researchers), 174
Battelle Technology Intelligence Program, 116
Baumgartner, Hans, 168
BBDO ad agency, 256
Bearden, William O., 23, 65
Beatty, Sharon E., 321, 397

Beck, John, 379
Belk, Ostergaard, and Groves (researchers), 219
Belk, Russ, 23, 189
Bell, Ho, and Tang (researchers), 411
Bem, Daryl J., 212
Benjamin, Jonathan, 57
Bentley, 101
Berners-Lee, Tim, 428
Bernier, 379
Better Business Bureau (http://www.bbbonline.org), 165, 222, 303
Bezos, Jeff, 425
Bickart and Schindler, 434
Bieberich, Doug, 389
Bill of Rights for Bystanders, 111
Bird's Eye, 67
BITNET, 428
Bix, 21
Bizrate (http://www.bizrate.com), 281, 284, 434
Bjorkman, Ingmar, 369
*Black Enterprise*, 48
Black Entertainment Television (BET), 48
*Bluetorch*, 52
*Bolt*, 52
Boston Consulting Group (BCG), 442
Bourne, Francis S., 65
Bove, Fred, 243
Bowen, John C., 213
Brand Loyalists, 291
Brillo cleaning pads, 159
British Telecom, 110
Broniarczyk, Susan M., 288
Bronson, Richard, 61
Brooks Brothers, 191
Brynjolfsson and Smith (researchers), 435, 436
Brynjolfsson, Erik, 10, 439
Bureau of the Census, 47
*Business Week*, 32
Business Women's Network (BWN), 98
Buy America Act, 347
buy.com, 438, 439
Buzzsaw.com, 446

Cacioppo, John T., 215
Cadillac Seville, 470
California Polytechnical State University, 134
Cambridgesoft, 445
Cancer Forum, 6
Carnegie Mellon University, 108
Carpoint (http://www.carpoint.com), 295
Catell, 58
Cell phone info (http://www.cellmania.com), 292

Centers for Disease Control (CDC), 159
CETSCALE, 202
CFI Group, 302
ChemACS.com, 445
ChemConnect's World Chemical Exchange (http://www.chemconnect.com), 295, 445
Chemdex, 438
*Chemical Engineering*, 169
Chen and Wells (researchers), 200
Child Online Privacy Protection Act (COPPA), 111
Children's Online Privacy Protection Act (COPPA), 440
Cialdini, Robert, 213
Clair Chemical Corporation (CCC), 379
Clinton, Bill, 75, 110
Clorox, 159
CNN, 169
Coco Pazzo, 21
Cohen, Joel B., 23, 58
Coleman, Richard P., 69
Colgate toothpaste, 396
Columbia Business School, 439
Columbia University, 289
*Commerce Business Daily (CBD)*, 345, 349
*Competitive Strategy*, 377
*Computer Economics*, 52, 102
Conference Board, 74
Consumer Confidence survey, 74
*Consumer Reports* (http://www.consumerreports.org), 13, 73, 153, 274, 284, 295, 320, 409
Coors beer, 58
Corporate Purchase card, 24
Coulter, Robin Higie, 239
Council for Better Business Bureaus (BBBonline), 440, 442
Coupey and Sandgathe (researchers), 132
Covinst, 352, 362
Cragmont cola, 139
Crush, 399
CSNET, 428
C-Span, 169
Cyber Dialogue, 243
Cyber Suite, 93
Cyberatlas.com, 258
Cybermoola.com, 320
*Cybermoola.com*, 52

Daniel, 21
Dartmouth College, 7
Datamonitor, 421
Dawson, Scott, 189, 190
Day, George S., 392

DDB Needham study, 263
DealPilot.com, 16
Dealtime.com, 281, 435
DeBono, Kenneth, 23
Del Monte, 236
Department of Defense (DOD), 165, 344, 345, 346, 351
Department of Energy (DOE), 46
Depend undergarments, 53
Dial soal, 58
Dichter, Ernest, 166
Dichter's list, 170
Dick, Alan, 408
Digitrends.net, 258
Dole, Bob, 21
Dollard, John, 141
Domenici, Senator Pete, 46
Dpreview.com., 436
Drucker, Peter F., 2, 4
Dyas, Robert, 200

Ebates.com, 291
*Ebony*, 48
Ebstein, Richard P., 57
*EcoMall.com*, 73
*Economist*, 447
e-coupons (www.e-coupon.com), 403
Edge razor blades, 215
EDI, 107
Edwards Personality Preference Schedule (EPPS), 58
Ekstrom, Karin, 321
Elf cola, 139
Elizabeth Taylor's Passion perfume, 465
EMarketer, 443
Emarketer.com, 258
*Emerge*, 48
Emeril, 21
End, William, 4
Engle, Randall W., 139
Englis and Solomon (researchers), 238
*Entertainment Weekly*, 169
Envirolink network (http://www.envirolink.netforchange.com), 72
Environmental Protection Agency (EPA), 77
EPA, 111
Erealty.com, 434
ESPNet, 6
*Essence*, 48
e-Steel B2B, 438, 444
Etzel, Michael J., 23, 65
European Free Trade Association (EFTA), 112
Evans, Franklin B., 58
ExpertCentral.com, 167
Eysenck, Hans, 56

Faber, Ronald J., 188

Fader, Peter S., 441
Fairfield Inn, 399
Fairfield Inn by Marriott, 399
Faller, Jim, 30
Federal Communications Commission (FCC), 111
Federal Procurement Policy Act, 347
Federal Trade Commission (http://www.ftc.gov), 76
FedEx Ship, 107
Fedex's NetReturn, 106
Fennel, Geraldine, 166
Festinger, Leon A., 213
Firestone/Bridgestone ATX tires, 460
FirstGov (http://firstgov.gov/), 110
Fishbein, Martin, 216, 217, 224
Food and Drug Administration, 434
Foodservice.com, 334
Foote, Cone, & Belding ad agency, 256
Ford Explorer, 460
Ford Mustang Cobra, 464
Ford Supplier Learning Institute (FSLI), 362
Ford Supplier Network (FSN), 362
Ford, Henry, 61
Ford's Lean Resource Center, 362
Ford's Total Cost Management (TCM), 362
Forrester Research, Inc., 258, 431, 439
Fortune 500, 32, 165, 475
Fossil watches, 28
Fournier, Susan, 392
Foxman, Ellen, 321
Freedom Group of Florida, 53
FreeMarkets (http://www.freemarkets.com), 444, 445, 446
Freud, Sigmund, 56, 166
Frontera Grill, 21
FTC, 111
FUD factor, 208
Fuji film, 406

Gallup poll, 263
Gallup study, 413
Ganesan, Shankar, 378
GardenWeb, 6
Gartner Group, 258
Gartner Research, 431
GE appliances, 367
GE Customer Awareness Center, 473
General Service Administration (GSA), 344
Generations, 51, 52

Genetic Confidentiality and Non-Discrimination Act, 46
Georgia State University, 320
Georgia State University's Center for Mature Consumer Studies, 52
Gifford, Kathie Lee, 198
Glazer, Rashi, 432
Gleevec, 434
Gofish, 445
Goldstar TV, 135
Gomez (http://www.gomez.com), 284
Google.com, 258
Gorn, Professor Gerald, 139
Grease, 139
Greene, Mean Joe, 466
Greenfield Online, 96, 243
Greenleaf, Eric A., 299
GreenMarketplace.com, 73
Gregson, Ric, 29
Griffin, Babin and Modianos (researchers), 415
Gurhan-Canli, Zeynep, 135
GUV survey of 1996, 148

Hagel, John III, 6
Haire, Mason, 236
Hanna, Janice, 167
Harley Davidson H.O.G. (Harley Owners Group), 176, 405
Harris Interactive, 169, 291
Harvard University Business School, 266
Harvard University, 141, 239
Hastings Institute, 466
Haubl and Trifts (researchers), 435
Head & Shoulders shampoo, 207, 399
Healthy Choice (http://www.healthychoice.com), 479
Heath, Chip, 278
Heathrow Airport in London, 110
Heider, 214
Henson, Jim, 159
Hermes, 149
Herzon Memorial Hospital, 57
Hippel, Eric Von, 147
Hires, 399
Hirschman, Elizabeth, 23, 187
Hispanic, 48, 49
Hispanic Business, 49
Hispanic Online (http://www.hispaniconline.com), 48
Hobrook, Morris, 289
Hoffman and Novak (researchers), 138
Hofstede, Geert, 61, 63
Holbrook, Morris, 23, 166
Holt, Douglas B., 190

Horney, Karen, 58
HoustonStreet.com, 445
Hoyer, Wayne D., 297
Hunter-Gatherers, 291
Hybels, William, 2

Icanbuy.com, 52, 320
ICG Commerce, 338
IMAC Apple computer, 130
IMF, 352
I-mode, (www.nttdocomo.com), 106
Import-Export Bank, 300
Industrial Marketing and Purchasing (IMP), 373, 385
Inetsurvey.com, 243
Information Acceleration, 266
Institute for the Future, 100
Intelliquest Inc., 399
International Mass Retail Association, 389
Internet Explorer, 439
Internet Tax Freedom Act, 75
Internet, 94
Ipsos-Reid, 440
iTurf, 52
iVillage.com, 50, 167

J. C. Williams Group, 434
J. D. Power and Associates, 434
Jackson, Mike, 29
Jacoby, Jacob, 391
Jaguar, 276
Jain, Arun K., 408
Jamias, Bruno, 21
Jaworski, Bernard J., 8, 23
Jewelry (http://www.bluenile.com), 292
Ji, Mindy, 324
Jiuan, Jung, Wirtz, and Keng (researchers), 186
Jobs, Steve, 389
Johar, J.S., 23
John, Deborah Roedder, 248, 323
Johnson, Eric, 439
Johnston and Johal (researchers), 63
Jordan, Michael, 63

Kahle, Lynn, 176, 397
Karsten, Yvonne Cariveau, 248
Kathie Lee clothing, 295
Katona, George, 74
Katz, Daniel, 220
Kelleher, Herbert D., 61
Kelley, Harold H., 169
Kelley, Robert, 242
Kellogg's Frosted Flakes, 323
Kelly repertory grid, 239
Kepferer, Jean, 23
Keri lotion, 159
Killarney, Ireland, 31

King Arthur Flour, 436, 437
Knowledge Systems & Research, 442
Kock, Soren, 369
Kodak film, 406
Kohli, Ajay K., 8
KOOL-AID, 289
Koop, William, 116
Korgaonkar, Pradeep K., 161
Kotler, Philip, 4, 5, 472
Krishnan, R., 134
Kristol, Irving, 69
Kwik coupons (www.kwikkoupon.com), 403

Laboratory of Clinical Science, 57
Lassar, Walfried, 26, 400
Laura Ashley, 180
Laurant, Gilles, 23
Lauren, Ralph, 180
Lee and Sternthal (researchers), 174
Lehmann, Donald R., 299
Lejander, Joe, 198
Leong, Siew Meng, 297
Levitt, Theodore, 19
Lewis, John (department stores), 201
Life cereal, 396
Life/Style Online, 238
Lifestyle Marketing Analysis, 258
Likert scales, 243
Liquidation.com, 446
Listerine, 76
London Institute, 408
Long Life (milk), 128
Los Angeles Century Plaza Hotel, 93
Lysol, 159

MacInnis, Debra, 23
MacWorld Expo, 389
Madisonville, Kentucky, 28
Maheswaran, Durairaj, 135, 214
Makino hydraulic controls, 207
Market Facts (http://www.marketfacts.com), 259
Marketing Challenges, 467
Marketing Simulation Lab, 266
Marlboro, 399
Maroone-Toyota dealership, 29
Martin, John E., 469
Maslow, Abraham, 159, 164, 176, 177, 180
Massie, Reverend James S. Jr., 389
Mateer, Bob, 363
Mazda Miata, 389
McDermott, Bill, 32

McKinsey & Company, 399
McLuhan, Marshall, 110
McMellon and Schiffman (researchers), 95
McNeal, James, 324
McQuarrie, Edward F., 233
Media Metrix, 258
Merill, David W., 59
Mesa Grill, 21
MetalSite, 445
Miata, 17
Miller, Neal E., 141
Millett, Stephen, 116
Milliman, Ronald E., 210
Milner, Peter, 168
Mine Expo, 28
Miniard, Paul, 23
MIT, 47, 245, 266, 439
Mittal, Banwari, 23, 26, 400
Moe, Wendy W., 441
Monroe, Kent B., 134
Moorthy, Ratchford, and Talukdar (researchers), 292
Morgan Stanley Dean Witter Technical Research, 144
Moschis, George P., 320
Motorola Digital DNA Laboratory, 105
*MTV Spring Break*, 204
MTV/Harris Interactive YouthPulse, 320
Multi-Channel Retail Report 2001, 434
Multiple Listing Services, 434
Munson, Jim, 23
Murray, Henry, 165
Murray's list, 170
MySimon.com, 281, 435
My-te-Fine cola, 139

NASA, 299, 351
National Consumer Council in UK, 151
*National Enquirer*, 169
National Institute of Health, 46
National Institute of Mental Health, 57
National Science Foundation (NSF), 428
National University of Singapore, 297
NatWest, 421
Nelson, Margaret C., 329
Nescafe (http://www.Nescafe.com), 395
Nescafe instant coffee, 236, 399
Netemeyer, Durvasula, and Lichtenstein (researchers), 202
New View Technologies (http://newview.com), 445
New York University, 391
Newbies, 291
Newman, Bruce, 23

*Newsweek*, 32
NexTag's Business exchange, 436
NFO Interactive, 243
NFO WorldGroup (http://www.nfow.com), 259
Nickelodeon, 320
Nielsen/Net Ratings, 428
Nielson TV, 263
n-Logue, 429
Nobel Prize, 138
Nolan, Kathleen, 466
North American Free Trade Agreement (NAFTA), 112, 421
Northwestern University, 4
Novartis AG, 434
NPD Group, 403
NPD, 243
NSFNET, 428

O'Guinn, C., 188
Old Spice, 58
Olds, James, 168
Olestra, 200
Oliver, Richard, 404
Omar, Ogenyi Ejye, 408
*OnHealth.com*, 50
Online/Harris Interactive KidPulse, 320
*Outbreak*, 159
*Oxygen.com*, 50

Park, C. W., 23, 318
Parvatiyar, Atul, 364
Patterson, Bill, 32
Pavlov, Ivan Petrovich, 138
PDA (Personal Digital Assistant), 104
Peapod, 291
Pechman, Cornelia, 208
Pentagon, 351
*People*, 169
People's Heritage Bank of Portland, Maine, 280
Peppers and Rogers Group, 100
Peppers, Don, 438
Peterson, Balasubramanian, and Bronnenberg (researchers), 430, 433
Petrus, Jim, 93
Petty, Richard E., 215
PlanetFeedback (http://www.planetfeedback.com), 303, 442
PlasticsNet.com, 445
Platform for Privacy Preferences Project (P3P), 439
Plax, 129
Plutchik, Robert, 171–173
*Popular Mechanics*, 169
Porter, Michael, 377
Portland State University, 189
Post-it notes, 10, 281

Prabhakar, Paul, 23
PrivaSeek, 5
Purchase Pooling Solutions, Inc. (http://www.transitpool.com), 445
*Purchasing*, 341

Rainwater, Lee P., 69
Raju, P. S., 168
Rangaswamy, Arvind, 403
Ratchford, Brian, 23
Ratneshwar, S., 208
Reichheld and Schefter, 403
Reiner, Bob, 54
Rembrandt, 464
Restaurantpro.com, 334
Retail Link, 334
Retirement+, 96
Richardson, Paul S., 408
Richins, Marsha, 173, 189, 190
Riesman's Social Character Theory, 180
Right Guard, 58
Rocketcash, 320
Rogers, Edward, 149
Rogers, Martha, 438
Rokeach, Milton, 176
Rosenberg, Milton, 216
Rosenbluth, Hal, 12

Saatchi & Saatchi, 55
Santa Clara University, 233
Sara Lee, 413
Schachter, Stanley, 171
Schaninger, Charles M., 58
School of Retail Studies, 408
Schumann, David, 215
*Science and Human Behavior*, 141
Sciglimpaglia, Donald, 59
Sciquest.com, 445
Scotch tape, 10
*Scour*, 52
Sears Gold Master Card, 11
Secure HyperText Transfer Protocol (S-HTTP), 440
Secure Sockets Layer (SSL), 440
Seelye, H. Ned, 368
Seelye-James, Alan, 368
SeniorNet, 96
SERVASSOR, 266
*Serving the Ageless Market*, 53
Shankar, Venhatesh, 403
Sharma, Arun, 400
Shasta cola, 139
Shavitt, Sharon, 23
Shaw, D. E., 425
Sheth, Jagdish N., 23, 104, 167, 237, 364
Sheth, Newman, and Gross, 166
Shimp and Sharma (researchers), 202
Shimp, Terence A., 139

Shopper.com, 435
Silk, Alvin J., 245
Simon, Herbert, 298
Sirgy, Joseph, 23
Sisodia, Rajendra S., 104
Skinner, B. F., 56, 141
Smith, Amy K., 403
Smith, Michael D., 10
*Snowball*, 52
Snyder, Mark, 23
Socratic Technologies, 243
Soft Bear, 159
Soll, Jack B., 278
Solomon, Michael, 23
Sony Clie, 104
Stanford Institute for the Quantitative Study of Society, 108
Steelkamp, Thomas T., 375
Steenkamp, Hofstede, and Wedel (researchers), 146
Steenkamp, Jan-Benedict E. M., 168
Sterling Commerce, 446
Strategy Analytics, 106
Stuart, Elnora W., 139
Sulloway, Frank, 47
Suntory brands, 421
Suntory Reserve, 421
SuperProfile, 5
Supplier Technical Assistance (STA), 362
Swedish School of Economics, 369
Szymanski and Hise (researchers), 302

Talpade, Salil, 321
Tamil Nadu Agricultural College and Research Institute, 429
Tamil Nadu Association for Veterinary and Animal Sciences, 429
Tang, 351
Tanshuhzj, Patria, 321
TechWeb, 149
Teenage Research Unlimited, 320
Teflon, 351
TeNet Group of IIT
Thatcher, Margaret, 110
*The Futurist*, 116
*ThriveOnline.com*, 50
TIGER (Topographically Integrated Geographic Coding and Referencing) system, 258
Tiger cola, 139
*Time*, 32
Tommy Boy, 465
Tommy Girl, 465
Tony the Tiger, 323
Toyota Camry, 458
Travelocity, 6

TRUSTe, 77, 440
Tversky, Amos, 296
Tylenol, 10

U.are.U Personal, 440
U.S. Bureau of Labor Statistics (http://www.bls.gov), 258
U.S. Census Bureau (http://www.census.gov), 257, 258
U.S. Department of Commerce, 48, 431
U.S. Department of Defense, 427
U.S. Federal Communications Commission, 415
U.S. Patent and Trademark Office (http://www.uspto.gov), 258
U.S. Postal Service, 441
U.S. Securities and Exchange Commission (http://www.sec.gov), 258
Uncover, Inc., 266
Uniform Contract Format (UCF), 346
United Nations, 352
University of British Columbia, 139

University of California at Irvine, 208
University of California at Los Angeles, 427
University of California at Santa Barbara, 428
University of Connecticut, 239
University of Florida, 208
University of Illinois, 134
University of Michigan Business School, 302
University of Michigan Survey Research Center, 74
University of Minnesota, 57
University of Missouri, 189
University of South Carolina, 139
University of Tennessee, 479
University of Texas at Austin, 297
University of Utah, 428
Urban, Glen L, 245, 266
Urban, Sultan, and Qualls (researchers), 441
USENET, 428

ValueSpace, 460
Van Gogh, 464

Vancouver Museum of Anthropology (MOA), 242
Vavra, Terry, 472
VerticalNet.com, 446
Virtualvineyards, 6
Virus, 159
Vyas, Niren, 339

Walkman, 94
Wall Street Journal, 465
Watson, Thomas, 61
Web of Trust (http://www.epinions.com), 284
Weber, Ernst, 134
Weber's Law, 410
WebMD.com, 96
Webster, Frederick E. Jr., 7
WebTV, 104
Welsh, Jack, 61
Westfall, 58
Wharton School, 392
Williams, Patti, 62
Willow Creek Community Church, 2
Wind and Rangaswamy (researchers), 438
Winthrop College, 139
Wired, 169
Wolfe, David B., 53

Wolin, Lori D., 161
Women.com, 50
Woodruff, Robert B., 479
Woods, 136
Woodside, Arch, 339
World Bank, 300, 352
World Health Organization, 258
World Wide Web Consorium, 439

Yankelovich Monitor, 259
YMCA, 64
YSB, 48

Zaltman, Gerald, 239
Zander, Dieter, 2
Ziprealty.com, 434
ZMET (http://www.hbs.edu/mml/zmet), 240
Zoomerang.com, 243

# Subject Index

Abstract vs. associative thinking, 63
Access, lack of, 16
Access to products, 105
Access value, 31
Accountability for decisions, 333
**Acculturation, 60**
Acquisition team, 347
**Actual self, 177**
**Adaptation, level of, 168**
**Addressability, 264**
Adopters, categories of, 144–145
Adopters of Internet technology for online shopping, 148
Adoption process, 147
**Adoption, 147**
Adults, young vs. mature, 53
Advanced Research Programs Agency (ARPA), 352
**Advertising,**
  **corrective, 76**
  **deceptive, 76**
**Advocate sources, 284**
**Affect, 203**
**Affective choice mode (ACM), 292**
**Affordability, 101**
  lack of, 17
African-American (race), 47, 48, 101, 431
Aftermarketing, 472
Age, 50
  influence of, 81
**Aggressive, 58**
Aging of the population, 95
AIO profiles, psychographics as, 180
Alaskan Eskimo race, 47
Alternative evaluation, 293, 435
Alzheimer's disease, 17, 46, 47
**Ambiguity, tolerance for, 168**
American Indian race, 47
**Annual purchasing agreements, 348**
**Approach motivation, 163**
Armed Service Procurement Act, 349
Arousal, need for, 168
**Arousal-seeking motive, 168**
Asian Americans, 48, 221, 431
Asian countries, lifestyle clusters in, 186
Asian Indians, 49
Asian race, 47
ASSESSOR, a simulation model, 245
**Assimilation and contrast, 134**

Associative vs. abstract thinking, 63
**Assortment, 406**
**Asymmetrical, 373**
**Atmospherics, 413**
**Atomistic family unit, 99**
**Attitude,**
  components in mutual interdependence, 207
  emotional hierarchy of, 204
  functional theory of, 220
  learning hierarchy of, 204
  low-involvement hierarchy of, 205
  **multiattribute models of, 216**
  three-component model of, 201, 203
Attitude change, and psychological processes, 211
Attitude formation, central and peripheral routes to, 215
**Attitude hierarchy, 203**
  degrees of involvement and types of, 206
**Attitude molding, 207**
  cognitive route, 207
  conative approach, 209
  incentives, 209
**Attitude persistence, 216**
Attitude research, 246
**Attitude strength, 206**
Attitude toward sites, measures for, 201
**Attitude valence, 206**
Attitude-based behavior, brand loyalty as, 392
**Attitudes, 200**
  applying the theory of, 222
  as evaluations, 200
  characteristics, 200
  conceptual framework, 199
  customer, 198, 217, 224–225
  defined, 200
  functions of, 221
  managing, 198
  molding customer, 207
**Attitudinal brand loyalty, 392**
**Attraction of alternatives, 397**
Attribution, need for, 168, 169
**Attribution motivation, 169**
Attribution processes, 212
**Attributions, 169**
**Authoritarian families, 320**
Authority, diffusion of, 350
Automated consumption, 107
Automated transaction recording, 475
Automation, 468
**Autonomous decisions, 317**
**Autonomy, 99**
Availability, limited, 464

**Avoidance motivation, 163**
Awarding the contract, 348
**Awareness set, 282**
Awareness, evoked, and consideration sets, 283

B2B, *see also* business-to-business
B2B
  business operating models, 444
  commerce, customer behavior, 443
  marketplace, learning new behaviors in, 446
  marketplaces, value creation in, 444
B2C, *see also* business-to-consumer
Baby Boomers, 52, 55
**Bargaining, 342**
Behavior,
  customer, 12
  understanding customer, 3
**Behavioral**
  **brand loyalty, 391**
  **compatibility, 148**
  incidents, description of, 249
  intention, Fishbein's extended model of, 217
**Behaviorally anchored scale, 248**
Behaviorism, 141
**Behaviorism theory, 56**
Behaviors in the B2B marketplace, learning new, 446
**Beliefs, 201**
Benefits of purchasing online, 148
Biases in the perceptual process, 132
Bid document, contents of, 346
Bid specifications, 345
**Biological determinism, 45**
Boredom, 143
**Borrowing power, 67**
Brain activity, 256
Brand, social and emotional identification with the, 394
**Brand belief, 202**
**Brand equity, 399**
  components of, 400
  measures of components of, 401
  two views of, 399
  vs. brand loyalty, 399
Brand Loyalists, 291
**Brand loyalty, 392**
  as attitude-based behavior, 392
  **attitudinal, 392**
  contributors to, 393
  definition and measurement, 391

framework for, 404
  illustrative measures of, 393
  model of, 393, 394
**Brand parity, 397**
Brand perceptions, differences in, 137
**Brand valuation, 399**
Browsers into buyers, turning, 441
**Budgeting, mental, 277**
Building relationships in Russia, 368
**Business, 332**
Business and government procurements compared, 348
Business and household buying compared, 333
Business buying, reasons for relationship development in, 374
Business buying behavior, 332, 355
  and perceived risk, 337
Business buying process, components of, 333
Business customer(s)
  decision making, 314
  innovators among, 147
  Maslow's needs for, 165
  personality of, 59
  trust and commitment from, 374
  use of the compensatory choice model, 294
Business customer's total costs, components of, 341
**Business cycle, 75**
Business decision making and customer roles, 353–354
**Business market, 12**
Business markets,
  intergenerational differences in, 55
  relationship buying and selling, 372
Business procedures, 210
Business process reengineering, 468
Business purchase(s)
  decision process, 339
  long-term contracts for repeat purchases, 339
  orientation, 338
  procurement costs, 341
  resources, 336
  rules and procedures, 339
Business purpose, fulfilling the, 480
Business size, 336
Business structure, 336
Buy American Act, 347
**Buy to Browse, 431**
**Buyclass, 334**
  buying behavior associated with, 335

**Buyer, 14**
Buyer/user/payer conceptual framework, 37
Buyers,
  creating market values for, 470
  self-concept as, 178
  turning browsers into, 441
**Buyers' remorse, 213**
Buyer-seller relationship, nutrients for, 378
**Buying, compulsive, 187**
Buying behavior,
  associated with buyclasses, 335
  business, 355
  government, 344, 355
  household, 316, 352
**Buying center, 338**
Buying center roles, varying influence of, 341
Buying decisions, family, 317
Buying power, lack of, 16
Buying procedures, government, 344
Buying process, formalization of the, 333
**Buy-side business models, 445**

Canada, 62
Car purchase information on the Internet, 285
Cash Management Account (CMA), 27
Caucasian race, 47
Central planning ideology, 110
**Central processing route, 214**
Central route to attitude formation, 215
CETSCALE, 202
**Change agent, 222**
**Change targets, 222**
**Changing demographics, 95**
Children's influence on family decisions, 320, 321
Children's Online Privacy Protection Act (COPPA), 77, 440
Children's role by family type, 322
Chinese Americans, 49
Choice,
  based on nonlocational criteria, 411
  deviation from the identified, 300
  of strategy, 223
**Classical conditioning, 139**
**Climate, 69**
**Cocooning, 100**
**Cognition, need for, 168**
Cognitive consistency theories, 213

**Cognitive dissonance, 213**
**Cognitive learning, 138**
**Collaborative filtering, 434–435**
Collectivism, 62
  vs. individualism, 62
Commercial data, selected sources, 259
**Commitment, 371**
  and trust, defined, 371
**Communicability, 148**
Communication and product support, 376
Comparative features of various choice models, 297
Compensatory choice model, use by a business customer, 294
**Compensatory model, 293**
**Competitive procurement, 344**
**Competitive promotional activity, 397**
Complaining, determinants of, 304
**Complexity, 148, 336**
  of requirements, 333
**Compliance, 76**
**Compliant, 58**
Complication, 142
**Complication, psychology of, 143**
Compulsive buyer defined, 188
**Compulsive buying, 187**
**Compulsive consumption, 187**
**Conation, 203**
**Concept-oriented families, 320**
**Concurrent protocols, 256**
**Conditioned stimulus (CS), 139**
Conflict,
  and resolution, business purchase, 342
  in family decisions, 327
  resolution, 328
  resolution techniques, 329
  types of, 328
**Conjunction model, 294**
**Consideration set, 282, 283**
**Consumer, 12**
Consumer Behavior Odyssey, 240
Consumer behavior, negligent, 76
Consumer involvement, illustrative measures of, 290
Consumer research, virtual reality techniques in, 265
Consumer research project, virtual-reality, 267
**Consumer socialization, 322–323**

**Consumers,**
  differences in Asian and Western, 137
  **passive, 108**
  socialization of Chinese children as, 324
**Consumption, compulsive, 187**
Consumption Emotions Set (CES), 173
Consumption motives, Dichter's, 166–167
**Content-based filtering, 435**
Context, 131
  personal, 59
Contract, awarding the, 348
Control and flexibility (of technology), 78
Control over information, increased, 104
Convenience, 407
**Convenience sampling, 232**
**Convenience value, 25, 474**
Convenient point of access, 474
Coproducers, customers as, 106
**Coproduction, 106, 438**
Corporate and brand perceptions, differences in, 137
Corporate crisis, protection against, 10
**Corporate image, 136**
**Corrective advertising, 76**
Cost efficiency from repeat customers, 8
Cost reduction, 380
Cost-benefit factors, 364
Council for Better Business Bureaus (BBBonline), 440
**Country-of-origin effects, 135**
Creating market values for buyers, 470
Creating market values for the customer, 457
Credit and financing value, 29, 469
  personal value, 24
**Credit value, 24**
Cross-cultural values, 61
Cuban Americans, 48
Culture, 60, 84
  abstract, 63
  characteristics of, 61
  Internet, 63
Cultural
  diversity, 102
  objects, 242
Curiosity, need for cognition, 168
Current solutions, forced irrelevance of, 143
**Customer(s), 2, 14**
  as a learner, 136

as a perceiver and learner, 128
as coproducers, 106
B2C defined, 430
classification of groups, 64
creating market values for, 457
determining supplier trust in, 376
established, 9
healthcare, 396
how they shop, 409
market values sought, 19
Maslow's needs for, 164–165
of products and services online, 432
passive, 111
repeat, 8
roles of, 14
satisfying the, 4
sources of information for, 284
Customer acceptance of change, 144
Customer attitudes
  and customer roles, 224–225
  cognitive and affective, 198
  example, Internet providers, 217
  molding, 207
**Customer behavior, 6, 12**
  and mental budgeting, 278
  benefits of anticipating trends, 94
  determinants of, 43
  impact on, 112
  implications for, 110
  in B2B commerce, 443
  influence of determinants, 80
  online, 425
  organizational, 343
  researching, 230
  understanding, 3
Customer behavior (online)
  and customer roles, 448–449
Customer behavior domain, 13
Customer behavior research
  and customer roles, 267–268
Customer characteristics, 131
**Customer conversion ratio, 428**
**Customer culture, 4**
**Customer decision(s), 277**
Customer decision making, individual, 274
Customer decision process, 277
Customer emotions, 159, 170
**Customer equity or goodwill, 372**
**Customer expectations, 74**
Customer factors, 397

Customer inference making, intuitive theories in, 288
Customer insight, 7, 53
**Customer loyalty, 400**
and customer roles, 417–418
importance of online, 402
to products, brands, and stores, 389
to stores, 405
**Customer militancy, 101**
Customer moods, 173
Customer motivation, 159
for relationship-based buying, 364
Customer needs, 159, 163
and wants, 17
Customer opportunity network, 5
**Customer orientation, 6**
and employee pride, 12
Customer outsourcing, 107
Customer perceptions
and preferences, methods of measuring, 251
of value delivery process, measuring, 481–483
Customer personality, 56
**Customer problem, 279**
Customer psychographics, 159
Customer relationship management and customer roles, 383
Customer responses in new technology, 106
Customer roles,
and household, business, and government decision making, 353–354
and individual customer decision making, 305–307
and loyalty to products and stores, 417–418
and online customer behavior, 448–449
and problem recognition, 281
customer attitudes and, 224–225
customer behavior research and, 267–268
customer relationship management and, 383
implications of the trends for, 113
in innovative adoption, 153
influence of demographics, 114
influence of public policy, 114
influence of technology, 114
learning the, 322
motivational processes and, 190–191
perceptual and learning process and, 151–152

personal characteristics and, 82–83
specialization of, 332
values and, 20
Customer satisfaction,
and loyalty to brands—international markets, 421
competitive advantage, 8
Customer segments by loyalty, 398
Customer value(s)
and hierarchy, 33
characteristics of, 32
delivery excellence, 476–478
diversity of, 33
fulfilling the business purpose by delivering, 480
linking product attributes to, 177
process for determining, 479–480
showcasing, 28
tools for creating, 459
variance, 34
**Customer visit, 233**
advantages of, 233
applications of, 234
Customer's final judgment, assessment of, 484
**Customerization, 438**
Customers' brand loyalty, model of, 394
**Customization, 27**
mass, 106
**Customized data, 259**
products and services, 79
**Cycle time, 468**

Data trail from shopping on the Internet, 266
Database research, 264
**Deceptive advertising, 76**
Decision confirmation, 301
Decision criteria, interplay of, 410
Decision maker,
individual, 275
psychology of, 342
roles of the, 276
Decision plan nets for a husband and wife, 319
Decision process, 330
and customer roles, 330
business purchase, 339
customer, 277
influences on, 330
Decision roles, husband-wife, 317
Decision-making process, family, 317
**Decisions,**
accountability for, 333

**customer, 277**
influence by spouse, 329
Declining middle class, 100
**Deep involvement, 175**
**Defense Acquisition Regulations (DARs), 345**
Defense mechanism, 56
Delay and delay closure, reasons for, 300
Delay in implementation, 299
**Democratic families, 322**
**Democratic justice, 325**
Demographic trends, 95
implications of, 113
**Demographics, changing, 95**
**Descriptive beliefs, 203**
**Detached, 58**
Determinants of
complaining, 304
customer behavior, 80
trust and commitment from business customers, 374
Deviation from the identified choice, 300
**Diagnosticity, 220**
Dichter's consumption motives, 166–167
Diffusion of authority, 350
**Diffusion process, 144**
Digital Generation, 54
Digital Signature and Electronic Authentication Law, 77
**Direct purchase, 344**
**Discretionary expenditures, 74**
**Disguised-nonstructured techniques, 237**
**Disguised-structured techniques, 235**
**Disintermediation, 107**
**Disjunctive model, 295**
Display or demonstration, 471
Dissatisfaction/satisfaction, 302
Distinct from income, 68
DNA, 45, 46, 57
Dominicans, 48
**Door-in-the-face strategy, 211**
**Drive, 161**

E. coli bacteria, 159
Echo Boomers, 54
**Ecological design, 210**
**Ecology, 71**
e-commerce, 52, 54, 73, 75, 96, 151, 200, 266, 426, 427
characteristics of the Internet that aid, 428
history of, 427
projections for, 428
**Economic integration, regional, 108**
motivation, 161
pragmatism, 352
over ideology, 108

Economies of scale, 467
**Economy, 73**
EDI, 107
**Effectiveness, 458**
**Efficiency, 458**
Egalitarianism, 62
**Ego, 56**
Ego defense function, 220
Electronic data interchange (EDI), 79
Elimination by Aspects (EBA) model, 308
**Elimination by aspects (EBA), 296**
**Emotional communications, 465**
**Emotional hierarchy, 204**
**Emotional value, 22**, 464
seeking, 174
**Emotions, 170**
and motivation, 163
defined, 170
model of, 171
types of, 171
**primary, 172**
Emotions typology, Plutchick's Circle, 172
**Enculturation, 60**
**Enduring involvement, 175, 289**
Envirolink network (http://www.envirolink.netforchange.com), 72
Environment, market, 69
Environmental characteristics, 18
**Environmental marketing, 73**
Environmental policies, promoting, 380
Environmental segments, 72
Environmentalism, business response to, 73
**Environmentally conscious consumers, 71**
**e-procurement, 445**
Established customers, premium prices from, 9
Ethnic diversity, 101
Ethnocentrism, 202
European Americans, 48
**Evaluated new unplanned purchases, 412**
Evaluation of alternatives, 435
**Evaluative beliefs, 203**
Evaluative consistency, 286
**Evoked set, 282**, 283
**Exchanges, 445**
Exclusive offerings, 465
Exit (future response), 303
**Expectations, 131**
and decision making, 342
**customer, 74**
measuring satisfaction in terms of, 303

Expenditures,
   discretionary, 74
   necessary, 74
Experience evaluation, 301
**Experience goods, 432**
Experiential consumption, 22
Experiment, 243
**Expertise, 145**, 289
   lack of, 16
**Exploratory shopping, 413**
Expressive nature of products
   and services, 292
**Extended problem solving,
   285**
**External attributions, 169**
**External stimuli, 279**
Eye movement, 255

Familiarity, 289
Families and households, 316
**Family, 316**
Family buying decisions, 317
   understanding, 330–331
Family characteristics, 332
   that influence IGI, 326
Family decision making,
   children's influence in, 320,
      321
   conflict in, 327
   process, 317
Family groups, 65
**Family life cycle concept,
   54**
   stage in, 319
**Family relationship, 326**
Family type, children's role
   by, 322
**Family unit, atomistic, 99**
**Family unit, nuclear, 99**
**Federal Acquisition Regu-
   lations (FARs), 345**
Federal Procurement Policy
   Act, 347
Federal Reserve, 75
Federal Trade Commission
   (http://www.ftc.gov), 76
Femininity vs. masculinity, 62
**Festinger's dissonance
   theory, 213**
**Financial well-being, 97**
Financing and credit, personal
   value, 24, 29
**Financing value, 24**, 469
Fiscal policy, 75
**Fishbein model, 216**
**Fishbein's extended
   model, 217–218**, 219
   schematic of, 218
Flexibility and control (of
   technology), 78
**Focus groups, 232**
**Foot-in-the-door strategy,
   211**
**Forced irrelevance, 143**
**Form utility, 470**

Formalization of the buying
   process, 333
**Forward buy, 413**
Free product or service, 17
Freedom of Information Act,
   350
FUD factor, 208
Fulfilling the business purpose
   by delivering customer
   value, 480
Functional theory, applications
   of the, 220
Functional vs. expressive nature
   of products and services,
   292
Future needs, meeting, 379
Future response, exit, voice,
   or loyalty, 303
Future technology and the
   Internet customer, 447

G.I. Bill, 52
G.I. Generation, 51–52
Gaining legitimacy in society, 4
Galvanic skin response (GSR),
   255
Gender, 50
   influence of, 81
**Gender-role orientation, 318**
Generation X, 52, 54, 55, 56
Generation Y, 52, 54, 55, 56
Genetic Confidentiality and
   Non-Discrimination Act,
   46
Genetics, 45, 57
   influence of, 80
**Geographic redistribution,
   102**
**Geographic variation, 71**
Germ scare, reacting to, 159
**Global sourcing, 444**
**Global warming, 71**
Globalization, 352
**Goal-object, 161**
Good citizenship, 380
**Government(s), 344**
   and business procurements
      compared, 348
   as customer, future of the,
      351
   buying behavior, 344, 355
   buying procedures, 344
   customer decision making,
      314
   decision making and cus-
      tomer roles, 353–354
   downsizing and restructur-
      ing, 351
   mandates, 210
   **policy, 75**
   compliance, 380
   procurement, U.S. laws
      governing, 350
   travails and rewards of sell-
      ing to the, 351

Great Depression, 52
**Green consumer, 71**, 72
Group influence,
   conditions for, 66
   types of, 66
**Group traits, 45**
Groups for household cus-
   tomers, classification of, 64
**Groups, 63**
   family, 65
   membership, 63–64
   primary, 63–64
   reference, 65
   religious, 65
   secondary, 63–64
   types of, 63–64
Guanxi in China, 369

**Habit, 150**
   and history, 396
**Habitual purchasing, 142**
Healthcare customers, cure
   quality vs. caring quality,
   396
Healthcare services, caring
   matters more than cure,
   395
**Hedonic consumption, 175**
   seeking emotional value, 174
**Heider's balance theory,
   214**
Hemophilia, 47
Heuristic search, 286
**Heuristics, 286**
   rapid, 297
Hierarchy components, con-
   sistency among, 206
High-involvement information-
   processing mode, 214
High-tech forecast, 116
History and habit, 396
Home health monitors, 116
Home Ownership and Equity
   Protection Act, 470
**Household, 316**
   and business buying com-
      pared, 333
   business, and government
      decision making and
      customer roles, 353–354
   single-person, 99
Household buying behavior,
   316, 352
Household customer decision
   making, 314
Household customers,
   classification of groups for, 64
   Maslow's needs for, 164
**Household market(s), 12**
   intergenerational differences
      in, 55
How factor, 407
Human Genome Project
   (HGP)(http://www.ornl.
   gov/hgmis/), 45–46

Hunter-Gatherers, 291
Huntington's chorea, 47
Husband-wife decision roles,
   317
Hybrid techniques, 238

**Id, 56**
Ideal points, perceptual map
   with, 253
**Ideal self, 177**
Identificational influence, 66
Identified choice, deviation
   from, 300
Ideology vs. economic prag-
   matism, 109
IGI across households, 327
IGI, see also intergenerational
   influence
**Ignorance paradox, 291**
**Imitation, 141**
**Imitative behavior, 141**
**Imitators, 145**
Implementation, delay in, 299
Importance of purchase, 319
**Importance of purchase,
   335**
Impulse behavior, 100
**Impulse purchases, 413**
Incentives to attitude molding,
   209
**Increased-productivity
   approach, 467**
**Index of Consumer Senti-
   ment, 74**
Individual characteristics, 330
Individual customer decision
   making, 274
   and customer roles, 305–307
Individual decision maker, 275
**Individual traits, 45**
Individual's decision, location
   and cost of, 276
Individualism vs. collectivism,
   62
Industrial Marketing and Pur-
   chasing (IMP), 373, 385
**Inference making, 212**
Influence of
   age, 81
   gender, 81
   genetics, 80
   personality, 81
   race, 80
Information,
   increased access to, 78
   increased control over, 104
   sources of, 284
**Information board, 254**
**Information content, 131**
Information for
   car buyers, 285
   customers, sources of, 284
**Information intensiveness
   continuum, 432**
Information motivation, 161

**Information overload, 292**
**Information processing mode (IPM), 292**
Information search, 282, 434
Information structuring, 211
Informational influence, 66
Information-processing modes, 214
**Information-processing research, 252**
**Innovation, 144**, 460
desirable characteristics of, 147
new product, 12
Innovation resistance, 149
typology of, 150
Innovative adoption, customer roles in, 153
Innovativeness, illustrative measures of, 146
Innovators among business customers, 147
**Innovators, 145**
Insight, customer, 53
**Instant gratification, 100**
**Instant marketing, 117**
Institution customer decision making, 314
**Institutions, 63**
and reference groups, 84
In-store factors, 413
In-store information and assistance, 407
**Instrumental conditioning, 141**
**Instrumentality of market values, 32**
Interactive control motivation, 161
Interactive Home Shopping (HIS), 283
**Interattribute inference, 286**
Intergenerational
class mobility, 68
differences in household and business markets, 55
**Intergenerational influence (IGI), 325, 327**
research findings on, 326
**Internal attributions, 169**
Internal capabilities, 333
Internal homogeneity, 68
**Internal stimuli, 279**
International markets, customer satisfaction and loyalty to brands, 421
Internet,
and culture, 63
and customer, and future technology, 447
data trail from shopping on, 266
history of, 427
in Asia, 121
in China, 123

in East Africa, 122
in Europe, 120
in Hungary, 121
in India, 121
in India, 429
in Russia, 122
shopping types, 291
status in different regions and countries, 120–123
technology for online shopping, early adoptors of, 148
tracking, and value for customers, 230
Interpersonal relationship, 475
**Interpretation, 130**
**Interpretive research, 240**
advantages and disadvantages, 242
Interspousal influence, factors influencing, 318
Intuitive theories in customer inference making, 288
**Invitation for bid (IFB), 344**
Invitation for bid procedure, 345
**Involvement, 175**, 289
consumer, 290

Japanese Americans, 49
**Joint decisions, 318**
**Just noticeable difference (j.n.d.), 134**

Karma, 49
Katona's classification of needs, 33
**Knowledge function, 220**
Knowledgeable salesperson, 471
Korean Americans, 49

**Laddering, 177**
**Lead users, 147**
Learner, customer as a, 136
**Learning, 129, 138**
mechanisms of, 138
Learning experience, ultimate, 144
**Learning hierarchy, 204**
Learning mechanisms, 323
Learning process,
and customer roles, 151–152
influence of, 152
Learning theories, 211
Legitimacy in society, gaining, 4
**Level of adaptation, 168**
**Lexicographic model, 295**
**Life cycle, family (concept), 54**
**Life-status change, 143**
Lifestyle clusters in Asian countries, 186
**Lifestyle retail brands, 180**

Lifestyle segments of the U.S., 181
**Lifestyles, 179**
**Lifetime revenue, 11, 51**
Limited availability, 464
**Limited problem solving, 286**
Linking product attributes to customer values, 177
Location and cost of an individual's decision, 276
Loneliness, 99
Long-term contracts, business purchases, 339
Low price from
increased productivity, 467
lower margins, 466
**Lower-margin approach, 466**
Lower margins, low price from, 466
**Low-involvement attitude hierarchy, 205**
Low-involvement information-processing mode, 214
Loyalty (future response), 305
Loyalty detractors, attraction of alternatives, 397
Loyalty needs attitude and behavior, 404

Maintenance/labor agreements, 348
Managerial uses of perceptual process, 134
**Mapping, perceptual and preference, 250**
Market context, 73, 85
Market environment, 69
Market factors, 397
**Market mavens, 169**
**Market orientation, 6**
Market success, key to, 2
Market traits, 69, 85
**Market value(s), 19**
classification of, 19
creating for buyers, 470
creating for payers, 466
creating for the customer, 457
creating for users, 459
sought by payers, 24
sought by users, 20
**Marketer sources, 284**
Marketers, and OSS
overall implications for, 117
**Marketing, environmental, 73**
Marketing communications, social-image-based, 465
**Marketing concept, 4**
adopting, 4
**Marketing myopia, 19**
Marketing scholars, needs identified by, 166

Markets, intergenerational differences in, 55
Masculinity vs. femininity, 62
**Maslow's hierarchy of needs,** 33, **164**, 170, 177, 180
Mason Haire Classic Study (instant coffee), 236
**Mass customization, 79**, 106, **463**
**Materialism, 187, 189**
scale to measure, 189
**Maturation, 143**
Mature adults, and young adults, 53
**Means-end chains, 177**
illustrated, 178
Measuring customer perceptions of value delivery process, 481–483
Membership groups, 63–64
**Mental budgeting, 277**
and customer behavior, 278
Merchandise quality, 406
Merchandise selection, ease of, 407
Mexicans, 48
Microbial Genome Project, 46
Middle class, declining, 100
Milleniums, 54
**Mobile commerce, 447**
**Modeling, 141**
Models,
comparative features of various choice, 297
how and when they are used, 296
Modernized plant, 467
**Modified rebuy, 334**, 446
Molding customer attitudes, 207
Monetary policy, 75
Monitoring services, selected trends measured by, 263
**Moods, 173**
Moon Festival Banquet, 50
**Motivation, 161**
process of, 162
Motivational processes and customer roles, 190–191
**Motivational research (MR)**
techniques for, 235
Motivations for Web usage, 161
Motorized vs. nonmotorized mobile homes, 241
Multiattribute attitude model, 219, 250
**Multiattribute models of attitude, 216**
Murray's list of psychogenic needs, 165–166
**Mutual goals, 376**

**National culture, 61**
**Nature, 47**

**Necessary expenditures, 74**
**Need, 17**
  categories, evaluation of, 170
  for arousal, 168
  for attribution, 168, 169
**Need for cognition, 168**
Needs,
  and motivation, 163
  and wants, determinants of, 18
  identified by marketing scholars, 166
**Negative cue, 287**
**Neglectful families, 320**
**Negligent consumer behavior, 76**
**Neo rich, 101**
**Networks, 367**
**Neutral marketplaces, 445**
Never-owned products, 116
New Class, The, 69
New product innovations, 12
New purchase, 446
**New task, 334**
Newbies, 291
Noncompensatory models, 294
**Nondisguised-nonstructured techniques, 235**
**Nondisguised-structured techniques, 235**
**Nonfamily household, 316**
Nonfood store shopping, 414
**Nonmarketer sources, 284**
**Norm of reciprocity, 213**
**Normative beliefs, 203**
Normative influence, 66
North American Free Trade Agreement (NAFTA), 421
**Nuclear family unit, 99**
**Nurture, 47**
Nurturing suppliers, advantages of, 381

Occupational Safety and Health Act (OSHA), 77
**Odd pricing, 134**
**One-stop shopping, 406**
  (OSS), 11, 415
  customer motivations for seeking, 416
  risks of, 416
Online customer behavior, 425
  and customer roles, 448–449
Online decision making,
  post-purchase stage, 442
  pre-purchase phase, 433
  purchase stage, 437
Online population by gender, 431
Online purchases,
  benefits of, 148
  of products and services, 432
  privacy concerns, 439
  satisfaction and loyalty, 442
  security concerns, 440

trust in, 440
Online satisfaction, 442
Open-access information, 349
**Opinion leadership, 145**
  illustrative measures of, 146
Opportunistic behavior, avoidance of, 376
Opportunity network, customer, 5
**Optimal level of stimulation, 168**
**Organization, 130**
Organizational
  characteristics, 336
  customer behavior, comprehensive model of, 343
Orientation, customer, 12
**Other-brand averaging, 287**
**Outsourced, 98**

Pacific Islander race, 47
**Partner-specific investments, 376**
**Passive consumers, 108**
Passive customers, rights of, 111
**Payer, 14**
Payers,
  creating market values for, 466
  product or service subsidized by, 17
  self-concept as, 178
PDA (Personal Digital Assistant), 104
People's Republic of China, 21
Perceived brand-performance fit, 393
Perceived corporate image, 136
**Perceived justice, 304**
**Perceived risk, 148, 287, 335, 365**
  and business buying behavior, 337
  and switching costs, combinations of, 366
**Perception, 129**
  and learning, 129
  factors that shape, 130
Perception process, influence of, 151
Perceptions and preferences, customer, 251
**Perceptual and preference mapping, 250**
**Perceptual distortion, 133**
Perceptual distortions, and decision making, 342
Perceptual map, 252
  with ideal points, 253
  with product attributes, 253
Perceptual process
  and customer roles, 151–152
  managerial uses of, 134
**Perceptual threshold, 134**

**Performance risk, 150**
**Performance value, 20, 459**
**Peripheral processing route, 214**
Peripheral route to attitude formation, 215
**Permissive families, 322**
Personal
  and environmental characteristics, 18
  characteristics and customer roles, 82–83
  context, 59, 84
  factors, 44
**Personal safety, 97**
Personal traits, 44, 80
**Personal value, 19**
  credit and financing, 24
Personal worth, 67, 85
  measurement of, 67
Personality, 56
  classification into social styles, 60
  customer, 56
  influence of, 81
  of business customer, 59
**Personality trait, 57, 58**
Personalization, 409, 438
  value, 31, 474
Personalized computers, 116
**Persuasion, 342**
**Phased decision strategy, 297**
Physical environment, structuring, 210
Pictorial scales to measure customer attitudes, 248
PIMS (Profit Impact of Marketing Strategies), 461
**Planned purchases, 412**
**Planned social change, 222**
Planned social change, typology of strategy mix for, 223
Plutchik's Circle, 172
Plutchik's emotions, scales to measure, 173
Point of access, convenient, 474
Political ideology, 109
**Politicking, 342**
**Popular culture, 61**
Population,
  aging of the, 95
  socioeconomic development of, 319
Post-purchase
  expectations, 148
experience, 301
  phase, service in the, 472
  stage, online decision making, 442
**Power dependence, 373**
Power distance, 62
Premium prices from established customers, 9

Preproposal conference, 347
Prepurchase service, 471
Pre-purpose stage of online decision making, 433
Prestige pricing, 464
Price, universal value, 24
Price perceptions, psychophysics of, 134
**Price value, 24, 406, 466**
Prices,
  premium, 9
  of products, increasing range of, 100
Pricing, prestige, 464
**Pricing proposal, 348**
**Primary demand, 281**
**Primary emotions, 172**
Primary groups, 63–64
Privacy concerns for online purchases, 439
Privately consumed
  luxuries, 65
  necessities, 66
Prizm, 260
Probability of purchase, 392
**Problem recognition, 278, 279, 280, 433**
  by customer role, 281
  situations for, 282
  stimuli for, 279
Problem resolution, 407
**Problem routinization, 142**
**Problem solving, 138, 285–286, 342**
**Problem, customer, 279**
Problems, typology of, 282
Procedural detail and paperwork, 350
Process for determining customer value, 479–480
Process of single-source data collection, 264
**Process-induced affect, 208**
**Processing by attributes, 296**
**Processing by brands, 296**
Procurement
  by state governments, 348
  costs, 341
  differences between government and business, 348
  similarities between government and business, 348
Product appeals, utilitarian vs. expressive, 23
Product attributes,
  linking to customer values, 177
  perceptual map with, 253
Product image, scale to measure, 179
Product innovation, 12, 78
Product maintenance, 474
Product on display or demonstration, 471

Product subsidized by payers, 17
Product support and communication, 376
Productivity, low price from increased, 467
**Products,**
  access to, 105
  customer loyalty to, 417–418
  increasing range of prices of, 100
  **smart, 105**
Products and services
  customers buy online, 432
  customized, 79
  functional vs. expressive nature, 292
Product-use advice and support, 472
Proportion of purchase, 391
Proposals, 347
**Proprietary data, 258**
**Protocol, 256**
Psychogenic needs, Murray's list of, 165–166
**Psychographics, 176**
  and motivation, 163
  as AIO profiles, 180
Psychological processes underlying attitude change, 211
**Psychology of complication, 143**
Psychology of simplification and complication, 142
Psychophysics of price perceptions, 134
Public data, 257
Public policy, 76
  implications of trends in, 115
  trends in, 108
Publicly consumed
  luxuries, 65
  necessities, 66
Purchase, 298
  and standardization, average size, 349
  importance of, 319
  nature of, 330, 334
  new, 446
  orientation of business, 338
  probability of, 392
  proportion of, 391
  resources of business, 336
  restrictions and compliance reviews, 349
  sequence of, 391
  stage, online decision making, 437
**Purchase-decision involvement, 289**
**Purposive behavior, 161**

**Qualitative research, 232**
Quality assurance, 380

**Quality cue, 134**
Quality improvement, 460
  program (FedEx), 461
**Quality of life, 103**
**Quantitative research, 242**
  applications of, 246
  methods, 242
  selected applications of, 247

Race, 47
  influence of, 80
Rank ordering, 68
Rapid heuristics, 297
**Reciprocity, 367**
**Recognition, problem, 279**
**Recommendation systems, 434**
**Recreational needs, 97**
**Redistribution, geographic, 102**
**Reengineering, 468**
  at Taco Bell, 469
Reference group(s), 65
  influence, conditions for, 65
  influence, types of, 66
  institutions and, 84
**Reference price, 134**
**Regional economic integration, 108**, 112
**Regional marketing, 71**
Relational buying, characteristics of, 373
Relationship buying
  and selling in business markets, 372
  by automobile makers, 375
  process of, 373
Relationship development
  in business buying, reasons for, 374
  steps in, 373
**Relationship-based buying,** 362, **364**
  customer motivation for, 364
  model of, 364
  nurturing suppliers, 377
  outcomes of, 372
Relationships in China, guanxi, 369
Relationships in Russia, building, 368
**Relative advantage, 147**
Relative brand uncertainty, 292
Relative permanence, 68
Religious groups, 65
Religious ideology, 109
Repeat customers, cost efficiency, 8
**Request for proposal (RFP), 345**
Research,
  advantages and disadvantages of subjective interpretive, 242

consumer, 265
database, 264
findings on intergenerational influence, 326
Researching customer behavior, 230
Resources, 181
**Restocking unplanned purchases, 412**
**Retail brands, lifestyle, 180**
**Retrospective protocols, 256**
Returns, online purchases, 443
Revenue, lifetime, 11, **51**
Reverse influence, 325
Riesman's Social Character Theory, 180
Rights of passive customers, 111
**Role formalness, 373**
**Role specialization, 14**
  reasons for, 15
**Roommate families, 98**
**Rosenberg model, 216**
**Rote memorization, 138**
**Routine problem solving, 285**
Rules and procedures, business purchases, 339

Safety, 97
Sale, more than just a, 362
Salesperson, knowledgeable, 471
Satisfaction
  and dissatisfaction, 302
  and loyalty, online purchasing, 442
  measuring in terms of expectations, 303
**Satisficing, 298**
**Schachter's two-factor theory, 171**
Schizophrenia, 47
Search, determinants of the amount of, 287
Search costs, 365
**Search goods, 432**
**Search strategy, 285**
**Secondary demand, 281**
Secondary groups, 63–64
**Secondary research, 257**
Security, 97
Security concerns in online purchases, 440
Segmented markets, 102
Selected trends measured by monitoring services, 263
Selective attention, 133
**Selective demand, 281**
Selective exposure, 132
Selective interpretation, 133
**Self-concept, 177**
  as users, payers, and buyers, 178

Self-image, scale to measure, 179
Self-orientation, 181
**Self-perception theory, 212**
Self-respect, 99
**Self-selection, 412**
Selling concept, 4
Selling to the government, travails and rewards, 351
**Sell-side business models, 445**
**Sensation, 130**
**Sensory, 130**
Sentence completion, 238
Sequence of purchase, 391
Service
  in the post-purchase phase, 472
  purchases, values sought, 26
  Quality Index (SQI), 461
  subsidized by payers, 17
**Service value, 25**, 30, 470
Services and products, customized, 79
  functional vs. expressive nature, 292
**Shopbots, 435**
Shopping motives, 414
Shopping,
  nonfood store, 414
  one-stop, 11
  types on the Internet, classification of, 291
Silent Generation, 52, 55
Simplification, 142
**Simulation, 245**
Single-person households, 99
**Single-source data, 263**
  collection, process of, 264
**Situational involvement, 175**
Size of business, 336
**Smart bots, 435**
**Smart products, 105**
Social and emotional
  identification with the brand, 394
  values, 464
**Social cause marketing, 465**
**Social class, 68**
  characteristics, 68
  in America, 69
Social escapism motivation, 161
**Social marketing, 222**
**Social orientation families, 320**
**Social risk, 150**
Social styles, and classification of personality, 60
**Social value, 21**
Social-image-based marketing communications, 465

Socialization,
early, 367
motivation, 161
of Chinese children as consumers, 324
outcomes, 325
Society, gaining legitimacy in, 4
Sociocultural factors, 367
Socioeconomic development of population, 319
Solicitation of sellers, 349
Specialization
of customer roles, 332
role, 14
Stage in family life cycle, 319
State government, procurement by, 348
**Stimulation, optimal level of, 168**
Stimuli for problem recognition, 279
**Stimulus, 130**
characteristics, 130
Store brand acceptance, determinants of, 408
Store brands, 407
Store choice, 409
decision process, flow chart of, 411
**Store image, 414**
**Store loyalty, 405**
measures of, 405
model of, 405
Store shopping, nonfood, 414
**Store visiting, 414**
Stores, customer loyalty to, 417–418
Story completion, 238
**Straight rebuy, 334, 445**
Strategy, choice of, 223
Structure of business, 336
**Subculture, 61**
**Subjective norms, 218**
Subjective research, advantages and disadvantages, 242
**Superego, 56**
Supplier partnering, factors for the growth of, 382
Supplier Technical Assistance (STA), 362
Supplier trust in customers, determinants of, 376

**Supplier-customer partnering, 381**
relationship, 370
Suppliers,
art of nurturing (relationship-based buying), 377
reasons for nurturing, 379
Survey, 242
Swap meet, psychology of buyers and sellers at a, 241
Switching costs and perceived risk, combinations of, 366
**Switching costs, 365**
**Syncratic decisions, 317**
**Syndicated data, 258**
**Systematic search, 286**

**Technical proposals, 347**
Technological trends, 104
implications of, 115
Technologies, new, 104
**Technology, 78**
flexibility and control, 78
**Technophiles, 79**
**Technophobes, 79**
**Techthusiasts, 79**
**Telematics, 447**
**Test marketing, 244**
**Thematic apperception test (TAT), 238**
Time pressure, 291, 319, 336
**Time shift, 98**
**Time shortage, 98**
Time, lack of, 16
**Tolerance for ambiguity, 168**
**Topography, 70**
Tracking services, 259
**Trait theory of personality, 58**
Transaction costs (Internet), 148
Transaction recording, automated, 475
**Transaction-specific investments/adaptations, 373**
**Trialability, 149**
**Trust, 370**
Trust and commitment, defined, 371
from business customers, determinants of, 374
Trust in online purchases, 440

**Trustworthiness, 145**
Two-stage choice process, 297
Typology of problems, 282

U.S. Department of Defense, 427
U.S. Government Publications, selected, 257
Uncertain avoidance, 62
**Unconditioned stimulus (UCS), 139**
Uniform Contract Format (UCF), 346
**Universal value, 19**
price, 24
**Unplanned purchases, 412**
**User, 14**
and buyer/payer roles, 15
roles, 15
self-concept as, 178
**Utilitarian function, 220**
Utilitarian vs. expressive product appeals, 23

VALS, 180, 181
American lifestyles, 182
applications of, 184
groups, 182
Japan, 185
questionnaire, 183
self survey (http://www.sric-bi.com/vals/presurvey.shtml), 182
Value, 457
**Value compatibility, 148**
Value creation in B2B marketplaces, 444
Value delivery process, measuring customer perceptions of, 481–483
**Value delivery, 458**
dimensions of, 458
measuring, 475
**Value expressive function, 220**
**Value synergy, 33**
Value-added benefits, 367
**Values, 176**
and customer roles, 20
are dynamic, 33
are hierarchical, 33
are role-specific, 34
are synergistic, 33

credit and financing, 469
social and emotional, 464
sought in service purchases, 26
varying, 34
Vendor relations in Japan and the U.S., 382
**Verbatim, 243**
**Verifiable benefit, 76**
**Virtual reality, 265**
as customer research tool, 265
Virtual reality techniques, advantages of, 266
in consumer research, 265
Virtual shopping, 265
Virtual test marketing, 266
Virtual vending machine (http://www.vendline.com), 267
Virtual-reality consumer research project, 267
**Visual image profile, 256**
Voice (future response), 303
**Voluntary simplicity, 190**

**Want, 17**
Warehouse clubs, 64
Warranties and guarantees, 463
Web pages by language, 103
**Weber's Law, 134**
Wellness, 96
What factor, 406
Wife's employment status, 318
Women in the workforce, 97
**Word association, 238**
Word of mouth, 11
Workforce, women in the, 97
World War II, 52
World Wide Web, history of, 427

**Zaltman metaphor elicitation technique (ZMET), 238**

**Anderson County Library**
300 North McDuffie Street
Anderson, South Carolina 29621
(864) 260-4500

Belton, Honea Path, Iva,
Lander Regional, Pendleton,
Piedmont, Powdersville,
Westside, Bookmobile